Mendenhall

Select problems in
Western Civilization.

Select Problems in Western Civilization

SELECT PROBLEMS IN WESTERN CIVILIZATION

THOMAS C. MENDENHALL
BASIL D. HENNING
ARCHIBALD S. FOORD
ARCHIBALD W. ALLEN
Department of History, Yale University

Holt, Rinehart and Winston
New York · Chicago · San Francisco
Toronto · London

25666-0916

Printed in the United States of America

PREFACE

Emboldened by the usefulness of the earlier volumes of Select Problems to history teachers, we have now assembled a relatively small group of Problems designed for the extensive time-span of the traditional course in Western civilization. New problems have been added, old ones have been lifted or adapted from earlier volumes, and a central theme—the individual and the state in the Western tradition—lends a real unity to the collection.

Of the following nine Problems, the first two are new. The first employs the death of Socrates as a device to study the Greek's concern for the relation of the individual to society, while the second examines the transition from Roman republic to empire in the same light. The next five Problems, taken largely from the earlier volumes of Select Problems, carry the examination of the central theme up through the Middle Ages, the Renaissance, the age of the new monarchies, the English Revolution of 1688, and the French Revolution. In the last two Problems, faced with the enormous complexity of the modern period, we have singled out some of the more influential ideas—laissez-faire, utilitarianism, socialism, nationalism, and science, for instance—and attempted in the selections to show the student some of the dimensions they have added to the Western tradition.

The systematic study of historical documents by undergraduates has long been possible either through "Readings in European History" or through organized problems in the sources. But the following Problems differ in purpose and method both from volumes of supplementary readings and from the earlier attempts to arrange these materials in problem form.

The purpose of these Problems is, first of all, to make the student aware of the complexity of history. Every survey course in Western civilization must impart a knowledge of events, of what happened in the long past. And no student can pretend to understand history without a grasp of its narrative. But in addition a comprehension of the interdependence of the many forces operating in society is essential; if the student learns only the narrative of events, his knowledge of history will be painfully superficial. It is believed that the study of these Problems, combined with the use of a textbook and the interpretation derived from lectures, will allow the student to obtain a fuller understanding of the complicated pattern of Western civilization. Only a genuine awareness of the sweep and the complexity of this civilization will enable the undergraduate to partake of the philosophical insight, of the serenity which comes with the broad perspective and the deep comprehension, and of the intellectual and moral inspiration which are the richest rewards of historical study.

The Problems are designed to demonstrate the principles of historical reasoning in such a way that the undergraduate may test them for himself. The student has had experience of the scientific method in the laboratory work accompanying courses in the natural sciences, but too often the historian has acted as if his techniques were a trade secret and has preferred to guard loyally his fellow guildsman's book from student attack. Often the undergraduate critic has had only common sense or principles drawn from another discipline with which to challenge the dogmatism of the textbook and the prejudices of the pedagogue. This is particularly to be regretted since the historian by his training is especially qualified to teach the student to seek and to find, to evaluate, and to interpret manmade evidence. These lessons are what the Problems are designed to teach, and it is here that they differ most from collections of supplementary readings, whose principal and laudable purpose is to enliven and enrich a text.

Each Problem has been divided into two or three Parts, each Part representing one assignment, though the instructor will find quickly that this division is sufficiently flexible to permit a different emphasis if desired. Each Problem is preceded by an introduction which sets the scene by indicating the reason for studying this specific subject and furnishing the necessary background. Included in each Problem are questions for study, designed to guide the student in handling and evaluating the very disparate material which he is called upon to study.

In teaching these Problems at Yale University, it has been the experience of the authors that college students enjoy working at the stuff of history for themselves, that these readings in original materials, if properly organized, can be made the central, rather than a supplementary part of a course, and that the techniques of the historian need not be taught at the extreme levels of either unimportant details or unsolvable enigmas but can contribute much to the intellectual powers of every undergraduate.

T. C. M.
B. D. H.
A. S. F.
A. W. A.

New Haven, Conn.
March 15, 1956

CONTENTS

[vii]

Select Problems in
Western
Civilization

I

Individualism and Authority in the Greek City-State

SOCRATES was the first philosopher to discuss the conduct of life; he was also the first to be condemned to death.

DIOGENES LAERTIUS, 3d cent. A.D.

CONTENTS

QUESTIONS FOR STUDY

PART I

1. How did Spartan discipline differ from Persian? How is it illustrated in the story of Aristodemus?

2. What moral and political issues are raised in the scene between Antigone and Ismene?

3. To what standards did Creon and Antigone appeal in justifying their acts?

4. Was a compromise possible between the principles of Creon and Antigone?

5. Does the conflict between Antigone and Creon suggest modern parallels?

6. How did Pericles associate the welfare of the individual with that of the state?

7. What importance did the "unwritten laws" have in Pericles' conception of government?

8. Does Pericles' vision of Athens present an ideal worthy of imitation today?

9. What serious suspicions of Socrates seem to lie behind the burlesque treatment of him in Aristophanes' *Clouds?*

PART II

10. Does the indictment against Socrates fit the picture of him given in the *Clouds?*

11. How did Socrates answer his "old accusers"?

12. How did he answer the charge of failing to honor the gods of the city?

13. How did he answer the charge of corrupting the young?

14. Why did he not take more part in Athenian political life?

15. How did he support his claim that his whole life had been devoted to the service of the god?

16. How did the "divine sign" affect his life?

17. What opportunities did he have to escape the death penalty?

18. What course did he consider to be open to an individual who believed that his country was unjustly governed?

19. At his trial Socrates argued his right to freedom of thought; when he had been condemned, he argued the right of Athens to execute the sentence against him. How did he reconcile these two arguments?

20. How does the problem faced by Socrates compare with that faced by a conscientious objector in this country? By a convinced communist facing a Soviet purge trial?

INTRODUCTION TO THE PROBLEM

A striking feature of Classical Greece is the simultaneous presence of extreme individualism and of extreme respect for social authority. Already in Homer's *Iliad,* the earliest monument of Greek (and European) literature, tension between these two attitudes is a central feature of the poem. Greek individualism is a trait which we can rather observe than explain, but there are identifiable historical factors which can help us to understand the strong sense of social solidarity. First, there is the small size of the Greek city-state. The small territory of Greece was, during its Classical period, divided into a multitude of completely sovereign states. The island of Melos, for example, is just twelve and a half miles long and six miles wide, yet it was fully independent until its conquest by Athens in 416 B.C. Athens itself had a territory somewhat smaller than the state of Rhode Island, and a population of perhaps 300,000, half of whom were slaves or resident aliens. Second, military tactics were such as to encourage a strong feeling of interdependence. Every man physically competent was liable to military service, and most took part in several campaigns. Armies fought in close infantry formation and every man's life depended on his neighbor. A few individuals breaking formation could produce immediate defeat, and it is characteristic of Greek battles that casualties were very light on the side of the victors, extremely heavy among the defeated. Finally, there was a close unity of interest among the inhabitants of the small states. An economic disaster such as a bad harvest was bound to be felt by the whole community. Any defeat in war—and wars were almost continuous—might mean total extinction. When Melos was conquered by Athens all men capable of bearing arms were put to death, and the rest of the population were sold into slavery. It is therefore not surprising that we find in Greek literature debates on the relation between the individual and society which have echoes in all subsequent discussions of the problem.

No single form of government was characteristic of Greece. Monarchy, oligarchy, and democracy all existed, as well as various combinations of these three basic types. No type was considered to be necessarily superior to the others, but a sharp distinction was usually made between a legitimate form of government (one based on the traditions of a people) and an illegitimate form (one imposed by violence, even though supported by a majority). Sparta had a mixed type of government, though it seems to modern judgment to have been predominantly oligarchical. Athens during much of the fifth century was a pure democracy (i.e., all adult male citizens participated directly in making laws, conducting the law courts, and choosing officials; all were eligible to hold office, and most offices were filled by lot). Sparta laid greatest stress on individual conformity to the group pattern, while Athens took particular pride in the freedom of her individual citizens.

The fifth century B.C. was the great period of Athenian history. At the beginning of the century she had taken over leadership of the Greek states in the defense against two invasions of Europe by the Persian Empire. Alone at Marathon (490 B.C.), and later with the support of some only of the tiny, divided, quarreling, and often treacherous Greek states (480–79 B.C.), she defended Greece against the greatest empire of the time. When the defensive stage of the war ended in 479, Sparta and most of the states of the Greek mainland withdrew, but Athens continued the war for thirty years, gradually liberating the Greek cities on the coast of Asia Minor from Persian rule; many of the smaller Greek states, chiefly those on the shores of the Aegean Sea, supported Athens with contributions of ships or money. When the war with Persia came to an end, Athens continued to demand these contributions, which were thus transformed into tribute. Since Athens also compelled states which attempted to withdraw from her alliance to remain, the alliance was in effect changed into an Athenian Empire. She eventually won for herself the invidious title "Tyrant City of Hellas." ("Hellas" is the native name for Greece; our name for Greece comes through Latin.) The aggressive conduct of Athens toward her neighbors led in 431 B.C. to a war between her and a coalition headed by Sparta and including most of the states of the Peloponnesus (the peninsula forming the southern part of Greece). The war lasted, with one short intermission, for twenty-seven years and extended even into Sicily when Athens attempted to conquer Syracuse, the strongest Greek city in the west. In 404 Athens, completely exhausted, had to admit defeat. She lost all possessions outside Attica itself and her walls were torn down. Her fleet had been destroyed, her treasury was empty, and a third of her people were dead. Moreover she had to accept a form of government imposed by Sparta. A body of thirty men was appointed to draw up a new constitution which would restrict political power to the richer citizens. This body was guilty of such violence, so many crudely disguised judicial murders, and such lack of respect for Athenian traditions, that they came to be known as the Thirty Tyrants; a civil war ensued, and a year after the surrender democracy was reestablished.

Soon after the restoration of the democracy, Socrates—the Athenian who "first called philosophy down from the sky and gave her a place in the cities of men" —was brought to trial on charges of impiety and of corrupting the youth of the city. This first Problem presents the question of individual freedom and its relation to the authority of society as this question was posed by the trial of Socrates. Part I gives a background to the charges made against him. Part II contains Socrates' words at his trial and in conversations which took place shortly after the trial.

THE PROBLEM

Part I. ## INDIVIDUALISM AND AUTHORITY
IN FIFTH CENTURY GREECE

A. ### THE NATURE OF AUTHORITY IN GREECE AND IN PERSIA

1. *A Conversation Between Xerxes and Demaratus.* Herodotus (c. 485–425 B.C.), a native of Halicarnassus, a Greek city on the coast of Asia Minor, wrote an account of the wars between the Greeks and Persians. At one point he presents a conversation between Xerxes, king of Persia, and Demaratus, an exiled Spartan king who had joined the Persians. This conversation, like all speeches in ancient historians, is the historian's own construction—an account of what he considered as fitting to have been spoken by the characters. The two kings are presented as speaking shortly before the battle of Thermopylae, where 300 Spartans under their King Leonidas, facing certain defeat by enormously superior numbers of Persians, chose to die rather than retreat. (In this translation "law" represents a Greek word which combines our idea of law with that of custom; it includes not only statutory laws but also laws based on the authority of generations of popular acceptance and approval.) Demaratus the Spartan is the first speaker.[1]

"Poverty is my country's inheritance from of old, but valor she won for herself by wisdom and the strength of law. By her valor Greece now keeps both poverty and bondage at bay. I think highly of all Greeks of Dorian descent, but what I am about to say will apply not to all Dorians, but to the Spartans only. First then, they will not under any circumstances accept terms from you which would mean slavery for Greece; secondly, they will fight you even if the rest of Greece submits. Moreover, there is no use in asking if their numbers are adequate to enable them to do this; suppose a thousand of them take the field—then that thousand will fight you; and so will any number, greater than this or less."

Xerxes laughed. "My dear Demaratus," he exclaimed, "what an extraordinary thing to say! Do you really suppose a thousand men would fight an army like mine? . . . Let me put my point as reasonably as I can—how is it possible that a thousand men, or ten thousand, or fifty thousand, should stand up to an army as big as mine, especially if they were not under a single master, but all perfectly free to do as they pleased? Suppose them to have five thousand men: in that case we should be more than a thousand to one! If, like ours, their troops were subject to the control of a single man, then possibly for fear of him, in spite of the disparity in numbers, they might show some sort of factitious courage, or let themselves be whipped into battle; but, as every man is free to follow his fancy, it is not conceivable that they should do either. Indeed, my own opinion is that even on equal terms the Greeks could hardly face the Persians alone. . . ."

"My lord," Demaratus answered, "I knew before I began that if I spoke the truth you would not like it. But, as you demanded the plain truth and nothing less, I told you how things are with the Spartans. Yet you are well aware that I now feel but little affection for my countrymen, who robbed me of my hereditary power and privileges and made me a fugitive without a home—whereas your father welcomed me at his court and gave me the means of livelihood and somewhere to live. Surely it is unreasonable to reject kindness; any sensible man will cherish it. Personally I do not claim to be able to fight ten men—or two; indeed I should prefer not even to fight with one. But should it be necessary—should there be some great cause to urge me on—then nothing would give me more pleasure than to stand up to one of those men of yours who claim to be a match for three Greeks. So it is with the Spartans; fighting singly, they are as good as any, but fighting together they are the best soldiers in the world. They are free—yes—but not entirely free; for they have a master, and that master is Law, which they fear much more than your subjects fear you. Whatever this master commands, they do; and his command never varies: it is never to retreat in battle, however great the odds, but always to stand firm, and to conquer or die. If, my lord, you think that what I have said is nonsense—very well; I am willing henceforward to hold my tongue."

2. *A Survivor of Thermopylae.* Aristodemus, one of the Spartan army under Leonidas, avoided the battle of Thermopylae (perhaps because of illness) and so survived. The fol-

lowing year (479 B.C.) he fought at the battle of Plataea, the decisive land battle which drove the Persians out of Greece. This is Herodotus' account of Aristodemus.[2]

He was met upon his return [from Thermopylae] with reproach and disgrace; no Spartan would give him a light to kindle his fire, or speak to him, and he was nicknamed the Trembler. However, he afterwards made amends for everything at the battle of Plataea. . . .

Much the greatest courage was shown [at Plataea], in my opinion, by Aristodemus—the man who had suffered the disgrace of being the sole survivor of the Three Hundred at Thermopylae. After him, the greatest personal distinction was won by the three Spartans, Posidonius, Philocyon, and Amompharetus. However, when, after the battle, the question of who had most distinguished himself was discussed, the Spartans present decided that Aristodemus had, indeed, fought magnificently, but that he had done so merely to retrieve his lost honor, rushing forward with the fury of a madman in his desire to be killed before his comrades' eyes; Posidonius, on the contrary, without any wish to be killed, had fought hardly less bravely, and was on that account the better man. It may, of course, have been envy which made them say this; in any case, the men I mentioned all received public honors except Aristodemus—Aristodemus got nothing, because he deliberately courted death for the reason already explained.

B.   CIVIC AND MORAL LAW

In speaking of Law Demaratus assumed no distinction between what we call statutory law, based on governmental authority, and customary law, based on moral conviction. The inquiring spirit of the fifth century B.C., however, raised the question of the proper course of action for the individual faced by a situation in which the two kinds of law are in conflict. About 441 B.C. the poet Sophocles (who was shortly afterward elected an Athenian general) presented a tragedy, the *Antigone,* which reflects the contemporary interest in these ideas. The scene of the tragedy is placed by Sophocles in the city of Thebes in the mythic past. There, after the death of King Oedipus, his son Eteocles had become king. Another son, Polyneices, had then attacked Thebes at the head of a foreign army from Argos. Both brothers were killed in battle, and the invaders were defeated. Creon, uncle of the brothers, then became king.

1. *The Individual in Conflict with the State.* In the opening scene of the tragedy Antigone and Ismene, the sisters of Eteocles and Polyneices, are talking privately at dawn on the day after the battle.[3]

Antigone. My sister, my Ismene, do you know
of any suffering from our fathers sprung
that Zeus does not achieve for us survivors?
There's nothing grievous, nothing free from doom,
not shameful, not dishonored, I've not seen.
Your sufferings and mine.
And now, what of this edict which they say
the commander has proclaimed to the whole people?
Have you heard anything? Or don't you know
that the foes' trouble comes upon our friends?
  Ismene. I've heard no word, Antigone, of our friends.
Not sweet nor bitter since that single moment
when we two lost two brothers
who died on one day by a double blow.
And since the Argive army went away
this very night, I have no further news
of fortune or disaster for myself.

An. I knew it well, and brought you from the house
for just this reason, that you alone may hear.
  Is. What is it? Clearly some news has clouded you.
  An. It has indeed. Creon will give the one
of our two brothers honor in the tomb;
the other none.
Eteocles, with just entreatment treated,
as law provides he has hidden under earth
to have full honor with the dead below.
But Polyneices' corpse who died in pain,
they say he has proclaimed to the whole town
that none may bury him and none bewail,
but leave him unwept, untombed, a rich sweet sight
for the hungry birds' beholding.
Such orders they say the worthy Creon gives
to you and me—yes, yes, I say to *me*—
and that he's coming to proclaim it clear
to those who know it not.
Further: he has the matter so at heart
that anyone who dares attempt the act
will die by public stoning in the town.
So there you have it and you soon will show
if you are noble, or fallen from your descent.

Is. If things have reached this stage, what can I do,
poor sister, that will help to make or mend?
　An. Think will you share my labor and my act.
　Is. What will you risk? And where is your intent?
　An. Will you take up that corpse along with me?
　Is. To bury him you mean, when it's forbidden?
　An. My brother, and yours, though you may wish he were not.
I never shall be found to be his traitor.
　Is. O hard of mind! When Creon spoke against it!
　An. It's not for him to keep me from my own.

. . . .

　Is. We must remember that we two are women
so not to fight with men.
And that since we are subject to strong power
we must hear these orders, or any that may be worse.
So shall I ask of them beneath the earth
forgiveness, for in these things I am forced,
and shall obey the men in power. I know
that wild and futile action makes no sense.
　An. I wouldn't urge it. And if now you wished
to act, you wouldn't please me as a partner.
Be what you want to; but that man shall I
bury. For me, the doer, death is best.
Friend shall I lie with him, yes friend with friend,
when I have dared the crime of piety.
Longer the time in which to please the dead
than that for those up here.
There shall I lie forever. You may see fit
to keep from honor what the gods have honored.
　Is. I shall do no dishonor. But to act
against the citizens, I cannot.

　2. *Duty to the State.* When Creon first appears he proclaims the principles he intends to practice as king.[4]

Creon. You cannot learn of any man the soul,
the mind, and the intent until he shows
his practice of the government and law.
For I believe that who controls the state
and does not hold to the best plans of all,
but locks his tongue up through some kind of fear,
that he is worst of all who are or were.
And he who counts another greater friend
than his own fatherland, I put him nowhere.
So I—may Zeus all-seeing always know it—
could not keep silent as disaster crept
upon the town, destroying hope of safety.
Nor could I count the enemy of the land
friend to myself, not I who know so well
that she it is who saves us, sailing straight,
and only so can we have friends at all.
With such good rules shall I enlarge our state.
And now I have proclaimed their brother-edict.

In the matter of the sons of Oedipus,
citizens, know: Eteocles who died,
defending this our town with champion spear,
is to be covered in the grave and granted
all holy rites we give the noble dead.
But his brother Polyneices whom I name
the exile who came back and sought to burn
his fatherland, the gods who were his kin,
who tried to gorge on blood he shared, and lead
the rest of us as slaves—
it is announced that no one in this town
may give him burial or mourn for him.
Leave him unburied, leave his corpse disgraced,
a dinner for the birds and for the dogs.
Such is my mind. Never shall I, myself,
honor the wicked and reject the just.
The man who is well-minded to the state
from me in death and life shall have his honor.
　Chorus. This resolution, Creon, is your own,
in the matter of the traitor and the true.
For you can make such rulings as you will
about the living and about the dead.

　3. *Duty to the Gods.* The following dialogue takes place when Antigone is brought before Creon, charged with attempting to bury the body of Polyneices in defiance of Creon's edict.[5]

Creon. You—tell me not at length but in a word.
You knew the order not to do this thing?
　Antigone. I knew, of course I knew. The word was plain.
　Cre. And still you dared to overstep these laws?
　An. For me it was not Zeus who made that order.
Nor did that Justice who lives with the gods below
mark out such laws to hold among mankind.
Nor did I think your orders were so strong
that you, a mortal man, could over-run
the gods' unwritten and unfailing laws.
Not now, nor yesterday's, they always live,
and no one knows their origin in time.
So not through fear of any man's proud spirit
would I be likely to neglect these laws,
draw on myself the gods' sure punishment.
I knew that I must die; how could I not?
even without your warning. If I die
before my time, I say it is a gain.
Who lives in sorrows many as are mine
how shall he not be glad to gain his death?
And so, for me to meet this fate, no grief.
But if I left that corpse, my mother's son,
dead and unburied I'd have cause to grieve
as now I grieve not.
And if you think my acts are foolishness
the foolishness may be in a fool's eye.

. . . .

Cre. This girl was expert in her insolence
when she broke bounds beyond established law.
Once she had done it, insolence the second,
to boast her doing, and to laugh in it.
I am no man and she the man instead
if she can have this conquest without pain. . . .
I hate it too when someone caught in crime
then wants to make it seem a lovely thing.

    An. Do you want more than my arrest and death?

    Cre. No more than that. For that is all I need.

    An. Why are you waiting? Nothing that you say
fits with my thought. I pray it never will.
Nor will you ever like to hear my words.
And yet what greater glory could I find
than giving my own brother funeral?
All these [citizens of Thebes] would say that they
  approved my act
did fear not mute them.
(A king is fortunate in many ways,
and most, that he can act and speak at will.)

    Cre. None of these others see the case this way.

    An. They see, and do not say. You have them cowed.

    Cre. And you are not ashamed to think alone?

    An. No, I am not ashamed. When was it shame
to serve the children of my mother's womb?

    Cre. It was not your brother who died against him, then?

    An. Full brother, on both sides, my parents' child.

    Cre. Your act of grace, in his regard, is crime.

    An. The corpse below would never say it was.

    Cre. When you honor him and the criminal just alike?

    An. It was a brother, not a slave, who died.

    Cre. Died to destroy this land the other guarded.

    An. Death yearns for equal law for all the dead.

    Cre. Not that the good and bad draw equal shares.

    An. Who knows that this is holiness below?

    Cre. Never the enemy, even in death, a friend.

    An. I cannot share in hatred, but in love.

    Cre. Then go down there, if you must love, and love
the dead. No woman rules me while I live.

    (The conflict between Antigone and Creon
    leads to tragedy for both. Antigone dies, and
    Haemon, Creon's son who was to have
    married her, kills himself. At the end Creon
    is broken and humiliated.)

C.   THE ATHENIAN IDEAL

In 431 B.C., when the war broke out between Athens and the Peloponnesian League under Sparta's leadership, Athens was at the height of her power and prestige. Her democratic institutions were fully developed, her empire was firmly established, and her economy was prosperous. The Parthenon had just been completed on the Acropolis. Sophocles, Euripides, and Aristophanes were presenting their tragedies and comedies in the Athenian theater. Herodotus and other intellectual leaders from the rest of Greece were visiting Athens as the intellectual capital of Greece. For some twenty years Pericles had been the most influential and respected Athenian political leader. At the end of the first year of the war Pericles delivered a funeral oration in honor of the dead. This speech, as found in the contemporary historian Thucydides, provides the classic Athenian interpretation of the relation of the individual to the state.[6]

. . . . Before I praise the dead, I should like to point out by what principles of action we rose to power, and under what institutions and through what manner of life our empire became great. For I conceive that such thoughts are not unsuited to the occasion, and that this numerous assembly of citizens and strangers may profitably listen to them.

Our form of government does not enter into rivalry with the institutions of others. We do not copy our neighbors, but are an example to them. It is true that we are called a democracy, for the administration is in the hands of the many and not of the few. But while the law secures equal justice to all alike in their private disputes, the claim of excellence is also recognised; and when a citizen is in any way distinguished, he is preferred to the public service, not as a matter of privilege, but as the reward of merit. Neither is poverty a bar, but a man may benefit his country whatever be the obscurity of his condition. There is no exclusiveness in our public life, and in our private intercourse we are not suspicious of one another, nor angry with our neighbor if he does what he likes; we do not put on sour looks at him which, though harmless, are not pleasant. While we are thus unconstrained in our private intercourse, a spirit of reverence pervades our public acts; we are prevented from doing wrong by respect for the authorities and for the laws, having an especial regard to those which are ordained for the protection of the injured as well as to those unwritten laws which bring upon the transgressor of them the reprobation of the general sentiment.

And we have not forgotten to provide for our weary spirits many relaxations from toil. . . . Because of the greatness of our city the fruits of the whole earth flow in upon us; so that we enjoy the goods of other countries as freely as of our own.

Then, again, our military training is in many respects superior to that of our adversaries. Our city is thrown open to the world, and we never expel a foreigner or prevent him from seeing or learning anything of which the secret if revealed to an enemy might profit him. We rely not upon management or trickery, but upon our own hearts and hands. And in the matter of education, whereas they from early youth are always undergoing laborious exercises which are to make them brave, we live at ease, and yet are equally ready to face the perils which they face. . . .

If then we prefer to meet danger with a light heart but without laborious training, and with a courage which is gained by habit and not enforced by law, are we not greatly the gainers? Since we do not anticipate the pain, although, when the hour comes, we can be as brave as those who never allow themselves to rest; and thus too our city is equally admirable in peace and in war.

For we are lovers of the beautiful, yet simple in our tastes, and we cultivate the mind without loss of manliness. Wealth we employ, not for talk and ostentation, but when there is a real use for it. To avow poverty with us is no disgrace; the true disgrace is in doing nothing to avoid it. An Athenian citizen does not neglect the state because he takes care of his own household; and even those of us who are engaged in business have a very fair idea of politics. We alone regard a man who takes no interest in public affairs, not as a harmless, but as a useless character; and if few of us are originators, we are all sound judges of a policy. The great impediment to action is, in our opinion, not discussion, but the want of that knowledge which is gained by discussion preparatory to action. . . .

To sum up: I say that Athens is the school of Hellas, and that the individual Athenian in his own person seems to have the power of adapting himself to the most varied forms of action with the utmost versatility. . . . We shall assuredly not be without witnesses; there are mighty monuments of our power which will make us the wonder of this and of succeeding ages. . . . Such is the city for whose sake these men nobly fought and died; they could not bear the thought that she might be taken from them; and every one of us who survive should gladly toil on her behalf.

I have dwelt upon the greatness of Athens because I want to show you that we are contending for a higher prize than those who enjoy none of these privileges, and to establish by manifest proof the merit of these men whom I am now commemorating. Their loftiest praise has been already spoken. For in magnifying the city I have magnified them, and men like them whose virtues made her glorious. . . .

I would have you day by day fix your eyes upon the greatness of Athens, until you become filled with the love of her; and when you are impressed by the spectacle of her glory, reflect that this empire has been acquired by men who knew their duty and had the courage to do it, who in the hour of conflict had the fear of dishonor always present to them, and who, if ever they failed in an enterprise, would not allow their virtues to be lost to their country, but freely gave their lives to her as the fairest offering which they could present at her feast. The sacrifice which they collectively made was individually repaid to them; for they received again each one for himself a praise which grows not old, and the noblest of all sepulchres—I speak not of that in which their remains are laid, but of that in which their glory survives, and is proclaimed always and on every fitting occasion both in word and deed. For the whole earth is the sepulchre of famous men; not only are they commemorated by columns and inscriptions in their own country, but in foreign lands there dwells also an unwritten memorial of them, graven not on stone but in the hearts of men. Make them your examples, and, esteeming courage to be freedom and freedom to be happiness, do not weigh too nicely the perils of war. . . .

D.   SOCRATES AND THE SOPHISTS

During the fifth century a great variety of new intellectual interests had permeated Greece. These interests were of many kinds: philosophy, theology, and poetry; astronomy, physics, and medicine; rhetoric, politics, and history. The distinctions between fields of knowledge which we recognize had not yet been established, and all of these topics were subjects of excited popular attention, based on a conviction that knowledge was the key to successful conduct of life. Men who taught the new ideas were called Sophists. (The name meant "teachers of wisdom.") Typical of the new ideas was a theory that all things are derived from a single basic substance, that this substance is something like air, from which more solid things are derived by a process of condensation, and that this substance—being eternal and indestructible—is "divine." Sophists also taught public speaking, a subject of particular interest to young men ambitious for a career in politics and the law-courts. Since one of their techniques was the delivery of speeches on both sides of the same question, an objection raised against them was that they taught intellectual dishonesty. The Sophists had both enthusiastic admirers and bitter opponents. Socrates insisted that he was not one of them, that he was an inquirer and not a teacher. But he was interested in the new ideas, he spent his life talking with all who wished to converse with him, and his reputation for wisdom brought people to him from all parts of Greece; so it is not unnatural that popular opinion classed him with the Sophists and he was compelled to share both the admiration and the hostility directed toward them. In the ninth year of the Peloponnesian War, when Socrates was about forty-seven years old, the poet Aristophanes presented a comedy in which Socrates was burlesqued as a typical Sophist operating a school of Sophistic wisdom. The plot concerns Strepsiades, an Athenian citizen who has fallen into debt through his son's passion for horses. Strepsiades has decided to become a pupil of Socrates in order to learn how to cheat his creditors. He is presented standing in front of Socrates' "thinking-house," where he sees a man hanging in the air in a basket.[7]

Strepsiades
Hallo! who's that? that fellow in the basket?
Student of Socrates
That's HE.
Strep.
                    Who's HE?
Stud.
                                Socrates.
Strep.
                                            Socrates!
You, sir, call out to him as loud as you can.
Stud.
Call him yourself: I have not leisure now.
Strep.
                            Socrates, Socrates!
Sweet Socrates!
Socrates.
                    Mortal! why call'st thou me?
Strep.
O, first of all, please tell me what you are doing.
Soc.
I walk on air, and contem-plate the Sun.
Strep.
O then from a basket you contemn the Gods,
And not from the earth, at any rate?
Soc.
                                        Most true.
I could not have searched out celestial matters
Without suspending judgment, and infusing
My subtle spirit with the kindred air.
If from the ground I were to seek these things,
I could not find: so surely doth the earth
Draw to herself the essence of our thought.
The same too is the case with water-cress.
Strep.
                    Hillo! what's that?
Thought draws the essence into water-cress?
Come down, sweet Socrates, more near my level,
And teach the lessons which I come to learn.
Soc.
And wherefore art thou come?

Strep.
                                    To learn to speak.
For owing to my horrid debts and duns,
My goods are seized, I'm robbed, and mobbed,
    and plundered.
Soc.
How did you get involved with your eyes open?
Strep.
A galloping consumption seized my money.
Come now: do let me learn the unjust Logic
That can shirk debts: now do just let me learn it.
Name your own price, by all the Gods I'll pay it.
Soc.
The Gods! why you must know the Gods with us
Don't pass for current coin.
Strep.
                            Eh? what do you use then?
Have you got iron, as the Byzantines have?
Soc.
Come, would you like to learn celestial matters,
How their truth stands?
Strep.
                            Yes, if there's any truth.
Soc.
And to hold intercourse with yon bright Clouds,
Our virgin Goddesses?
Strep.
                            Yes, that I should.

. . . .

Soc.
These, these then alone, for true Deities own,
            the rest are all Godships of straw.
Strep.
Let Zeus be left out: He's a God beyond doubt:
            come, that you can scarcely deny.
Soc.
Zeus, indeed! there's no Zeus: don't you be so
    obtuse.
Strep.
                    No Zeus up aloft in the sky!

Then, you first must explain, who it is sends the
rain;
        or I really must think you are wrong.
Soc.
Well then, be it known, these send it alone:
        I can prove it by arguments strong.
Was there ever a shower seen to fall in an hour
        when the sky was all cloudless and blue?
Yet on a fine day, when the Clouds are away,
        he might send one, according to you.
Strep.
Well, it must be confessed, that chimes in with
the rest:
        your words I am forced to believe.
Yet before, I had dreamed that the rain-water
streamed
        from Zeus and his chamber-pot sieve.
But whence then, my friend, does the thunder
descend?
        that does make me quake with affright!
Soc.
Why 'tis they, I declare, as they roll through the
air.
Strep.
        What the Clouds? did I hear you aright?
Soc.
Ay: for when to the brim filled with water they
swim,
        by Necessity carried along,
They are hung up on high in the vault of the sky,
        and so by Necessity strong
In the midst of their course, they clash with great
force,
        and thunder away without end.
Strep.
But it is not He who compels this to be?
        does not Zeus this Necessity send?
Soc.
No Zeus have we there, but a Vortex of air.
Strep.
        What! Vortex? that's something, I own.
I knew not before, that Zeus was no more,
        but Vortex was placed on his throne!

. . . .

Soc.
Now then you agree in rejecting with me
        the Gods you believed in when young,
And *my* creed you'll embrace *"I believe in wide
space,*
        in the Clouds, in the eloquent Tongue."
Strep.
If I happened to meet other Gods in the street,
        I'd show the cold shoulder, I vow.
No libation I'll pour: not one victim more
        on their altars I'll sacrifice now.
Clouds.
Now be honest and true, and say what we shall
do:
        since you never shall fail of our aid,

If you hold us most dear in devotion and fear,
        and will ply the philosopher's trade.

. . . .

Strep.
This then will I do, confiding in you,
        for Necessity presses me sore,
And so sad is my life, 'twixt my cobs and my wife,
        that I cannot put up with it more.
So now, at your word, I give and afford
My body to these, to treat as they please,
To have and to hold, in squalor, in cold,
In hunger and thirst, yea by Zeus, at the worst,
To be flayed out of shape from my heels to my
nape
So along with my hide from my duns I escape,
And to men may appear without conscience or
fear,
Bold, hasty, and wise, a concocter of lies,
A rattler to speak, a dodger, a sneak,
A regular claw of the tables of law,
A shuffler complete, well worn in deceit,
A supple, unprincipled, troublesome cheat;
A hang-dog accurst, a bore with the worst
In the tricks of the jury-courts thoroughly versed.

    But Strepsiades proves too old and stupid.
    He fails at Socrates' school, and sends his
    son Pheidippides instead. Pheidippides' suc-
    cess is proved in the following scene.

Strep.
                    Oh! Oh!
Help! Murder! Help! O neighbors, kinsfolk,
townsmen,
Help, one and all against this base assault,
Ah! Ah! my cheek! my head! O luckless me!
Wretch! do you strike your father?
Pheid.
                Yes, Papa.
Strep.
See! See! he owns he struck me.
Pheid.
               To be sure.
Strep.
Scoundrel! and parricide! and house-breaker!
Pheid.
Thank you: go on, go on: do please go on.
I am quite delighted to be called such names!

. . . .

Strep.
Strike you your father?
Pheid.
          O dear yes: what's more,
I'll prove I struck you justly.
Strep.
          Struck me justly!
Villain! how can you strike a father justly?

. . . .

Pheid.
How sweet it is these novel arts,
         these clever words to know,
And have the power established rules
         and laws to overthrow.
Why in old times when horses were
         my sole delight, 'twas wonder
If I could say a dozen words
         without some awful blunder!
But now that he has made me quit
         that reckless mode of living,
And I have been to subtle thoughts
         my whole attention giving,
I hope to prove by logic strict
         'tis right to beat my father.
Strep.
O! buy your horses back, by Zeus,
         since I would ten times rather
Have to support a four-in-hand,
         so I be struck no more.
Pheid.
Peace. I will now resume the thread
         where I broke off before.
And first I ask: when I was young,
         did you not strike me then?
Strep.
Yea: for I loved and cherished you.
Pheid.
         Well, solve me this again,
Is it not just that I your son
         should cherish you alike,
And strike you, since, as you observe,
         to cherish means to strike?

. . . .

Strep.
Good friends! I really think he has
         some reason to complain.
I must concede he has put the case
         in quite a novel light:
I really think we should be flogged
         unless we act aright!
Pheid.
Look to a fresh idea then.
Strep.
         He'll be my death I vow.
Pheid.
Yet then perhaps you will not grudge
         ev'n what you suffer now.
Strep.
How! will you make me like the blows
         which I've received to-day?

Pheid.
Yes, for I'll beat my mother too.
Strep.
         What! What is that you say!
Why, this is worse than all.
Pheid.
         But what, if as I proved the other,
By the same Logic I can prove
         'tis right to beat my mother?

. . . .

Strep.
Oh! fool, fool, fool, how mad I must have been
to cast away the Gods, for Socrates. . . .
And someone fetch me here a lighted torch,
And I'll soon see if, boasters as they are,
They won't repent of what they've done to me.
Student 1.
O dear! O dear!
Strep.
Now, now, my torch, send out a lusty flame.
Student 1.
Man! what are you at there?
Strep.
         What am I at? I'll tell you.
I'm splitting straws with your house-rafters here.
Student 2.
Oh me! who's been and set our house on fire?
Strep.
Who was it, think you, that you stole the cloak
  from?
Student 3.
O Murder! Murder!
Strep.
         That's the very thing,
Unless this pick prove traitor to my hopes
Or I fall down, and break my blessed neck.
Soc.
Hallo! what are you at, up on our roof?
Strep.
I walk on air, and contemplate the Sun.
Soc.
O! I shall suffocate. O, dear! O dear!
Student.
And I, poor devil, shall be burnt to death.
Strep.
For with what aim did ye insult the Gods,
And pry around the dwellings of the Moon?
Strike, smite them, spare them not, for many
  reasons,
BUT MOST BECAUSE THEY HAVE BLAS-
PHEMED THE GODS!

Part II.   THE TRIAL OF SOCRATES

A.   SOCRATES' SELF-DEFENSE

Two factors appear to have led the leaders of the newly restored Athenian democracy to bring Socrates to trial. One was his known friendship with some of the Thirty Tyrants who had aroused so much popular opposition. This could not, however, be included in the charges against him because an act of amnesty had been passed granting general pardon for past acts of a political nature. Nevertheless a strong residue of hatred for the supporters of the Tyrants remained; it was suspected that by years of secret treason they had been responsible for the lost war, and popular hostility was directed against all who were in any way associated with them. The result was that some of the bitterness following defeat and revolution was directed against Socrates. A second factor weighing against him was the conservative opposition to the new ideas of the Sophists—also associated with Socrates in the popular mind, as Aristophanes' *Clouds* shows. Socrates was seventy years old when he was brought to trial. It is generally believed that his enemies hoped that the threat of trial would cause him to go into exile; but he chose instead to use the trial as an opportunity to explain the principles which had guided the conduct of his life. The court before which he had to plead was representative of Athens. It consisted of 500 citizens who had been chosen by lot. They combined the functions of judge and of jury in an American court; they decided not only questions of fact, as do our juries, but also questions of law, as do our judges. The assignment of such broad responsibilities to ordinary citizens was possible because in Athens they could be assumed to have a thorough acquaintance with the law. They themselves debated and enacted the laws in the popular assembly. The laws were comparatively few and simple. They were inscribed on stone in places where they were constantly before men's eyes. Each case was decided solely with reference to the law and the facts; precedents in the form of previous decisions and interpretations were not binding. Since Athenian practice required that both prosecutors and defendants must plead their own cases, and since Athenians were notoriously fond of "going to court," prudence required that every man should be capable of serving as his own lawyer. It was therefore a highly sophisticated jury before which Socrates spoke.

1. *The Indictment.* The words of the indictment against Socrates have been reported as follows by Diogenes Laertius, a writer of late antiquity.[8]

This indictment is brought by Meletus, son of Meletus, of Pittheus against Socrates, son of Sophroniscus, of Alopece: Socrates is guilty of failing to honor the gods whom the city honors, and of introducing other new divinities; he is also guilty of corrupting the young.

2. *The Defense.* Meletus, Socrates' accuser, was supported in court by Lycon and Anytus. Meletus and Lycon are obscure persons, but Anytus was a leading figure in the reestablished democracy, with a reputation as a political moderate. We do not have an actual record of what Socrates said in his own defense, but we do have the speech of Socrates as it appears in the *Apology* of his younger friend Plato, who was present at the trial. We cannot know how closely Plato's version follows what Socrates in fact said. But it is in Plato's record that the memory of Socrates has lived and become a permanent part of European thought.[9]

How you, O Athenians, have been affected by my accusers, I cannot tell; but I know that they almost made me forget who I was—so persuasively did they speak; and yet they have hardly uttered a word of truth. . . .

First, I have to reply to the older charges and to my first accusers, and then I will go on to the later ones. For of old I have had many accusers, who have accused me falsely to you during many years; and I am more afraid of them than of Anytus and his associates, who are dangerous, too, in their own way. But far more dangerous are the others, who began when you were children, and took possession of your minds with their falsehoods, telling of one Socrates, a wise man, who speculated about the heaven above, and searched into the earth beneath, and made the worse appear the better cause. The disseminators of this tale are the accusers whom I dread; for their hearers are apt to fancy that such enquirers do not believe in the existence of the gods. And they are many, and their charges against me are of ancient date, and they were made by them in the days when you were more impressible than you are now—in childhood, or it may have been in youth—and the cause when heard went by default, for there was none to answer. And hardest of all, I do not know and cannot tell the names of my accusers; unless in the chance case of a comic poet. All who from envy and malice have persuaded you—some of them having first convinced themselves—all this class of men are most difficult to deal with; for I cannot have them up here, and cross-examine them, and therefore I must simply fight with shadows in my own defense, and argue when there is no one who answers. I will ask you then to assume with me, as I was saying, that my opponents are of two kinds; one recent, the other ancient: and I hope that you will see the propriety of my answering the latter first, for these accusations you heard long before the others, and much oftener. . . .

I will begin at the beginning, and ask what is the accusation which has given rise to the slander of me, and in fact has encouraged Meletus to prefer this charge against me. Well, what do the slanderers say? They shall be my prosecutors, and I will sum up their words in an affidavit: "Socrates is an evildoer, and a curious person, who searches into things under the earth and in heaven, and he makes the worse appear the better cause; and he teaches the aforesaid doctrines to others." Such is the nature of the accusation: it is just what you have yourselves seen in the comedy of Aristophanes, who has introduced a man whom he calls Socrates, going about and saying that he walks in air, and talking a deal of nonsense concerning matters of which I do not pretend to know either much or little—not that I mean to speak disparagingly of any one who is a student of natural philosophy. I should be very sorry if Meletus could bring so grave a charge against me. But the simple truth is, O Athenians, that I have nothing to do with physical speculations. . . .

As little foundation is there for the report that I am a teacher, and take money; this accusation has no more truth in it than the other. Although, if a man were really able to instruct mankind, to receive money for giving instruction would, in my opinion, be an honor to him. . . . Had I such wisdom I should have been very proud and conceited; but the truth is that I have no knowledge of the kind.

I dare say, Athenians, that some one among you will reply, "Yes, Socrates, but what is the origin of these accusations which are brought against you; there must have been something strange which you have been doing? All these rumors and this talk about you would never have arisen if you had been like other men: tell us, then, what is the cause of them, for we should be sorry to judge hastily of you." Now, I regard this as a fair challenge, and I will endeavor to explain to you the reason why I am called wise and have such an evil fame. Please to attend then. And although some of you may think that I am joking, I declare that I will tell you the entire truth. Men of Athens, this reputation of mine has come of a certain sort of wisdom which I possess. If you ask me what kind of wisdom, I reply, wisdom such as may perhaps be attained by man, for to that extent I am inclined to believe that I am wise; whereas the persons of whom I was speaking have a superhuman wisdom, which I may fail to describe, because I have it not myself; and he who says that I have, speaks falsely, and is taking away my character. And here, O men of Athens, I must beg you not to interrupt me, even if I seem to say something extravagant. For the word which I will speak is not mine. I will refer you to a witness who is worthy of credit; that witness shall be the god of Delphi—he will tell you about my wisdom, if I have any, and of what sort it is. You must have known Chaerephon; he was early a friend of mine, and also a friend of yours, for he shared in the recent exile of the people, and returned with you. Well, Chaerephon, as you know, was very impetuous in all his doings, and he went to Delphi and boldly asked the oracle to tell him whether—as I was saying, I must beg you not to interrupt—he asked the oracle to tell him whether any one was wiser than I was, and the Pythian prophetess answered, that there was no man wiser. Chaerephon is dead himself; but his brother, who is in court, will confirm the truth of what I am saying.

Why do I mention this? Because I am going to explain to you why I have such an evil name. When I heard the answer, I said to myself, What can the god mean? and what is the interpretation of his riddle? for I know that I have no wisdom, small or great. What then can he mean when he says that I am the wisest of men? And yet he is a god, and cannot lie; that would be against his nature. After long consideration, I thought of a method of trying the question. I reflected that if I could only find a man wiser than myself, then I might go to the god with a refutation in my hand. I should say to him, "Here is a man who is wiser than I am; but you said that I was the wisest." Accordingly I went to one who had the reputation of wisdom, and observed him—his name I need not mention; he was a politician whom I selected for examination—and the result was as follows: When I began to talk with him, I could not help thinking that he was not really wise, although he was thought wise by many, and still wiser by himself; and thereupon I tried to explain to him that he thought himself wise, but was not really wise; and the consequence was that he hated me, and his enmity was shared by several who were present and heard me. . . .

Then I went to one man after another, being not unconscious of the enmity which I provoked, and I lamented and feared this: but necessity was laid upon me—the word of God, I thought, ought to be considered first. And I said to myself, Go I must to all who appear to know, and find out the meaning of the oracle. And I swear to you, Athenians, by the dog I swear!—for I must tell you the truth—the result of my mission was just this: I found that the men most in repute were all but the most foolish; and that others less esteemed were really wiser and better. . . .

This inquisition has led to my having many enemies of the worst and most dangerous kind, and has given occasion also to many calumnies. And I am called wise, for my hearers always imagine that I myself possess the wisdom which I find wanting in others: but the truth is, O men of Athens, that God only is wise; and by his answer he intends to show that the wisdom of men is worth little or nothing; he is not speaking of Socrates, he is only using my name by way of illustration, as if he said, He, O men, is the wisest, who, like Socrates, knows that his wisdom is in truth worth nothing. And so I go about the world obedient to the god, and search and make enquiry into the wisdom of any one, whether citizen or stranger, who appears to be wise; and if he is not wise, then in vindication of the oracle I show him that he is not wise; and my occupation quite absorbs me, and I have no time to give either to any public matter of interest or to any concern of my own, but I am in utter poverty by reason of my devotion to the god.

There is another thing:—young men of the richer classes, who have not much to do, come about me of their own accord; they like to hear the pretenders examined, and they often imitate me, and proceed to examine others; there are plenty of persons, as they quickly discover, who think that they know something, but really know little or nothing; and then those who are examined by them instead of being angry with themselves are angry with me: This confounded Socrates, they say; this villainous misleader of youth!—and then if somebody asks them, Why, what evil does he practise or teach? they do not know, and cannot tell; but in order that they may not appear to be at a loss, they repeat the ready-made charges which are used against all philosophers about teaching things up in the clouds and under the earth, and having no gods,

and making the worse appear the better cause; for they do not like to confess that their pretence of knowledge has been detected—which is the truth; and as they are numerous and ambitious and energetic, and are drawn up in battle array and have persuasive tongues, they have filled your ears with their loud and inveterate calumnies. . . .

I have said enough in my defense against the first class of my accusers; I turn to the second class. They are headed by Meletus, that good man and true lover of his country, as he calls himself. Against these, too, I must try to make a defense:—Let their affidavit be read: it contains something of this kind: It says that Socrates is a doer of evil, who corrupts the youth; and who does not believe in the gods of the State, but has other new divinities of his own. Such is the charge; and now let us examine the particular counts. . . .

(In a part here omitted, Socrates questions Meletus, undertaking to show that the charge of corrupting the youth is nonsense and that of unorthodoxy false.)

I have said enough in answer to the charge of Meletus: any elaborate defense is unnecessary; but I know only too well how many are the enmities which I have incurred, and this is what will be my destruction if I am destroyed;—not Meletus, nor yet Anytus, but the envy and detraction of the world, which has been the death of many good men, and will probably be the death of many more; there is no danger of my being the last of them.

Some one will say: And are you not ashamed, Socrates, of a course of life which is likely to bring you to an untimely end? To him I may fairly answer: There you are mistaken: a man who is good for anything ought not to calculate the chance of living or dying; he ought only to consider whether in doing anything he is doing right or wrong—acting the part of a good man or of a bad. . . . Strange, indeed, would be my conduct, O men of Athens, if I, who, when I was ordered by the generals whom you chose to command me at Potidaea and Amphipolis and Delium, remained where they placed me, like any other man, facing death—if now, when, as I conceive and imagine, God orders me to fulfil the philosopher's mission of searching into myself and other men, I were to desert my post through fear of death, or any other fear; that would indeed be strange, and I might justly be arraigned in court for denying the existence of the gods, if I disobeyed the oracle because I was afraid of death, fancying that I was wise when I was not wise. For the fear of death is indeed the pretence of wisdom, and not real wisdom, being a pretence of knowing the unknown; and no one knows whether death, which men in their fear apprehend to be the greatest evil, may not be the greatest good. Is not this ignorance of a disgraceful sort, the ignorance which is the conceit that a man knows what he does not know? And in this respect only I believe myself to differ from men in general, and may perhaps claim to be wiser than they are:—that whereas I know but little of the world below, I do not suppose that I know: but I do know that injustice and disobedience to a better, whether God or man, is evil and dishonorable, and I will never fear or avoid a possible good rather than a certain evil. And therefore if you let me go now, and are not convinced by Anytus, who said that since I had been prosecuted I must be put to death; (or if not that I ought never to have been prosecuted at all); and that if I escape now, your sons will all be utterly ruined by listening to my words—if you say to me, Socrates, this time we will not mind Anytus, and you shall be let off, but upon one condition, that you are not to enquire and speculate in this way any more, and that if you are caught doing so again you shall die;—if this was the condition on which you let me go, I should reply: Men of Athens, I honor and love you; but I shall obey God rather than you, and while I have life and strength I shall never cease from the practice and teaching of philosophy, exhorting any one whom I meet and saying to him after my manner: You, my friend,—a citizen of the great and mighty and wise city of Athens,—are you not ashamed of heaping up the greatest amount of money and honor and reputation, and caring so little about wisdom and truth and the greatest improvement of the soul, which you never regard or heed at all? And if the person with whom I am arguing, says: Yes, but I do care; then I do not leave him or let him go at once; but I proceed to interrogate and examine and cross-examine him, and if I think that he has no virtue in him, but only says that he has, I reproach him with undervaluing the greater, and overvaluing the less. And I shall repeat the same words to every one whom I meet, young and old, citizen and alien, but especially to the citizens, inasmuch as they are my brethren. For know that this is the command of God; and I believe that no greater good has ever happened in the State than my service to the God. For I do nothing but go about persuading you all, old and young alike, not to take thought for your persons or your properties, but first and chiefly to care about the greatest improvement of the soul. I tell you that virtue is not given by money, but that from virtue comes money and every other good of man, public as well as private. This is my teaching, and if this is the doctrine which corrupts the youth, I am a mischievous person. But if any one says that this is not my teaching, he is speaking an untruth. Wherefore, O men of Athens, I say to you, do as Anytus bids or not as Anytus bids, and either acquit me or not; but whichever you do, understand that I shall never alter my ways, not even if I have to die many times.

Men of Athens, do not interrupt, but hear me; there was an understanding between us that you should hear me to the end: I have something more to say, at which you may be inclined to cry out; but I believe that to hear me will be good for you, and therefore I beg that you will not cry out. I would have you know, that if you kill such an one as I am, you will injure yourselves more than you will injure me. Nothing will injure me, not Meletus nor yet Anytus—they cannot, for a bad man is not permitted to injure a better than himself. I do not deny that Anytus may, perhaps, kill him, or drive him into exile, or deprive him of civil rights; and he may imagine, and others may imagine, that he is inflicting a great injury upon him: but there I do not agree. For the evil of doing as he is doing—the evil of unjustly taking away the life of another—is greater far.

And now, Athenians, I am not going to argue for my own sake, as you may think, but for yours, that you may not sin against the God by condemning me, who am his gift to you. For if you kill me you will not easily find a successor to me, who, if I may use such a ludicrous figure of speech, am a sort of gadfly, given to the State by God; and the State is a great and noble steed who is tardy in his motions owing to his very size, and requires to be stirred into life. I am that gadfly which God has attached to the State, and all day long and in all places am always fastening upon you, arousing and persuading and reproaching you. You will not easily find another like me, and therefore I would advise you to spare me. . . .

Some one may wonder why I go about in private giving advice and busying myself with the concerns of others, but do not venture to come forward in public and advise the State. I will tell you why. You have heard me speak at sundry times and in divers places of an oracle or sign which comes to me, and is the divinity which Meletus ridicules in the indictment. This sign, which is a kind of voice, first began to come to me when I was a child; it always forbids but never commands me to do anything which I am going to do. This is what deters me from being a politician. And rightly, as I think. For I am certain, O men of Athens, that if I had engaged in politics, I should have perished long ago, and done no good either to you or to myself. And do not be offended at my telling you the truth: for the truth is, that no man who goes to war with you or any other multitude, honestly striving against the many lawless and unrighteous deeds which are done in a State, will save his life; he who will fight for the right, if he would live even for a brief space, must have a private station and not a public one.

I can give you convincing evidence of what I say, not words only, but what you value far more—actions. . . . When the oligarchy of the Thirty was in power, they sent for me and four others into the rotunda, and bade us bring Leon the Salaminian from Salamis, as they wanted to put him to death. This was a specimen of the sort of commands which they were always giving with the view of implicating as many as possible in their crimes; and then I showed, not in word only but in deed, that, if I may be allowed to use such an expression, I cared not a straw for death, and that my great and only care was lest I should do an unrighteous or unholy thing. For the strong arm of that oppressive power did not frighten me into doing wrong; and when we came out of the rotunda the other four went to Salamis and fetched Leon, but I went quietly home. For which I might have lost my life, had not the power of the Thirty shortly afterwards come to an end. And many will witness to my words.

Now, do you really imagine that I could have survived all these years, if I had led a public life, supposing that like a good man I had always maintained the right and had made justice, as I ought, the first thing? No, indeed, men of Athens, neither I nor any other man. But I have been always the same in all my actions, public as well as private, and never have I yielded any base compliance to those who are slanderously termed my disciples, or to any other. Not that I have any regular disciples. But if any one likes to come and hear me while I am pursuing my mission, whether he be young or old, he is not excluded. . . . If I am or have been corrupting the youth, those of them who are now grown up and have become sensible that I gave them bad advice in the days of their youth should come forward as accusers, and take their revenge; or if they do not like to come themselves, some of their relatives, fathers, brothers, or other kinsmen, should say what evil their families have suffered at my hands. Now is their time. Many of them I see in the court. . . . Nay, Athenians, the very opposite is the truth. For all these are ready to witness on behalf of the corrupter, of the injurer of their kindred, as Meletus and Anytus call me; not the corrupted youth only—there might have been a motive for that—but their uncorrupted elder relatives. Why should they too support me with their testimony? Why, indeed, ex-

cept for the sake of truth and justice, and because they know that I am speaking the truth, and that Meletus is a liar.

Well, Athenians, this and the like of this is all the defense which I have to offer. Yet a word more. Perhaps there may be some one who is offended at me, when he calls to mind how he himself on a similar, or even a less serious occasion, prayed and entreated the judges with many tears, and how he produced his children in court, which was a moving spectacle, together with a host of relations and friends; whereas I, who am probably in danger of my life, will do none of these things. . . .

Setting aside the question of public opinion, there seems to be something wrong in asking a favor of a judge, and thus procuring an acquittal, instead of informing and convincing him. For his duty is, not to make a present of justice, but to give judgment; and he has sworn that he will judge according to the laws, and not according to his own good pleasure; and we ought not to encourage you, nor should you allow yourselves to be encouraged, in this habit of perjury—there can be no piety in that. Do not then require me to do what I consider dishonorable and impious and wrong, especially now, when I am being tried for impiety on the indictment of Meletus. For if, O men of Athens, by force of persuasion and entreaty I could overpower your oaths, then I should be teaching you to believe that there are no gods, and in defending should simply convict myself of the charge of not believing in them. But that is not so—far otherwise. For I do believe that there are gods, and in a sense higher than that in which any of my accusers believe in them. And to you and to God I commit my cause, to be determined by you as is best for you and me.

3. *The Verdict.* Socrates was found guilty by a vote of 280 to 220. The prosecution demanded the penalty of death. The law provided for the defendant to propose an alternate penalty; the jury had then to choose one of the two punishments proposed. It was expected that Socrates would propose exile, which would probably have been accepted by the court. Instead he suggested only a moderate fine, and coupled this with a suggestion that what he really deserved was support at public expense for the rest of his life, as a public benefactor. The judges were so annoyed by what appeared to them as arrogance that they voted a sentence of death by a majority of 360 to 140. After the sentence Socrates spoke again, concluding with words addressed to his friends.[10]

Friends, who would have acquitted me, I would like also to talk with you about the thing which has come to pass, while the magistrates are busy, and before I go to the place at which I must die. Stay then a little, for we may as well talk with one another while there is time. You are my friends, and I should like to show you the meaning of this event which has happened to me. O my judges—for you I may truly call judges—I should like to tell you of a wonderful circumstance. Hitherto the divine faculty of which the internal oracle is the source has constantly been in the habit of opposing me even about trifles, if I was going to make a slip or error in any matter; and now as you see there has come upon me that which may be thought, and is generally believed to be, the last and worst evil. But the oracle made no sign of opposition, either when I was leaving my house in the morning, or when I was on my way to the court, or while I was speaking, at anything which I was going to say; and yet I have often been stopped in the middle of a speech, but now in nothing I either said or did touching the matter in hand has the oracle opposed me. What do I take to be the explanation of this silence? I will tell you. It is an intimation that what has happened to me is a good, and that those of us who think that death is an evil are in error. For the customary sign would surely have opposed me had I been going to evil and not to good.

Wherefore, O judges, be of good cheer about death, and know of a certainty, that no evil can happen to a good man, either in life or after death. He and his are not neglected by the gods; nor has my own approaching end happened by mere chance. But I see clearly that the time had arrived when it was better for me to die and be released from trouble; wherefore the oracle gave no sign. For which reason, also, I am not angry with my condemners, or with my accusers; they have done me no harm, although they did not mean to do me any good; and for this I may gently blame them.

Still, I have a favor to ask of them. When my sons are grown up, I would ask you, O my friends, to punish them; and I would have you trouble them, as I have troubled you, if they seem to care about riches, or anything, more than about virtue; or if they pretend to be something when they are really nothing,—then reprove them, as I have reproved you, for not caring about that for which they ought to care, and thinking that they are something when they are really nothing. And if you do this, both I and my sons will have received justice at your hands.

The hour of departure has arrived, and we go our ways—I to die, and you to live. Which is better God only knows.

B.   ## SOCRATES' DEFENSE OF THE LAWS

Execution by administering hemlock poison usually followed conviction within twenty-four hours. But Socrates' trial had occurred just after a sacred ship had sailed to the island of Delos on an annual mission of religious purification; during its absence no executions were permitted. Socrates therefore waited in prison for a month, until the ship should return. He was permitted visits from his friends, and they made plans for his escape. In a dialogue of Plato, the *Crito*, Socrates is presented discussing with his friend Crito the question whether he should accept this opportunity offered to him.[11]

Socrates. Why have you come at this hour, Crito? it must be quite early?

Crito. Yes, certainly.

Soc. What is the exact time?

Cr. The dawn is breaking.

Soc. I wonder that the keeper of the prisoner would let you in.

Cr. He knows me, because I often come, Socrates; moreover, I have done him a kindness.

Soc. And are you only just arrived?

Cr. No, I came some time ago.

Soc. Then why did you sit and say nothing, instead of at once awakening me?

Cr. I should not have liked myself, Socrates, to be in such great trouble and unrest as you are—indeed I should not: I have been watching with amazement your peaceful slumbers; and for that reason I did not awake you, because I wished to minimize the pain. I have always thought you to be of a happy disposition; but never did I see anything like the easy, tranquil manner in which you bear this calamity. . . . But oh! my beloved Socrates, let me entreat you once more to take my advice and escape. . . . There are persons who are willing to get you out of prison at no great cost; and as for the informers, they are far from being exorbitant in their demands—a little money will satisfy them. My means, which are certainly ample, are at your service, and if you have a scruple about spending all mine, here are strangers who will give you the use of theirs; and one of them, Simmias the Theban, has brought a large sum of money for this very purpose; and Cebes and many others are prepared to spend their money in helping you to escape. . . . Nor can I think that you are at all justified, Socrates, in betraying your own life when you might be saved; in acting thus you are playing into the hands of your enemies, who are hurrying on your destruction. And further I should say that you are deserting your own children; for you might bring them up and educate them; instead of which you go away and leave them, and they will have to take their chance; and if they do not meet with the usual fate of orphans, there will be small thanks to you. No man should bring children into the world who is unwilling to persevere to the end in their nurture and education. But you appear to be choosing the easier part, not the better and manlier, which would have been more becoming in one who professes to care for virtue in all his actions, like yourself. And, indeed, I am ashamed not only of you, but of us who are your friends, when I reflect that the whole business will be attributed entirely to our want of courage. The trial need never have come on, or might have been managed differently; and this last act, or crowning folly, will seem to have occurred through our negligence and cowardice, who might have saved you, if we had been good for anything; and you might have saved yourself, for there was no difficulty at all. See now, Socrates, how sad and discreditable are the consequences, both to us and you. Make up your mind, then, or rather have your mind already made up, for the time of deliberation is over, and there is only one thing to be done, which must be done this very night, and if we delay at all will be no longer practicable or possible; I beseech you therefore, Socrates, be persuaded by me, and do as I say.

Soc. Dear Crito, your zeal is invaluable, if a right one; but if wrong, the greater the zeal the greater the danger; and therefore we ought to consider whether I shall or shall not do as you say. For I am and always have been one of those natures who must be guided by reason, whatever the reason may be which upon reflection appears to me to be the best; and now that this chance has befallen me, I cannot repudiate my own words: the principles which I have hitherto honored and revered I still honor, and unless we can at once find other and better principles, I am certain not to agree with you. . . . If I am clearly right in escaping, then I will make the attempt; but if not, I will abstain. The other considerations which you mention, of money and loss of character and the duty of educating one's children, are, I fear, only the doctrines of the multitude, who would be as ready to restore people to life, if they were able, as they are to put them to death—and with as little reason. But now, since the argument has thus far prevailed, the only question which remains to be considered is, whether we shall do rightly either in escaping

or in suffering others to aid in our escape and paying them in money and thanks, or whether in reality we shall not do rightly; and if the latter, then death or any other calamity which may ensue on my remaining here must not be allowed to enter into the calculation.

Cr. I think that you are right, Socrates; how then shall we proceed?

Soc. Let us consider the matter together, and do you either refute me if you can, and I will be convinced; or else cease, my dear friend, from repeating to me that I ought to escape against the wishes of the Athenians: for I highly value your attempts to persuade me to do so, but I may not be persuaded against my own better judgment. And now please to consider my first position, and try how you can best answer me.

Cr. I will.

Soc. Are we to say that we are never intentionally to do wrong, or that in one way we ought and in another way we ought not to do wrong, or is doing wrong always evil and dishonorable, as I was just now saying, and as has been already acknowledged by us? Are all our former admissions which were made within a few days to be thrown away? And have we, at our age, been earnestly discoursing with one another all our life long only to discover that we are no better than children? Or, in spite of the opinion of the many, and in spite of consequences whether better or worse, shall we insist on the truth of what was then said, that injustice is always an evil and dishonor to him who acts unjustly? Shall we say so or not?

Cr. Yes.

Soc. Then we must do no wrong?

Cr. Certainly not.

Soc. Nor when injured injure in return, as the many imagine; for we must injure no one at all?

Cr. Clearly not.

Soc. Again, Crito, may we do evil?

Cr. Surely not, Socrates.

Soc. And what of doing evil in return for evil, which is the morality of the many—is that just or not?

Cr. Not just.

Soc. For doing evil to another is the same as injuring him?

Cr. Very true.

Soc. Then we ought not to retaliate or render evil for evil to any one, whatever evil we may have suffered from him. But I would have you consider, Crito, whether you really mean what you are saying. For this opinion has never been held, and never will be held, by any considerable number of persons; and those who are agreed and those who are not agreed upon this point have no common ground, and can only despise one another when they see how widely they differ. Tell me, then, whether you agree with and assent to my first principle, that neither injury nor retaliation nor warding off evil by evil is ever right. And shall that be the premiss of our argument? Or do you decline and dissent from this? For so I have ever thought, and continue to think; but, if you are of another opinion, let me hear what you have to say. If, however, you remain of the same mind as formerly, I will proceed to the next step.

Cr. You may proceed, for I have not changed my mind.

Soc. Then I will go on to the next point, which may be put in the form of a question: Ought a man to do what he admits to be right, or ought he to betray the right?

Cr. He ought to do what he thinks right.

Soc. But if this is true, what is the application? In leaving the prison against the will of the Athenians, do I wrong any? or rather do I not wrong those whom I ought least to wrong? Do I not desert the principles which were acknowledged by us to be just—what do you say?

Cr. I cannot tell, Socrates; for I do not know.

Soc. Then consider the matter in this way: Imagine that I am about to play truant (you may call the proceeding by any name which you like), and the laws and the government come and interrogate me: "Tell us, Socrates," they say; "what are you about? are you not going by an act of yours to overturn us—the laws, and the whole State, as far as in you lies? Do you imagine that a State can subsist and not be overthrown, in which the decisions of law have no power, but are set aside and trampled upon by individuals?" What will be our answer, Crito, to these and the like words? Any one, and especially a rhetorician, will have a good deal to say on behalf of the law which requires a sentence to be carried out. He will argue that this law should not be set aside; and shall we reply, "Yes; but the State has injured us and given an unjust sentence." Suppose I say that?

Cr. Very good, Socrates.

Soc. "And was that our agreement with you?" the law would answer; "or were you to abide by the sentence of the State?" And if I were to express my astonishment at their words, the law would probably add: "Answer, Socrates, instead of opening your eyes—you are in the habit of asking and answering questions. Tell us, What complaint have you to make against us which justifies you in attempting to destroy us and the State? In the first place did we not bring you into existence? Your father married your mother by our aid and begat you. Say whether you have any objection to urge against those of us who regulate marriage?" None, I should reply. "Or against those of us who after birth regulate the nurture

and education of children, in which you also were trained? Were not the laws which have the charge of education, right in commanding your father to train you in music and gymnastic?" Right, I should reply. . . . "Because we think right to destroy you, do you think that you have any right to destroy us in return, and your country as far as in you lies? Will you, O professor of true virtue, pretend that you are justified in this? Has a philosopher like you failed to discover that our country is more to be valued and higher and holier far than mother or father or any ancestor, and more to be regarded in the eyes of the gods and of men of understanding? also to be soothed, and gently and reverently entreated when angry, even more than a father, and either to be persuaded, or if not persuaded, to be obeyed? And when we are punished by her, whether with imprisonment or stripes, the punishment is to be endured in silence; and if she lead us to wounds or death in battle, thither we follow as is right; neither may any one yield or retreat or leave his rank, but whether in battle or in a court of law, or in any other place, he must do what his city and his country order him; or he must change their view of what is just: and if he may do no violence to his father or mother, much less may he do violence to his country." What answer shall we make to this, Crito? Do the laws speak truly, or do they not?

Cr. I think that they do.

Soc. Then the laws will say: "Consider, Socrates, if we are speaking truly that in your present attempt you are going to do us an injury. For, having brought you into the world, and nurtured and educated you, and given you and every other citizen a share in every good which we had to give, we further proclaim to any Athenian by the liberty which we allow him, that if he does not like us when he has become of age and has seen the ways of the city, and made our acquaintance, he may go where he pleases and take his goods with him. None of us laws will forbid him or interfere with him. Any one who does not like us and the city, and who wants to emigrate to a colony or to any other city, may go where he likes, retaining his property. . . . There is clear proof," they will say, "Socrates, that we and the city were not displeasing to you. Of all Athenians you have been the most constant resident in the city, which, as you never leave, you may be supposed to love. For you never went out of the city either to see the games, except once when you went to the Isthmus, or to any other place unless when you were on military service; nor did you travel as other men do. Nor had you any curiosity to know other States or their laws: your affections did not go beyond us and our State; we were your special favorites, and you acquiesced in our government of you; and here in this city you begat your children, which is a proof of your satisfaction. Moreover, you might in the course of the trial, if you had liked, have fixed the penalty at banishment; the State which refuses to let you go now would have let you go then. But you pretended that you preferred death to exile, and that you were not unwilling to die. And now you have forgotten these fine sentiments, and pay no respect to us, the laws, of whom you are the destroyer; and are doing what only a miserable slave would do, running away and turning your back upon the compacts and agreements which you made as a citizen. And, first of all, answer this very question: Are we right in saying that you agreed to be governed according to us in deed, and not in word only? Is that true or not?" How shall we answer, Crito? Must we not assent?

Cr. We cannot help it, Socrates.

Soc. Then will they not say . . . "Just consider, if you transgress and err in this sort of way, what good will you do either to yourself or to your friends? That your friends will be driven into exile and deprived of citizenship, or will lose their property, is tolerably certain; and you yourself, if you fly to one of the neighboring cities, as, for example, Thebes or Megara, both of which are well governed, will come to them as an enemy, Socrates, and their government will be against you, and all patriotic citizens will cast an evil eye upon you as a subverter of the laws, and you will confirm in the minds of the judges the justice of their own condemnation of you. For he who is a corrupter of the laws is more than likely to be a corrupter of the young and foolish portion of mankind. Will you then flee from well-ordered cities and virtuous men? and is existence worth having on these terms? Or will you go to them without shame, and talk to them, Socrates? And what will you say to them? What you say here about virtue and justice and institutions and laws being the best things among men? Would

that be decent of you? Surely not. But if you go away from well-governed States to Crito's friends in Thessaly, where there is great disorder and licence, they will be charmed to hear the tale of your escape from prison, set off with ludicrous particulars of the manner in which you were wrapped in a goatskin or some other disguise, and metamorphosed as the manner is of runaways; but will there be no one to remind you that in your old age you were not ashamed to violate the most sacred laws from a miserable desire of a little more life? . . .

"Listen, then, Socrates, to us who have brought you up. Think not of life and children first, and of justice afterwards, but of justice first, that you may be justified before the princes of the world below. For neither will you nor any that belong to you be happier or holier or juster in this life, or happier in another, if you do as Crito bids. Now you depart in innocence, a sufferer and not a doer of evil; a victim, not of the laws but of men. But if you go forth, returning evil for evil, and injury for injury, breaking the covenants and agreements which you have made with us and wronging those whom you ought least of all to wrong, that is to say, yourself, your friends, your country, and us, we shall be angry with you while you live, and our brethren, the laws in the world below, will receive you as an enemy; for they will know that you have done your best to destroy us. Listen, then, to us and not to Crito."

This, dear Crito, is the voice which I seem to hear murmuring in my ears, like the sound of the flute in the ears of the mystic; that voice, I say, is humming in my ears, and prevents me from hearing any other. And I know that anything more which you may say will be vain. Yet speak, if you have anything to say.

Cr. I have nothing to say, Socrates.

Soc. Leave me then, Crito, to fulfil the will of God, and to follow whither he leads.

C.   THE EXECUTION

Two days after this conversation Socrates drank the hemlock. An account of his death is given by Plato, as narrated by Socrates' friend Phaedo.[12]

[Socrates] arose and went into a chamber to bathe; Crito followed him and told us to wait. So we remained behind, talking and thinking of the subject of discourse, and also of the greatness of our sorrow; he was like a father of whom we were being bereaved, and we were about to pass the rest of our lives as orphans. When he had taken the bath his children were brought to him (he had two young sons and an elder one); and the women of his family also came, and he talked

to them and gave them a few directions in the presence of Crito; then he dismissed them and returned to us.

Now the hour of sunset was near, for a good deal of time had passed while he was within. When he came out, he sat down with us again after his bath, but not much was said. Soon the jailer . . . entered and stood by him, saying:— To you, Socrates, whom I know to be the noblest and gentlest and best of all who ever came to this place, I will not impute the angry feeling of other men, who rage and swear at me, when, in obedience to the authorities, I bid them drink the poison—indeed, I am sure that you will not be angry with me; for others, as you are aware, and not I, are to blame. And so fare you well, and try to bear lightly what must needs be—you know my errand. Then bursting into tears he turned away and went out.

Socrates looked at him and said: I return your good wishes, and will do as you bid. Then turning to us, he said, How charming the man is: since I have been in prison he has always been coming to see me, and at times he would talk to me, and was as good to me as could be, and now see how generously he sorrows on my account. We must do as he says, Crito; and therefore let the cup be brought, if the poison is prepared: if not, let the attendant prepare some.

Yet, said Crito, the sun is still upon the hill-tops, and I know that many a one has taken the draught late, and after the announcement has been made to him, he has eaten and drunk, and enjoyed the society of his beloved: do not hurry —there is time enough.

Socrates said: Yes, Crito, and they of whom you speak are right in so acting, for they think that they will be gainers by the delay; but I am right in not following their example, for I do not think that I should gain anything by drinking the poison a little later; I should only be ridiculous in my own eyes for sparing and saving a life which is already forfeit. Please then to do as I say, and not to refuse me.

Crito made a sign to the servant, who was standing by; and he went out, and having been absent for some time, returned with the jailer carrying the cup of poison. Socrates said: You, my good friend, who are experienced in these matters, shall give me directions how I am to proceed. The man answered: You have only to walk about until your legs are heavy, and then to lie down, and the poison will act. At the same time he handed the cup to Socrates, who in the easiest and gentlest manner, without the least fear or change of color or feature, looking at the man with all his eyes, . . . as his manner was, took the cup and said: What do you say about making a libation out of this cup to any god? May I, or not? The man answered: We only

prepare, Socrates, just so much as we deem enough. I understand, he said: but I may and must ask the gods to prosper my journey from this to the other world—even so—and so be it according to my prayer. Then raising the cup to his lips, quite readily and cheerfully he drank off the poison. And hitherto most of us had been able to control our sorrow; but now when we saw him drinking, and saw too that he had fin-ished the draught, we could no longer forbear, and in spite of myself my own tears were flow-ing fast; so that I covered my face and wept, not for him, but at the thought of my own calamity in having to part from such a friend. Nor was I the first; for Crito, when he found himself unable to restrain his tears, had got up, and I followed; and at that moment, Apollodorus, who had been weeping all the time, broke out in a loud and passionate cry which made cowards of us all. Socrates alone retained his calmness: What is this strange outcry? he said. I sent away the women mainly in order that they might not misbehave in this way, for I have been told that a man should die in peace. Be quiet then, and have patience. When we heard his words we were ashamed, and refrained our tears; and he walked about until, as he said, his legs began to fail, and then he lay on his back, according to directions, and the man who gave him the poison now and then looked at his feet and legs; and after a while he pressed his foot hard, and asked him if he could feel; and he said, No; and then his leg, and so upwards and upwards, and showed us that he was cold and stiff. And he felt them himself, and said: When the poison reaches the heart, that will be the end. He was beginning to grow cold about the groin, when he uncovered his face, for he had covered himself up, and said—they were his last words—he said: Crito, I owe a cock to Asclepius; will you remember to pay the debt? The debt shall be paid, said Crito; is there anything else? There was no answer to this question; but in a minute or two a movement was heard, and the attendants uncovered him; his eyes were set, and Crito closed his eyes and mouth.

Such was the end . . . of our friend; concern-ing whom I may truly say, that of all men of his time whom I have known, he was the wisest and justest and best.

II

Rome: The Idea of Liberty

W E are all slaves of the laws in order that we may be free.

CICERO

Acton wanted to write the History of Man in terms of a History of the Idea of Freedom. But you cannot write a History of Freedom without at the same time writing a History of the Fact of Slavery. . . . Institutions are changed in an attempt to realize the Idea of Freedom. . . . Then the fact of the new slavery imposes itself on men's consciousness. It is perceived that the idea of freedom was not realized by the last change, that the new institutions are just as enslaving as the old. What is to be done? Change the new institutions for yet newer ones. And when *that* honeymoon is over? Change the yet newer for newer still.

ALDOUS HUXLEY (Eyeless in Gaza)

CONTENTS

[23]

QUESTIONS FOR STUDY

PART I

1. What were the powers of a) the consuls, b) the senate, c) the people? How did each provide a check on the others?
2. What protection for individual liberty was provided by the tribunes?
3. Does Livy's account of Titus Manlius' execution of his son support Lord Acton's statement that the Roman Republic disregarded the "rights of men"? How did Livy judge the act? Do you see a significant relation between the conduct of Manlius and that of Decius Mus?
4. How did the political situation described by Sallust differ from that described by Polybius? How had the exercise of popular liberty changed?
5. What reasons did Sallust give for avoiding political activity?
6. What kind of liberty did Lucretius consider valuable?
7. What reasons did Lucretius give for avoiding political activity?

PART II

8. How did Cicero answer such arguments as those of Sallust and Lucretius for abstaining from political activity?
9. How did Cicero's conception of the ideal form of government resemble the Roman government described by Polybius?
10. What meaning did Cicero attach to the words "power," "influence," and "liberty" in his description of the ideal form of government?
11. What did Cicero mean by "natural law"? How does natural law operate to secure justice in society?
12. What reasons did Caesar offer for rejecting the authority of the senate and the consuls?
13. Why did Cicero hesitate so long in leaving Italy? Why did he finally join Pompey?
14. What impression do Cicero's letters give of him as a man and as a statesman?
15. What did "liberty" mean for Cicero in his conflict with Antony?

PART III

16. What evidence does Augustus' statement offer to show that he attempted to preserve the formal structure of Republican government? What evidence that the structure of government had changed?
17. What facts presented by Augustus are made to appear in a different light by Tacitus' statement of them?
18. Does the author of the funeral oration in his wife's honor seem, in Tacitus' words, "ready to be a slave"?
19. For what acts of Trajan did Pliny praise him?
20. What did "liberty" mean for Pliny?
21. What part did Pontius Pilate have, as Roman governor, in the trial of Jesus?
22. What advantages did St. Paul derive from the fact of his Roman citizenship?
23. Under what circumstances did the first Roman persecution of Christians take place? How did Nero's action compare with the conduct of the Roman officials in Judaea?
24. What did "liberty" mean for Tertullian?
25. What did Eusebius regard as the divine purpose fulfilled by the Roman Empire?
26. How would Lucretius, Cicero, Pliny, Tertullian, and Eusebius compare in their judgment of the nature and value of liberty?

The Roman state was successively a monarchy, a republic, and an empire. According to the traditional chronology kings ruled for almost 250 years, from 753 B.C. to 509 B.C. Most of our information about this early period is uncertain, but we do know that Tarquin the Proud—last of the half-legendary kings—left as his legacy to the Roman Republic a hatred for the name of king. Livy, the historian of early Rome who lived at the beginning of the Empire, wrote of the Romans under the monarchy that "to be ruled by a king was their universal wish, for they had not yet tasted the sweetness of liberty" (Livy, I, xvii, 3). The history of the Republic was in Livy's eyes a history of liberty. After telling of the expulsion of Tarquin he began his account of the Republic by announcing as his subject henceforth: "the new liberty enjoyed by the Roman people, their achievements in peace and war, annual magistracies, and laws superior in authority to men" (II, i, 1). Yet at the very moment when the Republic had defeated all its external enemies it was succeeded by the Empire. After Caesar's conquest of Gaul, Roman control extended from the Atlantic to the Euphrates and from the Rhine to the Sahara desert. This was a far greater empire than the world had known before, and Rome faced the task of its control with political institutions which had originally been those of a small city-state. Athens, facing a similar challenge, though on a far smaller scale, had retained her institutions and lost her empire. The Roman Republic displayed an adaptability no Greek state was able to achieve, but by the middle years of the first century B.C. a crisis had been produced by Rome's continuing expansion. Between 49 and 31 B.C. three major civil wars were fought. When Augustus defeated Antony and Cleopatra at the Battle of Actium in 31 B.C. he was in fact sole ruler of Rome and the Republic had become the Empire. The Empire was to yield only to the impact of the Germanic invasions of the fifth century A.D., which brought the revolutionary changes which transformed the ancient into the medieval world.

For many Romans, even in imperial times, the Republic continued to be a symbol of liberty. Yet Lord Acton, writing in the nineteenth century on *The History of Freedom in Antiquity,* asserted: "The Roman Empire rendered greater services to the cause of liberty than the Roman Republic. . . . The Roman Empire possessed merits which, at a distance, and especially at a great distance of time, concern men more deeply than the tragic tyranny which was felt in the neighborhood of the Palace. The poor had what they had demanded in vain of the Republic. The rich fared better than during the Triumvirate. The rights of Roman citizens were extended to the people of the provinces. To the imperial epoch belong the better part of Roman literature and nearly the entire Civil Law; and it was the Empire that mitigated slavery, instituted religious toleration, made a beginning of the law of nations, and created a perfect system of the law of property. The Republic which Caesar overthrew had been anything but a free State. It provided admirable securities for the rights of citizens; it treated with savage disregard the rights of men; and allowed the free Roman to inflict atrocious wrongs on his children, on debtors and dependents, on prisoners and slaves."

Is it possible to reconcile these two ideas—one, that the cause of the Republic was the cause of liberty, and the other, that the Empire served liberty better than the Republic? Or do these ideas necessarily conflict? Perhaps there is no clear answer possible, since "liberty" is not a word of simple meaning. The way we understand it must affect the way we judge the changes which took place in the Roman government when the Republic was transformed into the Empire.

Part I.   THE REPUBLIC

"Republic" is the term commonly used of the Roman government in the period when it was exercised by "The Senate and Roman People," free from domination by king or emperor. The word can also be applied more widely in Latin, since *res publica* means literally "public possession," and may be translated as "republic," "commonwealth," or "state." The Emperor Hadrian could declare that he "would so govern the republic as to make evident that it was the possession not of himself but of the people." [1] Cicero denied the name to any government—monarchy, oligarchy, or democracy—conducted in the interest of an individual, party, or class.

A.   THE EARLY REPUBLIC

1. *The Republican Constitution* (unwritten, like that of modern England) achieved its most effective form in the opening years of the second century B.C., when Rome began to play a decisive role in the affairs of Greece. Polybius, a Greek who had taken part in the government of his own state, came to Rome as a hostage about 168 B.C. There he lived as a friend of leading Romans and became well acquainted with the working of their government. He wrote a history to explain "how it was and by virtue of what peculiar political institutions that in less than fifty-three years nearly the whole world was overcome and fell under the single dominion of Rome." [2] In the following passage he described the Roman constitution as it existed in his time.[3]

The three kinds of government [monarchy, aristocracy, democracy] all shared in the control of the Roman state. And such fairness and propriety in all respects was shown in the use of these three elements for drawing up the constitution and in its subsequent administration that it was impossible even for a native to pronounce with certainty whether the whole system was aristocratic, democratic, or monarchical. . . .

The consuls, previous to leading out their legions, exercise authority in Rome over all public affairs, since all the other magistrates except the tribunes are under them and bound to obey them, and it is they who introduce embassies to the senate. Besides this it is they who consult the senate on matters of urgency, they who carry out in detail the provisions of its decrees. Again as concerns all affairs of state administered by the people it is their duty to take these under their charge, to summon assemblies, to introduce measures, and to preside over the execution of the popular decrees. As for preparation for war and

the general conduct of operations in the field, here their power is almost uncontrolled; for they are empowered to make what demands they choose on the allies, to appoint military tribunes, to levy soldiers and select those who are fittest for service. They also have the right of inflicting, when on active service, punishment on anyone under their command; and they are authorized to spend any sum they decide upon from the public funds, being accompanied by a quaestor who faithfully executes their instructions. . . .

To pass to the senate. In the first place it has the control of the treasury, all revenue and expenditure being regulated by it. For with the exception of payments made to the consuls, the quaestors are not allowed to disburse for any particular object without a decree of the senate. And even the item of expenditure which is far heavier and more important than any other—the outlay every five years by the censors on public works, whether constructions or repairs—is under the control of the senate, which makes a grant to the censors for the purpose. Similarly crimes committed in Italy which require a public investigation, such as treason, conspiracy, poisoning, and assassination, are under the jurisdiction of the senate. Also if any private person or community in Italy is in need of arbitration or indeed claims damages or requires succor or protection, the senate attends to all such matters. It also occupies itself with the dispatch of all embassies sent to countries outside of Italy for the purpose either of settling differences, or of offering friendly advice, or indeed of imposing demands, or of receiving submission, or of declaring war; and in like manner with respect to embassies arriving in Rome it decides what reception and what answer should be given to them. . . .

It is the people which alone has the right to confer honors and inflict punishment, the only bonds by which kingdoms and states and in a word human society in general are held together. For where the distinction between these is overlooked or is observed but ill applied, no affairs can be properly administered. How indeed is this possible when good and evil men are held in equal estimation? It is by the people, then, in many cases that offenses punishable by a fine are tried when the accused have held the highest office; and they are the only court which may try on capital charges. . . . Again it is the people who bestow office on the deserving, the noblest reward of virtue in a state; the people have the power of approving or rejecting laws, and what is most important of all, they deliberate on the question of war and peace. Further in the case of alliances, terms of peace, and treaties, it is the people who ratify all these or the reverse. . . .

Having stated how political power is distributed among the different parts of the state, I will now explain how each of the three parts is enabled, if they wish, to counteract or cooperate with the others. The consul, when he leaves with his army invested with the powers I mentioned, appears indeed to have absolute authority in all matters necessary for carrying out his purpose; but in fact he requires the support of the people and the senate, and is not able to bring his operations to a conclusion without them. For it is obvious that the legions require constant supplies, and without the consent of the senate, neither corn, clothing, nor pay can be provided; so that the commander's plans come to nothing, if the senate chooses to be deliberately negligent and obstructive. It also depends on the senate whether or not a general can carry out completely his conceptions and designs, since it has the right of either superseding him when his year's term of office has expired or of retaining him in command. . . . It is the people which ratifies or annuls terms of peace and treaties, and what is most important, on laying down office the consuls are obliged to account for their actions to the people. So that in no respect is it safe for the consuls to neglect keeping in favor with both the senate and the people.

The senate again, which possesses such great power, is obliged in the first place to pay attention to the commons in public affairs and respect the wishes of the people, and it cannot carry out inquiries into the most grave and important offenses against the state, punishable with death, and their correction, unless the [decree of the senate] is confirmed by the people. . . . And what is most important is that if a single one of the tribunes interposes, the senate is unable to decide finally about any matter, and cannot even meet and hold sittings; and here it is to be observed that the tribunes are always obliged to act

as the people decree and to pay every attention to their wishes. Therefore for all these reasons the senate is afraid of the masses and must pay due attention to the popular will.

Similarly, again, the people must be submissive to the senate and respect its members both in public and in private. . . . The judges in most civil trials, whether public or private, are appointed from its members, where the action involves large interests. So that all citizens being at the mercy of the senate, and looking forward with alarm to the uncertainty of litigation, are very shy of obstructing or resisting its decisions. Similarly everyone is reluctant to oppose the projects of the consuls as all are generally and individually under their authority when in the field.

Such being the power that each part has of hampering the others or cooperating with them, their union is adequate to all emergencies, so that it is impossible to find a better political system than this.

2. *The Republican Aristocracy.* A feature of Roman public life not mentioned by Polybius is the role played in the government by a comparatively small number of aristocratic families. The same names recur generation after generation: Marcus Junius Brutus, the assassin of Julius Caesar in 44 B.C., was a descendant of Lucius Junius Brutus, who took a leading part in the expulsion of the kings in 509 B.C. It was difficult, though not impossible, for a "new man"—not belonging to one of the families which traditionally held office—to win election to positions leading to membership in the Senate and to the consulship. The near-monopoly of office by these families was based partly on wealth (since service in public office was unpaid), partly on the fact that they alone habitually prepared their sons for a career which demanded ability equally in administrative, judicial, and military activity, and partly on the prestige which they had gained by their tradition of public service. This tradition is illustrated by Livy's account of the conduct of Titus Manlius and Publius Decius Mus, consuls in 340 B.C., when Rome was engaged in war with a league of the other Latin cities. The issue was whether Rome should be on an equality with her immediate neighbors or should enjoy a predominant position over them.[4]

[The anxiety of the Romans] was sharpened by the fact that they must fight against the Latins, who were like themselves in language, customs, fashion of arms, and above all in military institutions; soldiers had mingled with soldiers, centurions with centurions, tribunes with tribunes, as equals and colleagues in the same garrisons and often in the same maniples. Lest this might betray the soldiers into some blunder, the consuls proclaimed that no man should quit his place to attack the foe.

It chanced that amongst the other squadron-leaders who had been sent off in all directions to reconnoitre, Titus Manlius, the consul's son, had ridden out with his troopers beyond the enemy's camp, till he was hardly the cast of a spear from their nearest outpost. There the Tusculan horse were stationed, under the command of Geminus Maecius, who enjoyed a reputation amongst his fellows for his achievements no less than for his noble birth. . . . Geminus rode out a little in front of his men, and asked, "Would you like . . . to do battle with me, yourself, that from the outcome of our duel men may see at once how far the Latin horse surpass the Roman?" The youth's bold heart was stirred, whether by anger, or by shame at the thought of refusing the combat, or by the irresistible force of destiny. And so, forgetting the commands of his father and the edict of the consuls, he allowed himself to be swept headlong into an encounter where it would make little difference to him whether he won or lost. They caused the rest of the horsemen to stand back, as though it had been a spectacle, and spurred their steeds against one another across the vacant space between. With lances levelled they rushed together; but the lance of Manlius glanced off the helmet of his enemy, and that of Maecius passed over the neck of the other's horse. Then, as they pulled their horses round, Manlius, who was the first to gather himself up for a second thrust, pricked his enemy's charger between the ears. The smart of this wound made the horse rear and toss his head so violently that he threw off his rider, who, raising himself with spear and shield, was struggling to his feet after the heavy fall, when Manlius plunged his lance into his throat so that it came out between the ribs and pinned him to the ground. He then gathered up the spoils and rode back to his troopers, who attended him with shouts of triumph to the camp, where he sought at once the headquarters of his father, knowing not what doom the future held for him, or whether praise or punishment were his appointed guerdon.

"Father," he said, "that all men might truly report me to be your son, I bring these equestrian spoils, stripped from the body of an enemy who challenged me." On hearing this, the consul straightway turned from his son and commanded a trumpet to sound the assembly. When the men had gathered in full numbers, the consul said, "Inasmuch, Titus Manlius, as you have held in reverence neither consular authority nor a father's dignity, and despite our edict have quitted your place to fight the enemy, and so far as in you lay, have broken military discipline, whereby the Roman state has stood until this day unshaken, thus compelling me to forget either the republic or myself, we will sooner endure the punishment of our wrong-doing than suffer the republic to expiate our sins at a cost so heavy to herself; we will set a stern example, but a salutary one, for the young men of the future. For my own part, I am moved, not only by a man's instinctive love of his children, but by this instance you have given of your bravery, perverted though it was by an idle show of honor. But since the authority of the consuls must either be established by your death, or by your impunity be forever abrogated, and since I think that you yourself, if you have a drop of my blood in you, would not refuse to raise up by your punishment the military discipline which through your misdemeanor has slipped and fallen—go, lictor, bind him to the stake."

All were astounded at so shocking a command; every man looked upon the axe as lifted against himself, and they were hushed with fear more than with reverence. And so, after standing, as if lost in wonder, rooted to the spot, suddenly, when the blood gushed from the severed neck, their voices burst out in such unrestrained upbraiding that they spared neither laments nor curses; and covering the young man's body with his spoils, they built a pyre outside the rampart, where they burned it with all the honors that can possibly attend a soldier's funeral; and the "orders of Manlius" not only caused men to shudder at the time, but became a type of severity with succeeding ages.

Nevertheless the brutality of the punishment made the soldiers more obedient to their general and not only were guard-duties, watches, and the ordering of outposts, everywhere more carefully observed, but in the final struggle, as well, when the troops had gone down into battle, that stern act did much good. . . .

[In the subsequent battle] Manlius commanded the right wing, Decius the left. In the beginning the strength of the combatants and their ardor were equal on both sides; but after a time the Roman [first line troops] on the left, unable to withstand the pressure of the Latins, fell back upon the [second line]. In the confusion of this movement Decius the consul called out to Marcus Valerius in a loud voice: "We have need of Heaven's help, Marcus Valerius. Come therefore, state pontiff of the Roman people, dictate the words, that I may devote myself to save the legions." The pontiff bade him don the purple-bordered toga, and with veiled head and one hand thrust out from the toga and touching his chin, stand upon a spear that was laid under his feet, and say as follows: "Janus, Jupiter, Father Mars, Quirinus, Bellona, Lares, divine Novensiles, divine Indigites, ye gods in whose power are both we and our enemies, and you divine Manes [spirits of the dead]—I invoke and worship you, I beseech and crave your favor, that you prosper the might and the victory of the Roman People of the Quirites, and visit the foes of the Roman people of the Quirites with fear, shuddering and death. As I have pronounced the words, even so in behalf of the republic of the Roman people of the Quirites, and of the army, the legions, the auxiliaries of the Roman people of the Quirites, do I devote the legions and auxiliaries of the enemy, together with myself, to the divine Manes and to Earth."

Having uttered this prayer he bade the lictors go to Titus Manlius and lose no time in announcing to his colleague that he had devoted himself for the good of the army. . . . Vaulting, armed, upon his horse he plunged into the thick of the enemy, a conspicuous object from either army and of an aspect more august than a man's, as though sent from heaven to expiate all anger of the gods, and to turn aside destruction from his people and bring it on their adversaries. Thus every terror and dread attended him, and throwing the Latin front into disarray, spread afterwards throughout their entire host. This was most clearly seen in that, wherever he rode, men cowered as though blasted by some baleful star; but when he fell beneath a rain of missiles, from that instant there was no more doubt of the consternation of the Latin cohorts. . . . At the same time the Romans—their spirits relieved of religious fears—pressed on as though the signal had just then for the first time been given, and delivered a fresh attack. . . .

Of all the citizens and allies, the chief glory of that war went to the consuls; of whom the one had drawn all the threats and menaces of the supernal and infernal gods upon himself alone, and the other had shown such valor and ability in the battle that it is readily agreed by both Romans and Latins who have handed down an account of this engagement that whichever side had been led by Titus Manlius would undoubtedly have been victorious.

B.   THE LATE REPUBLIC

During the last century of the Republic Rome had no serious rivals for power in the Mediterranean world. Civil war was feared, not foreign war. The constitution did not in theory differ essentially from Polybius' description of it, but in fact there had been important changes. Extension of citizenship to all Italians made the assemblies, which were always held at Rome, actually less representative of the whole body of citizens, and the assemblies were open to the pressure of bribery or of intimidation. The tribunes had come to act primarily in the interests of senators with whom they were in political alliance. The Senate now often represented rather a class than a national interest. The claim of the "nobles"—as the aristocratic families were sometimes called—to dominate political life had once been based on their real services to the state; many of them seem by this time to have felt that they ruled by inherited right. Provincial administration was often oppressive; border wars were begun or drawn out for the profit and glory of the governors. Among leading senators there were bitter personal rivalries leading to corrupt elections, bribed juries, and periods of rule by violence including wholesale murder of political opponents. By the middle of the first century B.C. it was clear that the claims of individuals to prestige and power were threatening the liberty of the whole people.

1. *A Contemporary Analysis of Political Life.* Sallust, who had entered on a political career, been a tribune, senator, and governor of the African province of Numidia, eventually withdrew to private life and the writing of history. This is his explanation of his retirement from public life, and his comment on political conditions in the middle years of the first century B.C.[5]

In my opinion, magistracies and military commands, in short all public offices, are least desirable in these times, since honor is not bestowed upon merit, while those who have gained it wrongfully are neither safe nor the more honorable because of it. For to rule one's country or subjects by force, although you both have the power to correct abuses, and do correct them, is nevertheless tyrannical; especially since all attempts at change foreshadow bloodshed, exile, and other horrors of war. Moreover, to struggle in vain and after wearisome exertion to gain nothing but hatred, is the height of folly, unless haply one is possessed by a dishonorable and pernicious passion for sacrificing one's personal honor and liberty to the power of a few men.

But among intellectual pursuits, the recording of the events of the past is especially serviceable; but of that it becomes me to say nothing, both because many men have already spoken of its value, and in order that no one may suppose that I am led by vanity to eulogize my own favorite occupation. I suppose, too, that since I have resolved to pass my life aloof from public affairs, some will apply to this arduous and useful employment of mine the name of idleness, certainly those who regard courting the people and currying favor by banquets as the height of industriousness. But if such men will only bear in mind in what times I was elected to office, what men of merit were unable to attain the same honor and what sort of men have since come into the senate, they will surely be convinced that it is rather from justifiable motives than from indolence that I have changed my opinion, and that greater profit will accrue to our country from my inactivity than from others' activity.

I have often heard that Quintus Maximus, Publius Scipio, and other eminent men of our country, were in the habit of declaring that their hearts were set mightily aflame for the pursuit of virtue whenever they gazed upon the masks of their ancestors. Of course they did not mean to imply that the wax or the effigy had any such power over them, but rather that it is the memory of great deeds that kindles in the breasts of noble men this flame that cannot be quelled until they by their own prowess have equalled the fame and glory of their forefathers.

But in these degenerate days, on the contrary, who is there that does not vie with his ancestors in riches and extravagance rather than in uprightness and diligence? Even the "new men," who in former times always relied upon worth to outdo the nobles, now make their way to power and distinction by intrigue and open fraud rather than by noble practices; just as if a praetorship, a consulship, or anything else of the kind were distinguished and illustrious in and of itself and were not valued according to the merit of those who live up to it. . . .

The institution of parties and factions, with all their attendant evils, originated at Rome . . . as the result of peace and of an abundance of everything that mortals prize most highly. For before the destruction of Carthage [in 146 B.C.] the people and senate of Rome together governed the republic peacefully and with moderation. There was no strife among the citizens either for glory or for power; fear of the enemy preserved the good morals of the state. But when the minds of the people were relieved of that dread, wantonness and arrogance naturally arose, vices which are fostered by prosperity. Thus the peace for which they had longed in time of adversity, after they had gained it proved to be more cruel and

bitter than adversity itself. For the nobles began to abuse their position and the people their liberty, and every man for himself robbed, pillaged, and plundered. Thus the community was split into two parties, and between these the state was torn to pieces.

But the nobles had the more powerful organization, while the strength of the commons was less effective because it was incompact and divided among many. Affairs at home and in the field were managed according to the will of a few men, in whose hands were the treasury, the provinces, public offices, glory and triumphs. The people were burdened with military service and poverty. The generals divided spoils of war with a few friends. Meanwhile the parents or little children of the soldiers, if they had a powerful neighbor, were driven from their homes. Thus, by the side of power, greed arose, unlimited and unrestrained, violated and devastated everything, respected nothing, and held nothing sacred, until it finally brought about its own downfall.

2. *Epicureanism.* Lucretius, in his poem *On the Nature of Things,* gave an exposition in Latin verse of Epicureanism, a Greek philosophy which had gained considerable influence in Rome. The Epicurean attitude toward participation in public life is expressed in the following passage.[6]

'Tis sweet, when, down the mighty main, the winds
Roll up its waste of waters, from the land
To watch another's laboring anguish far,
Not that we joyously delight that man
Should thus be smitten, but because 'tis sweet
To mark what evils we ourselves be spared;
'Tis sweet, again, to view the mighty strife
Of armies embattled yonder o'er the plains,
Ourselves no sharers in the peril; but naught
There is more goodly than to hold the high
Serene plateaus, well fortressed by the wise,
Whence thou may'st look below on other men
And see them ev'rywhere wand'ring, all dispersed
In their lone seeking for the road of life;
Rivals in genius, or emulous in rank,
Pressing through days and nights with hugest toil
For summits of power and mastery of the world.

O wretched minds of men! O blinded hearts!
In how great perils, in what darks of life
Are spent the human years, however brief!—
O not to see that nature for herself
Barks after nothing, save that pain keep off,
Disjoined from the body, and that mind enjoy
Delightsome feeling, far from care and fear!
Therefore we see that our corporeal life
Needs little, altogether, and only such
As takes the pain away, and can besides

Strew underneath some number of delights.
More grateful 'tis at times (for nature craves
No artifice nor luxury), if forsooth
There be no golden images of boys
Along the halls, with right hands holding out
The lamps ablaze, the lights for evening feasts,
And if the house doth glitter not with gold
Nor gleam with silver, and to the lyre resound
No fretted and gilded ceilings overhead,
Yet still to lounge with friends in the soft grass
Beside a river of water, underneath
A big tree's boughs, and merrily to refresh
Our frames, with no vast outlay—most of all
If the weather is laughing and the times of the
    year
Besprinkle the green of the grass around with
    flowers.
Nor yet the quicker will hot fevers go,
If on a pictured tapestry thou toss
Or purple robe, than if 'tis thine to lie
Upon the poor man's bedding.

                              Wherefore, since
Treasure, nor rank, nor glory of a reign
Avail us naught for this our body, thus
Reckon them likewise nothing for the mind:
Save then perchance, when thou beholdest forth
Thy legions swarming round the Field of Mars,
Rousing a mimic warfare—either side

Strengthened with large auxiliaries and horse,
Alike equipped with arms, alike inspired;
Or save when also thou beholdest forth
Thy fleets to swarm, deploying down the sea:
For then, by such bright circumstance abashed,
Religion pales and flees thy mind; O then
The fears of death leave heart so free of care.

But if we note how all this pomp at last
Is but a drollery and a mocking sport,
And of a truth man's dread, with cares at heels,
Dreads not these sounds of arms, these savage
    swords,
But among kings and lords of all the world
Mingles undaunted, nor is overawed
By gleam of gold nor by the splendor bright
Of purple robe, canst thou then doubt that this
Is aught, but power of thinking?—when, besides
The whole of life but labors in the dark.
For just as children tremble and fear all
In the viewless dark, so even we at times
Dread in the light so many things that be
No whit more fearsome than what children feign,
Shuddering, will be upon them in the dark.

This terror then, this darkness of the mind,
Not sunrise with its flaring spokes of light,
Nor glittering arrows of morning can disperse,
But only nature's aspect and her law.

Part II.   THE FALL OF THE REPUBLIC

A.   CICERO: A THEORY OF REPUBLICAN GOVERNMENT

Marcus Tullius Cicero was one of the foremost statesmen, orators, and prose writers of Rome. A "new man," he had attained the consulship in 63 B.C. During his consulship he crushed a conspiracy led by Catiline, a member of an ancient aristocratic family who had organized a plot to seize control of the government by force and introduce a program of radical economic reform, including general cancellation of debts. Toward the end of his life Cicero wrote two works of a political and philosophical nature, the *Republic* and the *Laws*. These were inspired by works of Plato, and also contain much that is derived from Stoic thought. By a combination of Greek theory and Roman historical experience he hoped to provide a program for restoring the stability of the Republic. The following selections from the *Republic* and the *Laws* present the principles on which Cicero believed that government must be based.

1. *The Problem Facing the Republic.*[7]

   The commonwealth of Rome is founded
        firm
   On ancient customs and on men of
        might.

Our poet [Ennius] seems to have obtained these words, so brief and true, from an oracle. For neither men alone, unless a State is supplied with customs too, nor customs alone, unless there have also been men to defend them, could ever have

been sufficient to found or to preserve so long a commonwealth whose dominion extends so far and wide. Thus, before our own time, the customs of our ancestors produced excellent men, and eminent men preserved our ancient customs and the institutions of their forefathers. But though the republic, when it came to us, was like a beautiful painting, whose colors, however, were already fading with age, our own time not only has neglected to freshen it by renewing the original colors, but has not even taken the trouble to preserve its configuration and, so to speak, its general outlines. For what is now left of the "ancient customs" on which he said "the commonwealth of Rome" was "founded firm"? They have been, as we see, so completely buried in oblivion that they are not only no longer practised, but are already unknown. And what shall I say of the men? For the loss of our customs is due to our lack of men, and for this great evil we must not only give an account, but must even defend ourselves in every way possible, as if we were accused of capital crime. For it is through our own faults, not by any accident, that we retain only the form of the commonwealth, but have long since lost its substance.

2. *The Duty of the Individual.*[8]

Marcus Cato, unknown and of obscure birth —by whom, as by a pattern for our emulation, all of us who are devoted to the same pursuits are drawn to diligence and valor—might surely have remained at Tusculum in the enjoyment of the leisurely life of that healthful spot so near to Rome. But he, a madman as our friends [the Epicureans] maintain, preferred, though no necessity constrained him, to be tossed by the billows and storms of our public life even to an extreme old age, rather than to live a life of complete happiness in the calm and ease of such retirement. I will not speak of the men, countless in number, who have each been the salvation of this republic. . . . I will content myself with asserting that Nature has implanted in the human race so great a need of virtue and so great a desire to defend the common safety that the strength thereof has conquered all the allurements of pleasure and ease. But it is not enough to possess virtue, as if it were an art of some sort, unless you make use of it. Though it is true that an art, even if you never use it, can still remain in your possession by the very fact of your knowledge of it, yet the existence of virtue depends entirely upon its use; and its noblest use is the government of the State, and the realization in fact, not in words, of those very things that the philosophers, in their corners, are continually dinning in our ears. For there is no principle enunciated by the philosophers—at least none that is just and honorable— that has not been discovered and established by those who have drawn up codes of law for States. For whence comes our sense of duty? From whom do we obtain the principles of religion? Whence comes the law of nations, or even that law of ours which is called "civil"? Whence justice, honor, fair-dealing? Whence decency, self-restraint, fear of disgrace, eagerness for praise and honor? Whence comes endurance amid toils and dangers? I say, from those men who, when these things had been inculcated by a system of training, either

confirmed them by custom or else enforced them by statutes. Indeed Xenocrates, one of the most eminent of philosophers, when asked what his disciples learned, is said to have replied: "To do of their own accord what they are compelled to do by the law." Therefore . . . since we feel a mighty urge to increase the resources of mankind, since we desire to make human life safer and richer by our thought and effort, and are goaded on to the fulfilment of this desire by Nature herself, let us hold to the course which has ever been that of all excellent men, turning deaf ears to those who, in the hope of even recalling those who have already gone ahead, are sounding the retreat.

As their first objection to these arguments, so well founded and so obviously sound, those who attack them plead the severity of the labor that must be performed in the defense of the State —surely a trifling obstacle to the watchful and diligent man, and one that merits only scorn, not merely with reference to matters of such moment, but even in the case of things of only moderate importance, such as a man's studies, or duties, or even his business affairs. Then too they allege the danger to which life is exposed, and confront brave men with a dishonorable fear of death. . . . In fact they now include my name also, and presumably because they think it was through my counsel and at my risk that their own peaceful life has been preserved to them, they complain even more bitterly and with greater kindness of the treatment I have received. . . . And yet my sufferings brought me more honor than trouble, more glory than vexation, and the joy I found in the affectionate longing felt for me by good citizens was greater than my grief at the exultation of the wicked. But, as I said before, if it had happened otherwise, how could I complain? For none of the misfortunes that fell to my lot in consequence of my great services was unexpected by me or more serious than I had foreseen. For such was my nature that, although, on account of the manifold pleasures I found in the studies which had engaged me from boyhood, it would have been possible for me, on the one hand, to reap greater profit from a quiet life than other men, or, on the other hand, if any disaster should happen to us all, to suffer no more than my fair share of the common misfortune, yet I could not hesitate to expose myself to the severest storms, and I might almost say, even to thunderbolts, for the sake of the safety of my fellow-citizens, and to secure, at the cost of my own personal danger, a quiet life for all the rest. . . .

Moreover we ought certainly not to listen to the other excuses to which these men resort, that they may be more free to enjoy the quiet life. They say, for example, that it is mostly worthless men who take part in politics, men with whom it is degrading to be compared, while to have conflict with them, especially when the mob is aroused, is a wretched and dangerous task. Therefore, they maintain, a wise man should not attempt to take the reins, as he cannot restrain the insane and untamed fury of the common herd; nor is it proper for a freeman, by contending with vile and wicked opponents, to submit to the scourgings of abuse or expose himself to wrongs which are intolerable to the wise—as if, in the view of good, brave, and high-minded men, there could be any nobler motive for entering public life than the resolution not to be ruled by wicked men and not to allow the republic to be destroyed by them, seeing that the philosophers themselves, even if they should desire to help, would be impotent.

3. *Definition of a Republic.*[9]

A commonwealth [*res publica*] is the property of a people. But a people is not any collection of human beings brought together in any sort of way, but an assemblage of people in large numbers associated in an agreement with respect to justice and a partnership for the common good. The first cause of such an association is not so much the weakness of the individual as a certain social spirit which nature has implanted in man.

4. *The Best Form of Government.*[10]

When the supreme authority is in the hands of one man, we call him a king, and the form of this State a kingship. When selected citizens hold this power, we say that the State is ruled by an aristocracy. But a popular government (for so it is called) exists when all the power is in the hands of the people. And any one of these three forms of government (if only the bond which originally joined the citizens together in the partnership of the State holds fast), though not perfect or in my opinion the best, is tolerable, though one of them may be superior to another. For either a just and wise king, or a select number of leading citizens, or even the people itself, though this is the least commendable type, can nevertheless, as it seems, form a government that is not unstable, provided that no elements of injustice or greed are mingled with it. But in kingships the subjects have too small a share in the administration of justice and in deliberation; and in aristocracies the masses can hardly have their share of liberty, since they are entirely excluded from deliberation for the common weal and from power; and when all the power is in the people's hands, even though they exercise it with justice and moderation, yet the resulting equality itself is inequitable. . . . The kingship, in my opinion, is by far the best of the three

primary forms, but a moderate and balanced form of government which is a combination of the three good simple forms is preferable even to the kingship. For there should be a supreme and royal element in the State, some power also ought to be granted to the leading citizens, and certain matters should be left to the judgment and desires of the masses. Such a constitution, in the first place, offers in a high degree a sort of equality, which is a thing free men can hardly do without for any considerable length of time, and secondly, it has stability. For the primary forms already mentioned degenerate easily into the corresponding perverted forms, the king being replaced by a despot, the aristocracy by an oligarchical faction, and the people by a mob and anarchy; but whereas these forms are frequently changed into new ones, this does not usually happen in the case of the mixed and evenly balanced constitution, except through great faults in the governing class. . . . Unless there is in the State an even balance of rights, duties, and functions, so that the magistrates have enough power, the counsels of the eminent citizens enough influence, and the people enough liberty, this kind of government cannot be safe from revolution.

5. *Justice.*[11]

The origin of Justice is to be found in Law, for Law is a natural force; it is the mind and reason of the intelligent man, the standard by which Justice and Injustice are measured. But since our whole discussion has to do with the reasoning of the populace, it will sometimes be necessary to speak in the popular manner, and give the name of law to that which in written form decrees whatever it wishes, either by command or prohibition. For such is the crowd's definition of law. But in determining what Justice is, let us begin with that supreme Law which had its origin ages before any written law existed or any State had been established.

6. *Natural Law.*[12]

True law is right reason in agreement with nature; it is of universal application, unchanging and everlasting; it summons to duty by its commands, and averts from wrongdoing by its prohibitions. And it does not lay its commands or prohibitions upon good men in vain, though neither have any effect on the wicked. It is a sin to try to alter this law, nor is it allowable to attempt to repeal any part of it, and it is impossible to abolish it entirely. We cannot be freed from its obligations by senate or people, and we need not look outside ourselves for an expounder or interpreter of it. And there will not be different laws at Rome and at Athens, or different laws now and in the future, but one eternal and un-changeable law will be valid for all nations and all times, and there will be one master and ruler, that is, God, over us all, for he is the author of this law, its promulgator, and its enforcing judge. Whoever is disobedient is fleeing from himself and denying his human nature, and by reason of this very fact he will suffer the worst penalties, even if he escapes what is commonly considered punishment. . . .

Since right reason is Law, we must believe that men have Law also in common with the gods. Further, those who share Law must also share Justice; and those who share these are to be re-garded as members of the same commonwealth. If indeed they obey the same authorities and powers, this is true in a far greater degree; but as a matter of fact they do obey this celestial system, the divine mind, and the God of transcendent power. Hence we must now conceive of this whole universe as one commonwealth of which both gods and men are members. . . . Out of all the material of the philosophers' discussions, surely there comes nothing more valuable than the full realization that we are born for Justice, and that

right is based, not upon men's opinions, but upon Nature. This fact will immediately be plain if you once get a clear conception of man's fel-lowship and union with his fellow-men. For no single thing is so like another, so exactly its counterpart, as all of us are to one another. Nay, if bad habits and false beliefs did not twist the weaker minds and turn them in whatever direc-tion they are inclined, no one would be so like his own self as all men would be like all others. . . . It is clear that, when a wise man shows to-ward another endowed with equal virtue the kind of benevolence which is so widely diffused among men, that will then have come to pass which, unbelievable as it seems to some, is after all the inevitable result—namely, that he loves himself no whit more than he loves another. . . . If Nature is not to be considered the foundation of Justice, . . . where then will there be a place for generosity, or love of country, or loyalty, or the inclination to be of service to others or to show gratitude for favors received? For these virtues originate in our natural inclination to love our fellow-men, and this is the foundation of Justice.

B.   CIVIL WAR

In 60 B.C. three leading political figures, Julius Caesar, Pompey, and Crassus, formed a personal alliance (later known as the First Triumvirate) to control political affairs. (Cicero was offered a partnership in the group, but refused, and was exiled in 58; the following year Pompey's influence secured his recall.) Caesar became consul in 59, and governor of Gaul in 58. In 50 he had for nine years been in command of the Gallic provinces. He had been extremely successful as a general, had grown very rich, and had a large and experi-enced army which was devoted to him personally. His political enemies held that he had been guilty of unconstitutional acts during his consulship in 59, and were waiting to attack him in the courts when he should return to the status of a private citizen. He there-fore wished to run in the elections of 49 for a second consulship, without laying down his military command while campaigning for office. This was contrary to usual practice and required permission of the Senate. The First Triumvirate had meanwhile dissolved: Crassus had died fighting the Parthians in Mesopotamia and Pompey had allied himself with the senatorial enemies of Caesar. The split between Caesar and Pompey was based in part on personal rivalry and in part on differences of political programs, since Pompey was supported by conservatives and Caesar by the popular party.

1. *The Crossing of the Rubicon.* In its first meetings of 49 B.C. the Senate discussed Cae-sar's proposal to be a candidate for consul in absentia. We have his account of the Senate's action, which the tribunes Antony (Marcus Antonius) and Cassius were illegally pre-vented from vetoing, and of the fateful move which Caesar made in consequence. (This translation of Caesar's report, in his *Commentaries on the Civil War,* uses the first person where Caesar wrote of himself in the third person.) [13]

Most of the senators, compelled by the consul's language, intimidated by the presence of the army and by the threats of Pompey's friends, against their will and yielding to pressure, adopted Scipio's proposal that I should disband my army before a fixed date, and that, if I failed to do so, I should be considered to be meditating treason against the Republic. . . .

Pompey, urged on by my enemies and by his desire that no one should be on the same level of authority with himself, had completely with-drawn himself from my friendship and become reconciled with our common enemies, most of whom he had himself imposed upon me at the time of our connection by marriage. Stirred, too, by the discredit attaching to his diversion of two legions from their route by Asia and Syria and his appropriation of them for his own power and supremacy, he was eager that the issue should be brought to the arbitrament of war.

For these reasons everything was done in hurry and confusion. My friends were allowed no time to inform me, nor were the tribunes given any opportunity of protesting against the peril that threatened them, nor even of retaining, by the exercise of their veto, the most fundamental of their rights. . . . Recourse was had to that extreme and ultimate decree of the Senate which had never previously been resorted to except when the city was at the point of destruction through the audacity of malefactors and all despaired of safety: "The consuls, the praetors, the tribunes, and all the proconsulars who are near the city shall take steps to see that the state incurs no harm." These resolutions were recorded by decree of the Senate on 7 January. . . . The tribunes at once fled from the city and came to me. I was at that time at Ravenna and was awaiting a reply to my very lenient demands, in the hope that by some sense of equity a peaceable conclusion might be reached. On the following days the Senate met outside the city. . . . Levies were held throughout Italy, arms were requisitioned, sums of money were extracted from the municipal towns and carried off from the temples, and all divine and human rights were thrown into confusion.

When this was known I addressed my troops. I related all the wrongs that my enemies had ever done me, and complained that Pompey had been led astray and corrupted by them through jealousy and a desire to detract from my credit, though he had himself always supported and aided my honor and dignity. I complained that a new precedent had been introduced into the state whereby the right of tribunicial intervention, which in earlier years had been restored by arms, was now being branded with ignominy and crushed by arms. . . . I exhorted them to defend from my enemies the reputation and dignity of the commander under whose guidance they had administered the state with unfailing good fortune for nine years, fought many successful battles, and pacified the whole of Gaul and Germany. Thereupon the men of the Thirteenth Legion, which was present—I had called this out at the beginning of the disorder: the rest had not yet assembled—exclaimed that they were ready to repel the wrongs of their commander and of the tribunes. Having thus learnt the disposition of the soldiers, I set out for [Ariminum] with that legion, and there met the tribunes who had fled to me.

2. *Cicero and Caesar.* Ariminum lies on the Adriatic coast of Italy, just south of the Rubicon River, which formed the southern boundary of Caesar's province. By crossing the Rubicon on the night of January 10, 49 B.C., Caesar put himself in the position of making war upon the Roman Republic. His military superiority became evident at once. Pompey had few troops at his disposal; he abandoned Rome immediately, withdrew to Brundisium in southern Italy, and on March 17 sailed with his small army for Greece. There he intended to gather sufficient forces to continue the war with Caesar. For Cicero the outbreak of civil war raised difficult questions: Could the Republic survive the victory of either Caesar or Pompey? Could he restore peace by mediating between the two enemies? Did personal loyalty require him to follow Pompey? His letters, which were published after his death by his secretary, Tiro, give a vivid sense of his agony of mind in the weeks following Caesar's invasion of Italy. He had himself recently returned from the province of Cilicia in Asia Minor, where he had been governor. The first of the following letters refers to his return to the neighborhood of Rome. Atticus, to whom most of these letters are addressed, was Cicero's closest personal friend, a wealthy Epicurean who avoided participation in public affairs.

[*Cicero to Tiro, Jan. 12.*] [14]

Although I miss your timely assistance at every turn, yet it is not on my own account so much as on yours that your illness grieves me. . . .

I approached the City on January 4. Nothing could be more complimentary than the way I was met by a procession. But my arrival coincided with a very conflagration of civil discord, or rather civil war; and though I had the eager desire, and I believe, the power to find a remedy for it, I was thwarted by the passionate desires of certain men; for there are those on both sides who desire to fight. To sum up, Caesar himself too, our former friend, has sent a threatening and disagreeable despatch to the Senate, and is still so insolent as to defy the Senate in retaining his army and province; and my old friend Curio eggs him on. Our friend Antony indeed and Quintus Cassius, though no violence was used in expelling them, set out in Curio's company to join Caesar, as soon as the Senate had formally charged the consuls, praetors, tribunes of the plebs, and us proconsuls with the duty of seeing that "the Republic suffered no injury."

Never was the State in greater danger; never have disloyal citizens had a better prepared man at their head. On the whole very careful preparations are being made on our side also. That is due to the influence and activity of our old friend Pompey, who, now that it is too late, is beginning to be afraid of Caesar. . . .

Again and again I beg you to take care of your health, and to send me a letter whenever you find a man to entrust with one. Again and again, good-bye.

[Cicero to Atticus, about Jan. 20.] [15]

What in the name of wonder is this? What is happening? I am in the dark. People say, "Cingulum is ours, Ancona is lost, Labienus has deserted from Caesar." Are we talking of a Roman officer or of Hannibal? Wretched madman never to have seen the shadow even of right! Yet all this, he says, is done to support his honor. Can there be honor without honesty: and is it honest to retain an army without sanction, to seize the cities of your country that you may strike the better at her heart, to contrive abolition of debts, the restoration of exiles, and scores of other crimes, "to win God's greatest gift, a crown?" Well, let him keep his fortune. For my part . . . better a thousand times to die than once to meditate such villainy. "Suppose you conceive a desire for it," you say. Desire is free to anyone; but I would rather be crucified than have such a desire. There is only one worse fate, to obtain your desire. But enough of this. It eases me to philosophize a trifle in our present straits. . . .

[Cicero to Atticus, Feb. 17.] [16]

. . . To my mind, no statesman or general has ever been guilty of conduct so disgraceful as Pompey's. I am sorry for him. He left Rome, his country, for which and in which it were glorious to die. You don't seem to me to realize what a disaster that is. You yourself are still in your own house; but you cannot stay there any longer without the consent of villains and traitors. It is the depth of misery and shame. We wander in want with wives and children. Our sole hope lies in the life of one man [Pompey], who falls dangerously sick every year. We are not driven, but summoned to leave our country. And our country which we have left will not be kept in safety against our return, but abandoned to fire and plunder. . . . My point is that I can gladly die for Pompey's sake—there is no one I hold dearer; but not in that way. In him I see no hope for the safety of the state. You express a view different from your usual view, that I must even leave Italy, if he does. That course seems to me of no

advantage to the state or to my children, and, moreover, neither right or honorable. But why do you say, "Will you be able to see a tyrant?" As if it mattered whether I hear of him or see him, or as if I wanted a better example than Socrates, who never set foot out of gate during the reign of the Thirty tyrants. . . .

[Cicero to Atticus, Feb. 27.] [17]

As you suppose, I am in great anxiety of mind. . . . But I fear, since lamentation is idle, I disgrace my philosophy and my works. So I spend my time considering the character of the ideal statesman, who is sketched clearly enough, you seem to think, in my books on the Republic. You remember then the standard by which our ideal governor was to weigh his acts. . . . "As a safe voyage is the aim of the pilot, health of the physician, victory of the general, so the ideal statesman will aim at happiness for the citizens of the state to give them material security, copious wealth, wide-reaching distinction and untarnished honor. This, the greatest and finest of human achievements, I want him to perform." Pompey never had this notion and least of all in the present cause. Absolute power is what he and Caesar have sought; their aim has not been to secure the happiness and honor of the community. Pompey has not abandoned Rome because it was impossible to defend, nor Italy on forced compulsion; but it was his idea from the first to plunge the world into war, to stir up barbarous princes, to bring savage tribes into Italy under arms, and to gather a huge army. . . . Or do you think that no agreement, no compromise between him and Caesar was possible? Why, it is possible to-day: but neither of them looks to our happiness. Both want to be kings. . . .

[Cicero to Atticus, March 1.] [18]

Let my secretary's handwriting be proof that I am suffering from inflammation of the eyes, and that is my reason for brevity, though now to be sure I have no news. I depend entirely on news from Brundisium. . . . Do you see the kind of man into whose hands the state has fallen? What foresight, what energy, what readiness! Upon my word, if he refrain from murder and rapine, he will be the darling of those who dreaded him most. The people of the country towns and the farmers talk to me a great deal. They care for nothing at all but their lands, their little homesteads and their tiny hoards. And see how public opinion has changed. They fear the man they once trusted [Pompey], and adore the man they once dreaded [Caesar]. It pains me to think of the mistakes and wrongs of ours that are responsible for this reaction. . . .

[*Cicero to Atticus, March 18.*] [19]

. . . I seem to myself to have been mad from the very beginning, and the one thing that tortures me is that I did not follow Pompey like a private soldier, when he was slipping or rather rushing to ruin. I saw he was terrified on the 17th of January: on that day I felt what he would do. Since then I have never approved his course, and he has never ceased to commit one blunder after another. Meantime not a letter to me, nothing but thoughts of flight. . . . If flight were his only object, I would have fled gladly enough. But I was aghast at warfare so cruel and desperate, the upshot of which is still unknown. What threats against the country towns, against the loyalists by name, in fact against all who should stay behind! . . . I shrank from a war of that kind, and also because I saw cruelty even greater was being planned and prepared [by the Pompeians]. Was it for me, whom some called the savior and father of Rome, to bring against her hordes of Getae, Armenians and Colchians? Was it for me to bring famine on my fellow-townsmen and devastation on Italy? In the first place I reflected that Caesar was mortal, and besides might be got rid of in many ways. But I thought that our city and our people should be preserved so far as in us lay for immortality; and anyhow I cherished a hope that some arrangement might be made before Caesar perpetrated such a crime or Pompey such iniquity. . . .

[*Caesar to Cicero, sometime in early March.*] [20]

Though I have only had a glimpse of our friend Furnius, and have not yet been able conveniently to speak to him or hear what he has to say, being in a hurry and on the march, yet I could not neglect the opportunity of writing to you and sending him to convey my thanks. Be sure I have often thanked you and I expect to have occasion to do so still more often in the future: so great are your services to me. First I beg you, since I trust that I shall quickly reach Rome, to let me see you there, and employ your advice, favor, position and help of all kinds. I will return to what I began with: pardon my haste and the shortness of my letter. All the other information you may get from Furnius.

[*Cicero to Caesar, March 19.*] [21]

On reading your letter, which I got from our friend Furnius, in which you told me to come near Rome, I was not much surprised at your wishing to employ "my advice and my position"; but I asked myself what you meant by my "influence" and "help." However, my hopes led me to think that a man of your admirable statesmanship would wish to act for the comfort, peace, and

agreement of the citizens, and for that purpose I considered my own character and inclination very suitable. If that is the case, and if you are touched by the desire to protect our friend Pompey and reconcile him to yourself and the State, I am sure you will find no one more suited for the purpose than I am. I have always advocated peace both with Pompey and the Senate ever since I have been able to do so, nor since the outbreak of hostilities have I taken any part in the war; I have considered that the war was attacking your rights in that envious and hostile persons were opposing a distinction conferred on you by the grace of the Roman people. But, as at that time I not only upheld your rights but urged others to assist you, so now I am greatly concerned with the rights of Pompey. It is many years since I chose you two men for my special respect, and to be my closest friends, as you are. So I ask you, or rather beseech and entreat you with all urgency, that in spite of all your anxieties you may devote some time to considering how I may be enabled by your kindness to be what decency and gratitude, nay good-feeling, require, in remembering my great debt to Pompey. If this only mattered to myself, I should yet hope to obtain my request; but to my mind it touches your honor and the public weal that I, a friend of peace and of both of you, should be so supported by you that I may be able to work for peace between you and peace amongst our fellow-citizens. . . .

[*Cicero to Atticus, March 26.*] [22]

Though I have nothing to write to you, still, not to miss a day, I send this letter. On the 27th of March Caesar will stop at Sinuessa, they say. . . . I had written praising to the skies his kindness, his clemency at Corfinium.* He replied as follows:

"You are right to infer of me (for I am well known to you) that there is nothing further from my nature than cruelty. Whilst I take great pleasure from that fact, I am proud indeed that my action wins your approval. I am not moved because it is said that those whom I let go have departed to wage war on me again, for there is nothing I like better than that I should be true to myself and they to themselves. I could wish you to meet me at Rome that I may avail myself of your advice and resources, as usual, in everything. You must know that nothing pleases me more than the presence of your relative Dolabella. This favor also I shall owe to him; for he will not be able to do otherwise than arrange it,

---

* Caesar had accepted the surrender of a senatorial army, freed the officers, and allowed the men to enlist in his own army.

such is his kindness, his feeling and goodwill towards me."

[Cicero to Atticus, March 28.] 23

In both respects I followed your advice. I spoke so as to gain Caesar's respect rather than his gratitude; and I persisted in my resolve not to go to Rome. We were mistaken in thinking he would be easy to manage. I have never seen anyone less easy. He kept on saying that my decision was a slur on him, and that others would be less likely to come, if I did not come.* I pointed out that my case was very unlike theirs. After much talk he said, "Well, come and discuss peace." "On my own terms?" I asked. "Need I dictate to you?" said he. "Well," said I, "I shall contend that the Senate cannot sanction your invasion of Spain or your going with an army into Greece, and," I added, "I shall lament Pompey's fate." He replied, "That is not what I want." "So I fancied," said I: "but I do not want to be in Rome, because either I must say that and much else, on which I cannot keep silent, if I am present, or else I cannot come." The upshot was that I was to think over the matter, as Caesar suggested, with a view to closing our interview. I could not refuse. So we parted. I am confident that he has no liking for me. But I like myself, as I have not for a long time. . . . Caesar's finale, which I had almost forgotten, was hateful:—"If I may not use your advice, I shall use the advice I can and go to any length." . . .

[Cicero to Atticus, April 14.] 24

. . . The war is not unjust on [Pompey's] part, nay, it is even righteous and necessary; but, unless he conquers, it will be fatal to his fellow-countrymen; and, even if he does conquer, it will be disastrous. These [Caesar and Pompey] are our great men; but I do not hold their achievements one whit superior to mine, nor even their fortune, though they may seem to have basked in fortune's smiles while I have met her frowns. For who can be happy, when he has caused his country to be deserted or enslaved? And if, as you admonish me, I was right in saying in those books of mine that nothing is good, save what is honorable, and nothing bad, save what is dishonorable, then certainly both of them are most miserable, since both of them have thought less of their country's safety and dignity than of their own high place and private interests. My conscience then is clear and helps to support me, when I think that I have always rendered my country good service, when I could, and assuredly have never harbored any but loyal thoughts, and that the State has

been wrecked by the very storm which I foresaw fourteen years ago. With a clear conscience then I shall depart, though the parting will cost me a bitter pang. . . .*

3. *Cicero and Antony.* The dictatorship of Caesar, which followed his defeat of Pompey, was short-lived. He was assassinated on March 15 (the Ides of March), 44 B.C. For a few months it seemed that the Republic might still be restored in its old form; but in the year after Caesar's death the Second Triumvirate was formed by Antony, Lepidus, and Octavian (Caesar's nephew and adopted son, later called Augustus). The efforts of the "Liberators," as Caesar's assassins called themselves, collapsed. Cicero and many others were put to death. Cicero had played a leading role in the final attempt to restore the Republic, attacking Antony with particular bitterness. The following passages from a speech against Antony express the spirit which animated Cicero's last efforts.25

The name of peace is dear to us and peace itself is a safe refuge; but between peace and slavery there is a great difference. Peace is undisturbed liberty, slavery is the ultimate evil from which war and even death must preserve us. . . .

If honor cannot lure you into right conduct [Mark Antony], cannot even fear summon you from acts of the utmost foulness? You do not fear our courts of law. If this is because of your innocence, you have my praise; but if it is because of your power, do you not understand what it is that a man must fear who for such a reason does not fear the courts? Even if you do not dread brave men and admirable citizens because they are kept from you by your weapons, your own supporters, believe me, will not put up with you for very long. What kind of a life is it that is spent in fear of friends every moment of the day and night? Do you hold them bound by greater services than he [Caesar] held some of those by whom he was killed? Or are you in any way to be compared with him? In him there were intelligence, judgment, memory, learning, devotion, deliberation, diligence; he had won victories which, though disastrous to the Republic, were still great; for many years he planned to become a tyrant, and with great effort and amid great dangers he had accomplished what he had designed. By giving entertainments, public buildings, doles, and food he had charmed the ignorant masses; he had bound his supporters by rewards and his opponents by a show of mercy. In short, partly by fear and partly by forebearance

---

* Caesar had asked Cicero to attend meetings of the senate.

* Cicero sailed to join Pompey a few weeks after writing this letter.

he had brought to a free people the habit of servitude.

I can compare you with him in your lust for power, but in other respects you are by no means his equal. Yet out of the many misfortunes which he inflicted on the Republic there has come one good thing: the Roman People has now learned how far to trust each individual, on whom to rely, against whom to be on guard. Do you not think of these things? Do you not understand that it is enough for brave men to have learned how splendid is the act, how welcome the benefit, how glorious the renown, of killing a tyrant? Or will men who could not bear him, endure you? There will be rivalry before long—believe me—in the rush to perform this act, there will be no lingering wait for opportunity. Return to your senses at last, I beg you. Consider those from whom you are descended, not those with whom you live. Do with me as you will, but make your peace with the Republic.

But it is for you to decide about yourself; I shall speak of my course. I defended the Republic when I was young, I shall not desert it when I am old; I scorned the swords of Catiline, I shall not fear yours. I would willingly offer my body if by my death the liberty of the Republic can be made real, so that at length the pain of the Roman People may bring to birth that with which it has so long been in travail. If indeed I declared almost twenty years ago in this very temple that death could not be untimely for one who had been a consul, how much more truly shall I declare this of an old man. For me, Senators, death is even welcome now that I have finished the tasks I undertook and have accomplished. There are two things I desire: first, that in dying I may leave the Roman People free (this is the greatest gift the immortal gods can grant me); and second, that each of us may fare as he has deserved of the Republic.

Part III.   THE EMPIRE

A.   AUGUSTUS

Augustus Caesar had been a boy of thirteen when the civil wars began. He was barely twenty when he joined Antony and Lepidus in the Second Triumvirate. Brutus and Cassius, the assassins of Caesar, were defeated and died at the battle of Philippi in 42 B.C. Lepidus was soon eliminated from power although he continued to hold the office of Pontifex Maximus. After some years of divided rule, while Antony controlled the East and Octavian (as Augustus was then called) held the West, a new civil war left Octavian in 31 B.C. victor without a rival. He succeeded, where Julius Caesar had failed, in securing general popular acquiescence in his power. In contrast to Julius Caesar, who had shown contempt for the traditional forms of government, Augustus respected the forms and titles of the Republic. He avoided any title which would suggest absolute power, and chose to be called by the informal title *Princeps,* a word familiar in the Republic to denote a leading citizen. (*Emperor*—in Latin, *imperator*—the term by which we usually designate Augustus and his successors, meant originally "commander of an army," and many men in Republican times had been *imperatores.* The term *Princeps* rather than *Emperor* is used as the title of office in the documents that follow.)

1. *The Accomplishments of Augustus.* Augustus continued in power until his death in 14 A.D. and was succeeded by his heir Tiberius. An account of the accomplishments of his life was prepared by himself and inscribed on many buildings throughout the empire. One copy has survived in Ankara, the modern capital of Turkey. Selections from it follow.[26]

(1) When I was nineteen years of age, on my own initiative as a private citizen and at my own expense, I raised the army by which I won liberty for the Republic, which had been subject to the tyranny of a party. In recognition of this the Senate honored me with membership during the consulship of Gaius Pansa and Aulus Hirtius [43 B.C.], and at the same time gave me the status of an ex-consul in debating issues and the right to military command. It ordered me . . . together with the consuls to "take action so that the Republic should suffer no harm." In the same year, when both the consuls had fallen in action, the people elected me to the consulship and to the Triumvirate for establishing order in the Republic.

(2) I forced my father's assassins into exile, punishing their crime by due process of law; when

they subsequently made war on the Republic I twice defeated them in battle.

(3) I engaged in civil wars on land and sea, and in foreign wars throughout the world. When I had won victory I spared all the citizens who survived the fighting. I chose rather to preserve than to destroy all foreign nations which could safely be pardoned. Approximately 500,000 Roman citizens served under my command. I established somewhat more than 300,000 of them in colonies or sent them back to their own municipalities after they had completed their periods of enlistment, and to all of these I gave lands which I had purchased or money in lieu of land. I captured 600 ships, exclusive of craft smaller than triremes.

(4) I twice received triumphal ovations, three times celebrated triumphs over foreign enemies, and was saluted as *Imperator* twenty-one times. . . . In my triumphs nine kings or children of kings were led before my chariot. At the time of writing this document I have been consul thirteen times and have held the tribunician power for thirty-seven years.

(5) I did not accept the dictatorship when it was offered me by the People and the Senate during the consulship of Marcus Marcellus and Lucius Arruntius [22 B.C.]. . . . When there was a serious shortage of grain I did not refuse the post of grain commissioner, and fulfilled this responsibility in such a way that within a few days I freed the whole people from fear and danger, at my own expense. I did not accept the permanent annual consulship offered me at the same time.

(6) . . . The Senate and the Roman People were in agreement that I should assume control of the laws and public morals, alone and with supreme authority. I declined to accept any office contrary to the customs of our ancestors. Instead I accomplished through my tribunician power the measures which the Senate then wished me to carry out. . . .

(12) . . . The Senate decreed that an altar of Augustan Peace should be consecrated in the Campus Martius, and ordered that the magistrates, priests, and Vestal virgins make annual sacrifice on it.

(13) Our ancestors have ordered that the gates of Janus Quirinus should be shut when peace with victory has been won on land and sea through the whole territory controlled by the Roman People: although before my birth this is only reported to have happened twice since the founding of the City, the Senate decreed the closing of the gates three times during my Principate.

(20) . . . I restored the aqueducts which were in many places crumbling with age. . . . In accordance with a decree of the Senate I repaired eighty-two temples of the gods in the City during my sixth consulship, omitting none which at that time needed repair. In my seventh consulship I rebuilt the Flaminian Road from the City to Ariminum, including all bridges except the Mulvian and the Minucian.

(22) I gave gladiatorial combats three times in my own name and five times in the name of my sons or grandsons; over 10,000 men fought in these combats. I presented to the people exhibitions of athletes gathered from all parts of the world, twice in my own name and a third time in the name of my grandson. I presented games four times in my own name and twenty-three times in the place of other magistrates. . . .

(25) I freed the sea from pirates. . . .

(26) I have extended the boundaries of every province of the Roman People on which border nations not subject to our rule. I have brought peace to the Gallic and Spanish provinces and to Germany—the shores of the Ocean from Cadiz to the mouth of the Elbe. . . . My fleet sailed through the Ocean from the mouth of the Rhine eastward as far as the lands of the Cimbri [in modern Denmark], where no Roman had gone before either by land or by sea. . . . At my command and under my auspices two armies were led at almost the same time into Ethiopia and into that part of Arabia which is called "Happy"; large forces of both these enemies were cut to pieces and many towns captured. In Ethiopia the army reached Nabata, near Meroe. In Arabia the army advanced into the Sabaean territory as far as Mariba [in the modern Yemen].

(27) I added Egypt to the empire of the Roman People. . . .

(28) I established colonies of soldiers in Africa, Sicily, Macedonia, both Spanish provinces, Achaea, Asia, Syria, Narbonese Gaul, and Pisidia. . . .

(29) I compelled the Parthians to return to me the spoils and standards of three Roman armies, and as suppliants to seek the friendship of the Roman People. The standards I placed in the inner sanctuary of the temple of Mars the Avenger.

(30) Through Tiberius Nero, then my son and lieutenant, I brought under Roman rule tribes of the Pannonians which no Roman army had approached before my Principate, and I extended the boundaries of Illyricum to the Danube. . . .

(31) Embassies from kings of India were frequently sent to me, although they had never before been seen in the camp of any Roman general. Our friendship was sought by envoys of the Bastarnae and the Scythians [in Rumania and southern Russia] and by the kings of the Sarma-

tians who live on both sides of the Don river, and by kings of the Albanians, the Iberians [both in the Caucasus], and the Medes [in Iran].

(34) In my sixth and seventh consulships [28 and 27 B.C.], when I had extinguished the fires of civil war after assuming absolute power by universal consent, I transferred the Republic from my control to the will of the Senate and the Roman People. In recognition of my services I was named Augustus by decree of the Senate, the door posts of my house were publicly decorated with laurel, the civic crown was fastened above my door, and a gold shield was placed in the Julian Senate House; the inscription on this shield bears witness that it was given me for my valor, clemency, justice, and piety. Since that time I have surpassed all other men in prestige, but have had no more power than those who have been my colleagues in office.

(35) During my thirteenth consulship [2 B.C.] the Senate, the knights, and the whole Roman People gave me the title "Father of his Country," and decreed that this title should be inscribed in the vestibule of my home, in the Senate House, and in the Forum of Augustus beneath the chariot which was set up in my honor by senatorial decree. I write this in my seventy-sixth year.

2. *Judgments on Augustus.* Historians have always differed sharply in their judgment of the life and character of Augustus. A century after his death Tacitus, one of the most brilliant and biting of Roman historians, began his history of the early Empire with a summary of contemporary opinions of Augustus.[27]

When after the destruction of Brutus and Cassius there was no longer any army of the Commonwealth, . . . when, with Lepidus pushed aside and Antonius slain, even the Julian faction had only [Augustus] Caesar left to lead it, then, dropping the title of triumvir, and giving out that he was a Consul, and was satisfied with a tribune's authority for the protection of the people, Augustus won over the soldiers with gifts, the populace with cheap corn, and all men with the sweets of repose, and so grew greater by degrees, while he concentrated in himself the functions of the Senate, the magistrates, and the laws. He was wholly unopposed, for the boldest spirits had fallen in battle, or in the proscription, while the remaining nobles, the readier they were to be slaves, were raised the higher by wealth and promotion, so that, aggrandised by revolution, they preferred the safety of the present to the dangerous past. Nor did the provinces dislike that condition of affairs, for they distrusted the government of the Senate and the people, because of the rivalries between the leading men and the rapacity of the officials, while the protection of the laws was unavailing, as they were continually deranged by violence, intrigue, and finally by corruption. . . .

[At the end of Augustus' life] at home all was tranquil, and there were magistrates with the same titles; there was a younger generation, sprung up since the victory of Actium, and even many of the older men had been born during the civil wars. How few were left who had seen the republic!

Thus the State had been revolutionised, and there was not a vestige left of the old sound morality. Stript of equality, all looked up to the commands of a sovereign without the least apprehension for the present, while Augustus in the vigor of life, could maintain his own position, that of his house, and the general tranquillity. When in advanced old age, he was worn out by a sickly frame, and the end was near and new prospects opened, a few spoke in vain of the blessings of freedom, but most dreaded and some longed for war. . . .

Then [on his death] followed much talk about Augustus himself. . . . People extolled the number of his consulships, . . . the continuance for thirty-seven years of the tribunitian power, the title of Imperator twenty-one times earned, and his other honors which had been either frequently repeated or were wholly new. Sensible men, however, spoke variously of his life with praise and censure. Some said "that dutiful feeling towards a father, and the necessities of the State in which laws had then no place, drove him into civil war, which can neither be planned nor conducted on any right principles. He had often yielded to Antonius, while he was taking vengeance on his father's murderers, often also to Lepidus. When the latter sank into feeble dotage and the former had been ruined by his profligacy, the only remedy for his distracted country was the rule of a single man. Yet the State had been organized under the name neither of a kingdom nor a dictatorship, but under that of a prince [*princeps*]. The ocean and remote rivers were the boundaries of the empire; the legions, provinces, fleets, all things were linked together; there was law for the citizens; there was respect shown to the allies. The capital had been embellished on a grand scale; only in a few instances had he resorted to force, simply to secure general tranquillity."

It was said, on the other hand, "that filial duty and State necessity were merely assumed as a mask. It was really from a lust of sovereignty that he had excited the veterans by bribery, had, when a young man and a subject, raised an army, tampered with the Consul's legions, and feigned an attachment to the faction of Pompeius. . . . Then, when Hirtius and Pansa were slain, . . . he at once possessed himself of both their armies, wrested the consulate from a reluctant Senate, and turned against the State the arms with which he had been intrusted against Antonius. Citizens were proscribed, lands divided, without so much as the approval of those who executed these deeds. Even granting that the deaths of Cassius and of the Bruti were sacrifices to a hereditary enmity (though duty requires us to waive private feuds for the sake of the public welfare), still Pompeius [the son of Julius Caesar's enemy] had been deluded by the phantom of peace, and Lepidus by the mask of friendship. Subsequently, Antonius had been lured on by . . . his marriage with the sister, and paid by his death the penalty of a treacherous alliance. No doubt, there was peace after all this, but it was a peace stained with blood.

3. *Private Life in the Period of Revolution.* An Italian inscription from the period of Augustus reveals the effect which the events of these years could have on the private lives of individuals. It is the eulogy by an unknown man of his wife, who had died after forty-one years of marriage.[28]

[During the war between Caesar and Pompey] you were suddenly left an orphan when both your parents were murdered in their place of retirement in the country. It was primarily because of you that the death of your parents did not remain unpunished, at a time when I had gone to the war in Macedon and your brother-in-law to Africa. . . . After the punishment of those responsible you moved to my mother's home, where you waited for my return. . . . With your jewels you provided me with ample means for my flight. . . . You took from yourself and gave to me all your gold and pearls; then, cleverly deceiving the guards set by our opponents, you made me comfortable in my absence by sending slaves, money, and provisions. After preserving my life when I was absent, as your courage urged you to do, your fidelity protected me by means of the clemency of those [the supporters of Julius Caesar] against whom you acted; yet you always spoke with firmness. At the same time you successfully kept off the guerrillas of Milo (whose house I had bought when he was in exile), when the civil war offered them an opportunity for breaking in and pillaging, and protected our house. . . .

[They were married after his pardon by Caesar. Then he fought in the army of Brutus and Cassius.]

I owe it no less to you than to Caesar [Augustus] himself that he allowed me to return to my country: if you had not taken measures for my safety and kept me alive so that he might preserve me, he would have promised his support in vain. So I owe my life as much to your fidelity as to the clemency of Caesar. Why should I now reveal our secret and hidden plans and private conversations?—how you prevented me from taking risks blindly and too boldly and, when I considered the situation more calmly, prepared a safe refuge for me and chose that your sister and her husband Gaius Cluvius should share your plans for procuring my safety, all of us sharing the same danger? I should never finish if I tried to mention everything. It is enough for you and me that I remained hidden in safety.

Yet I must confess that the most bitter experience of my life occurred in connection with you. When I was restored to my country, as a citizen no longer useless, by the generous decision of Caesar Augustus (who was then absent from Rome) you raised with Marcus Lepidus, his colleague, (then present in Rome) the question of my return. You threw yourself on the ground at his feet: not only were you not raised up; you were dragged and treated like a slave; your body was covered with bruises. Yet you continued with unbroken courage to remind him of Caesar's edict and Caesar's congratulations on my restoration. Even after you had heard his cutting words and felt his cruel blows you told people of his treatment, so that they might know who was responsible for my dangers. He suffered for this before long. What could be more effective than your courage? You offered Caesar an opportunity for clemency, and while preserving my life you drew attention to uncontrolled cruelty by your splendid endurance.

But what need is there of words? Let me be brief, since it is time to close. Let me not go on, treating of these admirable deeds in a way unworthy of them, since the fact that I am alive is proof of all that I owe to you.

When peace was brought to the whole world, and the Republic was restored, a calm and happy life came for us. . . .

You have deserved everything of me, and I have not been able to give you everything. Your wishes have been my law; I shall still do what lies within my power. May the spirits of the dead grant you peace and keep you safe.

B.   "PRINCIPATE AND LIBERTY"

During the first century A.D. the administration of the Empire was marred by periods of violent tyranny which, as in the closing years of Nero's reign, were felt chiefly by those nearest the ruler—especially by members of the Senate who considered themselves the defenders of Romans' ancient claim to liberty. During most of the second century, however, excellent relations existed between Senate and Princeps, while there was practically universal content with the existing order throughout the Empire. The historian Tacitus said of Nerva (whose brief rule from 96 to 98 A.D. introduced the period of the "five good emperors") that "he united things previously irreconcilable, principate and liberty" (*Agricola,* 3). Pliny's *Panegyric of Trajan,* delivered before the Senate in the year 100 A.D., expresses the attitude of a leading senator of this period. The speech was made on the occasion of Pliny's entrance upon the consulship; it is addressed both to the Senate and to Trajan, the princeps, who had himself held the consulship shortly before. (Trajan, like other successors of Augustus, was called Caesar Augustus.) Although Pliny eulogizes Trajan in terms which modern taste finds extravagant, we need not feel that his words lack sincerity.[29]

It is not a tyrant of whom we speak, but a fellow-citizen, not a master but a father; his excellence and pre-eminence among us are heightened by the very fact that he considers himself to be one of us and remembers that he is no less a man than a governor over men. Let us therefore understand our good fortune and prove ourselves worthy of him, and let us continually ask ourselves whether we should offer greater obedience to a princeps who delights in the servitude of citizens or to one who delights in their liberty. . . .

We are ruled by you [Pliny now addresses Trajan directly] and subject to you, but as we are subject to the laws. The laws curb our impulses and our desires, yet they exist with us and dwell with us. You are pre-eminent among us, you excel us, just as honor and power, though above men, nevertheless belong to men. Before you, those who held your office had forgotten how to walk because of scorn of us and something like a fear of equality. They were raised above our heads by the shoulders and necks of slaves; you are raised above them by glory, by the love of your fellow-citizens, and by liberty. You are lifted to the stars by this common earth you share with us, and by the footsteps of a princeps mingled with ours. . . .

There are statues of you such as once were dedicated to private individuals for their great services to the Republic; statues of Caesar are to be seen made of the same material as those of a Brutus, of a Camillus: and made for the same reason. They drove kings and a victorious enemy from our walls; he wards off and keeps far from us kingship itself and all the other evils defeat brings, and he occupies the place of a princeps in order that there may be no room for a master. . . .

I turn now to your consulship. . . . You were made a consul like one of us whom you make consuls. . . . The usual formalities of the elections had been completed—if one considered that this was the princeps—and the whole crowd had already begun to move away, when you, to the amazement of everyone, advanced to the seat of the presiding consul, and offered yourself to be bound by words unknown to a princeps except when he has compelled others to swear to them [i.e., the oath to obey the laws]. You see how essential it was that you should not refuse the consulship. If you had refused the office we could not have imagined that you would act as you did. I am amazed, fellow Senators, and cannot even yet believe my eyes and my ears, and still keep asking myself whether I really heard it, whether I really saw it. The Commander, Caesar, Augustus, the Pontifex Maximus, stood before the seated consul; the consul sat while the princeps stood before him, and he sat free from consternation, free from fear, as if this were a common occurrence. And further, seated he dictated the oath, and the princeps swore, spoke and proclaimed clearly the words by which he devoted himself and his house to the anger of the gods if he knowingly lied. . . . You made yourself subject to the laws, Caesar, to laws which no one has written for a princeps. But you wish that your rights be no greater than ours; the result is that we wish that your rights be greater than ours. I hear now for the first time, learn now for the first time—not "Princeps above Laws," but "Laws above Princeps"; and the same limitation is placed on the consul Caesar as on the rest of us. . . .

The first day of your consulship dawned; entering the Senate chamber you urged now individuals, now all of us to take back our liberty, to undertake the responsibilities of a shared command, to watch over the public welfare and rise to its demands. All before you have said the same things; no one before you has been believed. We had seen the shipwrecks of too many, shattered by an unexpected storm when they had sailed forth in a treacherous calm. What sea is so untrustworthy as the kindness of a princeps whose fickleness and guile are so great that it is easier to guard against his anger than against his favor? But we follow you wherever you call, eager and free from apprehension. You bid us be free; we shall be free. You bid us speak our thoughts in public; we shall proclaim them. We have not sat idle in the past because of cowardice and inborn apathy: terror and fear and an unhappy prudence born of peril warned us to turn our eyes, ears, and minds from the Republic (but there was indeed no Republic). But now relying and depending on your pledge and your promises we open mouths closed in long servitude and loosen tongues curbed by so many misfortunes.

C. THE EMPIRE AND EARLY CHRISTIANITY

Both the Republic and the Empire normally allowed complete toleration to all religious beliefs. The Romans, polytheistic themselves, had no compelling reasons for opposing new gods. Christianity, however, offered a special problem to the Roman authorities. In the beginning they were able to treat Christians like the adherents of any other religious sect, as we can see in the *Gospels* and the *Acts of the Apostles*. But Christianity soon acquired a status different from other religions, both because of the refusal of Christians to perform ritual acts of worship to the spirits of the emperors, and because of a widespread popular hostility to Christians; this hostility was kept alive by belief that Christians sacrificed babies and drank their blood, indulged in sexual debauchery under the guise of religious ceremony, and were engaged in a subversive conspiracy against the state. Several periods of persecution mark the century and a half between the reign of Nero and the Edict of Milan, which in 313 A.D. granted toleration to Christianity. Soon afterward, under the Emperor Constantine, it became the official religion of the Empire.

1. *The Trial of Jesus before Pilate.* In 30 A.D., when Jesus was brought to trial, Judaea was a minor Roman province governed by a Procurator, Pontius Pilate. He had the duty of maintaining order and safeguarding Roman interests; local government was in the hands of a High Priest assisted by a body called the Sanhedrin. Jesus, having been found guilty of blasphemy by the High Priest and the Sanhedrin, was brought to the court of the Procurator.[30]

Then they led Jesus from the house of Caiaphas [the High-Priest] to the praetorium [the office of Pontius Pilate, the Procurator]. It was early. They themselves did not enter the praetorium, so that they might not be defiled, but might eat the passover. So Pilate went out to them and said, "What accusation do you bring against this man?" They answered him, "If this man were not an evil-doer, we would not have handed him over." Pilate said to them, "Take him yourselves and judge him by your own law." The Jews said to him, "It is not lawful for us to put any man to death." This was to fulfill the word which Jesus had spoken to show by what death he was to die.

Pilate entered the praetorium again and called Jesus, and said to him, "Are you the King of the Jews?" Jesus answered, "Do you say this of your own accord, or did others say it to you about me?" Pilate answered, "Am I a Jew? Your own nation and the chief priests have handed you over to me; what have you done?" Jesus answered, "My kingship is not of this world; if my kingship were of this world, my servants would fight, that I might not be handed over to the Jews; but my kingship is not from the world." Pilate said to him, "So you are a king?" Jesus answered, "You say that I am a king. For this I was born, and for this I have come into the world, to bear witness to the truth. Every one who is of the truth hears my voice." Pilate said to him, "What is truth?"

After he had said this, he went out to the Jews again, and told them, "I find no crime in him. But you have a custom that I should release one man for you at the Passover; will you have me release for you the King of the Jews?" They cried out again, "Not this man, but Barabbas!" Now Barabbas was a robber.

Then Pilate took Jesus and scourged him. And the soldiers plaited a crown of thorns, and put it on his head, and arrayed him in a purple robe; they came up to him, saying, "Hail, King of the Jews!" and struck him with their hands. Pilate went out again, and said to them, "Behold I am bringing him out to you, that you may know that I find no crime in him." So Jesus came out, wearing the crown of thorns and the purple robe.

Pilate said to them, "Here is the man!" When the chief priests and the officers saw him, they cried out, "Crucify him, crucify him!" Pilate said to them, "Take him yourselves and crucify him, for I find no crime in him." The Jews answered him, "We have a law, and by that law he ought to die, because he has made himself the Son of God." When Pilate heard these words, he was the more afraid; he entered the praetorium again and said to Jesus, "Where are you from?" But Jesus gave no answer. Pilate therefore said to him, "You will not speak to me? Do you not know that I have power to release you, and power to crucify you?" Jesus answered him, "You would have no power over me unless it had been given you from above; therefore he who delivered me to you has the greater sin."

Upon this Pilate sought to release him, but the Jews cried out, "If you release this man, you are not Caesar's friend; every one who makes himself a king sets himself against Caesar." When Pilate heard these words, he brought Jesus out and sat down on the judgment seat at a place called The Pavement, and in Hebrew, Gabbatha. Now it was the day of Preparation for the Passover; it was about the sixth hour. He said to the Jews, "Here is your King!" They cried out, "Away with him, away with him, crucify him!" Pilate said to them, "Shall I crucify your King?" The chief priests answered, "We have no king but Caesar." Then he handed him over to them to be crucified.

2. *The Prosecution of St. Paul* for violation of Jewish law is recounted in the *Acts of the Apostles*, written about 63 A.D. As an inhabitant of Tarsus in Cilicia he was a Roman citizen. (Roman citizenship was gradually extended to non-Italians under the empire; it became universal in 212 A.D.)[31]

All the city [Jerusalem] was aroused, and the people ran together; they seized Paul and dragged him out of the temple, and at once the gates were shut. And as they were trying to kill him, word came to the tribune of the cohort that all Jerusalem was in confusion. He at once took soldiers and centurions, and ran down to them; and when they saw the tribune and the soldiers, they stopped beating Paul. Then the tribune came up and arrested him, and ordered him to be bound with two chains. He inquired who he was and what he had done. . . . They lifted up their voices and said, "Away with such a fellow from the earth! For he ought not to live." And as they cried out and waved their garments and threw dust into the air, the tribune commanded him to be brought into the barracks, and ordered him to be examined by scourging, to find out why they shouted thus against him. But when

they had tied him up with the thongs, Paul said to the centurion who was standing by, "Is it lawful for you to scourge a man who is a Roman citizen, and uncondemned?" When the centurion heard that, he went to the tribune and said to him, "What are you about to do? For this man is a Roman citizen." So the tribune came and said to him, "Tell me, are you a Roman citizen?" And he said, "Yes." The tribune answered, "I bought this citizenship for a large sum." Paul said, "But I was born a citizen!" So those who were about to examine him withdrew from him instantly; and the tribune also was afraid, for he realized that Paul was a Roman citizen and that he had bound him. . . .

[He was taken to Caesarea, seat of the Roman government in Judaea, and a long period of delay ensued until the Procurator Festus heard the case.] He took his seat on the tribunal and ordered Paul to be brought. And when he had come, the Jews who had gone down from Jerusalem stood about him bringing against him many serious charges which they could not prove. Paul said in his defense, "Neither against the law of the Jews, nor against the temple, nor against Caesar have I offended at all." But Festus, wishing to do the Jews a favor, said to Paul, "Do you wish to go up to Jerusalem, and there be tried on these charges before me?" But Paul said, "I am standing before Caesar's tribunal, where I ought to be tried; to the Jews I have done no wrong, as you know very well. If then I am a wrongdoer, and have committed anything for which I deserve to die, I do not seek to escape death; but if there is nothing in their charges against me, no one can give me up to them. I appeal to Caesar." Then Festus, when he had conferred with his council, answered, "You have appealed to Caesar; to Caesar you shall go."

Now when some days had passed, Agrippa the king and Bernice arrived at Caesarea to welcome Festus. And as they stayed there many days, Festus laid Paul's case before the king, saying, "There is a man left prisoner by Felix [the predecessor of Festus]; and when I was at Jerusalem, the chief priests and the elders of the Jews gave information about him, asking for sentence against him. I answered them that it was not the custom of the Romans to give up any one before the accused met the accusers face to face, and had opportunity to make his defense concerning the charge laid against him. . . . When Paul had appealed to be kept in custody for the decision of the emperor, I commanded him to be held until I could send him to Caesar."

. . . When we came into Rome, Paul was allowed to stay by himself, with the soldier that guarded him. . . . And he lived there two whole years at his own expense, and welcomed all who came to him, preaching the kingdom of God and teaching about the Lord Jesus Christ quite openly and unhindered.

3. *Roman Persecution of Christians.* The remaining events in the life of St. Paul are not known with certainty. It seems likely that he was eventually acquitted in Rome of the charges made in Judaea, and he may have died during the first persecution of Christians made by Roman authorities. This persecution is described by Tacitus in the course of his account of the great fire which devastated Rome in 64 A.D. under Nero.[32]

A disaster [occurred], whether accidental or treacherously contrived by the emperor, is uncertain, as authors have given both accounts, worse, however, and more dreadful than any which have ever happened to this city by the violence of fire. . . . All human efforts, all the lavish gifts of the emperor, and the propitiations of the gods, did not banish the sinister belief that the conflagration was the result of an order. Consequently, to get rid of the report, Nero fastened the guilt and inflicted the most exquisite tortures on a class hated for their abominations, called Christians by the populace. Christus, from whom the name had its origin, suffered the extreme penalty during the reign of Tiberius at the hands of one of our procurators, Pontius Pilatus, and a most mischievous superstition, thus checked for the moment, again broke out not only in Judaea, the first source of the evil, but even in Rome, where all things hideous and shameful from every part of the world find their center and become popular. Accordingly, an arrest was first made of all who pleaded guilty; then, upon their information, an immense multitude was convicted, not so much of the crime of firing the city, as of hatred against mankind. Mockery of every sort was added to their deaths. Covered with the skins of beasts, they were torn by dogs and perished, or were nailed to crosses, or were doomed to the flames and burnt, to serve as a nightly illumination, when daylight had expired. Nero offered his gardens for the spectacle, and was exhibiting a show in the circus, while he mingled with the people in the dress of a charioteer or stood aloft on a car. Hence, even for criminals who deserved extreme and exemplary punishment, there arose a feeling of compassion; for it was not, as it seemed, for the public good, but to glut one man's cruelty, that they were being destroyed.

4. *The Christian Martyrs.* Tertullian (c. 160– c. 225 A.D.) is one of the earliest Latin Christian writers. Among his many works is a communication addressed to Christians in prison, awaiting trial and almost certain martyrdom. The Christian attitude to the secular world appears in his contrast between the "liberty" of prison and of the world outside.[33]

Blessed Martyrs Designate—Along with the provision which our lady mother the church from her bountiful breasts, and each brother out of his private means, makes for your bodily wants in the prison, accept also from me some contribution to your spiritual sustenance. . . . As far as the prison gate . . . your relatives may have attended you. There and thenceforth you were severed from the world; how much more from the ordinary course of worldly life and all its affairs! Nor let this separation from the world alarm you. For if we reflect that the world is more really the prison, we shall see that you have gone out of a prison rather than into one. The world has the greater darkness, blinding men's hearts. The world imposes the more grievous fetters, binding men's very souls. The world breathes out the worst impurities—human lusts. The world contains the larger number of criminals, even the whole human race. Then, last of all, it awaits the judgment, not of the proconsul, but of God. Wherefore, O blessed, you may regard yourselves as having been translated from a prison to, we may say, a place of safety. . . . The Christian outside the prison has renounced the world, but in the prison he has renounced a prison too. It is of no consequence where you are in the world—you who are not of it. And if you have lost some of life's sweets, it is the way of business to suffer present loss, that after gains may be the larger. Thus far I say nothing of the rewards to which God invites the martyrs. Meanwhile let us compare the life of the world and of the prison, and see if the spirit does not gain more in the prison than the flesh loses. Nay, by the care of the church and the love of the brethren, even the flesh does not lose there what is for its good, while the spirit obtains besides important advantages. You have no occasion to look on strange gods, you do not run against their images; you have no part in heathen holidays, even by mere bodily mingling in them; you are not annoyed by the foul fumes of idolatrous solemnities; you are not pained by the noise of the public shows, nor by the atrocity or madness or immodesty of their celebrants; your eyes do not fall on stews and brothels; you are free from causes of offence, from temptations, from unholy reminiscences; you are free now from persecution too. The prison does the same service for the Christian which the desert did for the prophet. Our Lord Himself spent much of His time in seclusion, that He might have greater liberty to pray, that He might be quit of the world. It was in a mountain solitude, too, He showed His glory to the disciples. Let us drop the name of prison; let us call it a place of retirement. Though the body is shut in, though the flesh is confined, all things are open to the spirit. In spirit, then, roam abroad; in spirit walk about, not setting before you shady paths or long colonnades, but the way which leads to God. As often as in spirit your footsteps are there, so often you will not be in bonds.

5. *The Christian Empire.* The reign of the Emperor Constantine (who was sole emperor 324–37) presents a break with past Roman traditions. Outwardly this break was marked by transference of the capital of the Empire from Rome to Byzantium, renamed Constantinople. Constantine himself became a Christian, put an end to persecution, and favored Christians in official positions. In him also was fully realized the tendency to absolute monarchy which had been latent in the principate and had gradually become stronger since the death of Marcus Aurelius in 180 A.D. The emperors were now officially called *Dominus* ("Lord," "Master"), a word once used only by slaves, which Augustus would not allow to be addressed to him even jokingly. The absolutism of Constantine showed itself not only in secular but also in religious matters: the stage was set for the struggle between temporal and spiritual authority, which was to take place throughout the Middle Ages. But the conflict had not yet begun. Eusebius, bishop of Caesarea in Palestine, who baptized Constantine, saw in him only the ruler who released men from paganism.[34]

Invested as he is with a semblance of heavenly sovereignty, he (i.e., the Emperor Constantine) directs his gaze above, and frames his earthly government according to the pattern of that Divine original, feeling strength in its conformity to the monarchy of God. And this conformity is granted by the universal Sovereign to man alone of the creatures of this earth: for he only is the author of sovereign power, who decrees that all should be subject to the rule of one. And surely monarchy far transcends every other constitution and form of government: for that democratic equality of power, which is its opposite, may rather be described as anarchy and disorder. . . .

The Supreme Sovereign . . . ordained an invincible champion to be the minister of his heaven-sent vengeance (for our emperor's surpassing piety delights in the title of Servant of God), and him he has proved victorious over all that opposed him, having raised him up, an individual against many foes. For they were indeed numberless, being the friends of many evil spirits (though in reality they were nothing, and hence are now no more); but our emperor is one, appointed by, and the representative of, the one Almighty Sovereign. And they, in the very spirit of impiety, destroyed the righteous with cruel slaughter: but he, in imitation of his Savior, and knowing only how to save men's lives, has spared and instructed in godliness the impious themselves. And so, as truly worthy the name of Victor, he has subdued the twofold race of barbarians; soothing the savage tribes of men by prudent embassies, compelling them to know and acknowledge their superiors, and reclaiming them from a lawless and brutal life to the governance of reason and humanity; at the same time that he proved by the facts themselves that the fierce and ruthless race of unseen spirits had long ago been vanquished by a higher power. . . .

Of old the nations of the earth, the entire human race, were variously distributed into provincial, national, and local governments, subject to kingdoms and principalities of many kinds. The consequences of this variety were war and strife, depopulation and captivity, which raged in country and city with unceasing fury. Hence, too, the countless subjects of history, adulteries, and rapes of women; hence the woes of Troy, and the ancient tragedies, so known among all peoples. The origin of these may justly be ascribed to the delusion of polytheistic error. But when that instrument of our redemption, the thrice holy body of Christ, which proved itself superior to all Satanic fraud, and free from evil both in word and deed, was raised, at once for the abolition of ancient evils, and in token of his victory over the powers of darkness; the energy of these evil spirits was at once destroyed. The manifold forms of government, the tyrannies and republics, the siege of cities, and devastation of countries caused thereby, were now no more, and one God was proclaimed to all mankind. At the same time one universal power, the Roman empire, arose and flourished, while the enduring and implacable hatred of nation against nation was now removed: and as the knowledge of one God, and one way of religion and salvation, even the doctrine of Christ, was made known to all mankind; so at the self-same period, the entire dominion of the Roman empire being vested in a single sovereign, profound peace reigned throughout the world. And thus, by the express appointment of the same God, two roots of blessing, the Roman empire, and the doctrine of Christian piety, sprang up together for the benefit of men. For before this time the various countries of the world, as Syria, Asia, Macedonia, Egypt, and Arabia, had been severally subject to different rulers. The Jewish people, again, had established their dominion in the land of Palestine. And these nations, in every village, city, and district, actuated by some insane spirit, were engaged in incessant and murderous war and conflict. But two mighty powers, starting from the same point, the Roman empire, which henceforth was swayed by a single sovereign, and the Christian religion, subdued and reconciled these contending elements. Our Savior's mighty power destroyed at once the many governments and the many gods of the powers of darkness, and proclaimed to all men, both rude and civilized, to the extremities of the earth, the sole sovereignty of God himself. Meantime the Roman empire, the cause of multiplied governments being thus removed, effected an easy conquest of those which yet remained; its object being to unite all nations in one harmonious whole; an object in great measure already secured, and destined to be still more perfectly attained, even to the final conquest of the ends of the habitable world, by means of the salutary doctrine, and through the aid of that Divine power which facilitates and smooths its way. And surely this must appear a wondrous fact to those who will examine the question in the love of truth, and desire not to cavil at these blessings. The falsehood of demon superstition was convicted: the inveterate strife

and mutual hatred of the nations was removed: at the same time One God, and the knowledge of that God, were proclaimed to all: one universal empire prevailed; and the whole human race, subdued by the controlling power of peace and concord, received one another as brethren, and responded to the feelings of their common nature. Hence, as children of one God and Father, and owning true religion as their common mother, they saluted and welcomed each other with words of peace. Thus the whole world appeared like one well-ordered and united family: each one might journey unhindered as far as and whithersoever he pleased: men might securely travel from West to East, and from East to West, as to their own native country: in short, the ancient oracles and predictions of the prophets were fulfilled, more numerous than we can at present cite, and those especially which speak as follows concerning the saving Word. "He shall have dominion from sea to sea, and from the river to the ends of the earth." And again, "In his days shall righteousness spring up; and abundance of peace." "And they shall beat their swords into plough-shares, and their spears into sickles: and nation shall not take up sword against nation, neither shall they learn to war any more."

III

Canossa, 1077

THE creative spirits of the Roman Church who set themselves in the eleventh century to rescue our Western Society
from a feudal anarchy by establishing a Christian Republic
found themselves in the same dilemma as their spiritual
heirs who are attempting in our own day to replace an international anarchy by a world order. The essence of their aim
was to substitute authority for physical force, and the spiritual sword was the weapon with which their supreme victories
were won. But there were occasions on which it seemed as
though the established regime of physical force was in a
position to defy the spiritual sword with impunity; and it
was in such situations that the Roman Church Militant was
challenged to give its answer to the riddle of the Sphinx.
Was the soldier of God to deny himself the use of any but
his own spiritual arms at the risk of seeing his advance
brought to a standstill? Or was he to fight God's battle
against the Devil with the adversary's own weapons?

ARNOLD TOYNBEE

CONTENTS

[49]

QUESTIONS FOR STUDY

PART I

1. How had the position of the Papacy changed between 1046 and 1073? What were some of the stages in this change?

2. What reforms was Gregory attempting to effect? Why?

3. What were some of the difficulties facing the young Henry IV?

4. Describe the relations between Gregory and Henry from 1073 to 1076.

5. Why did Henry call the Council of Worms (January, 1076)?

6. How did Gregory justify his deposition of Henry?

7. What were the political implications of Gregory's action?

8. During the years 1046 to 1076 what correlation can be made between conditions in Germany and the papal policy of the German kings?

PART II

9. What were the provisions of the agreement at Oppenheim? Why did Henry agree to them?

10. Why did he decide to go to the pope in Italy?

11. Describe his journey. Why did he take the route he did?

12. How was he received in Italy?

13. How did the pope happen to be at Canossa?

14. Describe the meeting.

15. Compare and evaluate the accounts of the different chroniclers about Canossa.

16. What conditions did Henry have to meet before seeing the pope? On what conditions was he reconciled?

17. In your estimation, who triumphed at Canossa, pope or emperor?

18. What were the basic matters at issue?

19. In your estimation, how much importance should be attached to the personalities of the two protagonists in determining the cause of the conflict? In determining the result?

20. *To be handed in at class.* Write a 200-word narrative of one of the following, giving in the form of footnotes references for every statement of fact or opinion you make:
    a. Why Henry went to Canossa, or
    b. What happened at Canossa.

One of the most momentous themes in medieval history is the conflict between two standards of value—the temporal and the spiritual—for place and power in the world. King and prelate, merchant and priest, monastery and jousting place, or cathedral choir and peasant's close, the protagonists change and the locale is shifted, but the basic issue remains the same. This Problem is concerned with one crisis in this historic struggle: the young German king, Henry IV (1056–1106), and the mighty maker of Popes, now Pope himself, Gregory VII (1073–1085), are the main actors in the drama; Italy and Germany in the third quarter of the eleventh century provide the stage.

Although this conflict between the two cities, as St. Augustine defined it, pervades medieval civilization, it was possibly most apparent in the realm of politics. There the champions carried the most prestige, the stakes were highest, and the issues, in the end at least, best defined. Since the mid-fifth century under the headship of the Bishop of Rome or Pope, the Church, as it gradually supplanted the decaying Roman Empire, had asserted papal supremacy over religion and ultimate supremacy over the secular power. On the other hand, in the form of the emergent monarchies of the west, the state, as it struggled to reassert or recover its former authority, laid claim to a residuum of ultimate power which the Church would not let go unchallenged. Both parties had claims, rooted in history and theory, which if pressed would inevitably clash. Both had innumerable points of contact with each other, at all levels of local government and daily living where skirmishes, preliminary to the main battle, were constantly being fought.

Furthermore, their relationship during the troubled period between the disappearance of the Roman Empire in the west and the establishment of the feudal monarchies had been intimate and often cooperative. In their struggle against feudal anarchy the secular rulers had found in the Church a model and ally, while the latter had always preferred the wider authority of the growing monarchy to the particularism of the local warlords. At the top, the Papacy, as the spiritual reincarnation of Rome and successor to much of her power, was the transmitter of the greater part of the governmental heritage of the Middle Ages. For their part, the secular rulers, in the persons of the Frankish kings of the eighth century and the German kings two centuries later, had come to the rescue of the beleaguered Papacy, whose efforts to maintain its territorial independence amid the frequent turbulence of Italy had often necessitated non-Italian assistance.

The relationship between Church and state had been particularly close in tenth-century Germany. Both were firmly united against the ambitions of the dukes, the German church because the crown was a lesser threat to the local independence of the Church and a greater source of lands and power, the German kings because the bishops represented the finest source of administrative talent then available and the Church was for the moment more ally than threat to the monarchy. The results of this alliance were the establishment of powerful ecclesiastical principalities and the corresponding secularization of the Church through the evolution of a veritable "ecclesiastical feudalism" wherein the churchmen functioned in a way more befitting lay vassals of the crown than men of God. Finally, in 962, Otto I revived the ideal of imperial unity by having himself crowned emperor at Rome. The immediate result was the establishment of German sovereignty over central Italy and the reduction of the Papacy to a position comparable to that of a German bishop, both steps of immense significance for the future.

The stage was thus almost set for the great drama of the next century and only two further developments need be mentioned. The first is the adoption by the Papacy, in the second quarter of the eleventh century, of a reform program, largely Cluniac in inspiration. Founded in 910 in protest against the growing feudalization of the Church, the Burgundian monastery of Cluny found a ripe audience in many a prelate, with its insistence on a return to the earlier canons— on the celibacy of the clergy, methods of clerical election, and lay interference with church property. With the growing authority of the reformer, Hildebrand, in the councils of the Papacy after 1050, the implications of the movement for the position of the Papacy within the Church as well as its relations to temporal authority became momentous. At the same time the Empire was experiencing one of its fateful reversals of fortune, and the inheritance of the six-year-old Henry IV who succeeded his father in 1056 was hardly to be envied: "A Germany seething with discontent, a nobility on the point of rebellion, and in Italy the Papacy under the thumb of the reforming Hildebrand and his allies." [1]

Part I.
PAPACY AND EMPIRE

The roots of the controversy between Papacy and Empire lay deep in the past of both institutions. But the immediate background of the eleventh century furnishes many a clue as to the causes of the actual outbreak and even some indications prophetic of its outcome. In the first Part of the Problem the student is to examine the condition of the Papacy and the nature of the reform movement, the state of Germany during the early years of the young Henry, and finally the break between Pope and king. It is already clear that this was to be no passing quarrel; the intimate, historic relationship between the two parties and their central positions on the contemporary scene would combine to underline the significance of even the most trifling act. Mindful that the outcome of the rivalry was of vital importance to all who commented on it, the student must attempt to dissect the forces involved and judiciously assess their comparative importance.

A.
THE PAPACY IN THE ELEVENTH CENTURY

1. *The Papal Election of 1046.* In the following selection a contemporary chronicler describes the visit of Henry III (1017–1056) to Italy in 1046.[2]

The first and great synod was held at Pavia in the presence of the lord Henry, then king. The second at Sutri, at which in the presence of the king and according to the provisions of the canons two popes, the second and the third, were deposed. The third synod was held at Rome on the Tuesday and Wednesday before the Nativity of our Lord. At it Pope Benedict was canonically and synodically deposed; and by the unanimous election of the clergy and people Suidger, Bishop of Bamberg, was substituted for him. Suidger was consecrated pope with name of Clement [II] on the next day [December 25]; and, by the will and with the overwhelming approval of the Roman people, he crowned the lord Henry emperor.

2. *The Decree on Papal Elections, 1059.* At the Lateran Council, or synod, of 1059, the Pope, Nicholas II, promulgated a set of regulations redefining the organization of Papal elections. The first selection which follows is from a pro-papal version of the decree; the second, by a follower of the Emperor.[3]

[Papal Version] . . . we [Pope Nicholas II] decide and establish that, on the death of the pontiff of this Roman universal church, first of all the cardinal bishops shall discuss with most diligent consideration and then shall summon the cardinal clergy to join them; and afterwards the rest of the clergy and people shall give their assent to the new election. That, lest the disease of venality creep in by any means godly men shall take the chief part in the election of the pontiff, and the others shall follow their lead. [This method of election is then declared regular and in conformity with precedent, especially with the words of St. Leo.] "No argument," he says, "will permit them to be considered bishops who have not been elected by the clergy, nor demanded by the people, nor consecrated by the bishops of the province with the approval of the metropolitan." But since the apostolic see is raised above all churches in the world and therefore can have no metropolitan over it, the cardinal bishops without doubt perform the function of a metropolitan, when they raise the pontiff elect to the apostolic eminence. They shall elect someone from amongst this church [the Roman church] if a suitable candidate be found; if not, he shall be chosen from another church. Saving the honor and reverence due to our beloved son Henry, who at present is acknowledged King and, it is hoped, will be Emperor, if God permit; as we have granted to him and to such of his successors as obtain this right in person from the apostolic see. But, if the perversity of evil and wicked men shall make it impossible to hold a pure, sincere and uncorrupt election in the city, the cardinal bishops with the godly clergy and catholic laymen, even though few, shall have the lawful power to elect the pontiff of the apostolic see in any place which they shall consider more convenient. After an election has been clearly made, if the fierceness of war or the malignant endeavors of any man shall prevent him who is elected from being enthroned on the apostolic seat according to custom, the elect shall nevertheless have authority as Pope to rule the holy Roman church and to dispose of its resources, as we know that blessed Gregory did before his consecration. . . .

[*Imperial Version*] I, Nicholas, bishop of the holy, Catholic and apostolic Roman church, have signed this decree promulgated by us, as is set out above. I, Boniface, by God's grace bishop of Albano, have signed. I, Humbert, bishop of the holy church of Silva Candida, have signed. I, Peter, bishop of the church of Ostia, have signed. And 76 other bishops with priests and deacons have signed.

1. That, when the pontiff of this Roman church universal dies, the cardinals, after first conferring together with most diligent consideration—saving the honor and reverence due to our beloved son Henry, who is at present called king, and will be in the future, as it is hoped, emperor by God's grace, according as we now, by the mediation of his envoy W. the chancellor of Lombardy, have granted to him and to those of his successors who shall obtain this right personally from this apostolic see,—shall approach and consent to the new election.

2. That—lest the disease of venality creep in through any excuse whatever—the men of the church, together with our most serene son king Henry, shall be the leaders in carrying on the election of a pope, the others merely followers.

3. They shall make their choice, moreover, from the lap of this [Roman] church itself, if a suitable man is to be found there. But if not, one shall be chosen from another church.

4. But, if the perversity of depraved and wicked men shall so prevail that a pure, sincere and free election can not be held in Rome, they may have the right and power, even though few in numbers, of electing a pontiff for the apostolic see wherever it may seem to them, together with the most unconquerable king, Henry, to be most suitable.

3. *The Election of Gregory VII, 1073.* The conjunction of a man and a movement will always remain one of the most inflammatory forces in history. Hildebrand (1023–1085), the future Gregory VII, was born in Tuscany, entered a reformed (Cluniac) monastery and then began his more political career as chaplain to the exiled Gregory VI at Cologne, where he learned much of German politics. Returning to Rome in 1049 with Leo IX, he was employed by a succession of Popes on missions and negotiations of ever-increasing importance. In 1073 his turn came, as is described in the selection which follows.[4]

On the same day, after the body of the aforesaid pontiff [Alexander II, 1061–73] had been buried in the church of the Holy Savior [St. John Lateran], while the venerable Hildebrand was at-

tending to his burial, there rushed in all of a sudden a crowd of clerics, men and women: and a cry was raised, "Let Hildebrand be bishop!" On hearing this, the venerable archdeacon took alarm, and, desiring to quiet the people hurried to the pulpit. But Hugh the White anticipated him, and addressed the multitude thus: "Men and brethren, you know how from the days of Pope Leo [IX, 1048–54], Hildebrand has exalted the holy Roman church, and delivered our city. As it is impossible to find a better man, or his equal, whom we may elect, we elect him who has been ordained in our church, is well known to you as to us, and thoroughly approved." The Cardinal-bishops, priests and deacons, with the inferior clergy, after the accustomed manner, shouted "Blessed Peter has elected Gregory as Pope!" And forthwith, he was seized and carried off by the people to the church of St. Peter [ad Vincula]: where, though against his will, he was enthroned.

4. *The Church and Temporal Power, 1073.* Something of the extent of Gregory's claims can be realized from the following letter to the princes who were bent on conquering Spain. The letters of eminent men afford the historian a happy combination of personality and information. In the case of Gregory VII, a complete collection of his letters has been preserved. In using these letters the student must attempt to evaluate them both as official records and as personal documents.[5]

We suppose you know that the kingdom of Spain belonged of old to St. Peter, and that this right has never been lost, although the land has long been occupied by pagans. Therefore the ownership of this land inheres in the apostolic see alone, for whatever has come into the possession of the churches by the will of God, while it may be alienated from their use, may not by any lapse of time be separated from their ownership except by lawful grant. Count Evolus of Roceio, whose fame you must know, wishes to attack that land and rescue it from the heathen. Therefore we have granted him the possession of such territory as he may win from the pagans by his own efforts or with the aid of allies, on conditions agreed upon by us as the representative of St. Peter. You who join him in this undertaking should do so to the honor of St. Peter, that St. Peter may protect you from danger and reward your fidelity to him. But if any of you plan to attack that land independently with your own forces, you should do so in a spirit of devotion and with righteous motives. Beware lest after you have conquered the land you wrong St. Peter in the same way as the infidels do who now hold it. Unless you are prepared to recognize the rights

Magdeburg

Harzburg

Hersfeld

Mayence

Oppenheim

Bamberg

Worms

Forcheim

Spires

Toul

Regina

Augsburg

T H E

Besancon

E M P I R E

Geneva

Vercelli

Milan

Mt. Cenis

Pavia

Turin

Canossa

Sutri

Rome

STATES
OF THE
CHURCH

NORMAN

PRINCIPALITIES

Rhine R.

PAPACY AND EMPIRE, 1077

of St. Peter by making an equitable agreement with us, we will forbid you by our apostolic authority to go thither, that your holy and universal mother, the church, may not suffer from her sons the same injuries which she now suffers from her enemies, to the loss not only of her property, but also of the devotion of her children. To this end we have sent to Spain our beloved son, Hugo, cardinal priest of the holy Roman church, and he will inform you more fully of our terms and conditions.

5. *Gregory on the State of Christendom, 1075.* To ascertain more completely the motives behind Gregory's actions remains vital to any understanding of the matters at issue. Thus, his writings must always be scrutinized for all possible clues. The selections which follow are from a letter of Gregory's to Hugh, Abbot of Cluny, one of the inspirations for reform.[6]

If it were possible, I should like you fully to appreciate what great tribulation presses upon me, and what great labor, daily renewed tires me out and increases, to my deep distress. . . . For grievous sorrow and utter sadness surround me, because the Eastern Church, by suggestion of the devil, has abandoned the Catholic Faith; and the ancient foe by his members puts Christians to death on all sides: so that, by spiritually killing the head, he causes the members carnally to perish, lest at any time by divine grace they should repent.

Then again, if I take a mental survey, and look round upon the regions of west, south or north, I scarcely find any bishops lawfully appointed and of regular life who rule the people of God for the love of Christ and not for worldly ambition. And among all the secular princes there is hardly one who prefers the honor of God and righteousness to his own advantage. Those among whom I live—Romans, Lombards and Normans, as I often tell them, I count as worse somehow than Jews or pagans.

Returning to myself, I find myself so overburdened by the weight of my own doings, that no hope of salvation remains for me except in the sole mercy of Christ. For if I did not hope for a better life and to be of more profit to holy Church, I would not in any wise remain in Rome where, as God is witness, I have been obliged to live these five and twenty years. . . .

B. THE PAPACY AND REFORM

Although the reform movement of the eleventh-century church was to a considerable extent monastic in its origins and its early manifestations, it nevertheless came inevitably to involve the Papacy itself.

1. *Gregory VII to the Adherents of the Papacy in Lombardy, 1073.* In the selection which follows, the new Pope warns the Lombards of one of the evils besetting the Church.[7]

I desire you to know, beloved brethren, as many of you do know already, that we are so placed that, whether we will or no, we are bound to proclaim truth and righteousness to all peoples, especially to Christians, according to the word of the Lord: "Cry aloud; spare not, lift up thy voice like a trumpet and declare unto my people their transgressions!" And elsewhere: "If thou shalt not declare his wickedness unto the wicked, I will require his soul at thy hand." Also saith the prophet: "Cursed be he that keepeth back his sword from blood!" that is, he that keepeth back the word of preaching from reproving the carnally minded. We make this prelude because, among the many ills which afflict the whole world, certain ministers of Satan and heralds of Antichrist in Lombardy are striving to overturn even the Christian faith and thus are bringing down the wrath of God upon themselves.

As you well know, during the life of Guido, called archbishop of Milan, Godfrey had the audacity to purchase, like any vile wench, that church which once through the merits of Mary, most glorious Virgin and Mother of God, and through the fame of that most noted doctor, St. Ambrose, shone forth among the churches of Lombardy by its piety, its freedom and its own peculiar glory—that is to say, he prostituted the bride of Christ to the Devil and befouled her with the criminal heresy of Simony by trying to separate her from the catholic faith.

Hearing of this the Roman Church, mother of you and, as you know, mistress of all Christendom, called together a council from several countries and, supported by the approval of many priests and members of divers orders, through the authority of St. Peter, prince of the Apostles, pierced him with the lance of anathema as an enemy of the catholic faith and of the canon law, together with all those who took his part. This right of excommunication, as even the enemies of the Church cannot deny, was approved of old by holy fathers and has been confirmed and is still confirmed by Catholics through all the holy churches.

Wherefore, beloved brethren, in the name of

Almighty God, Father, Son and Holy Spirit, and of the blessed Peter and Paul, chiefs of the Apostles, we warn, exhort and command you to have no dealings whatever with the aforesaid heretic Godfrey, seeing that to side with him in this crime is to deny the faith of Christ. Resist him by whatever means you can as sons of God and defend the Christian faith whereby you are to be saved. And let no pride of men deter you; for he who is with us is greater than all, is ever unconquered, and it is his will that we labor for him, and he will give the crown to those who fight fairly, as the Apostle promises. For our captain [dux] is wont to crush the many and the proud by means of the few and the humble, and to confound the things that are strong by the things that are weak. Such is the will and pleasure of our invincible prince.

May Almighty God, who especially entrusted his sheep to St. Peter and gave him rule over all the Church, strengthen you in your devotion to him so that, delivered from your sins by his authority, you may have grace to withstand the enemies of God and win their hearts to repentance.

2. *Gregory VII and the Monk of Toul, 1074.* The reforming zeal of the Pope is seen in this order to the archbishop of Trier in October, 1074.[8]

We urge you, our brother, to give as prompt and careful attention to the matters we are entrusting to you as the nature of the case and the circumstances will permit. We hope that you will so consider both in the affair described below, that we may find you, as we believe you to be, our faithful and devoted fellow worker.

This monk of Toul, said to be a clerk, came to us and complained that his lord, said to be bishop of Toul, was enraged against him and that he had been driven into exile and deprived of all his goods, and he prayed to be relieved from his distress by apostolic charity. We inquired carefully how this had happened to him, and he replied that he had demanded of the bishop a certain benefice which he claimed as lawfully belonging to the office of *custos* which he held. The bishop, angered by this demand, not only refused him the benefice but forbade him upon his obedience to perform any duties of his office. To this he replied that he owed the bishop no duty of obedience because he [the bishop] had sold archdeaconates, consecrations of churches, and even churches themselves, and had thus made himself guilty of the heresy of Simony. Further, he charged that the bishop had lived in open relations with a certain woman, by whom he had had a child, and report had it that he had joined himself to her by a solemn promise and by a marriage after the man-

ner of laymen. Some said also that he had bought his way into the episcopal office.

When the bishop heard all this he spoke with this monk and also with others of the brethren about making amends as if he repented of the sins that had been brought to light, but finally broke out into a public display of anger against this man.

Shortly afterward in the absence of the bishop some of his men-at-arms, knowing his wishes, endangered the peace of this man and threatened him to his face within the cloister. When he learned that his life and honor were being plotted against he went away secretly, hoping that his absence would moderate the violence of this excitement. But the bishop straightway ordered that all his goods should be seized and sold, and he made his complaint that he had long been living in poverty and exile.

This seems to me against due order and very unjust. If the charges are true the bishop—nay the ex-bishop—hated, not this man, but his own conscience and ought to be brought to trial. But if they are false—as I hope they are—still it was not right that the man should be seized and flogged by soldiers but rather that he should be disciplined according to the law of the Church. Wherefore it is our will that you, my brother, being advised and supported by apostolic authority, invite our beloved colleague, Herman, the venerable bishop of Metz, to join with you in summoning the bishop of Toul to your presence. You are to order him to receive this clerk back into his cloister free from all danger to his life and safe from every form of insult. He shall restore to him the office of *custos* together with the benefice which he demanded, if he has a lawful claim to it, also all the other rights which lawfully belong to him, together with his provostship and his mastership of the scholars, and all the goods which were taken from him, and shall make good all the damage so unjustly inflicted upon him.

Then call the clergy of Toul together and give them strict orders upon their obedience and under penalty of anathema to disclose to you whatever they may know as to the life of the bishop and his accession to office, and after you have probed the truth from every side, fail not to inform us in writing at or before the synod which we are to hold during the first week of Lent what we ought to think of the matter. But if the bishop shall be proved innocent—as we hope he may be—of these many and grave charges we shall see to it with God's help that the rash offense of the clerk in seeking a hearing from us shall be duly corrected. If, however, the bishop shall not be able to clear himself of the charges brought against him, then in no wise is it to be endured that the wolf shall hold the shepherd's place.

3. *The Papal Decrees of 1074–75.* In the synods of 1074 and 1075 Gregory VII formally promulgated the principles of the reform movement. Earlier popes had denounced both simony and lay investiture and since the seventh century the Church in the west had been increasingly opposed to marriage for the clergy, for reasons of a theological as well as an economic nature. It is worth noting that the first three paragraphs quoted below are from Gregory's letters while the last decree survives only in the indirect reference by a Milanese historian.[9]

(1074) Those who have been advanced to any grade of holy orders, or to any office, through simony, that is, by the payment of money, shall hereafter have no right to officiate in the holy church. Those also who have secured churches by giving money shall certainly be deprived of them. And in the future it shall be illegal for anyone to buy or to sell [any ecclesiastical office, position, etc.].

Nor shall clergymen who are married say mass or serve the altar in any way. We decree also that if they refuse to obey our orders, or rather those of the holy fathers, the people shall refuse to receive their ministrations, in order that those who disregard the love of God and the dignity of their office may be brought to their senses through feeling the shame of the world and the reproof of the people. . . .

(1074) If there are any priests, deacons, or subdeacons who are married, by the power of omnipotent God and the authority of St. Peter we forbid them to enter a church until they repent and mend their ways. But if any remain with their wives, no one shall dare hear them [when they officiate in the church], because their benediction is turned into a curse, and their prayer into a sin. For the Lord says through the prophet, "I will curse your blessings" [Mal. 2:2]. Whoever shall refuse to obey this most salutary command shall be guilty of the sin of idolatry. For Samuel says: "For rebellion is as the sin of witchcraft, and stubbornness is as iniquity and idolatry" [1 Sam. 15:23]. Whoever therefore asserts that he is a Christian but refuses to obey the apostolic see, is guilty of paganism.

(1075) The Pope held a council at Rome and publicly forbade the King thenceforth to have any rights in the conferring of bishoprics, and he withdrew the investiture of churches from all lay persons.

C.   CONDITIONS IN GERMANY

The rise and fall of royal fortunes in Germany represents one of the more dramatic aspects of medieval history. The Saxon dynasty had died out in 1024; though elected according to the old practise, the first Franconian king, Conrad II (1024–39) proved to be unusually able. Carefully controlling the church he attempted to develop a loyal, secular administrative corps. He played off the lesser nobles against the all-powerful dukes and concentrated vacant dukedoms in his own family. Henry III (1039–46) appeared to touch new heights of royal power, but both his German policy of regranting the duchies out of his family and his papal policy of introducing the reformers to Rome boded ill for the future.

1. *The Early Years of Henry IV.* In the selection which follows a contemporary German chronicler describes the early years of Henry IV. Succeeding his father at the age of six, the young king was a minor in the custody of his mother from 1056 to 1065. Although his dates are occasionally confused, Ekkehard of Aurach is most informative on Henry's difficulties.[10]

In the year 1057 of the Incarnation of our Lord, and the year 1808 since the founding of the city, Henry IV, son of Emperor Henry, while still a boy, began to reign in the place of his father. At the time that this book is being written, he is reigning, in his forty-second year, as the eighty-seventh emperor since Augustus. . . .

In the year of our Lord 1058, Frederick, who as pope was called Stephen, died, and Alexander, bishop of Lucca, followed him. At that time Hildebrand, who later became pope, administered the office of archdeacon in Rome.

In the year of our Lord 1059, Pope Stephen died, and Gerhard followed him under the name of Nicholas [II]. Henry, king of France, died, and Philip, his son, reigned in his stead.

In the year of our Lord 1060, Luitpold, archbishop of Mayence, died and Siegfried, abbot of Fulda, followed him, who later allied himself with others in a conspiracy against his lord the king.

In the year of our Lord 1062, Archbishop Anno of Cologne, with the consent of the leaders of the empire, brought the prince [Henry IV], of whose person he had taken violent possession, under his control, and withdrew from the prince's mother the government of the empire, as if he felt it to be unworthy that the state should be ruled by the empress, who, though a woman, was enabled to exercise power after the manner of a man. After he had given an account before all of what he had done, he again gained the favor of his lord the king, and was again reconciled to the mother through the son. . . .

In the year of our Lord 1063, Pope Nicholas died and was followed by Bishop Alexander of Lucca. . . .

In the year of our Lord 1066, a comet glowed long over the whole earth. In the same year England was terribly desolated by the Norman William and finally subjugated, and he had himself made king. He then drove almost all the bishops of the said kingdom into banishment and had the nobles killed. The commons he gave over in bondage to his knights, and he compelled the wives of the natives to marry the invaders.

In the year of our Lord 1067, King Henry took to wife Bertha, daughter of a certain Otto, an Italian, and of Adelheid; and he celebrated the wedding at Tribur. Conrad, councilor of the church at Cologne, whom King Henry had designated as bishop of Trier, was taken prisoner by Theodoric, count of that city, and was carried into the forest by his followers and thrown down three times from the top of a mountain, but since he still remained unhurt, they dispatched him with a sword.

In the year of our Lord 1068, King Henry, with youthful recklessness, began to reside in Saxony alone of all the Roman Empire, to despise the princes, oppress the nobles, exalt the lowborn, and to devote himself (as was said) to the chase, to gaming and other occupations of this kind, more than to the administration of justice. He married the daughters of the nobles to his favorites of low origin, and, full of distrust against the powerful of the empire, he began to build certain castles. By thus recklessly sowing the seeds of discord it fell out that the number of those who proposed to deprive the king not only of his kingdom but even of his life grew rapidly. However, as he had not yet fully reached the years of maturity, many judged that the responsibility did not fall so much upon him as upon Archbishop Adelbert of Bremen, since everything was done on his advice.

In the year of our Lord 1069, the Empress Agnes, mother of King Henry, through vexation, or better, through divine inspiration, surrendered the duchy of Bavaria, and, discarding the reins of government in her devotion to Christ, betook herself to Rome, where, with marvelous humility, she brought forth the fruits of repentance and after a few years closed this earthly life in the Lord.

In the year of our Lord 1070, Margrave Teti, not without the connivance of the Saxon princes, established a tyranny directed against the king's followers. This was, however, suppressed through the intervention of the heavenly as well as the earthly majesty, for his castles of Beichlingen and Burgsheidungen were destroyed by the king; his son, likewise a warrior, was killed by some of his servants, and he himself soon died a natural death.

In the year of our Lord 1071, Duke Otto lost the duchy of Bavaria. He was a Saxon by origin, a man of excellent rank, to whom few could be compared in insight and military power. He enjoyed such respect among all the princes that the king, who was already an object of suspicion and hate to the Saxons, was fearful lest this Otto might, should the king's influence decline, attempt to win the royal throne itself.

A certain Egino, of mean origin and insignificant resources, took advantage of the situation for his evil ends. Although well known for his impudence and shameless conduct, he managed to slip into the court under the protection of certain of the king's adherents. He lied to the king, saying that great hero, Otto, who in reality had never known him, had conspired with him to murder the king. He offered himself, as was the custom, as a hostage until the truth of what he had said should be settled by a duel between him and the duke. What more need be said? After royal councils had been announced, one at Mayence and the other at Goslar, Otto disdained to fight with Egino,—the duke with the rogue, the prince with the common man,—nevertheless his innocence and Egino's shamelessness remained by no means concealed.

So Otto, guilty of lese-majesty, lost the duchy of Bavaria, which a certain Welf received, a distinguished, brave, warlike person, a Swabian by birth. From this seed, alas, did great dissension spring, which grew into the wretched fruit of continuous battles, of rebelliousness, robbery, and destruction, division in the Church, heresy, and many deaths.

In the year of our Lord 1072, the king followed Otto everywhere, destroyed as many of his fortresses as he could, wasted his lands, and strove completely to annihilate him, as an enemy of the state. Nevertheless, Otto, with a select following, and with his own stout arm and his heart full of bitter hate, since he might not fight directly with the royal troops, sought to avenge the injury which he had suffered, now by plundering, now by fire, now by the sword, wherever opportunity offered.

At his inspiration the Saxon people—of a very violent disposition as they are—ceased not, with one accord, to organize a conspiracy against the king; sent letters full of insulting and unheard-of accusations against the king to the apostolic see, and sought allies by letter and messenger throughout the whole German empire.

In the first place they made friends with Siegfried, the archbishop of Mayence, Adelbert of Worms, Adelberon of Würzburg, Gebhardt of Salzburg, and other bishops, as many as they could, and then through these they gained Pope Alexander. Many assert too that, last and greatest, Anno, archbishop of Cologne, was one of those privy to this conspiracy. Frightened at last by these intrigues, the king left Saxony and conducted the business of the empire in other regions.

In the year of our Lord 1073, the archbishop of Cologne and Herman of Babenberg were sent to Rome in order to get together the money which was owing the king there. They brought back, on their return, a letter from Pope Alexander, in which the king was ordered to give an account of his heresy, simony, and many other similar matters which called for improvement, rumors of which had reached him in Rome.

Thereupon the Saxons built many strongholds, for up to this time that country had had but few of them. Moreover they completely destroyed the castles which the king had built some time before. Among these they tore down the castle which was called Harzburg, the cathedral and the abbey which stood there, destroying all these in their rage and perversity, down to the very ground. Horrible to say, they took up the bones of the innocent son of the king, who had been buried there, and scattered them about as an insult to the father.

In the year of our Lord 1074, after Pope Alexander of blessed memory had died, Hildebrand, later called Gregory, followed him; by profession and rank he was a monk and archdeacon. Under him the Roman Empire and the whole Church began to be threatened by new and unheard-of divisions and turmoil. Since Gregory had reached this height of power without the king's permission, simply through the favor of the Romans, some asserted that he was not rightfully chosen, but had seized the papal dignity with his own hand. Therefore he was not recognized by some of the bishops. Gregory repeatedly summoned King Henry through messengers and letters to answer for his deeds before a synod.

In the year of our Lord 1074, Pope Gregory, after holding a synod, condemned the simonists, namely those who bought and sold the gift of the Holy Ghost, and provided that the Nicolaitae, that is to say, the priests who had married, should be removed from the service of the altar, and forbade the laity to attend masses performed by them.

In the year of the Lord 1075, King Henry moved against the Saxons, after he had collected a strong army from Alemannia, Bavaria, and Germania, and from Bohemia. He fought with the Saxons on the river Unstrut and after much blood had been shed on both sides, he finally returned home victorious.

Rudolph, duke of Alemannia and Burgundy, who later usurped the imperial crown, fought bravely there with his followers for the king. Bishop Herman of Babenberg was deposed, on account of his simoniacal practices, by command of Pope Hildebrand, and Ruotpert was put in his place by the king. In this year died Anno, archbishop of Cologne, rich in merits of piety, and was buried in the cloister of Siegburg, which he himself had built. He was followed by Hildolf.

2. *Gregory VII and the German Church, September 1075.* During the early years of his pontificate Gregory vigorously attempted to impose his reforming decrees on the German clergy. Three bishops were suspended for failing to appear at the Roman synod of February, 1075. The decrees of this synod were communicated to Archbishop Siegfried of Mainz who objected to enforcing them and to the calling of a synod of the German clergy. In the following letter the Pope replied to the reluctant archbishop.[11]

In your letter, my brother, you have brought forward many excuses [for not calling a German Council], plausible and from a human point of view valid, nor would they seem to me without force if such reasoning could excuse us before the judgment seat of God. It does indeed seem a reasonable explanation that the kingdom is in confusion, with wars, rebellions, hostile invasion, ruin of your property and the fear of death which seems to threaten our brethren from the hatred of the king, and also the dread lest men from different and mutually hostile sections coming together in one place might break out into violent conflict. All these seem to be amply sufficient excuses.

But, if we consider the wide difference between divine and human judgments, we find scarcely any pretext that we could safely offer in that last day for drawing back from the rescue of souls—not the loss of property, nor the assaults of the wicked, nor the wrath of the mighty, nor the sacrifice of our safety or of life itself. This is the difference between hirelings and shepherds: that when the wolf comes the hireling fears for himself, not for the sheep, abandons his flock and flees, leaving them to destruction; but the shepherd who truly loves his sheep does not desert them when danger approaches, and does not hesitate to sacrifice even his life for them. . . .

And now let us come to a matter which is at present weighing upon our mind and which is, as it were, the reason of this our discourse, namely, how we can bear with patience the reports we have received as to the conduct of our brother, the bishop of Strasbourg, not a few of which we know by trustworthy information to be true. We desire and command you, therefore, to investigate carefully one of them about which we are still in doubt, that is, the infection with the heresy of Simony. Whatever you discover with certainty upon this point, fail not to inform us at once, so that if the report be true the Church of Christ may be cleansed of this foulness and his soul may be rescued from destruction. But if, as we rather pray, it be false, then may this great calumny be turned away from him with the help of divine grace.

And now let those who say that the council which we have proclaimed ought to be postponed answer this question: What would the soldiers of a king do when they had been summoned to prepare for war and the enemy was already in the king's court with fire and sword? Let them say whether they ought to rush to arms and crush the enemy or idly watch what he is about? For what are those evil spirits doing but striving unceasingly to lay waste the Church of Christ with the flames of their vicious lives? And what ought those royal soldiers, the holy priests, to do, but to rise up against their fury, armed with the shield of priestly charity and girded with the sword of the divine word? As for what you say, that certain brethren cannot come to the council on account of the enmity of their prince, we say that it is enough for them if they send some of their clerks to answer for them.

But, since we are aware that you are being dissuaded by many carnally minded persons from working diligently and faithfully in the Lord's vineyard for the welfare of souls lest you suffer loss of fortune and incur the enmity of the powerful, we exhort and command you, in the name of Almighty God and by authority of St. Peter, that you venture not to turn aside from the straight way through fear or favor of anyone or through any loss of earthly goods, but that, so far as the Holy Spirit may grant, you shall diligently inquire into everything and report to us immediately whatever you ascertain. We ought to regard it as a shameful thing that the soldiers of this world daily stand up to fight for their earthly prince and shrink not from deadly conflict, while we, who are called priests of God, will not fight for our king who created all things out of nothing, and who did not hesitate to suffer death for us and has promised us an eternal reward.

This also we enjoin upon you, my brother, that you make diligent inquiry into the simoniac heresy and fornication of your clergy, as you have been instructed by the Apostolic See, and that whatever you find has been committed in the past you punish according to law and thoroughly root it out, and give strictest orders that it shall not occur in future.

D.
POPE AND KING

Henry IV was twenty-six years old in 1076 and Gregory VII was over fifty when at long last he came out from behind the scenes and became Pope himself. The contrast in their ages and characters was obviously to be one of the determining factors in the course and outcome of their encounter.

1. *The Young King Addresses the New Pope, 1073.* A few months after the election of Gregory VII in April 1073, the young king wrote to the Pope as follows.[12]

To the most watchful and best beloved lord, Pope Gregory, by divine will invested with the apostolic dignity, Henry, by the grace of God King of the Romans, presents his due and faithful service.

Kingdom and priesthood, if they are to be duly administered in Christ, need his continual support, and therefore, my beloved lord and father, they must never be in dissension but must inseparably cleave to each other in the bonds of Christ. For in this way and no other can the harmony of Christian unity and the institution of the Church be held in the bond of perfect love and peace.

But we, who by God's will have now for some time held the kingly office, have not in all respects shown toward the priesthood such reverence and honor as was due to it. Not without reason have we borne the sword of justice entrusted to us by God; but we have not always unsheathed it as we should have done against the guilty. Now, however, somewhat repentant and remorseful, we turn to your fatherly indulgence, accusing ourselves and trusting to you in the Lord that we may be found worthy of absolution by your apostolic authority.

Alas for me, guilty and unhappy that I am! Partly through the impulses of my deceitful youth, partly through the seductive counsels of my advisers, I have sinned against heaven and before you with fraudulent disloyalty and am no more worthy to be called your son. Not only have I encroached upon the property of the

Church, but I have sold churches themselves to unworthy persons, men poisoned with the gall of Simony, men who entered not by the gate but by other ways, and I have not defended the churches as I ought to have done.

But now, since I cannot regulate the churches alone, without authority from you, I most earnestly beg your advice and help in this and in all my affairs. Your directions shall be scrupulously followed in all respects. And first, in regard to the church of Milan, which has fallen into error through my fault, I beg that it may be restored according to law by your apostolic sentence and that then you will proceed to the regulation of other churches by your authority. I shall not fail you, so God will, and I humbly beseech your fatherly support in all my interests.

You will soon receive letters from me by the hands of most trustworthy messengers and from these you will, please God, learn more fully what remains to be said.

2. *The Pope Defines His Policy, 1073.* In the following letters Gregory announces his German policy to two of the German Dukes.[13]

(*To Duke Godfrey of Lorraine, May 1073.*) As regards the king, you may fully understand our purpose and our wishes. So far as God gives us to know, we believe there is no one more anxious or more desirous for his present and future glory than ourself. It is our wish at the first available opportunity to come to an understanding with him through our legates upon the matters which we think important for the welfare of the Church and the honor of his kingly office—with fatherly affection and admonition. If he will then listen to us we shall rejoice for his sake as well as for our own. Of a certainty he will find his profit in maintaining justice in accordance with our advice and warnings.

But if—which God forbid!—he shall repay our love with hate and show contempt toward Almighty God for the high office conferred upon him, then may the judgment which declares, "Cursed be he that keepeth back his sword from blood!" not fall upon us in the providence of God. For we are not free to set aside the law of God for the sake of any person, neither to draw back from the path of rectitude for any favor of men, according to the word of the Apostle, "If I were still pleasing men I should not be a servant of Christ."

(*To Duke Rudolph of Swabia, September 1073.*) Although your zeal in the past has made it clear that you are devoted to the honor of the Holy Roman Church, your recent letter shows your fervent affection for it and proves how greatly you surpass all the other princes of those parts in this respect. Among other welcome ex-pressions therein, this seemed especially calculated to advance the glory of the imperial government and also to strengthen the power of Holy Church, namely, that the empire and the priesthood should be bound together in harmonious union. For, as the human body is guided by two eyes for its physical illumination, so the body of the Church is guided and enlightened with spiritual light when these two offices work together in the cause of pure religion.

Wherefore we desire Your Excellency to know that we have no ill will toward King Henry, to whom we are under obligation because he was our choice as king, and because his father of honored memory, the Emperor Henry, treated me with especial honor among all the Italians at his court, and at his death commended his son to the Roman Church in the person of Pope Victor [II] of reverend memory. Nor, so God help us, would we willingly hate any Christian man, according to the word of the Apostle: "If I give my body to be burned, and if I bestow all my goods to feed the poor and have not love, I am nothing." But, since the harmony of Empire and Priesthood ought to be pure and free from all deceit, it seems to us highly important first to take counsel with you and the empress Agnes, the countess Beatrice, and Rainald, bishop of Como, and other God-fearing men. Then, after you have thoroughly understood our wishes, if our reasons seem sound to you, you may come to an agreement with us; but, if you find that anything should be added to our arguments or stricken from them, we shall be ready, with God's approval, to accept your advice.

3. *The New Pope Addresses the Young King, 1075–1076.* Five letters survive from Gregory to Henry in the three years 1073–76, before the outbreak of trouble. Selections from two of them follow. In the second letter (winter 1075–76) Gregory refers to Henry's investing of Tedold, rather than Gregory's candidate, with the archbishopric of Milan in the fall of 1075.[14]

Gregory . . . to King Henry, greeting . . . [July 20, 1075].

Among other praiseworthy actions, my beloved son, to which you are reported to have risen in your efforts at self-improvement, there are two that have specially commended you to your holy mother, the Roman Church: first, that you have valiantly withstood those guilty of Simony; and second, that you freely approve, and strenuously desire to enforce, the chastity of the clergy as servants of God. For these reasons you have given us cause to expect of you still higher and better things with God's help. Wherefore we earnestly pray that you may hold fast by these, and we beseech our Lord God that he may deign to increase your zeal more and more.

But now, as regards the church of Bamberg, which according to the ordinance of its founder [King Henry II] belongs to the Holy and Apostolic See as the shoulder to the head, that is, as a most intimate member, by a certain special bond of duty, we are greatly disturbed and we are forced by the obligation of our office to come to the rescue of its distress with all our powers. That simoniac so-called bishop Herman, summoned to a Roman synod this present year, failed to appear. He came within a short distance of Rome, but there halted and sent forward messengers with ample gifts, trying, with his well-known trickery, to impose upon our innocence and, if possible, to corrupt the integrity of our colleagues by a pecuniary bargain. But when this turned out contrary to his hopes, convinced of his own damnation he hastily retreated and, soothing the minds of the clergy who were with him by smooth and deceitful promises, declared that if he were able to regain his own country he would resign his bishopric and enter the monastic life.

How he kept these promises Your Highness, beloved son, well knows. With increasing audacity he plundered the clergy who were upholding the welfare and the honor of their church, and had not your royal power restrained him, as we are informed, he would have completely ruined them. After careful consideration of these outrages we removed him from his episcopal and priestly office. Further, as he dared to oppress the church of Bamberg, under the apostolic patronage of St. Peter, more cruelly and more harshly than before, we placed him in the bonds of anathema until he should lay down his usurped dignity and, nevertheless, present himself for trial before the Apostolic See.

Now, therefore, most excellent son, we ask Your Highness and urge you by our dutiful obligation to take counsel with men of piety and so to regulate the affairs of that church according to God's order, that you may be worthy of divine protection through the intercession of St. Peter, in whose name and under whose patronage the church was founded.

(Gregory to Henry, December 8, 1075, or January 8, 1076.) Considering and weighing carefully to how strict a judge we must render an account of the stewardship committed to us by St. Peter, prince of the Apostles, we have hesitated to send you the apostolic benediction, since you are reported to be in voluntary communication with men who are under the censure of the Apostolic See and of a synod. If this is true, you yourself know that you cannot receive the favor of God nor the apostolic blessing unless you shall first put away those excommunicated persons and

force them to do penance and shall yourself obtain absolution and forgiveness for your sin by due repentance and satisfaction. Wherefore we counsel Your Excellency, if you feel yourself guilty in this matter, to make your confession at once to some pious bishop who, with our sanction, may impose upon you a penance suited to the offense, may absolve you and with your consent in writing may be free to send us a true report of the manner of your penance.

We marvel exceedingly that you have sent us so many devoted letters and displayed such humility by the spoken words of your legates, calling yourself a son of our Holy Mother Church and subject to us in faith, singular in affection, a leader in devotion, commending yourself with every expression of gentleness and reverence, and yet in action showing yourself most bitterly hostile to the canons and apostolic decrees in those duties especially required by loyalty to the Church. Not to mention other cases, the way you have observed your promises in the Milan affair, made through your mother and through bishops, our colleagues, whom we sent to you, and what your intentions were in making them is evident to all. And now, heaping wounds upon wounds, you have handed over the sees of Fermo and Spoleto—if indeed a church may be given over by any human power—to persons entirely unknown to us, whereas it is not lawful to consecrate anyone except after probation and with due knowledge.

It would have been becoming to you, since you confess yourself to be a son of the Church, to give more respectful attention to the master of the Church, that is, to Peter, prince of the Apostles. To him, if you are of the Lord's flock, you have been committed for your pasture, since Christ said to him: "Peter, feed my sheep," and again: "To thee are given the keys of Heaven, and whatsoever thou shalt bind on earth shall be bound in Heaven, and whatsoever thou shalt loose on earth shall be loosed in Heaven." Now, while we, unworthy sinner that we are, stand in his place of power, still whatever you send to us, whether in writing or by word of mouth, he himself receives, and while we read what is written or hear the voice of those who speak, he discerns with subtle insight from what spirit the message comes. . . .

At a synod held at Rome during the current year, and over which Divine Providence willed us to preside, several of your subjects being present, we saw that the order of the Christian religion had long been greatly disturbed and its chief and proper function, the redemption of souls, had fallen low and through the wiles of the Devil had been trodden under foot. Startled by this danger and by the manifest ruin of the

Lord's flock we returned to the teaching of the holy fathers, declaring no novelties nor any inventions of our own, but holding that the primary and only rule of discipline and the well-trodden way of the saints should again be sought and followed, all wandering paths to be abandoned. For we know that there is no other way of salvation and eternal life for the flock of Christ and their shepherds except that shown by him who said: "I am the door and he who enters by me shall be saved and shall find pasture." This was taught by the Apostles and observed by the holy fathers and we have learned it from the Gospels and from every page of Holy Writ.

This edict [against lay investiture], which some who place the honor of men above that of God call an intolerable burden, we, using the right word, call rather a truth and a light necessary for salvation, and we have given judgment that it is to be heartily accepted and obeyed, not only by you and your subjects but by all princes and peoples who confess and worship Christ—though it is our especial wish and would be especially fitting for you, that you should excel others in devotion to Christ as you are their superior in fame, in station and in valor.

Nevertheless, in order that these demands may not seem to you too burdensome or unfair we have sent you word by your own liegemen not to be troubled by this reform of an evil practice but to send us prudent and pious legates from your own people. If these can show in any reasonable way how we can moderate the decision of the holy fathers [at the Council] saving the honor of the eternal king and without peril to our own soul, we will condescend to hear their counsel. It would in fact have been the fair thing for you, even if you had not been so graciously admonished, to make reasonable inquiry of us in what respect we had offended you or assailed your honor, before you proceeded to violate the apostolic decrees. But how little you cared for our warnings or for doing right was shown by your later actions.

However, since the long-enduring patience of God summons you to improvement, we hope that with increase of understanding your heart and mind may be turned to obey the commands of God. We warn you with a father's love that you accept the rule of Christ, that you consider the peril of preferring your own honor to his, that you do not hamper by your actions the freedom of that Church which he deigned to bind to himself as a bride by a divine union, but, that she may increase as greatly as possible, you will begin to lend to Almighty God and to St. Peter, by whom also your own glory may merit increase, the aid of your valor by faithful devotion.

Now you ought to recognize your special obligation to them for the triumph over your enemies which they have granted you, and while they are making you happy and singularly prosperous, they ought to find your devotion increased by their favor to you. That the fear of God, in whose hand is all the might of kings and emperors, may impress this upon you more than any admonitions of mine, bear in mind what happened to Saul after he had won a victory by command of the prophet, how he boasted of his triumph, scorning the prophet's admonitions, and how he was rebuked by the Lord as a reward for his humility in the midst of the tokens of his bravery.

Finally, as to what we have read in your letters and do not mention here we will give you no decided answer until your legates, Radbod, Adalbert and Odescalcus, to whom we entrust this, have returned to us and have more fully reported your decision upon the matters which we commissioned them to discuss with you.

E.   THE COUNCIL OF WORMS, JANUARY 1076

Gregory's last letter to Henry (December 1075–January 1076) was reinforced verbally by his envoys who delivered a virtual ultimatum to the king: compliance or else. Henry's reply was to summon the bishops of Germany to a council at Worms for January 24, 1076.

1. The Council to the Pope, January 24, 1076. With apparently little persuasion and less deliberation, the Council sent the following letter to the Pope.[15]

Siegfried, Archbishop of Mainz, Udo of Trier, William of Utrecht, Herman of Metz, Henry of Liège, Ricbert of Verden, Bibo of Toul, Hozemann of Speyer, Burckhard of Halberstadt, Werner of Strassburg, Burchard of Basel, Otto of Constance, Adalbero of Würzburg, Rodbert of Bamberg, Otto of Regensburg, Ellinard of Freising, Udalric of Eichstädt, Frederick of Münster, Eilbert of Minden, Hezil of Hildesheim, Benno of Osnabrück, Eppo of Naumburg, Imadus of Paderborn, Tiedo of Brandenburg, Burchard of Lausanne, Bruno of Verona—to brother Hildebrand.

Although, when thou didst first seize the control of the church, it was clear to us how unlawful and wicked a thing thou hadst presumed to do contrary to right and justice with thine usual arrogance; nevertheless we thought fit to cover the evil beginnings of thine inauguration with an indulgent silence, hoping that these iniquitous preliminaries would be emended and outweighed by the integrity and diligence of thy subsequent administration. But now, as the lamentable condition of the whole church sadly proclaims, thou art consistently and pertinaciously faithful to thine evil beginnings, in the increasing iniquity of thine actions and decrees. . . . The flame of discord, which thou didst arouse with bitter disputes in the Roman church, thou hast scattered with senseless fury throughout all the churches of Italy, Germany, Gaul and Spain. For to the utmost of thy power thou hast deprived the bishops of all the power, known to have been divinely given to them by the grace of the Holy Spirit, Who operates above all in ordinations. Thou hast given all oversight over ecclesiastical matters to the unstable mob. None is now acknowledged a bishop or a priest, unless by unworthy subservience he has obtained his office from thy magnificence. Thou hast thrown into wretched confusion all the life of the apostolic institution and that perfect interrelation of the members of Christ, which the teacher of the gentiles so often commends and inculcates.

Thus, because of thine ambitious decrees—with tears it must be said—the name of Christ has all but perished. Who is not outraged by thine unworthy conduct in arrogating to thyself a new and improper power in order to destroy the lawful rights of the whole brotherhood? For thou dost assert that, if the mere news of a sin committed by a member of our flocks reaches thee, none of us has thenceforth any power to bind or loose him, but thou only or he whom thou shalt specially delegate for the purpose. Who, that is learned in the sacred scriptures, does not see that this decree exceeds all madness? Wherefore . . . we have decided, by common consent of us all, to make known to thee that on which we have hitherto kept silence, namely why thou canst not now, nor ever could, preside over the apostolic see. Thou didst bind thyself with a corporal oath in the time of the Emperor Henry of blessed memory that never in the Emperor's lifetime, nor in that of his son, our present reigning and glorious King, wouldst thou thyself accept the papacy, or, as far as in thee lay, wouldst thou suffer another to accept it, without the consent and approval of the father, while he was alive, or of the son, while he lived. And there are to-day many bishops who witnessed that oath; who saw it with their eyes and heard it with their ears. Remember too how, when ambition to be pope moved several of the cardinals, to remove all rivalry on that occasion, thou didst bind thyself with an oath, on condition that they did the same, never to hold the papacy. See how faithfully thou hast kept both these oaths.

Further, when a synod was held in the time of Pope Nicholas, whereat 125 bishops assisted, it was established and decreed under pain of anathema that none should ever be made Pope except by the election of the cardinals, the approbation of the people and the consent and authorization of the king. And of that decision and decree thou thyself wast the author, promoter and signatory.

Also thou hast, as it were, filled the whole church with the stench of a grave scandal by associating more intimately than is necessary with a woman not of thy kin. This is a matter of propriety rather than of morality; and yet this general complaint is everywhere made, that at the apostolic see all judgments and all decrees are the work of women, and that the whole church is governed by this new senate of women. . . . And finally, no amount of complaint is adequate to express the insults and outrages you have heaped upon the bishops, calling them sons of harlots and other vile names. Therefore, since your pontificate was begun in perjury and crime, since your innovations have placed the church of God in the gravest peril, since your life and conduct are stained with infamy; we now renounce our obedience, which indeed was never legally promised to you. You have declared publicly that you do not consider us to be bishops; we reply that no one of us shall ever hold you to be the pope.

2. *The King to the Pope, January 24, 1076.* The King also wrote to the Pope describing the decision of the council.[16]

Henry, king not by usurpation, but by the holy ordination of God, to Hildebrand, not pope, but false monk.

This is the salutation which you deserve, for you have never held any office in the church without making it a source of confusion and a curse to Christian men instead of an honor and a blessing. To mention only the most obvious cases out of many, you have not only dared to touch the Lord's anointed, the archbishops, bishops, and priests; but you have scorned them and abused them, as if they were ignorant servants not fit to know what their master was doing. This you have done to gain favor with the vulgar crowd. You have declared that the bishops know nothing and that you know everything; but if you have such great wisdom you have used it not to build but to destroy. Therefore we believe that St. Gregory, whose name you have presumed to take, had you in mind when he said: "The heart of the prelate is puffed up by the abundance of subjects, and he thinks himself more powerful than all others." All this we have endured because of our respect for the papal office, but you have mistaken our humility for fear, and have dared to make an attack upon the royal and imperial authority which we received from God. You have even threatened to take it away, as if we had received it from you, and as if the empire and kingdom were in your disposal and not in the disposal of God. Our Lord Jesus Christ has called us to the government of the empire, but he never called you to the rule of the church. This is the way you have gained advancement in the church; through craft you have obtained wealth; through wealth you have obtained favor; through favor, the power of the sword; and through the power of the sword, the papal seat, which is the seat of peace; and then from the seat of peace you have expelled peace. For you have incited subjects to rebel against their prelates by teaching them to despise the bishops, their rightful rulers. You have given to laymen the authority over priests, whereby they condemn and depose those whom the bishops have put over them to teach them. You have attacked me, who, unworthy as I am, have yet been anointed to rule among the anointed of God, and who, according to the teaching of the fathers, can be judged by no one save God alone, and can be deposed for no crime except infidelity. For the holy fathers in the time of the apostate Julian did not presume to pronounce sentence of deposition against him, but left him to be judged and condemned by God. St. Peter himself said: "Fear God, honor the king" [1 Pet. 2:17]. But you, who fear not God, have dishonored me, whom He hath established. St. Paul, who said that even an angel from heaven should be accursed who taught any other than the true doctrine, did not make an exception in your favor, to permit you to teach false doctrines. For he says: "But though we, or an angel from heaven, preach any other gospel unto you than that which we have preached unto you, let him be accursed" [Gal. 1:8]. Come down, then, from that apostolic seat which you have obtained by violence; for you have been declared accursed by St. Paul for your false doctrines and have been condemned by us and our bishops for your evil rule. Let another ascend the throne of St. Peter, one who will not use religion as a cloak of violence, but will teach the life-giving doctrine of that prince of the apostles. I, Henry, king by the grace of God, with all my bishops, say unto you: "Come down, come down, and be accursed through all the ages."

F.   THE PAPAL REPLY, FEBRUARY 1076

The year 1075 had been a busy one for the Pope, culminating in December in the violent capture and imprisonment of Gregory by a Roman noble. An outraged Roman populace rescued him, and it was amid this outburst of enthusiasm that the news of Worms reached Rome. Henry and his German bishops had persuaded the Italian bishops to concur with the actions taken at Worms. An Italian bishop was then sent to convey the sentence of deposition to Rome. He arrived just as the Lenten Synod was commencing. Something of the effect produced by his message can be gathered from the documents which follow.

1. *The Lenten Synod of 1076.* The following excerpt from the Papal records should be compared with the decisions of the Council of Worms both as to tone and as to argument.[17]

In the year of the Incarnation 1075, our lord Pope Gregory held a synod at Rome in the church of Our Savior which is called the Constantiniana. A great number of bishops and abbots and clergy and laymen of various orders were present.

At this synod, among the decrees promulgated was the excommunication of Siegfried, archbishop of Mainz, in the following form:

In accordance with the judgment of the Holy Spirit and by authority of the blessed Apostles Peter and Paul, we suspend from every espiscopal function, and exclude from the communion of the body and blood of the Lord, Siegfried, archbishop of Mainz, who has attempted to cut off the bishops and abbots of Germany from the Holy Roman Church, their spiritual mother—unless perchance in the hour of death, and then only if he shall come to himself and truly repent. Those who voluntarily joined his schism and still persist in their evil deeds, we also suspend from all episcopal functions. Those, however, who consented against their will we allow time until the feast of St. Peter [August 1]; but if within that term they shall not have given due satisfaction in person or by messengers in our presence, they shall thenceforth be deprived of their episcopal office.

(*Excommunication of the bishops of Lombardy.*) The bishops of Lombardy who, in contempt of canonical and apostolic authority, have joined in a sworn conspiracy against St. Peter, prince of the Apostles, we suspend from their episcopal functions and exclude them from the communion of the Holy Church.

[Here follows a list of excommunications of prelates and laymen beyond the Alps, ending with the proclamation against King Henry IV.]

O blessed Peter, prince of the Apostles, mercifully incline thine ear, we [sic] pray, and hear me, thy servant, whom thou hast cherished from infancy and hast delivered until now from the hand of the wicked who have hated and still hate me for my loyalty to thee. Thou art my witness, as are also my Lady, the Mother of God, and the blessed Paul, thy brother among all the saints, that thy Holy Roman Church forced me against my will to be its ruler. I had no thought of ascending thy throne as a robber, nay, rather would I have chosen to end my life as a pilgrim than to seize upon thy place for earthly glory and by devices of this world. Therefore, by thy favor, not by any works of mine, I believe that it is and has been thy will, that the Christian people especially committed to thee should render obedience to me, thy especially constituted representative. To me is given by thy grace the power of binding and loosing in Heaven and upon earth.

Wherefore, relying upon this commission, and for the honor and defense of thy Church, in the name of Almighty God, Father, Son and Holy Spirit, through thy power and authority, I deprive King Henry, son of the emperor Henry, who has rebelled against thy Church with unheard-of audacity, of the government over the whole kingdom of Germany and Italy, and I release all Christian men from the allegiance which they have sworn or may swear to him, and I forbid anyone to serve him as king. For it is fitting that he who seeks to diminish the glory of thy Church should lose the glory which he seems to have.

And, since he has refused to obey as a Christian should or to return to the God whom he has abandoned by taking part with excommunicated persons, has spurned my warnings which I gave him for his soul's welfare, as thou knowest, and has separated himself from thy Church and tried to rend it asunder, I bind him in the bonds of anathema in thy stead and I bind him thus as commissioned by thee, that the nations may know and be convinced that thou art Peter and that upon thy rock the son of the living God has built his Church and the gates of hell shall not prevail against it.

2. *Gregory Explains His Action.* In the following circular letter, sent out shortly after the Lenten Synod, Gregory gave a more detailed description of his action.[18]

Gregory, Bishop, slave of the slaves of God, to all bishops, dukes, counts and others of the faithful, defenders of the Christian faith in the kingdom of Germans, greeting and apostolic benediction.

We have heard that some of you are in doubt and perplexity about the excommunication which we have inflicted on the king. . . . Wherefore we have carefully set forth before the eyes and minds of all, as accurately as possible (our conscience is our witness), how we were led to excommuni-

cate him; not so much, as it were with uplifted voice, publicly to proclaim the various causes (which alas! are but too well known), as to satisfy the minds of those, who think that we have drawn the spiritual sword rashly and more on the promptings of our own mind than through fear of God or zeal for righteousness.

Formerly, when we were occupying the post of deacon, there reached us an evil and very discreditable account of the king's actions. But from consideration for the imperial dignity and reverence for his father and mother, as also from the hope and desire for his correction, we frequently admonished him by letters and envoys to desist from his wickedness, and, mindful of his noble birth and dignity, to order his life with behavior fitting a king, and, if God permit, future Emperor. But since we in our unworthiness have been raised to the supreme pontificate, while his wickedness has increased with his advancing age, we have much more earnestly exhorted him in every way, arguing, entreating, rebuking, to amend his life—knowing that Almighty God would the more strictly require his soul at our hands, for that permission and authority to rebuke him had been given to us before all other men. He often sent us loyal salutations and letters . . . and in words has promised from day to day that he would most readily accept our warnings; but in fact and by the increase of his sins he has spurned them.

Meanwhile we summoned to repentance certain members of his court, through whose counsels and schemings he had defiled bishoprics and many monasteries with the simoniacal heresy, intruding, for money, wolves in place of shepherds; in order that, while amendment was possible, they should restore the property of the churches, which with sacrilegious hand they had obtained by this criminal commerce, to the venerable places to which it appertained, and that they themselves by heartfelt penitence should make satisfaction to God for the iniquity committed. But when we knew that they disregarded the grace afforded to them for fulfilling these duties and obstinately continued in their former wickedness, then, as was right, we separated them, as sacrilegious persons and as servants and members of the devil, from the communion and body of the whole church; and we admonished the king to dismiss them as excommunicates, from his house, his councils and all communion with himself.

Meanwhile the revolt of the Saxons against the king increased; and when he saw that the forces and defenders of the kingdom were for the more part prepared to abandon him, he again sent us a supplicatory letter, full of all humility. . . . And in this [i.e. ecclesiastical law] he promised us his entire obedience, consent and faithful support. And again later, when he was admitted to penance by our brothers and legates, Humbert, Bishop of Preneste, and Gerald, Bishop of Ostia, whom we sent to him, he repeated to them his promise and confirmed it on the sacred stoles which they wore upon their necks.

Some time later, after a battle with the Saxons, the king, in return for the victory gained, gave thanks and offerings to God thus—he continued to break the oaths which he had made about the amendment of his life; ignoring his promises, he admitted the excommunicates to the intimacy of his court; and he kept the churches in the same confusion as before. . . . [Gregory then dwells on his exhortation to Henry to amend his morals and to dismiss the excommunicates.]

He could not tolerate being reproved or criticized by anyone, and not only could not be induced to make amends for his offenses, but, overcome by yet greater madness of moral judgment, did not cease till he caused nearly all of the bishops in Italy and as many as he could in the German lands to make shipwreck concerning the faith of Christ, in that he forced them to deny to blessed Peter and the Apostolic See the obedience and honor due to them and granted by our Lord Jesus Christ.

Therefore, when we perceived that his wickedness had reached its climax, for the following causes—first because he refused to withdraw himself from intercourse with those who for sacrilege and conviction of simoniacal heresy had been excommunicated; further because he was unwilling—I do not say to undergo—but even to promise penance for the wickednesses of his life, thus giving the lie to the penitence which he had professed before our legates; and also because he did not shrink from dismembering the body of Christ, that is the unity of holy Church—for these offences, I say, we excommunicated him by sentence of a synod; in order that we may, with God's help, by severity recall to the way of salvation him, whom we could not move by gentleness, or, if he be unmoved—which God forbid—by the sentence of segregation. Our own soul at any rate may not incur the risk of negligence or cowardice.

If, therefore, anyone shall hold that this sentence has been unjustly or unreasonably pronounced, and if he be willing to apply his intellect to the sacred canons, let him communicate with us and, patiently hearing not what we, but what the divine authority teaches and commands, what the unanimous voice of the holy fathers decides, let him acquiesce. We do not think that any one of the faithful who knows the laws of the church is so mastered by this error as not to believe in his heart, even if he dare not publicly affirm his faith, that justice has been done.

Nevertheless, even if—which God forbid—we have thus bound him for insufficiently weighty cause or out of due order, the sentence, as the holy fathers assert, should not on that account be defied, but absolution should be sought with all humility. . . .

But if, inspired by God, he be willing to come to his senses, whatever he may attempt against us, he will always find us prepared to receive him into the holy communion, as your charity shall counsel us.

3. *The Royal Summons to a Diet at Worms, April–May, 1076.* Something of the effect of Gregory's actions on the leaders of the church in Germany can be gained from the following document, the summons of Henry to the bishops and princes of Germany to meet in a diet at Worms. Henry's efforts to convene this diet, as well as one at Mainz, were apparently unsuccessful.[19]

Henry, king by the grace of God, sends favor, greeting, love—not to all, but to a few.

In very important matters the wisest counsels of the greatest men are needed—men who shall both outwardly have the ability and inwardly shall not be without the will to give their best advice in a matter in which they are interested. For there is nothing whatever in the carrying out of which either ability without will or will without ability avails. Both of which thou, most faithful one, dost possess, as we think, in equal measure; or to speak more truly, although thou who art very great are not lacking in very great ability, —nevertheless, if we know thee rightly and have noted thy fidelity with proper care, thou dost abound with a good will greater even than this very great ability; to our own and to the country's advantage. For from the faithful services of the past we are led to hope for still more faithful services in the future. We rely moreover on thy love not to let thy faithfulness disappoint our expectations; for from the loyalty of none of the princes or bishops of the land do we hope for greater things than from thine, rejoicing, as we have done, not only in the showing of the past but also in what thou hast led us to expect from thee in the future. Let, therefore, thy timely good will be present now with thy ability; for it is called for not only by our own straits but also by those of all thy fellow-bishops and brothers— nay, of the whole oppressed church. Thou art not ignorant, indeed, of this oppression; only see to it that thou do not withdraw thy aid from the oppressed church, but that thou do give thy sympathy to the kingdom and the priesthood. For in both of these, even as the church has hitherto been exalted, so now, alas, in both it is humiliated and bereaved. Inasmuch as one man has claimed for himself both; nor has he helped the one, seeing that he neither would nor could help either. But, lest we keep from thee any longer the name of one who is known to thee, learn of whom we are speaking—Hildebrand, namely, outwardly, indeed, a monk; called pope, but presiding over the apostolic see rather with the violence of an invader than with the care of a pastor, and, from the seat of universal peace, sundering the chains of peace and unity—as thou thyself dost clearly know. For, to mention a few cases out of many, he usurped for himself the kingdom and the priesthood without God's sanction, despising God's holy ordination which willed essentially that they—namely the kingdom and the priesthood—should remain not in the hands of one, but, as two, in the hands of two. For the Saviour Himself, during His Passion, intimated that this was the meaning of the typical sufficiency of the two swords. For when it was said to Him: "Behold, Lord, here are two swords"—He answered: "It is enough," signifying by this sufficing duality that a spiritual and a carnal sword were to be wielded in the church, and that by them every thing evil was about to be cut off—by the sacerdotal sword, namely, to the end that the king, for God's sake, should be obeyed; but by the royal one to the end that the enemies of Christ without should be expelled, and that the priesthood within should be obeyed. And He taught that every man should be constrained so to extend his love from one to the other that the kingdom should neither lack the honor due to the priesthood, nor the priesthood the honor due to the kingdom. In what way the madness of Hildebrand confounded this ordinance of God thou thyself dost know, if thou hast been ready or willing to know. For in his judgment no one is rightfully priest save him who has bought permission from his own capricious self. Me also whom God called to the kingdom—not, however, having called him to the priesthood—he strove to deprive of my royal power, threatening to take away my kingdom and my soul, neither of which he had granted, because he saw me wishing to hold my rule from God and not from him—because he himself had not constituted me king. Although he had often, as thou dost know, thrown out these and similar things to shame us, he was not as yet satisfied with that but needs must inflict upon us from day to day new and ingenious kinds of confusion—as he recently proved in the case of our envoys. For a page will not suffice to tell how he treated those same envoys of ours, how cruelly he imprisoned them and afflicted them, when captive, with nakedness, cold, hunger and thirst and blows; and how at length he ordered them to be led like martyrs through the midst of the city, furnishing a spectacle for all; so that one would call him and believe him as mad as Decius the tyrant, and a burner of saints. Wherefore, beloved, be not tardy—may all in common not be tardy—to give ear to my request, and to that of thy fellow-bishops, that thou do come to Worms at Pentecost; and that thou there, with the other princes, do listen to many things a few of which are mentioned in this letter; and that thou do show what is to be done. Thou art asked to do this for love of thy fellow-bishops, warned to for the good of the church, bound to for the honor of our life and of the whole land.

Part II.

THE ROAD TO CANOSSA

The first Part of this Problem concentrated on the broad issues, the main lines of development which contributed to the controversy between Papacy and Empire. Now the focus changes. The particular question of lay investiture was to be settled in different ways all over Europe during the fifty years after 1075, and the general issue of spiritual versus temporal power was perhaps never to be definitively resolved. Nevertheless, the rest of this Problem is concerned primarily with the details of the immediate outcome of the dispute between Gregory VII and Henry IV which culminated in Henry's dramatic journey to Canossa. Canossa has something more than dramatic but passing importance; the student, aware of the larger matters at stake, can make of the most minute details a microcosm of a greater whole.

A.

THE PAPAL POSITION REAFFIRMED, AUGUST–SEPTEMBER 1076

1. *Gregory on the Excommunication of a King, August 1076.* Bishop Herman of Metz had apparently been forced to sign the decree of the bishops at Worms. In the following letter Gregory elaborates on the original papal position, in reply to some questions from the worried Herman who was desirous of strengthening his spirits for the battle ahead.[20]

You have asked a great many questions of me, a very busy man, and have sent me an extremely urgent messenger. Wherefore I beg you to bear with me patiently if my reply is not sufficiently ample.

There is no need to ask me who are the excommunicated bishops, priests, or laymen; since beyond a doubt they are those who are known to be in communication with the excommunicated King Henry—if, indeed, he may properly be called king. They do not hesitate to place the fear and favor of man before the commands of the eternal King nor to expose their king to the wrath of Almighty God by giving him their support.

He too feared not to incur the penalty of excommunication by dealing with followers who had been excommunicated for the heresy of Simony nor to draw others into excommunication through their dealings with him. How can we think of such things but in the words of the Psalmist: "The fool hath said in his heart there is no God," or again: "They are all gone astray in their wills."

Now to those who say: "A king may not be excommunicated," although we are not bound to reply to such a fatuous notion, yet, lest we seem to pass over their foolishness impatiently we will recall them to sound doctrine by directing their attention to the words and acts of the holy fathers. Let them read what instructions St. Peter gave to the Christian community in his ordination of St. Clement in regard to one who had not the approval of the pontiff. Let them learn why the Apostle said, "Being prompt to punish every disobedience"; and of whom he said, "Do not even take food with such people." Let them consider why Pope Zachary deposed a king of the Franks and released all his subjects from their oaths of allegiance. Let them read in the records [*registra*] of St. Gregory how in his grants to certain churches he not merely excommunicated kings and dukes who opposed him but declared them deprived of their royal dignity. And let them not forget that St. Ambrose not only excommunicated the emperor Theodosius but forbade him to stand in the room of the priests within the church.

But perhaps those people would imagine that when God commended his Church to Peter three times saying, "Feed my sheep," he made an exception of kings! Why do they not see, or rather confess with shame that, when God gave to Peter as leader the power of binding and loosing in heaven and on earth he excepted no one, withheld no one from his power? For if a man says that he cannot be bound by the ban of the Church, it is evident that he could not be loosed by its authority, and he who shamelessly denies this cuts himself off absolutely from Christ. If the

Holy Apostolic See, through the princely power divinely bestowed upon it, has jurisdiction over spiritual things, why not also over temporal things? When kings and princes of this world set their own dignity and profit higher than God's righteousness and seek their own honor, neglecting the glory of God, you know whose members they are, to whom they give their allegiance. Just as those who place God above their own wills and obey his commands rather than those of men are members of Christ, so those of whom we spoke are members of Antichrist. If then spiritual men are to be judged, as is fitting, why should not men of the world be held to account still more strictly for their evil deeds?

Perchance they imagine that royal dignity is higher than that of bishops, but how great the difference between them is, they may learn from the difference in their origins. The former came from human lust of power; the latter was instituted by divine grace. The former constantly strives after empty glory; the latter aspires ever toward the heavenly life. Let them learn what Anastasius the pope said to Anastasius the emperor regarding these two dignities, and how St. Ambrose in his pastoral letter distinguished between them. He said: "If you compare the episcopal dignity with the splendor of kings and the crowns of princes, these are far more inferior to it than lead is to glistening gold." And, knowing this, the emperor Constantine chose, not the highest, but the lowest seat among the bishops; for he knew that God resists the haughty, but confers his grace upon the humble.

Meantime, be it known to you, my brother, that, upon receipt of letters from certain of our clerical brethren and political leaders we have given apostolic authority to those bishops to absolve such persons excommunicated by us as have dared to cut themselves loose from the king. But as to the king himself, we have absolutely forbidden anyone to dare to absolve him until we shall have been made certain by competent witnesses of his sincere repentance and reparation; so that at the same time we may determine, if divine grace shall have visited him, in what form we may grant him absolution, to God's glory and his own salvation. For it has not escaped our knowledge that there are some of you who, pretending to be authorized by us, but really led astray by fear or the favor of men, would presume to absolve him if I [*sic*] did not forbid them, thus widening the wound instead of healing it. And if others, bishops in very truth, should oppose them, they would say that these were actuated, not by a sense of justice, but by personal hostility.

Moreover ordination and consecration by those bishops who dare to communicate with an excommunicated king become in the sight of God an execration, according to St. Gregory. For since they in their pride refuse to obey the Apostolic See, they incur the charge of idolatry, according to Samuel. If he is said to be of God who is stirred by divine love to punish crime, certainly he is not of God who refuses to rebuke the lives of carnal men so far as in him lies. And if he is accursed who withholds his sword from blood— that is to say, the word of preaching from destroying the life of the flesh—how much more is he accursed who through fear or favor drives his brother's soul into everlasting perdition! Furthermore you cannot find in the teaching of any of the holy fathers that men accursed and excommunicated can convey to others that blessing and that divine grace which they do not fear to deny by their actions.

2. *Gregory to the Faithful of Germany, September 1076.* In the following letter to his German supporters, the Pope suggests a policy for them to pursue in relation to King Henry.[21]

Gregory . . . to all the beloved brethren in Christ, fellow bishops, dukes, counts and all defenders of the Christian faith dwelling in the kingdom of Germany, greeting and absolution from all their sins through the apostolic benediction.

If you weigh carefully the decree in which Henry, king so-called, was excommunicated in a holy synod by judgment of the Holy Spirit, you will see beyond a doubt what action ought to be taken in his case. It will there be seen why he was bound in the bondage of anathema and deposed from his royal dignity, and that every people formerly subject to him is released from its oath of allegiance.

But because, as God knows, we are not moved against him by any pride or empty desire for the things of this world, but only by zeal for the Holy See and our common mother, the Church, we admonish you in the Lord Jesus and beg you as beloved brethren to receive him kindly if with his whole heart he shall turn to God, and to show toward him not merely justice which would prohibit him from ruling, but mercy which wipes out many crimes. Be mindful, I beg you, of the frailty of our common human nature and do not forget the pious and noble memory of his father and his mother, rulers the like of whom cannot be found in this our day.

Apply, however, the oil of kindness to his wounds in such a way that the scars may not grow foul by neglect of the wine of discipline and thus the honor of Holy Church and of the Roman Empire fall in widespread ruin through our indifference. Let those evil counselors be far removed from him, who excommunicated for the heresy of Simony, have not scrupled to infect their master with their own disease and by diverse crimes have seduced him into splitting our Holy Church in twain and have brought upon him the wrath of God and of Saint Peter. Let other advisors be given him who care more for his advantage than their own and who place God above all earthly profit. Let him no longer imagine that Holy Church is his subject or his handmaid but rather let him recognize her as his superior and his mistress. Let him not be puffed up with the spirit of pride and defend practices invented to check the liberty of Holy Church, but let him observe the teaching of the holy fathers which divine power taught them for our salvation.

But if he shall have given you reliable information as to these and other demands which may properly be made upon him, we desire that you give us immediate notice by competent messengers so that, taking counsel together, we may with God's help decide upon the right course of action. Above all, we forbid, in the name of St. Peter, that any one of you should venture to absolve him from excommunication until the abovementioned information shall have been given to us and you shall have received the consent of the Apostolic See and our renewed answer. We are distrustful of the conflicting counsels of different persons and have our suspicions of the fear and favor of men.

But now, if through the crimes of many [others] —which God forbid!—he shall not with whole heart turn to God, let another ruler of the kingdom be found by divine favor, such an one as shall bind himself by unquestionable obligations to carry out the measures we have indicated and any others that may be necessary for the safety of the Christian religion and of the whole empire. Further, in order that we may confirm your choice —if it shall be necessary to make a choice—and support the new order in our time, as we know was done by the holy fathers before us, inform us at the earliest possible moment as to the person, the character and the occupation of the candidate. Proceeding thus with pious and practical method you will deserve well of us in the present case and will merit the favor of the Apostolic See by divine grace and the blessing of St. Peter, prince of the Apostles.

As to the oath which you have taken to our best beloved daughter, the empress Agnes, in case her son should die before her, you need have no scruples, because, if she should be led by overfondness for her son to resist the course of justice or, on the other hand, should defend justice and consent to his deposition, you will know how to do the rest. This, however, would seem to be advisable: that when you have come to a firm decision among yourselves that he shall be removed, you should take counsel with her and with us as to the person to be entrusted with the government of the kingdom. Then either she will give her assent to the common judgment of us all, or the authority of the Apostolic See will release all bonds which stand in the way of justice.

B.   THE AGREEMENT AT OPPENHEIM, OCTOBER 1076

Which was to prevail, Pope or King? Each had ordered the other to descend from his lofty position. Part of the answer is to be found in the events leading up to Oppenheim on the Rhine in October 1076. At this point the student starts to make increasing use of the evidence of chroniclers, whose relative value, prejudice, and credibility must always be carefully appraised.

1. *Oppenheim: The Evidence of the Chroniclers.* Of the many chroniclers available for this momentous period in German history, two are of particular value. The first selection is from *The Annals of Berthold* which were compiled by a monk from the South German monastery of Reichenau, Baden. The *Annals,* rather voluminous in character and comparatively literary in flavor, were written shortly after the events described, to which the writer had not been an eyewitness. The second selection is from a work by a Saxon churchman, Bruno, *Concerning the Saxon War.* Bruno, who wrote his account about the year 1082, eventually received office from Rudolph Duke of Swabia, the leader of the Saxon opposition to Henry.[22]

(*Annals of Berthold*) In the anathema itself the lord pope had, on the part and in the name of the omnipotent Father, Son, and Holy Ghost, and by the authority of St. Peter, commanded all Christians not to obey the excommunicated king thenceforth as king in any way or serve him or keep an oath which they had made or were to make with him. This not the smallest part of the princes of the realm observed, and, though they were very often called to come to the king, they refused, striving diligently to have zeal for the Lord as they knew it. Even if they had known him to have been unjustly and uncanonically excommunicated, yet, according to the decree of the council of Sardica, they must not communicate with him in any way until they knew that he had been reconciled. Wherefore, fearing to associate with the king as yet unreconciled, since they could neither persuade him nor punish nor correct him, and since they shuddered to agree with him, they strove, as was fitting, to avoid him. Therefore the lords of the kingdom agreed, in the fall, to have a conference with him at Magdeburg, where they could by general council define what ought to be done about the matter of such great importance, and where they

might be allowed to serve their king and lord, when he had been admonished, turned to penance, and reconciled.

When they assembled there with no small force of soldiers, the king and his advisors were encamped on the other side of the Rhine at the town of Oppenheim with a considerable gathering of loyal men, threateningly and angrily wrought up. The princes of the realm, however, remained on this side of the Rhine; they questioned among themselves and, with God's assent, conferred more intimately one with another as to what conclusion they should reach in such an unusual matter. Thither had come the legates of the Apostolic See with letters pertaining to this matter, by which the pope had intrusted the bishop of Patavia, already long accepted as apostolic representative, to reconcile all canonically, the king excepted, who fittingly came to render satisfaction and do worthy penance, those namely who wished to stand on the side of St. Peter. Of these, the archbishop of Mainz with his knights, the bishops of Trier, of Strasburg, of Verdun, of Luttich, of Münster, the elect of Utrecht, of Spires, of Basel, of Constance, the one at Ulm, and several abbots, as well as a considerable host of more or less important personages who had been excommunicated because of the crime of associating with the king for disobedience or because they had received masses and offices from priests condemned for incontinence or the heresy of simony, were there reconciled and received into communion.

Finally, after they had spent ten days in such matters, the king, when he saw and heard that so many and such great men had yielded to the apostolic see, and that they were considering making another king in his place, pretended to yield, though unwilling and reluctant and no longer with any spirit beyond his grief, not only to the pope, but also to the princes of the realm, in all that they wished to impose on him or wanted him to observe. To them it then seemed, in addition to other things, that in the first place the see and city should be freely returned to the bishop of Worms, that the queen should leave it with all her following, that their hostages should be returned to the Saxons, and that the king should entirely separate himself from his excommunicated followers, and that he should also, without delay, send letters to pope Gregory, strongly intimating that he would perform due obedience, satisfaction, and fitting penance, and that he himself should await the apostolic answer and reconciliation, meanwhile abiding by their advice.

These and all the other matters the king performed there, though not with entire candor. From thence he despatched the letters, composed as they had agreed between themselves and sealed in their presence—he, nevertheless, later secretly altered and changed these to suit his will—to be presented to the pope at Rome by the archbishop of Trier. But the princes of the kingdom, fearing the tricks and the usual folly of the king's counselors, which they had so often experienced, likewise directed to Rome, in haste, trustworthy legates, who had been present at everything there enacted, so that the pope might not be deceived by their tricks, and to implore him, humbly supplicated through the mercy of God, to deign to come to these parts to settle this dissension. Furthermore, in order to constrain the king more perfectly to obedience to the Apostolic See, they took oath before they separated that if the king by his own fault remained excommunicated longer than a year they would no longer hold him as their king. Then, for fear of the king's future wrath and vengeance upon them, since many of them had left him, without visiting and greeting him, so that he was greatly angered with them, they pledged each other aid if anything should be done against them on this account, and returned, joyfully, each to his own home.

(*Bruno, Concerning the Saxon War*) And when they had already begun to confer about choosing a new king the Saxons wanted to choose one of the Swabians; the Swabians one of the Saxons. Over on the other bank of the Rhine the town of Mainz held Henry, all hope of holding his kingdom gone. Nevertheless, he sent messengers to arouse their pity that they might accord him the privilege of making reparation, for he had been punished enough. Our party, however, absolutely refused to deal with them until he had been absolved from the anathema by the papal legate. To hasten the account, they agreed to endure the humility of penance on the conditions which our party held out. When he had agreed to this our men proposed first that he reinstate in full authority the bishop of Worms, who had been long expelled from his city; secondly, that he should have letters written in which he admitted that he had unjustly afflicted the Saxons. These letters were to be looked over

by our men, were to be signed with the royal seal in their presence, and, thus sealed, were to be given to them and carried by their messengers throughout Germany and Italy. Then he himself was to go to Rome and, by making fitting amendment, free himself from the bonds of the anathema.

Accordingly, the bishop was installed in the city with great honor. The letters were written and signed in the presence of our men and sent by our messengers throughout Germany and Italy, while the king prepared in all haste to free himself from the bonds of the anathema through the indulgence of the pope. But every one of our men took oath that unless Henry IV, son of the emperor Henry, was absolved from the ban by the pope at the beginning of February, never would he be, or be called, their king. This oath the patriarch was the first to take, and when it was set down on parchment he placed it among the letters in his wallet. Nevertheless, he kept it better in writing than he did in deed, and, as was said shortly before, he suffered a cruel punishment.

Then the bishop of Patavia, legate of the Roman see, did likewise. After them all the bishops, dukes, counts, and all the other greater and lesser dignitaries who were present took the oath. But the bishops accomplished more than the others, for they kept it among their letters. Then they despatched a legate to the pope to have him come to Augsburg early in February in order to have the case considered carefully in the presence of all. There the pope might either absolve him from the ban or constrain him more closely than before. In the latter event they might then, with the pope's counsel, select another king who knew how to rule. When these matters had been accomplished the two armies separated with great friendship and marched home, rejoicing and singing the praise of the Lord.

2. *The Agreement at Oppenheim, October 1076.* The decisions of the diet at Oppenheim were formally recorded in two decrees, the promise of the king to the pope, and a general edict. Both decrees are printed below.[23]

(*Promise of the King to Offer Obedience to the Pope.*) Being admonished to do so by the counsel of our faithful ones, I promise to observe in all things the obedience due to the Apostolic See and to thee, Pope Gregory, and will take care devoutly to correct and to render satisfaction for anything whereby a derogation to the honor of that same see, or to thine, has arisen through us. Since, moreover, certain very grave charges are brought against us concerning attempts which I am supposed to have made against that same see and against thy reverence: these, at a suitable time, I will either refute by the help of innocence and by the favor of God, or, failing this, I will at length willingly undergo a suitable penance for them. It behooves thy holiness also, moreover, not to veil those things which, spread abroad concerning thee, cause scandal to the church—but rather, by removing this scruple too from the public conscience, to establish through thy wisdom the universal tranquillity of the church as well as of the kingdom.

(*Edict Cancelling the Sentence against Gregory VII, October, 1076.*) Henry, king by the grace of God, sends to the archbishops, bishops, margraves, counts and dignitaries of every rank the honorable distinction of his goodwill. Inasmuch as we have been brought to recognize, through the representations of our faithful ones, that we have been wanting in clemency, in some regards, towards the Apostolic See and its venerable bishop, Pope Gregory: it has pleased us, in accordance with healthful counsel, to change our former sentence and to observe, after the manner of our predecessors and progenitors, due obedience in all things to the holy see and to him who is known to preside over it, our master Gregory the Pope. And if we have presumed to act too severely against him we will atone for it by rendering fitting satisfaction. We will, moreover, that ye also, warned by our Highness's example, do not hesitate to render solemn satisfaction to St. Peter and to his vicar; and that those of you who understand themselves to be bound by his ban do strive to be solemnly absolved by him—by our master, namely, Gregory the Pope.

C. WHAT HAPPENED AT CANOSSA

His obvious plight seemed to Henry to warrant desperate measures. A variety of chroniclers described this famous series of events, and selections have been reprinted from several who contribute in an important way to the reconstruction of the actual narrative. In this task the student will find it necessary to compare the stories of two or more chroniclers and, sometimes, to reconcile conflicts in this evidence as best he can. The last selection contains Gregory's own version of the incident.

1. *The Annals of Augsburg.* These *Annals* are the record by the clerk of the town of the events of the year which seemed noteworthy. This determined their nature—terse, often crude or very local in character—and to a considerable extent their value. Such town annals were quite common in the Middle Ages and these of Augsburg may be taken as typical of their kind.[24]

A most disgraceful discord between pope and king, between bishops and dukes, between clergy and laymen. The pope, on account of his zeal for the house of God, is repudiated. At Rome the legates of the king are ill treated by the partisans of the pope. Priests are wretchedly thrown out by laymen for being married, or for buying their offices; everything, sacred and profane, is mingled in confusion. The pope, repudiated, retires to strongly fortified castles and other safe places. A conference between king and dukes at Oppenheim. The winter continuously severe, and an excess of snow from the Calends of November to the Calends of April so that the trees wither. So barren of fruits is the soil that even the seed fails. A council of the pope and dukes against the emperor.

King Henry, going into Italy, is received with all honor by the pope at Canossa, though before repudiated by a council of the dukes. After he is absolved from the ban he is honorably treated. While the king is staying in Italy Rudolph is made king at Foresheim, in an unhallowed spot on the estate of Pontius Pilate, in the middle of the Quadragesima. He, cursed with maledictions rather than consecrated, is anointed on the same day, contrary to the laws of the church. To add to his damnation, on that very day and in the same place—i.e., Mainz—a great many people are killed. King Henry, returning from Pavia, is received with all loyalty. Rudolph is driven into Saxony, his partisans in arms are visited with plunder, fires, and destruction of various kinds; his unhappy and sacrilegious followers suffer devastation and death. Laymen seize the possessions of churches and churchmen; both sides plunder and burn; many are deprived of their inheritance and benefices, many also of their lives. . . . King Henry spent the birthday of Mary in Augsburg [September 8].

2. *The Annals of Lambert.* In sharp contrast to the records of the town clerk are the *Annals* of Lambert, a monk of Hersfeld in Westphalia in northern Germany. Though not an eyewitness, his dramatic and readable description has always been popular. The monastery had had considerable contact with King Henry, once sheltering him in his youth, and was a frequent stopping-place for travellers of distinction. Lambert began his story with Adam and ended just before the election of the anti-king, Rudolph, in 1077.[25]

When Worms had been surrendered and the bishop was assured a most peaceful position the Saxons and Swabians returned home proudly happy. They had sent legates to the pope to insure his presence on the day set for calming the storms of civil war throughout Gaul [i.e., Germany]. The king, for his part, realized that his safety depended upon his obtaining absolution from the anathema before the year was up. Furthermore, for reasons of his own, he did not regard it as very safe to air his case before the pope in the presence of such hostile accusers. Under the circumstances, therefore, he came to the conclusion that it would be best to meet the pope in Italy just as he was setting out for Gaul. There he would try to gain absolution from the anathema in any way that he could. Once this was obtained, his other difficulties must be easily dispelled. No religious scruples would then interfere with his holding a meeting with the princes and obtaining the counsel and loyalty of his friends against his enemies.

Leaving Spires accordingly a few days before Christmas, he began the journey with his wife and young son. No German of any prominence, only one man of inferior rank, accompanied him on this journey out of the kingdom. In need of provisions for so long a journey he besought aid of many whom he had helped in his happier days. Only a few, grateful either for past favors or compassionate for his present condition, afforded him any assistance. To this state of calamity and misfortune had he suddenly fallen from the very height of rank and affluence. There were at the same time other excommunicates who were hurrying to Rome with a most ardent desire to obtain absolution; but either from fear of the princes or, even more, of the pope, they would not let the king join them.

The winter this year was consistently violent and inclement. The Rhine, ice-bound, remained passable for pedestrians from the Festival of St. Martin [November 11] almost to the Calends of April. The vines in most places withered up, their roots snapped off by the cold. King Henry, on his way to Italy, celebrated Christmas in Burgundy at a place called Besançon. He was received here magnificently enough, considering his condition at the time, and was entertained by his maternal uncle, count William, who had very large and prosperous holdings there. His reason for veering from the right road off into Burgundy was that he ascertained that all the roads and approaches into Italy, commonly called passes, had been closed with guards by the dukes Rudolph, Welf,

and Berthold for the very purpose of preventing his passage.

After a proper observance of Christmas he set out from there and came to a place called Cinis [Mt. Cenis]. Here he met his mother-in-law and her son, Amadeus, a man of eminent authority, extensive possessions, and very honorable reputation in these parts. At his approach they received him with honor. Nevertheless, they refused to grant him an escort through their territory unless he paid them the five adjacent Italian bishoprics as the price of the journey. This the counselors of the king regarded as excessive and intolerable. But, since it was absolutely necessary for him to procure passage in any way that he could, and since they were unaffected by any ties of relationship or compassion for his misfortune, it was reluctantly arranged, after much negotiation, that they were to receive a certain province of Burgundy that was rich in all things as the price of his passage. Thus did the indignation of the Lord turn from him persons bound to him not only by oath and many benefices, but actual friends and relatives. . . .

His trouble in getting permission to cross was followed by another difficulty. The winter was very bitter and the mountains through which the passage lay, stretching far and wide with peaks reared up almost to the clouds, were encumbered with masses of snow and ice. Passage by horse or footman over that slippery and precipitous descent was impossible without great danger. But the anniversary of the day on which the king had been excommunicated was threateningly near and would permit no delay in the journey. He knew that, unless he were absolved from the anathema by this day, it was decreed by a general sentence of the princes that his cause be forever lost and his kingdom gone without hope of restitution.

Accordingly he procured some of the natives, who were familiar with the country and accustomed to the rugged summit of the Alps, to go ahead and in every way possible mitigate the difficulties of the trip for his party. Under their guidance they reached the crest of the range with some difficulty, but the descent, precipitous and, as has been said, slippery with glacial ice, defied any farther advance. The men, however, were ready to brave all danger by strength. Now crawling on hands and feet, now leaning on the shoulders of their guides, staggering over the slippery places, falling sometimes, sliding more, and at a serious risk of their lives, they managed at last to reach the level land. The queen and the women in attendance on her were placed on the skins of oxen and dragged along by the guides in charge of the party. Of the horses, some were placed on certain contrivances, while the others were dragged along with their feet tied together. Many of them died while they were being dragged along, more sickened, while but few passed through the danger whole and unaffected.

When the rumor spread through Italy that the king was coming, that he had overcome the dangers of the mountains and was established within the confines of Italy, all the bishops and counts of the region crowded to him and received him with the greatest honor and magnificence as befitted a king. Within a few days he was surrounded by an innumerable host. For there were those who from the very beginning of his reign had desired this advent. Italy was constantly infested with wars, party strife, robberies, and assaults of various kinds on individuals. This and every other invasion upon the law and the rights of the many by the presumptuous few they expected him to correct with the royal censure. Then, too, it had been noised about that he was hastening in great anger to depose the pope. This also pleased many, for it would afford them the opportunity of obtaining fitting vengeance upon him who had so long suspended them from ecclesiastical communion.

Meantime, the pope was on his way to Germany. The princes who had met at Oppenheim had sent letters to him urging him to meet them at Augsburg on the day of the Purification of Saint Mary (February 2) to discuss the case of the king. Accordingly, in spite of the dissuasion of the Roman nobles who feared the uncertain outcome of the affair, he hastened his departure as much as he could in order to be there on the appointed day. His escort was furnished by the countess Matilda. . . . When he had started he learned unexpectedly that the king was already in Italy. At the urgence of Matilda, therefore, he retired into a certain highly fortified place called Canossa, to wait there until he had more carefully ascertained the purpose of the king's coming. He wished to know whether the king came to ask for pardon, or whether he was wrathfully seeking to avenge the excommunication by force.

King Henry, however, had a conference with the countess Matilda, and sent her to the pope, laden with prayers and promises. With her he sent also his mother-in-law, his son, likewise the margrave Azzo, the abbot of Cluny, as well as some of the princes of Italy who need not be mentioned. They begged the pope to absolve him from the excommunication and not rashly to place faith in the accusations of the German princes who were moved rather by the passion of spite than by the love of justice. When the pope heard this message he said that it was unfitting and quite contrary to ecclesiastical law to air the case of a defendant in the absence of the accusers. Nay, more, he told them that if the king were confident of his innocence he should lay aside

every scruple of fear and trustfully present himself at Augsburg on the day on which the princes had decided to come together. There, when the charges of both sides had been heard, he would receive most righteous justice on every point, without prejudice or favor, according to ecclesiastical law.

To this they answered that the king would never in the world evade a trial which he knew would be a most unassailable vindication and recommendation of his equity and innocence. But, they urged, the anniversary of the day on which the king had been excommunicated was drawing near, and the princes of the kingdom who had held aloof thus far pending the outcome of this affair were growing impatient. If he were not absolved before that day, according to Palatine law, he would be held unworthy of royal dignity and undeserving of any further hearing to prove his innocence. For this reason, they said, he seeks absolution so resolutely, and is ready to offer any form of satisfaction which the pope may demand in order only to be absolved from the anathema and to receive the grace of ecclesiastical communion. As for the charges which his accusers bring against him, he will be ready to make full answer, as if nothing had been done by this agreement, when and wherever the pope may ordain. Then, according to the pope's sentence, he will be ready to receive his kingdom again if he refute the charges, or resign with equanimity if his case is lost.

For a long time the pope refused to consider it, for he feared that the king was inconstant and of a disposition easily influenced by his immediate attendants. Overcome at last by the importunities of these zealous advocates as well as by the weight of their opinions, he said, "If he is truly penitent, let him give to our power his crown and other insignia of his kingdom as an evidence of truth and as an act of penance; and, after being so obstinate, let him profess himself unworthy of the kingdom." The envoys considered this too harsh, and they urged him strongly to temper his sentence and not utterly destroy a reed, already shattered, by the severity of his decision. Upon this exhortation he very reluctantly agreed that the king might come in person and, if he performed true penance for his admitted errors, the sin which he had committed by inflicting contumely upon the apostolic chair he might now expiate by obedience to it.

He came as he was ordered; the castle being inclosed by a triple wall, he himself was admitted within the inclosure of the second wall, while his attendants were left outside. There, his royal regalia laid aside and without any evidence of royalty or display of pomp, he stood as a humble penitent with bare feet from morning to night seeking the sentence of the pope. This he did on the next day, and again on the third. On the fourth he was finally admitted to the papal presence, and after much discussion on both sides he was at last absolved from excommunication on the following conditions.

First, that at the time and place which the pope should designate, he should appear before the German princes assembled in general council and should answer the charges preferred against him. There, with the pope as judge, if so it seemed to expedite matters, he should accept his decision, retain his kingdom if he refuted the charges, or give it up with equanimity if the charges were proven and he was held unworthy of the throne according to ecclesiastical law.

Second, that whether he retained or lost his kingdom, he should seek vengeance on no one for this trouble.

Third, that up to the day when, after proper discussion, his case had been ended, he should wear no ornaments of royal elegance, no insignia of royal dignity; he should not by his own right do anything in the administration as he was wont to do; decide nothing which ought rightly to be considered; and, finally, he should levy no royal or public taxes except for the sustenance of himself and his immediate servants.

Fourth, that all who had pledged loyalty to him by oath should meantime in the presence of God and men remain free and unhindered by the bonds of this oath and the obligations of loyalty.

Fifth, that he should forever dismiss from intimacy with himself Robert, bishop of Babenberg, Oudalric of Cosheim, and others by whose counsel he had betrayed himself and his state.

Sixth, that if the charges were refuted and he retained his kingdom, he should always be obedient to the Roman pontiff and comply with his decrees, and in accord with him stand forth as the worldly powerful co-operator in the correction of the abuses against the laws of the church which had by a pernicious custom grown up in the kingdom.

Last, that if he falsely agreed to any of these conditions the absolution which he had so earnestly sought would be endangered; nay, more, he would be considered as already convicted and confessed. He should then seek no further audience to prove his innocence, and the princes of the kingdom, thereby freed from all religious scruples in regard to their oath, would create another king upon whom they could agree.

These conditions the king accepted gratefully and promised with the most sacred assertions possible that he would observe all of them. And it was not a case of an acceptance of faith by one making rash promises, for the abbot of Cluny, though his monastic religion kept him from taking oath, interposed his faith before the eyes of the All-seeing God, while the bishop of Zeitz, the bishop of Vercelli, the margrave Azzo, and the other princes at the gathering confirmed by oath, over sacred relics, that the king would do as he had promised and would be led from his word neither by any temporary straits nor by a change in succeeding events.

When the excommunication was thus absolved the pope celebrated the solemn mass. When the sacred offering was ready he called the king and the rest of the people to the altar. Extending the body of the Lord with his hand, he said, "I have for some time received letters from you and your adherents in which you claim that I occupy the papal chair through the heresy of simony and that my life is spotted with various other crimes before as well as after I had received the episcopate, which, according to the canons, would have prevented all access to the sacred orders. This I could refute by the testimony of many suitable witnesses, both of those who are intimately acquainted with my career from the very beginning, as well as of those who are responsible for my elevation to the episcopacy. Yet, lest I seem to rely too much on human rather than on divine witness and in order to bring the whole scandal to short account before all, behold this body of the Lord which I am about to take. May it be for me this day the test of my innocence. May the Omnipotent God by His judgment either clear me of the crime charged against me if I am innocent or strike me with a sudden death if I am guilty."

With these and other terrible words he prayed the Lord to be most just judge of his case and asserter of his innocence, and then he took part of the sacred wafer and consumed it. This he did freely while the people acclaimed aloud their praises to God and offered thanks for his innocence. Then, commanding silence, he turned to the king and said: "Do therefore, my son, if it pleases you, what you have just seen me do. The princes of Germany have for days confused our ears with their accusations. They heap a great multitude of crimes upon you for which they think that you should not only be suspended from all administration of public affairs, but from ecclesiastical communion also, and even from any intercourse with secular life whatever for all time. They are especially anxious to fix a day and place and have an audience accorded them for the discussion of the charges which they bring against you. And you know best that human judgments often vacillate, and that falsity is sometimes more persuasive than truth. An untruth adorned with ornaments of words, with suavity, and by the genius and fluency of eloquent men, receives a more welcome hearing than the truth ungraced with eloquence which is often despised. Since, therefore, I wish you good counsel, all the more since you have in your calamities sought the patronage of the apostolic chair as a suppliant, so do as I admonish. If you know that you are innocent and that your reputation has been assailed with false charges by your enemies in a spirit of calumny, take the remainder of this sacred wafer and thus free, in a moment, the Church from the scandal of God and yourself from the uncertainty of a long dispute. Then your innocence will be proved by God's witness, every mouth turned against you in scandal will be stopped, and, with me as your advocate and the most vehement maintainor of your innocence, the princes will be reconciled to you, the kingdom restored, and the storms of civil war, with which it has been so long harassed, allayed."

The king, astonished at this unexpected situation, became very much embarrassed, looked around for excuses, and, drawing away from the multitude, he discussed with his friends how he might evade such an awful test, which was a matter of difficulty. When he had recovered his spirits he talked to the pope of the absence of the princes who had kept faith with him in his trouble; that without the accord of the accusers the effect of such a test would be destroyed, and that the incredulous would question a satisfaction rendered in the presence of the few here assembled. Therefore, he earnestly besought the pope to defer the whole matter to a general council where, while the accusers were gathered together and the accusations and the persons of the accusers were discussed according to the ecclesiastical law as the princes of the realm had proposed, he might refute the charges.

With great dignity the pope granted his petition, and when the solemn mass was ended he invited the king to dinner. And when this was ended and he had instructed him carefully as to what he must observe, the pope dismissed him with kindness and in peace to the men who had so long remained outside the walls. Furthermore, he sent out the bishop of Zeitz, Eppo, before him to absolve from their excommunication those who had incurred it by indifferently associating with the excommunicate before his absolution, kindly warning them not to occasion any stain upon the communion just newly received.

3. *The Annals of Berthold.* Berthold of Reichenau, to whom the student has already been introduced, furnishes an interesting comparison with Lambert; neither was an eyewitness and both wrote very shortly after the events they describe.[26]

When this colloquy had come to an end, about the Calends of November, a heavy snow, far greater than usual, began to cover the lands everywhere. This, an omen and sign of evil to come, greatly astounded not only the regions on this side of the Alps, but, which is more amazing, all Lombardy with its unheard-of amount. In fact, the Rhine and the Po alike, to say nothing of other streams, were so hardened by the excessive freezing cold that for a long time they afforded in themselves an icy road for all wanderers as though over land. Thus did the bitter and snow-laden winter continue with constant cold even to the Ides of March—that is, from the conference at Oppenheim to the colloquy which was held by the princes at Foresheim. Finally, on that very day, the snow began little by little to grow less, until after some time had elapsed it fairly flowed.

The king, however, when the said conference at Oppenheim had come to an end, remained for some time at Spires with the supporters and overseers whom the princes of the realm had assigned to him, and lived like a penitent. Then, suspecting on account of the aforesaid oath that their [the princes'] treachery and cunning would be turned against himself, he collected his counselors again from all sides and rashly disregarded the pleasure of the princes, and, to the end that he might not be deprived of his kingdom, he fortified himself most diligently with all the industry and attention of his own genius, with all the various investigations of his counselors, and by conferring on plans together.

The bishop of Toul, and also the one of Spires, with many others upon whom this had been imposed as a mark of obedience by the bishop of Patavia, soon hastened to Rome and gave themselves up to the pope as guilty, with due satisfaction and obedience. When these had been canonically reconciled he had them imprisoned in the jails of certain monasteries in order to test their obedience for some time, until by the intervention of the empress they were released therefrom and were permitted to return home with the grant of communion, but without having their rank restored.

Upon their footsteps the archbishop of Trier followed in great haste with the letters of the royal embassy, saluted the pope, and presented to him the falsified letters. These the pope was unwilling to have read except in the presence of the legates of the princes, so that they, who had also been present at the writing, might be witnesses at the reading. Accordingly, after these had been read, the legates recognizing the material as far other than that which had been composed and sealed in the presence of the princes of the realm, protested most freely by the Lord God that it was not the same, but that it had been altered and changed in places. So the archbishop of Trier, though at first he began to defend the letters, yet at length when he had been caught and reminded by these men confessed publicly that the fraud in these letters was not his, but the work of some one else whom he did not know. Thus the lord pope, together with the empress, watchfully discovered that all which this lying letter said of the obedience of the king was not a truth from the heart but was feigned statement full of deception. Thus what the king most anxiously entreated—namely, that he be permitted to come to Rome to be reconciled with the pope, the pope was unwilling to grant at all, but with apostolic authority commanded him to meet him at Augsburg in the presence of the princes of the realm, to be heard and reconciled by him, and he sent back word emphatically enough by the legates of both parties that he would come there to them about the feast of the Purification of St. Mary if God willed it. When they had received the letters of apostolic benediction in which, as is fitting, he admonished them very carefully, especially about his escort, about other necessaries, and about the peace, they returned joyfully to their fatherland to announce the coming of so great a guest.

Accordingly, when the princes had gratefully heard what these letters conveyed, they strove with every effort to make every preparation, not a little exhilarated by the great hope of restoring the ecclesiastical religion and observance. The heart of the king, stirred with far different intention, when he found out the proposition of the pope, strove industriously, with many consultations, to meet him before he entered our territory. For he proposed either to force the pope into flight in terror of the very great force of soldiers which he had gathered together at any price or, with the help of the Romans and his other counselors whom he had corrupted with such great gifts and thus made them each his supporter, to force the pope to his wish. If that failed, however, they, as warlike and angry as himself, should together fight to drive the pope unhurt from the church and substitute another after the heart of the king; and, thus elected and ordained as emperor by that pope, he would, with his wife, return to his fatherland in glory; that if, he however foolishly enough planned, by all these measures he succeeded in making the pope, overcome by the threats and blandishments of the Romans, compliant to himself, he would then be pious toward him, but very severe toward his adversaries.

Advised and encouraged by these and, as rumor has it, not a few other senseless proposals of his counselors, he obstinately set himself against the correction arranged by the princes and against the restoration of the church and did not cease to oppress their [the princes'] magistrates in every way and to free himself entirely from them as he

wished. To this purpose a certain margrave, Opertus by name, who came at this time from Lombardy, encouraged him more than the others. This man, magnificently loaded by him with gifts and honors, was seized with sudden death near Augsburg as he was on his way to his own country. He had fallen from his horse, and thus as he died a wretch condemned, he discovered how great a load the apostolic anathema was, although he had formerly regarded it as nothing.

The king celebrated the birth of the Lord at Besançon in Burgundy as best he could, for he remained there scarcely a day. Then after he had taken up his wife and son and also a whole host of followers, as had already been previously arranged, crossing the Rhone at Geneva, climbing and crawling over the Alps by the most difficult way, he entered Lombardy through the bishopric of Turin. There, collecting to himself also the host of excommunicated bishops, and as if to fortify their case by a sort of defensive majesty, he told them craftily that he would speak to the pope not only about the sentence of anathema on himself, but rather to have the harmful sentence over them investigated by him.

They, however, on the contrary, tried to dissuade the king from calling him pope, whom they had at his command cast forth from the church abjured, and whom they had forever separated from the body of the church as condemned by an anathema. Nevertheless, they thought it fitting to yield to time and comply, since he was constrained by the bond of such unavoidable necessity lest he, as false king, should rashly annul the pleasure of the princes entirely, and thus most justly incur their opposition; but then, that is to say, after this dispensation and the address to the pope, so necessary to him, he should, together with them, labor with every effort to free himself and the whole kingdom from so sacrilegious a man; but if he did not do this he should not ignore the fact that he himself would, by the most crafty spite and arrogance of him who bore the apostolic name, be deprived not only of his kingdom and honor but probably also of his life, and he should not in the least doubt that they, who had always been undaunted and prepared to go with him to death and destruction, would perish and be condemned likewise.

When, however, the legates of the king and of the princes had been dismissed by the pope and had begun their journey home, the pope, ever most ready to devote himself to his flock, at the appointed time went to the place which they had agreed upon; and there, as they had arranged, he awaited the escort for his march with impatience. But in vain; for when the princes found out about the stealthy and unexpected flight of the king over the Alps, they feared the wiles and assaults of the king; and though they were reluctant and unwilling, they ceased trying to send the agreed escort to meet the pope. So the pope waited for them some time at the castle of Canossa.

But when they, with difficulty, sent word to the pope that they could not come to him in the face of such dangers, then he was very much vexed that he had come there in vain, but not giving up hope of being later able to reach the Teutonic lands for the needs of the church, he was disposed to stop there for some time to wait for such an event. Then, reflecting that the journey of the king and his counselors was not of much advantage to the church and himself—nay, that it would render the Lombards, whom he had found rebellious to God and himself, much more rebellious; that it had troubled the people of Germany, distracted by no mean schism, and greatly worried them as to what they should do about so senseless a man; and that it had greatly disturbed the whole kingdom on all sides—he placed all his cares on the Lord, as befits an apostolic man, and prayed with tears day and night that the Divinity inspire him how he might rightly arrange to settle such a great matter synodically.

Then the king, accepting the wholesome advice of his men, laid aside the plan which he had with mad anger and malice conceived against the pope, and decided, with the intervention and aid of the countess lady Matilda, of his mother-in-law, marchioness Adelaide, of the abbot of Cluny, who had himself come there after he had just recently been reconciled at Rome for having associated with the king, and of all the others whom he could attract to his side, to meet the pope and submit, yield, obey, and agree with him in everything. With this intention, though he concealed it somewhat from the Lombards, he sent messengers to bring the aforesaid mediators to himself, and he himself followed them shortly to the aforesaid castle. These, meeting the king at the appointed place, aired the matter for which they had come together at great length, and considered it in every way with the usual consultations, but I know not what tricky and deceitful promises they gave in their most careful consideration, which they were quite afraid to bear as straightforward and true to the pope, who was, in truth, most experienced, for he had long been and was almost daily dealing with such cases. Nevertheless, since necessity so demanded it, they soon came back and related to the pope truthfully, and in order, everything which they thought colored and false.

The king, following hurriedly in their footsteps, came precipitately to the door of the castle with his excommunicated friends, though as yet unexpected and without the answer of the pope or a word of invitation, and, knocking sufficiently, he begged with all his strength to be allowed to enter. There, dressed in coarse woolen garments, with bare feet and freezing, he stayed outside the castle, even to the third day, with his friends, and thus, most strictly tested by many trials and temptations and found obedient as far as human judgment extends, he demanded with tears, as is the custom of penitents, the favor of Christian communion and the apostolic reconciliation.

The lord pope, however, who was most cautious and as unwilling to be deceived as to deceive, and who had so frequently been deluded by so many promises of the king, did not very easily credit his words. After much exchange of opinion he was at last persuaded that if the king would come most promptly to confirm by oath in person, or through others whom he might name as witnesses for himself, these conditions which he would now impose for the welfare of the holy church, and should in addition consent to give pledges into the hands of those intermediaries who were present for the observance of this oath and also of the empress, who was not yet there; if he should thus bind the compact he would not refuse to receive him again to the favor of Christian communion. The king with his followers, however, when he heard this answer of the pope, regarded the proposal as too harsh; but since he could not otherwise be reconciled, willing or unwilling, he agreed to it most sadly.

At length they intervened with the pope, who agreed that the king need not take the oath; two bishops, however, of Naumburg and Vercelli, besides other friends of his who would take oath, were chosen to take the oath for him. Who, that we may commemorate this most important oath, swore in this fashion—namely, that their lord Henry, whenever within the year pope Gregory should decide, would come into peace and concord with the princes of the realm either according to the judgment or the compassion of the pope, and that neither he nor any of his men would inflict any harm upon the pope or his legates into whatever parts of the kingdom they should come for the welfare of the church, nor should he capture or kill them; and if they were harmed by any other person, he should aid them in good faith as soon as he could; and if there were any obstacle in his way so that he could not meet the engagement which the pope had fixed, then as soon as possible he should meet it without further delay.

When this agreement had been made as before said, the king, weeping copiously, and the other excommunicates also in tears, were allowed access to the pope. What tears were shed by either party no one can easily say. When the pope, not a little moved for these lost sheep who were again seeking God with their pitiable lament, had delivered a suitable address on canonical reconciliation and apostolic consolation to them, after they had prostrated themselves with fitting humility and had confessed their rash presumption, and thus with apostolic indulgence and benediction, reconciled and restored to Christian communion, he took them into the church. Then, when he had made the customary oration and had greeted the king and the five bishops of Strasburg, Bremen, Lausanne, Basel, and Naumburg, and many others with the holy kiss, he called the king to the place of communion and extended to him the Eucharist which he had before forbidden him. The king, protesting that he was unworthy of participation in it, departed without the communion. Wherefore the pope not unwisely took it as an indication of impurity and an evidence of some hypocrisy latent in him, which the Spirit revealed, and after that he never presumed to place full faith in his words. But then when the dinner was quite ready they ate together at the same table and satisfied their wants with sober food; then, rising with the act of grace, they talked together about the most necessary matters of the promise of obedience, the pledges given, that the oath should not be violated, about the perfection of penance, as well as about avoiding contact with the excommunicated Lombards.

Then the king, after he had received the apostolic freedom and benediction, departed with all of his followers except the bishops, whom the pope ordered to be imprisoned as suited his good pleasure. Furthermore, the binding of this oath, which remained still to be done by the friends of the king, he insisted should be performed by them. This they tried to change from its agreed form, in fear that they would soon be taken by the pope as guilty of perjury; and in order not to swear they fled in every direction. One of them, the bishop of Augsburg, fled clandestinely at night without the permission of the pope and without being reconciled to him. Thus in the first compact which they had agreed upon these mendacious men left the pope craftily deluded and deceived.

About the same time that Roman Quintius, who to the addition of his damnation now held the bishop of Como captive, near the church of St. Peter at Rome, thought to visit the king at Pavia, and expected the king to treat him magnificently; nay, he didn't doubt at all that he deserved to have great gifts given to himself, not only for the capture of the bishop, but also for the sacrilegious seizure of the pope. When he came to the court the king did not dare to receive him with the kiss as he was wont to greet his friends, since Quintius was excommunicated, but feigned that on account of the many important affairs which now occupied him he could not receive him as was fitting and as he so much desired, and thus he put off meeting his friend for some days. Quintius, however, somewhat angered, proclaimed that he was being disdained and deceived until he at length extorted from the king the promise of favors and most certain evidences of a fitting reception. But on the night before the appointed day he was suffocated by a sudden deadly tumor in his neck, and without seeing or greeting the king he most quickly descended to the infernal regions, condemned to eternal death.

4. *Bruno, Concerning the Saxon War.* This Saxon churchman and author is already familiar to the student.[27]

The pope had, in accordance with the wishes of the princes, started toward Augsburg in order to reach there at the beginning of February in the year of our Lord 1077. Our men, too, were hastening there to receive him with due veneration when, lo! it was announced to the pope that Henry had entered Italy with a large army. It was furthermore reported that if he had come across the mountains with his original intention it was to set up another pope. Accordingly, he [the pope] sent an envoy to meet our men while he himself turned back with many fears to save Italy from fire and sword.

Henry, however, wandered through Italy, geographically, but even more was he uncertain in thought as to what he should do, for he feared that whatever he did he would lose his kingdom. If he did not come as a suppliant to the pope and receive absolution from the ban, he knew certainly that he was lost; if he did come as a suppliant to render satisfaction, he feared that the pope would deprive him of the kingdom on account of the enormity of his crimes; or, if he were disobedient to the pope the chains of papal restraint over him would be doubled. By such worries was he torn. Yet, though he felt that he was lost and would lose anyway, he selected that course as an alternative which offered most hope. Dressed in woolen garments and with bare feet he went to the pope and told him that he cared much more for the celestial than for the earthly kingdom, and offered to accept humbly whatever penance he would inflict. The pope was pleased at the extreme humility of so great a man. He bade him, therefore, not to wear the insignia of royalty until he himself permitted it, so that the contrition of his heart might be more acceptable to omnipotent God if his vile garments bore external evidence of it. He admonished him further to keep away from his court and counsel those who were excommunicated, lest the cleanliness gained by a proper conversion with the grace of God should become uncleanly by contagion with others. Both of these conditions he promised to observe, and was legally absolved. Then he was dismissed by the pope, though not without further admonitions not to lie to God, and that if he did not fulfil his promises not only would the former bonds not be taken off, but others even more stringent would be added.

So he went back to his people and began to dismiss the objectionable from his court. Thereupon they began to cause trouble, saying that if he now dismissed from his presence those by whose wisdom and courage he had thus far held his throne the pope could neither give him back that kingdom nor provide him with another. By such arguments his mind was changed. He returned to his former habits and bad counsel. He placed the golden crown upon his head and thus bound the anathema upon his heart with a grip stronger than that of iron. He held intercourse with the excommunicated, and from communion with the pious he was an outcast. It was therefore, manifest to all that his statement that he loved the celestial kingdom more than the earthly was not true. If he had but a moment remained in obedience he would not be holding his earthly kingdom in peace and when the time came would gain the celestial to hold without end. Now, however, that he is disobedient, he will now obtain this which he loves without great labor, and will not gain the other unless he greatly changes his whole life.

Meanwhile the Saxons and Swabians met at Foresheim, but there were present also legates from other regions who indicated that their people approved whatever these should suitably accomplish in regard to the republic. There was present likewise a legate of the pope who strengthened with the authority of the apostolic sublimity all the measures which our men took for the effective arrangement of the kingdom. From the many whom they brought forth in the election as of proven worth, nevertheless, the Saxons and Swabians with one accord chose Rudolph of the Swabians as their king.

But when they had to approve him as king one by one some of them wanted to impose some conditions, to elevate him as king over themselves according to this law, when he had made an especial promise to them of justification of their injuries. For Duke Otto was unwilling to make him his king until he should promise to restore the honor unjustly taken from him. In the same manner also many others interposed individual conditions which they wanted him to promise to correct. The apostolic legate, learning of this, kept it from being done, and pointing out that the king would be king not of single states, but of all, he regarded it sufficient if the king promised to be just to all. He said likewise, that if the king were elected in the manner in which they had begun, each exacting promises in advance, the election would not

be sincere, but would seem to be polluted with the poison of the heresy of simony. Nevertheless, certain cases were especially excepted which, because they had unjustly flourished, he ought to correct—namely, that he should not grant bishoprics for money or friendship, but to allow to each church the election by its members as the canons command.

This was likewise approved there by general assent and confirmed by the authority of the Roman pontiff, that the royal power should fall to no one by heredity, as the custom had been before, but that the son of a king, even if he were very worthy, should become king through a free election, rather than by lineal descent; on the other hand, if the son of a king were unworthy, or if the people didn't wish him, the people should have him in power whom they wished to make king.

After all these matters had been legally settled they conducted Rudolph, the king-elect, to Mainz with great honor, and supported him while he was receiving the royal consecration with veneration and with might, as was soon apparent. He was, however, consecrated by Siegfried, archbishop of the city of Mainz, in the presence and with the assistance of very many others in the year of the Lord 1077 on the 7th day from the Calends of April (26th of March).

5. *The Anonymous Life of the Emperor Henry IV.* This *Life* was probably written by a churchman and companion of the king shortly after the latter's death in 1106.[28]

Their [the Saxons'] conspiracy was further strengthened by the addition of some of the Lombards, Franks, Bavarians, and Swabians. Exchanging mutual pledges of faith, they combined to wage war on the king from all sides. They saw, however, that while they might wage war on him they could not dislodge or overcome him; nay, his strength was as yet unassailable. In order to weaken his power, therefore, they drew up a lot of fictitious charges against him. These charges were the foulest and worst that spite and malice could conceive, charges so foul that, should I set them down, they would nauseate me to write them, you to read them. Mingling truth with falsehood, they sent the indictment to Pope Gregory. It held that so disgraceful a person, better known for his crimes than by his name, was unfit to rule, especially since he had not obtained his royal dignity at Rome, that its rights in constituting kings ought to be returned to it, and that the pope and Rome should, with the counsel of the princes, select a king whose wisdom and conduct accorded with so great an honor.

The pope was both misled by this fraudulent representation and lured on by the honor of creating a king, which they so falsely held out to him. He placed the king under a ban and commanded the bishops and princes to abstain from all intercourse with the excommunicated sovereign. Furthermore, he announced that he would speedily come to the Teutonic lands to deal with the affairs of the church, and especially with those of the kingdom. Nay, he even went further. He absolved from their oath of fidelity all who were so bound to the king in order that this absolution might turn against him all whom that bond still held.

This displeased many—if, indeed, any one may be displeased at what the pope does—and they asserted that this deed was as ineffectively as it was illegally done. But I dare not set forth their assertions lest I seem with them to disapprove the deed of the pope. Soon most of the bishops who sided with the king either from affection or from fear withdrew from his side for fear of their positions. So, also, did most of their followers.

When the king saw his affairs in such a plight he secretly made a shrewd resolve. Suddenly and unexpectedly he set out to meet the pope. And thereby he accomplished two things—he received absolution from the ban and intercepted the suspicious conference of his enemies and the pope. As to the crimes charged against him he made no particular reply, for, he asserted, it was not for him to answer the accusation of his enemies, even if it were true. What advantage has it been to you to have had him put under the ban when, now released of that ban, he enjoys his power fully? What has it profited you to have accused him of fictitious charges when, with his easy answer, he has scattered your accusation like a puff of wind? Nay, what madness put you in arms against your king, the ruler of the world? Your malicious conspiracy has accomplished nothing, has profited nothing. Whom the hand of God has confirmed in his rule you cannot dethrone. Where is that loyalty which you swore to him? Wherefore have you been unmindful of the benefices which he conferred on you with royal favor? Henceforth employ wise counsel, not rage. Be penitent for your venture and thankful that he did not rise up in his might and conquer you; that he did not grind you in the dust under his feet and inflict that vengeance on you which would show to future ages what the hand of a king could do. At all events, O bishop, see that you do not wander from the paths of justice; see that you become not transgressors of your plighted faith. Nay, you know what the consequences will be to you.

6. *The Book of Bonizo to a Friend*. The author was bishop of Sutri and an intimate friend and partisan of Gregory. His *Book*,

in reality a church history, was written soon after Gregory's death in 1085.[29]

Meanwhile the venerable Gregory started with the grace of peace on his journey to Augsburg with the greatest difficulty on the march, for a most severe winter was then raging. The king, in truth, holding his oath of little account, very suddenly entered Italy. And there are those who say that he wished to capture the pope unaware. Which seems sufficiently like the truth, for Gregory, bishop of Vercelli, his chancellor in fact—he whom the princes had commanded to conduct the pope over the mountains—after he had crossed the yoke of the Apennines, heard that he had secretly come within the town of Vercelli. When he announced this to the pope the pope straightway went into Canossa, a most safely fortified camp of the most excellent Matilda.

The king, in the meantime, seeing that his schemes had been divulged, as was evident to every one, laid aside his ferocity, and approached Canossa clothed in dove-like simplicity. And, by suffering for several days with bare feet on the snow and ice, he deceived all the less wise, and from the venerable Gregory, who, nevertheless, was not ignorant of his tricks, he obtained the absolution which he sought, the Lord's sacrament taking a part in the celebration of the mass in this manner. For he made him a participant in the divine supper in the presence of the bishops, abbots, religious clerks, and laymen in this way, so that if the king had humiliated himself in mind as in body and believed him to be rightful pope, that he himself had been excommunicated after the example of Photius and Diocurus, and that he could be absolved through this sacrament, the supper would be to his salvation, but otherwise Satan would enter him after the host. What more? When the mass had been celebrated they had dinner together. Then he and all those absolved from the excommunication were commanded to avoid all association with the excommunicate. But there are some who say that he swore to the pope his life and his limb and his honor. But I do not at all affirm what I do not know.

7. *Donizo's Life of Matilda*. Matilda, countess of Tuscany, was heiress to lands of extreme strategic importance to Pope and German king alike. Her mother, Beatrice, had married Godfrey, Duke of Lorraine, as her second husband, whose opposition to the royal house was indefatigable. Matilda and Beatrice were friends and confidants of Gregory and Canossa was one of the countess' castles. Donizo was actually a monk in a monastery at Canossa, but his *Life* was not

completed until 1115 and remained essentially a paean in verse of the pious Matilda's virtues.[30]

Shortly after the death of her [Matilda's] mother the rumor spread through the world that the king had been condemned by the renowned pope. The brave and the powerful throughout the kingdom were indeed much wrought up, and said it was rash and arrogance not to yield sincerely and graciously to the Roman see, which holds the keys of heaven. Wherefore they rightly decided to shun him until he should yield; until he should strive to regain the peace of the pope. When the king realized that he could not otherwise recover his rule he sent word to his relation, Matilda. He begged her without fail to devise some plan to get the pope to come to Lombardy from the city that he himself might seek fitting indulgence.

And the pope, when he heard the prayers of Matilda, granted her request. The worthy shepherd left Rome, came to Canossa, and tarried there. Here she fittingly received him as the vicar of St. Peter, and was greeted by him. There, too, was the queen, wife of King Henry, accompanied by Matilda, and there was a great throng besides. Beyond me [i.e. at Canossa] there became a new Rome while these things were going on. O city, to your honor, behold! With me are king and pope alike, as well as the lords of Italy, and also of Gaul, Ultramontane, and Rome, effulgent with the pontifical garland. Many wise men, too, are here. Among them stands Hugh, abbot of Cluny, who was godfather of the baptism of the king.

These lords held discussions of peace, and, though they remained in discussion for three days, there was no peace. And the king, wishing to withdraw, went to the chapel of St. Nicholas and tearfully implored the pastor Hugh to become surety for his peace. To the king's entreaty the abbot replied, "This may not be." Then he asked it of Matilda, but she also replied, "This no one may do but you, I believe." Then on bended knees he said to her: "Unless you aid me greatly nevermore will I shatter a shield, for the pope has punished me severely. Go, powerful cousin, do me this favor." She raised him and pledged him her word. Then she left him and went up to the pope while the king remained below. She spoke to the pope, crying out against the end of the king, and in the earnestly spoken words of the venerable lady he put faith. Nevertheless, the recalled king was to swear to be faithful to the holy see and to do whatever the patron Gregory willed.

January this year was very cold, and there was a great deal of snow. Seven days before the end of the month the king, his naked feet nipped by the cold, was admitted to the presence of the pope. He threw himself on the cross, shouting again and again: "Spare me, blessed father! Holy father, spare me, I beseech thee." And the pope, gazing upon him crying, pitied him very much, and after having blessed him accorded him peace. Then he conducted mass himself and gave him the body of the Lord. They ate together in the castle of Canossa, and after he had taken his oath the pope dismissed him. He went to the city of Regina, where there was a great throng hostile to the pope and fearful that this peace would be made.

8. *Gregory to the German Princes, January 28, 1077.* Immediately after the events described by the chroniclers, the pope issued a circular letter to the princes of Germany, giving his version of the incident at Canossa. The text of his letter follows.[31]

Whereas, for love of justice you have made common cause with us and taken the same risks in the warfare of Christian service, we have taken special care to send you this accurate account of the king's penitential humiliation, his absolution, and the course of the whole affair from his entrance into Italy to the present time.

According to the arrangement made with the legates sent to us by you we came to Lombardy about twenty days before the date at which some of your leaders were to meet us at the pass and waited for their arrival to enable us to cross over into that region. But when the time had elapsed and we were told that on account of the troublous times—as indeed we well believe—no escort could be sent to us, having no other way of coming to you we were in no little anxiety as to what was our best course to take.

Meanwhile we received certain information that the king was on the way to us. Before he entered Italy he sent us word that he would make satisfaction to God and St. Peter and offered to amend his way of life and to continue obedient to us, provided only that he should obtain from us absolution and the apostolic blessing. For a long time we delayed our reply and held long consultations, reproaching him bitterly through messengers back and forth for his outrageous conduct, until finally, of his own accord and without any show of hostility or defiance, he came with a few followers to the fortress of Canossa where we were staying. There, on three successive days, standing before the castle gate, laying aside all royal insignia, barefooted and in coarse attire, he ceased not with many tears to beseech the apostolic help and comfort until all who were present or who had heard the story were so moved by pity and compassion that they pleaded his cause with prayers and tears. All marveled at our unwonted severity, and some even cried out that we were showing, not the seriousness of apostolic authority, but rather the cruelty of a savage tyrant.

At last, overcome by his persistent show of penitence and the urgency of all present, we released him from the bonds of anathema and received him into the grace of Holy Mother Church, accepting from him the guarantees described below, confirmed by the signatures of the abbot of Cluny, of our daughters, the countess Matilda and the Countess Adelaide, and other princes, bishops and laymen who seemed to be of service to us.

And now that these matters have been arranged, we desire to come over into your country at the first opportunity, that with God's help we may more fully establish all matters pertaining to the peace of the Church and the good order of the land. For we wish you clearly to understand that, as you may see in the written guarantees, the whole negotiation is held in suspense, so that our coming and your unanimous consent are in the highest degree necessary. Strive, therefore, all of you, as you love justice, to hold in good faith, the obligations into which you have entered. Remember that we have not bound ourselves to the king in any way except by frank statement—as our custom is—that he may expect our aid for his safety and his honor, whether through justice or through mercy, and without peril to his soul or to our own. . . .

The Oath of Henry, king of the Germans:

I, Henry, king, within the term which our lord Pope Gregory shall fix, will either give satisfaction according to his decision, in regard to the discontent and discord for which the archbishops, bishops, dukes, counts and other princes of the kingdom of Germany are accusing me, or I will make an agreement according to his advice— unless some positive hindrance shall prevent him or myself—and when this is done I will be prepared to carry it out.

Item: If the same lord Pope Gregory shall desire to go beyond the mountains or elsewhere he shall be safe, so far as I and all whom I can constrain are concerned, from all injury to life or limb and from capture—both he himself and all who are in his company or who are sent out by him or who may come to him from any place whatsoever—in coming, remaining, or returning. Nor shall he with my consent suffer any hindrance contrary to his honor; and if anyone shall offer such hindrance, I will come to his assistance with all my power.

IV

The Renaissance in Italy

T HERE is a certain justification for my plan of life. It may
be only glory that we seek here, but I persuade myself that,
so long as we remain here, that is right. Another glory awaits
us in heaven and he who reaches there will not wish even to
think of earthly fame. So this is the natural order, that
among mortals the care of things mortal should come first;
to the transitory will then succeed the eternal; from the first
to the second is the natural progression.

PETRARCH (1304–74)

CONTENTS

QUESTIONS FOR STUDY

PART I

1. How would a medieval ascetic have viewed the Genoa described by Aeneas Silvius Piccolomini?

2. What particular human qualities does Piccolomini single out for praise? What impresses him most about the city?

3. Why did Petrarch read the classic authors?

4. What is Petrarch's attitude to Cicero? How does it differ from that of the "old man" in the debate?

5. How does Salutati justify secular studies?

6. Why did Leonardo Bruni desert the law to study under Chrysoloras?

7. What does the description of the Duke of Urbino's library reveal about the interests of a Humanist book-lover? How did the Duke treat his books?

8. What were the content and purpose of Humanist education, as described by Guarino?

9. How does Guarino's approach to knowledge differ from that of St. Thomas Aquinas?

10. Why did Cellini love antiquities?

11. How did Cellini's approach to art differ from that of a medieval sculptor?

12. What did Aretino find enjoyable?

13. Having read the documents in Part I, formulate a definition of Humanism.

14. "They [the Humanists] shifted authorities, rather than freed men from them." Do you agree with this judgment?

PART II

15. Why did Cellini write his autobiography?

16. What made Alberti admirable in the eyes of his biographer?

17. What was the position of the artist in Renaissance society?

18. How did Nicolo Perotto obtain preferment in the Church?

19. What were the qualifications of the ideal courtier? How many were carried over from the medieval ideals?

20. How did Renaissance types differ from those of the Middle Ages? From those of today?

The Renaissance has been called "the most intractable problem child of historiography." [1] For the term, which means literally "Rebirth," is used to characterize both the period in history which immediately followed the Middle Ages, and an intellectual movement on a broad scale, which appeared in western Europe as the Middle Ages drew to a close. Among the basic difficulties in dealing with this "problem child," therefore, are to delimit accurately the historical period to which the term applies, and to determine the nature and character of the intellectual movement.

Any attempt to set precise terminal dates for the Renaissance involves the delicate decision as to the point at which one age ends and another begins. History flows continuously, and the transition from age to age is gradual and often imperceptible. Moreover, history flows unevenly, and some areas of the world make the transition to a new age considerably in advance of others. Thus, the terminal dates of an historical period can be stated only approximately and with careful qualifications as to locale.

Now in one sense the transition from Middle Ages to Renaissance was a transformation of the basis of western culture from a rural agrarian economy to an urban commercial economy. Viewed in this way, the Renaissance was the fulfillment of the promise of the Middle Ages, for the small and often insecure medieval town grew to be the dynamic economic factor in western civilization; and the point at which the men and methods of the city came to dominate those of the countryside was the dividing line between the two ages. The transformation occurred first in Italy. Here the medieval towns, which had grown wealthy on the Mediterranean trade that revived with the launching of the Crusades, became the prosperous center of a network of trade routes extending all over Europe. In the general neighborhood of the year 1300 Italy had come to be dominated by her vigorous city-states. That date may be taken as the beginning of the Renaissance.

The transition was delayed by a century or more in northern Europe. The towns of the northern countries, unable to exploit fully the commercial advantages of their geographical positions until after the great voyages of discovery, developed more slowly than those of Italy. But by the latter half of the fifteenth century it was clear that the Middle Ages had closed and the Renaissance begun in the north. The Hanseatic League of German cities grew opulent on the Baltic trade; the Netherlands flourished as the entrepôt of the west; and the towns of France and England throve and expanded with the aid and protection of their kings. Thus the age of the Renaissance came gradually into being in the fourteenth and fifteenth centuries. By the end of the sixteenth century the Renaissance had drawn to a close, as further developments and new factors effected the transition to the modern age. Thus, at its greatest extent, the Renaissance is said to span the years from 1300 to 1600.

To determine the nature and character of the Renaissance as an intellectual movement is also a task of considerable complexity. For it was a movement which vitally affected a wide range of man's activities. On the one hand, it touched the development of the fine arts: painting, sculpture, and architecture. On the other, it touched many fields of thought: education, literature, and philosophy. The movement is alternately termed Humanism. But though it can be denominated by a word, it cannot so easily be defined. Its manifold character demands careful investigation and analysis.

The purpose of this problem is to arrive at a definition of Humanism by the examination of documents illustrating the growth of the movement in Italy.

Humanism first appeared in the writings of Italian authors in the fourteenth and fifteenth centuries. Inspired by their own works, they first spoke of themselves as leading a *Rinascimento* or Renaissance, and throughout much of the period they held the position of leadership in the Humanist movement. Men of other lands caught the spirit of Humanism from Italy, which enjoyed a cultural pre-eminence unequalled since the days of ancient Rome. The documents in the following pages are selected from the works of prominent writers in the three centuries of the Italian Renaissance.

Part I.   ITALIAN HUMANISM

A.   THE SETTING OF THE HUMANIST MOVEMENT

Genoa in 1432. The milieu in which the Humanist movement took place—the cities of Italy—is pictured in the following document. It is a selection from a letter written by Aeneas Silvius Piccolomini (afterwards Pope Pius II), in which he describes the city of Genoa in 1432.² He had traveled widely on the continent, also visiting England.

Would you were with me! You would see a city which has no equal anywhere on earth. It lies upon a hill over which rude mountains tower, while the lower city is washed by the waves of the sea. The harbor is bow-shaped so that the storms can not do the ships any harm. . . . It constitutes thus a thoroughly reliable anchorage sought by ships big as hills, triremes and countless other craft. And what a coming and going there is! From the east they hail and from the west, so that you may see daily people of the most different sort with unimaginable rough manners and customs and traders with every conceivable ware. Right at the shore arise the most magnificent palaces, heaven-scaling, built of marble, decorated with columns and often too with sculptures. Under them runs an arcade for the length of a thousand steps where every conceivable object is for sale.

The rest of the city winds upward along the side of the hill. In this section the houses are so large and distinguished that a king or a prince might be content with any one of them. For they are all of royal magnificence though they stand closely together and the streets are narrow to the point of permitting only two or three people to pass abreast. The churches, beautiful as they are, do not seem to me to be worthy of such a city. However, they are not without splendor and boast more particularly some handsome sepulchral monuments in honor of deceased noblemen. Certain relics enjoy considerable veneration. I examined the emerald bowl, from which, according to the legend, our Savior ate with his disciples, and found it marvelously luminous. The city is notably well supplied with water from mountain sources which is distributed to the individual houses and is of especial excellence of taste.

Now as to the life and customs of the population. The men are substantial, well-grown, and impressive, carry themselves proudly and are in fact proud. They are a gifted folk, not likely to be found inferior to any other people in the quality of their mind. Strenuous labors, night-watches, and self-denials they bear easily. Their deeds of bravery at sea are incredible; incredible too the perils they confront and the difficulties they master. Our helmsman, a certain Ottobono Imperiali, who has been living at sea now for twenty-three years, has never slept between walls, and never, as he told us, did he change his clothes, even when he was drenched with water. The advantages that come with profits and riches offer compensation for past hardships. In case of a war at sea one does well to take their experience and skill into account, for victory depends solely on them. Should they desire it, victory is certain; should they be contrary-minded, there is no prospect of success since they are the lords of the sea and every one trembles before them.

They dress nobly and elegantly. As for their women, they let them do as they please, for rather may it be said that the women wield the scepter than the other way about. They are not afflicted with thirst for education, though they learn languages as they need them. For other elements of the Liberal Arts they have little use, except as a possible relief from business. Every man selects a woman to whom he pays court. A strange thing is that they maintain irregular relations with other men's wives and at the same time are not in the least offended with the carryings-on of their own wives. Thus it happens that the women of this city enjoy great freedom; indeed it would not be an exaggeration to designate Genoa as the paradise of women. . . . Their dresses are luxurious, loaded with gold and silver trimmings and with jewels. On their fingers sparkle emeralds and diamonds supplied by India and Persia. For where it is a question of adornment they fear no expense. They bother neither about the household nor about needle and dishes, for every house enjoys abundant service. I remember a woman who was not even a woman of rank—when her son-in-law asked her what she had prepared for his breakfast, she made answer that she had not been in the kitchen for seven years. These women are all very easy-going, refuse to make an effort, and do not wait for the holidays to enjoy themselves with their admirers. They are always showing themselves in their best clothes. Indeed the more I reflect upon this city, the more I am convinced that Venus in our time no longer dwells in Cyprus or on Cytheron but in this city of Genoa. Here seems to me to be her shrine. . . .

Even the nuns are not held to a rigorous stand-ard. They go about at pleasure whither they will. It is incredible that this should not distract them from their purpose. Nor do they, as is said to be the case with us [i.e., the Sienese], curse their parents who confined them in the cloister. They are very numerous and much more merry than the married women, evidently because they do not bear the yoke of matrimony. . . .

B.   THE CULT OF THE CLASSICS

1. *Petrarch on Homer.* Francesco Petrarca (1304–74), or, as he is commonly known, Petrarch, was the most famous of the earliest Humanists in Italy. He was born in Arezzo, where his family had been exiled from Florence, and spent much of his life in the towns of Italy and southern France. He was destined for the law, but his introduction to the Latin classics, particularly Cicero and Vergil, so charmed him that he forsook law and embraced literature. He produced much, in both Latin and the vernacular, which won him such fame throughout Europe that in 1341 Rome revived an old office by conferring upon Petrarch the crown of poet laureate. Following is a selection from one of Petrarch's letters, the spirit and content of which are typical of early Humanism.[3]

You ask me finally to lend you the copy of Homer that was on sale at Padua, if, as you suppose, I have purchased it; since, you say, I have for a long time possessed another copy; so that our friend Leo may translate it from Greek into Latin for your benefit and for the benefit of our other studious compatriots. I saw this book, but neglected the opportunity of acquiring it, because it seemed inferior to my own. It can easily be had with the aid of the person to whom I owe my friendship with Leo; a letter from that source would be all-powerful in the matter, and I will myself write him.

If by chance the book escape us, which seems to me very unlikely, I will let you have mine. I have been always fond of this particular translation and of Greek literature in general, and if fortune had not frowned upon my beginnings, in the sad death of my excellent master, I should be perhaps today something more than a Greek still at his alphabet. I approve with all my heart and strength your enterprise, for I regret and am indignant that an ancient translation, presumably the work of Cicero, the commencement of which Horace inserted in his *Ars Poetica,* should have been lost to the Latin world, together with many other works. It angers me to see so much solicitude for the bad and so much neglect of the good.

But what is there to be done? We must be resigned. If the zeal of strangers shall come to rouse us from our lethargy, then may the Muses and our Apollo help it on! The Chinese, the Arabs and the Red Sea offer in my eyes no more valuable merchandise [*merx*]. I am not unaware of what I say. I know that this nominative [*merx*] is not used to-day by our grammarians; but it was used by the ancients, possibly not by the very earliest, whose style the ignorance of our times blushes to imitate; but by those nearest to us and the first in science and ability, whom blind and loquacious pride has not yet dared to set aside. In their writings, and notably in Horace, I remember that the nominative of which I speak is often found. Let us put it again into use, I beg of you, if we may; for I do not know why we should not dare to recall from unmerited exile this word banished from the Latin country, and introduce it into the tongue to which we are devoting all our time.

I wish to take this opportunity of warning you of one thing, lest later on I should regret having passed it over in silence. If, as you say, the translation is to be made literally in prose, listen for a moment to the opinion of St. Jerome as expressed in his preface to the book, *De Temporibus,* by Eusebius of Caesarea, which he translated into Latin. Here are the very words of this great man, well acquainted with these two languages, and indeed with many others, and of especial fame for his art of translating: "If any one," he says, "refuses to believe that translation lessens the peculiar charm of the original, let him render Homer into Latin, word for word; I will say further, let him translate it into prose in his own tongue, and he will see a ridiculous array and the most eloquent of poets transformed into a stammerer." I tell you this for your own good, while it is yet time, in order that so important a work may not prove useless.

As for me, I wish the work to be done, whether well or ill. I am so famished for literature that just as he who is ravenously hungry is not inclined to quarrel with the cook's art, so I await with lively impatience whatever dishes are to be set before my soul. And in truth, the morsel in which the same Leo, translating into Latin prose the beginning of Homer, has given me a foretaste of the whole work, although it confirms the sentiment of St. Jerome, does not displease me. It possesses, in fact, a secret charm, as certain viands, which have failed to take a moulded shape, although they are lacking in form, nevertheless preserve their taste and odor. May he continue with the aid of Heaven, and may he give us Homer, who has been lost to us!

In asking of me the volume of Plato which I have with me, and which escaped the fire at my trans-Alpine country house, you give me proof of your ardor, and I shall hold this book at your disposal, whenever the time shall come. I wish to aid with all my power such noble enterprises. But beware lest it should be unbecoming to unite in one bundle these two great princes of Greece, lest the weight of these two spirits should overwhelm mortal shoulders. Let your messenger undertake, with God's aid, one of the two, and first him who has written many centuries before the other. Farewell. (Milan, Aug. 18, 1360.)

2. *Petrarch on Cicero.* Following is another of Petrarch's letters, in which he describes the scholarly labors of a Humanist.[4]

Your copy of Cicero has been in my possession four years and more. There is a good reason, though, for so long a delay; namely, the great scarcity of copyists who understand such work. It is a state of affairs that has resulted in an incredible loss to scholarship. Books that by their nature are a little hard to understand are no longer multiplied, and have ceased to be generally intelligible, and so have sunk into utter neglect, and in the end have perished. This age of ours consequently has let fall, bit by bit, some of the richest and sweetest fruits that the tree of knowledge has yielded; has thrown away the results of the vigils and labors of the most illustrious men of genius,—things of more value, I am almost tempted to say, than anything else in the whole world. . . .

But I must return to your Cicero. I could not do without it, and the incompetence of the copyists would not let me possess it. What was left for me but to rely on my own resources, and press these weary fingers and this worn and ragged pen into the service? The plan that I followed was this. I want you to know it, in case you should ever have to grapple with a similar task. Not a single word did I read except as I wrote. But how is that, I hear some one say; did you write without knowing what it was that you were writing? Ah! but from the very first it was enough for me to know that it was a work of Tullius, and an extremely rare one too. And then as soon as I was fairly started, I found at every step so much sweetness and charm, and felt so strong a desire

to advance, that the only difficulty which I experienced in reading and writing at the same time came from the fact that my pen could not cover the ground so rapidly as I wanted it to, whereas my expectation had been rather that it would outstrip my eyes, and that my ardor for writing would be chilled by the slowness of my reading.

So the pen held back the eye, and the eye drove on the pen, and I covered page after page, delighting in my task, and committing many and many a passage to memory as I wrote. For just in proportion as the writing is slower than the reading does the passage make a deep impression and cling to the mind. . . .

And yet I must confess that I did finally reach a point in my copying where I was overcome by weariness; not mental, for how unlikely that would be where Cicero was concerned, but the sort of fatigue that springs from excessive manual labor. I began to feel doubtful about this plan that I was following, and to regret having undertaken a task for which I had not been trained; when suddenly I came across a place where Cicero tells how he himself copied the orations of— someone or other; just who it was I do not know, but certainly no Tullius, for there is but one such man, one such voice, one such mind. These are his words: "You say that you have been in the habit of reading the orations of Cassius in your idle moments. But I," he jestingly adds, with his customary disregard of his adversary's feelings, "have made a practice of *copying* them, so that I might *have* no idle moments."

As I read this passage I grew hot with shame, like a modest young soldier who hears the voice of his beloved leader rebuking him. I said to myself, "So Cicero copied orations that another wrote, and you are not ready to copy his? What ardor! what scholarly devotion! what reverence for a man of godlike genius!" These thoughts were a spur to me, and I pushed on, with all my doubts dispelled. If ever from my darkness there shall come a single ray that can enhance the splendor of the reputation which his heavenly eloquence has won for him, it will proceed in no slight measure from the fact that I was so captivated by his ineffable sweetness that I did a thing in itself most irksome with such delight and eagerness that I scarcely knew I was doing it at all.

So then at last your Cicero has the happiness of returning to you, bearing you my thanks. And yet he also stays, very willingly, with me; a dear friend to whom I give the credit of being almost the only man of letters for whose sake I would go to the length of spending my time, when the difficulties of life are pressing on me so sharply and inexorably and the cares pertaining to my literary labors make the longest life seem far too short, in transcribing compositions not my own.

I may have done such things in former days, when I thought myself rich in time, and had not learned how stealthily it slips away: but I now know that this is of all our riches the most uncertain and fleeting; the years are closing in upon me now, and there is no longer any room for deviation from the beaten path. I am forced to practise strict economy; I only hope that I have not begun too late. But Cicero! he assuredly is worthy of a part of even the little that I still have left. Farewell.

3. *A Humanist Debate on Cicero.* In the following passage, Petrarch describes how he introduced two critical letters he had written on Cicero into a heated scholarly debate in 1351.[5]

These two [letters] you read while the others listened; and then the strife of words grew warmer. Some approved of what I had written, admitting that Cicero deserved my censure. But the old man stood his ground more stubbornly even than before. He was so blinded by love of his hero and by the brightness of his name that he preferred to praise him even when he was in the wrong; to embrace faults and virtues together rather than make any exceptions. He would not be thought to condemn anything at all in so great a man. So instead of answering our arguments he rang the changes again and again upon the splendor of Cicero's fame, letting authority usurp the place of reason. He would stretch out his hand and say imploringly: "Gently, I beg you, gently with my Cicero." And when we asked him if he found it impossible to believe that Cicero had made mistakes, he would close his eyes and turn his face away and exclaim with a groan, as if he had been smitten, "Alas! alas! Is my beloved Cicero accused of doing wrong?" just as if he were speaking not of a man but of some god. I asked him accordingly whether in his opinion Tullius was a god or a man like others. "A god," he replied; and then realizing what he had said, he added, "a god of eloquence."

4. *Salutati on Secular Studies.* Notable among the early Humanists was Coluccio Salutati (1331–1406), who, though for thirty years chancellor of the city of Florence, found time for considerable literary output. Following is a selection from a letter he wrote to a certain Brother John of San Miniato in 1406.[6]

I read recently, Venerable Father in Christ, the letter which you wrote to that very dear son of mine, Angelo Corbinelli, and was greatly amused by it. You are trying, according to your habit, to draw him away from poetry and secular studies; or, to put it more exactly, to frighten him away

from them. Whether you are right in so doing is your affair, and I leave you to the reproaches of my distinguished friend, John of Ravenna, and the many others who hold a contrary opinion [that is, the whole body of the humanists]. . . .

What right have you, I beg you, to forbid my friend Angelo to indulge his taste for oratory, poetry, and philosophy? What rights have you over any one outside your monastery? True, it is right for you and for every one to encourage and even command that which is honorable and to prohibit the contrary, but what is there in these things which makes it right to forbid them? I know and read daily in St. Jerome, St. Ambrose, and St. Augustine splendid passages from the philosophers and orators and verses from the poets which shine out like stars from those most sacred writings, and I do not suppose you condemn this in them as a crime. If things true and holy, decorous and beautiful, are found in those doctors [of the Church] and may be read there without harm, why should these same things be called profane and infamous in the original writings of their authors? Why are they forbidden to us if they were permitted to holy doctors? . . .

5. *Bruni on Greek Letters.* A friend and admirer of Salutati, Leonardo Bruni (1370–1444) was inspired by him to pursue classical studies. In the following selection from Bruni's *History of His Own Times in Italy* he describes an event that extended Humanist study of the ancients.[7]

Then first came the knowledge of Greek letters, which for seven hundred years had been lost among us. It was the Byzantine, Chrysoloras, a nobleman in his own country and most skilled in literature, who brought Greek learning back to us. Because his country was invaded by the Turks, he came by sea to Venice; but as soon as his fame went abroad, he was cordially invited and eagerly besought to come to Florence on a public salary to spread his abundant riches before the youth of the city. [This took place in 1396.] At that time I was studying Civil Law. But my nature was afire with the love of learning and I had already given no little time to dialectic and rhetoric. Therefore at the coming of Chrysoloras I was divided in my mind, feeling that it was a shame to desert the Law and no less wrong to let slip such an occasion for learning Greek. And often with youthful impulsiveness I addressed myself thus: "When you are privileged to gaze upon and have converse with Homer, Plato, and Demosthenes as well as the other poets, philosophers, and orators of whom such wonderful things are reported, and when you might saturate yourself with their admirable teachings, will you turn your back and flee? Will you permit this opportunity, divinely offered you, to slip by? For seven hundred years now no one in Italy has been in possession of Greek and yet we agree that all knowledge comes from that source. What great advancement of knowledge, enlargement of fame, and increase of pleasure will come to you from an acquaintance with this tongue! There are everywhere quantities of doctors of the Civil Law and the opportunity of completing your study in this field will not fail you. However, should the one and only doctor of Greek letters disappear, there will be no one from whom to acquire them."

Overcome at last by these arguments, I gave myself to Chrysoloras and developed such ardor that whatever I learned by day, I revolved with myself in the night while asleep. I had many fellow-students, two of the number who were particularly proficient belonging to the Florentine nobility. . . .

C.   THE CULT OF BOOK COLLECTING

The Library of Frederick, Duke of Urbino. One aspect of Humanism was the love of books. The following description of the library of Frederick, Duke of Urbino (1422–82), written by a contemporary Florentine bookseller, indicates the nature and extent of the interests of a book lover of that day.[8]

We come now to consider in what high esteem the Duke held all Greek and Latin writers, sacred as well as secular. He alone had a mind to do what no one had done for a thousand years or more; that is, to create the finest library since ancient times. He spared neither cost nor labor, and when he knew of a fine book, whether in Italy or not, he would send for it. It is now fourteen or more years ago since he began the library, and he always employed, in Urbino, in Florence and in other places, thirty or forty scribes in his service. He took the only way to make a fine library like this: by beginning with the Latin poets, with any comments on the same which might seem merited; next the orators, with the works of Tully and all Latin writers and grammarians of merit; so that not one of the leading writers in this faculty should be wanted. He sought also all the known works on history in Latin, and not only those, but likewise the histories of Greek writers done into Latin, and the orators as well. The Duke also desired to have every work on moral and natural philosophy in Latin, or in Latin translations from Greek.

As to the sacred Doctors in Latin, he had the works of all four, and what a noble set of letters and writings we have here; bought without regard of cost. After the four Doctors, he was set on having the works of St. Bernard and of all the Doctors of old, without exception, Tertullian, Hilarius, Remigius, Hugh de St. Victor, Isidore, Anselm, Rabanus and all the rest. After Latin works came Greek writings done into Latin, Dionysius the Areopagite, Basil, Cyril, Gregory, Nazianzen, John of Damascus, John Chrysostom, Gregory of Nicea, all the works of Eusebius, of Ephrem the monk, and of Origen, an excellent writer. Coming to the Latin Doctors in philosophy and theology, all the works of Thomas Aquinas, and of Albertus Magnus; of Alexander ab Alexandro, of Scotus, of Bonaventura, of Richard of Mediavilla, of the Archbishop of Antoninus and of all the recognized modern Doctors, down to the *Conformità* of St. Francis: all the works on civil law in the finest text, the lectures of Bartolo written on goat-skin.

He had an edition of the Bible made in two most beautiful volumes, illustrated in the finest possible manner and bound in gold brocade with rich silver fittings. It was given this rich form as the chief of all writings. With it are all the commentaries of the Master of the Sentences, of Nicola di Lira, and of all the Greek and Latin Doctors, together with the literal glossary of Nicola di Lira. Likewise all the writers on astrology, geometry, arithmetic, architecture and *De re Militari;* books on painting, sculpture, music and canon law, and all the texts and lectures on the *Summa* of Ostiensis and other works in the same faculty. In medicine all the works of Avicenna, Hippocrates, Galen, the *Continenti* of Almansor and the complete works of Averroes in logic and natural philosophy. A volume of all the Councils, held since ancient times, and the logical, philosophical and musical works of Boethius.

There were all the works of modern writers beginning with Pope Pius; of Petrarch and Dante in Latin and in the vulgar tongue, of Boccaccio in Latin; of Coluccio and of Lionardo d'Arezzo, original and translations; of Fra Ambrogio, of Giannozzo Manetti and Guerrino; the prose and poetical works of Panormita, and Francesco Filelfo, and Campano; as well as everything written by Perrotto, Maffeo Vegio, Nicolò Secondino (who was interpreter of Greek and Latin at the Council of the Greeks in Florence), Pontano, Bartolomeo Fazi, Gasparino, Pietro Paolo Vergerio, Giovanni Argiropolo (which includes the Philosophy and Logic of Aristotle and the Politics besides), Francesco Barbaro, Lionardo Giustiniano, Donato Acciaiuoli, Alamanno, Rinuccini, Cristofano da Prato, Vecchio, Poggio, Giovanni Tortello, Francesco d'Arezzo and Lorenzo Valla.

He added to the books written by ancient and modern doctors on all the faculties all the books known in Greek, also the complete works of Aristotle and Plato (written on the finest goat-skin) ; of Homer in one volume, the *Iliad*, the *Odyssey*, and the *Batrachomiomachia;* of Sopho-cles, Pindar and Menander, and all the other Greek poets; a fine volume of Plutarch's lives and his moral works, the *Cosmography* of Ptolemy illustrated in Greek, and the writings of Herodo-tus, Pausanius, Thucydides, Polybius, Demos-thenes, Æschines and Plotinus. All the Greek comments, such as those upon Aristotle, the *Physica de Plantis* and Theophrastus; all the Greek vocabulists—Greek into Latin; the works of Hippocrates, Galen, Xenophon, St. Basil, St. John Chrysostom, St. Athanasius, St. John Damascenas, St. Gregory Nazianzen, St. Gregory of Nicea, Origen, Dionysius the Areopagite, John Climacus, St. Ephrem the monk, Æneas the Sophist, the Collations of John Cassianus, the book of Para-dise, *Vitae sanctorum patrum ex Ægypto,* the Life of Barlaam and Josaphat, a wonderful psalter in Hebrew, Greek and Latin, verse by verse, and all the Greek works on geometry, arithmetic, and astrology.

Finding that he lacked a vast number of Greek books by various writers, he sent to seek them so that nothing in that tongue which could be found should be lacking; also whatever books which were to be had in Hebrew, beginning with the Bible and all those dealt with by the Rabbi Moses and other commentators. And besides the Holy Scriptures, there are books in Hebrew on medicine, philosophy and the other faculties.

The Duke, having completed this noble work at the great cost of thirty thousand ducats, be-side the many other excellent provisions that he made, determined to give every writer a worthy finish by binding his work in scarlet and silver. Beginning with the Bible, as the chief, he had it covered with gold brocade, and then he bound in scarlet and silver the Greek and Latin doctors and philosophers, the histories, the books on medicine and the modern doctors, a rich and magnificent sight. In this library all the books are superlatively good, and written with the pen, and had there been one printed volume it would have been ashamed in such company. They were beautifully illuminated and written on parch-ment.

This library is remarkable amongst all others in that, taking the works of all writers, sacred and profane, original and translated, there will be found not a single imperfect folio. No other library can show the like, for in all of them the works of certain authors will be wanting in places. A short time before the Duke went to Ferrara it chanced that I was in Urbino with His Lordship, and I had with me the catalogues of the principal Italian libraries: of the papal library, of those of San Marco at Florence, of Pavia, and even of that of the University of Oxford, which I had procured from England. On comparing them with that of the Duke I remarked how they all failed in one respect; to wit, they possessed the same work in many examples, but lacked the other writings of the author; nor had they writers in all the faculties like this library.

D.   HUMANIST EDUCATION

> *Guarino on Teaching and Studying.* Battista Guarino (1370–1460) was, like his father, the head of a famous academy at Ferrara. In *De Ordine Docendi et Studendi,* 1459, Guarino laid down the educational princi-ples upon which he and his father conducted the academy.[9]

In offering this short treatise for your accept-ance, I am fully aware that you need no incen-tive to regard the pursuit of letters as the most worthy object of your ambition. But you may find what I have written a not unwelcome re-minder of our past intercourse, whilst it may prove of use to other readers into whose hands it may fall. For I have had in view not only stu-dents anxious for guidance in their private read-ing, but masters in search of some definite prin-ciples of method in teaching the classics. Hence I have treated both of Greek and of Latin letters and am confident that the course I have laid down will prove a thoroughly satisfactory train-ing in literature and scholarship. I should re-mind you that the conclusions presented in this little work are not the result of my own expe-rience only. It is indeed a summary of the theory and practice of several scholars, and especially does it represent the doctrine of my father, Guarino of Verona; so much so, that you may suppose him to be writing to you by my pen and giving you the fruit of his long and ripe expe-rience in teaching. May I hope that you will yourself prove to be one more example of the high worth of his precepts?

Let me, at the outset, begin with a caution. No master can endow a careless and indifferent nature with the true passion for learning. That a young man must acquire for himself. But once the taste begins to develop, then in Ovid's words "the more we drink, the more we thirst." For when the mind has begun to enjoy the pleasures of learning, the passion for fuller and deeper knowledge will grow from day to day. But there can be no proficiency in studies unless there be first the desire to excel. Wherefore let a young man set forward eagerly in quest of those true, honorable, and enduring treasures of the mind which neither disease nor death has power to destroy. Riches, which adventurers seek by land and sea, too often win men to pleasure rather than to learning; for self-indulgence is a snare from whose enticements it is the bounden duty of parents to ween their children, by kind words, or by severity if need arise. Perchance then in later years the echo of a father's wise advice may linger and may avail in the hour of temptation. . . .

As regards the course of study. From the first, stress must be laid upon distinct and sustained enunciation, both in speaking and in reading. But at the same time utterance must be perfectly natural; if affected or exaggerated the effect is unpleasing. The foundation of education must be laid in grammar. Unless this be thoroughly learnt, subsequent progress is uncertain,—a house built upon treacherous ground. . . .

Now these rules can be most satisfactorily learnt from the Compendium written by my father which briefly sets out the more important laws of composition. In using this or a similar textbook the pupil must be practised both in written and in oral exercises. Only by rapid practise in oral composition can fluency and readiness be gained. And this will be further secured if the class is accustomed to speak in Latin. . . .

I have said that ability to write Latin verse is one of the essential marks of an educated person. I wish now to indicate a second, which is of at least equal importance, namely, familiarity with the language and literature of Greece. The time has come when we must speak with no uncertain voice upon this vital requirement of scholarship. I am well aware that those who are ignorant of the Greek tongue decry its necessity for reasons which are sufficiently evident. But I can allow no doubt to remain as to my own conviction that, without a knowledge of Greek, Latin scholarship itself is, in any real sense, impossible. . . .

But whilst a beginning is being thus made with Greek, continued progress must at the same time be secured in Latin. For instance, the broader rules of grammar which sufficed in the earlier stages must give place to a more complete study of structure, such as we find in Priscian, and irregularities or exceptions, hitherto ignored, must be duly noted. At the same time the Epistles

of Cicero should be taken in hand for purposes of declamation. Committed to memory they serve as one of the finest possible aids to purity, directness, and facility of style, and supply admirable matter in no less admirable form for adaptation to our own uses. Yet I would not be understood to claim the *Letters* of Cicero as alone offering a sufficient training in style. For distinction of style is the fruit of a far wider field of study. To quote Horace:

> Of writing well, be sure, the secret lies
> In wisdom: therefore study to be wise.

But we are now passing from the first, or elementary to the second, or more advanced, stage of grammar which I called "historices" and which is concerned with the study of continuous prose authors, more particularly the historians. Here we begin with a short but comprehensive view of general history, which will include that of the Roman people by such writers as Justin or Valerius Maximus. The latter author is also valuable as affording actual illustrations of virtuous precepts couched in attractive style. The scholar will now devote his attentions to the historians in regular order. By their aid he will learn to understand the manners, laws, and institutions of different types of nations, and will examine the varying fortune of individuals and states, the sources of their success and failure, their strength and their weakness. . . .

Side by side with the study of history a careful reading of the poets will be taken in hand. The true significance of poetic fiction will now be appreciated. It consists, as Cicero says, in the exhibition of the realities of our own life under the form of imaginary persons and situations. Thus Jerome could employ Terence in bringing home his exhortations to temperance. Let us not forget that Virgil as a subject of deep and regular study must always stand not first, but alone. Here we have the express authority of Augustine, who urges the supreme claim of the great poet to our life-long companionship. Lucian may perhaps with good reason be postponed to a later stage. Quintilian regarded him as the "rhetorical poet"; and undoubtedly his poem has much affinity with certain aspects of the forensic art. There is a certain strain of the keen debator in particular portions of his work. So I should advise that Virgil be followed by Statius, whose *Thebais*, fashioned upon the *Aeneid*, will be found easy reading. The *Metamorphoses* of Ovid form a useful introduction to the systematic knowledge of mythology—a subject of wide literary application and as such deserves close attention.

The course of study which I have thus far sketched out will prove an admirable preparation for that further branch of scholarship which constitutes rhetoric, including the thorough examination of the great monuments of eloquence. . . . The first work to claim our attention in this subject is the *Rhetoric* of Cicero, in which we find all the points of oratory concisely but comprehensively set forth. The other rhetorical writings of Cicero will follow; and the principles therein laid down must be examined in the light of his own speeches. Indeed the student of eloquence must have his Cicero constantly in his hand; the simplicity, the lofty moral standard, the practical temper of his writings render them a peculiarly noble training for a public speaker. Nor should the admirable Quintilian be neglected in this same connection.

It will be desirable also to include the elements of logic in our course of studies, and with that the *Ethics* of Aristotle and the *Dialogues* of Plato. For these are necessary aids to the proper understanding of Cicero. . . .

Before I bring this short treatise to a close I would urge you to consider the function of letters as an adornment of leisure. Cicero, as you may remember, declares learning to be the inspiration of youth, the delight of age, the ornament of happy fortunes, the solace of adversity. A recreation in the study, abroad it is no hindrance. In our work, in our leisure, whether we keep vigil or whether we court sleep, letters are ever at hand as our surest resource. Do we seek refreshment for our minds? Where can we find it more happily than in a pursuit which affords alike utility and delight? If others seek recreation in dice, in ball-play, in the theatre, do you seek it in acquir-

ing knowledge. There you will see nothing which you may not admire; you will hear nothing which you would gladly forget. For good books give no offense, call forth no rebuke; they will stir you, but with no empty hopes, no vain fears. Finally, through books, and books alone, will your converse be with the best and greatest, nay, even with the mighty dead themselves. . . .

Let us, then, heeding these great names, see to it that we allow not our short working years to pass idly away. To each species of creatures has been allotted a peculiar and instinctive gift. To horses galloping, to birds flying comes naturally. To man is given the desire to learn. Hence what the Greeks called παιδεία, we call *studia humanitatis*. For learning and training in virtue are peculiar to man; therefore our forefathers called them *humanitas*, the pursuits and activities proper to mankind. And no branch of knowledge embraces so wide a range of subjects as that learning which I have here attempted to describe.

I will end as I began. If this little work fulfills, perhaps more than fulfills, the promise which I held out, it is because it does but exhibit that order and method of study which my learned and revered father has followed for so many years in his own school. For as from the Trojan Horse of old the Greek heroes spread over the captured city, so from that famous Academy of my father has proceeded the greater number of those scholars who have carried learning, not merely throughout Italy, but far beyond her borders.

E.   THE CULT OF ANTIQUITY

Cellini on Antique Remains. Besides an interest in ancient literature, the Humanists had an enormous enthusiasm for the physical remains of Greek and Roman civilization. The following selections from the autobiography of the famous goldsmith and sculptor, Benvenuto Cellini (1500–71), illustrate this enthusiasm for the antique.[10]

[Rome] At this period, when I was still a youth of about twenty-three years of age, a pestilential disease broke out of such unparalleled virulence that there died in Rome many thousands per day. Somewhat terrified by this, I began to take up certain amusements such as my fancy directed, caused moreover by a circumstance that I shall relate. For I enjoyed on feast-days visiting the antiquities [of the city], copying them either in wax models or by drawing from them; and since these said antiquities are all in ruins, and amid these same ruins build a great

many pigeons, the desire came upon me to employ against them my fowling-piece; and in order to avoid intercourse with anyone, being afraid of the plague, I put my gun upon the shoulder of my boy Pagolino, and he and I went alone to the said ruins. It resulted therefore that very many times I returned laden with very plump pigeons. I did not care to load my gun with more than a single ball, and it was therefore by real skill in that art that I made such large bags. I had a straight fowling-piece made by my own hands; and (so bright was it) both within and without there was never seen a mirror like it. I made besides with my own hands the finest gunpowder, in the composition of which I discovered the finest secrets that have ever up to today been discovered by anyone. . . .

By means of this diversion of mine, I acquired the friendship of certain curiosity-hunters who watched out for those Lombard peasants, who came to Rome at that season to till the vines.

These latter in the course of their tilling the earth often found antique medals, agates, chrysoprases, cornelians, cameos; they found besides precious stones, that is to say, emeralds, sapphires, diamonds, and rubies. These same curio-hunters sometimes got from those peasants for very small sums some of these things; for which I—meeting these curio-hunters occasionally, nay, very often—gave as many gold *scudi* for a thing which they had frequently just bought for scarcely as many pence (*giuli*). This circumstance, exclusive of the great profit that I procured out of it, which was tenfold or more, set me besides in high favor with almost all the Roman cardinals.

Of these objects I will only speak of the notable and rarest examples. There fell into my hands, among so many other things, a dolphin's head as large as a big balloting bean. Amongst the other treasures, not only was this the most beautiful, but nature in this case had far surpassed art; for this emerald was of such fine color that the man who bought it of me for some tens of *scudi* had it set after the fashion of an ordinary stone to wear in a ring; set thus he sold it for some hundreds. I had besides another variety of stone: this was a head made of the most beautiful topaz that the world ever saw. In this object art had equalled nature. It was as big as a large filbert, and the head upon it was as well executed as it is possible to imagine: it represented *Minerva*. There was besides another stone differing from these. This was a cameo; upon it was cut a *Hercules binding the three-jawed Cerberus*. This was of such beauty and fashioned with such fine skill, that our great Michelagniolo protested that he had never seen anything so wonderful. There were besides, among many bronze medals, one that fell into my hands, upon which was the head of *Jove*. This medal was much larger than any that I had ever seen. The head was so beautifully executed that such a medal had never been seen. It had a most beautiful reverse side, with some small figures likewise superbly executed. . . .

[Florence] One feast day among others I went into the Palace after dinner, and when I came up into the Hall of the Clock I saw the door of the Wardrobe open; and when I approached it a little the duke [of Florence, Cosimo de' Medici] called to me, and, with a kindly greeting, said to me: "You are welcome indeed. Look at this chest which has been sent as a present to me by the lord Stefano of Pilestina! Open it, and let us see what the thing is." Having immediately opened it, I said to the Duke: "My Lord! this is a figure in Greek marble, and a wondrous thing. I tell you that for a boy's figure I do not recollect that I have ever seen among the antiques so fine a work, nor one of so beautiful a fashion. Wherefore I offer to Your Most Illustrious Excellency

to restore it, and the head and the arms and the feet. And I will make an eagle in order that it may be labeled as a *Ganymede*. And although it is not customary for me to patch up statues—for that is the art of certain bunglers, who do it very badly—yet the excellence of this great master calls me to assist him." The Duke was pleased that the statue was so beautiful, and asked me many questions, saying to me: "Tell me distinctly, my Benvenuto! in what consists the great talent of this master, which causes you so much admiration." Thereupon I demonstrated to His Most Illustrious Excellency after the best method that I knew in order to make him understand such beauty, and the intellectual skill, and the rare manner [of the fragment]; upon which questions I discoursed very much and I did it the more willingly, realizing that therein His Excellency took very great pleasure.

While I was thus agreeably entertaining the Duke, it chanced that a page went out of the Wardrobe, and as the said [page] went out Bandinello [a rival sculptor] entered. When the Duke saw him he was half disturbed, and with a severe expression he said to him: "What are you doing here?" The said Bandinello, without making any other reply, immediately cast his eyes upon that chest, wherein lay the said uncovered statue, and with one of his evil chuckles, shaking his head, he said, turning towards the Duke: "My Lord! These are some of those things of which I have so often spoken to Your Most Illustrious Excellency. Know that these ancient [sculptors] understood nothing at all about anatomy, and for this reason their works are quite full of faults." I remained quiet and paid no attention to anything that he was saying; rather I had turned my back on him.

Directly that this animal had finished his disagreeable chatterings, the Duke said: "Oh! Benvenuto! This is exactly the opposite to that which you with so many fine arguments have but now so well demonstrated to me. Therefore defend it a little." At these words of the Duke, conveyed to me with so much charm, I immediately responded, and said: "My Lord! Your Most Illustrious Excellency ought to know that Baccio Bandinelli is composed entirely of evil, and so he always has been: in such a way that whatever he gazed upon, to his disapproving eyes immediately, although the thing may be altogether good in a superlative degree, it is immediately converted into the worst evil. But I who am drawn only towards the good, perceive the truth more divinely; in such a fashion that what I have said to Your Most Illustrious Excellency about this most beautiful statue is altogether the simple truth, and that which Bandinello has said is altogether that evil of which alone he is composed."

The Duke stood listening to me with much pleasure; and while I was saying these things Bandinello fidgeted and made the ugliest grimaces of his countenance—which was [itself] the most ugly—that it is possible to imagine in the world. The Duke immediately moved away, proceeding through certain lower chambers and the said Bandinello followed him. And the Chamberlain took me by the cloak and led me after him. And thus we followed the Duke, so that when His Most Illustrious Excellency reached a certain chamber he sat down, and both Bandinello and I stood, one upon the right, and the other upon the left, of His Most Illustrious Excellency. I remained silent, and those who were around us—several servants of His Excellency—all gazed fixedly at Bandinello, somewhat sniggering with one another at those words which I had uttered in that chamber above. So the said Bandinello began to chatter, and he said: "My Lord! When I uncovered my *Hercules and Cacus* I certainly believe that more than one hundred ballads were made upon me, which they say were the worst that one could possibly imagine in the world from this mob."

I thereupon answered and said: "My Lord, when our Michelagniolo Buonaroti unveiled his Sacristy, where may be seen so many beautiful figures, this admirable and talented School, the friend of truth and of the excellent, made more than one hundred sonnets upon him, competing with one another which could speak the best of him. And so just as that work of Bandinello's deserved so much ill said as he says has been spoken about it, so that of Buonaroti deserved as much good as was said of him." At these words of mine Bandinello fell into such a fury that he was bursting, and he turned to me and said: "And what do you know that you can say about it?" "I will tell you if you have sufficient patience to know how to listen to me." Says he: "Speak up then now." The Duke and the others who were there, all listened eagerly.

I began, and in the first place I said: "Do you know that it pains me to have to tell you of the defects of that work of yours; but I will not speak of such things, rather I will tell you all that this most talented School says about it." And because this wretched man kept now saying something disagreeable, and now moving about his hands and his feet, he caused me to fall into such a rage that I began in a much more unpleasant manner than I should have done if he had acted otherwise.

"This talented School says that if one were to shave the hair off *Hercules,* there would not remain noddle sufficient to contain his brain;

and that as regards that face of his one would not know whether it was the countenance of a man or of a lion-ox: and that he is not paying any attention to what he is doing: and that it is badly attached to its neck, with so little skill and with so bad a grace, that one has never seen anything worse: and that those two ugly shoulders of his resemble the two pommels of an ass's packsaddle; and that his breasts and the rest of his muscles are not copied from those of a man, but are drawn from an old sack full of melons, which has been set upright propped against a wall. So [also] the loins seem to be copied from a sack full of long gourds; one does not know by what method the two legs are attached to that ugly body; for one does not know upon which leg he is standing, or upon which he is making any display of pressure: still less does he appear to be resting upon both, as it is customary sometimes for those masters who know something about the representation [of figures]. It is easy to see that he is falling forward more than a third of a *braccio* [balance]; for this alone is the greatest and most intolerable fault that those wretched masters of the common herd commit. Of the arms they say that they are both stretched downwards without any grace: nor is there any artistic sense to be perceived in them, as if you had never seen living nudes: and that the right leg of *Hercules* and that of *Cacus* make a mixture in the calves of their legs; so that if one of the two were removed from the other, not only one of them, but rather both would remain without calves at that point where they touch: and they say that one of the feet of *Hercules* is buried and the other appears to have fire under it."

The man could not restrain himself to be patient, so that I might tell him also the great defects of *Cacus*. For one thing was that I was speaking truly, and another was that I was making it known clearly to the Duke and to the others who were in our presence, so that they made very great expressions and acts of astonishment, and then realized that I was telling the very truth. All at once this wretched man said: "Ah! you wicked lying tongue! Oh! where do you leave my design?" I replied "that he who designs well can never work out that design badly. Consequently I can believe that your design is like your work." Now when he saw from those ducal and other countenances that with their looks and with their gestures they were despising him, he allowed himself to be too much overcome by his insolence, and turning towards me with his most hideous ugly face, he all of a sudden said to me: "Oh! be silent! You b. . . . b. . . . you!"

F.   THE CULT OF BEAUTY

1. *Cellini and the Pope's Button.* Love of
the antique inspired men of the Renaissance
to the creation of new things of beauty. The
passage from Benvenuto Cellini's autobiography quoted below reveals the Renaissance
approach to art and the artist.[11]

[Cellini had been engaged to reset some jewels
for Pope Clement VII.] Since that was not, however, a work in which I could gain great reputation, the pope was resolved, he said, to employ
me in an undertaking of the last importance, in
which I should have opportunity of displaying
my abilities. "The work I have in mind," he
added, "is the button for the pontifical cape,
which is made round, and in the form of a
trencher and as big as a small trencher; in this
I would have God the Father represented in half
relievo, and in the midst of it I would have the
edge of the large diamond set, with many other
jewels of the greatest value. Go then and draw a
fine design of it." Thereupon he caused all his
jewels to be shown me, and I left him, highly
pleased with my success.

[Several of Cellini's rivals, hearing of this undertaking, had a number of other designs made,
which were submitted to the pope at the same
time as his.] It so fell out that all those who had
drawn those designs had laid the fine large and
beautiful diamond in the middle of the breast of
God the Father. The pope, who was a person
of great genius, having noticed this blunder,
would proceed no farther in examining their performances. After he had examined about ten, he
threw the rest upon the ground and desired me
to give him my model, that he might see whether
I had committed the same mistake. Thereupon I
came forward and opened a little round box,
when instantly there seemed to flash from it a
luster which dazzled the pope himself, and he
cried out with a loud voice, "Benvenuto, had you
been my very self, you could not have designed
this with greater propriety." Then calling to
Trojano, his gentleman of the bedchamber, he
ordered him to fetch five hundred ducats.

Whilst they were bringing the money, he examined more minutely the ingenious artifice by
which I had placed that fine diamond and God
the Father in a proper position. I had laid the
diamond exactly in the middle of the work, and
over it I represented God the Father sitting in a
sort of free, easy attitude, which suited admirably
well with the rest of the piece, and did not in
the least crowd the diamond; his right hand was
lifted up, giving his blessing. Under the diamond
I had drawn three little boys, who supported it

with their arms raised aloft. Round it was a
number of figures of boys placed amongst other
glittering jewels. The remainder of God the
Father was covered with a cloak which wantoned
in the wind, from whence issued several figures
of boys, with other striking ornaments, most
beautiful to behold.

[While Cellini was engaged on this work and
other orders for the pope, his brother was killed
in a street brawl between some soldiers and
young gallants, such as occurred almost daily on
any provocation, or none.] Meanwhile I exerted
my utmost efforts to finish the work in gold which
I was employed in by Pope Clement; still thinking day and night of the musketeer that shot my
brother. Perceiving that my solicitude and anxious
desire of revenge deprived me both of sleep and
appetite, which threw me into a lingering disorder, and not caring to have recourse to any
treacherous or dishonorable means, one evening I
prepared to put an end to my disquietude.

Just after sunset, as this musketeer stood at
his door with his sword in his hand, when he
had done supper, I with great address came close
up to him with a long dagger and gave him a
violent back-handed stroke which I had aimed
at his neck; that instant he turned about, and
the blow falling directly upon his left shoulder,
broke the whole bone of it; upon which he
dropped his sword, quite overcome by the pain,
and took to his heels. I pursued and in four
steps came up with him, when, raising the dagger
over his head which he lowered down, I hit exactly upon his collar bone and the middle of the
neck; the weapon penetrated so deep into both
that though I made a great effort to recover it
again, I found it impossible; for at that same
instant there issued out of a neighboring house
four soldiers, with their swords drawn, so that I
was obliged to draw mine also in my own defense.

[He takes refuge with his protector, Duke
Alexander de' Medici, in whose palace he stays
under cover for eight days. At the end of that
time the pope sends for him, the messenger saying that the pope] knew all that had happened,
that his Holiness was very much my friend, and
desired me to go on with my business without
giving myself any uneasiness. When I came into
the presence of the pontiff, he frowned on me
very much, and with angry looks seemed to repri-
mand me; but, upon viewing my performance,
his countenance grew serene and he praised me
highly, telling me that I had done a great deal
in a short time; then looking attentively at me,
he said, "Now that you have recovered your
health, Benvenuto, take care of yourself." I un-

derstood his meaning, and told him that I should not neglect his advice.

2. *Letters of Aretino*. Another aspect of Humanist love of beauty is to be found in the following selections from the letters of Pietro Aretino (1492–1556). He was a biting satirist, whose sharp pen caused his banishment from both Arezzo and Rome and caused him to take up his residence at Venice, where he lived on the bounty of patrons who infinitely preferred supporting him to becoming the subjects of his satire.[12]

(*To his landlord.*) I should think it a sin of ingratitude, gentle sir, if I did not repay with praise a part of my debt to the divine site on which your house is built and where I dwell with the utmost pleasure in life, for it is set in a place which neither hither nor thither nor higher nor lower could better. Certainly, whoever built it gave it the most proper and pre-eminent place on the whole Grand Canal, and, as this is the patriarch of all avenues and Venice the Pope of all cities, I may truthfully say that I enjoy the most beautiful street and the most delightful view in the world. I never go to the window but I see thousands of people and as many gondolas going to market. The *piazze* to my right are the Beccarie and the Pescaria; on the left, the Bridge and the Fondaco dei Tedeschi; while, facing them both, rises the Rialto, crowded with traders. Here I see boats full of grapes, game and birds in the shops, and kitchen gardens on the pavements. Rivers and irrigated fields I no longer care to see, now that I can watch the water at dawn covered with every manner of thing that is in season. It is a joy to study the bearers of this grand plenty of fruits and greens and to watch them dispensing them to the porters who carry them to their stalls.

But all this is nothing to the sight of twenty or twenty-five sail-boats, heaped up with melons like a little island, and the multitude thronging about them to reckon and weigh and smell their beauty. Of the beautiful housewives shining in silks and gold and jewels, and seated proudly under the poop, I will say nothing, lest I slight their pomp. But I will say that I hold my sides when I listen to the boatmen shouting, jeering, and roaring at those who are rowed by lackeys without scarlet hose. And what man could hold his water if he saw, as Giulio Camillo and I saw, a boatload of Germans upset in the dead of winter, just as they came out of a tavern? Giulio is a wag and he says that the side-door of this house, being dark, narrow, and brutal to climb, is like the terrible name I have made for myself by venting the truth; but he adds: anyone who knows

me finds in my pure, frank, and natural friendship the same calm contentment that he feels when he comes out on the portico of my palace and leans on my balcony. Moreover, to add to the delight of my eye, here are the orange groves that gild the base of the Palazzo dei Camerlinghi on one side, and on the other the *rio* and bridge of San Giovanni Grisostomo; and the winter sun cannot rise without saluting my bed, my study, my kitchen; my chambers, and my hall. . . .

In sum, if I could satisfy touch and the other senses as I satisfy sight, the house would be a heaven, for I enjoy every recreation here that can please the eye. Nor must I forget the great gentlemen, both foreign and native, who pass my door, nor my heavenly rapture when the Bucentaur goes by, nor the regattas, nor the festivals which convert the Canal into a continual triumph for my eye, which is lord of all it surveys. And what shall I say of the lights which appear in the evening like scattered stars? Or of the night music which tickles my ear with sweet harmonies? It would be easier to describe your profound judgment in letters and public affairs than to exhaust the delights that I enjoy merely in gazing. Therefore, if there be any faint breath of talent in the trifles I have written, I owe it to the influence, neither of shadow nor of light nor yet of verdure nor of violets, but to the joy I feel in the airy felicity of your mansion, in which God grant me to number, in vigor and health, the years a respectable man may hope to live.

(*To Titian.*) My dear gossip, having in contempt of my custom supped alone, or rather in company of this tedious fever which lets me relish no food, I rose from table, surfeited with the despondency with which I sat down to it. And resting both arms flat on the window-sill, and leaning my whole body on it, I abandoned myself to the marvellous spectacle of the multitude of boats. . . . And when the crowds had dispersed, I, like a man weary of himself and with nothing to occupy his mind, raised my eyes to the heavens which, since God made them, were never so lovely with light and shadow. The atmosphere was such as men like myself, who envy you because they cannot be you, would render it. First, the buildings in the foreground, although of stone, seemed to be of some plastic material; and beyond them you beheld the air, in some parts pure and alive, in other murky and sallow.

Fancy, too, how I marvelled at the clouds, dense with moisture, lying half in the foreground over the roofs and half in the gloaming, for on the right everything was a *sfumato* darkening down into gray-black. I was spellbound by the variety of hues they revealed. The nearest burned with the embers of the sunset; the farthest glowed with a dimmer, leaden hue. Ah, how beautifully the hand of Nature hatched the air, making it fade and recede from the palaces, as Titian does in his landscapes! Here was a blue-green and there a green-blue, truly conceived by the caprice of Nature, that master of masters! She melted and modelled with light and shadow in a manner which made me exclaim more than once: O Titian, where are you? Upon my word, if you had painted what I report, you would confound men with the wonder that astounded me; and in gazing on what I have told you I nourished my soul on it, for the wonder of such paintings does not endure.

Part II.   TYPES OF THE ITALIAN RENAISSANCE

The Humanist movement produced many colorful individuals. An examination of their lives gives a clear insight into the effect of the Renaissance upon man's approach to living and the things of this world. Three selections in this part, therefore, are drawn from the lives of notable Renaissance types, and a fourth represents the ideal man as the age envisaged him.

A.   THE ARTIST AS AN INDIVIDUALIST

Following are the opening passages from the autobiography of Benvenuto Cellini, the famous sculptor and goldsmith, whose work was quoted in other connections in the first part of this problem.[13]

All men of every sort, who have done anything that is meritorious, or that indeed resembles merit, ought, if they be truthful persons and of good report, to set forth their lives with their own hand: but they should not commence so noble an undertaking before they have passed the age of forty years. Recognizing such a fact, now that I have travelled along my life's span for full fifty-eight years, and am in Florence, my native place, whilst recalling the many afflictions which befall those who live, and being troubled with these same afflictions less than I have ever been before up to this age: even it would seem to me that I am in greater content of mind and health of body that I have ever been in times past: and remembering certain agreeable blessings and certain incalculable calamities; looking back upon these I am struck with astonishment that I should have arrived at this age of 58 years, in which I am, by the grace of God, so happily proceeding onwards.

Although these men, inasmuch as they have labored with the very smallest trace of merit, have made themselves known to the world, the fact alone ought to be sufficient for them, that they see themselves men of mark; but because they must live in the same manner as others live, we experience in this respect a certain amount of worldly curiosity, which arises upon many different points. The first duty is to make known to others that the hero traces his descent from persons of merit and very ancient lineage. I am called Benvenuto Cellini, the son of Giovanni d'Andrea di Christofano Cellini; my mother was Elisabetta, daughter of Stefano Granacci: and both of them were Florentine citizens.

We find it set out in the chronicles made by our most ancient and reliable Florentines, according to what Giovanni Villani writes, that we may observe how the city of Florence is constructed in imitation of the beautiful city of Rome, and some traces may be discovered of the Colosseum and of the Baths. These traces are near to Santa Croce; the Capital was where the Mercato Vecchio stands today; the Rotonda is entirely standing, which was made for a temple of Mars, and today is dedicated to our patron, San Giovanni. That this was so can be very clearly seen and cannot be denied: but the said edifices are much smaller than those in Rome. They say that the man who caused them to be built was Julius Caesar, together with certain other Roman nobles, who having conquered and taken Fiesole, erected a city on that spot; and each of them undertook one of these remarkable structures. Julius Caesar had a brave chief captain who was called Fiorino da Cellino (which is a fortress about two miles from Monte Fiasconi). This Fiorino having taken up his abode below Fiesole, on the spot where Florence now is, in order to be near the river Arno for the convenience of his army, all his soldiers and such other persons as had dealings with this said captain used to say: "Let us go to Fiorenze," because the said captain bore the name of Fiorino, and because in that place where he had his said dwelling, from the natural features of the place, there grew a vast quantity of flowers. So in giving a commencement to the city, since this seemed to Julius Caesar a most beautiful name, and one appropriately given to it, and because flowers bring good omen, he gave this name of Fiorenze to the said city; and in order besides to confer a sort of favor upon his brave captain; since he liked him so much the more, because he had drawn him from a very humble condition, and because so brave a man had been created by himself. . . .

We find that there are some of our Cellini in Ravenna, the most ancient city in Italy, and there they are great nobles; they are also in Pisa, and I have found them in many places throughout Christendom; and in this very State there also remain some of the stock, addicted, moreover, to the profession of arms; for it is not so many years back that a youth named Luca Cellini, a beardless lad, entered into combat with a soldier, a skilled and very valiant man, who had fought on previous occasions in the lists, called Francesco da Vicorati. This Luca, by his own valor, sword in hand, conquered and slew him with so much bravery and skill, that he made every one marvel, since they had expected the opposite result. So that I boast of having my descent from brave men.

Now as regards such honor as I have acquired for my house, under the known conditions of our life today and by means of my profession, which is not a matter of great consequence, I will speak of it in its own place, glorying much more in that having been born in humble circumstances I have added some honorable foundation to my family, than if I had sprung from high lineage and by base qualities had stained or extinguished it. I will therefore commence with how it pleased God that I should be born.

B. THE ARTIST-SCHOLAR

The following account of the life and talents of Leon Battista Alberti (1404–72) is taken from Giorgio Vasari's *Lives of Seventy of the Most Eminent Painters, Sculptors, and Architects*. Vasari, a contemporary of Cellini, was himself a talented painter, but he is remembered more as a biographer. His life of Alberti reveals the versatility of the Renaissance artist.[14]

The knowledge of letters and the study of the sciences are without doubt of the utmost value to all, and offer the most important advantages to every artist who takes pleasure therein; but most of all they are serviceable to sculptors, painters, and architects, for whom they prepare the path to various inventions in all the works executed by them; and be the natural qualities of a man what they may, his judgment can never be brought to perfection if he be deprived of the advantages resulting from the accompaniment of learning. . . . Since theory, when separated from practice, is, for the most part, found to avail very little; but when theory and practice chance to be happily united in the same person, nothing can be more suitable to the life and vocation of artists, as well because art is rendered much richer and more perfect by the aid of science, as because the councils and writings of learned artists have, in themselves, a greater efficacy, and obtain a higher degree of credit, than can be accorded to the words or works of those who know nothing beyond the simple process they use, and which they put in practice, well or ill, as it may chance.

Now that all this is true is seen clearly in the instance of Leon Battista Alberti, who, having given his attention to the study of Latin as well as to that of architecture, perspective, and painting, has left behind him books, written in such a manner, that no artist of later times has been able to surpass him in his style and other qualities as an author, while there have been numbers, much more distinguished than himself in the practice of art, although it is very generally supposed (such is the force of his writings, and so extensive has been their influence on the pens and words of the learned, his contemporaries and others), that he was, in fact, superior to all those who have, on the contrary, greatly surpassed him in their works. We are thus taught, by experience, that, in so far as regards name and fame, the written word is that which, of all things has the most effectual force, the most vivid life, and the longest duration; for books make their way to all places, and everywhere they obtain the credence of men, provided they be truthful and written in the spirit of candor. We are therefore not to be surprised if we find the renowned Leon Battista to be better known by his writings than by the works of his hand.

This master was born in Florence, of the most noble family of the Alberti, concerning which we have already spoken in another place. He gave his attention, not only to the acquirement of knowledge in the world of art generally, and to the examination of works of antiquity in their proportions, etc., but also, and much more fully, to writing on these subjects, to which he was by nature more inclined than to the practice of art.

Leon Battista was well versed in arithmetic, and a very good geometrician; he wrote ten books respecting architecture in the Latin tongue, which were published in 1481; they may now be read in the Florentine language, having been translated by the Rev. Messer Cosimo Bartoli, provost of San Giovanni, in Florence. He likewise wrote three books on painting, now translated into the Tuscan by Messer Ludovico Domenichi, and composed a dissertation of tractile forces, containing rules for measuring heights. Leon Battista was moreover the author of the *Libri della vita civile*, with some other works of an amatory character, in prose and verse: he was the first who attempted to apply Latin measures to Italian verse. . . .

At the time when Nicholas V had thrown the city of Rome into utter confusion with his peculiar manner of building, Leon Battista Alberti arrived in that city, where, by means of his intimate friend Biondo da Forli, he became known to the pontiff. The latter had previously availed himself of the counsel of Bernardo Rossellino, a Florentine sculptor and architect, as will be related in the life of Antonio, his brother; and Bernardo, having commenced the restoration of the papal palace, with other works in Santa Maria Maggiore, thenceforward proceeded by the advice of Leon Battista, such being the will of the Pope. Thus the pontiff with the counsel of one of these two, and the execution of the other, brought many useful and praiseworthy labors to conclusion: among these was the Fountain of the Acqua Vergine, which had been ruined, and was restored by him. He likewise caused the fountain of the Piazza de' Trevi to be decorated with the marble ornaments which we now see there, among which are the arms of Pope Nicholas himself, and those of the Roman people. . . .

It is said that the same architect produced the design for the palace and gardens, erected by the Rucellai family in the Via della Scala, an edifice constructed with much judgment, and which is therefore exceedingly commodious. Besides many other convenient arrangements, there are two galleries or *loggie,* one towards the south, the other to the west, both very beautiful, and raised upon the columns without arches; which method is the true and proper one, according to the ancients, because the architraves, which are placed immediately upon the capitals of the columns, stand level, while a rectangular body, such as is the arch turned into a vault in the upper part, cannot stand on a round column, without having the angles out of square or awry; this considered, the best mode of construction requires that the architraves should be placed upon the columns, or that, when it is resolved to construct arches, the master should employ pillars instead of columns. . . .

Leon Battista Alberti was a man of refined habits and praiseworthy life, a friend of distinguished men, liberal and courteous to all. He lived honorably and like a gentleman, as he was, all the course of his life, and finally, having attained to a tolerably mature age, he departed content and tranquil to a better life, leaving behind him a most honorable name.

C.   THE SCHOLAR-CHURCHMAN

The life of Nicolò Perotto (d. 1480), which follows, was written by Vespasiano da Bisticci, a Florentine bookseller who recorded the lives of many of the notable Humanists with whom he came into contact in his business.[15]

Messer Nicolò Perotto, born of poor parentage, was learned in Greek and Latin, having been sent in his youth to study under Guerino at Ferrara, where by his ready intellect he soon became a fine scholar and master of an elegant style in writing. While he was at Ferrara, William Gray, Bishop of Ely, and of royal descent, was also a student there, and, having been told of the good qualities of Messer Nicolò, he asked him to lodge with him. He was so conscious of the virtues of Nicolò that he gave him as much as he needed for the purchase of books.

After several years of assiduous study had passed, the King of England wrote to Gray and directed him to go to Rome as his proctor, whereupon he took Nicolò in his train. Here Gray was fully occupied with his duties, and Nicolò, being anxious to go on with his Greek studies, although he was already well versed in the language, begged his patron to arrange with Cardinal Niceno that he might acquire still fuller knowledge of it. When he learned Nicolò's wishes Gray procured his admission to the cardinal's house when he was twenty years old. Here he studied Greek day and night till he became a profound scholar, and the cardinal, who was greatly attached to men of worth, showed him much favor and affection. He ultimately determined to become a priest, and by the cardinal's aid he got a benefice. His father was very poor, but Nicolò, who enjoyed certain emoluments and was able to live well, managed to have him made a *cavaliere* whereby he obtained an income from the state. Thus he was able to do good service to his family.

Messer Nicolò won great honor at the court for his writings, and the beauty of his style. Pope Nicolas, having seen some of his compositions, begged him to translate *Polibio Megalopolitano* from Greek into Latin, which work he executed with such skill that all who read it were astonished, declaring that no writer during the present pontificate had written with such elegance and erudition. He then presented it to the Pope, who, when he saw it, was so greatly pleased that he gave Nicolò a purse of six hundred ducats. This work was of such excellence that, when it appeared in Florence, Messer Poggio and other scholars of the time praised it highly. It happened that, before this, Messer Poggio had differed sharply with Messer Nicolò, but now—so great is the power of truth—he was constrained to praise it unreservedly, saying he had never read a finer or more coherent style.

This work brought him fame at the court of Rome and throughout Italy. He spent several years in Rome and had charge of the household of the Cardinal of Niceno. Nevertheless, he still found time for study, and when the bishopric of Sipontino became vacant the Pope gave it to him. Then, when he had established a suitable household for himself, he found posts for his father and all his brothers. He translated several works of St. Basil, *De Odio et Invidia,* Plutarch's

De fortuna populi Romani et Virtute Alexandri, and others. He wrote a book on the rules of verse, and a grammar for the use of Latin students. Last, he wrote a great and intricate work on all the Latin and Greek authors which, though he called it the *Commento di Marziale,* is really an alphabetical list of all Latin writers, and much longer than the ten books of Livy, a work which he was able to complete without grammar or vocabulary so great was his knowledge of Latin. He wrote it at the request of the Duke of Urbino, who afterwards preserved him from disaster.

Up to the time of Pope Sixtus, Nicolò was very prosperous, and was nominated to several state offices, but this Pope at once began to persecute him; to lay hands on him, to rob him of all he had and even worse. And if the Duke of Urbino had not remembered him favorably and had not come to his rescue—like a protector of all men of merit—he would have fared badly. As it was Nicolò was only saved because the Duke had a strong hold over the Pope. Nicolò was in no respect culpable, he was only attacked through envy and jealousy. He lost heavily through this molestation and, finding himself debarred from all enjoyment of the fruit of his labor, he fell ill of grief and died. He left a number of writings which are not mentioned here.

D.   THE COURTIER

One of the most famous works of the Renaissance was *The Book of the Courtier* by Baldassare Castiglione (1478–1529). Written in 1508, the book reports conversations held in the court of the Duke of Urbino. Castiglione was himself a diplomat and courtier, and the following selections from his work indicate the ideal of the early sixteenth century.[16]

". . . I would that this evening's game might be, that we select some one of the company and give him the task of portraying a perfect Courtier, explaining all the conditions and special qualities requisite in one who deserves this title; and as to those things that shall not appear sound, let everyone be allowed to contradict as in the schools of the philosophers it is allowed to contradict anyone who proposes a thesis. . . ."

"I wish, then, that this Courtier of ours should be nobly born and of gentle race; because it is far less unseemly for one of ignoble birth to fail in worthy deeds, than for one of noble birth, who, if he strays from the path of his predecessors, stains his family name, and not only fails to achieve but loses what has been achieved already; for noble birth is like a bright lamp that manifests and makes visible good and evil deeds, and kindles and stimulates to virtue both by fear of shame and by hope of praise. And since this splendor of nobility does not illumine the deeds

of the humbly born, they lack that stimulus and fear of shame, nor do they feel any obligation to advance beyond what their predecessors have done; while to the nobly born it seems a reproach not to reach at least the goal set them by their ancestors. . . ."

"It is true that, by favor of the stars or of nature, some men are endowed at birth with such graces that they seem not to have been born, but rather as if some god had formed them with his very hands and adorned them with every excellence of mind and body. So too there are many men so foolish and rude that one cannot but think that nature brought them into the world out of contempt or mockery. Just as these can usually accomplish little even with constant diligence and good training, so with slight pains those others reach the highest summit of excellence. And to give you an instance: you see my lord Don Ippolito d'Este, Cardinal of Ferrara, who has enjoyed such fortune from his birth, that his person, his aspect, his words, and all his movements are so disposed and imbued with this grace, that—although he is young—he exhibits among the most aged prelates such weight of character that he seems fitter to teach than to be taught; likewise in conversation with men and women of every rank, in games, in pleasantry and in banter, he has a certain sweetness and manners so gracious, that whoso speaks with him or even sees him, must needs remain attached to him forever.

"But to return to our subject: I say that there is a middle state between perfect grace on the one hand and senseless folly on the other; and those who are not thus perfectly endowed by nature, with study and toil can in great part polish and amend their natural defects. Besides his noble birth, then, I would have the Courtier favored in this regard also, and endowed by nature not only with talent and beauty of person and feature, but with a certain grace and (as we say) air that shall make him at first sight pleasing and agreeable to all who see him; and I would have this an ornament that should dispose and unite all his actions, and in his outward aspect give promise of whatever is worthy the society and favor of every great lord."

Here, without waiting longer, my lord Gaspar Pallavicino said:

"In order that our game may have the form prescribed, and that we may not seem to slight the privilege given us to contradict, I say that this nobility of birth does not appear to me so essential in the Courtier; and if I thought I were saying what was new to any of us, I should cite instances of many men born of the noblest blood who have been full of vices; and on the other hand, of many men among the humbly born who by their virtue have made their posterity illustrious. And if what you just said be true, namely that there is in everything this occult influence of the original seed, then we should all be in the same case, because we had the same origin, nor would any man be more noble than another. But as to our differences and grades of eminence and obscurity, I believe there are many other causes: among which I rate fortune to be chief; for we see her holding sway in all mundane affairs, often amusing herself by lifting to heaven whom she pleases (although wholly without merit), and burying in the depths those most worthy to be exalted.

"I quite agree with what you say as to the good fortune of those endowed from birth with advantages of mind and body: but this is seen as well among the humbly born, since nature has no such subtle distinctions as these; and often, as I said, the highest gifts of nature are found among the most obscure. Therefore. since this

nobility of birth is won neither by talent nor by strength nor by craft, and is rather the merit of our predecessors than our own, it seems to me too extravagant to maintain that if our Courtier's parents be humbly born, all his good qualities are spoiled, and that all those other qualifications that you mentioned do not avail to raise him to the summit of perfection; I mean talent, beauty of feature, comeliness of person, and that grace which makes him always charming to everyone at first sight. . . ."

"But to come to some details, I am of opinion that the principal and true profession of the Courtier ought to be that of arms; which I would have him follow actively above all else, and be known among others as bold and strong, and loyal to whomsoever he serves. And he will win a reputation for these good qualities by exercising them at all times and in all places, since one may never fail in this without severest censure. And just as among women, their fair fame once sullied never recovers its first luster, so the reputation of a gentleman who bears arms, if once it be in the least tarnished with cowardice or other disgrace, remains forever infamous before the world and full of ignominy. Therefore the more our Courtier excels in this art, the more he will be worthy of praise; and yet I do not deem essential in him that perfect knowledge of things and those other qualities that befit a commander; since this would be too wide a sea, let us be content, as we have said, with perfect loyalty and unconquered courage, and that he be always seen to possess them. . . .

"Not that we would have him look so fierce, or go about blustering, or say that he has taken his cuirass to wife, or threaten with those grim scowls that we have often seen in Berto; because to such men as this, one might justly say that which a brave lady jestingly said in gentle company to one whom I will not name at present; who, being invited by her out of compliment to dance, refused not only that, but to listen to the music, and many other entertainments proposed to him,—saying always that such silly trifles were not his business; so that at last the lady said, 'What is your business, then?' He replied with a sour look, 'To fight.' Then the lady at once said, 'Now that you are in no war and out of fighting trim, I should think it were a good thing to have yourself well oiled, and to stow yourself with all your battle harness in a closet until you be needed, lest you grow more rusty than you are'; and so, amid much laughter from the bystanders, she left the discomfited fellow to his silly presumption.

"Therefore let the man we are seeking be very bold, stern, and always among the first, where the enemy are to be seen; and in every other place, gentle, modest, reserved, above all things avoiding ostentation and that impudent self-praise by which men ever excite hatred and disgust in all who hear them."

Then my lord Gaspar replied:

"As for me, I have known few men excellent in anything whatever, who do not praise themselves; and it seems to me that this may well be permitted them; for when anyone who feels himself to be of worth, sees that he is not known to the ignorant by his works, he is offended that his worth should lie buried, and needs must in some way hold it up to view, in order that he may not be cheated of the fame that is the true reward of worthy effort. Thus among the ancient authors, whoever carries weight seldom fails to praise himself. They indeed are insufferable who do this without desert, but such we do not presume our Courtier to be."

The Count then said:

"If you heard what I said, it was impudent and indiscriminate self-praise that I censured: and as you say, we surely ought not to form a bad opinion of a brave man who praises himself modestly, nay we ought rather to regard such praise as better evidence than if it came from the mouth of others. I say, however, that he, who in praising himself runs into no error and incurs no annoyance or envy at the hands of those that hear him, is a very discreet man indeed and merits praise from others in addition to that which he bestows upon himself; because it is a very difficult matter."

Then my lord Gaspar said:

"You must teach us that."

The Count replied:

"Among the ancient authors there is no lack of those who have taught it; but to my thinking, the whole art consists in saying things in such a way that they shall not seem to be said to that end, but let fall so naturally that it was impossible not to say them, and while seeming always to avoid self-praise, yet to achieve it; but not after the manner of those boasters, who open their mouths and let the words come forth haphazard. Like one of our friends a few days ago, who, being quite run through the thigh with a spear at Pisa, said he thought it was a fly that had stung him; and another man said he kept no mirror in his room because, when angry, he became so terrible to look at, that the sight of himself would have frightened him too much."

Everyone laughed at this, but messer Cesare Gonzaga added:

"Why do you laugh? Do you not know that Alexander the Great, on hearing the opinion of a philosopher to be that there was an infinite number of worlds, began to weep, and being asked why he wept, replied, 'Because I have not yet conquered one of them'; as if he would fain have vanquished all? Does not this seem to you a greater boast than that about the fly-sting?"

Then the Count said:

"Yes, and Alexander was a greater man than he who made the other speech. But extraordinary men are surely to be pardoned when they assume much; for he who has great things to do must needs have daring to do them, and confidence in himself, and must not be abject or mean in spirit, yet very modest in speech, showing less confidence in himself than he has, lest his self-confidence lead to rashness."

The Count now paused a little, and messer Bernardo Bibbiena said, laughing:

"I remember what you said earlier, that this Courtier of ours must be endowed by nature with beauty of countenance and person, and with a grace that shall make him so agreeable. Grace and beauty of countenance I think I certainly possess, and this is the reason why so many ladies are ardently in love with me, as you know; but I am rather doubtful as to the beauty of my person, especially as regards these legs of mine, which seem to me decidedly less well proportioned than I should wish: as to my bust and other members however, I am quite content. Pray, now, describe a little more in particular the sort of body that the Courtier is to have, so that I may dismiss this doubt and set my mind at rest."

After some laughter at this, the Count continued:

"Of a certainty that grace of countenance can be truly said to be yours, nor need I cite further example than this to show what manner of thing it is, for we unquestioningly perceive your aspect to be most agreeable and pleasing to everyone, albeit the lineaments of it are not very delicate. Still it is of a manly cast and at the same time full of grace; and this characteristic is to be found in many different types of countenance. And of such sort I would have our Courtier's aspect; not so soft and effeminate as is sought by many, who not only curl their hair and pluck their brows, but gloss their faces with all those arts employed by the most wanton and unchaste women in the world; and in their walk, posture and every act, they seem so limp and languid that their limbs are like to fall apart; and they pronounce their words so mournfully that they appear about to expire upon the spot: and the more they find themselves with men of rank, the more they affect such tricks. Since nature has not made them women, as they seem to wish to appear and be, they should be treated not as good women but as public harlots, and driven not merely from the courts of great lords but from the society of honest men.

"Then coming to the bodily frame, I say it is enough if this be neither extremely short nor tall, for both of these conditions excite a certain contemptuous surprise, and men of either sort are gazed upon in much the same way that we gaze on monsters. Yet if we must offend in one of the two extremes, it is preferable to fall a little short of the just measure of height than to exceed it, for besides often being dull of intellect, men thus huge of body are also unfit for every exercise of agility, which thing I should much wish in the Courtier. And so would I have him well built and shapely of limb, and would have him show strength and lightness and suppleness, and know all bodily exercises that befit a man of war: whereof I think the first should be to handle every sort of weapon well on foot and on horse, to understand the advantages of each, and especially to be familiar with those weapons that are ordinarily used among gentlemen; for besides the use of them in war, where such subtlety in contrivance is perhaps not needful, there frequently arise differences between one gentleman and another, which afterwards result in duels often fought with such weapons as happen at the moment to be within reach: thus knowledge of this kind is a very safe thing. Nor am I one of those who say that skill is forgotten in the hour of need; for he whose skill forsakes him at such a time, indeed gives token that he has already lost heart and head through fear.

"Moreover I deem it very important to know how to wrestle, for it is a great help in the use of all kinds of weapons on foot. Then, both for his own sake and for that of his friends, he must understand the quarrels and differences that may arise, and must be quick to seize an advantage, always showing courage and prudence in all things. Nor should he be too ready to fight except when honor demands it; for besides the great danger that the uncertainty of fate entails, he who rushes into such affairs recklessly and without urgent cause, merits the severest censure even though he be successful. But when he finds himself so far engaged that he cannot withdraw without reproach, he ought to be most deliberate, both in the preliminaries to the duel and in the duel itself, and always show readiness and daring. . . .

"Even in time of peace weapons are often used in various exercises, and gentlemen appear in public shows before the people and ladies and great lords. For this reason I would have our Courtier a perfect horseman in every kind of seat; and besides understanding horses and what pertains to riding, I would have him use all possible care and diligence to lift himself a little beyond the rest in everything, so that he may be ever recognized as eminent above all others.

And as we read of Alcibiades that he surpassed all the nations with whom he lived, each in their particular province, so I would have this Courtier of ours excel all others, and each in that which is most their profession. And as it is the especial pride of the Italians to ride well with the rein, to govern wild horses with consummate skill, and to play at tilting and jousting,—in these things let him be among the best of the Italians. In tourneys and in the arts of defence and attack, let him shine among the best in France. In stick-throwing, bull-fighting, and in casting spears and darts, let him excel among the Spaniards. But above everything he should temper all his movements with a certain good judgment and grace, if he wishes to merit that universal favor which is so greatly prized.

"There are also many other exercises, which although not immediately dependent upon arms, yet are closely connected therewith, and greatly foster manly sturdiness; and one of the chief among these seems to me to be the chase, because it bears a certain likeness to war: and truly it is an amusement for great lords and befitting a man at court, and furthermore it is seen to have been much cultivated among the ancients. It is fitting also to know how to swim, to leap, to run, to throw stones, for besides the use that may be made of this in war, a man often has occasion to show what he can do in such matters; whence good esteem is to be won, especially with the multitude, who must be taken into account withal. Another admirable exercise, and one very befitting a man at court, is the game of tennis, in which are well shown the disposition of the body, the quickness and suppleness of every member, and all those qualities that are seen in nearly every other exercise. Nor less highly do I esteem vaulting on horse, which although it be fatiguing and difficult, makes a man very light and dexterous more than any other thing; and besides its utility, if this lightness is accompanied by grace, it is to my thinking a finer show than any of the others.

"Our Courtier having once become more than fairly expert in these exercises, I think he should leave the others on one side: such as turning somersaults, rope-walking, and the like, which savor of the mountebank and little befit a gentleman.

"But since one cannot devote himself to such fatiguing exercises continually, and since repetition becomes very tiresome and abates the admiration felt for what is rare, we must always diversify our life with various occupations. For this reason I would have our Courtier sometimes descend to quieter and more tranquil exercises, and in order to escape envy and to entertain himself agreeably with everyone, let him do whatever others do, yet never departing from praiseworthy deeds, and governing himself with that good judgment which will keep him from all folly; but let him laugh, jest, banter, frolic, and dance, yet in such fashion that he shall always appear genial and discreet, and that everything he may do or say shall be stamped with grace. . . ."

"I would have him more than passably accomplished in letters, at least in those studies that are called the humanities, and conversant not only with the Latin language but with the Greek, for the sake of the many different things that have been admirably written therein. Let him be well versed in the poets, and not less in the orators and historians, and also proficient in writing verse and prose, especially in this vulgar tongue of ours; for besides the enjoyment he will find in it, he will by this means never lack agreeable entertainment with ladies, who are usually fond of such things. And if other occupations or want of study prevent his reaching such perfection as to render his writings worthy of great praise, let him be careful to suppress them so that others may not laugh at him, and let him show them only to a friend whom he can trust: because they will at least be of this service to him, that the exercise will enable him to judge the work of others. For it very rarely happens that a man who is not accustomed to write, however learned he may be, can ever quite appreciate the toil and industry of writers, or taste the sweetness and excellence of style, and those latent niceties that are often found in the ancients.

"Moreover these studies will also make him fluent, and as Aristippus said to the tyrant, confident and assured in speaking with everyone. . . ."

"My lords, you must know that I am not content with the Courtier unless he be also a musician and unless, besides understanding and being able to read notes, he can play upon divers instruments. For if we consider rightly, there is to be found no rest from toil or medicine for the troubled spirit more becoming and praiseworthy in time of leisure, than this; and especially in courts, where besides the relief from tedium that music affords us all, many things are done to please the ladies, whose tender and gentle spirit is easily penetrated by harmony and filled with sweetness. Thus it is no marvel that in both ancient and modern times they have always been inclined to favor musicians, and have found refreshing spiritual food in music. . . ."

". . . I wish to discuss another matter, which I deem of great importance and therefore think our Courtier ought by no means to omit: and this is to know how to draw and to have acquaintance with the very art of painting.

"And do not marvel that I desire this art, which today may seem to savor of the artisan and little to befit a gentleman; for I remember having read that the ancients, especially throughout Greece, had their boys of gentle birth study painting in school as an honorable and necessary thing, and it was admitted to the first rank of the liberal arts; while by public edict they forbade that it be taught to slaves. Among the Romans too, it was held in highest honor, and the very noble family of the Fabii took their name from it; for the first Fabius was given the name *Pictor,* because,—being indeed a most excellent painter, and so devoted to painting that when he painted the walls of the temple of Health,—he inscribed his own name thereon; for although he was born of a family thus renowned and honored with so many consular titles, triumphs and other dignities, and although he was a man of letters and learned in the law, and numbered among the orators,—yet he thought to add splendor and ornament to his fame by leaving a memorial that he had been a painter. Nor is there lack of many other men of illustrious family, celebrated in this art; which besides being very noble and worthy in itself, is of great utility, and especially in war for drawing places, sites, rivers, bridges, rocks, fortresses, and the like; since however well we may keep them in memory (which is very difficult), we cannot show them to others.

"And truly he who does not esteem this art, seems to me very unreasonable; for this universal fabric that we see,—with the vast heaven so richly adorned with shining stars, and in the midst the earth girdled by the seas, varied with mountains, valleys and rivers, and bedecked with so many divers trees, beautiful flowers and grasses, —may be said to be a great and noble picture, composed by the hand of nature and of God; and whoever is able to imitate it, seems to me deserving of great praise: nor can it be imitated without knowledge of many things, as he knows well who tries. Hence the ancients greatly prized both the art and the artist, which thus attained the summit of highest excellence; very sure proof of which may be found in the antique marble and bronze statues that yet are seen. And although painting is different from sculpture, both the one and the other spring from the same source, which is good design. Therefore, as the statues are divine, so we may believe the pictures were also; the more indeed because they are susceptible of greater skill."

V

The New Monarchy

T HE motive of domination became a reigning force in Europe; for it was an idea which monarchy would not willingly let fall after it had received a religious and an international consideration. For centuries it was constantly asserted as a claim of necessity and of right. It was the supreme manifestation of the modern state according to the image which Machiavelli had set up, the state that suffers neither limit nor equality, and is bound by no duty to nations or to men, that thrives on destruction and sanctifies whatever things contributed to increase of power.

LORD ACTON

CONTENTS

QUESTIONS FOR STUDY

PART I

1. Why did Machiavelli write *The Prince?* For what audience did he design it?

2. What assumptions did Machiavelli make about the nature of man and human history? How did these assumptions affect his recommendations to a prince?

3. What policies did Machiavelli recommend for a ruler?

4. What kinds of argument did he employ to justify his policies?

5. In the Machiavellian state, what were the rights and liberties of the subject?

6. What system of international politics would ensue if Machiavelli's policies were followed by all princes?

7. What similarities, either in approach or method, do you find between Bodin and Machiavelli?

PART II

8. What is Luther's attitude toward temporal power? What factors in German history and German conditions in Luther's time helped to shape his ideas on church and state?

9. Is there any difference between the attitudes of Luther and Calvin on civil government?

10. In what sense did Knox extend the arguments of Calvin concerning civil government to their logical conclusion? What would the Papacy have said of Knox's arguments?

11. What, according to Knox, is the source of "right knowledge"?

12. In what different ways did the rulers of France, England, and Spain attempt to solve the relation of church and state? Why did they differ?

13. What common assumption underlies all the solutions?

14. How do these religious settlements implement Bodin's ideas on the state?

The medieval world lived under the dominance of a single unifying ideal. From the ninth through the fifteenth centuries Western Europeans subscribed with remarkable accord to the well-articulated concept of a *Respublica Christiana*, a universal society ruled by God's will through His chosen instrument, the Church, and its secular arm, the civil state. Based upon the assumption that the purpose of life in this world is salvation in the next, the medieval ideal pictured the Church as the interpreter of the divine law, and the kings and princes as its executioners. The ever-present hand of God assured the harmonious operation of His plan for the government of men over all the earth.

Within the narrow limits of the West, the *Respublica Christiana* approached realization about as closely as do most such politico-religious ideals. In a predominantly agrarian society, strikingly uniform in its major aspects, all men were of the same faith, and the secular rulers regularly gave lip service to the doctrine that support and maintenance of the Church Universal was their highest function. But harmony and homogeneity were unattainable. Feudal government was primarily local in character, and central authority was weak. Provincial necessities and practical considerations often overrode universal spiritual ideals. Furthermore, the Church was more than the repository of the Faith; it was also a human institution, embodied in a clerical hierarchy, descending from pope to priest, which possessed wealth, power, and a claim to the loyalty of every individual. The interests of the clerical hierarchy often conflicted with those of civil rulers. Hence it was that throughout the Middle Ages pope and bishop contended unceasingly with king and emperor for temporal sway and earthly riches as well as for the maintenance of faith and dogma. As long, however, as Western society remained primarily agrarian and Western government remained decentralized, there were no forces strong enough to challenge the ascendancy or disrupt the unity of the Church Universal, and the ideal of the *Respublica Christiana* retained its grip upon the minds of men.

Alterations in the economic and political structure of Europe produced a new situation. By the end of the fifteenth century the high development of commerce and industry, after more than five centuries of slow revival, had established the preponderance of urban over rural life. In the process the intrinsic character of society was changed. The great majority of bondsmen gradually acquired free status, and the rising middle class came to challenge the landed nobility as the dominant social element. Economic revival opened up new sources of fluid wealth and created large accumulations of capital, which made possible greater concentrations of power. Ambitious princes, ever eager to extend the area of their control, were thereby enabled to increase their strength at the expense either of their overlords or their underlings.

At the opening of the sixteenth century, therefore, the political structure of Europe had evolved from a congeries of petty lordships, nominally under the control of greater suzerains, to a collection of independent states ruled by vigorous sovereigns, the so-called "New Monarchs," who willingly accepted no limitations upon their power. The kings of France, England, and Spain had, by subjecting all forces within their realms to the royal authority, created large political units with extensive economic resources. In Italy and Germany, where central government had broken down, there existed numerous smaller states, each centered upon the domains of a territorial princeling, lay or ecclesiastical, or upon the wealth and influence of a commercial city. Whether or not they owed allegiance to a higher authority, as did the German magnates to the Holy Roman Emperor, the rulers of these lesser realms formulated and executed their policies with a practical independence comparable to that of the greater sovereigns.

Upon this scene burst the Protestant Reformation. It was a product of historical forces long in operation. Wealth, ease, and internal dissension had corrupted the clerical hierarchy of the Church to the disgust of the pious. The development of the new urban culture, customarily termed the Renaissance, was secular in character, infused with a worldly and individualistic spirit antipathetic to the asceticism and formalism of medieval faith. When in 1517 Martin Luther broke out into open revolt against Catholic dogma, therefore, he found immediate and widespread support in Northern Europe. Within a few years Zwingli at Zurich and Calvin at Geneva also developed new doctrines which penetrated into all the lands of the West. The unity of the Church Universal had been irrevocably destroyed.

With the appearance of the sovereign state and the Protestant Reformation, there ceased to exist the political and religious conditions amid which the ideal of the *Respublica Christiana* had flourished. The old concept lost any application to reality, and statesmen were driven inevitably to seek new ones that offered solutions to the practical problems of their age. How was the "New Monarch" to cope with a world wherein competing states threatened the existence of his own, rivals menaced his power within the realm, and contending religions rent the loyalty of his subjects? Many men gave searching thought to these questions, and some brought forth spectacular answers which, in the nature of their recommendations, typified the thought and action of the period. The purpose of this Problem is to examine the ideology of the "New Monarchy" as seen in the writings of some of its greatest proponents.

In Part I the student encounters two different kinds of political thinkers. The first, Niccolo Machiavelli (1469–1527), was a clear-minded realist who had served as secretary to the governing body of the Florentine Republic during the early years of the French invasions when Italy was the "cockpit of Europe." Trained in the hard school of diplomacy, Machiavelli made his classic work, *The Prince,* not a theoretical treatise but a practical handbook for the guidance of an Italian ruler. On the other hand, Jean Bodin (1530–1596) was a French lawyer with scholarly tastes and a keen interest in the juridical aspects of the state. His *Six Books Concerning the State* was an endeavor to work out a comprehensive political system at the highest level of theory. The works of Machiavelli and Bodin complement each other and make clear the main trends of sixteenth-century political thought.

Part II deals with the problems of church and state created by the Protestant Reformation. In the first section the reformers themselves, Luther, Calvin, and Knox, reveal their attitude to the relationship between the pious subject and his ruler. The second section contains the religious settlements imposed upon their subjects by three of the "New Monarchs."

The whole problem should be approached not only as an examination of the nature of sixteenth-century statecraft but also as a study in the historical origins of the issues facing the modern state. For it may truly be said of all these documents, as was said of Machiavelli's alone, that their authentic interpretator is "the whole of later history."

Part I.   THE SECULAR THEORY OF THE STATE

A.   THE PRINCE

The Prince was the product of Machiavelli's exile from Florence and public service. For almost twenty years, from 1494 to 1512, he had been busy as a diplomat in the service of the Republic. The return of the Medici in 1512 meant exile from his native city, and as time showed, an end to his public employment. The first product of this new leisure was the essay, *The Prince,* which was not published until after his death. Its purpose is made clear with only a modicum of polite restraint in the first section quoted below. The first eleven chapters of the work describe the various kinds of principalities as Machiavelli distinguishes them—civil, religious, hereditary, those acquired by arms or ability or good fortune, and those acquired by wickedness. Then follow three chapters on the armed forces and the act of war as far as they concern the prince. Chapters XV–XXIII provide a detailed analysis of the conduct proper to a prince. The last three concern primarily contemporary Italy and Machiavelli's solutions for its troubles.[1]

(*Preface*) Niccolo Machiavelli to the Magnificent Lorenzo di Piero de' Medici: Those who strive to obtain the good graces of a prince are accustomed to come before him with such things as they hold most precious, or in which they see him take most delight: whence one often sees horses, arms, cloth of gold, precious stones, and similar ornaments presented to princes, worthy of their greatness.

Desiring therefore to present myself to your Magnificence with some testimony of my devotion towards you, I have not found among my possessions anything which I hold more dear than, or value so much as, the knowledge of the actions of great men, acquired by long experience in contemporary affairs, and a continual study of antiquity; which, having reflected upon it with great and prolonged diligence, I now send, digested into a little volume, to your Magnificence. . . .

Seventh Chapter. Concerning New Principalities which are Acquired Either by The Arms of Others or by Good Fortune: Those who solely by good fortune become princes from being private citizens have little trouble in rising, but much in keeping atop; they have not any difficulties on the way up, because they fly, but they have many when they reach the summit. Such are those to whom some state is given either for money or by the favor of him who bestows it; as happened to many in Greece, in the cities of Ionia and of the Hellespont, where princes were made by Darius, in order that they might hold the cities both for his security and his glory; as also were those emperors who, by the cor-

ruption of the soldiers, from being citizens came to empire. Such stand simply upon the goodwill and the fortune of him who has elevated them—two most inconstant and unstable things. Neither have they the knowledge requisite for the position; because, unless they are men of great worth and ability, it is not reasonable to expect that they should know how to command, having always lived in a private condition; besides, they cannot hold it because they have not forces which they can keep friendly and faithful.

States that rise unexpectedly, then, like all other things in nature which are born and grow rapidly, cannot have their foundations and correspondencies fixed in such a way that the first storm will not overthrow them; unless, as is said, those who unexpectedly become princes are men of so much ability that they know they have to be prepared at once to hold that which fortune has thrown into their laps, and that those foundations, which others have laid *before* they became princes, they must lay *afterwards.*

Concerning these two methods of rising to be a prince by ability or fortune, I wish to adduce two examples within our own recollection, and these are Francesco Sforza and Cesare Borgia. Francesco, by proper means and with great ability, from being a private person rose to be Duke of Milan, and that which he had acquired with a thousand anxieties he kept with little trouble. On the other hand, Cesare Borgia, called by the people Duke Valentino, acquired his state during the ascendency of his father, and on its decline he lost it, notwithstanding that he had taken every measure and done all that ought to be done by a wise and able man to fix firmly his roots in the states which the arms and fortunes of others had bestowed on him.

Because, as is stated above, he who has not first laid his foundations may be able with great ability to lay them afterwards, but they will be laid with trouble to the architect and danger to the building. If, therefore, all the steps taken by the duke be considered, it will be seen that he laid solid foundations for his future power, and I do not consider it superfluous to discuss them, because I do not know what better precepts to give a new prince than the example of his actions; and if his dispositions were of no avail, that was not his fault, but the extraordinary and extreme malignity of fortune.

Alexander the Sixth, in wishing to aggrandize the duke, his son, had many immediate and prospective difficulties. Firstly, he did not see his way to make him master of any state that was not a state of the Church; and if he was willing to rob the Church he knew that the Duke of Milan and the Venetians would not consent, because Faenza and Rimini were already under the protection of the Venetians. Besides this, he saw the arms of Italy, especially those by which he might have been assisted, in hands that would fear the aggrandizement of the Pope, namely, the Orsini and the Colonnesi and their following. It behooved him, therefore, to upset this state of affairs and embroil the powers, so as to make himself securely master of part of their states. This was easy for him to do, because he found the Venetians, moved by other reasons, inclined to bring back the French into Italy; he would not only not oppose this, but he would render it more easy by dissolving the former marriage of King Louis. Therefore the king came into Italy with the assistance of the Venetians and the consent of Alexander. He was no sooner in Milan than the Pope had soldiers from him for the attempt on the Romagna, which yielded to him on the reputation of the king. The duke, therefore, having acquired the Romagna and beaten the Colonnesi, while wishing to hold that and to advance further, was hindered by two things: the one, his forces did not appear loyal to him, the other, the goodwill of France: that is to say, he feared that the forces of the Orsini, which he was using, would not stand to him, that not only might they hinder him from winning more, but might themselves seize what he had won, and that the king might also do the same. Of the Orsini he had a warning when, after taking Faenza and attacking Bologna, he saw them go very unwillingly to that attack. And as to the king, he learned his mind when he himself, after taking the Duchy of Urbino, attacked Tuscany, and the king made him desist from that under-

taking; hence the duke decided to depend no more upon the arms and the luck of others.

For the first thing he weakened the Orsini and Colonnesi parties in Rome, by gaining to himself all their adherents who were gentlemen, making them his gentlemen, giving them good pay, and, according to their rank, honoring them with office and command in such a way that in a few months all attachment to the factions was destroyed and turned entirely to the duke. After this he awaited an opportunity to crush the Orsini, having scattered the adherents of the Colonna house. This came to him soon and he used it well; for the Orsini, perceiving at length that the aggrandizement of the duke and the Church was ruin to them, called a meeting at Magione in Perugia. From this sprung the rebellion at Urbino and the tumults in the Romagna, with endless dangers to the duke, all of which he overcame with the help of the French. Having restored his authority, not to leave it at risk by trusting either to the French or other outside forces, he had recourse to his wiles, and he knew so well how to conceal his mind that, by the mediation of Signor Pagolo—whom the duke did not fail to secure with all kinds of attentions, giving him money, apparel, and horses— the Orsini were reconciled, so that their simplicity brought them into his power at Sinigalia. Having exterminated the leaders, and turned their partisans into his friends, the duke had laid sufficiently good foundations to his power, having all the Romagna and the Duchy of Urbino; and the people now beginning to appreciate their prosperity, he gained them all over to himself. And as this point is worthy of notice, and to be imitated by others, I am not willing to leave it out.

When the duke occupied the Romagna he found it under the rule of weak masters, who rather plundered their subjects than ruled them, and gave them more cause for disunion than for union, so that the country was full of robbery, quarrels, and every kind of violence; and so, wishing to bring back peace and obedience to authority, he considered it necessary to give it a good governor. Thereupon he promoted Messer Ramiro d'Orco, a swift and cruel man, to whom he gave the fullest power. This man in a short time restored peace and unity with the greatest success. Afterwards the duke considered that it was not advisable to confer such excessive authority, for he had no doubt but that it would become odious, so he set up a court of judgment in the country, under a most excellent president, wherein all cities had their advocates. And because he knew that the past severity had caused some hatred against himself, so, to clear himself in the minds of the people, and gain them entirely to himself, he desired to show that, if any cruelty had been practised, it had not originated with him, but in the natural sternness of the minister. Under this pretence he took Ramiro, and one morning caused him to be executed and left on the piazza at Cesena with the block and a bloody knife at his side. The barbarity of this spectacle caused the people to be at once satisfied and dismayed.

But let us return whence we started. I say that the duke, finding himself now sufficiently powerful and partly secured from immediate dangers by having armed himself in his own way, and having in a great measure crushed those forces in his vicinity that could injure him if he wished to proceed with his conquest, had next to consider France, for he knew that the king, who too late was aware of his mistake, would not support him. And from this time he began to seek new alliances and to temporize with France in the expedition which she was making towards the kingdom of Naples against the Spaniards who were besieging Gaeta. It was his intention to secure himself against them, and this he would have quickly accomplished had Alexander lived.

Such was his line of action as to present affairs. But as to the future he had to fear, in the first place, that a new successor to the Church might not be friendly to him and might seek to take from him that which Alexander had given him, so he decided to act in four ways. Firstly, by exterminating the families of those lords whom he had despoiled, so as to take away that pretext from the Pope. Secondly, by winning to himself all the gentlemen of Rome, so as to be able to curb the Pope with their aid, as has been observed. Thirdly, by converting the college [of Cardinals] more to himself. Fourthly, by acquiring so much power before the Pope should die that he could by his own measures resist the first shock. Of these four things, at the death of Alexander, he had accomplished three. For he had killed as many of the dispossessed lords as he could lay hands on, and few had escaped; he had won over the Roman gentlemen, and he had the most numerous party in the college. And as to any fresh acquisition, he intended to become master of Tuscany, for he already possessed Perugia and Piombino, and Pisa was under his protection. And as he had no longer to study France (for the French were already driven out of the kingdom of Naples by the Spaniards, and in this way both were compelled to buy his goodwill), he pounced down upon Pisa. After this, Lucca and Siena yielded at once, partly through hatred and partly through fear of the Florentines; and the Florentines would have had no remedy had he continued to prosper, as he was prospering the year that Alexander died, for he had acquired so

much power and reputation that he would have stood by himself, and no longer have depended on the luck and forces of others, but solely on his own power and ability.

But Alexander died five years after he had first drawn the sword. He left the duke with the state of Romagna alone consolidated, with the rest in the air, between two most powerful hostile armies, and sick unto death. Yet there were in the duke such boldness and ability, and he knew so well how men are to be won or lost, and so firm were the foundations which in so short a time he had laid, that if he had not had those armies on his back, or if he had been in good health, he would have overcome all difficulties. And it is seen that his foundations were good, for the Romagna awaited him for more than a month. In Rome, although but half alive, he remained secure; and whilst the Baglioni, the Vitelli, and the Orsini might come to Rome, they could not effect anything against him. If he could not have made Pope him whom he wished, at least the one whom he did not wish would not have been elected. But if he had been in sound health at the death of Alexander, everything would have been easy to him. On the day that Julius the Second was elected, he told me that he had thought of everything that might occur at the death of his father, and had provided a remedy for all, except that he had never anticipated that, when the death did happen, he himself would be on the point to die.

When all the actions of the duke are recalled, I do not know how to blame him, but rather it appears to me, as I have said, that I ought to offer him for imitation to all those who, by the fortune or the arms of others, are raised to government. Because he, having a lofty spirit and far-reaching aims, could not have regulated his conduct otherwise, and only the shortness of the life of Alexander and his own sickness frustrated his designs. Therefore, he who considers it necessary to secure himself in his new principality, to win friends, to overcome either by force or fraud, to make himself beloved and feared by the people, to be followed and revered by the soldiers, to exterminate those who had power or reason to hurt him, to change the old order of things for new, to be severe and gracious, magnanimous and liberal, to destroy a disloyal soldiery and to create new, to maintain friendship with kings and princes in such a way that they must help him with zeal and offend with caution, cannot find a more lively example than the actions of this man.

Only can he be blamed for the election of Julius the Second, in whom he made a bad choice, because, as is said, not being able to elect a Pope to his own mind, he could have hindered any other from being elected Pope; and he ought never to have consented to the election of any cardinal whom he had injured or who had cause to fear him if they became pontiffs. For men injure either from fear or hatred. Those whom he had injured, amongst others, were San Pietro ad Vincula, Colonna, San Giorgio, and Ascanio. The rest, in becoming Pope, had to fear him, Rouen and the Spaniards excepted; the latter from their relationship and obligations, the former from his influence, the kingdom of France having relations with him. Therefore, above everything, the duke ought to have created a Spaniard Pope, and, failing him, he ought to have consented to Rouen and not San Pietro ad Vincula. He who believes that new benefits will cause great personages to forget old injuries is deceived. Therefore, the duke erred in his choice, and it was the cause of his ultimate ruin. . . .

Eleventh Chapter. Concerning Ecclesiastical Principalities: It only remains now to speak of ecclesiastical principalities, touching which all difficulties are prior to getting possession, because they are acquired either by capacity or good fortune, and they can be held without either; for they are sustained by the ancient ordinances of religion, which are so all-powerful, and of such a character that the principalities may be held no matter how their princes behave and live. These princes alone have states and do not defend them, they have subjects and do not rule them; and the states, although unguarded, are not taken from them, and the subjects, although not ruled, do not care, and they have neither the desire nor the ability to alienate themselves. Such principalities only are secure and happy. But being upheld by powers, to which the human mind cannot reach, I shall speak no more of them, because, being exalted and maintained by God, it would be the act of a presumptuous and rash man to discuss them. . . .

Fifteenth Chapter. Concerning Things for Which Men, and Especially Princes, Are Praised or Blamed: It remains now to see what ought to be the rules of conduct for a prince towards subject and friends. And as I know that many have written on this point, I expect I shall be considered presumptuous in mentioning it again, especially as in discussing it I shall depart from the methods of other people. But, it being my intention to write a thing which shall be useful to him who apprehends it, it appears to me more appropriate to follow up the real truth of a matter than the imagination of it; for many have pictured republics and principalities which in fact have never been known or seen, because how one lives is so far distant from how one ought to live, that he who neglects what is done for what ought to be done, sooner effects his ruin than his preservation; for a man who wishes to act entirely up to his professions of virtue soon meets with what destroys him among so much that is evil.

Hence it is necessary for a prince wishing to hold his own to know how to do wrong, and to make use of it or not according to necessity. Therefore, putting on one side imaginary things concerning a prince, and discussing those which are real, I say that all men when they are spoken of, and chiefly princes for being more highly placed, are remarkable for some of those qualities which bring them either blame or praise; and thus it is that one is reputed liberal, another miserly, using a Tuscan term (because an avaricious person in our language is still he who desires to possess by robbery, whilst we call one miserly who deprives himself too much of the use of his own); one is reputed generous, one rapacious; one cruel, one compassionate; one faithless, another faithful; one effeminate and cowardly, another bold and brave; one affable, another haughty; one lascivious, another chaste; one sincere, another cunning; one hard, another easy; one grave, another frivolous; one religious, another unbelieving, and the like. And I know that every one will confess that it would be most praiseworthy in a prince to exhibit all the above qualities that are considered good; but because they can neither be entirely possessed nor observed, for human conditions do not permit it, it is necessary for him to be sufficiently prudent that he may know how to avoid the reproach of those vices which would lose him his state; and also to keep himself, if it be possible, from those which would not lose him it; but this not being possible, he may with less hesitation abandon himself to them. And again, he need not make himself uneasy at incurring a reproach for those vices without which the state can only be saved with difficulty, for if everything is considered carefully, it will be found that something which looks like virtue, if followed, would be his ruin; whilst something else, which looks like vice, yet followed brings him security and prosperity. . . .

Sixteenth Chapter. Concerning Liberality and Meanness: Commencing then with the first of the above-named characteristics, I say that it would be well to be reputed liberal. Nevertheless, liberality exercised in a way that does not bring you the reputation for it, injures you; for if one exercises it honestly and as it should be exercised, it may not become known, and you will not avoid the reproach of its opposite. Therefore, any one wishing to maintain among men the name of liberal is obliged to avoid no attribute of magnificence; so that a prince thus inclined will consume in such acts all his property, and will be compelled in the end, if he wish to maintain the name of liberal, to unduly weigh down his people, and tax them, and do everything he can to get money. This will soon make him odious to his subjects, and becoming poor he will be little valued by any one; thus, with his liberality, having offended many and rewarded few, he is affected by the very first trouble and imperilled by whatever may be the first danger; recognizing this himself, and wishing to draw back from it, he runs at once into the reproach of being miserly.

Therefore, a prince, not being able to exercise this virtue of liberality in such a way that it is recognized, except to his cost, if he is wise he ought not to fear the reputation of being mean, for in time he will come to be more considered than if liberal, seeing that with his economy his revenues are enough, that he can defend himself against all attacks, and is able to engage in enterprises without burdening his people; thus it comes to pass that he exercises liberality towards all from whom he does not take, who are numberless, and meanness towards those to whom he does not give, who are few.

We have not seen great things done in our time except by those who have been considered mean; the rest have failed. Pope Julius the Second was assisted in reaching the papacy by a reputation for liberality, yet he did not strive afterwards to keep it up, when he made war on the King of France; and he made many wars without imposing any extraordinary tax on his subjects; for he supplied his additional expenses out of his long thriftiness. The present King of Spain would not have undertaken or conquered in so many enterprises if he had been reputed liberal. A prince, therefore, provided that he has not to rob his subjects, that he can defend himself, that he does not become poor and abject, that he is not forced to become rapacious, ought to hold of little account a reputation for being mean, for it is one of those vices which will enable him to govern. . . .

Seventeenth Chapter. Concerning Cruelty and Clemency, and Whether it is Better to be Loved than Feared: Coming now to the other qualities mentioned above, I say that every prince ought to desire to be considered clement and not cruel. Nevertheless he ought to take care not to misuse this clemency. Cesare Borgia was considered cruel; notwithstanding, his cruelty reconciled the Romagna, unified it, and restored it to peace and loyalty. And if this be rightly considered, he will be seen to have been much more merciful than the Florentine people, who, to avoid a reputation for cruelty, permitted Pistoia to be destroyed. Therefore a prince, so long as he keeps his subjects united and loyal, ought not to mind the reproach of cruelty; because with a few exam-

ples he will be more merciful than those who, through too much mercy, allow disorders to arise, from which follow murder or robbery; for these are wont to injure the whole people, whilst those executions which originate with a prince offend the individual only.

And of all princes, it is impossible for the new prince to avoid the imputation of cruelty, owing to new states being full of dangers. Hence Virgil, through the mouth of Dido, excuses the inhumanity of her reign owing to its being new, saying: —

Res dura, et regni novitas me talia cogunt
Moliri, et late fines custode tueri.

Nevertheless he ought to be slow to believe and to act, nor should he himself show fear, but proceed in a temperate manner with prudence and humanity, so that too much confidence may not make him incautious and too much distrust render him intolerable.

Upon this a question arises: whether it be better to be loved than feared or feared than loved? It may be answered that one should wish to be both, but, because it is difficult to unite them in one person, it is much safer to be feared than loved, when, of the two, either must be dispensed with. Because this is to be asserted in general of men, that they are ungrateful, fickle, false, cowards, covetous, and as long as you succeed they are yours entirely; they will offer you their blood, property, life, and children, as is said above, when the need is far distant; but when it approaches they turn against you. And that prince who, relying entirely on their promises, has neglected other precautions, is ruined; because friendships that are obtained by payments, and not by greatness or nobility of mind, may indeed be earned, but they are not secured, and in time of need cannot be relied upon; and men have less scruple in offending one who is beloved than one who is feared, for love is preserved by the link of obligation which, owing to the baseness of men, is broken at every opportunity for their advantage; but fear preserves you by a dread of punishment which never fails.

Nevertheless a prince ought to inspire fear in such a way that, if he does not win love, he avoids hatred; because he can endure very well being feared whilst he is not hated, which will always be as long as he abstains from the property of his citizens and subjects and from their women. But when it is necessary for him to proceed against the life of some one, he must do it on proper justification and for manifest cause, but above all things he must keep his hands off the property of others, because men more quickly forget the death of their father than the loss of their patrimony. Besides, pretexts for taking away the property are never wanting; for he who has once begun to live by robbery will always find pretexts for seizing what belongs to others; but reasons for taking life, on the contrary, are more difficult to find and sooner lapse. But when a prince is with his army, and has under control a multitude of soldiers, then it is quite necessary for him to disregard the reputation of cruelty, for without it he would never hold his army united or disposed to its duties. . . .

Eighteenth Chapter. Concerning the Way in Which Princes Should Keep Faith: Every one admits how praiseworthy it is in a prince to keep faith, and to live with integrity and not with craft. Nevertheless our experience has been that those princes who have done great things have held good faith of little account, and have known how to circumvent the intellect of men by craft, and in the end have overcome those who have relied on their word. You must know there are two ways of contesting, the one by the law, the other by force; the first method is proper to men, the second to beasts; but because the first is frequently not sufficient, it is necessary to have recourse to the second. Therefore it is necessary for a prince to understand how to avail himself of the beast and the man. This has been figuratively taught to princes by ancient writers, who describe how Achilles and many other princes of old were given to the Centaur Chiron to nurse, who brought them up in his discipline; which means solely that, as they had for a teacher one who was half beast and half man, so it is necessary for a prince to know how to make use of both natures, and that one without the other is not durable. A prince, therefore, being compelled knowingly to adopt the beast, ought to choose the fox and the lion; because the lion cannot defend himself against snares and the fox cannot defend himself against wolves. Therefore, it is necessary to be a fox to discover the snares and a lion to terrify the wolves. Those who rely simply on the lion do not understand what they are about. Therefore a wise lord cannot, nor ought he to, keep faith when such observance may be turned against him, and when the reasons that caused him to pledge it exist no longer. If men were entirely good this precept would not hold, but because they are bad, and will not keep faith with you, you too are bound not to observe it with them. Nor will there ever be wanting to a prince legitimate reasons to excuse this non-observance. Of this endless modern examples could be given, showing how many treaties and engagements have been made void and of no effect through the faithlessness of princes; and he who has known best how to employ the fox has succeeded best.

But it is necessary to know well how to disguise this characteristic, and to be a great pretender and dissembler; and men are so simple, and so subject to present necessities, that he who seeks to deceive will always find some one who will allow himself to be deceived. One recent example I cannot pass over in silence. Alexander the Sixth did nothing else but deceive men, nor ever thought of doing otherwise, and he always found victims; for there never was a man who had greater power in asserting, or who with greater oaths would affirm a thing, yet would observe it less; nevertheless his deceits always succeeded according to his wishes, because he well understood this side of mankind.

Therefore it is unnecessary for a prince to have all the good qualities I have enumerated, but it is very necessary to appear to have them. And I shall dare to say this also, that to have them and always to observe them is injurious, and that to appear merciful, faithful, humane, religious, upright, and to be so, but with a mind so framed that should you require not to be so, you may be able and know how to change to the opposite.

And you have to understand this, that a prince, especially a new one, cannot observe all those things for which men are esteemed, being often forced, in order to maintain the state, to act contrary to fidelity, friendship, humanity, and religion. Therefore it is necessary for him to have a mind ready to turn itself accordingly as the winds and variations of fortune force it, yet, as I have said above, not to diverge from the good if he can avoid doing so, but, if compelled, then to know how to set about it.

For this reason a prince ought to take care that he never lets anything slip from his lips that is not replete with the above-named five qualities, that he may appear to him who sees and hears him altogether merciful, faithful, humane, upright, and religious. There is nothing more necessary to appear to have than this last quality, inasmuch as men judge generally more by the eye than by the hand, because it belongs to everybody to see you, to few to come in touch with you. Every one sees what you appear to be, few really know what you are, and those few dare not oppose themselves to the opinion of the many, who have the majesty of the state to defend them; and in the actions of all men, and especially of princes, which it is not prudent to challenge, one judges by the result.

For that reason, let a prince have the credit of conquering and holding his state, the means will always be considered honest, and he will be praised by everybody; because the vulgar are always taken by what a thing seems to be and by what comes of it; and in the world there are only the vulgar, for the few find a place there only when the many have no ground to rest on.

One prince of the present time, whom it is not

well to name, never preaches anything else but peace and good faith, and to both he is most hostile, and either, if he had kept it, would have deprived him of reputation and kingdom many a time.

Nineteenth Chapter. That One Should Avoid Being Despised and Hated: Now, concerning the characteristics of which mention is made above, I have spoken of the more important ones, the others I wish to discuss briefly under this generality, that the prince must consider, as has been in part said before, how to avoid those things which will make him hated or contemptible; and as often as he shall have succeeded he will have fulfilled his part, and he need not fear any danger in other reproaches.

It makes him hated above all things, as I have said, to be rapacious, and to be a violater of the property and women of his subjects, from both of which he must abstain. And when neither their property nor honor is touched, the majority of men live content, and he has only to contend with the ambition of a few, whom he can curb with ease in many ways.

It makes him contemptible to be considered fickle, frivolous, effeminate, mean-spirited, irresolute, from all of which a prince should guard himself as from a rock; and he should endeavor to show in his actions greatness, courage, gravity, and fortitude; and in his private dealings with his subjects let him show that his judgments are irrevocable, and maintain himself in such reputation that no one can hope either to deceive him or to get round him.

That prince is highly esteemed who conveys this impression of himself, and he who is highly esteemed is not easily conspired against; for, provided it is well known that he is an excellent man and revered by his people, he can only be attacked with difficulty. For this reason a prince ought to have two fears, one from within, on account of his subjects, the other from without, on account of external powers. From the latter he is defended by being well armed and having good allies, and if he is well armed he will have good friends, and affairs will always remain quiet within when they are quiet without, unless they should have been already disturbed by conspiracy; and even should affairs outside be disturbed, if he has carried out his preparations and has lived as I have said, as long as he does not despair, he will resist every attack, as I said Nabis the Spartan did.

But concerning his subjects, when affairs outside are disturbed he has only to fear that they will conspire secretly, from which a prince can easily secure himself by avoiding being hated and despised, and by keeping the people satisfied with him, which it is most necessary for him to

accomplish, as I said above at length. And one of the most efficacious remedies that a prince can have against conspiracies is not to be hated and despised by the people, for he who conspires against a prince always expects to please them by his removal; but when the conspirator can only look forward to offending them, he will not have the courage to take such a course, for the difficulties that confront a conspirator are infinite. And as experience shows, many have been the conspiracies, but few have been successful; because he who conspires cannot act alone, nor can he take a companion except from those whom he believes to be malcontents, and as soon as you have opened your mind to a malcontent you have given him the material with which to content himself, for by denouncing you he can look for every advantage; so that, seeing the gain from this course to be assured, and seeing the other to be doubtful and full of dangers, he must be a very rare friend, or a thoroughly obstinate enemy of the prince, to keep faith with you.

And to reduce the matter into a small compass, I say that, on the side of the conspirator, there is nothing but fear, jealousy, prospect of punishment to terrify him; but on the side of the prince there is the majesty of the principality, the laws, the protection of friends and the state to defend him; so that, adding to all these things the popular goodwill, it is impossible that any one should be so rash as to conspire. For whereas in general the conspirator has to fear before the execution of his plot, in this case he has also to fear the sequel to the crime; because on account of it he has the people for an enemy, and thus cannot hope for any escape.

Endless examples could be given on this subject, but I will be content with one, brought to pass within the memory of our fathers. Messer Annibale Bentivogli, who was prince in Bologna (grandfather of the present Annibale), having been murdered by the Canneschi, who had conspired against him, not one of his family survived but Messer Giovanni, who was in childhood: immediately after his assassination the people rose and murdered all the Canneschi. This sprung from the popular goodwill which the house of Bentivogli enjoyed in those days in Bologna; which was so great that, although none remained there after the death of Annibale who were able to rule the state, the Bolognese, having information that there was one of the Bentivogli family in Florence, who up to that time had been considered the son of a blacksmith, sent to Florence for him and gave him the government of their city, and it was ruled by him until Messer Giovanni came in due course to the government.

For this reason I consider that a prince ought to reckon conspiracies of little account when his people hold him in esteem; but when it is hostile to him, and bears hatred towards him, he ought to fear everything and everybody. And well-ordered states and wise princes have taken every care not to drive the nobles to desperation, and to keep the people satisfied and contented, for this is one of the most important objects a prince can have.

Among the best ordered and governed kingdoms of our times is France, and in it are found many good institutions on which depend the liberty and security of the king; of these the first is the parliament and its authority, because he who founded the kingdom, knowing the ambition of the nobility and their boldness, considered that a bit in their mouths would be necessary to hold them in; and, on the other side, knowing the hatred of the people, founded in fear, against the nobles, he wished to protect them, yet he was not anxious for this to be the particular care of the king; therefore, to take away the reproach which he would be liable to from the nobles for favoring the people, and from the people for favoring the nobles, he set up an arbiter, who should be one who could beat down the great and favor the lesser without reproach to the king. Neither could you have a better or a more prudent arrangement, or a greater source of security to the king and kingdom. From this one can draw another important conclusion, that princes ought to leave affairs of reproach to the management of others, and keep those of grace in their own hands. And further, I consider that a prince ought to cherish the nobles, but not so as to make himself hated by the people.

It may appear, perhaps, to some who have examined the lives and deaths of the Roman emperors that many of them would be an example contrary to my opinion, seeing that some of them lived nobly and showed great qualities of soul, nevertheless they have lost their empire or have been killed by subjects who have conspired against them. Wishing, therefore, to answer these objections, I will recall the characters of some of the emperors, and will show that the causes of their ruin were not different to those alleged by me; at the same time I will only submit for consideration those things that are noteworthy to him who studies the affairs of those times. . . .

But returning to the subject of our discourse, I say that whoever will consider it will acknowledge that either hatred or contempt has been fatal to the above-named emperors, and it will be recognized also how it happened that, a number of them acting in one way and a number in another, only one in each way came to a happy end and the rest to unhappy ones. Because it would have been useless and dangerous for Pertinax and Alexander, being new princes, to imitate Marcus,

who was heir to the principality; and likewise it would have been utterly destructive to Caracalla, Commodus, and Maximinus, to have imitated Severus, they not having sufficient valor to enable them to tread in his footsteps. Therefore a prince, new to the principality, cannot imitate the actions of Marcus, nor, again, is it necessary to follow those of Severus, but he ought to take from Severus those parts which are necessary to found his state, and from Marcus those which are proper and glorious to keep a state that may already be stable and firm. . . .

Twenty-First Chapter. How a Prince Should Conduct Himself so as to Gain Renown: Nothing makes a prince so much esteemed as great enterprises and setting a fine example. We have in our time Ferdinand of Aragon, the present King of Spain. He can almost be called a new prince, because he has risen, by fame and glory, from being an insignificant king to be the foremost king in Christendom; and if you will consider his deeds you will find them all great and some of them extraordinary. In the beginning of his reign he attacked Granada, and this enterprise was the foundation of his dominions. He did this quietly at first and without any fear of hindrance, for he held the minds of the barons of Castille occupied in thinking of the war and not anticipating any innovations; thus they did not perceive that by these means he was acquiring power and authority over them. He was able with the money of the Church and of the people to sustain his armies, and by that long war to lay the foundation for the military skill which has since distinguished him. Further, always using religion as a plea, so as to undertake greater schemes, he devoted himself with a pious cruelty to driving out and clearing his kingdom of the Moors; nor could there be a more admirable example, nor one more rare. Under this same cloak he assailed Africa, he came down on Italy, he has finally attacked France; and thus his achievements and designs have always been great, and have kept the minds of his people in suspense and admiration and occupied with the issue of them. And his actions have arisen in such a way, one out of the other, that men have never been given time to work steadily against him.

Again, it much assists a prince to set unusual examples in internal affairs, similar to those which are related of Messer Bernabo da Milano, who, when he had the opportunity, by any one in civil life doing some extraordinary thing, either good or bad, would take some method of rewarding or punishing him, which would be much spoken about. And a prince ought, above all things, always to endeavor in every action to gain for himself the reputation of being a great and remarkable man.

A prince is also respected when he is either a true friend or a downright enemy, that is to say, when, without any reservation, he declares himself in favour of one party against the other; which course will always be more advantageous than standing neutral; because if two of your powerful neighbors come to blows, they are of such a character that, if one of them conquers, you have either to fear him or not. In either case it will always be more advantageous for you to declare yourself and to make war strenuously; because, in the first case, if you do not declare yourself, you will invariably fall a prey to the conqueror, to the pleasure and satisfaction of him who has been conquered, and you will have no reasons to offer, nor anything to protect or to shelter you. Because he who conquers does not want doubtful friends who will not aid him in the time of trial; and he who loses will not harbor you because you did not willingly, sword in hand, court his fate.

Antiochus went into Greece, being sent for by the Aetolians to drive out the Romans. He sent envoys to the Acheans, who were friends of the Romans, exhorting them to remain neutral; and on the other hand the Romans urged them to take up arms. This question came to be discussed in the council of the Acheans, where the legate of Antiochus urged them to stand neutral. To this the Roman legate answered: "As for that which has been said, that it is better and more advantageous for your state not to interfere in our war, nothing can be more erroneous; because by not interfering you will be left, without favor or consideration, the guerdon of the conqueror." Thus it will always happen that he who is not your friend will demand your neutrality, whilst he who is your friend will entreat you to declare yourself with arms. And irresolute princes, to avoid present dangers, generally follow the neutral path, and are generally ruined. But when a prince declares himself gallantly in favor of one side, if the party with whom he allies himself conquers, although the victor may be powerful and may have him at his mercy, yet he is indebted to him, and there is established a bond of amity; and men are never so shameless as to become a monument of ingratitude by oppressing you. Victories after all are never so complete that the victor must not show some regard, especially to justice. But if he with whom you ally yourself loses, you may be sheltered by him, and whilst he is able he may aid you, and you become companions in a fortune that may rise again.

In the second case, when those who fight are of such a character that you have no anxiety as to who may conquer, so much the more is it greater prudence to be allied, because you assist at the destruction of one by the aid of another, who, if he had been wise, would have saved him; and conquering, as it is impossible that he should not with your assistance, he remains at your discretion. And here it is to be noted that a prince ought to take care never to make an alliance with one more powerful than himself for the purpose of attacking others, unless necessity compels him, as is said above; because if he conquers you are at his discretion, and princes ought to avoid as much as possible being at the discretion of any one. The Venetians joined with France against the Duke of Milan, and this alliance, which caused their ruin, could have been avoided. But when it cannot be avoided, as happened to the Florentines when the Pope and Spain sent armies to attack Lombardy, then in such a case, for the above reasons, the prince ought to favor one of the parties.

Never let any government imagine that it can choose perfectly safe courses; rather let it expect to have to take very doubtful ones, because it is found in ordinary affairs that one never seeks to avoid one trouble without running into another; but prudence consists in knowing how to distinguish the character of troubles, and for choice to take the lesser evil.

A prince ought also to show himself a patron of ability, and to honor the proficient in every art. At the same time he should encourage his citizens to practice their callings peaceably, both in commerce and agriculture, and in every other following, so that the one should not be deterred from improving his possessions for fear lest they be taken away from him or another from opening up trade for fear of taxes; but the prince ought to offer rewards to whoever wishes to do these things and designs in any way to honor his city or state.

Further, he ought to entertain the people with festivals and spectacles at convenient seasons of the year; and as every city is divided into guilds or into societies, he ought to hold such bodies in esteem, and associate with them sometimes, and show himself an example of courtesy and liberality; nevertheless, always maintaining the majesty of his rank, for this he must never consent to abate in anything.

Twenty-Second Chapter. Concerning the Secretaries of Princes: The choice of servants is of no little importance to a prince, and they are good or not according to the discrimination of the prince. And the first opinion which one forms of a prince, and of his understanding, is by observing the men he has around him; and when they are capable and faithful he may always be considered wise, because he has known how to recognize the capable and to keep them faithful. But when they are otherwise one cannot form a good opinion of him, for the prime error which he made was in choosing them.

There were none who knew Messer Antonio da Venafro as the servant of Pandolfo Petrucci, Prince of Siena, who would not consider Pandolfo to be a very clever man in having Venafro for his servant. Because there are three classes of intellects: one which comprehends by itself; another which appreciates what others comprehend; and a third which neither comprehends by itself nor by the showing of others; the first is the most excellent, the second is good, the third is useless. Therefore, it follows necessarily that, if Pandolfo was not in the first rank, he was in the second, for whenever one has judgment to know good or bad when it is said and done, although he himself may not have the initiative, yet he can recognize the good and the bad in his servant, and the one he can praise and the other correct; thus the servant cannot hope to deceive him, and is kept honest.

But to enable a prince to form an opinion of his servant there is one test which never fails; when you see the servant thinking more of his own interests than of yours, and seeking inwardly his own profit in everything, such a man will never make a good servant, nor will you ever be able to trust him; because he who has the state of another in his hands ought never to think of himself, but always of his prince, and never pay any attention to matters in which the prince is not concerned.

On the other hand, to keep his servant honest the prince ought to study him, honoring him, enriching him, doing him kindnesses, sharing with him the honors and cares; and at the same time let him see that he cannot stand alone, so that many honors may not make him desire more, many riches make him wish for more, and that many cares may make him dread changes. When, therefore, servants, and princes towards servants, are thus disposed, they can trust each other, but when it is otherwise, the end will always be disastrous for either one or the other.

Twenty-Third Chapter. How Flatterers Should Be Avoided: I do not wish to leave out an important branch of this subject, for it is a danger from which princes are with difficulty preserved, unless they are very careful and discriminating. It is that of flatterers, of whom courts are full, because men are so self-complacent in their own affairs, and in a way so deceived in them, that they are preserved with difficulty from this pest, and if they wish to defend themselves they run the danger of falling into contempt. Because there is no other way of guarding oneself from flatterers except letting men understand that to tell you the truth does not offend you; but when every one may tell you the truth, respect for you abates.

Therefore a wise prince ought to hold a third course by choosing the wise men in his state, and giving to them only the liberty of speaking the truth to him, and then only of those things of which he inquires, and of none others; but he ought to question them upon everything, and listen to their opinions, and afterwards form his own conclusions. With these councillors, separately and collectively, he ought to carry himself in such a way that each of them should know that, the more freely he shall speak, the more he shall be preferred; outside of these, he should listen to no one, pursue the thing resolved on, and be steadfast in his resolutions. He who does otherwise is either overthrown by flatterers, or is so often changed by varying opinions that he falls into contempt.

I wish on this subject to adduce a modern example. Fra Luca, the man of affairs to Maximilian, the present emperor, speaking of his majesty, said: He consulted with no one, yet never got his own way in anything. This arose because of his following a practice the opposite to the above; for the emperor is a secretive man—he does not communicate his designs to any one, nor does he receive opinions on them. But as in carrying them into effect they become revealed and known, they are at once obstructed by those men whom he has around him, and he, being pliant, is diverted from them. Hence it follows that those things he does one day he undoes the next, and no one ever understands what he wishes or intends to do, and no one can rely on his resolutions.

A prince, therefore, ought always to take counsel, but only when he wishes and not when others wish; he ought rather to discourage every one from offering advice unless he asks it; but, however, he ought to be a constant inquirer, and afterwards a patient listener concerning the things of which he inquired; also, on learning that any one, on any consideration, has not told him the truth, he should let his anger be felt.

And if there are some who think that a prince who conveys an impression of his wisdom is not so through his own ability, but through the good advisers that he has around him, beyond doubt they are deceived, because this is an axiom which never fails: that a prince who is not wise himself will never take good advice, unless by chance he has yielded his affairs entirely to one person who happens to be a very prudent man. In this case indeed he may be well governed, but it would not be for long, because such a governor would in a short time take away his state from him.

But if a prince who is not experienced should take counsel from more than one he will never get united counsels, nor will he know how to unite them. Each of the counsellors will think of his own interests, and the prince will not know how to control them or to see through them. And they are not to be found otherwise, because men will always prove untrue to you unless they are kept honest by constraint. Therefore it must be inferred that good counsels, whencesoever they come, are born of the wisdom of the prince, and not the wisdom of the prince from good counsels. . . .

Twenty-Fifth Chapter. What Fortune Can Effect in Human Affairs, and How to Withstand Her: It is not unknown to me how many men have had, and still have, the opinion that the affairs of the world are in such wise governed by fortune and by God that men with their wisdom cannot direct them and that no one can even help them; and because of this they would have us believe that it is not necessary to labor much in affairs, but to let chance govern them. This opinion has been more credited in our times because of the great changes in affairs which have been seen, and may still be seen, every day, beyond all human conjecture. Sometimes pondering over this, I am in some degree inclined to their opinion. Nevertheless, not to extinguish our free will, I hold it to be true that fortune is the arbiter of one half of our actions, but that she still leaves us to direct the other half, or perhaps a little less.

I compare her to one of those raging rivers, which when in flood overflows the plains, sweeping away trees and buildings, bearing away the soil from place to place; everything flies before it, all yield to its violence, without being able in any way to withstand it; and yet, though its nature be such, it does not follow therefore, that men, when the weather becomes fair, shall not make provision, both with defenses and barriers, in such a manner that, rising again, the waters may pass away by canal, and their force be neither so unrestrained nor so dangerous. So it happens with fortune, who shows her power where valor has not prepared to resist her, and thither she turns her forces where she knows that barriers and defenses have not been raised to constrain her.

And if you will consider Italy, which is the seat of these changes, and which has given to them their impulse, you will see it to be an open country, without barriers and without any defense. For if it had been defended by proper valor, as are Germany, Spain, and France, either this invasion would not have made the great changes it has made or it would not have come at all. And this I consider enough to say concerning resistance to fortune in general.

But confining myself more to the particular, I say that a prince may be seen happy to-day and ruined tomorrow without having shown any change of disposition or character. This, I believe, arises firstly from causes that have already been discussed at length, namely, that the prince who relies entirely upon fortune is lost when it changes. I believe also that he will be successful who directs his actions according to the spirit of the times, and that he whose actions do not accord with the times will not be successful. Because men are seen, in affairs that lead to the end which every man has before him, namely, glory and riches, to get there by various methods; one with caution, another with haste; one by force, another by skill; one by patience, another by its opposite; and each one succeeds in reaching the goal by a different method. One can also see of two cautious men the one attain his end, the other fail; and similarly, two men by different observances are equally successful, the one being cautious, the other impetuous; all this arises from nothing else than whether or not they conform in their methods to the spirit of the times. This follows from what I have said, that two men working differently bring about the same effect, and of two working similarly, one attains his object and the other does not.

Changes in estate also issue from this, for if, to one who governs himself with caution and patience, times and affairs converge in such a way that his administration is successful, his fortune is made; but if times and affairs change, he is ruined if he does not change his course of action. But a man is not often found sufficiently circumspect to know how to accommodate himself to the change, both because he cannot deviate from what nature inclines him to, and also because, having always prospered by acting in one way, he cannot be persuaded that it is well to leave it; and, therefore, the cautious man, when it is time to turn adventurous does not know how to do it, hence he is ruined; but had he changed his conduct with the times fortune would not have changed.

Pope Julius the Second went to work impetuously in all his affairs, and found the times and circumstances conform so well to that line of action that he always met with success. Consider his first enterprise against Bologna, Messer Giovanni Bentivogli being still alive. The Venetians were not agreeable to it, nor was the King of Spain, and he had the enterprise still under discussion with the King of France; nevertheless he personally entered upon the expedition with his accustomed boldness and energy, a move which made Spain and the Venetians stand irresolute and passive, the latter from fear, the former from desire to recover all the kingdom of Naples; on the other hand, he drew after him the King of France, because that king, having observed the movement, and desiring to make the Pope his friend so as to humble the Venetians, found it impossible to refuse him soldiers without manifestly offending him. Therefore Julius with his impetuous action accomplished what no other pontiff with simple human wisdom could have done; for if he had waited in Rome until he could get away, with his plans arranged and everything fixed, as any other pontiff would have done, he would never have succeeded. Because the King of France would have made a thousand excuses, and the others would have raised a thousand fears.

I will leave his other actions alone, as they were all alike, and they all succeeded, for the shortness of his life did not let him experience the contrary; but if circumstances had arisen which required him to go cautiously, his ruin would have followed, because he would never have deviated from those ways to which nature inclined him.

I conclude therefore that, fortune being changeful and mankind steadfast in their ways, so long as the two are in agreement men are successful, but unsuccessful when they fall out. For my part I consider that it is better to be adventurous than cautious, because fortune is a woman, and if you wish to keep her under it is necessary to beat and ill-use her; and it is seen that she allows herself to be mastered by the adventurous rather than by those who go to work more coldly. She is, therefore, always, woman-like, a lover of young men because they are less cautious, more violent, and with more audacity command her.

B.   Bodin on the Nature and Functions of Sovereignty

The Six Books Concerning the State first appeared in French in 1576. The book systematically considers such general problems as the "principal end of a well-ordered commonwealth" as well as the more detailed questions of institutions and forms of government. It is Bodin's practice to announce an idea and then illustrate his arguments by evidence drawn from ancient and modern history. In the following selection he is analysing the central problem of sovereignty.[2]

Sovereignty is supreme power over citizens and subjects, unrestrained by laws. . . . Since we have already defined the state as the rightful government of a number of families in their common affairs, with a supreme and perpetual power, it should now be explained what is meant by supreme and perpetual power. We say that the power must be perpetual; for supreme power over citizens may be given to some one or several not perpetually, but for a brief period at the expiration of which the authority ceases. Such persons cannot be called sovereign rulers; they are rather custodians of sovereignty until such time as the sovereign prince or people may withdraw the power intrusted, of which they are the true owners and possessors, as those who have lent or pawned their goods to another; just as those who have conferred upon others powers of judgment and command for a certain time, or to be withdrawn at will, do not cease to be masters and possessors of the jurisdiction and authority. So the jurist has said that the prefect of the Roman emperor surrendered his authority upon demand of the magistrate. It makes no difference whether greater or less power is thus conferred; for if the high power conceded by a prince to his lieutenant to be withdrawn at will, be called sovereignty, the power might be used against the prince himself, to whom nothing but an empty title would then remain; so also a servant might command his master, than which nothing more absurd can be imagined. When authority is granted to a magistrate or to a private individual the person of the prince is always excepted. Whatever authority the sovereign gives to another is less than that which he reserves to himself by virtue of his sovereignty; and he is never so divested of his sovereignty that he may not undertake an examination of the affairs committed to his magistrates or officers, by way of prevention, concurrence, or challenge, or that he may not withdraw power altogether from them. Wherefore, the Roman dictator, the harmosts of the Lacedaemonians, the esymnet of Thessaly, the archons of Malta, or the ancient bailly of Florence (when it had popular government), or those who among us are called regents, or any magistrate or officer to whom is conceded power which though supreme is not perpetual—no such official can be said to have sovereignty.

But suppose that supreme power, unlimited by laws, and without protest or appeal, be granted by the people to some one or few, shall we say that the latter have sovereignty? For he has sovereignty who, after God, acknowledges no one greater than himself. I hold that sovereignty resides not in such persons, but in the people, at whose pleasure they hold their power, or to whom they must return their authority at the expiration of the period designated. The people cannot be considered as having divested themselves of their power when they intrust supreme authority, unrestrained by laws, to one or a few, if the commitment is for a certain period of time, or at the pleasure of the people; for in either case the holders of the supreme authority must render account of their doings to the prince or people, who, being sovereign, are required to give account to no one, save immortal God. What if supreme power be conferred for a period of ten years; as in Athens one archon, whom they called judge, stood thus preëminent in power in the city? Still the sovereignty of the state did not rest in him; he was rather curator or deputy for the people, and had to render account to them. What if the high power of which I speak be given to one or more for a year, with no requirement that account of their actions be given to any one? So the Cnidians every year chose sixty citizens whom they called *amymones*, that is, men superior to any limitation or censure. Sovereignty, nevertheless, was not in them, since they were compelled, at the expiration of the year, to surrender their authority.

But what if the people have given supreme and perpetual power to any one for life: If the power is given unlimited by laws, and without the name of magistrate, deputy, governor, or guardian, and not at the pleasure of any one, certainly it must be confessed that sovereign rights have been conceded to such a one. The people in such case have despoiled themselves of their authority, in order to give to another all the privileges of sovereignty, without conditions; in like manner as any one might by pure gift surrender to another the ownership and possession of his property; such a perfect donation contains no conditions.

As a prince is bound by no laws of his predecessor, much less is he bound by his own laws. One man may receive a command from another, but no man can command himself. Pomponius says that no obligation can exist if it must receive its sanction from the will of him who makes the promise; this shows conclusively that a prince can in no way be bound by his own laws and orders. As the Pope, according to the jurists, cannot bind his own hands, so the supreme prince, or even the lowest magistrate, or a private person, cannot issue commands to himself. Thus we see at the end of every law, "because it has so pleased us," in order that all may understand that laws, however just in themselves, depend for their force solely upon the will of him who makes the law.

As for the laws of God and of nature, princes and people are equally bound by them, so that no one who attempts to abrogate or weaken them can escape the judgments of divine sovereignty. What we have said as to the freedom of sovereignty from the binding force of law does not have reference to divine or natural law. That Pope who best of all knew the rights of sovereignty and who brought under his sway almost all Christian emperors and princes, said "sovereignty pertains to him who can derogate from ordinary law"; the latter expression I interpret to mean the laws of the country. But is a prince bound by the laws of his country if he has sworn to observe them? Here it is necessary to make a distinction. If the prince has sworn to himself, no obligation exists; he is not bound by an oath made to himself; just as private persons are not bound by oaths which they make in mutual contract, if the contract be such as the law does not make binding, however honorably the agreements may have been made. If a prince swears to another ruler not to abrogate the laws made by himself or by his predecessors, he is bound, if the prince to whom he makes the promise has interest in the matter. . . .

Likewise we say that a prince who has made sworn promises to his subjects is bound by them, if the promises are reasonable; but this is true not because he has sworn or because he is bound by his own laws, but because any one is bound by his just covenants, if they are made with another who has any interest, whether the promises be made with or without oath. Moreover, as a private person may be relieved of his obligation if he has been circumvented by fraud, deceit, error, or threat, so a prince may be released not only in those cases which tend to impair his sovereignty, but also where his private convenience and domestic affairs are disturbed.

This, then, I hold: A prince may abrogate, modify, or replace a law made by himself and without the consent of his subjects; such action is fully permissible where justice seems to demand it; the abrogation, modification, or substitution, however, must not be obscure or ambiguous, but must be set forth in clear detail. If there is no probable reason for abrogating the law, he is acting contrary to the duty of a good prince in seeking such abrogation. However, he is not bound by any obligation assumed by his predecessors, further than what is compatible with his own interest. . . .

We must not confuse laws and contracts. Law depends upon the will of him who holds supreme power in the state, and who can bind subjects by his law, but cannot bind himself. A contract between a prince and his subjects has mutual binding force, so that it cannot be departed from save with the consent of both parties; in this the prince seems to have nothing above his subjects, except that the purpose of a law to which he has sworn having ceased to exist, he is no longer bound either by the law or by the oath which he took with regard to the law. A well-advised prince will not suffer himself to be bound by oath to observe the laws, for in such case he does not possess the supreme authority in the commonwealth.

As to laws concerning the supreme power, the prince cannot abrogate or modify them, since they are attached to the very sovereignty with which he is clothed; such as the Salic law, which is the foundation of our monarchy.

The sovereignty of a prince is manifest in the fact that when the estates and orders of the people, with humble mien, present their requests to him they are exercising no authority of commanding, forbidding, or concurring; but the prince by his own judgment and will directs everything; whatever he desires and orders has the force of law. The opinion of those who in books scattered broadcast have written that the king is bound by the popular command, must be disregarded; such doctrine furnishes seditious men with material for revolutionary plots, and leads to disturbance in the commonwealth. No reasonable ground can be adduced why subjects should control princes, or why power should be attributed to popular assemblies—except in the infancy, madness, or captivity of the prince, when a guardian or deputy may be created by the suffrages of the people. If princes were restrained by laws made by these assemblies or by the commands of the people, the power of the prince would be worthless and the royal name a vain thing.

The approval and promulgation of laws, which is commonly done in an assembly or senate, does not imply that the sovereignty of the realm resides in such assembly or senate, but only a species of authority without which laws issued by the king might be called in question at his death, or before the senate when it acts judicially. I hold, therefore, that the sovereignty of the prince is in no degree diminished by calling together the assemblies or estates, though indeed a prince grants many things to the assembled people which he would not so readily grant to individuals; this is because the voices of individuals are not heard so clearly as the voice of the multitude; or it is because the prince, accustomed to use the eyes and ears of others, in the assembly sees and hears the people directly, and so, impelled by shame, religious fear, or his own good disposition, he grants their requests. But the highest privilege of sovereignty consists primarily in giving laws not only to individuals but also to the people as a whole, without their consent.

We may hold that a king who by lawful right assumes the kingship is bound by the contracts and promises of his predecessors, in so far as such contracts were made for the benefit of the commonwealth. This is especially true if they were made with the judgment and consent of the entire people or of the greater assemblies; for their good faith is at stake, which it is not only appropriate but necessary for the king to respect, even though the state may be harmed thereby. But when a prince has contracted with strangers or with citizens concerning matters pertaining to the commonwealth without the consent of the people, if serious injury would come upon the commonwealth from the performance of the contracts, his successor is not bound by them, especially if he obtains his authority through election by the people or the senate; in such case he has received none of his privileges from his predecessor. It would be otherwise if he had acquired authority by grant from another; then he would be bound by the latter's promises, unless express exception had been made. But by whatever right a prince obtains his authority, whether by law, testament, popular election, or lot, it is just to fulfil those obligations which were undertaken for the good of the state. Otherwise it would be permissible for him, through evil practices, contrary to the laws of nature, to draw profit to himself out of hardships endured by others. It is of concern to the citizenship to keep the public faith to the best of its ability, lest when the state is in extreme danger all means of relief should be cut off. . . .

But why, some one may ask, are the foregoing distinctions necessary, since all princes are bound by the law of nations? For in that law compacts and testaments are included. This is not true, if we mean every kind of contract or testament. But admitting it to be true, it does not follow that a prince is more bound by the law of nations than by his own laws, except in so far as the former are in agreement with the laws of nature and of God; to these latter laws all that we have said concerning the obligation of princes must be referred. If certain of the laws of nations are unjust, the prince may abrogate them and forbid his subjects to follow them. This we showed in relation to slavery; this institution was established in many states, by pernicious examples, yet in accord with the law of almost every nation; but through salutary decrees of several princes it has been abolished, in conformity to the laws of nature. What has been said of one thing may be extended to other things of like kind; for a proviso in the whole argumentation is that nothing be sanctioned which is contrary to the laws of God or of nature. For if justice is the end of the law, and law is the command of the prince, and the prince is the image of the almighty God, then the laws of the prince should bear the stamp of divine laws.

The first and principal function of sovereignty is to give laws to the citizens generally and individually, and, it must be added, not necessarily with the consent of superiors, equals, or inferiors. If the consent of superiors is required, then the prince is clearly a subject; if he must have the consent of equals, then others share his authority; if the consent of inferiors—the people or the senate—is necessary, then he lacks supreme authority. . . .

It may be objected that custom does not get its power from the judgment or command of the prince, and yet has almost the force of law, so that it would seem that the prince is master of law, the people of custom. Custom, insensibly, yet with the full compliance of all, passes gradually into the character of men, and acquires force with the lapse of time. Law, on the other hand, comes forth in one moment at the order of him who has the power to command, and often in opposition to the desire and approval of those whom it governs. Wherefore, Chrysostom likens law to a tyrant and custom to a king. Moreover, the power of law is far greater than that of custom, for customs may be superseded by laws, but laws are not supplanted by customs; it is within the power and function of magistrates to restore the operation of laws which by custom are obsolescent. Custom proposes neither rewards nor penalties; laws carry one or the other, unless it be a permissive law which nullifies the penalty of some other law. In short, a custom has compelling force only as long as the prince, by adding his endorsement and sanction to the custom, makes it a law.

It is thus clear that laws and customs depend for their force upon the will of those who hold supreme power in the state. This first and chief mark of sovereignty is, therefore, of such sort that it cannot be transferred to subjects, though the prince or people sometimes confer upon one

of the citizens the power to frame laws, which then have the same force as if they had been framed by the prince himself. The Lacedaemonians bestowed such power upon Lycurgus, the Athenians upon Solon; each stood as deputy for his state, and the fulfilment of his function depended upon the pleasure not of himself but of the people; his legislation had no force save as the people confirmed it by their assent. The former composed and wrote the laws, the people enacted and commanded them.

Under this supreme power of ordaining and abrogating laws, it is clear that all other functions of sovereignty are included; so that it may be truly said that supreme authority in the state is comprised in this one thing—namely, to give laws to all and each of the citizens, and to receive none from them. For to declare war or make peace, though seeming to involve what is alien to the term law, is yet accomplished by law, that is by decree of the supreme power. It is also the prerogative of sovereignty to receive appeals from the highest magistrates, to confer authority upon the greater magistrates and to withdraw it from them, to allow exemption from taxes, to bestow other immunities, to grant dispensations from the laws, to exercise power of life and death, to fix the value, name and form of money, to compel all citizens to observe their oaths: all of these attributes are derived from the supreme power of commanding and forbidding—that is, from the authority to give law to the citizens collectively and individually, and to receive law from no one save immortal God. A duke, therefore, who gives laws to all his subjects, but receives law from the emperor, Pope, or king, or has a co-partner in authority, lacks sovereignty.

Part II.   CHURCH AND STATE

A.   THE NEW CHURCHMEN

The Protestant reformers had little political experience, but since European monarchs had traditionally employed the power of the state to maintain the prevailing faith, the reformers were obliged to face the political implications of their work. The following selections indicate their views upon the crucial problem of the relationship between the new religions and the New Monarchy.

1. *Luther*, On Secular Authority, *1523.* Martin Luther (1483–1546) opened his assault on the Catholic Church in 1517, and the rapid acceptance of his views by many German princes led to political turmoil in the Holy Roman Empire. After his *Address to the German Nobility* in 1520 had failed to improve the situation, Luther further

expounded his theories three years later in a pamphlet entitled *On Secular Authority,* excerpts from which are printed below.[3]

. . . For this reason God has ordained the two governments; the spiritual, which by the Holy Spirit under Christ makes Christians and pious people; the secular, which restrains the unchristian and wicked so that they must needs keep the peace outwardly, even against their will. So Paul interprets the secular sword, Romans xiii, and says it is not a terror to good works, but to the evil. And Peter says it is for the punishment of evil doers. . . .

For this reason these two kingdoms must be sharply distinguished, and both be permitted to remain; the one to produce piety, the other to bring about eternal peace and prevent evil deeds; neither is sufficient in the world without the other. For no one can become pious before God by means of the secular government, without Christ's spiritual rule. Hence Christ's rule does not extend over all, but Christians are always in the minority and are in the midst of non-Christians. Where there is only secular rule or law, there, of necessity, is sheer hypocrisy, though the commandments be God's very own. Without the Holy Spirit in the heart no one becomes really pious, he may do as fine works as he will. Where, on the other hand, the spiritual government rules alone over land and people, there evil is given free rein and the door is opened for every kind of knavery; for the natural world cannot receive or comprehend spiritual things. . . .

But perhaps you will say, since Christians do not need the secular sword and the law, why does Paul say to all Christians, in Romans xiii, "Let all souls be subject to power and authority?" And St. Peter says, "Be subject to every human ordinance," etc., as quoted above. I answer, as I have said, that Christians, among themselves and by and for themselves, need no law or sword, since it is neither necessary nor profitable for them. Since, however, a true Christian lives and labors on earth not for himself, but for his neighbor, therefore the whole spirit of his life impels him to do even that which he need not do, but which is profitable and necessary for his neighbor. Because the sword is a very great benefit and necessary to the whole world, to preserve peace, to punish sin and to prevent evil, he submits most willingly to the rule of the sword, pays tax, honors those in authority, serves, helps, and does all he can to further the government, that it may be sustained and held in honor and fear. Although he needs none of these things for himself and it is not necessary for him to do them, yet he considers what is for the good and profit of others, as Paul teaches in Ephesians v.

He serves the State as he performs all other works of love, which he himself does not need. He visits the sick, not that he may be made well; feeds no one because he himself needs food; so he also serves the State not because he needs it, but because others need it,—that they may be protected and that the wicked may not become worse. He loses nothing by this, and such service

in no way harms him, and yet it is of great profit to the world. If he did not do it, he would be acting not as a Christian but contrary even to love, and would also be setting a bad example to others, who like him would not submit to authority, though they were no Christians. In this way the Gospel would be brought into disrepute, as though it taught rebellion and made self-willed people, unwilling to benefit or serve any one, when in reality it makes a Christian the servant of every one. Thus in Matthew xvii, Christ gave the tribute money that He might not offend them, although He did not need to do it. . . .

Worldly government has laws which extend no farther than to life and property and what is external upon earth. For over the soul God can and will let no one rule but Himself. Therefore, where temporal power presumes to prescribe laws for the soul, it encroaches upon God's government and only misleads and destroys the souls. We desire to make this so clear that every one shall grasp it, and that our junkers, the princes and bishops, may see what fools they are when they seek to coerce the people with their laws and commandments into believing one thing or another.

> 2. *Calvin*, On Civil Government, *1536.* John Calvin (1509–1564) produced his great work *The Institutes of the Christian Religion* in 1536. At the outset he realized the necessity of stating clearly the nature of the relationship of church to state, and so the *Institutes* contain a chapter entitled "On Civil Government," selections from which follow.[4]

Having already stated that man is the subject of two kinds of government, and having sufficiently discussed that which is situated in the soul, or the inner man, and relates to eternal life,—we are, in this chapter, to say something of the other kind, which relates to civil justice, and the regulation of the external conduct. For, though the nature of this argument seems to have no connection with the spiritual doctrine of faith which I have undertaken to discuss, the sequel will show that I have sufficient reason for connecting them together, and, indeed, that necessity obliges me to it; especially since, on the one hand, infatuated and barbarous men madly endeavor to subvert this ordinance established by God; and, on the other hand, the flatterers of princes, extolling their power beyond all just bounds, hesitate not to oppose it to the authority of God Himself. Unless both these errors be resisted the purity of the faith will be destroyed. . . .

But for speaking of the exercise of civil polity,

there will be another place more suitable. At present we only wish it to be understood, that to entertain a thought of its extermination, is inhuman barbarism; it is equally as necessary to mankind as bread and water, light and air, and far more excellent. For it not only tends to secure the accommodations arising from all these things, that men may breathe, eat, drink, and be sustained in life, though it comprehends all these things while it causes them to live together, yet, I say, this is not its only tendency; its objects also are, that idolatry, sacrileges against the name of God, blasphemies against His truth, and other offenses against religion, may not openly appear and be disseminated among the people; that the public tranquillity may not be disturbed; that every person may enjoy his property without molestation; that men may transact their business together without fraud or injustice; that integrity and modesty may be cultivated among them; in short, that there may be a public form of religion among Christians, and that humanity may be maintained among men.

Nor let any one think it strange that I now refer to human polity the charge of the due maintenance of religion, which I may appear to have placed beyond the jurisdiction of men. For I do not allow men to make laws respecting religion and the worship of God now, any more than I did before; though I approve of civil government, which provides that the true religion which is contained in the law of God, be not violated, and polluted by public blasphemies, with impunity. . . .

It now remains for us, as we proposed, in the last place, to examine what advantage the common society of Christians derives from laws, judgments, and magistrates; with which is connected another question—what honor private persons ought to render to magistrates, and how far their obedience ought to extend. . . .

We owe these sentiments of affection and reverence to all our rulers, whatever their characters may be; which I the more frequently repeat, that we may learn not to scrutinize the persons themselves, but may be satisfied with knowing that they are invested by the will of the Lord with that function, upon which He has impressed an inviolable majesty. But it will be said, that rulers owe mutual duties to their subjects. That I have already confessed. But he who infers from this that obedience ought to be rendered to none but just rulers, is a very bad reasoner. . . .

Wherefore, if we are inhumanly harassed by a cruel prince; if we are rapaciously plundered by an avaricious or luxurious one; if we are neglected by an indolent one; or if we are persecuted, on account of piety, by an impious and sacrilegious one,—let us first call to mind our transgressions against God, which He undoubtedly chastises by these scourges. Thus our impatience will be restrained by humility. Let us, in the next place, consider that it is not our province to remedy these evils, and that nothing remains for us, but to implore the aid of the Lord, in whose hand are the hearts of kings and the revolutions of kingdoms. It is "God" who "standeth in the congregation of the mighty," and "judgeth among the gods"; Whose presence shall confound and crush all kings and judges of the earth who shall not have kissed His Son; "that decree unrighteous decrees, to turn aside the needy from judgment, and to take away the right from the poor, that widows may be their prey, and that they may rob the fatherless. . . ."

But in the obedience which we have shown to be due to the authority of governors, it is always necessary to make one exception, and that is entitled to our first attention,—that it do not seduce us from obedience to Him, to Whose will the desires of all kings ought to be subject, to Whose decrees all their commands ought to yield, to Whose majesty all their scepters ought to submit. And, indeed, how preposterous it would be for us, with a view to satisfy men, to incur the displeasure of Him on whose account we yield obedience to men! The Lord, therefore, is the King of Kings; Who, when He has opened His sacred mouth, is to be heard alone, above all, for all, and before all; in the next place, we are subject to those men who preside over us; but no otherwise than in Him. If they command any thing against Him, it ought not to have the least attention; nor, in this case, ought we to pay any regard to all that dignity attached to magistrates; to which no injury is done when it is subjected to the unrivalled and supreme power of God. . . .

3. *Calvinism in Scotland.* Calvin's ideas were brought to Scotland by John Knox (1505–1572), who applied them to practical politics in the reign of Mary, Queen of Scots, a Catholic. The following description of one of Knox's arguments with the queen is taken from his *History of the Reformation in Scotland*. In it Knox speaks of himself in the third person, but otherwise he is hardly retiring.[5]

Whether it was by counsel of others, or the queen's own desire, we know not; but the queen spake with John Knox, and had long reasoning with him, none being present, except the lord James—two gentlemen stood in the other end of the house. The sum of their reasoning was this. . . .

"But yet," said she, "ye have taught the people to receive another religion, than their princes can allow: and how can that doctrine be of God, seeing, that God commands subjects to obey their princes?"

"Madam," said he, "as that right religion takes neither original nor authority from worldly princes, but from the eternal God alone, so are not subjects bound to frame their religion according to the appetite of their princes; for oft it is, that princes are the most ignorant of all others in God's true religion, as we may read as well in the histories before the death of Christ Jesus, as after. If all the seed of Abraham should have been of the religion of Pharaoh, to whom they were long subjects, I pray you, madam, what religion should there have been in the world? For, if all men, in the days of the apostles, should have been of the religion of the Roman emperors, what religion should have been upon the face of the earth? Daniel and his fellows were subjects to Nebuchadnezzar, and unto Darius, and yet, madam, they would not be of their religion, neither of the one nor of the other: for the three children said, 'We make it known unto thee, O king, that we will not worship thy gods.' And Daniel did pray publicly unto his God, against the express commandment of the king. And so, madam, ye may perceive, that subjects are not bound to the religion of their princes, albeit they are commanded to give them obedience."

"Yea," said she, "none of those men raised the sword against their princes." "Yet, madam," said he, "ye cannot deny but that they resisted: for these that obey not the commandments that are given, in some sort they resist." "But yet," said she, "they resisted not by the sword." "God," said he, "madam, had not given unto them the power and the means." "Think ye," said she, "that subjects having power may resist their princes?" "If their princes exceed their bounds," said he, "madam, and do against that wherefore they should be obeyed, it is no doubt but they may be resisted, even by power. . . ."

At these words, the queen stood as it were amazed, more than a quarter of an hour; her countenance altered, so that lord James began to entreat her, and to demand, "What has offended you, madam?" At length, she said, "Well, then, I perceive, that my subjects shall obey you, and not me; and shall do what they list, and not what I command: and so must I be subject to them, and not they to me." "God forbid," answered he, "that ever I take upon me to command any to obey me, or yet to set subjects at liberty to do what pleases them. But my travail is, that both princes and subjects obey God. And

think not," said he, "madam, that wrong is done unto you, when you are willed to be subject unto God: for, it is He that subjects the people under princes, and causes obedience to be given unto them; yea, God craves of kings, 'That they be, as it were, foster-fathers to His kirk, and commands queens to be nurses unto His people.' And this subjection, madam, unto God, and unto His troubled kirk, is the greatest dignity that flesh can get upon the face of the earth, for it shall carry them to everlasting glory."

"Yea," said she, "but ye are not the kirk that I will nurse. I will defend the kirk of Rome, for it is, I think, the true kirk of God."

"Your will," said he, "madam, is no reason; neither doth your thought make that Roman harlot to be the true and immaculate spouse of Jesus Christ. And wonder not, madam, that I call Rome a harlot; for that kirk is altogether polluted with all kind of spiritual fornication, as well in doctrine as in manners. Yea, madam, I offer myself farther to prove, that the kirk of the Jews, that crucified Christ Jesus, when that they manifestly denied the Son of God, was not so far degenerated from the ordinances and statutes which God gave by Moses and Aaron unto His people, as that the kirk of Rome is declined, and more than five hundred years hath declined from the purity of that religion, which the apostles taught and planted."

"My conscience," said she, "is not so." "Conscience, madam," said he, "requires knowledge; and I fear that right knowledge you have none." "But," said she, "I have both heard and read." "So, madam," said he, "did the Jews who crucified Christ Jesus, read both the law and the prophets, and heard the same interpreted after their manner. Have ye heard," said he, "any teach, but such as the pope and the cardinals have allowed? And ye may be assured, that such will speak nothing to offend their own estate." "Ye interpret the scriptures," said she, "in one manner, and they in another; whom shall I believe, and who shall be judge?" "You shall believe God," said he, "that plainly speaketh in His word: and farther than the word teacheth you, you neither shall believe the one nor the other. The word of God is plain in the self; and if there appear any obscurity in any place, the Holy Ghost, who is never contrarious to Himself, explains the same more clearly in other places: so that there can remain no doubt, but unto such as will remain obstinately ignorant."

B.   THE NEW MONARCHS

The Protestant Reformation forced all the new monarchs to seek answers to the telling questions asked by Mary, Queen of Scots: "Whom shall I believe, and who shall be judge?" The answers given by the rulers of three great Western kingdoms may be discovered in the following selections.

1. *England*. Henry VIII broke with the Papacy and established a state church under his own control in 1534. Twenty years later his daughter Mary restored Catholic rule in England. When his daughter Elizabeth ascended the throne in 1558, her country was beset with religious unrest and uncertainty. The course she determined to follow was set by the Act of Supremacy, 1559, excerpts from which follow.[6]

The Act of Supremacy

Most humbly beseech your most excellent majesty your faithful and obedient subjects, the Lords spiritual and temporal, and the Commons, in this your present Parliament assembled, that where in time of the reign of your most dear father, of worthy memory, King Henry VIII, divers good laws and statutes were made and established, as well for the utter extinguishment and putting away of all usurped and foreign powers and authorities out of this your realm, and other your highness's dominions and countries, as also for the restoring and uniting to the imperial crown of this realm the ancient jurisdictions, authorities, superiorities, and pre-eminences to the same of right belonging and appertaining, by reason whereof we, your most humble and obedient subjects, from the five-and-twentieth year of the reign of your said dear father [1534] were continually kept in good order, and were disburdened of divers great and intolerable charges and exactions before that time unlawfully taken and exacted by such foreign power and authority as before that was usurped, until such time as all the said good laws and statutes, by one Act of Parliament made in the first and second years of the reigns of the late King Philip and Queen Mary, your highness's sister, entitled, An Act repealing all statutes, articles, and provisions made against the See Apostolic of Rome since the twentieth year of King Henry VIII, and also for the establishment of all spiritual and ecclesiastical possessions and hereditaments conveyed to the laity, were all clearly repealed and made void, as by the same Act of repeal more at large does and may appear; by reason of which Act of repeal, your said humble subjects were eftsoons brought under an usurped foreign power and authority, and do yet remain in that bondage, to the intolerable charges of your loving subjects, if some redress, by the authority of this your High Court of Parliament, with the assent of your highness, be not had and provided:

II. May it therefore please your highness, for the repressing of the said usurped foreign power and the restoring of the rights, jurisdictions, and pre-eminences appertaining to the imperial crown of this your realm, that it may be enacted by the authority of this present Parliament, that the said Act made in the said first and second years of the reigns of the said late King Philip and Queen Mary, and all and every branches, clauses, and articles therein contained (other than such branches, clauses, and sentences as hereafter shall be excepted) may, from the last day of this session of Parliament, by authority of this present Parliament, be repealed, and shall from thenceforth be utterly void and of none effect. . . .

XVI. And to the intent that all usurped and foreign power and authority, spiritual and temporal, may for ever be clearly extinguished, and never to be used or obeyed within this realm, or any other your majesty's dominions or countries, may it please your highness that it may be further enacted by the authority aforesaid, that no foreign prince, person, prelate, state, or potentate, spiritual or temporal, shall at any time after the last day of this session of Parliament, use, enjoy, or exercise any manner of power, jurisdiction, superiority, authority, pre-eminence or privilege, spiritual or ecclesiastical, within this realm, or within any other your majesty's dominions or countries that now be, or hereafter shall be, but from thenceforth the same shall be clearly abolished out of this realm, and all other your highness's dominions for ever; any statute, ordinance, custom, constitutions, or any other matter or cause whatsoever to the contrary in any wise notwithstanding.

XVII. And that also it may likewise please your highness, that it may be established and enacted by the authority aforesaid, that such jurisdictions, privileges, superiorities, and pre-eminences, spiritual and ecclesiastical, as by any spiritual or ecclesiastical power or authority hath heretofore been, or may lawfully be exercised or used for the visitation of the ecclesiastical state and persons, and for reformation, order, and correction of the same, and of all manner of errors, heresies, schisms, abuses, offences, contempts, and enormities, shall for ever, by authority of this present Parliament, be united and annexed to the imperial crown of this realm.

XVIII. And that your highness, your heirs and successors, kings or queens of this realm, shall have full power and authority by virtue of this Act, by letters patent under the great seal of England, to assign, name, and authorize, when and as often as your highness, your heirs or successors, shall think meet and convenient, and for such and so long time as shall please your highness, your heirs or successors, such person or persons being natural-born subjects to your highness, your heirs or successors, as your majesty, your heirs or successors, shall think meet, to exercise, use, occupy, and execute under your highness, your heirs and successors, all manner of jurisdictions, privileges, and pre-eminences, in any wise touching or concerning any spiritual or ecclesiastical jurisdiction, within these your realms of England and Ireland, or any other your highness's dominions or countries; and to visit, reform, redress, order, correct, and amend all such errors, heresies, schisms, abuses, offences, contempts, and enormities whatsoever, which by any manner of spiritual or ecclesiastical power, authority, or jurisdiction, can or may lawfully be reformed, ordered, redressed, corrected, restrained, or amended, to the pleasure of Almighty God, the increase of virtue, and the conservation of the peace and unity of this realm; and that such person or persons so to be named, assigned, authorized, and appointed by your highness, your heirs or successors, after the said letters patent to him or them made and delivered, as is aforesaid, shall have full power and authority, by virtue of this Act, and of the said letters patent, under your highness, your heirs and successors, to exercise, use, and execute all the premises, according to the tenor and effect of the said letters patent; any matter or cause to the contrary in any wise notwithstanding.

XIX. And for the better observation and maintenance of this Act, may it please your highness that it may be further enacted by the authority aforesaid, that all and every archbishop, bishop, and all and every other ecclesiastical person, and other ecclesiastical officer and minister, of what estate, dignity, pre-eminence, or degree soever he or they be or shall be, and all and every temporal judge, justice, mayor, and other lay or temporal officer and minister, and every other person having your highness's fee or wages, within this realm, or any your highness's dominions, shall make, take, and receive a corporal oath upon the evangelist, before such person or persons as shall please your highness, your heirs or successors, under the great seal of England to assign and

name, to accept and to take the same according to the tenor and effect hereafter following, that is to say: 'I, A. B., do utterly testify and declare in my conscience that the queen's highness is the only supreme governor of this realm, and of all other her highness's dominions and countries, as well in all spiritual or ecclesiastical things or causes, as temporal, and that no foreign prince, person, prelate, state or potentate, hath, or ought to have, any jurisdiction, power, superiority, pre-eminence, or authority, ecclesiastical or spiritual, within this realm; and therefore I do utterly renounce and forsake all foreign jurisdictions, powers, superiorities, and authorities, and do promise that from henceforth I shall bear faith and true allegiance to the queen's highness, her heirs and lawful successors, and to my power shall assist and defend all jurisdictions, pre-eminences, privileges, and authorities granted or belonging to the queen's highness, her heirs and successors, or united and annexed to the imperial crown of this realm. So help me God, and by the contents of this book.' . . .

XXIII. And that it may likewise be further enacted by the authority aforesaid, that if any such person or persons, as at any time hereafter shall be promoted, preferred, or collated to any such promotion spiritual or ecclesiastical, benefice, office, or ministry, or that by your highness, your heirs or successors, shall be promoted or preferred to any temporal or lay office, ministry, or service, shall and do peremptorily and obstinately refuse to take the same oath so to him to be offered; that then he or they so refusing shall presently be judged disabled in the law to receive, take, or have the same promotion spiritual or ecclesiastical, the same temporal office, ministry, or service within this realm, or any other your highness's dominions, to all intents, constructions, and purposes. . . .

XXVII. And for the more sure observation of this Act, and the utter extinguishment of all foreign and usurped power and authority, may it please your highness, that it may be further enacted by the authority aforesaid, that if any person or persons dwelling or inhabiting within this your realm, or in any other your highness's realms or dominions, of what estate, dignity, or degree soever he or they be, after the end of thirty days next after the determination of this present Parliament, shall by writing, printing, teaching, preaching, express words, deed or act, advisedly, maliciously, and directly affirm, hold, stand with, set forth, maintain, or defend the authority, pre-eminence, power or jurisdiction, spiritual or ecclesiastical, of any foreign prince, prelate, person, state, or potentate whatsoever, heretofore claimed, used, or usurped within this realm, or any dominion or country being within or under the power, dominion, or obeisance of your highness; or shall advisedly, maliciously, and directly put in use or execute anything for the extolling, advancement, setting forth, maintenance, or defence of any such pretended or usurped jurisdiction, power, pre-eminence, or authority, or any part thereof; that then every such person and persons so doing and offending, their abettors, aiders, procurers, and counsellors, being thereof lawfully convicted and attainted, according to the due order and course of the common laws of this realm, for his or their first offence shall forfeit and lose unto your highness, your heirs and successors, all his and their goods and chattels, as well real as personal. . . .

XXIX. And that also all and every the benefices, prebends, and other ecclesiastical promotions and dignities whatsoever, of every spiritual person so offending, and being attainted, shall immediately after such attainder be utterly void to all intents and purposes, as though the incumbent thereof were dead; and that the patron and donor of every such benefice, prevend, spiritual promotion and dignity, shall and may lawfully present unto the same, or give the same, in such manner and form as if the said incumbent were dead; and if any offender or offenders, after such conviction or attainder, do eftsoons commit or do the said offences, or any of them, in manner and form aforesaid, and be thereof duly convicted and attainted, as is aforesaid; that then every such offender and offenders shall for the same second offence incur into the dangers, penalties, and forfeitures ordained and provided by the statute of Provision and *Praemunire,* made in the sixteenth year of the reign of King Richard II.

XXX. And if any such offender or offenders, at any time after the said second conviction and attainder, do the third time commit and do the said offences, or any of them, in manner and form aforesaid, and be thereof duly convicted and attainted, as is aforesaid; that then every such offence or offences shall be deemed and adjudged high treason, and that the offender and offenders therein, being thereof lawfully convicted and attainted, according to the laws of this realm, shall suffer pains of death, and other penalties, forefeitures, and losses, as in cases of high treason by the laws of this realm. . . .

2. *France.* Since the Concordat of Bologna in 1516, the French kings had exercised strict control over the Catholic Church within their realm. The appearance of a strong Calvinist movement in the middle of the sixteenth century threatened to upset the existing settlement. Royal policy wavered, and 1562 France embarked upon thirty-five years of religious civil war. In 1598 Henry IV finally restored order and imposed religious peace by the Edict of Nantes. The Edict is a lengthy document consisting of 92 clauses, 56 supplementary clauses, and several additional proclamations. Selections which indicate the nature of the monarch's settlement are printed below.[7]

Henry, by the Grace of God, King of France and Navarre. To all that are and shall be, greeting:

The most signal and remarkable mercy, among the infinite ones which it has pleased God to vouchsafe to us, is the having given us virtue and firmness sufficient to prevent our granting any thing under the influence of the dreadful trouble, discord and confusion which prevailed at the period of our accession to the throne. The kingdom was divided into many parts and factions, so many that the orderly portion was, perhaps, one of the smallest. We have been supported so as to withstand this great storm, we have overcome it, and now at last have reached the haven of safety and repose. . . .

In the conflicting claims for pre-eminence amongst the various important and perilous affairs which pressed upon us, and which could not all receive attention at once, we resolved upon the following course. In the first place to deal with such as required to be settled by main force, delaying for a while such as could be regulated by principles of reason and justice; as, for example, the general differences amongst our good subjects, and some particular hardships, complained of by the more healthy portions of the state, which we believe may be the more effectually relieved by our having first put an end to the civil war, which was one chief cause.

By the grace of God, we have happily so far succeeded that hostilities have ceased throughout the kingdom. We hope for equal success in composing those differences that yet remain to be adjusted, and then will be accomplished the great object of our prayers, and we shall be rewarded for all our labors, by once more beholding peace and tranquillity within our borders. Amongst the most important of said affairs, the consideration of which we were obliged to postpone, were the complaints of various Catholic towns and provinces that the Catholic Religion had not been universally re-established, in conformity with the Edicts formerly passed for the pacification of religious troubles; also, the petitions and remonstrances of our subjects of the pretended Reformed Religion, complaining of the non-performance of what had been promised to them by the said Edicts, and begging for further enactments to secure to them that liberty of conscience, personal safety and security of property which the late disturbances have made them believe to be in jeopardy, giving them reason to fear that plans were laid for their ruin. . . .

Being fully sensible of the great importance of this subject, and the necessity of bestowing deep consideration upon it, we have carefully looked over the folios of complaints from our Catholic subjects, and we have permitted our subjects of the aforesaid pretended Reformed Religion to assemble by deputy to prepare their list of grievances. We have conferred with both parties various times, and carefully examined all former Edicts, and now we have concluded that one general, clear, plain and absolute law must be enacted, for the government of all our subjects, and by which they shall be regulated in the settlement of all differences which have already arisen, or which may in future arise. With this, all must rest satisfied, as the best that the state of the times allows, us having, in our deliberations, had no other end in view than zeal for the service of God and a desire to see it manifested by our said subjects, amongst whom we hope to establish a firm and durable peace. . . .

Accordingly, with the advice and assistance of the Princes of the Blood, the Princes and Officers of the Crown, and other great and important personages of our Council of State, we have duly weighed and considered all this matter; and we have, by this perpetual and irrevocable Edict, said, declared and ordered, and we do say, declare and order,

1st.—That the memory of the past, on both sides, from the beginning of March, 1585, to the date of our accession to the throne, shall be buried in oblivion; and it shall be unlawful for our Attorney General, or any other person, public or private, at any time, or for any purpose whatsoever, to make mention of the former troubles in any process or law suit, in any Court or Jurisdiction whatever.

2d.—We forbid all our subjects, whatever may be their rank or condition, to revive the recollection of the past, or to attack, resent, injure or provoke by reproaches, under any pretext whatever; and they must not dispute, quarrel, outrage or offend one another, by word or deed, but must restrain themselves, and live in peace as brothers, friends and fellow citizens, upon penalty to the disobedient of being punished as disturbers of the peace.

3d.—We command that in all places of this our kingdom and country of our obedience, where the exercise of the Apostolic Roman Catholic religion has been interrupted, it shall be re-established, to be there freely exercised wthout trouble or hin-

drance. We forbid expressly, all persons, of whatsoever rank, degree or condition, upon the above named penalty, to molest or disturb the clergymen in the celebration of Divine Service, the enjoyment and collection of tithes, first fruits and revenues from their benefices, or any other rights and duties appertaining thereto. All persons, who, during the troubles, became possessed of churches, houses, property and revenues belonging to the said clergymen, and who retain and occupy them, shall give up the same to the clergy, with the entire possession and peaceable enjoyment of all rights, privileges and securities which they had before they were seized upon. It is expressly forbidden, to those of said pretended Reformed Religion, to preach or perform any service according to said religion in the churches, houses, or places of abode of said clergymen. . . .

6th.—And in order to leave no opening for discord and divisions amongst our subjects, we have permitted and do permit those of the pretended Reformed Religion to live and remain in all cities and places within this our kingdom and country of our obedience without being disturbed, vexed, molested or forced to do any thing against their conscience on the subject of religion, neither can their houses or places of abode be searched on that score; provided that in all things they conform to what is contained in our present Edict. . . .

9th.—We also permit those of the said religion to continue the exercise of it in all cities and places under our government, where it was established and publicly practised at different times in the year 1596, and before the end of August 1597, notwithstanding any decrees or decisions to the contrary.

10th.—The said exercise shall likewise be established and restored in all cities and places where it was established, or had the right to be so, by the Edict of Pacification, passed in the year 1577, or by the secret articles and conferences of Nérac and Fleix, without the said establishment being prevented in places of the domain given in the said Edict, though they may since have been made over to Catholic persons. Let it then be understood that the said exercise may be always re-established in places of the said domain which have formerly been in the possession of those who professed the pretended Reformed Religion, in which it would have been placed in consideration of their persons, or because of their feudal rights, even if the said fiefs should now be possessed by persons of the said Apostolical Roman Catholic Religion. . . .

13th.—We expressly forbid any of the said religion having any religious exercise whatever, either ministerial, or for discipline or public in-

struction of children and others in this our kingdom; except in those places permitted and
granted by the present Edict.

14th.—As also having any exercises of said religion within our Court and Suite, nor likewise in
our lands and territories beyond the Alps, nor
in our city of Paris, neither within five leagues
of the said city: nevertheless, those of the said
religion living in the said country beyond the
Alps, and in our said city, and within five leagues
around it, shall not be subject to espionage in
their houses, nor compelled to do any thing on
account of their religion against their consciences,
if they in all things act in conformity with the
provisions of the present Edict.

15th.—The public exercise of the said religion
cannot be permitted in the army, except at the
quarters of those Generals who profess it, always
excepting those occupied by our own person. . . .

17th.—We forbid all preachers, readers, and
others who speak in public, using any words or
discourse tending to excite sedition among the
people, but on the contrary we enjoin upon them
the practice of forbearance and meekness, saying
nothing but what is for the instruction and edifi-
cation of their hearers, and suited to the maintenance of that peace and tranquillity which we
have established in our said kingdom, under
penalties prescribed in former Edicts. We expressly enjoin our attorneys general and their
substitutes to give official information against
those who violate it, under the penalty of being
answerable for the same in their own names and
persons, and being ejected from office.

18th.—We also forbid all our subjects, of whatsoever rank or condition, carrying off children by
force, or persuasion, against the will of their
parents of the said religion, in order to have them
baptized or confirmed in the Apostolical Roman
Catholic Church: the same prohibition extends to
those of the said pretended Reformed Religion,
all being subject to exemplary punishment for
such offenses. . . .

27th.—In order the better to promote that
union which we wish to see prevail amongst our
subjects, and to take away all cause of complaint,
we declare that all those who have made or shall
make profession of the pretended Reformed
Religion shall be eligible for all public offices or
employments, whether royal, manorial, or civic,
in all parts of our dominions, and shall be impartially appointed thereto, our courts of Parle-
ment confining themselves in the matter to inquiries as to the piety, morality, and integrity of
those nominated for offices, as much those of one
religion as the other, without requiring from them
any other oath than that they will faithfully serve
the King and obey the laws. In case of vacancies

occurring in any of said offices in our disposal, we
shall without partiality appoint capable persons
to such offices. Let it also be understood, that
those of said pretended Reformed Religion can
be admitted and received into all councils, assemblies, and meetings, which follow from the aforesaid offices, without rejection on account of said
religion. . . .

82d.—Likewise, those of said religion must
forbear and desist from all devices, negotiations
and correspondence as well within as without
our kingdom; and the assemblies formed in the
provinces must be dissolved immediately; all
leagues and associations formed, or to be formed,
under any pretext whatsoever, contrary to our
present Edict, shall be broken and annulled, as
we do break and annul such; we expressly forbid
all our subjects from this day forth, holding
clubs, raising money without permission, making
fortifications, enlisting men, congregating and
assembling otherwise than permitted by this
Edict, and without arms, all of which we prohibit
and forbid under pain of being severely punished,
as despisers and breakers of our commands and
ordinances. . . .

Additional Edict

This day, the last of April, 1598, the King
being at Nantes, wishing to content his subjects
of the pretended Reformed Religion as much as
possible, and to grant all their requests to him,
for such things as they considered to be essential
for the safety of their persons, property, and
estates; and for the confidence that His Majesty
reposes in their fidelity, and their sincere affection with some other important considerations
affecting the tranquillity of the state; His said
Majesty, in addition to what is contained in the
Edict he has lately resolved upon, and which
ought to be published, for the regulation of what
concerns them, has granted, and promised to
them that a list of all places, cities, and castles, of
which they had possession until the end of the
month of August last, in which they shall have
garrisons, shall be drawn up and signed by His
Majesty; and [that these places] shall remain in
their keeping, under the authority of His Majesty,
for the space of eight years, to count from the day
of publication of the Edict. For other places
which they hold, where they shall have no garri-
son, there shall be no change or innovation. . . .

And for the support of the said garrisons,
which are to be maintained in the said cities,
places and castles, His said Majesty has granted
the sum of one hundred and eighty thousand
crowns, without including those in the Province
of Dauphiny, for which there shall otherwise be
provided the sum of one hundred and eighty

thousand crowns annually: promising and assuring, that appropriations shall be made of the most available and undoubted nature, where the said garrisons are established. And if these shall not be sufficient, the said sum shall be made up from other sources, and shall be completely paid.

His Majesty likewise promises that when he makes up the list, or establishment for the said garrisons, he will call around him those of the said religion, to take their opinion, and listen to their complaints, before he gives his orders, which he will always do in a manner to be as satisfactory to them as he possibly can. . . .

And after this term of eight years has expired, although His Majesty's promise will be redeemed, and the places restored to him, yet he promises, that if garrisons shall be continued there, and governors remain to command them, he will not dispossess those who shall be in office there, to appoint any others. He likewise declares that it is his intention, as well during the said eight years, as after them, to gratify those of the said religion, and to give them a share of the offices, governments and other honors that he will have to bestow; and to distribute them without favor or partiality, according to the rank and merit of the persons, as to his other Catholic subjects; without, however, the places and cities which may be hereafter intrusted to their command, besides those they now have, being considered, in consequence of that, to be more particularly appropriated to those of the said religion.

3. *Spain*. The monarchs of united Spain traditionally followed two strong lines of religious policy: to maintain the purity of the Catholic faith and to exercise the greatest possible control over the clerical hierarchy within their state. Despite the vigilance of the Inquisition, however, Protestant doctrines seeped into Spain, and at the same time the Popes were prone to regard with jealousy the royal authority over the personnel and property of the Spanish clergy. To indicate how the kings dealt with these problems, two documents from the reign of Philip II (1556–98) are printed below. The first is an edict issued after the Council of Trent had formulated definitive Catholic dogma. The second is an order to the Viceroy of New Spain, in which Philip extended to his dominions overseas the clerical policy to which he rigidly adhered at home.[8]

Royal Decree of July 12, 1564

It is certain and well known that Christian kings and princes have the obligation to obey, keep, and comply with, and to see that in their kingdoms, states, and dominions and decrees and commandments of the Holy Mother Church be obeyed, kept, and complied with; and that they should assist, aid, and favor the execution and conservation of the same, as obedient children and protectors and defenders of the Church. Likewise they have an obligation to comply with and carry out [the decrees of] the general councils which have been legitimately and canonically convoked . . . with the authority of the Holy Apostolic See of Rome. . . . One of these councils (first instigated by my father the Emperor and after many and great difficulties ordered and convoked by Paul III, Roman Pontiff of happy memory) is that which was lately convened at Trent for the extirpation of heresies and errors which have been so extended in Christendom in these times, and for the reformation of abuses, excesses and disorders, of which there was such need. . . . It has been continued and prosecuted to a conclusion and end in which all of Christendom took part, especially so many and so notable prelates and many other persons of great knowledge, religion and example, from our kingdoms, and also the ambassadors of the Emperor our uncle, and our own, and those of the other kings and princes and of the states and potentates of Christendom; and in it, with the grace of God and the assistance of the Holy Spirit, many holy and catholic decrees were made for the faith and religion, and likewise were made and ordered for the reformation [of the Church] many things very holy and very just and very convenient and important for the service of our Lord God and the good of His Church and of the government and ecclesiastical policy.

And now, his Holiness having sent to us the decrees of the said holy council printed in authentic form, we, as Catholic king and true and obedient son of the Church, wishing to satisfy . . . the obligation which we have, in accordance with the example of the kings our ancestors of glorious memory, . . . do accept and receive the said sacrosanct council, and we desire that in these our kingdoms it be kept, complied with and executed, and we shall give and lend our help and favor for the said execution and compliance, and for the conservation and defense of what has been ordered in it, interposing for that purpose our authority and royal arm, and whatever may be necessary and convenient.

And we charge and order our archbishops and bishops and other prelates, and the generals, provincials and priors (guardians of the [religious] orders) and whomsoever this may . . . concern, that they immediately publish and make public in their churches, districts and dioceses, and in the other parts and places where it may be convenient, the [decrees of] the said holy council, and that they keep and obey them and make others keep, obey and execute them with the care, zeal and diligence that an affair so much to the service of God and the good of the Church requires.

And we command our council, the president of our audiencias, our governors, corregidores, and any other of our judges, that they give and lend whatever favor and aid is necessary for the execution of and compliance with the said council and of that which has been ordered in it. And we shall have great concern and shall wish . . . to know and understand how the above mentioned is kept, complied with and executed, so that in a business of such great importance to the service of God and the good of His Church there be no carelessness or negligence.

Royal Decree of June 1, 1574

The King. To our viceroy of New Spain, or the person or persons who shall, for the time being, be exercising the government of that country: As you know, the right of the ecclesiastical patronage belongs to us throughout the realm of the Indies—both because of having discovered and acquired that new world, and erected there and endowed the churches and monasteries at our own cost, or at the cost of our ancestors, the Catholic sovereigns; and because it was conceded to us by bulls of the most holy pontiffs, conceded of their own accord. For its conservation, and that of the right that we have to it, we order and command that the said right of patronage be always preserved for us and our royal crown, singly and *in solidum*, throughout all the realm of the Indies, without any derogation therefrom, either in whole or in part; and that we shall not concede the right of patronage by any favor or reward that we or the kings our successors may confer.

Further, no person or persons, or ecclesiastical or secular communities, or church or monastery, shall be able to exercise the right of patronage by custom privilege, or any other title, unless it be the person who shall exercise it in our name, and with our authority and power; and no person, whether secular or ecclesiastical, and no order, convent, or religious community, of whatever state, condition, rank, and pre-eminence he or they may be, shall for any occasion and cause whatever, judicially or extra-judicially, dare to meddle in any matter touching my royal patronage, to injure us in it—to appoint to any church, benefice, or ecclesiastical office, or to be accepted if he shall have been appointed—in all the realm of the Indies, without our presentation, or that of the person to whom we commit it by law or by letters-patent. He who shall do the contrary, if he be a secular person, shall incur the loss of the concessions that shall have been made to

him by us in all the realm of the Indies, shall be unable to hold and obtain others, and shall be exiled perpetually from all our kingdoms and seigniories; and if he shall be an ecclesiastical person, he shall be considered as a foreigner, and exiled from all our kingdoms, and shall not be able to hold or obtain any benefice or ecclesiastical office, and shall incur the other penalties established against such by laws of these my kingdoms. And our viceroys, audiencias, and royal justices shall proceed with all severity against those who thus shall infringe or violate our right of patronage; and they shall proceed officially, either at the petition of our fiscals, or at that of any party who demands it; and in the execution of it great diligence shall be exercised.

We desire and order that no cathedral church, parish church, monastery, hospital, votive church, or any other pious or religious establishment be erected, founded, or constructed, without our express consent for it, or that of the person who shall exercise our authority; and further, that no archbishopric, bishopric, dignidad, canonry, racion, media-racion, rectorial or simple benefice, or any other ecclesiastical or religious benefice or office, be instituted, or appointment to it be made, without our consent or presentation, or that of the person who shall exercise our authority; and such presentation or consent shall be in writing, in the ordinary manner.

The archbishopric and bishoprics shall be appointed by our presentation, made to our very holy father (i.e., the Roman pontiff) who shall be at that time, as has been done hitherto.

The dignidades, canonries, racions and media-racions of all the cathedral churches of the Indies shall be filled by presentation made by our royal warrant, given by our royal Council of the Indies, and signed by our name, by virtue of which the arch-bishop or bishop of the church where the said dignidad, canonry, or racion shall be shall grant to him collation and canonical installation, which shall also be in writing, sealed with his seal and signed with his hand. Without the said presentation, title, collation, and canonical installation, in writing, he shall not be given possession of such dignidad, canonry, racion, or media-racion; neither shall he accept the benefits and emoluments of it, under the penalties contained in the laws against those who violate our royal patronage. . . .

No prelate, even though he have an authentic relation and information that we have presented any person to a dignidad, canonry, racion, or any other benefice, shall grant him collation or canonical installation, or shall order that he be given possession of it, unless our original warrant of the said presentation be first presented; and our viceroys or audiencias shall not meddle by making them receive such persons without the said presentation.

After the original warrant of our presentation has been presented, appointment and canonical installation shall be made without any delay; and order will be given to assign to him the emoluments, unless there is some legitimate objection against the person presented, and one which can be proved. If there is no legitimate objection, or if any such be alleged that shall not be proved, and the prelate should delay the appointment, installation, and possession, he shall be obliged to pay to such person the emoluments and incomes, costs, and interests, that shall have been incurred by him. . . .

No general, commissary-general, visitor, provincial, or any other superior of the religious orders, shall go to the realm of the Indies, without first showing in our royal Council of the Indies the powers that he bears and giving us relation of them; and without the Council giving him our decree and permission so that he may go, and a warrant so that our viceroys, audiencias, justices, and our other vassals may admit and receive him to the exercise of his office, and give him all protection and aid in it. . . .

In order that we may better make the presentation that shall become necessary of prelacies, dignidades, prebends, and the other ecclesiastical offices and benefices, we ask and charge the said diocesan prelates and the provincials of the religious orders, and we order our viceroys, presidents, audiencias, and governors, each one of them, separately and distinctly by himself, without communicating one with another, to make a list of all the dignidades, benefices, missions, and ecclesiastical offices in his province, noting those of them that are vacant, and those that are filled. Likewise they shall make a list of all the ecclesiastical and religious persons, and of the sons of citizens and Spaniards who are studying for the purpose of becoming ecclesiastics, and of the good character, learning, competency and qualities of each one, stating clearly his good parts and also his defects, and declaring, so that prelacies,

dignidades, benefices, and ecclesiastical offices shall be suitably filled, both those that shall be at present found vacant, and those that shall become vacant hereafter. Those relations shall be sent us closed and sealed, in each fleet, and in different ships; and what shall be deemed advisable to add to or to suppress from the preceding ones that shall have been sent before, shall be added or suppressed; so that no fleet shall sail without its relation. We charge the consciences of one and all straitly with this matter. . . .

Inasmuch as it is our will that the above-contained be observed and obeyed, for we believe that such procedure is expedient for the service of God and for our own, I order you to examine the above, and to observe and obey it, and cause it to be observed and obeyed in all those provinces and villages, and their churches, *in toto*, and exactly as is contained and declared, for what time shall be our will. You shall accomplish and fulfil it, in the ways that shall appear most advisable to you. You shall take for this purpose such measures and precautions as shall be advisable, in virtue of this my decree; and I give you for that complete authority in legal form. Accordingly we request and charge the very reverend father in Christ, the archbishop of that city, and member of our Council, and the reverend fathers in Christ, the archbishop of New Spain, the venerable deans and cabildo of the cathedral churches of that country, and all the curas, beneficiaries, sacristans, and other ecclesiastical persons, the venerable and devout fathers provincial, guardians, priors, and other religious of the orders of St. Dominic, St. Augustine, St. Francis, and of all the other orders, that in what pertains to, and is incumbent on them, they observe and obey this decree, acting in harmony with you, for all that shall be advisable. Given in San Lorenzo el Real, June first, one thousand five hundred and seventy-four.

I THE KING
By order of his Majesty:
ANTONIO DE ERASO

VI

The "Glorious" Revolution of 1688

A PEOPLE may let a king fall, yet still remain a people; but if a king let his people slip from him, he is no longer a king.

GEORGE SAVILE, first Marquis of Halifax

CONTENTS

QUESTIONS FOR STUDY

PART I

1. Evaluate the importance of the personalities of Charles and James in the fall of the House of Stuart.

2. How would Machiavelli have appraised Charles and James as princes?

3. What were Louis XIV's interests in England?

4. Who stood to gain more by the Treaty of Dover, Louis or Charles?

5. How well do the terms of the Declaration of Indulgence of 1673 indicate that Charles understood the prejudices of his subjects?

6. What was the principal objection of the Commons to Charles' Declaration?

7. "James II, in his Declaration of Indulgence (1687), tried to play both ends against the middle." Explain.

8. "James II behaved as if the civil wars had never been fought." Explain.

9. What rights did James infringe on, in his dealings with the Universities?

10. "James might have had his army if it had not been for his religion." Explain.

11. After 1688 the Whigs claimed all the credit for effecting the Glorious Revolution. How far do they rightfully deserve that credit?

12. "Nobody loves a failure." How far do you think this is responsible for posterity's judgment of the Stuarts?

PART II

13. What clues do you find as to why the revolution of 1688 has been called "glorious"?

14. What is the constitutional importance of the first act of the Convention Parliament?

15. What major points of conflict between crown and parliament during the previous ninety years were settled in 1688–1690?

16. What is the importance of the Act of Settlement of 1701?

17. How does Locke define political power? Did it exist in the state of nature?

18. What is the basis of the inviolability of property? What is the importance of Locke's concept of property for his political thought?

19. How do political societies come into existence? What protection do subjects have against an unjust or tyrannical government?

20. To what extent are the circumstances of the Glorious Revolution reflected in Locke's *Treatise?*

The Restoration of Charles II in 1660 seemed to many Englishmen little short of a miracle: "This day," wrote John Evelyn in his diary, "His Majesty Charles the Second came to London after a sad and long exile and calamitous suffering both of the king and the Church. . . . This was also his birthday, and with a triumph of above 20,000 horse and foot, brandishing their swords and shouting with inexpressible joy; the ways strewed with flowers, the bells ringing, the streets hung with tapestries, fountains running with wine; trumpets, music, and myriads of people flocking. . . . I stood in the Strand and beheld it, and blessed God. And all this was done without one drop of blood shed, and by that very army which rebelled against him; but it was the Lord's doing, for such a restoration was never mentioned in any history, ancient or modern, since the return of the Jews from the Babylonian captivity; nor so joyful a day and so bright ever seen in this nation, this happening when to expect or effect it was past all human policy." [1]

The "inexpressible joy" with which most Englishmen greeted the Restoration did not endure. The return of Charles II solved the immediate problem of re-establishing a stable government, but the terms upon which Charles II ascended the throne left open numerous vital issues which had brought on the Civil Wars. Many of the religious and financial questions of the earlier reigns remained unsettled, and the king accepted few formal limitations upon his powers with regard to the law and to the "rights and privileges" of the parliament.

Moreover, a new element of conflict was added in the form of Catholicism in the royal family. The queen was a Catholic. "The king never committed himself until he lay on his death-bed, but his sympathies were not concealed." The king's brother, who ascended the throne as James II in 1685, was an avowed Catholic who converted his first wife and married a Catholic as his second. A Catholic royal family as head of a Protestant Church and an overwhelmingly Protestant state was an anomalous situation inevitably fraught with friction and irritation.

The Restoration did not, therefore, allay domestic strife. Old issues and new produced a continuation of internal quarrels, which were, to a great extent, canalized into a new form of conflict, the rivalry of political parties. The politically potent subjects of the crown were not all agreed, but tended rather to align themselves on either side of questions of great importance. Thus there came into existence the two historic factions of Whigs and Tories, which, though agreed on numerous fundamental points, fought on opposite sides on many of the major issues of the day and struggled for power and influence in the state.

To the domestic issues and party struggles were added the problems of foreign policy. Across the Channel, France and Holland were continually at swords' points. England was drawn to Holland by the religious tie of Protestantism, but repelled from her by a bitter commercial rivalry. France was not yet a serious business competitor, but she was a Catholic state with grandiose ambitions on the continent which might threaten England's security. Thus England had points of enmity and friendship with both countries, and Englishmen were continually torn between a desire to destroy their commercial rival and a growing dread of extending the power of the ambitious Louis XIV. The policy of the state alternated between war with the Dutch and alliance with the Dutch against France, and the natural dilemma as to which cause was to the true interest of England became involved with the political, religious and financial issues at home.

The period of the Restoration was thus an era in which were prolonged the struggles of earlier reigns, complicated and intensified by new questions. So explosive were the issues that they eventually burst forth in a new political over-turn, the "Glorious" Revolution of 1688.

While the whole period may be regarded as critical, two specific crises have been selected to introduce the student to the major issues and partisans involved. The documents illustrating these crises make up Part I of this Problem; those in Part II indicate the nature of the Revolutionary Settlement and conclude with selections from John Locke's great defense of it.

Part **I.** THE COMING OF REVOLUTION

A. THE ROYAL BROTHERS

The seventeenth century in England is famous for the character study. Bishop Burnet, in intimate contact with the affairs of his time, began his *History of His Own Time* in 1683 and in it included character sketches.

1. *Charles II, by Burnet.*[1]

The king was then thirty years of age, and, as might have been supposed, past the levities of youth and the extravagance of pleasure. He had a very good understanding. He knew well the state of affairs both at home and abroad. He had a softness of temper that charmed all who came near him, till they found how little they could depend on good looks, kind words, and fair promises; in which he was liberal to excess, because he intended nothing by them, but to get rid of importunities, and to silence all further pressing upon him. He seemed to have no sense of religion: Both at prayers and sacrament he, as it were, took care to satisfy people, that he was in no sort concerned in that about which he was employed. So that he was very far from being an hypocrite, unless his assisting at those performances was a sort of hypocrisy (as no doubt it was).

But he was sure not to increase that by any the least appearance of religion. He said once to myself, he was no atheist, but he could not think God would make a man miserable only for taking a little pleasure out of the way. He disguised his Popery to the last. But when he talked freely, he could not help letting himself out against the liberty that under the Reformation all men took of inquiring into matters of religion: For from their inquiring into matters of religion they carried the humor farther, to inquire into matters of state. He said often, he thought government was a much safer and easier thing where the authority was believed infallible, and the faith and submission of the people was implicit: About which I had once much discourse with him.

He was affable and easy, and loved to be made so by all about him. The great art of keeping him long was, the being easy, and the making everything easy to him. He had made such observation on the French Government, that he thought a king who might be checked, or have his ministers called to an account by a parliament, was but a king in name. He had a great compass of knowledge, tho' he was never capable of much application or study. He understood the Mechanics and

Physic; and was a good chemist, and much set on several preparations of mercury, chiefly the fixing it. He understood navigation well: But above all he knew the architecture of ships so perfectly, that in that respect he was exact rather more than became a prince. His apprehension was quick, and his memory good.

He was an everlasting talker. He told his stories with a good grace: But they came in his way too often. He had a very ill opinion of men and women; and did not think that there was either sincerity or chastity in the world out of principle, but that some had either the one or the other out of humor or vanity. He thought that nobody did serve him out of love: And so he was quits with all the world, and loved others as little as he thought they loved him. He hated business, and could not be easily brought to mind any: But when it was necessary, and he was set to it, he would stay as long as his ministers had work for him. The ruin of his reign, and of all his affairs, was occasioned chiefly by his delivering up at his first coming over to a mad range of pleasure. . . .

And, in the state his affairs were then in [when he was in exile] he accustomed himself to say to every person, and upon all occasions, that which he thought would please most: So that words or promises went very easily from him. And he had so ill an opinion of mankind, that he thought the great art of living and governing was, to manage all things and all persons with a depth of craft and dissimulation. And in that few men in the world could put on the appearance of sincerity better than he could: Under which so much artifice was usually hid, that in conclusion he could deceive none, for all were become mistrustful of him. He had great vices, but scarce any virtues to correct them: He had in him some vices that were less hurtful, which corrected his more hurtful ones.

He was during the active part of life given up to sloth and lewdness to such a degree, that he hated business, and could not bear the engaging in any thing that gave him much trouble, or put him under any constraint. And, tho' he desired to become absolute, and to overturn both our religion and our laws, yet he would neither run the risk, nor give himself the trouble, which so great a design required. He had an appearance of gentleness in his outward department: But he seemed to have no bowels nor tenderness in his nature: And in the end of his life he became cruel. He was apt to forgive all crimes, even blood itself: Yet he never forgave any thing that was done against himself, after his first and general act of indemnity, which was to be reckoned as done rather upon maxims of state than inclinations of mercy.

2. *James II, by Burnet.*[2]

I will digress a little to give an account of the Duke's character, whom I knew for some years so particularly, that I can say much upon my own knowledge. He was very brave in his youth, and so much magnified by Monsieur Turenne, that, till his marriage lessened him he really clouded the King, and pass'd for the superior genius. He

was naturally candid and sincere, and a firm friend, till affairs and his religion wore out all his first principles and inclinations. He had a great desire to understand affairs: And in order to that he kept a constant journal of all that pass'd of which he showed me a great deal.

The Duke of Buckingham gave me once a short but severe character [sketch] of the two brothers. It was the more severe, because it was true: The King (he said) could see things if he would, and the Duke would see things if he could. He had no true judgment, and was soon determined by those whom he trusted: But he was obstinate against all other advices. He was bred with high notions of kingly authority, and laid it down for a maxim, that all who opposed the King were rebels in their hearts. He was perpetually in one amour or other, without being very nice in his choice: Upon which the King said once, he believed his brother had his mistresses given him by his priests for penance. . . .

B.   THE CRISIS OF 1670–74

After the Restoration the management of affairs of state was largely in the hands of the Lord Chancellor, Edward Hyde, Earl of Clarendon. It was he who engineered much of the Restoration Settlement, part of which—the Clarendon Code—bears his name. His power and his personality bred opposition, however, and in 1667 he fell from power. The immediate cause of his downfall was the war with the Dutch. This war, ended by the Peace of Breda in 1667, while it brought to England, New York and New Jersey, had been by no means a completely successful venture for England, and Clarendon was chosen as a scapegoat. The banishment of Clarendon marked a turning point both in domestic and foreign policy. Charles II gave to no single minister as much power as the Chancellor had possessed; after 1667 he chose five advisers ("the cabal"), an arrangement which allowed him to pursue his own policies with considerable freedom.

1. *The Secret Treaty of Dover, 22 May 1670.* In 1668 England turned to her old enemies the Dutch, and with them and with Sweden formed the Triple Alliance, a league designed primarily to check French ambitions in the Low Countries. But the king of England had other policies and other motives. Alliance with the Dutch was distasteful to him. As republicans, and as commercial and naval rivals, they seemed to threaten his policies and his kingdom, and the Triple Alliance was scarcely concluded before Charles embarked on another course. The negotiations which led up to the Treaty of Dover were extraordinarily secret, and only a very few of Charles' ministers were admitted to his confidence. The text of the treaty was not published until 1830.[3]

For the perpetual union and friendship between the two kings and their states, articles so secret and advantageous to both monarchs have

been agreed upon that a treaty of similar importance can hardly be found in any period of history.

The King of England, being convinced of the truth of the Roman Catholic religion is resolved to declare it, and to reconcile himself with the Church of Rome as soon as the state of his country's affairs permit. He has such confidence in the fidelity and affection of his subjects that none of them, not even those who (as yet) have been denied a full outpouring of divine grace, will fail in their due obedience to their sovereign. But as there are always unquiet spirits who mask their designs under the guise of religion, the King of England, for the peace of his kingdom, will avail himself of the assistance of the King of France, who, on his part, as he is anxious to contribute to a design glorious not only for the King of England but for the whole of Catholic Christendom, promises to pay to the King of England, the sum of two million livres tournois, the first half payable three months after ratification of the present treaty, the other half three months later. In addition, the King of France undertakes to provide, at his own expense, 6,000 troops for the execution of this design, if they should be required. The time for the declaration of Catholicism is left entirely to the discretion of the King of England.

The King of France will never violate the peace which he has concluded with Spain, nor will he do anything inconsistent with the terms of the treaty of Aix-la-Chapelle; so that it will be possible for the King of England to act in conformity with the conditions of the Triple Alliance.

If the King of France should acquire any fresh claims or rights on the Spanish dominions, the King of England will assist him by land and sea to enforce these rights.

Each of the contracting sovereigns has a sufficiently large population to justify their joint resolution to humble the pride of the States General [of Holland], and to destroy the power of a people which has not only shown ingratitude to those who have helped it to create its republic, but has had the insolence to set itself up as a sovereign arbiter among other states. Accordingly both sovereigns will jointly declare war on the States General, and neither will engage in a treaty or truce without the other. . . .

In the joint hostilities agreed upon the King of France will defray all the expenses of the campaign by land, the King of England agreeing to supply at his charge 6,000 foot.

For the war by sea the King of England will arm at least 60 men-of-war and 10 fireships, to be joined by a French auxiliary fleet of at least 30 good ships, the whole to be under the command of the Duke of York. To assist the King of England to defray the costs of the campaign, the King of France undertakes to pay him each year the sum of three million livres tournois, for so long as the war may last. The English share of the conquests from the Dutch shall be Walcheren, Sluys and Cadsand. . . .

After the King of England has made the declaration specified in article 2, it will be free for the King of France to decide the time for the joint declaration of war.

Should there be found in any treaty of either crown with another state any clause inconsistent with the terms of this treaty, such clause shall be null and void. . . .

2. *The Declaration of Indulgence.* The first indication of Charles' new policy can be seen in the following declaration issued on March 15, 1672. At the time Parliament was not in session.[4]

Charles Rex.
Our care and endeavors for the preservation of the rights and interests of the Church, have been sufficiently manifested to the world, by the whole course of our government since our happy restoration, and by the many and frequent ways of coercion that we have used for reducing all erring or dissenting persons, and for composing the unhappy differences in matters of religion, which we found among our subjects upon our return; but it being evident by the sad experience of twelve years, that there is very little fruit of all these forcible courses, we think ourselves obliged to make use of that supreme power in ecclesiastical matters, which is not only inherent in us, but hath been declared and recognized to be so, by several statutes and acts of Parliament; and therefore we do now accordingly issue this our declaration, as well for the quieting of our good subjects in these points, as for inviting strangers in this conjecture to come and live under us; and for the better encouragement of all to a cheerful following of their trades and callings, from whence we hope, by the blessing of God, to have many good and happy advantages to our government; as also for preventing for the future the danger that might otherwise arise from private meetings and seditious conventicles.

And in the first place, we declare our express resolution, meaning and intention to be, that the Church of England be preserved, and remain entire in its doctrine, discipline and government, as now it stands established by law; and that this be taken to be, as it is, the basis, rule, and standard of the general and public worship of God, and that the orthodox conformable clergy do receive and enjoy the revenues belonging thereunto, and that no person, though of a different opinion and persuasion, shall be exempt from paying his tithes or dues whatsoever. And further we declare, that no person shall be capable of holding any benefice, living, or ecclesiastical dignity or preferment of any kind, in this our kingdom of England, who is not exactly conformable.

We do in the next place declare our will and pleasure to be, that the execution of all, and all manner of penal laws in matters ecclesiastical, against whatsoever sort of nonconformists or recusants, be immediately suspended, and they are hereby suspended; and all judges, judges of assize and jail delivery, sheriffs, justices of peace, mayors, bailiffs and other officers whatsoever, whether ecclesiastical or civil, are to take notice of it, and pay due obedience thereto.

And that there may be no pretense for any of our subjects to continue their illegal meetings and conventicles, we do declare, that we shall from time to time allow a sufficient number of places as they shall be desired, in all parts of this our kingdom, for the use of such as do not conform to the Church of England, to meet and assemble in order to their public worship and devotion, which places shall be open and free to all persons.

But to prevent such disorders and inconveniences as may happen by this our indulgence, if not duly regulated; and that they may be the better protected by the civil magistrate; our express will and pleasure is, that none of our subjects do presume to meet in any place, until such places be allowed, and the teacher of that congregation be approved by us.

And lest any should apprehend that this restriction should make our said allowance and approbation difficult to be obtained, we do further declare, that this our indulgence as to the allowance of the public places of worship, and approbation of the preachers, shall extend to all sorts of nonconformists and recusants, except the recusants of the Roman Catholic religion, to whom we shall in no wise allow public places of worship, but only indulge them their share in the common exemption from the penal laws, and the exercise of their worship in their private houses only.

And if after this our clemency and indulgence any of our subjects shall pretend to abuse this liberty, and shall preach seditiously, or to the derogation of the doctrine, discipline or government of the established church, or shall meet in places not allowed by us, we do hereby give them warning, and declare we will proceed against them with all imaginable severity. And we will let them see, we can be as severe to punish such offenders when so justly provoked, as we are indulgent to truly tender consciences.

Given at our court at Whitehall this 15th day of March, in the four and twentieth year of our reign.

3. *Declaration of War on the Dutch.* On March 17, 1672, two days after the issuance of the Declaration of Indulgence, Charles declared war on the Dutch. "Incidents" had already occurred; in the summer of 1671, an English yacht had fired on Dutch ships in the Channel for failing to salute the English flag, and early in March, 1672 a small English force had attacked a large Dutch convoy off the Isle of Wight.[5]

We have been always so zealous for the quiet of Christendom and so careful not to invade any Kingdom or State, that we hope you will do us the justice to believe, that it is nothing but inevitable necessity which forces us to the Resolution of taking up arms.

[Account here follows of the causes of the First Dutch War, 1665-7, and the subsequent violation of the Treaty of Breda by the Dutch in Surinam.]

But it is no wonder that they venture these outrages upon our subjects in remote parts when they dare be so bold with Our Royal Person and the honor of this nation so near us as in their own country, there being scarce a town within their territories, that is not filled with abusive pictures and false historical medals and pillars. . . .

The right of the flag is so ancient . . . it was never questioned and it was expressly acknowledged in the Treaty of Breda, and yet this last summer it was not only violated by their commanders at sea, and that violation afterwards justified at the Hague, but it was also represented by them in most Courts of Christendom as ridiculous for us to demand. . . . An ungrateful insolence. . . .

We have therefore thought fit to declare and do hereby declare, that we will prosecute war both by sea and land against the States General of the United Provinces and all their subjects and inhabitants, . . . willing and requiring all our subjects to take notice of the same.

4. *The Commons and the Declaration of Indulgence.* When Parliament convened in February, 1673, the provisions of the Declaration of Indulgence had been in effect for almost a year. The passages which follow indicate the reaction of the Commons to Charles' religious policy. The first selection, an account of the debates on February 10, 1673, is taken from a diary kept by Sir Edward Dering, M.P. for East Retford and a moderate supporter of the king. The remaining selections are from the *Journals* of the Lords and Commons.[6]

(*Commons' Debates, February 10, 1673.*) This day according to order we were to take into consideration the King's declaration concerning tender consciences, and that clause particularly which did declare all the penal laws in matters of religion to be suspended.

The speaker put them in mind of the debate adjourned to this day, and for long time no man stood up at all to speak.

At last Sir George Reeves stood up, and said he perceived that those gentlemen that were so warm for this debate on Saturday were now grown cool in it, and therefore desired the House would proceed to something else.

Then Sir Thomas Meres stood up, and said though they were willing to proceed very calmly in this business yet they should find they were not cool in it, though there be always too many gentlemen in this House that are but luke-warm in matters of religion, or to that effect; words that from another man would not have passed without some exception taken to them.

But he moved nothing at all, and again a long silence was in the House, till at last Sir Thomas Lee moved for reading the King's declaration, which was to be the subject matter of the debate; which was done and after that a long and unusual silence in the House a third time, till the speaker putting them in mind that time was precious, and it was now half past eleven, my Lord Cavendish then stood up, and desired that the reasons of the House given to his Majesty upon the like occasion in March 1662 might be read, which being seconded by Sir John Mounson, was done, and those reasons read, which were indeed direct to the matter in hand, and full against all indulgence to dissenters in religion; one reason among others being that there were laws of uniformity in force, which could not be dispensed with but by act of parliament, and that his Majesty's declaration from Breda, or any otherwise, could not bind him against the advice of his people tendered in parliament, with other things to this purpose.

Then Mr. Waller stood up and made a long premeditated speech concerning the power of the King in ecclesiastical matters; the usefulness to the people of his power of dispensing, instanced particularly in the dispensing of keeping of Lent, which because it pleased us, we did not complain of.

Then Mr. Powle made a long speech to the contrary, showing that the King could not dispense, much less suspend, the laws in being.

Mr. Seymour, Sir Robert Howard, and Sir George Downing spoke for the declaration. Colonel Strangways, Sergeant Seys, and Mr. Whorwood and Sir Thomas Meres against it.

Mr. Attorney General opened at large the King's power in ecclesiastical matters; that it was the same with what it was in temporal; that his supremacy as head of the church was chiefly negative, and exclusive of all others, particularly of the Pope, and so it was put in the 39 Articles, and so in the oath of supremacy; that the convocation could make no canons without the King's consent, and yet even then they did not bind without authority of parliament; but that in particular cases the King might judge of the expediency of many laws, and dispense with them *pro bono publico;* that he might pardon the penalties of any laws after they were broken was known by all; that in many cases he might dispense with the law before it was broken, as in the act of navigation, when we wanted provisions to set out our fleet, and could not have them but in foreign bottoms, he had done, and with very just reason. . . .

But the debate quickly went off from justifying and maintaining the clause to the manner of laying it asleep; the words of the question moved by many being that we should vote it illegal. Others, thinking that too harsh, would have us proceed by petition to the King that he would be pleased to consider the consequences of those words; that they gave us some apprehensions of invalidating our laws without the due proceedings which we conceive ought to be by acts of parliament; and that he would please to declare that the laws in matters of religion and uniformity were still in force, notwithstanding the said declaration; and for the wording of it, it might be done with more respect to his Majesty, and with more full security of what we desired by a petition than it could be done by a vote; and therefore moved that a committee might be appointed to draw up such an address to his Majesty. This was moved by Sir Robert Carr, seconded by Mr. Secretary, myself, Mr. Attorney General, and Sir Thomas Osborne; but opposed by Sir Thomas Meres, Sir Thomas Lee, Sergeant Seys, and others.

That which I said was to this purpose: that we were told on all sides that this was a very nice question, and so indeed it was; that many a good man there, and desirous to do his duty to his King and his country, might yet be very doubtful what to advise them to; that I was no advocate for that clause in the declaration which was now under debate because that I did not see any material difference between an universal indefinite, unlimited suspension of laws, as this seemed to be by the declaration, and a total repeal and abrogation, which no man had yet affirmed the King had power to do. But yet I did most willingly join with these gentlemen who had made it their desires that it might be suffered at least *decenter cadere* [to perish decently]; that there might pass no vote upon this occasion which might so much as in appearance lessen the entire happy harmony that was between the King and this House; that if we did look back what our ancestors had done in this place, it might be some directions to us what to do; that I should not look further back than to 3rd *Caroli* [1628], a parliament that was zealous enough for the liberty of those who sent them thither, and which had been already often cited in the debates of this day.

They had then many reasons to complain of the violation of their laws, and in matters of supreme importance. . . . That yet all this produced but a petition and address commonly known by the name of the Petition of Right; and that secured them. That thanks be to God the case was now very different, no man could yet say that anyone's liberty or property had been invaded in the least, or that suffered to the value of a hair of his head. That what we complained of was rather what we feared than what we felt; that I would not deny but these fears were worthy of our consideration by men in the trust under which we were, but I would not have any jealousy from a doubtful word or unweighed expression put us upon anything that might be inconvenient or so much as ungrateful to his Majesty. That we all agreed in the end, and I, as much as any man, aimed at the security of our laws, only debated about the means of coming to it. That it was yet but 4 days since Mr. Speaker had, in the name of the House, desired leave of his Majesty to address ourselves to him in all cases of difficulty and importance; that I did not know any case more important likely to happen than this, and therefore thought it proper to make use of that liberty we had asked and his Majesty had granted; that from so gracious a King to so dutiful and loyal a parliament we could no ways doubt of a satisfactory answer; and therefore humbly moved them to name a committee to draw up an address to his Majesty upon the subject matter of this debate.

At last, the question being stated and called for, it was moved that the previous question should be put; *viz.*, whether the question should be put or not. And the House being divided, the yeas that stayed in were 168, the noes that went out were 116.

After this the main question was put in these words, "whether the penal statutes of this kingdom in matters ecclesiastical can be suspended otherwise than by act of parliament," and carried full in the negative without dividing the House. Then they ordered a committee to draw up an address to the King upon this vote and the debate of the House. And Tuesday being Shrove Tuesday and Wednesday Ash Wednesday, the House adjourned to Thursday.

(*14 February.*) . . . Mr. Powle reports from the committee appointed to prepare and draw up a petition and address to his majesty the said petition and address; which he read in his place and, after, delivered the same in at the clerk's table. And the same, being again twice read, is as followeth, *viz.:*—

Most gracious sovereign: We, your majesty's most loyal and faithful subjects, the commons assembled in parliament, do in the first place, as in all duty bound, return your majesty our most humble and hearty thanks for the many gracious promises and assurances, which your majesty hath several times during this present parliament given to us, that your majesty would secure and maintain unto us the true reformed Protestant religion, our liberties, and properties; which most gracious assurances your majesty hath out of your great goodness been pleased to renew unto us more particularly at the opening of this present session of parliament.

And further we crave leave humbly to represent that we have with all duty and expedition taken into our consideration several parts of your maj-

esty's last speech to us, and withal the declaration therein mentioned for indulgence to dissenters, dated the 15th of March last. And we find ourselves bound in duty to inform your majesty that penal statutes in matter ecclesiastical cannot be suspended but by act of parliament. We therefore, . . . do most humbly beseech your majesty that the said laws may have their free course until it shall be otherwise provided for by act of parliament; and that your majesty would graciously be pleased to give such directions herein, that no apprehensions or jealousies may remain in the hearts of your majesty's good and faithful subjects.

Resolved, etc., that this house doth agree with the committee in the petition and address by them drawn up to be presented to his majesty. . . .

(*24 February.*) . . . Mr. Secretary Coventry reports and presents in writing from his majesty his answer to the humble petition and address of this house, which . . . is as followeth, *viz.:*—

Charles R. His majesty hath received an address from you, and he hath seriously considered of it, and returneth you this answer: that he is very much troubled that that declaration which he put out for ends so necessary to the quiet of his kingdom, and especially in that conjuncture, should have proved the cause of disquiet in this house of commons and give occasion to the questioning of his power in ecclesiastics; which he finds not done in the reigns of any of his ancestors. He is sure he never had thoughts of using it otherwise than as it hath been entrusted in him—to the peace and establishment of the Church of England and the ease of all his subjects in general.

Neither doth he pretend to the right of suspending any laws where in the properties, rights, or liberties of any of his subjects are concerned, nor to alter anything in the established doctrine or discipline of the Church of England; but his only design in this was to take off the penalties the statutes inflict upon the dissenters, and which he believes, when well considered of, you yourselves would not wish executed according to the rigor and letter of the law. Neither hath he done this with any thought of avoiding or precluding the advice of his parliament; and, if any bill shall be offered him which shall appear more proper to attain the aforesaid ends and secure the peace of the church and kingdom, when tendered in due manner to him, he will show how readily he will concur in all ways that shall appear good for the kingdom. . . .

(*26 February.*) . . . Mr. Powle reports . . . an answer agreed by the committee . . . , which . . . is as followeth, *viz.:*—

Most gracious sovereign: We, your majesty's

most humble and loyal subjects, the knights, citizens, and burgesses in this present parliament assembled, do render to your sacred majesty our most dutiful thanks for that, to our unspeakable comfort, your majesty hath been pleased so often to reiterate unto us those gracious promises and assurances of maintaining the religion now established and the liberties and properties of your people. And we do not in the least measure doubt but that your majesty had the same gracious intentions in giving satisfaction to your subjects by your answer to our last petition and address.

Yet, upon a serious consideration thereof, we find that the said answer is not sufficient to clear the apprehensions that may justly remain in the minds of your people by your majesty's having claimed a power to suspend penal statutes in matters ecclesiastical, and which your majesty does still seem to assert . . . to be entrusted in the crown and never questioned in the reigns of any of your ancestors—wherein we humbly conceive your majesty hath been very much misinformed; since no such power was ever claimed or exercised by any of your majesty's predecessors, and, if it should be admitted, might tend to the interrupting of the free course of the laws and altering the legislative power, which hath always been acknowledged to reside in your majesty and your two houses of parliament.

We do therefore, with an unanimous consent, become again most humble suitors unto your sacred majesty that you would be pleased to give us a full and satisfactory answer to our said petition and address, and that your majesty would take such effectual order that the proceedings in this matter may not for the future be drawn into consequence or example.

. . . Resolved, etc., that the whole address be agreed to as it was brought in by the committee. . . .

(8 *March*.) . . . His majesty sitting in his royal throne, adorned with his crown and regal ornaments, commanded the gentleman usher of the black rod to give notice to the house of commons that they attend his majesty presently. The commons being come with their speaker, his majesty made this short speech following: "My lords and gentlemen: . . . If there be any scruple remain with you concerning the suspension of penal laws, I here faithfully promise you that what hath been done in that particular shall not for the future be drawn either into consequence or example. . . ."

Next the lord chancellor reported . . . that his majesty had the last night, in pursuance of what he then intended and declared this morning concerning the suspension of penal laws not being for the future drawn either into consequence or example, caused the original declaration under the great seal to be cancelled in his presence;

whereof himself and several other lords of the council were witnesses. . . .

5. *The Religious Policy of the Commons.* The withdrawal of the Declaration of Indulgence was not enough to satisfy the Commons. In the previous session there had been introduced a bill to prevent the growth of popery. This bill, later to be known as the "Test Act," received the royal assent on March 29, 1673.[7]

An act for preventing dangers which may happen from popish recusants. For preventing dangers which may happen from popish recusants and quieting the minds of his majesty's good subjects: be it enacted . . . that all and every person or persons, as well peers as commoners, that shall bear any office or offices civil or military; or shall receive any pay, salary, fee, or wages by reason of any grant from his majesty; or shall have command or place of trust from or under his majesty or from any of his majesty's predecessors . . . within the realm of England, . . . or in his Majesty's navy, . . . or shall be of the household or in the service or employment of his majesty or of his royal highness the duke of York, who shall inhabit, reside, or be within the city of London or Westminster or within thirty miles distant from the same . . . ; the said person and persons shall personally appear . . . in his majesty's high court of chancery or in his majesty's court of king's bench, and there in public . . . take the several oaths of supremacy and allegiance. . . . And the said respective officers aforesaid shall also receive the sacrament of the Lord's Supper according to the usage of the Church of England . . . in some parish church upon some . . . Sunday immediately after divine service and sermon. . . .

[The next article provides similar tests to be taken by every new appointee to such office within stated times after his appointment.]

And be it further enacted . . . that all . . . that do . . . refuse to take the said oaths and sacrament in the said courts and places . . . shall be *ipso facto* adjudged incapable and disabled in law . . . to have . . . the said office or offices. . . . And be it further enacted that all . . . that shall . . . refuse to take the said oaths or the sacrament as aforesaid . . . , and yet after such neglect and refusal shall execute any of the said offices or employments after the said times expired . . . , and being thereupon lawfully convicted . . . , shall be disabled from thenceforth to sue or use any action, bill, plaint, or information in course of law, or to prosecute any suit in any court of equity or to be guardian of any child or executor or administrator of any person or capable of any legacy or deed or gift, or to bear any office within this realm of England, . . . ; and shall forfeit the sum of £500, to be recovered by him that shall sue for the same. . . .

And be it further enacted that, if any person or persons, not bred up by his or their parent or parents from their infancy in the popish religion and professing themselves to be popish recusants, shall breed up, instruct, or educate his or their child or children, or suffer them to be instructed or educated, in the popish religion, every such person, being thereof convicted, shall be thenceforth disabled of bearing any office or place of trust or profit in church or state. . . .

And be it further enacted . . . that at the same time when the persons concerned in this act shall take the aforesaid oaths of supremacy and allegiance, they shall likewise make and subscribe this declaration following, under the same penalties and forfeitures as by this act is appointed: "I, A.B., do declare that I do believe that there is not any transubstantiation in the sacrament of the Lord's Supper, or in the elements of bread and wine, at or after the consecration thereof by any person whatsoever."

6. *The Commons and the Dutch War.* On October 27, 1673 Charles asked Parliament for additional funds with which to carry on the war. In the selections which follow, the reaction of the Commons is demonstrated. The first selection is taken from an account of proceedings in the House of Commons written by Anchitel Grey, M.P. for Derby; the others are from the *Journals* of the Commons.[8]

Mr. Russell. The business of this day is "Money." . . . Would not vote things hand over head; let us consider what we give this money for, and consider what we give as destructive to the nation (by maintaining this war) and the Protestant religion. The French king calls this war a "Catholic war" and seeing we are upon so wrong a bottom, and if betrayed by those about the king let us tell him plainly of it. Former Parliaments have done it; and moves to pass a negative vote upon "Money."

Mr. Secretary Coventry. Knows not that ever the House of Austria had the name of Huguenot among them, though Holland joined with them. We can have war with Holland without religion in the case, they once had with the French as we have now. . . . Consider they [the Dutch] have provided a great fleet against the summer, and you will give no money, and so have no fleet; which way will you secure the plantations [colonies] and Tangier?

Mr. Sacheverell. Is one of those that think "giving of money" one of the greatest grievances. It

seems to him that those villainous counsellors, that persuaded the king to make this war, have deceived him in this speech; do not they know of the unpaid taxes granted this last session with the prizes and the customs? . . . It was said before . . . "Give money and grievances shall be redressed." . . . The army is so insolent that they may turn you out of doors. . . . If redress of grievances be an argument for "Money" you will never want grievances. Will you not heighten France by giving more money, . . . that he may have dominion at sea which we now contend for? And by this negative we may deliver ourselves both from France and Rome.

Mr. Attorney Finch. This is an English and no other war. . . . The king may engage in a war; but when his people shall storm him out of it, the hour will come that his enemies wish for, for the Dutch will now be upon greater terms, having ever desired such a storm as the king could not allay.

Mr. Powle. Shall never think that privilege of Parliament is not violated so long as a Privy Councilor sits in the Chair. He that was contriver of the Declaration [of Indulgence] made Lord Privy Seal and another as much concerned made chief governor of Scotland. This is to bring in popery in triumph.

Sir William Coventry. Thinks it better we had no fleet; thinks not so highly of the Dutch nor meanly of ourselves but that we may do well without the King of France. . . . The French interest is to keep us from being masters of the sea; the French have pursued that interest well; moves to insert in the question, "unless it shall appear that the obstinacy of the Dutch shall make a supply necessary."

[The Commons then refuse a supply.]

(*January 24, 1674.*) A message from His Majesty by Sir Edward Carteret, Usher of the Black Rod.

Mr. Speaker, His Majesty commands this honorable House to attend him immediately in the House of Peers.

And accordingly Mr. Speaker, with the House went up to attend His Majesty.

Mr. Speaker reports that, because he would not trust his memory, His Majesty had been pleased to deliver to him his speech in writing: which he read to the House; which is as follows, *viz.:*—

My Lords and Gentlemen,

At the beginning of this session I told you (as I thought I had reason to do), that the States General had not yet made me any proposals which could be imagined with intent to conclude, but only to amuse.

To avoid this imputation they have now sent me a letter by the Spanish ambassador, offering me some terms of peace, upon conditions formerly drawn up, and in a more decent style than before.

It is upon this that I desire your speedy advice: For, if you shall find the terms such as may be embraced, your advice will have great weight with me: And if you find them defective, I hope you will give me your advice and assistance how to get better terms.

Upon the whole matter I doubt not but you will have a care of my honor, and the honor and safety of the nation, which are now so deeply concerned.

(*January 27, 1674.*) The House then resolved into a Committee of the whole House to proceed in the consideration of His Majesty's last speech.

Mr. Speaker left the Chair.

Sir Charles Harbord took the Chair of the Committee.

Mr. Speaker resumed the Chair.

Sir Charles Harbord reports from the Committee of the whole House a vote and resolve of the Committee to be presented to the House: which was delivered in at the clerk's table; and is as follows; *viz.:*—

That, upon consideration of His Majesty's gracious speech, and the proposals from the States General of the United Provinces, this committee is of opinion that His Majesty be humbly advised to proceed in a treaty with the said States, in order to a speedy peace.

7. *The Treaty of Westminster, February 9, 1674.*[9]

It is concluded and agreed that from this day there shall be a firm and inviolable peace, union and friendship betwixt His Majesty the King of Great Britain and the High and Mighty Lords the States General of the United Provinces, and betwixt all their subjects whether within Europe or without, in all regions and places whatsoever. . . .

IV. That the aforesaid States General of the United Provinces in due acknowledgment on their part of the King of Great Britain's right to have his flag respected in the seas hereafter mentioned, shall and do declare and agree, that whatsoever ships or vessels belonging to the United Provinces whether vessels of war or others or whether single or in fleets, shall meet in any of the seas from Cape Finisterre to the middle point of the land Van Staten in Norway, with any ships or vessels belonging to his Majesty of Great Britain, whether those ships be single or in greater number, if they carry His Majesty of Great Britain's flag or jack, the aforesaid Dutch vessels or ships shall strike their flag and lower their top sail, in the same manner and with as much respect as hath at any time or in any place been formerly practised towards any ships of His Majesty of Great Britain or his predecessors, by any ships of the States General or their predecessors.

C. THE CRISIS OF 1685–88

In 1685, Charles II, having fulfilled his primary policy of "never going again on his travels," died in his bed at Whitehall. The last years of his reign had not been peaceful. In 1678 England had been convulsed with the hysteria of the Popish Plot, the principal results of which had been a violent increase of anti-Catholic feeling, and a serious attempt to exclude Charles' brother James, an avowed Catholic, from the succession. The attempt at exclusion failed and Charles, favored by a popular revulsion against the violent measures of the Exclusionists, or "Whigs," built up a strong party of Anglican Tories around the monarchy. Thus he passed to James a reasonably stable throne.

1. *Catholics in the Army: the King and the Parliament.* In the spring of 1685 James II had to face rebellion. The Duke of Monmouth, an illegitimate son of Charles II, was put forward by the Whig extremists as the rightful heir to the throne and the protector of the Protestant interest. Monmouth attracted relatively few adherents, and the militia, stiffened by the tiny regular army, put down the rebellion with little trouble. Parliament, summoned before the rebellion, had given James agreeable evidence of its loyalty by voting funds; in their second session, James went before them confidently

with a request for more money. The selections which follow are taken from Anchitel Grey's *Debates.*[10]

(*The king's speech, November 9, 1685.*) My Lords and Gentlemen,

After the storm that seemed to be coming upon us when we parted last, I am glad to meet you all again in so great peace and quietness; God Almighty be praised, by whose blessing that Rebellion was suppressed! But when we reflect what an inconsiderable number of men began it, and how long they carried it on without any opposition, I hope everybody will be convinced that the militia, which hath hitherto been so much depended on, is not sufficient for such occasions; and that there is nothing but a good force of well-disciplined troops in constant pay that can defend us from such as, either at home or abroad, are disposed to disturb us: And, in truth, my concern for the peace and quiet of my subjects, as well as for the safety of the Government, made me think it necessary to increase the number to the proportion I have done: That I owed as well to the honor as the security of the nation; whose reputation was so infinitely exposed to all our neighbors, by having so evidently lain open to this late wretched attempt, that it is not to be repaired without keeping such a body of men on foot that none may ever have the thought of finding us again so miserably unprovided.

It is for the support of this great charge, which is now more than double to what it was, that I ask your assistance in giving me a supply answerable to the expenses it brings along with it: and I cannot doubt, but what I have begun, so much for the honor and defense of the Government, will be continued by you with all the cheerfulness and readiness that is requisite for a work of so great importance.

Let no man take exception that there are some officers in the army not qualified, according to the late tests, for their employments: The gentlemen, I must tell you, are most of them well-known to me: And, having formerly served with me on several occasions and always approved the loyalty of their principles by their practice, I think them now fit to be employed under me. And I will deal plainly with you, that, after having had the benefit of their service in such a time of need and danger, I will neither expose them to disgrace, nor myself to the want of them, if there should be another rebellion to make them necessary to me.

(*The Commons debate, November 12.*) Sir Winston Churchill. Some other than the militia is necessary to be found: I move a supply for the army.

Lord Preston. We have lately had an unfortunate proof, how little we are to depend upon the militia, and therefore we must all approve of His Majesty's increasing the forces to what they are. France is formidable, now Holland's forces are greatly increased, and we must be strong in proportion, for preservation of ourselves and Flanders and toward that, the good harmony betwixt the King and this House hath greatly contributed. It has had two other great effects abroad. 1. The French King's army last spring was marching towards Germany; Crequi was far advanced; but when the King of France heard the kindness of this House to the King, and the defeat of Mon-

mouth, he recalled them. 2. The French and Spaniards had also a difference about Haye and Fonterabia: The French advanced their troops and recalled them on this news. This is the noble effect of the harmony between the King and this House who have (I hope) brought the same Heart and Loyalty they had the last time here. Hence we may conclude, these levies made by the King are just, reasonable, and necessary. And so let us vote a supply to answer His Majesty's present occasions.

Earl of Ranelagh. The question is, whether a supply or not? I do not intend to arraign the militia, but seeing a soldier is a trade and must (as all other trades are) be learned, I will show you where the militia has failed; *viz.,* at Chatham; and in June last, when the late Duke of Monmouth landed and had but eighty-three men, and £300 in money, who, in spite of the militia, nay in spite of such other force as the King could spare hence, brought it so far as he did. If the King of France had landed then, what would have become of us? I say, the militia is not insignificant, but an additional force is necessary and so a supply that is answerable to it. . . .

Sir Thomas Clarges. If it shall appear to you that the King's revenue that he hath already be sufficient to supply all the occasions what then need we give him more? It is moved that we should proceed by paragraphs. To come first to the militia, who (let me tell you) did considerable service in the late Rebellion, and if a great nobleman of this Kingdom had been supplied and assisted, it had soon been quelled. A confidence betwixt the King and his people is absolutely needful, let it come whence it will; our happiness consists in it. His Majesty, on his first entrance on the Crown, told us, "he had been misrepresented, and that he would preserve the Government in Church and State now established by law, and would maintain us in all our just rights and privileges."

Over-joyed at this, we ran hastily in to him; we gave four millions (reckoning what we added to him for life was worth) at once. The present revenue is £1,900,000, or two millions, yearly; the charge of the Government (admitting this army kept up) is but £1,300,000 yearly: And pray let us not forget that there was a Bill of Exclusion debated in this House; I was here, and showed myself against it; the arguments for it were, "That we should, in case of a Popish successor, have a Popish army." You see the Act of the Test already broken, but pray remember what the late Lord Chancellor told you, when the late King (of blessed memory) passed that Act: The words were to this effect; "By this Act you are provided against Popery, that no Papist can possibly creep into any employment."

I am afflicted greatly at this breach of our liberties, and seeing so great difference betwixt this speech and those heretofore made, cannot but believe this was by some other advice. This, struck at here, is our all, and I wonder there have been any men so desperate as to take any employment not qualified for it; and I would therefore have the question, "That a standing army is destructive to the country." . . .

Sir William Trumbull. The Kingdom is guarded by law; we are now in perfect peace; the King is both feared and loved; an army little needed; men justly afraid: That which made the last rebellion as it was, the man that headed it was a favorite of the faction, and though he had got such a number, he was beaten by 1800 men only. I am against an army.

Mr. Seymour. This last rebellion has contributed to our future peace and those engaged in it have sung their penitential psalm and their punishment rejoiced at by all good persons. I do not commend the militia, yet it is not to be rejected, but to be new modeled; and for my part, I had rather pay double to these, [meaning for keeping up the militia] from whom I fear nothing, than half so much to those, of whom I must ever be afraid; and, say what you will, it is a standing army. The last force preserved the peace and was sufficient to do it, in the late King's time, and is now; all the profit and security of this nation is in our ships; and had there been the least ship in the Channel, it would have disappointed him.

Supporting an army is maintaining so many idle persons to lord it over the rest of the subjects. The King declared, "That no soldiers should quarter in private houses"; but that they did: "That they should pay for all things they took"; but they paid nothing for almost all they took. And for officers to be employed not taking the tests, it is dispensing with all the laws at once; and if these men be good and kind, we know not whether it proceeds from their generosity or principles: For we must remember, it is treason for any man to be reconciled to the Church of Rome; for the Pope, by law, is declared an enemy to this Kingdom.

A supply given, as moved for, is a kind of an establishing an army by Act of Parliament; and when they have got the power into their hands, we are then to derive it from their courtesy; and therefore I would have the question be, "That the safety of the Kingdom doth not consist with a standing force": And this, it may be, well disappoint these persons that make it their business this way, to make themselves useful. . . .

Sir Richard Temple. I must concur with the King that the militia is not sufficient: I am for mending the militia, and to make it such as the King and Kingdom may confide in it; to trust to mercenary force alone is to give up all our liberties at once. If you provide a constant supply to support them by setting up an army, Sir Thomas Meres has turned it into a supply for the navy. There is no country in the world that has a law to set up an army. We have already made an ample supply for the Government. It is for kings to come to the House, from time to time, on extraordinary occasions; and if this army be provided for by law, they will never more come to this House.

I am for giving for the extraordinary charge past. Armies are useful when occasion is for them; but if you establish them, you can disband them no more. I am for a supply, but not on this score of the militia: There was not a company formed till 1588; and as soon as Queen Elizabeth had done with her army, she disbanded it. Armies have been fatal often to princes. The Army, in the late King's time, often turned out their leaders. I am for going to the House for leave for a bill to mend the militia.

Sir Winston Churchill. The Beef-Eaters [Tower of London guards], at this rate, may be called an army.

Sir Thomas Hussey. The colonel may say what he will of the Beef-Eaters, as he nick-names them; but they are established by Act of Parliament. . . .

The question being put, that a supply be given to His Majesty,

Sir Thomas Clarges moved, that the words, "towards the support of the additional forces," may be added: which was carried in the negative, 225 to 156; and then these votes passed:

Resolved, *Nemine contradicente,* That a supply be given to His Majesty; and that the House be moved to give leave to bring in a bill to render the militia useful.

Which were agreed to by the House.

(*The Commons' address, November 16.*) We your Majesty's most loyal and faithful subjects, the Commons in Parliament assembled, do in the first place (as in duty bound) return your Majesty our most humble and hearty thanks for your great care and conduct in supporting the late Rebellion, which threatened the overthrow of this Government both in Church and State, and the utter extirpation of our religion as by law established, which is most dear unto us, and which your Majesty hath been pleased to give us repeated assurances you will always defend and support; which with all grateful hearts we shall ever acknowledge.

We farther crave leave to acquaint your Majesty that we have, with all duty and readiness, taken into our consideration your Majesty's gracious speech to us: And as to that part of it, relating to the officers in the army, not qualified for their employments, according to an Act of Parliament made in the 25th year of the reign of your Majesty's Royal Brother, entitled, An Act for preventing Dangers which may happen from Popish Recusants, we do, out of our bounden duty, humbly represent unto your Majesty, that those officers cannot by law be capable of their employments; and that the incapacities they bring upon themselves thereby, can no way be taken off but by an Act of Parliament.

Therefore, out of that great deference and duty we owe unto your Majesty, who have been graciously pleased to take notice of their services to you, we are preparing a bill to pass both Houses for your royal assent, to indemnify them from the penalties they have now incurred: and because the continuing of them in their employments may be taken to be a dispensing with that law without Act of Parliament (the consequence of which is of the greatest concern to the rights of all your Majesty's subjects, and to all the laws made for security of their religion) we therefore, the knights, citizens, and burgesses of your Majesty's House of Commons, do most humbly beseech your Majesty that you would be graciously pleased to give such directions therein that no apprehensions or jealousies may remain in the hearts of your Majesty's good and faithful subjects.

2. Catholics in the Army: the King and Courts.
After his failure in Parliament, James turned to the law courts. In 1686 a test case was arranged in which Sir Edward Hales, a Catholic holding a colonel's commission, was sued by his coachman Godden according to the provisions of the Test Act. In defense Hales pleaded that he had received the King's letters patent dispensing with the oaths in his case. The speech of the Lord Chief Justice follows.[11]

. . . In the case of Godden and Hales, wherein the defendant pleads a dispensation from the king, it is doubted whether or no the king had such a prerogative. Truly, upon the argument before us, it appeared as clear a case as ever came before this court; but, because men fancy I know not what difficulty when really there is none, we were willing to give so much countenance to the question in the case as to take the advice of all the judges of England.

They were all assembled at Serjeants' Inn, and this case was put to them. . . . And I must tell you that there were ten upon the place that clearly delivered their opinions. . . . My brother Powell said he was inclined to be of the same opinion, but he would rather have some more time to consider of it. But, he has since sent by

my brother Holloway to let us know that he does concur with us. To these eleven judges there is one dissenter, brother Street, who yet continues his opinion that the king cannot dispense in this case. But that's the opinion of one single judge against the opinion of eleven.

We were satisfied in our judgments before and, having the concurrence of eleven out of twelve, we think we may very well declare the opinion of the court to be that the king may dispense in this case. And the judges go upon these grounds: —(1) that the kings of England are sovereign princes; (2) that the laws of England are the king's laws; (3) that therefore 'tis an inseparable prerogative in the kings of England to dispense with penal laws in particular cases and upon particular necessary reasons; (4) that of those reasons and those necessities, the king himself is sole judge; and then, which is consequent upon all; (5) that this is not a trust invested in, or granted to, the king by the people, but the ancient remains of the sovereign power and prerogative of the kings of England; which never yet was taken from them, nor can be. And therefore, such a dispensation appearing upon records to come [in] time enough to save him from the forfeiture, judgment ought to be given for the defendant.

3. Catholics in the Universities.
James hoped to introduce his co-religionists not only into the army but also into the universities and even into the Church of England. The following account of these activities is taken from Bishop Burnet's *History of His Own Times*. Burnet was a firm Protestant, but while his writings against popery incurred the enmity of the court party, his deprecation of the persecution of papists gained him the hatred of the extreme anti-Catholic faction. He held various ecclesiastical offices, but in 1684 thought it advisable to go into voluntary exile on the continent. In 1689 William made him Bishop of Salisbury.[12]

Jefferies [the Lord Chief Justice] was much sunk at court and Herbert was the most in favor. But now [1686] Jefferies, to recommend himself, offered a bold and illegal advice, for setting up an ecclesiastical commission, without calling it the high commission, pretending it was only a standing court of delegates. The act that put down the high commission in the year 1640, had provided by a clause, as full as could be conceived, that no court should be ever set up for those matters, besides the ordinary ecclesiastical courts. Yet, in contempt of that, a court was erected, with full power to proceed in a summary and arbitrary way in all ecclesiastical matters, without limitations to any rule of law in their proceedings. This stretch of the supremacy, so contrary to law, was assumed by a king, whose religion made him condemn all that supremacy that the law had vested in the crown. . . .

The deanery of Christ's Church [College], the most important post in the university [of Oxford], was given to Massey, one of the new converts [to Catholicism], though he had neither the gravity, the learning, nor the age that was suitable to such a dignity. But all was supplied by his early conversion: and it was set up for a maxim, to encourage all converts. He at first went to prayers in the chapel. But soon after, he declared himself more openly. Not long after this, the president of Magdalen college died. That is esteemed the richest foundation in England, perhaps in Europe; for though their certain rents are but about £4 or £5000 yet it is thought that the improved value of the estate belonging to it is about £40,000. So it was no wonder that the priests studied to get this endowment into their hands.

They had endeavored to break in upon the university of Cambridge in a matter of less importance, but without success: and now they resolved to attack Oxford by a strange fatality in their counsels. In all nations the privileges of colleges and universities are esteemed such sacred things, that few will venture to dispute these, much less to disturb them, when their title is good, and their possession is of a long continuance: for in these, not only the present body espouses the matter, but all who have been of it, even those that have only followed their study in it, think themselves bound in honor and gratitude to assist and support them. . . .

They began with Cambridge upon a softer point, which yet would have made way for all the rest. The king sent his letter, or *mandamus,* to order F. Francis, an ignorant Benedictine monk, to be received a master of arts; once to open the way for letting them into the degrees of the university.

The truth is, the king's letters were scarce ever refused in conferring degrees: and when ambassadors or foreign princes came to those places, they usually gave such degrees to those who belonged to them as were desired. The Morocco ambassador's secretary, that was a Mahometan, had that degree given him; but a great distinction was made between honorary degrees given to strangers, who intended not to live among them, and those given to such as intended to settle among them: for every master of arts having a vote in the convocation, they reckoned that, if they gave this degree, they must give all that should be pretended to on the like authority: and they knew all the king's priests would be let in upon them, which might occasion in present great distraction and contentions among them;

and in time they might grow to be a majority in the convocation, which is their parliament.

They refused the *mandamus* with great unanimity, and with a firmness that the court had not expected from them. New and repeated orders, full of severe threatenings in case of disobedience, were sent to them: and this piece of raillery was everywhere set up, that a papist was reckoned worse than a Mahometan, and that the king's letters were less considered than the ambassador from Morocco had been.

Some feeble or false men of the university tried to compound the matter, by granting this degree to F. Francis, but enacting at the same time, that it should not be a precedent for the future for any other of the like nature. This was not given way to: for it was said, that in all such cases the obedience that was once paid would be a much stronger argument for continuing to do it, as oft as it should be desired, than any such proviso could be against it.

Upon this the vice-chancellor was summoned before the ecclesiastical commission to answer this contempt. He was a very honest, but a very weak man. He made a poor defense. . . . But he having acted only as the chief person of that body, all that was thought fit to be done against him was to turn him out of his office. . . . The university chose another vice-chancellor, who was a man of much spirit: and in his speech, which in course he made upon his being chosen, he promised that, during his magistracy, neither religion nor the rights of the body should suffer by his means. . . .

And now all people began to see that they had taken wrong measures of the king, when they thought that it would be easy to engage him into bold things, before he could see into the ill consequences that might attend them, but that being once engaged he would resolve to go through with them at all adventures. When I knew him, he seemed to have set up that for a maxim, that a king when he made a step was never to go back, nor to encourage faction and disobedience by yielding to it.

After this unsuccessful attempt upon Cambridge, another was made upon Oxford, that lasted longer and had greater effects; which I shall set all down together, though the conclusion of this affair ran far into the year after this that I now write of. The presidentship of Magdalen was given by the election of the fellows. So the king sent a *mandamus* requiring them to choose one Farmer, an ignorant and vicious person, who had not one qualification that could recommend him to so high a post besides that of changing his religion. *Mandamus* letters had no legal authority in them: but all the great preferments of the church being in the king's disposal, those who did pretend to favor were not apt to refuse his recommendation, lest that should be afterwards remembered to their prejudice.

But now, since it was visible in what channel favor was like to run, less regard was had to such a letter. The fellows of that house did upon this choose Dr. Hough, one of their body, who, as he was in all respects a statutable man, so he was a worthy and a firm man, not apt to be threatened out of his right. They carried their election, according to their statutes, to the bishop of Winchester, their visitor: and he confirmed it. So that matter was legally settled. This was highly resented at court. . . .

The cause was brought before the ecclesiastical commission. The fellows were first asked why they had not chosen Farmer in obedience to the king's letter? And to that they answered by offering a list of many just exceptions against him. The subject was fruitful, and the scandals he had given were very public. The court was ashamed of him and insisted no more on him: but they said that the house ought to have shown more respect to the king's letter than to have proceeded to an election in contempt of it.

The ecclesiastical commission took upon them to declare Hough's election null, and to put the house under suspension. And, that the design of the court in this matter might be carried on without the load of recommending a papist, Parker, bishop of Oxford, was now recommended: and the fellows were commanded to proceed to a new election in his favor.

They excused themselves, since they were bound by their oaths to maintain their statutes: and by these, an election being once made and confirmed, they could not proceed to a new choice, till the former was annulled in some court of law: church benefices and college preferments were freeholds, and could only be judged in a court of record: and since the king was now talking so much of liberty of conscience, it was said, that the forcing men to act against their oaths seemed not to agree with those professions. In opposition to this it was said that the statutes of colleges had been always considered as things that depended entirely on the king's good pleasure; so that no oaths to observe them could bind them, when it was in opposition to the king's command.

This did not satisfy the fellows: and, though the king, as he went through Oxford in his progress in the year 1687, sent for them and ordered them to go presently and choose Parker for their president, in a strain of language ill suited to the majesty of a crowned head (for he treated them with foul language pronounced in a very angry tone), yet it had no effect on them. They insisted still on their oaths, though with a humility and submission that they hoped would have mol-

lified him. They continued thus firm. A subaltern commission was sent from the ecclesiastical commission to finish the matter. Bishop Cartwright was the head of this commission, as Sir Charles Hedges was the king's advocate to manage the matter. . . .

The new president was turned out. And, because he would not deliver the keys of his house, the doors were broken open: and Parker was put in possession. The fellows were required to make their submission, to ask pardon for what was past, and to accept of the bishop for their president. They still pleaded their oath: and were all turned out, except two that submitted. So that it was expected to see that house soon stocked with papists. The nation, as well as the university, looked on all this proceeding with a just indignation. It was thought an open piece of robbery and burglary, when men, authorized by no legal commission, came and forcibly turned men out of their possession and freehold.

4. *King James' Declaration of Indulgence, 1687.* A further twist in James' religious policy can be seen in the Declaration of Indulgence issued on April 4, 1687, selections from which follow.[18]

His Majesty's gracious Declaration to all his loving subjects for liberty of conscience.

. . . We cannot but heartily wish, as it will easily be believed, that all the people of our dominions were members of the Catholic Church, and yet we humbly thank Almighty God, it is and has of long time been our constant sense and opinion, . . . that conscience ought not to be constrained nor people forced in matters of mere religion. . . .

[Opening clause of Declaration promises to protect the clergy of the Church of England in the free exercise of their religion and in the enjoyment of their possessions.] . . . We do likewise declare that it is our royal will and pleasure that . . . the execution of all . . . penal laws . . . be immediately suspended.

And . . . we straightly charge and command all our loving subjects, that—like as we do freely give them leave to meet and serve God after their own way . . . be it in private houses or places publicly hired or built for that use— we . . . do hereby command that no disturbance of any kind be made or given unto them under pain of our displeasure. . . .

We do hereby further declare that . . . the oaths commonly called "the oaths of supremacy and allegiance," and also the several tests and declarations mentioned in the Acts of Parliament made in the five and twentieth and thirtieth years of the reign of our late royal brother, King Charles II, shall not . . . hereafter be required to be taken, declared or subscribed by any person . . . whatsoever, who is or shall be employed in any office or place of trust, either civil or military, under us or in our Government . . . and . . . we do hereby give our free and ample pardon unto all nonconformists, recusants and other our loving subjects for all crimes and things . . . done contrary to the penal laws. . . .

5. *The King and a Future Parliament.* King James was well aware that he could not govern indefinitely without calling a Parliament, and he was also aware that the members of the last House of Commons were not in sympathy with his current activities. He sought, therefore, to find means of providing himself with a sympathetic House. The following account of his method of proceeding is taken from the diary of Sir John Reresby, an M.P. and Governor of York.[14]

The king caused the lord lieutenants of most if not all counties of England to call together all their deputy lieutenants and the justices of the peace, and to ask them these three questions:

1. In case the King should call a Parliament and they should be chosen of it, would they give their votes to take away the test and the penal laws?

2. Would they give their votes for the choosing of such members as they believed would be for the taking them away?

3. Would they live peaceably with such as dissented from them in religion, as good Christians ought to do?

Several lord lieutenants that refused to execute this order were turned out, and papists put in their places; and the deputy lieutenants and justices of the peace that did not give a satisfactory answer were generally displaced. This was indeed putting the thing too far, and the wonder of all men to what purpose it was done. For what answer could a man give that was to be a member of Parliament till he heard the reasons and debates of the House? And who could tell the temper of intention of him that was voted for till he came into the House? And if men had a mind to deceive the king, how easy (nay, how likely) was it for them to pretend to be of one judgment now and of another when they were of the House?

Besides, it struck at the very foundation of Parliaments to pre-engage men before they came there, where they were to be allowed the freedom both of their speech and judgments. The most general answer that was given by Protestants of the Church of England was this, that they would give their votes so, if of the House, as the reasons of the debate directed them; that they would vote for such as they thought would do so; and that they would live quietly with all men as good Christians and loyal subjects.

There was about this time great removes of officers, military and civil, and most corporations were purged of their Church of England aldermen, and papists or dissenters put in their places.

6. *The King and the Seven Bishops.* In May, 1688, James issued a second Declaration of Indulgence, repeating the substance of the first and adding a promise that a Parliament should meet before fall. He also issued an order in council to the bishops, instructing them to have the Declaration read in all parish churches throughout the kingdom. The results of these acts are described by John Evelyn, the celebrated diarist.[15]

May 18th. The king, enjoining the ministers to read his Declaration for giving liberty of conscience (as it was styled) in all the churches of England, this evening, 6 bishops, Bath and Wells, Peterborough, Ely, Chichester, St. Asaph, and Bristol, in the name of all the rest of the bishops, came to his majesty to petition him that he would not impose the reading of it to the several congregations within their dioceses; not that they were averse to the publishing it for want of due tenderness towards dissenters, in relations to whom they should be willing to come to such a temper as should be thought fit, when that matter might be considered and settled in parliament and convocation; but that, the Declaration being founded on such a dispensing power as might at pleasure set aside all laws ecclesiastical and civil, it appeared to them illegal, as it had done to the Parliament in 1661 and 1672, and that it was a point of such consequences, that they could not so far make themselves parties to it as the reading of it in church in time of divine service amounted to.

The king was so far incensed at this address that he with threatening expressions commanded them to obey him in reading it at their perils, and so dismissed them.

20th. I went to Whitehall Chapel, where, after the morning lessons, the Declaration was read by one of the choir who used to read the chapters. I hear it was in the Abbey Church, Westminster, but almost universally forborn throughout all London: the consequence of which a little time will show.

25th. All the discourse now was about the bishops refusing to read the injunctions for the abolition of the Test, etc. It seems the injunctions came so crudely from the secretary's office that it was neither sealed nor signed in form, nor had any lawyer been consulted, so as the bishops who took all imaginable advice, put the Court to great difficulties how to proceed against them. Great were the consults, and a proclamation expected all this day, but nothing was done. The action of the bishops was universally applauded and reconciled many adverse parties, papists only excepted, who were now exceedingly perplexed, and violent courses were every moment expected. Report was that the Protestant secular lords and nobility would abet the clergy. . . .

June 8th. This day the Archbishop of Canterbury, with the bishops of Ely, Chichester, St. Asaph, Bristol, Peterborough, and Bath and Wells, were sent from the Privy Council prisoners to the Tower, for refusing to give bail for their appearance, on their not reading the declaration for liberty of conscience; they refused to give bail, as it would have prejudiced their peerage. The concern of the people for them was wonderful, infinite crowds on their knees begging their blessing, and praying for them as they passed out of the barge along the Tower wharf.

10th. A young prince born, which will cause disputes.

About 2 o'clock we heard the Tower ordnance discharged, and the bells ringing for the birth of a Prince of Wales. This was very surprising, it having been universally given out that her majesty did not look till the next month.

13th. I went to the Tower to see the bishops, visited the Abp. and Bps. of Ely, St. Asaph, and Bath and Wells.

14th. Dined with my Lord Chancellor.

15th. Being the first day of term, the bishops were brought to Westminster on habeas corpus, when the indictment was read, and they were called on to plead; their counsel objected that the warrant was illegal, but after long debate it was over-ruled, and they pleaded. The court then offered to take bail for their appearance, but this they refused, and at last were dismissed on their own recognizances to appear that day fortnight; the Abp. in £200, the bishops £100 each.

29th. They appeared; the trial lasted from 9 in the morning to past 6 in the evening, when the jury retired to consider of their verdict, and the courts adjourned to 9 the next morning. The jury were locked up till that time, 11 of them being for an acquittal, but one (Arnold a brewer) would not consent. At length he agreed with the others. The Chief Justice Wright behaved with great moderation and civility to the bishops. Alibone, a papist, was strongly against them; but Holloway and Powell, being of opinion in their favor, they were acquitted. When this was heard, there was great rejoicing; and there was a lane of people from the King's Bench to the water side, on their knees, as the bishops passed and repassed, to beg their blessing. Bonfires were made that night, and bells rung, which was taken very ill at Court, and an appearance of near 60 earls and lords, &c. on the bench, did not a little comfort them, but indeed they were all along full of comfort and cheerful.

Note, they denied to pay the Lieut. of the Tower (Hales, who used them very surlily) any fees, alleging that none were due.

17th. Was a day of thanksgiving in London and 10 miles about for the young prince's birth; and a form of prayer made for the purpose by the Bp. of Rochester.

The night was solemnized with bonfires and other fire-works, &c.

July 2nd. The two judges, Holloway and Powell, were displaced.

7. *The Invitation to William of Orange, 30 June 1688.* On the night of the acquittal of the seven bishops the following letter was sent to William of Orange.[16]

We have great satisfaction to find by 35 [Russell] . . . that your Highness is so ready and willing to give us such assistances as . . . [he has] related to us. We have great reason to believe, we shall be every day in a worse condition than we are and less able to defend ourselves. . . . The people are so generally dissatisfied with the present conduct of the government in relation to their religion, liberties, and properties (all of which have been greatly invaded) . . . that your Highness may be assured, there are nineteen parts out of twenty of the people . . . who would contribute to it, if, they had such protection to countenance their rising as would secure them from being destroyed before they could get to be in a position able to defend themselves. . . .

Much the greatest part of the . . . gentry are as much dissatisfied . . . many of the officers [are] so discontented that they continue in their service only for a subsistence . . . and very many of the common soldiers do daily show such an aversion to the Popish religion, that there is the greatest probability imaginable of great numbers of deserters which would come from them, should there be such an occasion; and amongst the seamen, it is almost certain, there is not one in ten who would do them any service in such a war. . . . If upon a due consideration of all these circumstances, Your Highness shall think fit to adventure upon the attempt . . . there must be no time lost, in letting us know your resolution concerning it, and in what time we may depend that all the preparations will be ready.

(signed)

Shrewsbury	[Protestant convert from Catholicism]
Devonshire	[Whig]
Danby	[Tory]
Lumley	[Protestant convert from Catholicism]
Bishop of London	[Tory]
Russell	[Whig]
Sydney	[Whig]

Part II.   THE REVOLUTIONARY SETTLEMENT

The invitation to William of Orange in June was followed by William's invasion of England in November, 1688. But no battle took place. James wavered and procrastinated, as his adherents gradually deserted him, until he finally took refuge in flight. After one unsuccessful attempt to flee, James finally made his way into France without having struck a blow in his own defense, and William was left master of the kingdom. By a series of legislative acts, Parliament then endeavored to eradicate the sources of domestic conflict. The Bill of Rights, passed immediately after the Revolution, was succeeded by further enactments in the next fifteen years, by which Parliament circumscribed the power of the Crown and did much to establish the supremacy of Parliament in English government. The following documents illustrate the means taken by Parliament to secure the "rights and privileges" for which they had fought so long.

A.   THE REVOLUTIONARY SETTLEMENT, 1689–1701

William of Orange, who had been invited on June 30, 1688, landed on November 5; on December 10 James first tried to leave the country. Meanwhile, the peers, under Halifax, had set up a provisional government. On December 23 William was authorized by a group of peers and commons to hold elections for a Convention Parliament, to meet on January 22, 1689.

1. *The First Act of the Convention Parliament, 1689.* The following document was the first act of the Convention Parliament and appears in the statute book as 1 Will. and Mary, cap. 1, 1689.[17]

An Act for removing and preventing All Questions and Disputes concerning the Assembling and Sitting of the Present Parliament.

For preventing all doubts and scruples which may in any wise arise concerning the meeting, sitting and proceeding of this present Parliament, be it declared and enacted . . .

II. That the Lords Spiritual and Temporal and Commons convened at Westminster, the two and twentieth day of January in the year of Our Lord one thousand six hundred eighty nine, and there sitting on the thirteenth day of February following, are the two Houses of Parliament, and so shall be and are hereby declared, enacted and adjudged to be to all intents, constructions, and purposes whatsoever, notwithstanding any want of writ or writs of summons or any other defect of form or default whatsoever, as if they had been summoned according to the usual form, and that this Present Act and all other Acts, to which the royal assent shall at any time be given before the next prorogation after the said thirteenth of February, shall be understood, taken and adjudged in law to begin and commence upon the said thirteenth of February on which day their said Majesties at the request and by the advice of the Lords and Commons did accept the crown and royal dignity of King and Queen of England, France and Ireland, and the dominions and territories thereunto belonging. . . .

2. *The Bill of Rights, 1689.* Like most pieces of legislation, the Bill of Rights, which follows, is as much a résumé of the past as it is a prophecy for the future.[18]

Whereas the said late King James II having abdicated the government, and the throne being thereby vacant, his Highness the prince of Orange (whom it hath pleased Almighty God to make the glorious instrument of delivering this kingdom from popery and arbitrary power) did (by the advice of the lords spiritual and temporal, and diverse principal persons of the Commons) cause letters to be written to the lords spiritual and temporal, being Protestants, and other letters to the several counties, cities, universities, boroughs, and Cinque Ports, for the choosing of such persons to represent them, as were of right to be sent to parliament, to meet and sit at Westminster upon the two and twentieth day of January, in this year 1689, in order to such an establishment as that their religion, laws, and liberties might not again be in danger of being subverted; upon which letters elections have been accordingly made.

And thereupon the said lords spiritual and temporal and Commons, pursuant to their respective letters and elections, being now assembled in a full and free representation of this nation, taking into their most serious consideration the best means for attaining the ends aforesaid, do in the first place (as their ancestors in like case have usually done), for the vindication and assertion of their ancient rights and liberties, declare:

1. That the pretended power of suspending laws, or the execution of laws, by regal authority, without consent of parliament, is illegal.

2. That the pretended power of dispensing with the laws, or the execution of law by regal authority, as it hath been assumed and exercised of late, is illegal.

3. That the commission for erecting the late court of commissioners for ecclesiastical causes, and all other commissions and courts of like nature, are illegal and pernicious.

4. That levying money for or to the use of the crown by pretense of prerogative, without grant of parliament, for longer time or in other manner than the same is or shall be granted, is illegal.

5. That it is the right of the subjects to petition the king, and all commitments and prosecutions for such petitioning are illegal.

6. That the raising or keeping a standing army within the kingdom in time of peace, unless it be with consent of parliament, is against law.

7. That the subjects which are Protestants may have arms for their defense suitable to their conditions, and as allowed by law.

8. That election of members of parliament ought to be free.

9. That the freedom of speech, and debates or proceedings in parliament, ought not to be impeached or questioned in any court or place out of parliament.

10. That excessive bail ought not to be required, nor excessive fines imposed, nor cruel and unusual punishments inflicted.

11. That jurors ought to be duly impaneled and returned, and jurors which pass upon men in trials for high treason ought to be freeholders.

12. That all grants and promises of fines and forfeitures of particular persons before conviction are illegal and void.

13. And that for redress of all grievances, and for the amending, strengthening, and preserving of the laws, parliament ought to be held frequently.

And they do claim, demand, and insist upon all and singular the premises, as their undoubted rights and liberties; and that no declarations, judgments, doings, or proceedings, to the prejudice of the people in any of the said premises, ought in any wise to be drawn hereafter into consequence or example.

To which demand of their rights they are particularly encouraged by the declaration of his Highness the prince of Orange, as being the only means for obtaining a full redress and remedy therein.

Having therefore an entire confidence that his said Highness the prince of Orange will perfect the deliverance so far advanced by him, and will still preserve them from the violation of their rights, which they have here asserted, and from all other attempt upon their religion, rights, and liberties:

The said lords spiritual and temporal, and commons, assembled at Westminster, do resolve that William and Mary, prince and princess of Orange, be, and be declared, king and queen of England, France, and Ireland, the dominions thereunto belonging, to hold the crown and royal dignity of the said kingdoms and dominions to them the said prince and princess during their lives, and the life of the survivor of them; and that the sole and full exercise of the regal power be only in, and executed by, the said prince of Orange, in the names of the said prince and princess, during their joint lives; and after their deceases, the said crown and royal dignity of the said kingdoms and dominions to be to the heirs of the body of the said princess; and for default of such issue to the princess Anne of Denmark, and the heirs of her body; and for default of such issue to the heirs of the body of the said prince of Orange. And the lords spiritual and temporal, and commons, do pray the said prince and princess to accept the same accordingly. . . .

Upon which their said Majesties did accept the crown and royal dignity of the kingdoms of England, France, and Ireland, and the dominions thereunto belonging, according to the resolution and desire of the said lords and commons contained in the said declaration.

3. *The Mutiny Act, 1689.* To all students of English and continental history in the seventeenth century, the position of the Mutiny Act in the settlement of 1689 is clearly central. The pertinent sections are quoted below.[19]

Whereas the raising or keeping a standing army within this kingdom in time of peace, unless it be with consent of parliament, is against law; and whereas it is judged necessary by their Majesties and this present parliament that during this time of danger several of the forces which are now on foot should be continued, and others raised, for the safety of the kingdom, for the common defense of the Protestant religion, and for the reducing of Ireland.

And whereas no man may be forejudged of life or limb, or subjected to any kind of punishment, by martial law or in any other manner than by the judgment of his peers and according to the known and established laws of this realm, yet nevertheless it being requisite for retaining such forces as are or shall be raised during this exigence of affairs in their duty, an exact discipline be observed, and that soldiers who shall mutiny or stir up sedition or shall desert their Majesties' service be brought to more exemplary and speedy punishment than the usual forms of law will allow. . . .

II. Be it therefore enacted by the king's and queen's most excellent Majesties, by and with the advice and consent of the lords spiritual and temporal and commons in this parliament assembled, and by authority of the same, that, from and after the twelfth of April in the year of our Lord one thousand six hundred eighty-nine, every person being in their majesties' service in the army and being mustered and in pay as an officer or soldier, who shall at any time before the tenth day of November in the year of our Lord one thousand six hundred eighty-nine excite, cause, or join in any mutiny or sedition in the army, or shall desert their majesties' service in the army, shall suffer death or such other punishment as by a court marshal shall be inflicted. . . .

VII. Provided always, that this act or anything therein contained shall not extend or be anywise construed to extend to or concern any the militia forces of this kingdom.

VIII. Provided always, that this act shall continue and be in force until the said tenth of November in the said year of our Lord one thousand six hundred eighty-nine, and no longer. . . .

X. And no sentence of death shall be given against any offender in such case by any court unless nine of thirteen officers present shall concur therein, and if there be a greater number of officers present, then the judgment shall pass by the concurrence of the greater part of them so sworn, and not otherwise, and no proceedings, trial, or sentence of death shall be had or given against any offender but between the hours of eight in the morning and one in the afternoon.

4. *The Toleration Act, 1689.* Although it bears comparison with such contemporary events as the Revocation of the Edict of Nantes (1685), the Toleration Act of 1689 must be studied primarily as a solution to the question of freedom of worship as it had developed in England during the preceding century and a half. In this connection it is important for what it leaves unsettled as well as for its more permanent accomplishments.[20]

An Act for exempting their Majesties' Protestant Subjects, differing from the Church of England, from the Penalties of certain Laws.

Forasmuch as some ease to scrupulous consciences in the exercise of religion may be an effectual means to unite their Majesties' protestant subjects in interest and affections: . . .

II. Be it enacted . . . That neither the statute made in the three and twentieth year of the reign of the late Queen Elizabeth, intituled An act to retain the Queen's Majesty's subjects in their due obedience; nor the statute made in the twenty-ninth year of the said Queen intituled An act for the more speedy and due execution of certain branches of the statute made in the three and twentieth year of the Queen's Majesty's reign, *viz.* the aforesaid act; nor that branch or clause of a statute made in the first year of the reign of the said Queen intituled, An act for the uniformity of common prayer and service in the church . . . by all person, having no lawful or reasonable excuse to be absent, are required to resort to their parish church or chapel, or some usual place where the common prayer shall be used, upon pain of punishment by the censures of the church, and also upon pain that every person so offending shall forfeit for every such offense twelve pence; nor the statute made in the third year of the reign of the late King James the first, intituled, An act for the better discovering and repressing popish recusants; nor that other statute made in the same year, intituled An act to prevent and avoid dangers which may grow by popish recusants; nor any other law or statute of this realm made against papists or popish recusants; except . . . the statute made in the thirtieth year of . . . King Charles the second, intituled an act for the more effectual preserving the King's person and government by disabling papists from sitting in either house of parliament; shall be construed to extend to any person or persons dissenting from the Church of England, that shall take the oaths mentioned in a statute made by this present parliament . . . and that shall make and subscribe the declaration mentioned in a statute made in the thirtieth year of the reign of King Charles the second . . . which oaths and declaration the justices of peace at the general sessions of the peace . . . are hereby required to tender and administer to such persons as shall offer themselves to take, make, and subscribe the same, and thereof to keep a register; and likewise none of the persons aforesaid shall give or pay, as any fee or reward, to any officer or officers belonging to the court aforesaid, above the sum of sixpence, nor that more than once, for his or their entry of his taking the said oaths, and making and subscribing the said declaration; nor above the further sum of sixpence for any certificate of the same, to be made out and signed by the officer or officers of the said court.

III. And be it further enacted . . . That all . . . persons already convicted or prosecuted in order to conviction of recusancy . . . grounded upon the aforesaid statutes, or any of them, that shall take the said oaths mentioned in the said statute in this present parliament, and make and subscribe the declaration aforesaid . . . and to be thence respectively certified into the Exchequer, shall be thenceforth exempted and discharged from all the penalties, seizures, forfeitures, judgments, and executions, incurred by force of any of the aforesaid statutes, without any composition, fee, or further charge whatsoever.

IV. And be it further enacted . . . That all . . . persons that shall take the said oaths, and make and subscribe the declaration aforesaid, shall not be liable to any pains, penalties, or forfeitures, mentioned in an act made in the five and thirtieth year of the reign of the late Queen Elizabeth . . . nor an act made in the two and twentieth year of the reign of the late King Charles the second . . . nor shall any of the said persons be prosecuted in any ecclesiastical court, for or by reason of their nonconforming to the Church of England.

V. Provided always . . . That if any assembly of persons dissenting from the Church of England shall be had in any place for religious worship with the doors locked, barred, or bolted, during any time of such meeting . . . , shall not receive any benefit from this law, but be liable to all the pain and penalties of all the aforesaid laws recited in this act, for such their meeting, notwithstanding his taking the oaths, and making and subscribing the declaration aforesaid.

VI. Provided always, That nothing herein contained shall . . . exempt any of the persons aforesaid from paying of tithes or other parochial duties, or any other duties to the church or minister, nor from any prosecution in any ecclesiastical court, or elsewhere for the same. . . .

XVII. Provided always . . . That neither this act, nor any clause, article, or thing herein contained, shall . . . extend to give any ease, benefit, or advantage to any papist or popish recusant whatsoever, or any person that shall deny in his preaching or writing the doctrine of the Blessed Trinity, as it is declared in the aforesaid articles of religion.

5. *The Act of Settlement, 1701.* Although it occurs over ten years later the Act of Settlement may well be taken as the essence of the Revolutionary Settlement.[21]

An Act for the further Limitation of the Crown and better securing the Rights and Liberties of the Subject.

I. Whereas in the First Year of the Reign of Your Majesty and of our late most gracious Sovereign Lady Queen Mary (of blessed Memory) An Act of Parliament was made intituled An Act for declaring the Rights and Liberties of the Subject and for settling the Succession of the Crown wherein it was (amongst other things) enacted, established, and declared, That the Crown and Regal Government of the Kingdoms of England, France, and Ireland, and the Dominions thereunto belonging should be and continue to Your Majesty and the said late Queen during the joint lives of Your Majesty and the said Queen and to the Survivor.

And that after the Decease of Your Majesty and of the said Queen the said Crown and Regal Government should be and remain to the Heirs of the Body of the said late Queen, and for Default of such Issue to her Royal Highness the Princess Ann of Denmark and the Heirs of her Body, and for Default of such Issue to the Heirs of the Body of Your Majesty and it was thereby further enacted that all and every Person and Persons that then were or afterwards should be reconciled to or shall hold Communion with the See or Church of Rome or should profess the Popish Religion or marry a Papist should be excluded and are by that Act made forever incapable to inherit, possess, or enjoy the Crown and Government of this Realm and Ireland and the Dominions thereunto belonging, or any part of the same, or to have, use, or exercise any regal Power, Authority, or Jurisdiction within the same.

And in all and every such Case or Cases the People of these Realms shall be and are thereby absolved of their allegiance. And that the said Crown and Government shall from time to time descend to and be enjoyed by such Person or Persons being Protestants as should have inherited and enjoyed the same in case the said Person or Persons so reconciled, holding Communion, professing, or marrying, as aforesaid, were naturally dead. . . . And your Majesty's said Subjects having Daily Experience of Your Royal Care and Concern for the present and future welfare of these Kingdoms and particularly recommending from your Throne a further provision to be made for the Succession of the Crown in the Protestant Line for the Happiness of the Nation and the Security of our Religion.

And it being absolutely necessary for the Safety, Peace, and Quiet of this Realm to obviate all Doubts and Contentions in the same by reason of any pretended Titles to the Crown, and to maintain a Certainty in the succession thereof to which your Subjects may safely have Recourse for their Protection in case the Limitations in the said recited Act should determine. Therefore for a further Provision of the Succession to the Crown in the Protestant Line We, Your Majesty's most dutiful and Loyal Subjects, the Lords Spiritual and Temporal and Commons in this present Parliament assembled, do beseech Your Majesty that it may be enacted and declared, and be it enacted and declared by the King's most Excellent Majesty by and with the Advice and Consent of the

Lords Spiritual and Temporal and Commons in this Present Parliament assembled, and by the authority of the same, that the most Excellent Princess Sophia, Electress and Duchess Dowager of Hanover, Daughter of the most Excellent Princess Elizabeth, late Queen of Bohemia, Daughter of our late Sovereign Lord King James the First of happy Memory, be and is hereby declared to be the next in Succession in the Protestant Line to the Imperial Crown and Dignity to the said Realms of England, France, and Ireland, and of the Dominions thereunto belonging, after His Majesty and the Princess Ann of Denmark, and in Default of Issue of the said Princess Ann and of His Majesty respectively, and that from and after the Deceases of His said Majesty our now Sovereign Lord, and of Her Royal Highness the Princess Ann of Denmark, and for Default of Issue of the said Princess Ann and of His Majesty respectively, the Crown and Regal Government of the said Kingdoms of England, France, and Ireland, and of the Dominions thereunto belonging, with the Royal State and Dignity of the said Realms, and all the Honors, Styles, Titles, Regalities, Prerogatives, Powers, Jurisdictions, and Authorities to the same belonging and appertaining, shall be, remain, and continue to the said most Excellent Princess Sophia and the Heirs of her Body being Protestants.

And thereunto the said Lords Spiritual and Temporal and Commons shall and will in the Name of all the People of this Realm . . . do faithfully promise That after the Deceases of His Majesty and Her Royal Highness and the failure of the Heirs of their respective Bodies, to stand, to maintain and defend the said Princess Sophia and the Heirs of her Body being Protestants according to the Limitation and Succession of the Crown in this Act specified and contained, to the utmost of their Powers, with their Lives and Estates, against all Persons whatsoever that shall attempt anything to the contrary. . . .

III. And Whereas it is requisite and necessary that some further Provision be made for securing our Religion, Laws, and Liberties from and after the Death of His Majesty and the Princess Ann of Denmark, and in Default of Issue of the Body of the said Princess and of his Majesty respectively, Be it enacted by the King's most excellent Majesty by and with the Advice and Consent of the Lords Spiritual and Temporal and Commons in Parliament assembled, and by the Authority of the same.

That whosoever shall hereafter come to the Possession of this Crown shall join in Communion with the Church of England as by Law established.

That in case the Crown and Imperial Dignity of this Realm shall hereafter come to any Person not being a Native of this Kingdom of England, this Nation be not obliged to engage in any War for the Defense of any Dominions or Territories which do not belong to the Crown of England, without the consent of Parliament.

That no Person who shall hereafter come to the possession of the Crown shall go out of the Dominions of England, Scotland, and Ireland, without the consent of Parliament.

That from and after the Time that the further Limitation by this Act all Matters and Things relating to the well governing of this Kingdom which are properly cognizable in the Privy Council by the Laws and Customs of this Realm shall be transacted there and all Resolutions taken thereupon shall be signed by each of the Privy Council as shall advise and consent to the same.

That after the said Limitation shall take Effect as aforesaid, no Person born out of the Kingdoms of England, Scotland, or Ireland, or the Dominions thereunto belonging (although he be naturalized and made a Denizen) (except such as are born of English parents) shall be capable to be of the Privy Council, or a Member of either House of Parliament, or to enjoy any Office or Place of Trust, either Civil or Military, or to have any Grant of Lands, Tenements, or Hereditaments, from the Crown to himself or to any other or others in trust for Him.

That no Person who has an Office or Place of Profit under the King, or receives a Pension from the Crown, shall be capable of serving as a Member of the House of Commons.

That after the said Limitation shall take Effect as aforesaid, Judges Commissions be made *Quam diu se bene Gesserint,* and their Salaries ascertained and established, but upon the Address of both Houses of Parliament it may be lawful to remove them.

That no pardon under the Great Seal of England be pleadable to an Impeachment by the Commons in Parliament.

IV. And whereas the laws of England are the birthright of the people thereof and all the Kings and Queens who shall ascend the throne of this realm ought to administer the Government of the same according to the said laws and all their officers and ministers ought to serve them respectively according to the same the said Lords Spiritual and Temporal and Commons do therefore humbly pray that all the laws and statutes of this realm for securing the established religion and rights and liberties of the people thereof and all other laws and statutes of the same now in force may be ratified and confirmed. And the same are by his Majesty by and with the advice and consent of the said Lords Spiritual and Temporal and Commons and by authority of the same ratified and confirmed accordingly.

B.   JOHN LOCKE AND THE GLORIOUS REVOLUTION

John Locke (1652–1704) was the son of a Puritan soldier in the English civil wars. Educated at Oxford, he became a physician by profession, but for fifteen years he served as secretary to the Earl of Shaftesbury, a stormy petrel in politics and founder of the Whig party. Locke's connection with Shaftesbury twice forced him into exile, whence he returned the second time after his friend William of Orange had secured the throne. His philosophical works, especially his *Essay Concerning Human Understanding* (1690) profoundly influenced the thought of the eighteenth century. Out of the same philosophical position came his *Two Treatises on Civil Government* (1690). Having replied in the *First Treatise* to the supporters of divine right, Locke proceeded in the *Second Treatise* to deal with the "true original extent and end of civil government" and to suggest a philosophical defense of the revolutionary settlement.[22]

Chapter I

Political power . . . I take to be a right of making laws, with penalties of death, and consequently all less penalties for the regulating and preserving of property, and of employing the force of the community in the execution of such laws, and in the defense of the commonwealth from foreign injury, and all this only for public good.

Chapter II: Of the State of Nature

To understand political power aright, and derive it from its original, we must consider what estate all men are naturally in, and that is, a state of perfect freedom to order their actions, and dispose of their possessions and persons as they think fit, within the bounds of the law of nature, without asking leave or depending upon the will of any other man.

A state also of equality, wherein all the power and jurisdiction is reciprocal, no one having more than another, there being nothing more evident than that creatures of the same species and rank, promiscuously born to all the same advantages of nature, and the use of the same faculties, should also be equal one amongst another, without subordination or subjection, unless the Lord and Master of them all should, by any manifest declaration of His will, set one above another, and confer on him, by an evident and clear appointment, an undoubted right to dominion and sovereignty. . . .

But though this be a state of liberty, yet it is not a state of licence; though man in that state have an uncontrollable liberty to dispose of his person or possessions, yet he has not liberty to destroy himself, or so much as any creature in his possession, but where some nobler use than its bare preservation calls for it. The state of nature has a law of nature to govern it, which obliges every one, and reason, which is that law, teaches all mankind who will but consult it, that being all equal and independent, no one ought to harm another in his life, health, liberty or possessions; for men being all the workmanship of one omnipotent and infinitely wise Maker; all the servants of one sovereign Master, sent into the world by His order and about His business; they are His property, whose workmanship they are made to last during His, not one another's pleasure. And, being furnished with like faculties, sharing all in one community of nature, there cannot be supposed any such subordination among us that may authorize us to destroy one another, as if we were made for one another's uses, as the inferior ranks of creatures are for ours. Every one as he is bound to preserve himself, and not to quit his station wilfully, so by the like reason, when his own preservation comes not in competition, ought he as much as he can to preserve the rest of mankind, and not unless it be to do justice on an offender, take away or impair the life, or what tends to the preservation of the life, the liberty, health, limb, or goods of another.

And that all men may be restrained from invading others' rights, and from doing hurt to one another, and the law of nature be observed, which willeth the peace and preservation of all mankind, the execution of the law of nature is in that state put into every man's hands, whereby every one has a right to punish the transgressors of that law to such a degree as may hinder its violation. For the law of nature would, as all other laws that concern men in this world, be in vain if there were nobody that in the state of nature had a power to execute that law, and thereby preserve the innocent and restrain offenders; and if any one in the state of nature may punish another for any evil he has done, every one may do so. For in that state of perfect equality, where naturally there is no superiority or jurisdiction of one over another, what any may do in prosecution of that law, every one must needs have a right to do.

And thus, in the state of nature, one man comes by a power over another, but yet no absolute or arbitrary power to use a criminal, when he has got him in his hands, according to the passionate heats or boundless extravagancy of his own will, but only to retribute to him so far as calm reason and conscience dictate, what is proportionate to his transgression, which is so much as may serve for reparation and restraint. For these two are the only reasons why one man may lawfully do harm to another, which is that we call punishment. In transgressing the law of nature, the offender declares himself to live by another rule than that of reason and common equity, which is that measure God has set to the actions of men for their mutual security, and so he becomes dangerous to mankind; the tie which is to secure them from injury and violence being slighted and broken by him, which being a trespass against the whole species, and the peace and safety of it, provided for by the law of nature, every man upon this score, by the right he hath to preserve mankind in general, may restrain, or where it is necessary destroy things noxious to them, and so may bring such evil on any one who hath transgressed that law, as may make him repent the doing of it, and thereby deter him, and, by his example, others from doing the like mischief. And in this case, and upon this ground, every man hath a right to punish the offender, and be executioner of the law of nature. . . .

To this strange doctrine—viz., that in the state of nature every one has the executive power of the law of nature—I doubt not but it will be objected that it is unreasonable for men to be judges in their own cases, that self-love will make men partial to themselves and their friends; and, on the other side, ill-nature, passion, and revenge will carry them too far in punishing others, and hence nothing but confusion and disorder will follow, and that therefore God hath certainly appointed government to restrain the partiality and violence of men. I easily grant that civil government is the proper remedy for the inconveniences of the state of nature, which must certainly be great where men may be judges in their own case, since it is easy to be imagined that he

who was so unjust as to do his brother an injury will scarce be so just as to condemn himself for it. But I shall desire those who make this objection to remember that absolute monarchs are but men; and if government is to be the remedy of those evils which necessarily follow from men being judges in their own cases, and the state of nature is therefore not to be endured, I desire to know what kind of government that is, and how much better it is than the state of nature, where one man commanding a multitude has the liberty to be judge in his own case, and may do to all his subjects whatever he pleases without the least question or control of those who execute his pleasure? and in whatsoever he doth, whether led by reason, mistake, or passion, must be submitted to? which men in the state of nature are not bound to do one to another. And if he that judges, judges amiss in his own or any other case, he is answerable for it to the rest of mankind. . . .

Chapter IV: Of Slavery

The natural liberty of man is to be free from any superior power on earth, and not to be under the will or legislative authority of man, but to have only the law of nature for his rule. The liberty of man in society is to be under no other legislative power but that established by consent in the commonwealth, nor under the dominion of any will, or restraint of any law, but what that legislative shall enact according to the trust put in it. Freedom, then, is not what Sir Robert Filmer tells us: "A liberty for every one to do what he lists, to live as he pleases, and not to be tied by any laws"; but freedom of men under government is to have a standing rule to live by, common to every one of that society, and made by the legislative power erected in it. A liberty to follow my own will in all things where that rule prescribes not, not to be subject to the inconstant, uncertain, unknown, arbitrary will of another man, as freedom of nature is to be under no other restraint but the law of nature.

This freedom from absolute, arbitrary power is so necessary to, and closely joined with, a man's preservation, that he cannot part with it but by what forfeits his preservation and life together. For a man, not having the power of his own life, cannot by compact or his own consent enslave himself to any one, nor put himself under the absolute arbitrary power of another to take away his life when he pleases. Nobody can give more power than he has himself, and he that cannot take away his own life cannot give another power over it. Indeed, having by his fault forfeited his own life by some act that deserves death, he to whom he has forfeited it may, when he has him in his power, delay to take it, and make use of him to his own service; and he does him no injury by it. For, whenever he finds the hardship of his slavery outweigh the value of his life, it is in his power, by resisting the will of his master, to draw on himself the death he desires.

Chapter V: Of Property

Whether we consider natural reason, which tells us that men, being once born, have a right to their preservation, and consequently to meat and drink and such other things as nature affords for their subsistence, or "revelation," which gives us an account of those grants God made of the world to Adam, and to Noah and his sons, it is very clear that God, as King David says (Psalm CXV. 16), "has given the earth to the children of men," given it to mankind in common. But, this being supposed, it seems to some a very great difficulty how any one should ever come to have a property in anything, I will not content myself to answer, that, if it be difficult to make our "property" upon a supposition that God gave the world to Adam and his posterity in common, it is impossible that any man but one universal monarch should have any "property" upon a supposition that God gave the world to Adam and his heirs in succession, exclusive of all the rest of his posterity; but I shall endeavor to show how men might come to have a property in several parts of that which God gave to mankind in common, and that without any express compact of all the commoners.

God, who hath given the world to men in common, hath also given them reason to make use of it to the best advantage of life and convenience. The earth and all that is therein is given to men for the support and comfort of their being. And though all the fruits it naturally produces, and beasts it feeds, belong to mankind in common, as they are produced by the spontaneous hand of nature, and nobody has originally a private dominion exclusive of the rest of mankind in any of them, as they are thus in their natural state, yet being given for the use of men, there must of necessity be a means to appropriate them some way or other before they can be of any use, or at all beneficial, to any particular men. The fruit or venison which nourishes the wild Indian, who knows no enclosure, and is still a tenant in common, must be his, and so his—*i.e.,* a part of him, that another can no longer have any right to it before it can do him any good for the support of his life.

Though the earth and all inferior creatures be common to all men, yet every man has a "property" in his own "person." This nobody has any right to but himself. The "labor" of his body and the "work" of his hands, we may say, are properly his. Whatsoever, then, he removes out of the state that nature hath provided and left it in, he hath mixed his labor with it, and joined to it something that is his own, and thereby makes it his property. It being by him removed from the common state nature placed it in, it hath by this labor something annexed to it that excludes the common right of other men. For this "labor" being the unquestionable property of the laborer, no man but he can have a right to what that is once joined to, at least where there is enough, and as good left in common for others. . . .

It will, perhaps, be objected to this, that if gathering the acorns or other fruits of the earth, etc., makes a right to them, then any one may engross as much as he will. To which I answer, Not so. The same law of nature that does by this means give us property, does also bound that property too. "God has given us all things richly." Is the voice of reason confirmed by inspiration? But how far has He given it us—"to enjoy"? As much as any one can make use of to any advantage of life before it spoils, so much he may by his labor fix a property in. Whatever is beyond this is more than his share, and belongs to others. Nothing was made by God for man to spoil or destroy. And thus considering the plenty of natural provisions there was a long time in the world, and the few spenders, and to how small a part of that provision the industry of one man could extend itself and engross it to the prejudice of others, especially keeping within the bounds set by reason of what might serve for his use, there could be then little room for quarrels or contentions about property so established.

But the chief matter of property being now not the fruits of the earth and the beasts that subsist on it, but the earth itself as that which takes in and carries with it all the rest, I think it is plain that property in that too is acquired as the former. As much land as a man tills, plants, improves, cultivates, and can use the product of, so much is his property. He by his labor does, as it were, enclose it from the common. Nor will it invalidate his right to say everybody else has an equal title to it, and therefore he cannot appropriate, he cannot enclose, without the consent of all his fellow-commoners, all mankind. God, when He gave the world in common to all mankind, commanded man also to labor, and the penury of his condition required it of him. God and his reason commanded him to subdue the earth—*i.e.,* improve it for the benefit of life and therein lay out something upon it that was his own, his labor. He that, in obedience to this command of God, subdued, tilled, and sowed any part of it, thereby annexed to it something that was his property, which another had no title to, nor could without injury take from him.

Nor was this appropriation of any parcel of land, by improving it, any prejudice to any other man, since there was still enough and as good left, and more than the yet unprovided could use. . . .

God gave the world to men in common, but since He gave it them for their benefit and the greatest conveniencies of life they were capable to draw from it, it cannot be supposed He meant it should always remain common and uncultivated. He gave it to the use of the industrious and rational (and labor was to be his title to it); not to the fancy or covetousness of the quarrelsome and contentious. He that had as good left for his improvement as was already taken up needed not complain, ought not to meddle with what was already improved by another's labor. . . .

Now of those good things which nature hath provided in common, every one hath a right (as hath been said) to as much as he could use, and had a property in all he could effect with his labor; all that his industry could extend to, to alter from the state nature had put it in, was his. He that gathered a hundred bushels of acorns or apples had thereby a property in them; they were his goods as soon as gathered. He was only to look that he used them before they spoiled, else he took more than his share, and robbed others. And, indeed, it was a foolish thing, as well as dishonest, to hoard up more than he could make use of. If he gave a part to anybody else, so that it perished not uselessly in his possession, these he also made use of. And if he also bartered away plums that would have rotted in a week, for nuts that would last good for his eating a whole year, he did no injury; he wasted not the common stock; destroyed no part of the portion of goods that belonged to others, so long as nothing perished uselessly in his hands. Again, if he would give his nuts for a piece of metal, pleased with its color, or exchange his sheep for shells, or wool for a sparkling pebble or a diamond, and keep those by him all his life, he invaded not the right of others; he might heap up as much of these durable things as he pleased; the exceeding of the bounds of his just property not lying in the largeness of his possession, but the perishing of anything uselessly in it.

And thus came in the use of money; some lasting thing that men might keep without spoiling, and that, by mutual consent, men would take in exchange for the truly useful but perishable supports of life.

And as different degrees of industry were apt to give men possessions in different proportions, so this invention of money gave them the opportunity to continue and enlarge them. . . .

Thus, in the beginning, all the world was America, and more so than that is now; for no such thing as money was anywhere known. Find out something that hath the use and value of money amongst his neighbors, you shall see the same man will begin presently to enlarge his possessions.

But since gold and silver, being little useful to the life of man, in proportion to food, raiment, and carriage, has its value only from the consent of men—whereof labor yet makes in great part the measure—it is plain that the consent of men have agreed to a disproportionate and unequal possession of the earth—I mean out of the bounds of society and compact; for in governments the laws regulate it; they having, by consent, found out and agreed in a way how a man may, rightfully and without injury, possess more than he himself can make use of by receiving gold and silver, which may continue long in a man's possession without decaying for the overplus, and agreeing those metals should have a value. . . .

Chapter VI: Of Paternal Power

Though I have said above "that all men by nature are equal," I cannot be supposed to understand all sorts of "equality." Age or virtue may give men a just precedency. Excellency of parts and merit may place others above the common level. Birth may subject some, and alliance or benefits others, to pay an observance to those to whom nature, gratitude, or other respects, may have made it due; and yet all this consists with the equality which all men are in in respect of jurisdiction or dominion one over another, which was the equality I there spoke of as proper to the business in hand, being that equal right that every man hath to his natural freedom, without being subjected to the will or authority of any other man. . . .

The freedom then of man, and liberty of acting according to his own will, is grounded on his having reason, which is able to instruct him in that law he is to govern himself by, and make him know how far he is left to the freedom of his own will. To turn him loose to an unrestrained liberty, before he has reason to guide him, is not the allowing him the privilege of his nature to be free, but to thrust him out amongst brutes, and abandon him to a state as wretched and as much beneath that of a man as theirs. This is that which puts the authority into the parents' hands to govern the minority of their children. God hath made it their business to employ this care on their offspring, and hath placed in them suitable inclinations of tenderness and concern to temper this power, to apply it as His wisdom designed it, to the children's good as long as they should need to be under it.

Chapter VII: Of Political or Civil Society

Man being born, as has been proved, with a title to perfect freedom and an uncontrolled enjoyment of all the rights and privileges of the law of nature, equally with any other man, or number of men in the world, hath by nature a power not only to preserve his property—that is, his life, liberty, and estate—against the injuries and attempts of other men, but to judge of and punish the breaches of that law in others, as he is persuaded the offense deserves, even with death itself, in crimes where the heinousness of the fact, in his opinion, requires it. But because no political society can be, nor subsist, without having in itself the power to preserve the property, and in order thereunto punish the offenses of all those of that society, there, and there only, is political society where every one of the members hath quitted this natural power, resigned it up into the hands of the community in all cases that exclude him not from appealing for protection to the law established by it. And thus all private judgment of every particular member being excluded, the community comes to be umpire, and by understanding indifferent rules and men authorized by the community for their execution, decides all the differences that may happen between any members of that society concerning any matter of right, and punishes those offenses which any member hath committed against the society with such penalties as the law has established; whereby it is easy to discern who are, and are not, in political society together. Those who are united into one body, and have a common established law and judicature to appeal to, with authority to decide controversies between them and punish offenders, are in civil society one with another; but those who have no such common appeal, I mean on earth, are still in the state of nature, each being where there is no other, judge for himself and executioner; which is, as I have before showed it, the perfect state of nature.

Chapter VIII: Of the Beginning of Political Societies

Men being, as has been said, by nature all free, equal, and independent, no one can be put out of this estate and subjected to the political power of another without his own consent, which is done by agreeing with other men, to join and unite into a community for their comfortable, safe, and peaceable living, one amongst another, in a secure enjoyment of their properties, and a greater security against any that are not of it. This any number of men may do, because it injures not the freedom of the rest; they are left, as they were, in the liberty of the state of nature. When any number of men have so consented to make one community or government, they are thereby presently incorporated, and make one body politic, wherein the majority have a right to act and conclude the rest.

For, when any number of men have, by the consent of every individual, made a community, they have thereby made that community one body, with a power to act as one body, which is only by the will and determination of the majority. For that which acts [moves] any community, being only the consent of the individuals of it, and it being one body, must move one way, it is necessary the body should move that way whither the greater force carries it, which is the consent of the majority, or else it is impossible it should act or continue one body, one community, which the consent of every individual that united into it agreed that it should; and so every one is bound by that consent to be concluded by the majority. And therefore we see that in assemblies empowered to act by positive laws where no number is set by that positive law which empowers them, the act of the majority passes for the act of the whole, and of course determines as having, by the law of nature and reason, the power of the whole. . . .

Whosoever, therefore, out of a state of nature unite into a community, must be understood to give up all the power necessary to the ends for which they unite into society to the majority of the community, unless they expressly agreed in any number greater than the majority. And this is done by barely agreeing to unite into one political society, which is all the compact that is, or needs be, between the individuals that enter into or make up a commonwealth. And thus, that which begins and actually constitutes any political society is nothing but the consent of any number of freemen capable of majority, to unite and incorporate into such a society. And this is that, and that only, which did or could give beginning to any lawful government in the world.

To this I find two objections made: 1. That there are no instances to be found in story of a company of men, independent and equal one amongst another, that met together, and in this way began and set up a government. 2. It is impossible of right that men should do so, because all men, being born under government, they are to submit to that, and are not at liberty to begin a new one.

To the first there is this to answer: . . . if we may not suppose men ever to have been in the state of nature, because we hear not much of them in such a state, we may as well suppose the armies of Salmanasser or Xerxes were never children, because we hear little of them till they were men and embodied in armies. Government is everywhere antecedent to records. . . .

Chapter IX: *Of the Ends of Political Society and Government*

If man in the state of nature be so free as has been said, if he be absolute lord of his own person and possessions, equal to the greatest and subject to nobody, why will he part with his freedom, this empire, and subject himself to the dominion and control of any other power? To which it is obvious to answer, that though in the state of nature he hath such a right, yet the enjoyment of it is very uncertain and constantly exposed to the invasion of others; for all being kings as much as he, every man his equal, and the greater part no strict observers of equity and justice, the enjoyment of the property he has in this state is very unsafe, very insecure. This makes him willing to quit this condition which, however free, is full of fears and continual dangers; and it is not without reason that he seeks out and is willing to join in society with others who are already united, or have a mind to unite for the mutual preservation of their lives, liberties, and estates, which I call by the general name—property.

The great and chief end, therefore, of men uniting into commonwealths, and putting themselves under government, is the preservation of their property; to which in the state of nature there are many things wanting.

Firstly, there wants an established, settled, known law, received and allowed by common consent to be the standard of right and wrong, and the common measure to decide all controversies between them. . . .

Secondly, in the state of nature there wants a known and indifferent judge, with authority to determine all differences according to the established law. . . .

Thirdly, in the state of nature there often wants power to back and support the sentence when right, and to give it due execution. . . .

And so, whoever has the legislative or supreme power of any commonwealth, is bound to govern by established standing laws, promulgated and known to the people, and not by extemporary decrees, by indifferent and upright judges, who are to decide controversies by those laws; and to employ the force of the community at home only in the execution of such laws, or abroad to prevent or redress foreign injuries and secure the community from inroads and invasion. And all this to be directed to no other end but the peace, safety, and public good of the people.

Chapter XVIII: *Of Tyranny*

Wherever law ends, tyranny begins, if the law be transgressed to another's harm; and whosoever in authority exceeds the power given him by the law, and makes use of the force he has under his command to compass that upon the subject which the law allows not, ceases in that to be a magistrate, and acting without authority may be opposed, as any other man who by force invades the right of another. This is acknowledged in subordinate magistrates. He that hath authority to seize my person in the street may be opposed as a thief and a robber if he endeavors to break into my house to execute a writ, notwithstanding that I know he has such a warrant and such a legal authority as will empower him to arrest me abroad. And why this should not hold in the highest, as well as in the most inferior magistrate, I would gladly be informed. Is it reasonable that the eldest brother, because he has the greatest part of his father's estate, should thereby have a right to take away any of his younger brothers' portions? Or that a rich man, who possessed a whole country, should from thence have a right to seize, when he pleased, the cottage and garden of his poor neighbor? The being rightfully possessed of great power and riches, exceedingly beyond the greatest part of the sons of Adam, is so far from being an excuse, much less a reason for rapine and oppression, which the endamaging another without authority is, that it is a great aggravation of it. For exceeding the bounds of authority is no more a right in a great than a petty officer, no more justifiable in a king than a constable. But so much the worse in him as that he has more trust put in him, is supposed, from the advantage of education and counsellors, to have better knowledge and less reason to do it, having already a greater share than the rest of his brethren.

Chapter XIX: *Of the Dissolution of Government*

There is, therefore, . . . another way whereby governments are dissolved, and that is, when the legislative, or the prince, either of them act contrary to their trust. . . .

Whensoever, therefore, the legislative shall transgress this fundamental rule of society, and either by ambition, fear, folly, or corruption, endeavor to grasp themselves, or put into the hands of any other, an absolute power over the lives, liberties, and estates of the people, by this breach of trust they forfeit the power the people had put into their hands for quite contrary ends, and it devolves to the people, who have a right to resume their original liberty, and by the establishment of a new legislative (such as they shall think fit), provide for their own safety and security, which is the end for which they are in society. What I have said here concerning the legislative in general holds true also concerning the supreme executor, who having a double trust put in him, both to have a part in the legislative and the supreme execution of the law, acts against both, when he goes about to set up his own arbitrary will as the law of the society. He acts also contrary to his trust when he employs the force, treasure, and offices of the society to corrupt the representatives and gain them to his purposes, when he openly pre-engages the electors, and prescribes, to their choice, such whom he has, by solicitation, threats, promises, or otherwise, won to his designs, and employs them to bring in such who have promised beforehand what to vote and what to enact.

VII
Liberalism and Nationalism in the French Revolution

Y̲E sons of France, awake to glory,
The sun of victory soon will rise;
Though the tyrant's standard all gory
Is upreared in pride to the skies,
Is upreared in pride to the skies.
Do ye not hear in every village,
Fierce soldiers who spread war's alarms?
Who even in our sheltering arms,
Slay our sons and give our homes to pillage?
To arms, ye brave, to arms!
We'll form battalions strong.
March on, March on!
Their blood impure
Shall bathe our thresholds soon!

And would that horde of slavish minions
Conspire our freedom to overthrow,
Say for whom these gyves were intended,
Which their craft prepared long ago,
Which their craft prepared long ago.
What righteous rage should now excite us,
For Frenchmen what shame is so great?
They even dare to meditate
To enslave, but this they will unite us.
To arms, ye brave, to arms!
We'll form battalions strong.
March on, march on!
Their blood impure
Shall bathe our thresholds soon!

ROUGET DE L'ISLE, 1792

CONTENTS

[173]

QUESTIONS FOR STUDY

PART I

1. Mirabeau said that the revolutionaries meant to draw up not so much a declaration of rights as a declaration of war against tyrants. What qualities of the Declaration does this judgment underline?

2. Mirabeau's conception of property has both a destructive and a conservative purpose. Explain.

3. What liberal principle does the *Loi le Chapelier* try to establish? What other liberal principle is thereby opposed?

4. What general problem of the early phase of the Revolution is foreshadowed by Arthur Young's description of the French press in 1789?

5. According to Condorcet's plan, what should be the aim of a national system of education? How is this aim best fulfilled?

6. How did the local and regional administrative structure established by the legislation of 1789 compare with that of the *ancien régime*?

7. How democratic was the Constitution of 1791? Is there any contradiction between the provisions of the Constitution and the principles of the Declaration of the Rights of Man? What does the section on constitutional revision reveal concerning the intentions of the early revolutionary leaders in 1791?

8. What stage in the development of nationalism is revealed in the attitudes of the early revolutionaries toward internal differences and foreign peoples?

PART II

9. Compare the Constitutions of 1791 and 1793. Which was the more democratic? The more idealistic? The more practical? How does the Jacobin ideal differ from the aims of the early revolutionary leaders?

10. How does Robespierre justify revolutionary dictatorship? What specific circumstances are adduced by St. Just to explain its necessity? How far is Jacobin dictatorship consistent with its general theories of government?

11. What was the status of individual rights under the Jacobin regime? In what respects did the authority for state action differ from that which justified such action before 1789?

12. Was the Law of the Maximum a frankly collectivist measure? To what extent was its passage dictated by circumstances and to what extent by new principles concerning the role of property? What would Adam Smith have said of the measure?

13. Which government was more concerned for the rights of the individual, the revolutionary government before 1792 or the Jacobin dictatorship?

14. What instruments of propaganda were employed by the Jacobins at home, and what was the purpose of their employment?

15. How did the Jacobin system of administration differ from that established by the revolutionaries before 1792?

16. What was the Jacobin attitude toward France's role in the European community of states?

17. "Most wars begin as a crusade but all end as a business." Apply this statement to French foreign policy, 1791–93.

18. "Although Americans have completely accepted their Revolution of 1776, it is still difficult for Frenchmen to be objective about the French Revolution." What evidence in this Problem substantiates this statement?

Alexis de Tocqueville, the nineteenth-century French political theorist, viewed the French Revolution primarily as a reconstitution of the dominant elements of the collapsed *ancien régime*. Contemporary observers, like the German writer Johann Wolfgang Goethe, saw in it the dawn of a new age. Both conceptions find justification in the Revolution, for in retrospect it is Janus-faced. It looks out both upon the past and the future. If it synthesized the growing authority of the centralized state with rival liberal ideas, both of which characterized the eighteenth century, it foreshadowed at the same time the very different pattern of development to be followed by political life in the century to come. For already in the Revolution itself not only was the struggle for civil liberty, political and social equality, and national security transferred from the realm of ideas to the real world of ballot boxes and barricades, but the obstacles blocking the full realization of such ideals were at least visible. The bridge between the Revolution as the product of the past and the Revolution as harbinger of the future is to be found in its own history. Here the dynamic was created which has completely transformed the public life of France and all Europe.

The question at once arises: What lay behind this dynamic which drove the Revolution beyond the solution of its immediate problems into issues which belonged to the future? What kept its forward wave ever on the rise for the five long years between May 1789 and July 1794? More concretely, the question may be posed in terms of the social force which was to carry the Revolution almost from its inception until its end—the fortunes of the French middle class. While the first breach in the structure of the old France was initiated by the aristocracy, which desired a political function to buttress its waning social and economic predominance, the middle class assumed political power as early as June 17, 1789, when the Third Estate worked the transformation of the feudal Estates General into the National Assembly. By September 30, 1791, when this body was dissolved, a social revolution establishing the dominance of the *bourgeoisie* had been consummated by the enactment of an institutional and legal framework responsive to its interests. But although the middle class retained political control—the successive dominant parties, Feuillants, Girondists, and Jacobins, were all *bourgeois* —the Revolution continued on its course of ever more violent change.

The elements to be evaluated in explaining this later phase of the Revolution may be gathered under three categories: the role of ideas, the role of social classes, and the role of practical circumstances. The ideas which were factors can be summed up in the revolutionary slogan "Liberty, Equality, Fraternity," the variations in whose relative importance almost epitomize the Revolution. The growing power of the so-called *sans-culottes*, a loosely defined social group including great masses of the petty *bourgeoisie* and the workers of the cities, is indicative of further strains in the class structure. Finally, concrete circumstances making for a continuous state of crisis added their contribution to the explosive situation: the complete breakdown of authority at the start of the Revolution; the counterrevolutionary machinations of partisans of the old order, breaking out sporadically into actual civil war; the constant threat of war, which became actuality in 1792; the location of the government in radical Paris; the continuing economic crisis.

From the very beginning the Revolution was hastened on by the interaction of these elements. In the study of this first large-scale attempt to put liberal and national ideals into practice the student should evaluate for himself the participation of the ideals, of social groups, and of circumstances in the end product. He should pay particular attention to the development which these ideals undergo when subjected to the iron test of reality.

Part I.   THE LIBERAL PHASE

In the period between the convocation of the Estates General in 1789 and the abolition of the monarchy in September 1792 the liberal ideas as developed by the *philosophes* during the preceding half-century were put into practice in France. Indeed much that was to prove most permanent in the revolutionary achievement, much that has continued as constituent elements in French public life down to the present day, dates from this period. The following documents illustrate the impact of these liberal ideas and the extent of their penetration into the fabric of French society.

A.   LIBERALISM AND THE INDIVIDUAL: THE DECLARATION
              OF THE RIGHTS OF MAN AND OF THE CITIZEN

This Declaration which was passed by the National Assembly on August 27, 1789, and later served as preamble to the Constitution of 1791, was designed to remove the rights and liberties of the individual from any threat of interference by the government. While the extent of its indebtedness to specific precedents such as the American Declaration of Independence and the various bills of rights of American state constitutions has been disputed, the general climate of opinion in which these documents all shared is readily apparent. (1)

The representatives of the people of France, formed into a National Assembly, considering that ignorance, neglect, or contempt of human rights, are the sole causes of public misfortunes and corruptions of government, have resolved to set forth in a solemn declaration, these natural, imprescriptible, and inalienable rights: that this declaration being constantly present to the minds of the members of the body social, they may be forever kept attentive to their rights and duties; that the acts of the legislative and executive powers of government, being capable of being every moment compared with the end of political institutions, may be more respected; and also, that the future claims of the citizens, being directed by simple and incontestable principles, may always tend to the maintenance of the Constitution, and the general happiness.

For these reasons, the National Assembly doth recognize and declare, in the presence of the Supreme Being, and with the hope of His blessing and favor, the following *sacred* rights of men and citizens:

I. Men are born, and always continue, free and equal in respect of their rights. Civil distinctions, therefore, can be founded only on public utility.

II. The end of all political associations is the preservation of the natural and imprescriptible rights of man; and these rights are liberty, property, security, and resistance of oppression.

III. The nation is essentially the source of all sovereignty; nor can any individual, or any body of men, be entitled to any authority which is not expressly derived from it.

IV. Political liberty consists in the power of doing whatever does not injure another. The exercise of the natural rights of every man, has no other limits than those which are necessary to secure to every *other* man the free exercise of the same rights; and these limits are determinable only by law.

V. The law ought to prohibit only actions hurtful to society. What is not prohibited by the law, should not be hindered; nor should anyone be compelled to that which the law does not require.

VI. The law is an expression of the will of the community. All citizens have a right to concur, either personally, or by their representatives, in its formation. It should be the same to all, whether it protects or punishes; and all being equal in its sight, are equally eligible to all honors, places, and employments, according to their different abilities, without any other distinction than that created by their virtues and talents.

VII. No man should be accused, arrested, or held in confinement, except in cases determined by the law, and according to the forms which it has prescribed. . . .

VIII. The law ought to impose no other penalties but such as are absolutely and evidently necessary; and no one ought to be punished, but in virtue of a law promulgated before the offense, and legally applied.

IX. Every man being presumed innocent till he has been convicted, whenever his detention becomes indispensable, all rigor to him, more than is necessary to secure his person, ought to be provided against by the law.

X. No man ought to be molested on account of his opinions, not even on account of his *religious* opinions, provided his avowal of them does not disturb the public order established by the law.

XI. The unrestrained communication of thoughts and opinions being one of the most precious rights of man, every citizen may speak, write, and publish freely, provided he is responsible for the abuse of this liberty, in cases determined by the law.

XII. A public force being necessary to give security to the rights of men and of citizens, that force is instituted for the benefit of the community and not for the particular benefit of the persons to whom it is intrusted.

XIII. A common contribution being necessary for the support of the public force, and for defraying the other expenses of government, it ought to be divided equally among the members of the communtiy, according to their abilities.

XIV. Every citizen has a right, either by himself or his representative, to a free voice in determining the necessity of public contributions, the appropriation of them, and their amount, mode of assessment, and duration.

XV. Every community has a right to demand of all its agents an account of their conduct.

XVI. Every community in which a separation of powers and a security of rights is not provided for, wants a constitution.

XVII. The right to property being inviolable and sacred, no one ought to be deprived of it, except in cases of evident public necessity, legally ascertained, and on condition of a previous just indemnity.

B. ECONOMIC LIBERALISM

1. The Concept of Property. In the effort to resuscitate the national finances, the opportunistic Talleyrand, Bishop of Autun, introduced into the National Assembly a measure calling for the confiscation of Church lands. In the course of the debate on this bill, Count Mirabeau, the most influential of the early revolutionary leaders, developed the following theory of property rights to meet these new conditions. (2)

[Mirabeau to the National Assembly, November 2, 1789]

If I consider property, in its relation to individuals, in its nature, in its effects, and its relation to the sanction of law, I discover:

(1) That each individual possesses by virtue of this right of possession which he has given to others and which all have given to an individual; and this first quality does not fit the properties of the Church or of any corporation;

(2) That the right on which private properties is founded is, so to speak, coexistent with the establishment of the society, since it has its source in this faculty which every individual has of participating in the advantages which all the other members with whom he is forming a political association will have; and this second quality also does not fit the goods of the clergy nor of any corporation; having been established only after the society has been formed, they can have no right which is coexistent with it and which in some way constitutes part of the social pact;

(3) That special laws are not necessary to assure the domain of private property, for, by want of ordering in principle a community of possessions, the establishment and the guarantee of individual possessions are a necessary consequence of the very foundation of society: and this third quality is again alien to the possessions of the clergy and of anybody whatsoever. It is clear that with respect to them the capacity for acquisition can only be the work of the legislature and the law.

Finally, I discover that each individual enjoys his property not by title of contract, since he can dispose of it; nor as depositary, since he can dissipate it; nor as usufructer, since he can destroy it; but as absolute master, just as he can dispose of his will, his arms, his thought. And none of these qualities fit the clergy. . . .

The property of corporations cannot be founded on that right which every man who enters a society has to have exclusive of possessions if he and if all permit such possession; for corporations are not, like individuals, the primary elements of society; they do not precede its existence, they cannot have rights at the very instant it is formed.

2. Economic Individualism in Action. In the early stages of the Revolution the National Assembly swept away many of the restrictions which the *ancien régime* had placed or maintained on trade and industry. The Assembly translated into law the principle of free economic activity by the abolition of the guilds and similar measures. A partial result was an artificial boom, further stimulated by the financial legislation of the Assembly. The collapse of the boom in the spring of 1791, with consequent unemployment and high prices, led the carpenters of Paris to form strike organizations (*coalitions*) as a means of raising their wages. In the months of April and May 1791 the Paris Commune, which exercised municipal authority in that city, attempted to deal with the specific problem of the Parisian carpenters, and in June the National Assembly met the issue in general terms with the passage of the *Loi le Chapelier* (named for its proposer, a lawyer and deputy from Rennes). The first selection which follows is from the records of the Paris Commune on the subject of the labor federations. The second is from the preamble and first section of the *Loi le Chapelier.* (3)

[*Warning Issued by the Paris Commune, April 29, 1791*]

The municipal authorities have learned that the workers in some trades are meeting daily in great numbers and are combining instead of spending their time at work; that they are debating and making decrees by which they are arbitrarily setting a day's wages; that many of them are circulating around in the various shops and spreading their supposed decrees to those who had not cooperated and are using threats and violence against these others in order to make them join the movement and stop work.

The suppression [of tolls on foodstuffs entering towns] is of benefit to all citizens. To lower the pay of workers because of this suppression, on the grounds that their food is now cheaper and that their masters will have to pay the taxes which of necessity will have to replace the tolls, this would be to put things back where they were and to betray the will of the nation by making the law work only to the advantage of the rich. The employers and masters certainly do not suggest this injustice.

But if it is just and reasonable that the workers should gain by the ending of tolls, is it right that they should take this opportunity to burden the owners or employers, by forcing them to raise wages? All citizens have equal rights but they are not (nor will they ever be) equal in ability or in talents; nature has not wished it. It is thus impossible that they should hope to make the same gains. A law which would fix their rate of pay and which would remove the hope of making more than the next fellow would thus be an unjust law. A coalition of workmen to fix a uni-

form daily pay and to force their fellow workmen to submit to this scale would obviously be against their real interests. In addition such a coalition would be a violation of the law, the annihilation of public order, a threat to the public interest, and the means of reducing those who advocated it to poverty by means of the halt or cessation of work which would result. In every respect the result would be a tragedy. . . .

[*Chapelier to the National Assembly, June 14, 1791*]

I come in the name of your constitutional committee to refer to you a violation of the constitutional principles which suppress guilds, violation of which carries great danger for the public peace; several people have attempted to revive the forbidden guilds, by forming associations of arts and trades, in which they name presidents, secretaries, managers, and other officers. The object of these associations, which are increasing throughout the kingdom, and which are already in touch with one another, is to force the people who contract for the work, heretofore the masters, to raise the price of a day's work, to prevent the workmen and the men who employ them from coming to a friendly agreement, to make them give written records that they will submit to the daily rate for work as set by these associations, and other regulations that they make. They even use violence to enforce these regulations. . . .

The first group of workmen who met together obtained permission to do so from the municipal government of Paris. In this respect the city seems to have been in error. All citizens should without doubt be allowed to hold meetings, but it is not necessary to allow citizens of certain professions to meet for their pretended common benefit. There are no more guilds in the country; now there is only the particular interest of each individual, and the welfare of the public. No one is allowed to suggest to the citizens an intermediate interest, to separate them from the public cause by the spirit of the guilds.

The associations which I am discussing at present presented, to obtain the municipal authorization, some specious reasons for meeting; they said their object was to help members of the same profession who were ill or unemployed; these funds for aid seemed useful; but let us not be misunderstood on this statement; it is up to the nation, up to the public officials in the name of the state, to provide work for the needy, and aid for the ill. These particular distributions of assistance, when they are not made dangerous by bad management, tend at the least to revive the guilds; they necessitate frequent meetings of individuals of the same occupation, the nomination of managers and other officers, the forming of rules, the exclusion of those who will not submit to these rules. Thus are revived the privileges, the controls, etc. Your committee believes that the prevention of the progress of this disorder is urgent. The unfortunate groups have taken the place in Paris of a society which was already established there under the name of "Society of Duties." Those who didn't do their duty, didn't live up to the rules of the society, were harassed in all sorts of ways. We have the strongest reasons to believe that the forming of these assemblies was suggested to the workers, less with the end in mind of raising, by uniting together, their daily pay, than with the secret intention of stirring up trouble.

It is necessary then to return to the principle that it is up to free agreements, person to person, to set the day's pay for each workman; it is then up to the worker to keep the agreement made with his employer. Without taking into consideration what ought reasonably to be the pay for a day's work, and saying only that it should be a

little higher than at present, what I have stated above is very true; for in a free nation, salaries should be large enough so that those who receive them keep out of that absolute dependency which results from the lack of the primary necessities, and which is practically slavery. It is thus that English workmen are paid better than the French. I say then that without setting here the exact price of a day's work, a price which should be reached by free agreement between the individuals concerned, the committee on constitution has thought it necessary to submit to you the following outline for a decree, whose object is to prevent the coalitions formed by workers to raise the rate of daily wages, as well as those formed by employers to lower them:

ARTICLE I. The abolition of all kinds of associations of citizens of the same occupation or profession being one of the fundamental bases of the French Constitution, it is forbidden to reestablish them under any pretext or in any form. . . .

C. LIBERTY OF THE PRESS

Among the civil liberties they deemed desirable, the *philosophes* had given special emphasis to freedom of thought and expression. During the early course of the Revolution the emphasis on these freedoms gave rise to a host of publications, representing the widest possible diversities of political views. The following letter, written by the Englishman Arthur Young, describes the situation of the French press in June 1789. (4) The writer, an agricultural reformer, had traveled extensively in France just before the outbreak of the Revolution.

The business going forward at present in the pamphlet shops of Paris is incredible. I went to the Palais Royal to see what new things were published, and to procure a catalogue of all. Every hour produces something new. Thirteen came out today, sixteen yesterday, and ninety-two last week. We think sometimes that Debrett's or Stockdale's shops at London are crowded, but they are mere deserts compared to Desein's, and some others here, in which one can scarcely squeeze from the door to the counter. The price of printing two years ago was from 27 livres to 30 livres per sheet, but now it is from 60 livres to 80 livres. This spirit of reading political tracts, they say, spreads into the provinces so that all the presses of France are equally employed.

Nineteen twentieths of these productions are in favor of liberty, and commonly violent against the clergy and nobility; I have today bespoke many of this description that have reputation; but inquiring for such as had appeared on the other side of the question, to my astonishment I find there are but two or three that have merit enough to be known. Is it not wonderful, that

while the press teems with the most levelling and even seditious principles, that if put into execution would overturn the monarchy, nothing in reply appears, and not the least step is taken by the court to restrain this extreme licentiousness of publication? It is easy to conceive the spirit that must thus be raised among the people. But the coffeehouses in the Palais Royal present yet more singular and astonishing spectacles; they are not only crowded within, but other expectant crowds are at the doors and windows, listening *à gorge déploye* [with open mouths] to certain orators, who from chairs or tables harangue each his little audience: the eagerness with which they are heard, and the thunder of applause they receive for every sentiment of more than common hardiness or violence against the present government, cannot easily be imagined. I am all amazement at the ministry permitting such nests and hotbeds of sedition and revolt which disseminate among the people, every hour, principles that by and by must be opposed with vigor, and therefore it seems little short of madness to allow the propagation at present.

D. ## THE LIBERALS AND EDUCATION

Popular education was a constant concern of the revolutionary legislators. Not only was it an element in the liberal creed, but the condition of French schools called pressingly for action. The pre-revolutionary system, which had been dominated by the Church, was thoroughly disorganized by the ecclesiastical measures of the National Assembly. Various plans of education were submitted, none of which, however, was immediately acted upon. The most important of these was Condorcet's *Report on the General Organization of Public Instruction,* which he presented to the Legislative Assembly, April 20, 1792. It constituted the most notable expression of revolutionary liberalism on the subject of education, and, though tabled by the Assembly, it was used in the enactment of later legislation. Extracts from this report follow. (5)

To offer to all individuals of the human race the means of providing for their needs, of assuring their welfare, of knowing and exercising their rights, of understanding and fulfilling their obligations. To assure each one the facility of perfecting his skill, of rendering himself capable of the social functions to which he has the right to be called, of developing to the fullest extent those talents with which nature has endowed him; and thereby to establish among all citizens an actual equality, thus rendering real the political equality recognized by the law. This should be the first aim of any national education; and, from such a point of view, this education is for the government an obligation of justice.

To direct the teaching in such a manner that the perfecting of the industries shall increase the pleasures of the generality of the citizens and the welfares of those who devote themselves to them, that a greater number of men shall be capable of exercising the functions necessary to society, and that the ever-increasing progress of enlightenment shall provide an inexhaustible source of help in our needs, of remedies for our ills, of means of individual happiness and of general prosperity. In short, to cultivate in each generation the physical, intellectual, and moral faculties, and thereby contribute to the general and gradual improvement of the human race—which should be the final aim of every social institution. This likewise should be the object of education, and it is for the government a duty imposed on it by the common interest of society, by that of all mankind.

As the first requisite of all education is that only the truth be taught, all institutions established by the government should be as free as possible from all political control, and, since this independence cannot be absolute, it results from the same principle that they must depend only on the Assembly of the Representatives of the People. . . .

So far, we have spoken, both for children and for adults, only of direct instruction; as this is the only kind of teaching whose procedure, arrangement, and extent must be determined before undertaking the organization of the institutions for public education. Other educational means will be considered in another part of our work.

Thus, for instance, the national holidays, by recalling the glorious epochs of liberty, by perpetuating the memory of men whose virtues have honored their country, by celebrating acts of sacrifice and courage of which it has been the scene, will teach all men, in the cities and in the country alike, to cherish the duties which have been made known to them. Besides, in the schools, care will be taken to teach the children to be good and just. They will be made to put in practice, in their relations with each other, the principles which have been taught them. In this manner, while they are being made to acquire the habits of regulating their conduct according to these principles, they will learn to understand them better and to feel more profoundly their usefulness and justice. Books will be especially prepared both for adults and for children: books which they will find easy to read and will be disposed to procure for themselves because of their utility or their interest. Place before the simplest men interesting and easily acquired information, above all, useful information, and they will profit by it. It is the discouraging difficulty of most studies; it is the uselessness of those to which a preconceived opinion had given the preference that indisposed men to learning. . . .

The principles of ethics that will be taught in the institutes will be those which, being founded on natural sentiments and on reason, are common to all men. The Constitution, by recognizing the right of each individual to choose his religion, by establishing a complete equality among all the inhabitants of France, does not permit the introduction into public instruction of any teaching which, by excluding the children of a part of the citizens, would destroy the quality of social advantages, and give to particular dogmas an advantage contrary to the liberty of opinions. . . . Each religion should be taught in its own temples and by its own ministers. Parents can then, whatever may be their opinions concerning the necessity of one religion or another, send, without reluctance, their children to the national schools; and the government will not have usurped rights over consciences under pretext of enlightening and guiding them. . . .

Above the primary schools, education ceases to be absolutely general. But we have felt that the double objective of assuring the country all the talents that could serve it, and of not depriving any individual of the advantage of developing those with which he has been endowed would be attained, if the children who show the most aptitude in a given grade of instruction should be chosen to enter the next higher; and maintained at the expense of the national treasury; they would be called National Scholars. According to the plan proposed by the committee, 3850

children, or thereabouts, would receive a sum sufficient for their maintenance. Of these, 1000 would attend the institutes and 600 the lyceums. About 400 would come out each year to take up useful employments in society or to devote themselves to the sciences. Never in any country has the government opened for the poorer classes a more abundant source of prosperity and learning; never has it used more powerful means to maintain the natural equality of men. Not alone will the study of the sciences be encouraged, but also that modest industry, which seeks only to make easier the admittance to a laborious profession, will not be neglected. As it is desirable that there be also rewards for diligence, for love of work, and for integrity, even when not accompanied by brilliant qualities, the government will provide for other National Scholars their apprenticeship in industries of general utility. . . .

E. LIBERALISM AND GOVERNMENT

A total reorganization of the governmental and administrative structure was required both by the practical need to replace the system of the *ancien régime*, which had broken down at the outset of the Revolution, and by the liberal demand for popular participation in government. The organs of the new local and regional administration were created by the legislation of December 1789. The central government was administered by the King and the National Assembly until the final passage of the Constitution of 1791 which, it was hoped, would provide a permanent government for France.

1. *Law on Municipalities, December 14, 1789* (6)

ART. I. The municipalities currently existing in each town, borough, parish or community, under the title of town halls, mayoralties, shrievalties, consulates, and generally under whatever title and qualification it be, are suppressed and abolished; however, the municipal officers currently on duty will continue their functions until they have been replaced.

II. The officers and members of the present municipalities will be replaced through election.

III. The rights of presentation, nomination, or confirmation, and the rights of presidency or of presence at municipal assemblies, claimed or exercised as attached to the possession of certain lands, to the function of commandant of a province or town, to bishops or archbishops, and generally to whatever other title it can be, are abolished. . . .

V. All the active citizens of each town, borough, parish, or community, can assemble for the election of the members of the municipal corporation. . . .

2. *Law on Local Government, December 22, 1789* (7)

ART. I. There will be a new division of the kingdom into departments, both for representation and for administration. These departments will be from 75 to 85 in number.

II. Each department will be divided into districts whose number, which cannot be less than three nor more than nine, will be regulated by the National Assembly, according to the need and convenience of the department, after having heard the deputies of the provinces.

III. Each district will be divided into divisions called cantons, of about four square leagues (ordinary French leagues). . . .

VIII. The representatives named to the National Assembly by the departments cannot be regarded as representatives of a particular department, but as the representatives of the totality of the departments, that is, of the entire nation

SECTION II: OF THE FORMATION AND ORGANIZATION OF THE ADMINISTRATIVE ASSEMBLIES

ART. II. After having named the representatives to the National Assembly, the same electors will elect in each department the thirty-six members who will compose the department administration.

III. The electors of each district will then meet in the capital of their district and name the twelve members who will compose the district administration. . . .

VI. To be eligible to the department and the district administration, it will be necessary to have, in addition to the conditions required to be an active citizen, that of paying a larger direct tax, which amounts to at least the local value of ten days' labor. . . .

XIV. In each department administration there will be an attorney general and in each district administration a public prosecutor. They will be named by individual ballot and by absolute plurality of the votes simultaneously with the members of each administration and by the same electors. . . .

XXVIII. The administrations and the directories of the district will be completely subordinated to the administrations and directories of the departments. . . .

SECTION III: OF THE FUNCTIONS OF THE ADMINISTRATIVE ASSEMBLIES

ART. I. The department administrations are charged, under the inspection of the legislative body and by virtue of its decrees:

1. To distribute all the direct taxes imposed on each department. . . .

3. To regulate and supervise all that concerns both the collection and the payment of the taxes and the service of the agents in charge of it. . . .

II. The department administrations are also charged, under the authority and inspection of the king, as supreme chief of the nation and of the general administration of the kingdom, with all parts of this administration. . . .

VIII. From the day that the department and district administrations will be formed, the provincial estates, provincial assemblies, and subordinate assemblies which exist at present, will be suppressed and will entirely cease to function.

IX. There will be no intermediary between the department administration and the supreme executive power. The replaced commissioners, intendants, and their subdelegates will cease all functions as soon as the department administrations will have entered into activity.

3. *The Constitution of 1791* (8)

FUNDAMENTAL REGULATIONS GUARANTEED BY THE CONSTITUTION

The Constitution guarantees, as natural and civil rights,

1. That all the citizens are admissible to places and employments, without any other distinction than that of virtue and talents.

2. That all taxes shall be equally divided among all the citizens, in proportion to their abilities.

3. That the same crimes shall be subject to the same punishments, without any distinction of persons.

The Constitution in like manner guarantees, as natural and civil rights, liberty to every man to go, stay, or depart, without being arrested or detained, except according to the forms of the Constitution.

Liberty to every man to speak, write, print, and publish his thoughts, without the writings being subjected to censure or inspection before their publication, and to exercise the religious worship to which he is attached.

Liberty to address, to the constituted authorities, petitions signed by individuals.

The legislative power can make no law which would attack, or impede, the exercise of the natural and civil rights expressed in the present title, and guaranteed by the Constitution; but as liberty consists only in the power of doing whatever neither injures the rights of another, nor the public safety, the law may establish penalties against acts, which, attacking either the rights of others, or the public safety, would be injurious to society.

The Constitution guarantees the inviolability of property, or a just and previous indemnity for that of which public necessity, legally proved, shall require the sacrifice.

Property destined to the expense of worship, and to all services of public utility belongs to the nation, and shall at all times be at its disposal.

The Constitution guarantees all the alienations which have been, or which shall be made according to the forms established by the law.

The citizens have a right to elect and choose the ministers of their religions.

There shall be created and organized a general establishment of *public aid* for the education of deserted children, to relieve the infirm poor, and to procure work for the healthy poor who have not been able to find it for themselves.

There shall be created and organized a *public instruction*, common to all citizens, gratuitous with regard to those parts of instruction indispensable for all men, and of which the establishments shall be gradually distributed, in a proportion combined with the division of the kingdom.

There shall be established national festivals, to preserve the remembrance of the French Revolution, to keep up fraternal affection amongst the citizens, and attachment to the Constitution, the country, and the laws.

There shall be drawn up a code of civil laws, common to all the kingdom.

OF THE PUBLIC POWERS

I. The sovereignty is one, indivisible, inalienable, and imprescriptible; it belongs to the nation; no section of the people, nor any individual, can assume to itself the exercise of it.

II. The nation, from which alone flow all the powers, cannot exercise them but by delegation. The French Constitution is representative; the representatives are the legislative body and the king.

III. The legislative power is delegated to a national assembly, composed of temporary representatives freely chosen by the people, to be exercised by this assembly with the sanction of the king, in manner afterwards determined.

IV. The government is monarchical; the executive power is delegated to the king, to be exercised under his authority, by ministers and other responsible agents, in manner afterwards determined.

V. The judicial power is delegated to judges chosen for a time by the people.

CHAPTER I: OF THE LEGISLATIVE ASSEMBLY

I. The National Assembly, forming the legislative body, is permanent, and consists of one chamber only.

II. It shall be formed by new elections every two years. Each period of two years shall form one legislature.

III. The dispositions of the preceding articles shall not take place with respect to the ensuing legislative body, whose powers shall cease the last day of April 1793. . . .

V. The legislative body cannot be dissolved by the king. . . .

Section I: Number of Representatives— Bases of Representatives

I. The number of representatives in the legislative body is 745, on account of the eighty-three departments of which the kingdom is composed, and independent of those that may be granted to the colonies.

II. The representatives shall be distributed among the eighty-three departments, according to the three proportions of territory, of population, and of direct contribution.

III. Of the 745 representatives, 247 are distributed according to territory.

Of these each department shall nominate three, except the department of Paris, which shall only nominate one.

IV. Two hundred and forty-nine representatives are attributed to the population.

V. The sum total of the direct contribution of the kingdom is likewise divided into 249 parts; and each department nominates as many deputies as it pays parts of the contribution.

Section II: Primary Assemblies—Nomination of Electors

I. In order to form a National Legislative Assembly, the active citizens shall meet every two years, in primary assemblies, in the towns and cantons. . . .

II. To be an active citizen it is necessary,

To be born, or to have become, a Frenchman;

To be twenty-five years of age complete;

To have resided in the city or canton during the time determined by the law;

To pay, in any part of the kingdom, a direct contribution, at least equal to the value of three days' labor, and to produce the acquittance;

Not to be in a menial capacity; namely, that of a servant receiving wages;

To be inscribed, in the municipality of the place of residence, in the list of the national guards;

To have taken the civic oath.

III. Every six years the legislative body shall fix the *minimum* and the *maximum* of the value of a day's labor, and the administrators of the departments shall determine the rate for every district.

IV. None shall exercise the rights of an active citizen in more than one place, nor employ another as a substitute.

V. Those shall be excluded from the rights of an active citizen,

Who are in a state of accusation;

Who, after having been constituted in a state of failure, or insolvency proved by authentic documents, shall not produce a general discharge from their creditors.

VI. The primary assemblies shall name electors in proportion to the number of active citizens residing in the town or canton.

There shall be named one elector for 100 active citizens present, or not, in the assembly.

There shall be named two for 151 to 250; and so on in this proportion.

VII. No man can be named elector, if, to the conditions necessary in order to be an active citizen, he does not join the following: In towns of more than 6000 inhabitants, that of being proprietor or life-renter of a property valued on the rolls of the contribution at a revenue equal to the local value of 150 days' labor.

VIII. In towns below 6000 inhabitants, that of being proprietor or life-renter of a property valued, on the rolls of contribution, at a revenue equal to the local value of 150 days' labor; or of renting a house valued, on the same rolls, at a revenue equal to the value of 100 days' labor.

And in the country, that of being proprietor or life-renter of a property valued on the rolls of contribution at a revenue equal to the local value of 150 days' labor, or of being a farmer of lands valued, on the same rolls, at the value of 400 days' labor.

With respect to those who shall be at the same time proprietors or life-renters on one hand, and taxpayers or farmers on the other, their powers on these different accounts shall be added together, to establish their eligibility.

Section III: Electoral Assemblies—Nomination of Representatives

I. The electors named in each department shall convene in order to choose that number of representatives whose nomination shall belong to their department, and a number of substitutes equal to a third of the representatives.

The electoral assemblies shall form themselves, of full right, the last Sunday of March, if they have not been convoked sooner by the public officers established by law.

II. The representatives and substitutes shall be chosen by an absolute majority of votes, and cannot be chosen but from among the active citizens in the department.

III. All the active citizens, whatever be their condition, possession, or contribution, may be chosen representatives of the nation.

IV. These, however, shall be obliged to decide between one or other situation—ministers, and other agents of the executive power, removable at pleasure . . . and those who, under any denomination whatever, are attached to the employ of the military or civil household of the king.

V. The exercise of judiciary functions shall be incompatible with those of a representative of the nation, during all the continuance of the legislature.

The judges shall be replaced by their substitutes, and the king shall provide, by briefs of commission, for the replacing of his commissaries at the tribunals.

VI. The members of the legislative body may be re-elected to the next legislature; but not afterward, until after an interval of one legislature.

VII. The representatives named in the departments shall not be representatives of a particular department, but of the whole nation, and no mandate can be given them.

OF THE REVISION OF CONSTITUTIONAL DECREES

I. The National Constituent Assembly declares that the nation has an imprescriptible right to change its constitution; and nevertheless, considering that it is most suitable to the national interest to make use of the right of reforming those articles which experience shall demonstrate the inconvenience of only by means appointed by the Constitution itself, decrees that the assembly of revision shall proceed in the following manner:

II. When three successive legislatures shall have declared a uniform wish for the change of any constitutional article, the revision demanded shall take place.

III. The ensuing legislature [that commencing in 1791] cannot propose the reform of any constitutional article. . . .

F.   LIBERAL NATIONALISM

Although many evidences of national consciousness were to be found in the *cahiers* (the lists of grievances), which were drawn up in the electoral assemblies to accompany the delegates to the Estates General in May 1789, this consciousness was in general, during the early period of the Revolution, still in the process of formation. The two sections which follow show two aspects of this process.

1. *Fraternity and Federalism.* The first Festival of the Federations was held on the first anniversary of Bastille Day, July 14, 1790. The federations which met then were local defense groups which had been formed throughout France during the unrest of the summer in 1789 and which had already then taken up some measure of contact with one another for mutual assistance. In addition all the national guards and army corps had been ordered present by the decree of May 27, 1790, which established the occasion as a national convocation. Following are two eyewitness accounts of the celebration. (9)

Meanwhile, more than 300,000 people of both sexes, from Paris and the environs, had been assembled since six in the morning at the Champ-de-Mars. Sitting on turf seats, which formed an immense circus, drenched, draggled, sheltering themselves with parasols from the torrents of rain which descended upon them, and at the least ray of sunshine adjusting their dresses, they waited, laughing and chatting, for the federates and the National Assembly.

A spacious amphitheater had been erected for the King, the royal family, the ambassadors, and the deputies. The federates, who first arrived, began to dance farandeles; those who followed joined them, forming a round which soon embraced part of the Champ-de-Mars. A sight worthy of the philosophic observer was that exhibited by this host of men, who had come from the most opposite parts of France, hurried away by the impulse of the national character, banishing all remembrance of the past, all idea of the present, all fear of the future, and indulging in a delicious thoughtlessness. Three hundred thousand spectators, of all ages and of both sexes, followed their motions, beating time with their hands, forgetting the rain, hunger, and the weariness of long waiting. At length, the whole procession having entered the Champ-de-Mars, the dance ceased, each federate repaired to his banner. The Bishop of Autun prepared to perform mass at an altar in the antique style, erected in the center of the Champ-de-Mars. Three hundred priests in white surplices, girt with broad tricolored scarfs, ranged themselves at the four corners of the altar. The Bishop of Autun blessed the oriflamme and the eighty-three banners: he struck up the *Te Deum*. Twelve hundred musicians played that hymn. . . .

The enthusiasm and the festivities were not confined to the day of the federation. During the stay of the federates at Paris, there was one continued series of entertainments, of dances, and of rejoicing. People again went to the Champ-de-Mars, where they drank, sang, and danced. M. de La Fayette reviewed part of the national guard of the departments and the army of the line. The King, Queen, and the Dauphin were present at this review. They were greeted with acclamations. The Queen, with a gracious look, gave the federates her hand to kiss, and showed them the Dauphin. The federates, before they quitted the capital, went to pay homage to the King: all of them testified the most profound respect, the warmest attachment. The chief of the Bretons dropped on his knee, and presented his sword to Louis XVI. "Sire," said he, "I deliver to you, pure and sacred, the sword of the faithful Bretons: it shall never be stained but with the blood of your enemies." "That sword cannot be in better hands than those of my dear Bretons," replied Louis XVI,

raising the chief of the Bretons, and returning him his sword. "I have never doubted their affection and fidelity. Assure them that I am the father, the brother, the friend, of all the French." The King, deeply moved, pressed the hand of the chief of the Bretons, and embraced him. A mutual emotion prolonged for some moments this touching scene. The chief of the Bretons was the first to speak. "Sire," he said "all the French, if I may judge from our hearts, love and will love you, because you are a citizen king."

2. *Liberal France and the War.* On April 20, 1792, the Legislative Assembly declared war on Austria, in part from internal political motives which made the rising Girondists the war party and in part in response to what the French felt to be a grave threat posed by the monarchical powers of Europe to the revolution in France. The following selection has been taken from this declaration of war. (10)

The National Assembly declared that the French nation, faithful to the principles consecrated by the Constitution "not to undertake any war with a view of making conquests, and never to employ its forces against the liberty of any people," takes up arms only for the maintenance of its liberty and independence; that the war which it is obliged to undertake is not a war of nation against nation, but the just defense of a free people against the unjust aggression of a king;

That the French will never confuse their brothers with their real enemies; that they will neglect nothing to soften the scourge of war, to care for and preserve property, and to cause the miseries inseparable from war to fall only on those who are allied against its liberty;

That it adopts in advance all foreigners who, renouncing the cause of its enemies, will come to stand under its banners and to consecrate their efforts to the defense of liberty; that it will even favor, by all the means in its power, their establishment in France. . . .

Part II.   THE NATIONAL PHASE

Despite the realization of the liberal program in the early period of the Revolution and the constant efforts of moderates to call a halt, the increased pace of the Revolution inexorably played into the hands of the more radical groups. Many factors entered into this development: the intrigues of the *émigrés;* the constant threat represented by the hostile courts of Europe culminating in the French declaration of war in April 1792; internal resistance, led by priests and conservative peasants, to revolutionary enactments, especially in the provinces of the north and west, breaking forth ultimately in open insurrections like that of the Vendée in March 1793; the continued economic crisis, accompanied from the middle of 1791 by high prices, food shortages, and unemployment; the successive rise to power of political groups like the Girondins and the Jacobins, with a republican and equalitarian emphasis which gave a different interpretation of the liberal ideal from that of the early revolutionaries. Although the trend to the Left was a continuous one, the break came with the convocation of the Convention on September 20, 1792, and the abolition of the monarchy on the following day. The ideas, measures, and policies dominant in this period have been characterized as "Jacobin," for, after their struggle with the Girondists for power in the Convention ended with the arrest of the outstanding Girondist deputies on June 2, 1793, the leaders of the Jacobin clubs, under Robespierre, assumed control of the Convention. As the Party of the Mountain, they determined the internal and foreign policy of France for the fourteen months which constituted the extreme phase of the Revolution, until their overthrow, July 27, 1794 (the famous "9th of Thermidor") .

A. THE JACOBIN IDEAL

The Constitution of 1793, passed by the Convention under the auspices of the Mountain on June 24, 1793, was a Jacobin revision of the constitutional draft which had been worked out by Condorcet and the Girondists. Though approved by popular referendum in July, the constitution never went into effect, for its execution was suspended in favor of the revolutionary government of the committees created by the Convention. It nevertheless remains as the theoretical political testament of the Jacobins. (11)

The Constitution of 1793

The French people, convinced that forgetfulness of, and contempt for, the natural rights of man are the only causes of the misfortunes of the world, have resolved to expose, in a declaration, their sacred and inalienable rights, in order that all citizens, being able always to compare the acts of the government with the end of every social institution, may never suffer themselves to be oppressed and degraded by tyranny; and that the people may always have before their eyes the basis of their liberty and happiness; the magistrates the rules of their duty; and the legislature the object of their mission.

They acknowledge therefore and proclaim, in the presence of the Supreme Being, the following

DECLARATION OF THE RIGHTS OF MAN AND OF THE CITIZEN

ARTICLE I. The end of society is common happiness. Government is instituted to secure to man the enjoyment of his natural and imprescriptible rights.

II. These rights are equality, liberty, safety, and property.

III. All men are equal by nature, and before the law.

IV. The law is the free and solemn expression of the general will. It ought to be the same for all, whether it protects or punishes. It cannot order but what is just and useful to society. It cannot forbid but what is hurtful.

V. All citizens are equally admissible to public employments. Free people avow no other mo-

tives of preference in their elections than virtues and talents.

VI. Liberty is that power which belongs to a man of doing everything that does not hurt the rights of another: its principle is nature; its rule is justice; its protection the law; and its moral limits are defined by the maxim, "Do not to another what you would not wish done to yourself."

VII. The right of manifesting one's thoughts and opinions, either by the press, or in any other manner; the right of assembling peaceably; and the free exercise of religious worship cannot be forbidden. The necessity of announcing these rights supposes either the presence or the recent remembrance of despotism. . . .

VIII. The right of property is that right which belongs to every citizen to enjoy and dispose of according to his pleasure his property, revenues, labor, and industry.

XVIII. No kind of labor, culture, or commerce can be forbidden to the industrious citizen.

XIX. Every man may engage his services and his time, but he cannot sell himself — his person is not alienable property. The law does not acknowledge servitude; there can exist only an engagement of care and acknowledgment between the man who labors and the man who employs him.

XX. No one can be deprived of the smallest portion of his property without his consent, except when the public necessity, legally ascertained, evidently requires it, and on condition of a just and previous indemnification.

XXI. No contribution can be established but

for general utility, and to relieve the public wants. Every citizen has the right to concur in the establishment of contributions, to watch over the use made of them, and to call for a statement of their expenditure.

XXII. Public aids are a sacred debt. Society is obliged to provide for the subsistence of the unfortunate, either by procuring them work, or by securing the means of existence to those who are unable to labor.

XXIII. Instruction is the want of all, and society ought to favor, with all its power, the progress of public reason; and to place instruction within the reach of every citizen. . . .

XXVI. The sovereignty resides in the people. It is one and indivisible, imprescriptible and inalienable.

XXVII. No portion of the people can exercise the power of the whole, but each section of the sovereign assembled ought to enjoy the right of expressing its will in perfect liberty. Every individual who arrogates to himself the sovereignty, or who usurps the exercise of it, ought to be put to death by free men.

XXVIII. A people have always the right of revising, amending, and changing their constitution. One generation cannot subject to its laws future generations.

XXIX. Every citizen has an equal right of concurring in the formation of the law, and in the nomination of his mandatories or agents. . . .

XXX. Public functions cannot be considered as distinctions or rewards, but as duties. . . .

CONSTITUTIONAL ACT OF THE REPUBLIC

ARTICLE I. The French Republic is one and indivisible.

Of the Division of the People

II. The French people are divided, for the exercise of the sovereignty, into primary assemblies of cantons.

III. For the administration of justice they are divided into departments, districts, and municipalities.

Of the State of Citizens

IV. Every man born and resident in France of the age of twenty-one years complete, every foreigner aged twenty-one years complete who has resided a year in France, who has acquired property, married a French woman, adopted a child, or maintained an aged person; in short, every foreigner who shall be judged by the legislative body to have deserved well by his humanity shall be admitted to exercise the rights of a French citizen.

V. The exercise of the rights of citizens shall be lost by being naturalized in a foreign country, by accepting functions or favors from a government not popular, and by condemnation to disgraceful or penal punishments. . . .

Of the Sovereignty of the People

VII. The sovereign people are the generality of the French citizens.

VIII. They shall immediately name the deputies.

IX. They shall delegate to electors the choice of administrators, public arbitrators, criminal judges, and judges of repeal.

X. They shall deliberate on laws.

Of Primary Assemblies

XI. Primary assemblies shall be composed of citizens who have resided six months in each canton.

XII. They shall consist of two hundred citizens at least, or six hundred at most, called to vote. . . .

Of the National Representation

XXI. Population is the only basis of national representation.

XXII. There shall be a deputy for every 40,000 inhabitants.

Of Electoral Assemblies

XXXVII. The citizens united in primary assemblies shall name an elector for every 200 citizens, present or not, two for from 201 to 400, and three for from 401 to 600.

XXXVIII. The holding of the electoral assemblies, and the mode of election, shall be the same as for the primary assemblies.

Of the Legislative Body

XXXIX. The legislative body is one, indivisible, and permanent.

XL. Its time of sitting shall be one year.

Of the Functions of the Legislative Body

LIII. The legislative body shall propose laws and pass decrees.

LIV. Under the general name of *laws* are comprehended acts of the legislative body concerning civil and criminal legislation; the general administration of the revenues and ordinary expenses of the Republic; the nature, amount, and collecting of the contributions; the declaring of war; every new division of the French territories; public instruction; and the public honors granted to the memory of great men.

LV. Under the particular name of *decrees* are comprehended acts of the legislative body concerning the annual establishment of the sea and land forces; permitting or prohibiting the passage of foreign troops through the French territories;

the introduction of foreign naval forces into parts of the Republic; measures of general safety and tranquillity; the annual and temporary distribution of aids and public labors; orders for the coining of money of every kind; unforeseen and extraordinary expenses; measures peculiar and local to one administration, commune, or kind of public works; the defense of territory; the ratification of treaties; the nomination and suspensions of commanders in chief of the armies; the enforcing of the responsibility of members of the council, or public functionaries; the accusing of persons guilty of forming plots against the general safety of the Republic; every change in the partial division of the French territory; and national rewards.

On the Formation of a Law

LVI. Every plan of a law shall be preceded by a report.

LVII. The discussion cannot begin, and the law cannot be provisionally decreed, until fifteen days after the report.

LVIII. The plan shall be printed and sent to all the communes of the Republic, under the title of *a law proposed.*

LIX. Forty days after the plan has been published and distributed, if in one half of the departments, plus one, a tenth part of the primary assemblies of each of them, regularly formed, have not remonstrated against the plan, it shall be considered as accepted, and shall become a *law.*

LX. If there be a remonstrance, the legislative body shall convoke the primary assemblies. . . .

Of the Executive Council

LXII. There shall be an executive council composed of twenty-four members.

LXIII. The electoral assembly of each department shall name a candidate, and the legislative body shall from the general list choose the members of the council.

LXIV. One half of the members shall be renewed each legislature, in the last months of the session.

LXV. The council is charged with the direction and inspection of the general administration. It cannot act but to execute laws and decrees of the legislative body.

LXVI. It appoints from outside its own body the principal agents of the general administration of the Republic.

LXVII. The legislative body determines the number and the duties of these agents. . . .

2. *Robespierre on the Aim of the Revolution.* Maximilian Robespierre (1758–94), in the very midst of the Terror, on February 5, 1794, set forth before the Convention in the name of the Committee of Public Safety the following vision toward which his Jacobin group purportedly strove. (12)

It is time to mark clearly the aim of the Revolution. . . .

We wish an order of things where all low and cruel passions are enchained by the laws, all beneficent and generous feelings awakened; where ambition is the desire to deserve glory and to be useful to one's country; where distinctions arise only from equality itself; where the citizen is subject to the magistrate, the magistrate to the people, the people to justice; where the country secures the welfare of each individual, and each individual proudly enjoys the prosperity and glory of his country; where all minds are enlarged by the constant interchange of republican sentiments and by the need of earning the respect of a great people; where industry is an adornment to the liberty that ennobles it, and commerce the source of public wealth, not simply of monstrous riches for a few families.

We wish to substitute in our country morality for egotism, probity for a mere sense of honor, principle for habit, duty for etiquette, the empire of reason for the tyranny of custom, contempt for vice for contempt for misfortune, pride for insolence, large-mindedness for vanity, the love of glory for the love of money, good men for good company, merit for intrigue, talent for conceit, truth for show, the charm of happiness for the tedium of pleasure, the grandeur of man for the triviality of grand society, a people magnanimous, powerful, and happy for a people lovable, frivolous, and wretched—that is to say, all the virtues and miracles of the Republic for all the vices and puerilities of the monarchy.

We wish in a word to fulfill the course of nature, to accomplish the destiny of mankind, to make good the promises of philosophy, to absolve Providence from the long reign of tyranny and crime. May France, illustrious formerly among peoples of slaves, eclipse the glory of all free peoples that have existed, become the model to the nations, the terror of oppressors, the consolation of the oppressed, the ornament of the universe; and in sealing our work with our blood may we ourselves see at last the dawn of universal felicity gleam before us! That is our ambition. That is our aim.

B.   THE THEORY OF REVOLUTIONARY GOVERNMENT

To bridge the gap between their ideal and their practice, the Jacobins invoked a theory of emergency government by which they sought to justify their actions by reference to the extraordinary circumstances of the times. The student should examine this theory and decide which—if any—elements of the Jacobin ideal have been carried over into it, particularly in respect to the liberal and national components of that ideal.

1. *Saint Just and the Need for Revolutionary Government.* On October 10, 1793, Saint Just, the young radical doctrinaire of the Jacobins, delivered a report to the Convention in the name of the Committee of Public Safety proposing a decree which would give legal sanction to virtually unlimited authority for the Committee. (13)

It is time to announce a truth which henceforth should never be forgotten by those who govern: the Republic will be founded only when the will of the sovereign will have checked the monarchical minority and will reign over it by right of conquest. You should no longer humor the enemies of the new order of things, and liberty must conquer at any price.

Your Committee of Public Safety . . . has worked out the causes of the public misfortunes; it has found them in the weakness with which your decrees are executed, in the lack of economy of administration, in the instability of the views of the state, in the shifting of the passions which influence the government. Therefore it has resolved to reveal the condition of things to you and to present the means it believes appropriate for consolidating the revolution, defeating federalism, relieving the people and procuring abundance for them, fortifying the armies, and purging the conspiracies which infest them. No prosperity can be hoped for so long as the last enemy of liberty breathes. You must punish not only the traitors but also those who are indifferent; you must punish all who are passive in the Republic and do nothing for it. For since the French people have manifested its will, all who are beyond the sovereign are enemies.

If the conspiracies had not troubled this empire, if *la patrie* had not been a thousand times a victim of indulgent laws, it would be easy to rule by maxims of peace and natural justice; these maxims are good among friends of liberty, but between the people and its enemies there is nothing in common but the sword. Those who cannot be governed by justice must be governed by iron; it is necessary to crush tyrants. You have had the energy; the public administration has lacked it. You have desired economy; the accounting offices have not seconded your efforts. Everybody has robbed the state. The generals

have made war on their armies; the owners of manufactures and goods and all the vices of the monarchy have joined against the people and you. A people has but one dangerous enemy, and that is its government; yours has constantly made war upon you with impunity. . . .

The rich have become wealthier since the taxes, which have been made primarily in favor of the people; they have doubled the value of their holdings; they have doubled their means of seduction. Wealthy men contribute—do not doubt it—to the prolongation of the war. It is they who are everywhere in competition with the state in its purchases. They put their money in the hands of unfaithful administrations, commissioners, agents; the government is leagued with them. . . . It is necessary that you charge wealth with tribute; you must establish a tribunal so that all those who for four years have handled the revenues of the Republic account for their fortunes. . . . The public treasury must be filled with the restitutions of the thieves and justice must reign in its turn. . . . The bread which the rich give is bitter; it compromises liberty; bread belongs to the people by right in a wisely ruled state. . . . One of the best ways to lower the price of goods is to diminish the excess in fortunes and to force him who has too much to economy. . . .

Let us glance at commerce and the exchange. . . . Many goods have become scarce; they are those which our country does not produce; these goods can become scarcer still through the difficulty of procuring them; foreign exchange no longer exists but it is better to do without luxury goods than those of courage and virtue. . . .

Your committee had had the idea of employing men who were justly suspect for repairing [roads], deepening the Saint-Quentin and Orleans canals, transporting wood for the navy, dredging the rivers. . . . In a Republic no consideration should prevail over social utility: it would be just for the people to rule in its turn over the oppressors, and that sweat wash the pride from their faces. . . .

In the circumstances in which the Republic finds itself, the Constitution cannot be put in force; it would be used to destroy itself. It would become the guarantee of crimes against liberty because it would lack the violence necessary to repress them. . . . You are too far from all the crimes, the sword of the laws must go everywhere quickly and your arm must be present everywhere to stop crime. You ought to guarantee the independence of the administrations, divide authority, identify it with the revolutionary movement and yourselves, and multiply it. . . . It is impossible for the revolutionary laws to be executed if the government itself does not become revolutionary.

You cannot hope for prosperity if you do not establish a government which, gentle and moderate toward the people, will be terrible toward itself through the energy of its reports; this government should weigh on itself and not on the people. Every injustice toward the citizens, every treason, every act of indifference toward *la patrie*, all softness, should be repressed in it. It must specify duties, place the sword everywhere against abuses, so that everything be free in the Republic save those who conspire against it and who govern badly. . . .

2. *Robespierre and the Principles of Revolutionary Government.* On December 25, 1793, Robespierre, again on behalf of the Committee of Public Safety, delivered a report to the Convention in which he sought to provide a theoretical foundation for a rule which clearly contravened the political philosophy of the Jacobins. (14)

The theory of the revolutionary government is as new as the Revolution itself, from which this government was born. . . . The goal of a constitutional government is the protection of the Republic; that of a revolutionary government is the establishment of the Republic. The Revolution is the war waged by liberty against its foes—but the Constitution is the regime of victorious and peaceful freedom. The revolutionary government will need to put forth extraordinary activity, because it is at war. It is subject to no constant laws, since the circumstances under which it prevails are those of a storm, and change with every moment. This government is obliged unceasingly to disclose new sources of energy to oppose the rapidly changing face of danger.

Constitutional government is concerned principally with civil liberty, and revolutionary government with public liberty. Under the constitutional regime it suffices to protect individuals against the abuse of the public power. Under the revolutionary regime the public power itself is obliged to defend itself against all the factions which attack it. The revolutionary government owes a national protection to good citizens; to its foes it owes only death. . . .

Is the revolutionary government, because its course is more rapid and movements more free than ordinary government, therefore less just and less legitimate? No, it is based on the most sacred of all laws, on the general weal and on the iron-clad law of necessity! It too has its rules, all drawn from justice and public order. This government has nothing in common with anarchy or with disorder; on the contrary, its goal requires the destruction of anarchy and disorder in order to realize a dominion of law. It has nothing in common with autocracy, for it is not inspired by personal passions, but by the public interest.

C.   THE JACOBINS IN ACTION

An examination of Jacobin theory in action, of the legislative acts and administrative practices of Jacobin rule, serves to make clear the revolutionary novelty of the forces at work in France.

1. *The Jacobins and Government.* The governmental system, as created by the Jacobins, operated chiefly through three instruments: the Committees of Public Safety and General Security at the apex, the representatives on mission for regional coordination, and the extra-official Jacobin clubs in local administration. The selections which follow deal with the powers and activities of these organs. (15)

[*Decree of the Convention Creating the Committee of Public Safety, April 6, 1793*]

ART. I. There will be formed, by roll call of the Convention, a Committee of Public Safety, composed of nine members of the National Convention.

II. This Committee will deliberate secretly; it will be charged with supervising and accelerating the action of the administration entrusted to the provisional executive council (a body of ministers charged with the executive power), whose decrees it can even suspend when it believes them contrary to the national interest, with the duty of informing the Convention of it immediately.

III. It is authorized to take, in urgent circumstances, measures of general external and internal defense; and its decrees, signed by the majority of its members present, which cannot be under two thirds, will be executed immediately by the provisional executive council. It can in no case issue writs of arrest, save against its own agents and then with the duty of accounting for it to the Convention immediately. . . .

V. Each week it will make a general report, in writing, of its operations and of the situation of the Republic. . . .

VII. The Committee is established only for one month. . . .

[*Decree on the Revolutionary Government Passed by the Convention, October 10, 1793*]

ART. I. The provisional government of France is revolutionary until the peace.

II. The provisional executive council, the ministers, the generals, the constituted corporations are placed under the supervision of the Committee of Public Safety, which will report to the Convention every eight days.

III. Every security measure should be taken by the provisional executive council, under the authorization of the Committee, which will report on it to the Convention.

IV. The revolutionary laws should be executed rapidly. The government will correspond directly with the districts in matters of public safety. . . .

VI. Since the inertia of the government is the cause of reverses, deadlines for the execution of laws and measures of public safety will be set; violation of the deadlines will be punished as an attack against liberty. . . .

[*Decree Creating the Post of Representatives on Mission to the Armies Passed April 9, 1793*]

ART. I. There will constantly be three representatives of the people deputized to each of the armies of the Republic; each month one of the three will be replaced.

II. They will exercise the most active kind of supervision over the operations of the agents of the executive council, over the conduct of the generals, officers, and soldiers of the army; they will examine daily into the condition of the warehouses of supplies, food, and munitions; they will investigate most severely the operations and the conduct of all the suppliers and contractors of the armies of the republic. . . .

IV. The representatives deputized to the armies are invested with unlimited powers for the exercise of the functions which are delegated to them by the present decrees; they can employ as many agents as they find feasible; the extraordinary expenses which they will authorize will be paid by the public treasury on accounts endorsed by them; their decrees will be executed provisionally, with the duty of addressing them in twenty-four hours to the National Convention, and for those that are to be secret, to the Committee of Public Safety.

V. All civil and military agents are enjoined to obey the demands of the commissioners of the National Convention, with the right to make to the Convention any complaints they believe well founded. . . .

[*Notes on a Meeting of the Jacobin Club of Perpignan late in 1793*]

Deputation to headquarters [of the army] to get it to give orders for the distribution of wood to the soldiers to be so made that they may use it without having to split it, for not every soldier has an ax.

First deputation to the district to get it to order the commissioners around the Canigou to continue to burn charcoal and to come to Perpignan to sell it as they used to, in as much as the village governments seem to be . . . [in conspiracy] not to burn any or at least not to come to Perpignan to sell it.

The members of the deputation reported that the *procureur syndic* had already busied himself with the matter, and orders to bring in charcoal have been given.

Second deputation to the district to get it to order the communes to bury any corpses left on their territory. [This was on the Spanish frontier, where the Republican armies were engaged with the Spanish.]

First deputation to the city government to request it to make at once requisitional visits to all cobblers and shoemakers to see whether any have stocks of shoes they refuse to sell. This measure is essential, as some brothers-in-arms lack shoes. The members of the deputation having returned said that they would report tomorrow. Second deputation to the city government to get the pavements repaired and to keep the streets clean. Third deputation to the city government to have the *fleur de lis* removed from the steeple of the Church of St. John. Fourth deputation to the city government to get it to search in private houses to find surplus candles.

Second deputation to headquarters to get it to order the captains to inspect weekly the booty gathered by the soldiers. If any soldiers are discovered selling or possessing extra boots, they should be arrested. The deputation, having returned, reported that there was no one at headquarters.

[*Extract of a Letter from the Committee of Public Safety to the Popular Societies (Jacobin Clubs) of France, February 4, 1794*]

It is in the bosom of the Popular Societies that the spirit of liberty was born, grew, and finally reached its height. Alert sentinels, more or less the advance guard of public opinion, they sounded the alarm for all dangers and traitors.

The Republic awaits new services from the Popular Societies. The revolutionary government, organized into its different parts, is going to develop strongly; and, overcoming all resistance, it should be able to catch all the enemies of the people. The National Convention calls upon you for communal work, for combined effort, to establish this edifice upon a firm foundation.

You will be our most powerful auxiliaries. The last thread of conspiracy will be snapped; we will sweep out the impure dregs of federalism, which still taint a large part of the administration. Unveil the intrigue which has besmirched public offices; tear the masks from hypocrites who profess patriotism; cut away and burn out all superstition; follow in their labyrinth the tortuous maneuvers of the agents, the accomplices, the emissaries of the tyrants; crush the last heads of treason with which the hydra seeks to strengthen its straggling and disunited parts; denounce the false and lying agent, and the coward who deserts his post, and the corrupt person who sells his ideals and trafficks with his conscience, and the egoist who has no country; shine on all public figures that torch which in your hands throws such a bright light, in whose brilliance all those who are guilty become pale; use also another kind of denunciation, no less useful: the search for virtues which live in obscurity; hunt for, discover, encourage modest talents, point out their calling, show to your country all who may, in some way, work for and support the plans for regeneration and the revolutionary order; put to work those who are pure, enlightened, courageous, tired of tyranny (and you are the nursery where the Republic will go to look for them) : that is what the Convention, the Committee of Public Safety, and all good citizens expect of you. Representatives have been sent to the different departments to purge and reorganize the present authorities: light their way. Chosen by the people, charged with the people's interests, they wish only to see through the eyes of the people and act for them.

2. *Jacobin Nationalism and the Individual.* The relationship of the state to its citizens is revealed in two famous Jacobin decrees of 1793, the *Levée en Masse* and the Law on Suspects. In the third selection here a young conscript soldier informs his mother of his feelings toward his country. (16)

[*The Levée en Masse, August 23, 1793*]

1. From this moment until that in which the enemy shall have been driven from the soil of the Republic, all Frenchmen are in permanent requisition for the service of the armies.

The young men shall go to battle; the married men shall forge arms and transport provisions; the women shall make tents and clothing and shall serve in the hospitals; the children shall turn old linen into lint; the aged shall betake themselves to the public places in order to arouse the courage of the warriors and preach the hatred of kings and the unity of the Republic.

2. The national buildings shall be converted into barracks, the public places into workshops for arms, the soil of the cellars shall be washed in order to extract therefrom the saltpeter.

3. The arms of the regulation caliber shall be reserved exclusively for those who shall march against the enemy; the service of the interior shall be performed with hunting pieces and side arms.

4. The saddle horses are put into requisition to complete the cavalry corps; the draft horses, other than those employed in agriculture, shall convey the artillery and the provisions.

5. The Committee of Public Safety is charged to take all the necessary measures to set up without delay an extraordinary manufacture of arms of every sort which corresponds with the ardor and energy of the French people. It is, accordingly, authorized to form all the establishments, factories, workshops, and mills which shall be deemed necessary for the carrying on of these works as well as to put in requisition, within the entire extent of the Republic, the artists and workingmen who can contribute to their success. . . .

6. The representatives of the people sent out for the execution of the present law shall have the same authority in their respective districts, acting in concert with the Committee of Public Safety; they are invested with the unlimited powers assigned to the representatives of the people to the armies.

7. Nobody can get himself replaced in the service for which he shall have been requisitioned. The public functionaries shall remain at their posts.

[*The Law on Suspects, September 17, 1793*]

1. Immediately after the publication of the present decree all the suspect persons who are in the territory of the Republic and who are still at liberty shall be placed under arrest.

2. These are accounted suspect persons: 1st, those who by their conduct, their connections, their remarks, or their writings show themselves the partisans of tyranny or federalism and the enemies of liberty; 2d, those who cannot, in the manner prescribed by the decree of March 21st last, justify their means of existence and the performance of their civic duties; 3d, those who have been refused certificates of civism; 4th, public functionaries suspended or removed from their functions by the National Convention or its com-

missioners and not reinstated, especially those who have been or shall be removed in virtue of the decree of August 14th last; 5th, those of the former nobles, all of the husbands, wives, fathers, mothers, sons or daughters, brothers or sisters, and agents of the *émigrés,* who have not constantly manifested their attachment to the revolution; 6th, those who have emigrated from France in the interval from July 1, 1789, to the publication of the decree of March 30–April 8, 1792, although they may have returned to France within the period fixed by that decree or earlier.

3. The committees of surveillance established according to the decree of March 21st last, or those which have been substituted for them, either by the orders of the representatives of the people sent with the armies and into the departments, or in virtue of special decrees of the National Convention, are charged to prepare, each in its district, the list of suspect persons, to issue warrants of arrest against them, and to cause seals to be put upon their papers. The commanders of the public force to whom these warrants shall be delivered shall be required to put them into execution immediately, under penalty of removal.

4. The members of the committee without being seven in number and an absolute majority of votes cannot order the arrest of any person.

9. The committees of surveillance shall send without delay to the committee of general security of the National Convention the list of the persons whom they shall have caused to be arrested, with the reasons for their arrest and the papers which shall have been seized with them as suspect persons.

10. The civil and criminal tribunals can, if there is need, cause to be arrested and sent into the above-mentioned jails persons accused of offenses in respect of whom it may have been declared that there was no ground for accusation, or who may have been acquitted of the accusations brought against them.

[Conscript Joliclerc to his Mother, December 13, 1793]

When *la patrie* calls us for her defense, we should fly to it as I should run to a good meal. Our life, our properties, and our talents do not belong to us. It is to the nation, to *la patrie* that all that belongs. Well do I know that you and all the other inhabitants of our village do not share these sentiments. They are insensible to the cries of this outraged *patrie,* and all they do for it they do by compulsion. But I, who have been raised in liberty of conscience and of thought, who have always been a republican in my soul, although obliged to live in a monarchy, these principles of love for *la patrie,* for Liberty, for the Republic, have not only been engraved on my heart

but are inlaid in it and they will remain in it so long as it will please that Supreme Being who govern all to maintain a breath of life in me. . . .

[May 30, 1794] About my lot? I am at my post, I am where I ought to be. . . . Should I perish there you ought to rejoice about it. Can one make a finer sacrifice than to sacrifice oneself for one's country? Can one sacrifice oneself for anything more glorious, more just, and more equitable? No, my dear mother. Think that I am at my post and you will be consoled. If your conscience makes you some reproach, sell even the last of your petticoats for *la patrie.* It should be our sole rudder, for it guides us and gives us happiness. I told you in my last letter that our Lieutenant David was in jail at Nantes. Well, he was guillotined with two of our captains about three weeks ago. . . .

3. *Jacobin Economic Nationalism.* The Jacobins, like the other revolutionary groups, began as advocates of *laissez faire* in economic matters. Until late 1792 they refused to press for a national grain tax and other restrictions on the freedom of internal trade, and even thereafter it was only slowly, under the pressure of the growing food crisis in the cities and the agitation of the urban masses, that they changed. Thus the development of a control system proceeded by half measures, beginning with the reinstitution of regional regulation of grain on December 8, 1792 and proceeding through provisions for subsidies (April 5, 1793), the establishment of a maximum price for grain (May 4), a law against monopoly (July 20), the creation of public granaries (August 9), extensions of the power of requisition (August 14 and 15), establishment of maximum prices on fuels (August 19) and oats (August 23), and the abolition of trade in grain (September 11), to the general Law of the Maximum, the capstone of the system, on September 29, 1793. The following selections include Jacobin petitions and speeches which give some indication of the Jacobin economic doctrine. The final selection is the report on and the text of the Law of the Maximum. (17)

[Chaumette, in the Name of the Paris Commune, to the Convention, February 27, 1793]

The public misery is the basis of the selfish speculation of an infinite number of capitalists. . . . The poor, like the rich and more than the rich, have made the Revolution. Everything has changed around the poor, only they have remained in the same situation; they have won from the Revolution only the right to complain of their misery. . . . The Revolution, in procuring liberty for the rich, has made them a great gift; it has also given liberty and equality to the poor, but to live in freedom one must live, and if a reasonable proportion between the wages of the poor and the price of the goods necessary to their existence is no longer present the poor cannot live. Citizens, re-establish this salutary proportion. Do more, make the Revolution change this proportion to the benefit of the poor; it is the only means of making them love the Revolution; it is the only means of giving to the poor the hope of becoming a proprietor some day, and perhaps the Revolution will be truly consolidated only at that happy time. Then the poor man will no longer regard himself as a mere tenant in his *patrie.*

[*Speech of Robespierre to the Convention, December 2, 1792*]

Liberty of commerce is necessary, but only to the point at which homicidal cupidity begins to abuse it. The authors of the theory [of free trade] have considered the goods most necessary to life as ordinary merchandise; they have marked no difference between trade in grain and trade in indigo; they have expatiated more on trade in grain than on the subsistence of the people; and for want of having the latter enter into their calculations they have made a false application of principles which are in general evident. . . .

Even less have they adapted it to the stormy circumstances which a revolution brings; and their vague theory, even were it good in ordinary times, could find no application to the immediate measures which moments of crisis can require from us. They have counted the profits of merchants and proprietors for much, the lives of men for nothing. And why? It was the great, the ministers, the rich, who wrote and who governed. . . .

Common sense shows, for example, that the goods which are not required for the primary needs of life can be abandoned to the most unlimited speculations of the merchant . . . and it is enough that in general the unlimited liberty of this trade redounds to the greater profit of the state. But the lives of men cannot be submitted to the same chances. . . .

The first of rights is the right to exist. Therefore the primary social law is that which guarantees to all members of society the means of existence; all other rights are subordinated to this. It is in order to live that one has property. It is no longer true that property can ever be in opposition to the food of men, which is as sacred as life itself. Everything necessary to maintain it is a property common to the entire society; only the surplus is individual property and is left to the industry of merchants.

[*Herault de Seschelles to the Convention, August 20, 1793*]

It is not sufficient for the French Republic to be founded on equality; it is still necessary that its laws and the customs of its citizens tend by a happy accord to banish the inequality of pleasures. A happy existence must be assured to all Frenchmen. Henceforth the love of riches must yield to the sublime love of *la patrie* and the rich must be less the proprietors than the fortunate depositaries of the surplus of the wealth belonging to their fellow citizens.

[*Report by Couppé (de l'Oise) of the Subsistence Committee to the Convention, September 28, 1793*]

This law is awaited with the greatest impatience; and malevolence and cupidity, combining their detestable operations with those of our foreign enemies, do not permit us to defer it. We have been conscious of all the difficulties and the extent of them; even some of our colleagues have been frightened by them. We are small in numbers, sustained less by confidence in our forces than by our good will.

In ordinary times the price of goods is formed naturally by the reciprocal interests of the sellers and buyers; this balance is infallible. It is useless, even for the best government, to mix in it. However enlightened, however well intentioned it be, it never hits the point squarely enough and it runs the risk of altering it by touching it. But when a general conspiracy of malevolence, of perfidy, of unexampled fury, joins to break this natural equilibrium, in order to famish us, to despoil us, the safety of the people becomes the supreme rule.

Society has the right to resist this war of trade and tyrants, to re-establish and to assure with a firm hand the balance which ought to exist between our production and our needs. . . . However, an intelligent calculation is necessary; we must content ourselves with establishing, by a maximum, salutary and fair limits which it will not be permitted to exceed. It is fitting to permit activity to legitimate commerce and to manage the relationships of interests. . . .

[*Extract from the Law of the Maximum Passed by the Convention, September 29, 1793*]

1. The articles which the Convention has decided to be of prime necessity and for which it has believed that it ought to fix the *maximum* or highest price are: fresh meat, salt meat and bacon, butter, sweet oil, cattle, salt fish, wine, brandy, vinegar, cider, beer, firewood, charcoal,

mineral coal, candles, combustible oil, salt, soda, sugar, honey, white paper, skins, iron, brass, lead, steel, copper, hemp, linen, wool, woolens, fabrics, the raw materials which serve for fabrics, sabots, shoes, cabbages, and turnips, soap, potash, and tobacco.

2. For the articles included in the above list, the *maximum* of price for firewood of the first quality, that of charcoal and of mineral coal are the same as in 1790, plus a twentieth of the price. The decree of August 19th upon the determination by the departments of the prices of firewood, coal, and peat is repealed. . . .

7. All persons who may sell or purchase the articles of merchandise included in Article I above the *maximum* of the price settled and posted in each department shall pay by way of the municipal police a fine, for which they shall be jointly and severally liable, of double the value of the article sold and payable to the informer: they shall be enrolled upon the list of suspected persons and treated as such. The purchaser shall not be subject to the penalties provided above, if he denounces the offense of the seller; and each merchant shall be required to have a list displayed in his shop, bearing the *maximum* or highest price of his merchandise.

8. The *maximum* or highest price belonging to salaries, wages, and manual labor in each place shall be fixed, to commence from the publication of this law until the month of September next, by the general councils of the communes at the same amount as in 1790, to which there shall be added half of that price in addition.

9. The municipalities shall put into requisition and punish, according to circumstances, with three days' imprisonment the workingmen, factory operatives, and various laboring persons who may refuse without legitimate reasons to engage in their accustomed labors. . . .

17. During the war all exportation of articles of merchandise or commodities of prime necessity, under any name or commission whatsoever, is prohibited upon all the frontiers, salt excepted.

4. *The Jacobins and the Press.* Jacobin policy called for new regulations on the press. The unlimited freedom which accompanied the early years of the Revolution (see Part I, C) had already been given some limitation on August 23, 1791, when the National Assembly passed a law guaranteeing freedom of written opinion but providing for prosecution of libel or agitation for resistance to established law. Under Jacobin impetus the Convention enacted a press decree on March 29, 1793. Following is an extract from the speech introducing the decree to the Convention and the decree itself. (18)

[*To the Convention, March 29, 1793*]

Liberty of the press and liberty of opinion should be protected in every government that is not arbitrary; but it is clear to all that this liberty does not consist in the power to disturb the public order established by law with impunity through the dissemination of thoughts and writings. It is clear that this liberty will never consist in the power to provoke—unpunished—discord, civil war, the overthrow of liberty, the reign of tyranny, and the massacre of the representatives of the people. Each citizen has the right to speak and to write, but if, instead of using this sacred right to save *la patrie,* he abuses it in order to destroy it, he is clearly responsible for it in the eyes of the nation and the law.

From another point of view, it is certain that in revolutionary moments all kinds of individual liberty should suffer some modification. And let it not be said, as some people have repeated so often, that the principles are violated. No, citizens, they are not: these are just exceptions required by the public security, and they do not violate principle, for they are as fundamental, as useful, as sacred, as the principle itself. . . .

[*The Decree*]

ART. I. Whoever shall be convicted of having written or printed writings which propose the reestablishment of royalty in France or the dissolution of the national representation will be arraigned before the revolutionary tribunal and punished with death.

II. The death punishment for those who incite, in their writings, to murder or pillage.

III. The vendors, distributors, and hawkers of these works or writings shall be condemned to an imprisonment which shall not exceed three months, if they declare the authors, printers, or other persons from whom they have obtained them; if they refuse to make this declaration, they shall be punished by two years in prison.

5. *The Jacobins and Public Opinion.* The concern of the Jacobins to influence public opinion manifested itself in many ways. In popular education, for instance, through a steady stream of decrees, the Convention continuously agitated for the establishment of a public school system. Since implementation lagged far behind intent, the net result in this respect was negligible; yet the purpose and techniques of these propaganda efforts remain significant. The following selections show some of the methods utilized by the Jacobins "to win friends and influence people." It should be noticed that the decrees

use the months of the new Republican calendar: *"nivose," "germinal,"* etc. (19)

[*Order of the Committee of Public Safety, February 15, 1794*]

The Committee of Public Safety, considering the resolution of the Committee of Public Instruction, dated 29 *nivose* last, regarding a project of the artists who compose the music for the National Guard of Paris, who propose to have patriotic songs printed and to distribute issues each month throughout the Republic; considering that this enterprise, apart from the useful possibility which it presents to music to become an instrument of public instruction, is an important measure with regard to the morale of the Revolution, in that it tends to raise the spirits of the people by the spreading of republican hymns and songs, to rouse in this way the courage of the nation's defenders, at the same time giving to the public festivals, which can never be too numerous, one of their most important attractions, which very effectively raises the people's morale; considering, on the other hand, the conditions of membership and subscription proposed by the musicians of the National Guard of Paris, decrees: 1st, that the organization of these musicians will receive a draft on the national treasury for the sum of 33,000 livres to assist them in their efforts to spread patriotic music; 2d, that they will be obliged, for a full year starting 1 *germinal* next, to give each month to the Committee of Public Safety 550 copies of the booklet of music which they are going to publish, which shall contain one symphony, one hymn or chorus, one military march, one rondeau or *pas redouble,* and at least one patriotic song, totaling 50 or 60 pages; 3d, these booklets will be distributed in all the districts by the Committee of Public Safety for use in civic festivals, in such a way that they will be made available to the greatest possible number of citizens.

[*Barère, in the Name of the Committee of Public Safety, to the Convention, January 27, 1794*]

Citizens, the allied tyrants have said: Ignorance has always been our most important auxiliary; we must maintain ignorance; ignorance makes fanatics, it makes more counterrevolutionaries, let us push France back to barbarism; let us make use of poorly educated people or those who speak a different dialect from that taught in the schools. The Committee has understood this conspiracy of ignorance and despotism.

Today I want to call your attention to the most beautiful European language, that which first consecrated the rights of man and of the citizen, that which must transmit to the world the most sublime ideals of liberty and the greatest theories of the science of government. For a long time this language was a slave, it flattered kings, corrupted courts, and enslaved the people; for a long time it was dishonored in the schools, and made to lie in the textbooks; crafty in the courts, fanatic in the churches, barbarous in diplomacy, made effeminate by the poets, corrupted in the theaters, it seemed to wait for, even to hunt, a more worthy destiny. Made pure finally, and smoothed by several dramatists, ennobled and made brilliant in the discourses of a few orators, it was just gathering strength and freedom through the pens of several philosophers who had been honored by persecution before the Revolution of 1789.

But the language still seemed to belong only to certain classes of society; it had been colored by the usages of the nobility; and courtiers, not content to be distinguished by their vices and depravities, wanted also to be set apart by a different language. One would have said there were several nations rather than just one. . . .

These puerile distinctions have disappeared along with the ridiculous courtiers and the toys of a perverse court. Even pride in an accent more or less pure has disappeared, since citizens from all parts of the country have expressed in their national assemblies their wish for liberty and their ideas for common legislation. Heretofore, they were brilliant slaves of various shadings; they argued about the pre-eminence of custom and of language. Free men are all alike; and the vigorous accent of liberty and equality is the same whether it comes from the mouth of an inhabitant of the Alps or the Vosges, the Pyrenees or the Cantal, Mont-Blanc or Mont-Terrible, whether it derives from men of the central countries, the maritime countries, or the frontiers.

Only four parts of the Republic merit the attention of the revolutionary legislator regarding dialects which seem the most contrary to the spreading of public spirit and present obstacles to the understanding and execution of the laws of the republic.

Among the ancient languages, Welsh, Gascon, Celtic, Visigoth, *Phocéen,* or Oriental, which color the dialects of the various citizens and of the districts forming the territory of our Republic, we have observed (and the reports of our representatives agree on this point with those of agents sent into the departments) that the low-Breton dialect, the Basque dialect, and the German and Italian languages, have perpetuated the reign of fanaticism and superstition, assured the domination of the priests, nobles, and practitioners, kept the Revolution from penetrating into nine important departments, and could be of help to the enemies of France. . . .

For three years the national assemblies have talked about and discussed public education; for a long time we have felt the need for primary schools; they are a form of moral support needed in the country; but perhaps we are still too academic and too far from the people to give them the institutions best adapted to their present needs.

The laws of education make provision for teaching artisans, artists, experts, scholars, and public functionaries; but the first laws of education should provide for the preparation of citizens; now, to be a citizen, one must obey the laws, and to obey them one must know them. The people must then be given first an education which enables them to understand the voice of the legislator. What a contradiction presents itself in the departments of Haut-Rhin and Bas-Rhin, Morbihan, Finistère, Ille-et-Vilaine, Loire-Inférieure, Côtes-du-Nord, Basse-Pyrénées, and Corsica. The legislator speaks a language which cannot be understood by those who should enforce and obey the laws. The ancients never knew such striking and dangerous contrasts.

We must popularize the language; we must destroy that aristocracy of language which seems to establish a polite nation in the midst of a barbarous one. We have revolutionized government, laws, customs, habits, clothing, trade, and even thought; let us also revolutionize the language, an instrument in daily use. Federalism and superstition speak low-Breton; emigration and the hatred of the Republic speak German; the counterrevolution speaks Italian, and fanaticism speaks Basque. Let us break these weapons of shame and error.

The Committee therefore proposes . . . to give to each commune in the above departments an instructor in the French language, in charge of teaching to the young people of both sexes, and of reading, each Decadi, to all the other citizens in the commune, the laws, the decrees, and the instructions of the convention. . . . Rome taught its youth to read from the laws of the twelve tables; France will teach part of its citizens the French language in the book of the Declaration of Rights. . . .

Good patriots and enlightened men, there are the first qualities necessary for teachers. The Popular Societies [clubs] will list the candidates . . . and the representatives of the people sent for the purpose to these communes will choose the instructors. . . .

If I were to speak to a tyrant, he would blame me . . . for a despot has need of carefully isolating people and separating the regions, of dividing interests and preventing communication. . . . In a democracy, on the other hand, the supervision of the government is confided to each citizen; in order to supervise it, he must recognize it, and, especially, he must speak its language. . . .

How much money have we spent in having the laws of the first two assemblies translated into the different dialects spoken in France. . . . Citizens, the speech of a free people should be the same for all. As soon as men think, as soon as they can organize their thoughts, the dominion of the priests, the despots, and the plotters is ruined. Let us then give to the citizens the weapon of public opinion, the most certain agent of the Revolution, a common tongue. Let us have pride in the pre-eminence of the French language, now that it is republican, and do our duty. . . .

Here then is the decree: The National Convention . . . decrees:

1. Within ten days there will be established an instructor in the French language in each rural commune in the Departments of Morbihan, Finistère, Côtes-du-Nord, and that part of the Loire-Inférieure where they speak low-Breton.

2. [Same for] Haut-Rhin and Bas-Rhin, Corsica, and parts of Moselle, Nord, Mont-Terrible, Alpes-Maritimes, and Basses-Pyrénées. . . . This decree was passed.

[Account of the Youth Festival March 30, 1794, Written by Theobald Wolfe Tone, an Irish Émigré in France]

Went today to the Church of St. Roch, to the *Fête de la Jeunesse:* all the youth of the district, who have attained the age of sixteen, were to present themselves before the municipality, and receive their arms, and those who were arrived at twenty-one were to be enrolled in the list of citizens, in order to ascertain their right of voting in the assemblies. The church was decorated with the national colors, and a statue of Liberty, with an altar blazing before her. At the foot of the statue the municipality were seated, and the sides of the church were filled with a crowd of spectators, the parents and friends of the young men, leaving a space vacant in the center for the procession. It consisted of the État-Major of the sections composing the district, of the National Guards under arms, of the officers of the sections, and, finally, of the young men who were to be presented. The guard was mounted by veterans of the troops of the line, and there was a great pile of muskets and of sabers before the municipality. When the procession arrived, the names of the two classes were enrolled, and, in the meantime, the veterans distributed the arms amongst the parents and friends and mistresses of the young men. When the enrollment was finished, an officer pronounced a short address to the youths of sixteen, on the duty which they owed to their country, and the honor of bearing arms in her defense, to which they were about to be admitted. They then ran among the crowd of spectators, and received their firelocks and sabers, some from their fathers, some from their mothers, and many, I could observe, from their lovers. When they were armed, their parents and mistresses embraced them, and they returned to their station. It is impossible to conceive anything more interesting than the spectacle was at that moment; the pride and pleasure in the countenance of the parents: the *fierté* of the young soldiers; and above all, the expression in the features of so many young females, many of them beautiful, and all interesting from the occasion. I was in an enthusiasm. I do not at all wonder at the miracles which the French army has wrought in the contest for their liberties.

6. *Jacobin Nationalism and Europe.* War was a constant factor conditioning the development of Jacobin nationalism. Hence it is not surprising that along with the internal effects of the heightened national consciousness went a changed conception of the relationships of revolutionary France to other nations. Jacobin views are illustrated in the Convention's occupation policy, quoted first below. The final selection is from a speech of Lazare Carnot (1753–1823), an upright and virtuous republican, "Organizer of Victory" for the Committee of Public Safety. (20)

[*Decree for Proclaiming the Liberty and Sovereignty of All Peoples, Passed by the Convention, December 15, 1792*]

The National Convention, after having heard the report of its united committees of finances, war, and diplomacy, faithful to the principles of the sovereignty of the people, which do not permit it to recognize any of the institutions which bring an attack upon it, and wishing to settle the rules to be followed by the generals of the armies of the Republic in the countries where they shall carry its arms, decrees:

1. In the countries which are or shall be occupied by the armies of the Republic, the generals shall proclaim immediately, in the name of the French nation, the sovereignty of the people, the suppression of all the established authorities and of the existing imposts and taxes, the abolition of the tithe, of feudalism, of seignorial rights, both feudal and *censuel,* fixed or precarious, of *banalités,* of real and personal servitude, of the privileges of hunting and fishing, of *corvées,* of the nobility, and generally of all privileges.

2. They shall announce to the people that they bring them peace, assistance, fraternity, liberty, and equality, and that they will convoke them directly in primary or communal assem-

blies, in order to create and organize an administration and a provisional judiciary; they shall look after the security of persons and property; they shall cause the present decree and the proclamation herewith annexed to be printed in the language or idiom of the country, and to be posted and executed without delay in each commune. . . .

4. The generals shall directly place under the safeguard and protection of the French Republic all the movable and immovable goods belonging to the public treasury, to the prince, to his abettors, adherents, and voluntary satellites, to the public establishments, to the lay and ecclesiastical bodies and communities; they shall cause to be prepared without delay a detailed list of them, which they shall dispatch to the executive council, and shall take all the measures which are in their power that these properties may be respected.

5. The provisional administration selected by the people shall be charged with the surveillance and control of the goods placed under the safeguard and protection of the French Republic; it shall look after the security of persons and property; it will cause to be executed the laws in force relative to the trial of civil and criminal suits and to the police and the public security; it shall be charged to regulate and to cause the payment of the local expenses and those which shall be necessary for the common defense; it may establish taxes, provided, however, that they shall not be borne by the indigent and laboring portion of the people.

6. When the provisional administration shall be organized the National Convention shall appoint commissioners from within its own body to go to fraternize with it.

7. The executive council shall also appoint national commissioners, who shall repair directly to the places in order to cooperate with the generals and the provisional administration selected by the people upon the measures to be taken for the common defense, and upon the means employed to procure the clothing and provisions necessary for the armies, and to meet the expenses which they have incurred and shall incur during their sojourn upon its territory. . . .

9. The provisional administration selected by the people and the functions of the national commissioners shall cease as soon as the inhabitants after having declared the sovereignty and independence of the people, liberty, and equality, shall have organized a free and popular form of government.

10. There shall be made a list of the expenses which the French Republic shall have incurred for the common defense and of the sums which it may have received, and the French nation shall

make arrangements with the government which shall have been established for that which may be due; and in case the common interest should require that the troops of the Republic remain beyond that time upon the foreign territory, it shall take suitable measures to provide for their subsistence.

11. The French nation declares that it will treat as enemies the people who, refusing liberty and equality, or renouncing them, may wish to preserve, recall, or treat with the prince and the privileged castes; it promises and engages not to subscribe to any treaty, and not to lay down its arms until after the establishment of the sovereignty and independence of the people whose territory the troops of the Republic have entered upon and who shall have adopted the principles of equality, and established a free popular government.

[*Report by Carnot to the Diplomatic Committee, February 13, 1793*]

Nations are, among themselves, in the political order what individuals are in the social order: like the latter they have their respective rights; these rights are independence, security abroad, unity at home, national honor, primary interests . . . which a people can lose only by force and which it can always take back again when the occasion for it arises. . . .

No annexation, increase, diminution, or change of any territory whatsoever can take place in the extent of the Republic unless it is recognized: 1. that this change is not contrary to the interests of the state; 2. that the local administrations have asked for it by a free and formal vote or that the general security of the Republic makes it indispensable. . . .

To say that sovereignty resides in the universality of the human species is to say that France is only a portion of the sovereign, that it has not the right . . . to enact at home the laws which are fitting to it; and we have as a principle that every people, however small its territory, is absolutely master at home; that it is equal in right to the largest, and that no other can legitimately attack its independence, unless its own is visibly compromised. . . .

Let us follow then the law of preservation written in the hearts of all men, and let us try not to abuse it; may the national honor and French generosity be for all the people of the earth the certain guarantees of justice which you owe them and which you wish to give to them. . . .

The old and natural frontiers of France are the Rhine, the Alps, and the Pyrenees; the parts which have been taken from it have been taken by usurpation; there will be, then, following the ordinary rules, no injustice in taking them back; it will not be ambition to recognize as brothers those who were such formerly, to re-establish the bonds which were only broken by ambition itself.

But these diplomatic claims, founded on old possession, are as nothing to our eyes as are those of reason. The right of each nation is to live isolated if it pleases, or to unite with others if they wish it, for the common interest. We French recognize as sovereigns only the people themselves; our system is not domination, but fraternity. . . .

D. A REVOLUTIONARY TESTAMENT

In 1798 Carnot, then one of the Directors, was implicated in a conspiracy to overthrow the government. His speech of May 7, 1798, indignantly denying his complicity in the plot, ended as follows. (21)

My aim was to make the Republic loved by founding it on genuine liberty rather than on mocking words. . . . If I took advantage of the general enthusiasm to prosecute the war with a new vigor, my only purpose was to end that much more quickly the state of crisis into which this very enthusiasm was dragging the nation. . . .

I have never used the power entrusted to me to make my fortune or to raise my relations to fat jobs; my hands are clean and my heart is pure. . . . I have never ceased to work for my country; no one can deny me that status of citizen which is mine by the Constitution, which I have merited by my love of country and my zeal to serve her. I will never recognize arbitrary acts or tyrannical deeds: I demand a proper, constitutional trial and I fear neither the severity of a judge nor the vigor of a jury; whatever they may be, I feel confident that I am as republican as they are. . . . My only crime, I repeat, and no one can accuse me of any other, is to have sought to prevent the French people from acquiring tyrants. . . .

Oh France, oh my country, oh great, truly great people! It is on your soil that I had the good fortune to be born; I can only cease to belong to you by ceasing to exist. You encompass all the objects of my affection: the great work which my hands helped to found; the honest parents who brought me into the world; a family without suspicion; friends who know the very bottom of my heart; who will testify that my heart never held any other feeling save the happiness of my fellow Frenchmen; that it has had no other wish but the immortal glory and continuous prosperity of France. Accept this vow which I repeat each day, which I now address to all virtuous and honest souls, to all those who have in themselves the sacred spark of liberty; and I close with the Spartan prayer:

OH GOD, MAKE US ABLE TO SUFFER INJUSTICE!

VIII

The Nineteenth Century:
The Age of the Isms

T HE great conquerors, from Alexander to Caesar, and from Caesar to Napoleon, influenced profoundly the lives of subsequent generations. But the total effect of this influence shrinks to insignificance, if compared to the entire transformation of human habits and human mentality produced by the long line of men of thought from Thales to the present day, men individually powerless, but ultimately the rulers of the world.

A. N. WHITEHEAD

CONTENTS

QUESTIONS FOR STUDY

PART I

1. Why does Adam Smith oppose economic regulation by the state? Under what circumstances may economic regulation be justified?
2. How does Smith reconcile economic individualism with social utility?
3. What are the fundamental postulates in Malthus's thesis? Are they valid? What argument does he derive from them?
4. What was the natural effect of the Malthusian "iron law of population" upon the development of liberal ideas?
5. Define Bentham's "principle of utility." According to Bentham, how should it be defined to legislation in theory? How in practice?
6. How could a conflict arise between the application of the "principle" in theory and in practice? Did Bentham observe the possibility of such a conflict?
7. How did John Stuart Mill view liberal principles in 1873? Did he consider that the "principle of utility" was enough?

PART II

8. For Acton what is the relation of nationality to liberty?
9. Why does Acton consider the theory of nationality "a retrograde step in history"?
10. What is Marx's philosophy of history? How does it differ from other philosophies of history with which you are familiar?
11. Why does Marx think the bourgoisie has played historically a most revolutionary part?
12. According to Marx, is a socialist society inevitable?
13. To what extent is Marx indebted to Adam Smith and Malthus?
14. Upon what scientific principle does Büchner base his whole position?
15. What branches of natural science contributed most to Büchner's thesis?
16. Does Büchner see any way to reconcile faith and science?
17. After reading the passages from Büchner formulate a definition of materialism. What, if anything, would such a definition have in common with nationalism or Marxism?

PART III

18. What, to Comte, is the relationship of the positive stage to the other two stages of the human mind?
19. What is the difference between social statics and social dynamics? Why are both necessary to social physics?
20. What, according to Spencer, has contributed to the development of social structures? Where does he differ from Comte here?
21. How would he define "civilized" or "savaged"?
22. What is Huxley's theory of the growth of civilized society? What tends to check its growth?
23. What is the effect of Huxley's concluding argument upon the doctrines of liberalism?
24. According to Pearson, what is "the natural history view of mankind"? Does he consider this view to be good or evil?
25. What is the effect of Pearson's concluding arguments upon nationalism?

26. What resentment did Freud consider would be aroused by psychoanalysis? Why?
27. Why does he believe that psychoanalysis will lead to a "new orientation in the world and in science"?
28. Compare the view of human nature taken by the philosophic radicals with that taken by Freud. What significance do you see in the differences?
29. How do you account for the multiplicity of "isms" produced in the nineteenth century?
30. How would the different authors in this Problem define progress?
31. What are some of the implications of liberalism, nationalism, socialism, and nineteenth-century science and social science for the relation of Europe to the world?

Every generation either constructs a new periodization of the past or puts a different emphasis on the one it has inherited. As our age has gained more perspective on the nineteenth century, our interpretation of it and particularly our location of it in the sweep of history have undergone profound change. To many moderns the previous century now bulks as the great watershed in the panorama of western civilization, towering over the decline of the ancient world, the Middle Ages, the Renaissance, or even the eighteenth century. Thus, Jane Austen and Sir Walter Scott now seem further away from us than they in turn might have felt from Shakespeare, Chaucer, Beowulf, Vergil, Homer, or the Pharaohs. Even those who feel an affinity for the world of *Mansfield Park* and *Old Mortality* must acknowledge their remoteness from the present. To explore this considerable foreground to the atomic age is the purpose of this problem.

As is always the case, the roots of nineteenth century change lay deep in the past, but they cluster together in two main areas. Out of the Renaissance and Enlightenment stem that optimistic confidence in man and his reason, a belief which underwent all the trials and tribulations of experience in the course of the French Revolution. Of equal importance for the nineteenth century are the earlier developments in pure and applied science. Slower to take shape than some of the changes in politics and religion that heralded the advent of modern Europe, the scientific revolution achieved its first great synthesis with Newton and thereafter proceeded to capture an increasing share of man's efforts and imagination as he progressively employed it to understand and exploit the world around him. These two root systems were intertwined in a common past: reason contributed to the scientific advance which in turn fortified the optimism of the Enlightenment. And in the next century this intimacy would continue, for man's increased understanding of himself and his world would at once chasten and strengthen his earlier optimism.

The materials in the first part of the Problem help to mark the transition from the age of the *philosophe* to the age of the machine. Though Adam Smith applied the yardstick of reason to economic institutions in the best philosophic tradition, his book appeared during one revolution and its doctrine was to provide a rallying point for economic theory and governmental policy during the next century. The political ideals of the Enlightenment were to experience the harsh test of reality in the French Revolution which served also to make them a part of the general inheritance of modern Europe. Bentham, Malthus, and Mill pointed up future possibilities and problems to a liberalism which already had to live with its own past.

Meanwhile, the future was increasingly shaped by the forces of economic change. The sharp rise in the rate of population increase after 1750, the growth of towns, the interaction of science and technology, and their dramatic transformation of human life all combined to effect changes, as extensive as they were rapid and continuous, on the entire fabric of European civilization. A thoroughgoing materialism in philosophy, with its own dour notions of progress, arose to rival idealism and romanticism. With this materialism as his premise and the glaring inequalities of the new system of production as his inspiration, Karl Marx called on all workers to unite and win the brave new world by force. But another faith was bidding for their loyalty. The new nation-state, which came of age after 1789 as an end in itself, provided not only the material goal of political and territorial unity, but also the idea of nationalism as a corporate ideal.

It was science which at some point or other stimulated all these other developments, science which was proliferating from its older centers in mathematics and physics into the great synthesizing ventures in geology, chemistry, biology, and physics. Although the successive steps here belong more properly to a history of science, the repercussions of this highly technical development quickly became noticeable in religion, politics, and society in general. In particular the study of man came to be studied as scientifically as the world around him. To Comte and Spencer social science was a science, while Freud sought to establish psychology upon the same foundation as physics or any other science.

If science thus provides the key to so much in nineteenth-century thought and life, the individual and society or man and the state will still represent the two poles around which to order its history and put it into perspective with the more distant past.

Part I.   LAISSEZ-FAIRE AND UTILITARIANISM

If the seventeenth century—that "Age of Genius"—effected significant syntheses in mathematics, natural science, philosophy and political theory, the great thinkers of the eighteenth century adapted, expanded and publicized the ideas of their predecessors. Determined to relate his knowledge to the life of mankind, inspired by his belief in reform through reason, and supremely confident of the outcome, the *philosophe* both hastened the disintegration of the *ancien régime* and helped to shape its successor. In the area of social, economic, and political reform the ideas of the Enlightenment combine to make the credo of liberalism whose economic tenets are best summarized in the laissez-faire of Adam Smith. During the age of revolutions the liberal credo underwent both compromise and defeat, a bitter experience for any doctrinaire movement. But if Malthus was unsparing in his criticism of this aspect of liberalism, his contemporaries Bentham and the Utilitarians were perfecting a formula whereby the initial vigor of the movement would be recovered. As a result Reform England remains to a considerable extent a monument to liberalism's ability to renew its strength at the source.

A.   Adam Smith's "Wealth of Nations"

Adam Smith (1723–1790) was a Scot, who, having studied at Oxford and traveled on the Continent, returned to his native land to become a professor at Glasgow University. Though he occupied successively the chairs of logic and moral philosophy, he turned his mind for a time to contemporary economic problems, perhaps as a result of his contact with the French physiocrats abroad, and in 1776 he published *An Inquiry into the Nature and Causes of the Wealth of Nations*. The book won for Smith an immediate and enduring fame and established him as one of the outstanding thinkers of his time. As representative of the economic thought of the Enlightenment, portions of the *Wealth of Nations* follow.[1]

The property which every man has in his own labor, as it is the original foundation of all other property, so it is the most sacred and inviolable. The patrimony of a poor man lies in the strength and dexterity of his hands; and to hinder him from employing this strength and dexterity in what manner he thinks proper without injury to his neighbor is a plain violation of this most sacred property. It is a manifest encroachment upon the just liberty both of the workman and of those who might be disposed to employ him. As it hinders the one from working at what he thinks proper, so it hinders the other from employing whom they think proper. To judge whether he is fit to be employed may surely be trusted to the discretion of the employers whose interest it so much concerns. The affected anxiety of the law giver lest they should employ an improper person is evidently as impertinent as it is oppressive.

The institution of long apprenticeships can give no security that insufficient workmanship shall not frequently be exposed to public sale. When this is done it is generally the effect of fraud, and not of inability; and the longest apprenticeship can give no security against fraud. Quite different regulations are necessary to pre-

vent this abuse. The sterling mark upon plate, and the stamps upon linen and woolen cloth, give the purchaser much greater security than any statute of apprenticeship. He generally looks at these, but never thinks it worth while to inquire whether the workman had served a seven years' apprenticeship. . . .

People of the same trade seldom meet together, even for merriment and diversion, but the conversation ends in a conspiracy against the public or in some contrivance to raise prices. It is impossible indeed to prevent such meetings by any law which either could be executed or would be consistent with liberty and justice. But though the law cannot hinder people of the same trade from sometimes assembling together, it ought to do nothing to facilitate such assemblies, much less to render them necessary.

The pretense that corporations are necessary for the better government of the trade is without any foundation. The real and effectual discipline which is exercised over a workman is not that of his corporation, but that of his customers. It is the fear of losing their employment which restrains his frauds and corrects his negligence. An exclusive corporation necessarily weakens the force of this discipline. A particular set of workmen must then be employed, let them behave well or ill. . . .

Though anciently it was usual to rate wages, first by general laws extending over the whole kingdom, and afterwards by particular orders of the justices of peace in every particular county, both these practices have now gone entirely into disuse. "By the experience of above four hundred years," says Doctor Burn, "it seems time to lay aside all endeavors to bring under strict regulations, what in its own nature seems incapable of minute limitation; for if all persons in the same kind of work were to receive equal wages, there would be no emulation, and no room left for industry or ingenuity."

Particular acts of Parliament, however, still attempt sometimes to regulate wages in particular trades and in particular places. Thus the 8th [Act] of George III prohibits under heavy penalties all master tailors in London, and five miles round it, from giving, and their workmen from accepting, more than two shillings and seven pence halfpenny a day, except in the case of a general mourning. Whenever the legislature attempts to regulate the differences between masters and their workmen, its counselors are always the masters. When the regulation, therefore, is in favor of the workmen, it is always just and equitable; but it is sometimes otherwise when in favor of the masters. Thus the law which obliges the masters in several different trades to pay their workmen in money and not in goods is quite just and equitable. It imposes no real hardships upon the masters. It only obliges them to pay that value in money, which they pretended to pay, but did not always really pay, in goods. This law is in favor of the workmen; but the 8th of George III is in favor of the masters. When masters combine together in order to reduce the wages of their workmen, they commonly enter into a private bond or agreement not to give more than a certain wage under a certain penalty. Were the workmen to enter into a contrary combination of the same kind, not to accept of a certain wage under a certain penalty, the law would punish them very severely; and if it dealt impartially, it would treat the masters in the same manner. But the 8th of George III enforces by law that very regulation which masters sometimes attempt to establish by such combinations. The complaint of the workmen, that it puts the ablest and most industrious upon the same footing with an ordinary workman, seems perfectly well founded.

In ancient times, too, it was usual to attempt to regulate the profits of merchants and other dealers, by rating the price both of provisions and other goods. The assize of bread is, so far as I know, the only remnant of this ancient usage. Where there is an exclusive corporation, it may perhaps be proper to regulate the price of the first necessary of life. But where there is none, the competition will regulate it much better than any assize. . . .

Though the profusion of government must, undoubtedly, have retarded the natural progress of England toward wealth and improvement, it has not been able to stop it. . . . England . . . as it has never been blessed with a very parsimonious government, so parsimony has at no time been the characteristical virtue of its inhabitants. It is the highest impertinence and presumption, therefore, in kings and ministers, to pretend to watch over the economy of private people, and to restrain their expense either by sumptuary laws, or by prohibiting the importation of foreign luxuries. They are themselves always, and without any exception, the greatest spendthrifts in the society. Let them look well after their own expense, and they may safely trust private people with theirs. If their own extravagance does not ruin the state, that of their subjects never will. . . .

In some countries the interest of money has been prohibited by law. But as something can everywhere be made by the use of money, something ought everywhere to be paid for the use of it. This regulation, instead of preventing, has been found from experience to increase the evil of usury, the debtor being obliged to pay, not only for the use of the money, but for the risk which his creditor runs by accepting a compensation for that use. He is obliged, if one may say so, to insure his creditor, from the penalties of usury. . . .

The different progress of opulence in different ages and nations has given occasion to two different systems of political economy with regard to enriching the people. The one may be called a system of commerce, the other that of agriculture. I shall . . . begin with the system of commerce. It is the modern system, and is best understood in our own country and in our own times. . . .

This commercial or "mercantile" system is based on the false but popular notion that wealth consists in money, or in gold and silver. . . . Some of the best English writers upon commerce set out with observing that the wealth of a country consists, not in gold and silver only, but in its lands, houses, and consumable goods of all different kinds. In the course of their reasonings, however, the lands, houses, and consumable goods seem to slip out of their memory, and the strain of their argument frequently supposes that all wealth consists in gold and silver, and that to multiply those metals is the great object of national industry and commerce.

The two principles being established, however, that wealth consisted in gold and silver, and that those metals could be brought into a country which had no mines only by the balance of trade, or by the exporting to a greater value than it imported, it necessarily became the great object of political economy to diminish as much as possible the importation of foreign goods for home consumption, and to increase as much as possible the exportation of the produce of domestic industry. Its two great engines for enriching the country, therefore, were restraints upon importation, and encouragements to exportation. . . .

By restraining, either by high duties, or by absolute prohibitions, the importation of such goods from foreign countries as can be produced at home, the monopoly of the home market is more or less secured to the domestic industry employed in producing them. . . .

That this monopoly of the home market frequently gives great encouragement to that particular species of industry which enjoys it, and frequently turns toward that employment a greater share of the labor and stock of the society than would otherwise have gone into it, cannot be doubted. But whether it tends either to increase the general industry of the society, or to give it the most advantageous direction, is not, perhaps, altogether so evident.

The general industry of the society never can exceed what the capital of the society can employ. As the number of workmen that can be kept in employment by any particular person must bear a certain proportion to his capital, so the number of those who can be continually employed by all the members of a great society must bear a certain proportion to the whole capital of that society, and never can exceed that proportion. No regulation of commerce can increase the quantity of industry in any given society beyond what its capital can maintain. It can only divert a part of it into a direction into which it might not otherwise have gone; and it is by no means certain that this artificial direction is likely to be more advantageous to the society than that into which it would have gone of its own accord.

Every individual is continually exerting himself to find out the most advantageous employment for whatever capital he can command. It is his own advantage, indeed, and not that of the society, which he has in view. But the study of his own advantage, naturally, or rather necessarily, leads him to prefer that employment which is most advantageous to the society.

First, every individual endeavors to employ his capital as near home as he can, and consequently as much as he can in the support of domestic industry; provided always that he can thereby obtain the ordinary, or not a great deal less than the ordinary profits of stock. . . .

Secondly, every individual who employs his capital in the support of domestic industry, necessarily endeavors so to direct that industry that its produce may be of the greatest possible value.

The produce of industry is what it adds to the subject or materials upon which it is employed. In proportion as the value of this produce is great or small, so will likewise be the profits of the employer. But it is only for the sake of profit that any man employs a capital in the support of industry, and he will always, therefore, endeavor to employ it in the support of that industry of which the produce is likely to be of the greatest, or to exchange for the greatest quantity either of money or of other goods.

But the annual revenue of every society is always precisely equal to the exchangeable value of the whole annual produce of its industry, or rather is precisely the same thing with that exchangeable value. As every individual, therefore, endeavors as much as he can both to employ his capital in the support of domestic industry, and so to direct that industry that its produce may be of the greatest value; every individual necessarily labors to render the annual revenue of the society as great as he can. He generally, indeed, neither intends to promote the public interest, nor knows how much he is promoting it. By preferring the support of domestic to that of foreign industry, he intends only his own security; and by directing that industry in such a manner that its produce may be of the greatest value, he intends only his own gain, and he is in this, as in many other cases, led by an invisible hand to promote an end which was no part of his intention. Nor is it always the worse for the society that it was no part of it. By pursuing his own interest he frequently promotes that of the society more effectually than when he really intends to promote it. I have never known much good done by those who affected to trade for the public good. It is an affectation, indeed, not very common among merchants, and very few words need be employed in dissuading them from it.

What is the species of domestic industry which his capital can employ, and of which the produce is likely to be of the greatest value, every individual, it is evident, can, in his local situation, judge much better than any statesman or lawgiver can do for him. The statesman who should attempt to direct private people in what manner they ought to employ their capitals would not only load himself with a most unnecessary attention, but assume an authority which could safely be trusted, not only to no single person, but to no council or senate whatever, and which would nowhere be so dangerous as in the hands of a man who had folly and presumption enough to fancy himself fit to exercise it.

To give the monopoly of the home market to the produce of domestic industry, in any particular art or manufacture, is in some measure to direct private people in what manner they ought to employ their capitals, and must, in almost all cases, be either a useless or a hurtful regulation. If the produce of domestic can be brought there as cheap as that of foreign industry, the regulation is evidently useless. If it cannot, it must generally be hurtful. It is the maxim of every prudent master of a family never to make at home what it will cost him more to make than to buy. The tailor does not attempt to make his own shoes, but buys them of the shoemaker. The shoemaker does not attempt to make his own clothes, but employs a tailor. The farmer attempts to make neither the one nor the other, but employs those different artificers. All of them find it to their interest to employ their whole industry in a way in which they have some advantage over their neighbors, and to purchase with a part of its produce, or what is the same thing, with the price of a part of it, whatever else they have occasion for.

What is prudence in the conduct of every private family can scarce be folly in that of a great kingdom. If a foreign country can supply us with a commodity cheaper than we ourselves can make it, better buy it of them with some part of the produce of our own industry employed in a way in which we have some advantage. The general industry of the country, being always in proportion to the capital which employs it, will not thereby be diminished, no more than that of the above-mentioned artificers; but only left to find out the way in which it can be employed with the greatest advantage. It is certainly not employed to the greatest advantage when it is thus directed toward an object which it can buy cheaper than it can make. The value of its annual produce is certainly more or less diminished when it is thus turned away from producing commodities evidently of more value than the commodity which it is directed to produce. According to the supposition, that commodity could be purchased from foreign countries cheaper than it can be made at home. It could, therefore, have been purchased with a part only of the commodities, or, what is the same thing, with a part only of the price of the commodities, which the industry employed by an equal capital would have produced at home, had it been left to follow its natural course. The industry of the country, therefore, is thus turned away from a more to a less advantageous employment, and the exchangeable value

of its annual produce, instead of being increased, according to the intention of the lawgiver, must necessarily be diminished by every such regulation.

By means of such regulations, indeed, a particular manufacture may sometimes be acquired sooner than it could have been otherwise, and after a certain time may be made at home as cheap or cheaper than in the foreign country. But though the industry of the society may be thus carried with advantage into a particular channel sooner than it could have been otherwise, it will by no means follow that the sum total, either of its industry, or of its revenue, can ever be augmented by any such regulation. The industry of the society can augment only in proportion as its capital augments, and its capital can augment only in proportion to what can be gradually saved out of its revenue. But the immediate effect of every such regulation is to diminish its revenue, and what diminishes its revenue is certainly not very likely to augment its capital faster than it would have augmented of its own accord had both capital and industry been left to find out their natural employments.

Though for want of such regulations the society should never acquire the proposed manufacture, it would not, upon that account, necessarily be the poorer in any one period of its duration. In every period of its duration its whole capital and industry might still have been employed, though upon different objects, in the manner that was most advantageous at the time. In every period its revenue might have been the greatest which its capital could afford, and both capital and revenue might have been augmented with the greatest possible rapidity.

The natural advantages which one country has over another in producing particular commodities are sometimes so great that it is acknowledged by all the world to be in vain to struggle with them. By means of glasses, hotbeds, and hot walls, very good grapes can be raised in Scotland, and very good wine too can be made of them at about thirty times the expense for which at least equally good can be brought from foreign countries. Would it be a reasonable law to prohibit the importation of all foreign wines merely to encourage the making of claret and burgundy in Scotland? But if there would be a manifest absurdity in turning toward any employment thirty times more of the capital and industry of the country than would be necessary to purchase from foreign countries an equal quantity of the commodities wanted, there must be an absurdity, though not altogether so glaring, yet exactly of the same kind, in turning toward any such employment a thirtieth, or even a three-hundredth part more of either. Whether the advantages which one country has over another be natural or acquired is in this respect of no consequence. As long as the one country has those advantages, and the other wants them, it will always be more advantageous for the latter rather to buy of the former than to make. It is an acquired advantage only, which one artificer has over his neighbor, who exercises another trade; and yet they both find it more advantageous to buy of one another than to make what does not belong to their particular trades. . . .

There seem, however, to be two cases in which it will generally be advantageous to lay some burden upon foreign for the encouragement of domestic industry.

The first is, when some particular sort of industry is necessary for the defense of the country. The defense of Great Britain, for example, depends very much upon the number of its sailors and shipping. The Act of Navigation, therefore, very properly endeavors to give the sailors and shipping of Great Britain the monopoly of the trade of their own country, in some cases by absolute prohibitions and in others by heavy burdens upon the shipping of foreign countries. . . .

The second case, in which it will generally be advantageous to lay some burden upon foreign for the encouragement of domestic industry is, when some tax is imposed at home upon the produce of the latter. In this case, it seems reasonable that an equal tax should be imposed upon the like produce of the former. This would not give the monopoly of the home market to domestic industry, nor turn toward a particular employment a greater share of the stock and labor of the country than what would naturally go to it. It would only hinder any part of what would naturally go to it from being turned away by the tax into a less natural direction, and would leave the competition between foreign and domestic industry, after the tax, as nearly as possible upon the same footing as before it. In Great Britain, when any such tax is laid upon the products of domestic industry, it is usual at the same time, in order to stop the clamorous complaints of our merchants and manufacturers that they will be undersold at home, to lay a much heavier duty upon the importation of all foreign goods of the same kind. . . .

The case in which it may sometimes be a matter of deliberation how far it is proper to continue the free importation of certain foreign goods is, when some foreign nation restrains by high duties or prohibitions the importation of some of our manufactures into their country. Re-

venge in this case naturally dictates retaliation, and that we should impose the like duties and prohibitions upon the importation of some or all of their manufactures into ours. Nations, accordingly, seldom fail to retaliate in this manner. . . .

There may be good policy in retaliations of this kind, when there is a probability that they will secure the repeal of the high duties or prohibitions complained of. The recovery of a great foreign market will generally more than compensate the transitory inconvenience of paying dearer during a short time for some sorts of goods. To judge whether such retaliations are likely to produce such an effect does not, perhaps, belong so much to the science of a legislator, whose deliberations ought to be governed by general principles which are always the same, as to the skill of that insidious and crafty animal, vulgarly called a statesman or politician, whose councils are directed by the momentary fluctuations of affairs. When there is no probability that any such repeal can be procured, it seems a bad method of compensating the injury done to certain classes of our people to do another injury ourselves, not only to those classes, but to almost all the other classes of them. . . .

Every system which endeavors, either by extraordinary encouragements to draw toward a particular species of industry a greater share of the capital of the society than what would naturally go to it, or, by extraordinary restraint, force from a particular species of industry some share of the capital which would otherwise be employed in it, is in reality subversive of the great purpose which it means to promote. It retards, instead of accelerating, the progress of the society toward real wealth and greatness; and diminishes, instead of increasing, the real value of the annual produce of its land and labor.

All systems either of preference or restraint, therefore, being thus completely taken away, the obvious and simple system of natural liberty establishes itself of its own accord. Every man, as long as he does not violate the laws of justice, is left perfectly free to pursue his own interest his own way, and to bring both his industry and capital into competition with those of any other man, or order of men. The sovereign is completely discharged from a duty, in the attempting to perform which he must always be exposed to innumerable delusions, and for the proper performance of which no human wisdom or knowledge could ever be sufficient; the duty of superintending the industry of private people, and of directing it toward the employments most suitable to the interest of the society.

B.   MALTHUS ON POPULATION

"Philosophic radicals" is the title given to a small group of English thinkers in the late eighteenth and early nineteenth centuries. Their approach was peculiarly English, for it combined a love of "clear and self-evident reasoning," as advocated by the French *philosophes,* with a strong native dislike for abstractions. The weight of their influence, as was later observed by John Stuart Mill, was derived from "the air of strong conviction with which they wrote when scarcely anyone else seemed to have an equally strong faith in as definite a creed; the boldness with which they tilted against the very front of both existing parties," Whig and Tory alike; and "their uncompromising profession of opposition of many of the generally received opinions."

Thomas Robert Malthus (1766–1834) was a curate and professor in a college near London who reacted against the exuberant optimism and belief in the perfectibility of mankind which were characteristic of Condorcet and of such English supporters of the French Revolution as Thomas Paine and William Godwin. As an answer to this enthusiasm of the *philosophes* he published his *Essay on Population* in 1798. The sections quoted below illustrate the main reasons advanced by Malthus to contradict their optimism.[2]

The great and unlooked-for discoveries that have taken place of late years in natural philosophy; the increasing diffusion of general knowledge from the extension of the art of printing; the ardent and unshackled spirit of inquiry that prevails throughout the lettered, and even unlettered world; the new and extraordinary lights that have been thrown on political subjects, which dazzle and astonish the understanding; and particularly that tremendous phenomenon in the political horizon, the French Revolution, which, like a blazing comet, seems destined either to inspire with fresh life and vigor, or to scorch up and destroy the thinking inhabitants of the earth, have all concurred to lead able men into the opinion, that we were touching upon a period big with the most important changes, changes that would in some measure be decisive of the future fate of mankind.

It has been said that the great question is now at issue whether man shall henceforth start forwards with accelerated velocity toward illimitable and hitherto unconceived improvement; or be condemned to a perpetual oscillation between happiness and misery and after every effort remain still at an immeasurable distance from the wished-for goal.

Yet, anxiously as every friend of mankind must look forward to the termination of this painful suspense; and, eagerly as the inquiring mind would hail every ray of light that might assist its view into futurity, it is much to be lamented that the writers on each side of this momentous question still keep far aloof from each other. Their mutual arguments do not meet with a candid examination. The question is not brought to rest on fewer points and even in theory scarcely seems to be approaching to a decision.

The advocate for the present order of things is apt to treat the sect of speculative philosophers either as a set of artful and designing knaves, who preach up ardent benevolence, and draw captivating pictures of a happier state of society, only the better to enable them to destroy the present establishments, and to forward their own deep-laid schemes of ambition, or, as wild and mad-headed enthusiasts, whose silly speculations, and absurd paradoxes, are not worthy the attention of any reasonable man.

The advocate for the perfectibility of man, and of society, retorts on the defender of establishments a more than equal contempt. He brands him as the slave of the most miserable, and narrow prejudices; or, as the defender of the abuses of civil society, only because he profits by them. He paints him either as a character who prostitutes his understanding to his interest; or as one whose powers of mind are not of a size to grasp anything great and noble; who cannot see above five yards before him; and who must therefore be utterly unable to take in the views of the enlightened benefactor of mankind.

In this unamicable contest, the cause of truth cannot but suffer. The really good arguments on each side of the question are not allowed to have their proper weight. Each pursues his own theory, little solicitous to correct, or improve it, by an attention to what is advanced by his opponents.

The friend of the present order of things condemns all political speculations in the gross. He will not even condescend to examine the grounds from which the perfectibility of society is inferred. Much less will he give himself the trouble in a fair and candid manner to attempt an exposition of their fallacy.

The speculative philosopher equally offends against the cause of truth. With eyes fixed on a happier state of society, the blessings of which he paints in the most captivating colors, he allows himself to indulge in the most bitter invectives against every present establishment, without applying his talents to consider the best and safest means of removing abuses, and without seeming to be aware of the tremendous obstacles that threaten, even in theory, to oppose the progress of man toward perfections.

It is an acknowledged truth in philosophy that a just theory will always be confirmed by experiment. Yet so much friction, and so many minute circumstances occur in practice, which it is next to impossible for the most enlarged and penetrating mind to foresee, that on few subjects can any theory be pronounced just that has not stood the test of experience. But an untried theory cannot be advanced as probable, much less as just, till all the arguments against it have been maturely weighed and clearly and consistently confuted.

I have read some of the speculations on the perfectibility of man and of society with great pleasure. I have been warmed and delighted with the enchanting picture which they hold forth. I ardently wish for such happy improvements. But I see great and, to my understanding, unconquerable difficulties in the way to them. These difficulties it is my present purpose to state, declaring, at the same time, that so far from exulting in them, as a cause of triumphing over the friends of innovation, nothing would give me greater pleasure than to see them completely removed. . . .

In entering upon the argument I must premise that I put out of the question, at present, all mere conjectures; that is, all suppositions, the probable realization of which cannot be inferred upon any just philosophical grounds. A writer may tell me that he thinks man will ultimately become an ostrich. I cannot properly contradict him. But before he can expect to bring any reasonable person over to his opinion he ought to show that the necks of mankind have been gradually elongating; that the lips have grown harder and more prominent; that the legs and feet are daily altering their shape; and that the hair is beginning to change into stubs of feathers. And till the probability of so wonderful a conversion can be shown, it is surely lost time and lost eloquence to expatiate on the happiness of man in such a state; to describe his powers, both of running and flying; to paint him in a condition where all narrow luxuries would be condemned: where he would be employed, only in collecting the necessaries of life; and where, consequently, each man's share of labor would be light, and his portion of leisure ample.

I think I may fairly make two postulata.

First, That food is necessary to the existence of man.

Secondly, That the passion between the sexes is necessary, and will remain nearly in its present state.

These two laws, ever since we have had any knowledge of mankind, appear to have been fixed laws of our nature; and, as we have not hitherto seen any alteration in them, we have no right to conclude that they will ever cease to be what they are now, without an immediate act of power in that Being who first arranged the system of the universe, and for the advantage of His creatures, still executes, according to fixed laws, all its various operations.

I do not know that any writer has supposed that on this earth man will ultimately be able to live without food. But Mr. Godwin has conjectured that the passion between the sexes may in time be extinguished. As, however, he calls this part of his work a deviation into the land of conjecture, I will not dwell longer upon it at present than to say that the best arguments for the perfectibility of man are drawn from a contemplation of the great progress that he has already made from the savage state and the difficulty of saying where he is to stop. But toward the extinction of the passion between the sexes, no progress whatever has hitherto been made. It appears to exist in as much force at present as it did two thousand or four thousand years ago. There are individual exceptions now as there always have been. But as these exceptions do not appear to increase in number, it would surely be a very unphilosophical mode of arguing, to infer merely from the existence of an exception, that the exception would in time become the rule and the rule the exception.

Assuming, then, my postulata as granted, I say that the power of population is indefinitely greater than the power in the earth to produce subsistence for man.

Population, when unchecked, increases in a geometrical ratio. Subsistence only increases in an arithmetical ratio. A slight acquaintance with numbers will show the immensity of the first power in comparison of the second.

By that law of our nature which makes food necessary to the life of man, the effects of these two unequal powers must be kept equal.

This implies a strong and constantly operating check on population from the difficulty of subsistence. This difficulty must fall somewhere and must necessarily be severely felt by a large portion of mankind.

Through the animal and vegetable kingdoms, nature has scattered the seeds of life abroad with the most profuse and liberal hand. She has been comparatively sparing in the room and the nourishment necessary to rear them. The germs of existence contained in this spot of earth, with ample food and ample room to expand it, would fill millions of worlds in the course of a few thousand years. Necessity, that imperious, all-pervading law of nature, restrains them within the prescribed bounds. The race of plants and the race of animals shrink under this great restrictive law. And the race of man cannot, by any efforts of reason, escape from it. Among plants and animals its effects are waste of seed, sickness, and premature death. Among mankind, misery and vice. The former, misery, is an absolutely necessary consequence of it. Vice is a highly probable consequence, and we therefore see it abundantly prevail; but it ought not, perhaps, to be called an absolutely necessary consequence. The ordeal of virtue is to resist all temptation to evil.

This natural inequality of the two powers of population and of production in the earth, and that great law of our nature which must constantly keep their effects equal, form the great difficulty that to me appears insurmountable in the way to perfectibility of society. All other arguments are of slight and subordinate consideration in comparison of this. I see no way by which man can escape from the weight of this law which pervades all animated nature. No fancied equality, no agrarian regulations in their utmost extent, could remove the pressure of it even for a single century. And it appears, therefore, to be decisive against the possible existence of a society, all the members of which should live in ease, happiness, and comparative leisure; and feel no anxiety about providing the means of subsistence for themselves and their families.

Consequently, if the premises are just, the argument is conclusive against the perfectibility of the mass of mankind.

I have thus sketched the general outline of the argument; but I will examine it more particularly; and I think it will be found that experience, the true source and foundation of all knowledge, invariably confirms its truth. . . .

The ultimate check to population appears then to be a want of food, arising necessarily from the different ratios according to which population and food increase. But this ultimate check is never the immediate check, except in cases of actual famine.

The immediate check may be stated to consist in all those customs, and all those diseases, which seem to be generated by a scarcity of the means of subsistence; and all those causes, independent of this scarcity, which tend prematurely to weaken and destroy the human frame.

These checks to population, which are con-

stantly operating with more or less force in every society, and keep down the number to the level of the means of subsistence, may be classed under two general heads—the preventive and the positive checks.

The preventive check, as far as it is voluntary, is peculiar to man, and arises from that distinctive superiority in his reasoning faculties which enables him to calculate distant consequences. The checks to the indefinite increase of plants and irrational animals are all either positive, or, if preventive, involuntary. But man cannot look around him and see the distress which frequently presses upon those who have large families; he cannot contemplate his present possessions or earnings, which he now nearly consumes himself, and calculate the amount of each share, when with very little addition they must be divided, perhaps, among seven or eight, without feeling a doubt whether, if he follow the bent of his inclinations, he may be able to support the offspring which he will probably bring into the world. In a state of equality, if such can exist, this would be the simple question. In the present state of society other considerations occur. Will he now lower his rank in life, and be obliged to give up in great measure his former habits? Does any mode of employment present itself by which he may reasonably hope to maintain a family? Will he not at any rate subject himself to greater difficulties and more severe labor than in his single state? Will he not be unable to transmit to his children the same advantages of education and improvement that he had himself possessed? Does he even feel secure that, should he have a large family, his utmost exertions can save them from rags and squalid poverty and their consequent degradation in the community? And may he not be reduced to the grating necessity of forfeiting his independence and of being obliged to the sparing hand of charity for support?

The positive checks to population are extremely various, and include every cause, whether arising from vice or misery, which in any degree contributes to shorten the natural duration of human life. Under this head, therefore, may be enumerated all unwholesome occupations, severe labor and exposure to the seasons, extreme poverty, bad nursing of children, great towns, excesses of all kinds, the whole train of common diseases and epidemics, wars, plague, and famine.

On examining these obstacles to the increase of population which I have classed under the heads of preventive and positive checks, it will appear that they are all resolvable into moral restraint, vice, and misery.

Of the preventive checks, the restraint from marriage which is not followed by irregular gratifications may properly be termed moral restraint.

Promiscuous intercourse, unnatural passions, violations of the marriage bed, and improper arts to conceal the consequences of irregular connections, are preventive checks that clearly come under the head of vice.

Of the positive checks, those which appear to arise unavoidably from the laws of nature may be called exclusively misery; and those which we obviously bring upon ourselves, such as wars, excesses, and many others which it would be in our power to avoid, are of a mixed nature. They are brought upon us by vice, and their consequences are misery. . . .

In every country some of these checks are, with more or less force, in constant operation; yet, notwithstanding their general prevalence, there are few states in which there is not a constant effort in the population to increase beyond the means of subsistence. This constant effort as constantly tends to subject the lower classes of society to distress and to prevent any great permanent melioration of their condition.

C.   BENTHAM ON THE PRINCIPLE OF UTILITY

Jeremy Bentham (1748–1832) was the son of a wealthy London solicitor, whose private income made it possible for him to devote his long lifetime to a career of speculation and writing. He produced a prodigious volume of work, and one of his earliest books was *An Introduction to the Principles of Morals and Legislation,* privately printed in 1780 and published in 1789. The principles which Bentham laid down in this work were fundamental to all his thinking and exercised a profound influence upon that of his contemporaries. The following selection is from the first chapter of this work.[3]

I. Nature has placed mankind under the governance of two sovereign masters, *pain* and *pleasure*. It is for them alone to point out what we ought to do, as well as to determine what we shall do. On the one hand the standard of right and wrong, on the other the chain of causes and effects, are fastened to their throne. They govern us in all we do, in all we say, in all we think: every effort we can make to throw off our subjection, will serve but to demonstrate and confirm it. In words a man may pretend to abjure their empire, but in reality he will remain subject to it all the while. The *principle of utility* recognizes this subjection, and assumes it for the foundation of that system, the object of which is to rear the fabric of felicity by the hands of reason and of law. Systems which attempt to question it deal in sounds instead of sense, in caprice instead of reason, in darkness instead of light.

But enough of metaphor and declamation: it is not by such means that moral science is to be improved.

II. The principle of utility is the foundation of the present work: it will be proper therefore at the outset to give an explicit and determinate account of what is meant by it. By the principle of utility is meant that principle which approves or disapproves of every action whatsoever, according to the tendency which it appears to have to augment or diminish the happiness of the party whose interest is in question: or, what is the same thing in other words, to promote or to oppose that happiness. I say of every action whatsoever; and therefore not only of every action of a private individual, but of every measure of government.

III. By utility is meant that property in any object whereby it tends to produce benefit, advantage, pleasure, good, or happiness (all this in the present case comes to the same thing), or (what comes again to the same thing) to prevent the happening of mischief, pain, evil, or unhappiness to the party whose interest is considered: if that party be the community in general, then the happiness of the community; if a particular individual, then the happiness of that individual.

IV. The interest of the community is one of the most general expressions that can occur in the phraseology of morals: no wonder that the meaning of it is often lost. When it has a meaning, it is this. The community is a fictitious body, composed of the individual persons who are considered as constituting as it were its members. The interest of the community then is—what? The sum of the interests of the several members who compose it.

V. It is in vain to talk of the interest of the community without understanding what is the interest of the individual. A thing is said to promote the interest, or to be for the interest of an individual, when it tends to add to the sum total of his pleasures; or, what comes to the same thing, to diminish the sum total of his pains.

VI. An action then may be said to be conformable to the principle of utility, or, for shortness sake, to utility (meaning with respect to the community at large), when the tendency it has to augment the happiness of the community is greater than any it has to diminish it.

VII. A measure of government (which is but a particular kind of action, performed by a particular person or persons) may be said to be con formable to or dictated by the principle of utility, when in like manner the tendency which it has to augment the happiness of the community is greater than any which it has to diminish it.

VIII. When an action, or in particular a measure of government, is supposed by a man to be conformable to the principle of utility, it may be convenient, for the purposes of discourse, to imagine a kind of law or dictate, called a law or dictate of utility; and to speak of the action in question as being conformable to such law or dictate.

IX. A man may be said to be a partisan of the principle of utility, when the approbation or disapprobation he annexes to any action, or to any measure, is determined by and proportioned to the tendency which he conceives it to have to augment or to diminish the happiness of the community; or in other words, to its conformity or unconformity to the laws or dictates of utility.

X. Of an action that is conformable to the principle of utility, one may always say either that it is one that ought to be done, or at least that it is not one that ought not to be done. One may say also that it is right it should be done—at least that it is not wrong it should be done; that it is a right action—at least that it is not a wrong action. When thus interpreted, the words *ought*, and *right* and *wrong*, and others of that stamp have a meaning: when otherwise, they have none.

XI. Has the rectitude of this principle been ever formally contested? It should seem that it had, by those who have not known what they have been meaning. Is it susceptible of any direct proof? It should seem not; for that which is used to prove everything else cannot itself be proved: a chain of proofs must have their commencement somewhere. To give such proof is as impossible as it is needless.

XII. Not that there is or ever has been that human creature breathing, however stupid or perverse, who has not on many, perhaps on most occasions of his life, deferred to it. By the natural constitution of the human frame, on most occasions of their lives men in general embrace this principle, without thinking of it; if not for the ordering of their own actions, yet for the trying of their own actions, as well as of those of other men. There have been, at the same time, not many perhaps even of the most intelligent, who have been disposed to embrace it purely and without reserve. There are even few who have not taken some occasion or other to quarrel with it, either on account of their not understanding always how to apply it, or on account of some prejudice or other which they were afraid to examine into, or could not bear to part with. For such is the stuff that man is made of: in principle and in practice, in a right track and in a wrong one, the rarest of all human qualities is consistency.

XIII. When a man attempts to combat the principle of utility, it is with reasons drawn, without his being aware of it, from that very principle itself. His arguments, if they prove anything, prove not that the principle is *wrong*, but that according to the applications he supposes to be made of it, it is *misapplied*. Is it possible for a man to move the earth? Yes; but he must first find out another earth to stand upon.

D.   BENTHAM ON POLITICAL ECONOMY

Among Bentham's voluminous works was his *Manual of Political Economy*, which, though published only in part before his death, contained an incisive summary of the manner in which Bentham believed that his principle of utility should be applied. Bentham's manner of application, as set forth in this work, was typical of the philosophic radicals as a whole. Following is a selection from the opening chapter of the *Manual*.[4]

Political Economy is at once a science and an art. The value of the science has for its efficient cause and measure its subserviency to the art.

According to the principle of utility in every branch of the art of legislation, the object or end in view should be the production of the maximum of happiness in a given time in the community in question.

In the instance of this branch of the art, the object or end in view should be the production of that maximum of happiness, in so far as this more general end is promoted by the production of the maximum of wealth and the maximum of population.

The practical questions, therefore, are—how far the measures respectively suggested by these two branches of the common end agree?—how far they differ, and which requires the preference?—how far the end in view is best promoted by individuals acting for themselves?—and in what cases these ends may be best promoted by the hands of government? . . .

With the view of causing an increase to take place in the mass of national wealth, or with a view to increase of the means either of subsistence or enjoyment, without some special reason, the general rule is, that nothing ought to be done or attempted by government. The motto, or watchword of government, on these occasions, ought to be—*Be quiet.*

For this quietism there are two main reasons:

1. Generally speaking, any interference for this purpose on the part of government is needless. The wealth of the whole community is composed of the wealth of the several individuals belonging to it taken together. But to increase his particular portion is, generally speaking, among the constant objects of each individual's exertions and care. Generally speaking, there is no one who knows what is for your interest so well as yourself—no one who is disposed with so much ardor and constancy to pursue it.

2. Generally speaking, it is moreover likely to be pernicious, viz., by being unconducive, or even obstructive, with reference to the attainment of the end in view. Each individual, bestowing more time and attention upon the means of preserving and increasing his portion of wealth than is or can be bestowed by government, is likely to take a more effectual course than what, in his instance and on his behalf, would be taken by government.

It is, moreover, universally and constantly pernicious in another way, by the restraint or constraint imposed on the free agency of the individual. Pain is the general concomitant of the sense of such restraint, wherever it is experienced. . . .

With few exceptions, and these not very considerable ones, the attainment of the maximum of enjoyment will be most effectually secured by leaving each individual to pursue his own maximum of enjoyment, in proportion as he is in possession of the means. Inclination in this respect will not be wanting on the part of anyone. Power, the species of power applicable to this case—viz., wealth, pecuniary power—could not be given by the hand of government to one without being taken from another; so that by such interference there would not be any gain of power upon the whole. . . .

We have seen above the grounds on which the general rule in this behalf—*Be quiet*—rests. Whatever measures, therefore, cannot be justified as exceptions to that rule, may be considered as *non agenda* on the part of government. The art, therefore, is reduced within a small compass: security and freedom are all that industry requires. The request which agriculture, manufactures, and commerce present to governments is modest and reasonable as that which Diogenes made to Alexander: "Stand out of my sunshine." We have no need of favor—we require only a secure and open path.

E. JOHN STUART MILL REVALUATES LIBERALISM, 1873

John Stuart Mill (1806–73) had been brought up a strict "utilitarian" by his father, an intimate of Jeremy Bentham and a prominent member of the philosophic radicals. All his life Mill had been deeply interested in reform and had written much on the question of freedom in society. In the following selection from his autobiography, written in the last year of his life, Mill revaluates the principles he had learned in his youth.[5]

In those days I had seen little further than the old school of political economists into the possibilities of fundamental improvement in social arrangements. Private property, as now understood, and inheritance, appeared to me, as to them, the *dernier mot* of legislation: and I looked no further than to mitigating the inequalities consequent on these institutions, by getting rid of primogeniture and entails. The notion that it was possible to go further than this in removing the injustice—for injustice it is, whether admitting of a complete remedy or not—involved in the fact that some are born to riches and the vast majority to poverty, I then reckoned chimerical, and only hoped that by universal education, leading to voluntary restraint on population, the portion of the poor might be made more tolerable. In short, I was a democrat, but not the least of a socialist.

We were now much less democrats than I had been, because so long as education continues to be so wretchedly imperfect, we dreaded the ignorance and especially the selfishness and brutality of the mass: but our ideal of ultimate improvement went far beyond democracy, and would class us decidedly under the general designation of socialists. While we repudiated with the greatest energy that tyranny of society over the individual which most socialistic systems are supposed to involve, we yet looked forward to a time when society will no longer be divided into the idle and the industrious; when the rule that they who do not work shall not eat, will be applied not to paupers only, but impartially to all; when the division of the produce of labor, instead of depending, as in so great a degree it now does, on the accident of birth, will be made by concert on an acknowledged principle of justice; and when it will no longer either be, or be thought to be, impossible for human beings to exert themselves strenuously in procuring benefits which are not to be exclusively their own, but to be shared with the society they belong to.

The social problem of the future we considered to be, how to unite the greatest individual liberty of action, with a common ownership in the raw material of the globe, and an equal participation of all in the benefits of combined labor. We had not the presumption to suppose that we could already foresee by what precise form of institutions these objects could most effectually be attained, or at how near or how distant a period they would become practicable. We saw clearly that to render any such social transformation either possible or desirable, an equivalent change of character must take place both in the uncultivated herd who now compose the laboring masses, and in the immense majority of their employers. Both these classes must learn by practice to labor and combine for generous, or at all events for public and social purposes, and not, as hitherto, solely for narrowly interested ones. But the capacity to do this has always existed in mankind, and is not, nor is ever likely to be, extinct. Education, habit, and the cultivation of the sentiments, will make a common man dig or weave for his country, as readily as fight for his country. True enough, it is only by slow degrees, and a system of culture prolonged through successive generations, that men in general can be brought up to this point. But the hindrance is not in the essential constitution of human nature.

Interest in the common good is at present so weak a motive in the generality, not because it can never be otherwise, but because the mind is not accustomed to dwell on it as it dwells from morning till night on things which tend only to personal advantage. When called into activity, as only self-interest now is, by the daily course of life, and spurred from behind by the love of distinction and the fear of shame, it is capable of producing, even in common men, the most strenuous exertions as well as the most heroic sacrifices. The deep-rooted selfishness, which forms the general character of the existing state of society, is so deeply rooted only because the whole course of existing institutions tends to foster it; and modern institutions in some respects more than ancient, since the occasions on which the individual is called on to do anything for the public without receiving its pay, are far less frequent in modern life than in the smaller commonwealths of antiquity.

These considerations did not make us overlook the folly of premature attempts to dispense with the inducements of private interest in social affairs, while no substitute for them has been or can be provided: but we regarded all existing institutions and social arrangements as being (in a phrase I once heard from Austin) "merely provisional," and we welcomed with the greatest pleasure and interest all socialistic experiments by select individuals (such as the cooperative societies), which, whether they succeeded or failed, could not but operate as a most useful education of those who took part in them, by cultivating their capacity of acting upon motives pointing directly to the defects which render them and others incapable of doing so.

Part II. MATERIALISM, SOCIALISM, AND NATIONALISM

Among the most important legacies of the French Revolution to the nineteenth century were liberalism and nationalism. The former, despite the disillusionment of the Napoleonic imperium and the reaction of the Vienna settlement, had not lost its appeal. Both in England and on the continent, liberal thinkers and statesmen were advocating individual liberties under law, constitutionalism, or laissez-faire as the answer to the political and social problems of the day. But often they found conservative forces in power and so opposed to any changes that the liberals resorted to conspiracy and even revolution. Outbreaks in 1820 and 1830 were ultimately put down, not without changes in regime or in the territorial map of Vienna, but in 1848 a revolution in Paris against the increasingly conservative government of Louis Phillipe set off similar movements throughout Italy, Germany, and much of the Habsburg empire. Though the liberal elements often scored initial victories over the defenders of the status quo, in the long run they proved too few, too undecisive, and too lacking in mass appeal to maintain control. Instead, Bismarck or Napoleon III, leaders with more avowedly nationalist aims and autocratic inclinations, proved the ultimate victors. The achievement of unified nation-states in Italy and Germany by 1870 shows the potency of these nationalist ideas, which a contemporary observer, Lord Acton, was among the first to perceive and analyze. The liberal failure in 1848, however, was caused not only by their underestimating the appeal of nationalism but also by their virtual obliviousness to the growing movement of social protest, inspired at once by the ideas of the French Revolution and the grim realities of urbanism and industrialism. Although Karl Marx was not the first to verbalize this protest, his writing would soon become by far the most influential. Underlying both the triumphant nationalism and incipient socialism of the mid-century was a growing materialism based in large part on the new synthesis and conclusions in science which spread rapidly to the general reading public through the efforts of such philosopher-popularizers as Ludwig Büchner, a selection of whose writings conclude this Part of the Problem.

A.   ACTON ON NATIONALISM

No more cosmopolitan observer of nineteenth century nationalism than Lord Acton (1834–1902) could be imagined. Born of an English catholic gentry family with close relatives among the noble families of Germany and Italy, he was educated in England, Scotland, and on the continent, and traveled as far as Russia and the United States. Active as a critic of the more extreme catholic, papal policies, member of Parliament and intimate of Gladstone, Acton finally became Regius Professor of Modern History at Cambridge in 1895. Though he never finished his great work on the history of liberty, his essays have long shown the almost prophetic character of his insights. The following selection is from his essay on nationality written in 1862.[6]

In pursuing the outward and visible growth of the national theory we are prepared for an examination of its political character and value. The absolutism which has created it denies equally that absolute right of national unity which is a product of democracy, and that claim of national liberty which belongs to the theory of freedom. These two views of nationality, corresponding to the French and to the English systems, are connected in name only, and are in reality the opposite extremes of political thought. In one case, nationality is founded on the perpetual supremacy of the collective will, of which the unity of the nation is the necessary condition, to which every other influence must defer, and against which no obligation enjoys authority, and all resistance is tyrannical. The nation is here an ideal unit founded on the race, in tradition and of existing rights. It overrules the rights and wishes of the inhabitants, absorbing their divergent interests in a fictitious unity; sacrifices their several inclinations and duties to the higher claim of nationality, and crushes all natural rights and all established liberties for the purpose of vindicating itself. Whenever a single definite object is made the supreme end of the State, be it the advantage of a class, the safety or the power of the country, the greatest happiness of the greatest number, or the support of any speculative idea, the State becomes for the time inevitably absolute. Liberty alone demands for its realization the limitation of the public authority, for liberty is the only object which benefits all alike, and provokes no sincere opposition. In supporting the claims of national unity, governments must be subverted in whose title there

is no flaw, and whose policy is beneficent and equitable, and subjects must be compelled to transfer their allegiance to an authority for which they have no attachment, and which may be practically a foreign domination. Connected with this theory in nothing except in the common enmity of the absolute state, is the theory which represents nationality as an essential, but not a supreme element in determining the forms of the State. It is distinguished from the other because it tends to diversity and not to uniformity, to harmony and not to unity; because it aims not at an arbitrary change, but at careful respect for the existing conditions of political life, and aspirations of an ideal future. While the theory of unity makes the nation a source of despotism and revolution, the theory of liberty regards it as the bulwark of self government, and the foremost limit to the excessive power of the State. Private rights, which are sacrificed to the unity, are preserved by the union of nations. No power can so efficiently resist the tendencies of centralization, of corruption, and of absolutism, as that community which is the vastest that can be included in a State, which imposes on its members a consistent similarity of character, interest, and opinion, and which arrests the action of the sovereign by the influence of a divided patriotism. The presence of different nations under the same sovereignty is similar in its effect to the independence of the Church in the State. . . .

The difference between nationality and the State is exhibited in the nature of patriotic attachment. Our connection with the race is merely natural or physical, whilst our duties to the political nation are ethical. One is a community of affections and instincts infinitely important and powerful in savage life, but pertaining more to the animal than to the civilized man; the other is an authority governing by laws, imposing obligations, and giving a moral sanction and character to the natural relations of society. Patriotism is in political life what faith is in religion, and it stands to the domestic feelings and to home-sickness as faith to fanaticism and to superstition. It has one aspect derived from private life and nature, for it is an extension of the family affections, as the tribe is an extension of the family. But in its real political character, patriotism consists in the development of the instinct of self-preservation into a moral duty which may involve self-sacrifice. Self-preservation is both an instinct and a duty, natural and involuntary in one respect, and at the same time a moral obligation. By the first it produces the family; by the last the State. If the nation could exist without the State, subject only to the instinct of self-preservation, it would be incapable of denying, controlling, or sacrificing itself; it would be an end and a rule to itself. But in the political order moral purposes are realized and public ends are pursued to which private interests and even existence must be sacrificed. The great sign of true patriotism, the development of selfishness into sacrifice, is the product of political life. That sense of duty which is supplied by race is not entirely separated from its selfish and instinctive basis; and the love of country, like married love, stands at the same time on a material and a moral foundation. The patriot must distinguish between the two causes or objects of his devotion. The attachment which is given only to the country is like obedience given only to the State—a submission to physical influences. The man who prefers his country before every other duty shows the same spirit as the man who surrenders every right to the State. They both deny that right is superior to authority . . .

The great importance of nationality in the State consists in the fact that it is the basis of political capacity. The character of a nation determines in great measure the form and vitality of the State. Certain political habits and ideas belong to particular nations, and they vary with the course of the national history. A people just emerging from barbarism, a people effete from the excesses of a luxurious civilization, cannot possess the means of governing itself; a people devoted to equality, or to absolute monarchy, is incapable of producing an aristocracy; a people averse to the institution of private property is without the first element of freedom. Each of these can only by the contact of a superior race, in whose power will lie the future prospects of the State. A system which ignores these things,

and does not rely for its support on the character and aptitude of the people, does not intend that they should administer their own affairs, but that they should simply be obedient to the supreme command. The denial of nationality, therefore, implies the denial of political liberty.

The greatest adversary of the rights of nationality is the modern theory of nationality. By making the State and the nation commensurate with each other in theory, it reduces practically to a subject condition all other nationalities that may be within the boundary. It cannot admit them to an equality with the ruling nation which constitutes the State, because the State would then cease to be national, which would be a contradiction of the principle of its existence. According, therefore, to the degree of humanity and civilization in that dominant body which claims all the rights of the community, the inferior races are exterminated, or reduced to servitude, or outlawed, or put in a condition of dependence.

If we take the establishment of liberty for the realization of moral duties to be the end of civil society, we must conclude that those states are substantially the most perfect which, like the British and Austrian Empires, include various distinct nationalities without oppressing them. Those in which no mixture of races has occurred are imperfect; and those in which its effects have disappeared are decrepit. A State which is incompetent to satisfy different races condemns itself; a State which labours to neutralize, to absorb, or to expel them, destroys its own vitality; a State which does not include them is destitute of the chief basis of self-government. The theory of nationality, therefore, is a retrograde step in history. It is the most advanced form of the revolution, and must retain its power to the end of the revolutionary period, of which it announces the approach. Its great historical importance depends on two chief causes.

First, it is a chimera. The settlement at which it aims is impossible. As it can never be satisfied and exhausted, and always continues to assert itself, it prevents the government from ever relapsing into the condition which provoked its rise. The danger is too threatening, and the power over men's minds too great, to allow any system to endure which justifies the resistance of nationality. It must contribute, therefore, to obtain that which in theory it condemns—the liberty of different nationalities as members of one sovereign community. This is a service which no other force could accomplish; for it is a corrective alike of absolute monarchy, of democracy, and of constitutionalism, as well as of the centralization which is common to all three. Neither the monarchical, nor the revolutionary, nor the parliamentary system can do this; and all the ideas which have excited enthusiasm in past times are impotent for the purpose except nationality alone.

And secondly, the national theory marks the end of the revolutionary doctrine and its logical exhaustion. In proclaiming the supremacy of the rights of nationality, the system of democratic equality goes beyond its own extreme boundary, and falls into contradiction with itself. Between the democratic and the national phase of the revolution, socialism had intervened, and had already carried the consequences of the principle to an absurdity. But that phase was passed. The revolution survived its offspring, and produced another further result. Nationality is more advanced than socialism, because it is a more arbitrary system. The social theory endeavors to provide for the existence of the individual beneath the terrible burdens which modern society heaps upon labour. It is not merely a development of the nation of equality, but a refuge from real misery and starvation. However false the solution, it was a reasonable demand that the poor should be saved from destruction; and if the freedom of the State was sacrificed to the safety of the individual, the more immediate object was, at least

in theory, attained. But nationality does not aim either at liberty or prosperity, both of which it sacrifices to the imperative necessity of making the nation the mould and measure of the State. Its course will be marked with material as well as moral ruin, in order that a new invention may prevail. There is no principle of change, no phase of political speculation conceivable, more comprehensive, more subversive, or more arbitrary than this. It is a confutation of democracy, because it sets limits to the exercise of the popular will, and substitutes for it a higher principle. It prevents not only the division, but the extension of the State, and forbids to terminate war by conquest, and to obtain a security for peace. Thus, after surrendering the individual to the collective will subject to conditions which are independent of it, and rejects all law, only to be controlled by an accident.

Although, therefore, the theory of nationality is more absurd and more criminal than the theory of socialism, it has an important mission in the world, and marks the final conflict, and therefore the end, of two forces which are the worst enemies of civil freedom,—the absolute monarchy and the revolution.

B.   KARL MARX AND THE COMMUNIST MANIFESTO

Karl Marx (1818–83) came of a well-to-do German Jewish family, but when he was six years old his father embraced Christianity and Marx was brought up in that faith. He was a brilliant student and was educated at the universities of Bonn, Jena, and Berlin. At this last seat of learning he was introduced to the philosophic method of Hegel, a fact of great importance in shaping his subsequent ideas. Briefly, the Hegelian dialectic conceived that change took place through the struggle of antagonistic elements or ideas and their resolution into a synthesis in which a new and higher idea or concept was formed by virtue of the union of contradictory elements.

After receiving his doctorate Marx entered journalism and in 1843 went to Paris to practice that profession. It was there that he met his lifetime friend and collaborator, Friedrich Engels, a German businessman who also was the highly successful operator of spinning mills in England. It was Engels, himself the author of a book entitled *The Condition of the Working Class in 1844,* who had in his firsthand knowledge of working conditions in the early days of technological change the wherewithal to supply Marx with much of his factual materials. Ousted from France at the request of the Prussian government, Marx went to Brussels and thence in January 1847 to London, where he and Engels composed *The Communist Manifesto.*

In November 1847 the Communist League held a congress in London. Although the League was then composed exclusively of German workingmen, the meeting had to be held outside Germany to avoid the attention of the German police. This congress asked Marx and Engels to draw up a complete program for the League; *The Communist Manifesto* was the result. It was written in German the following January and went to press shortly before the outbreak of the revolutions of 1848. While it was produced jointly by Marx and Engels, the latter admitted that the principal ideas were developed by Marx. The *Manifesto* has been translated into almost all languages and has run through many editions. The selections which follow are taken from an English translation authorized and edited by Engels.[7]

A specter is haunting Europe—the specter of communism. All the powers of old Europe have entered into a holy alliance to exorcise this specter; Pope and Czar, Metternich and Guizot, French radicals and German police spies.

Where is the party in opposition that has not been decried as communistic by its opponents in power? Where the opposition that has not hurled back the branding reproach of communism against the more advanced opposition parties, as well as against its reactionary adversaries?

Two things result from this fact.

I. Communism is already acknowledged by all European powers to be in itself a power.

II. It is high time that communists should openly, in the face of the whole world, publish their views, their aims, their tendencies, and meet this nursery tale of the specter of communism with a manifesto of the party itself.

To this end the communists of various nationalities have assembled in London, and sketched the following manifesto to be published in the English, French, German, Italian, Flemish, and Danish languages.

I: Bourgeois and Proletarians

The history of all hitherto existing society is the history of class struggles.

Freeman and slave, patrician and plebeian, lord and serf, guild master and journeyman, in a word, oppressor and oppressed, stood in constant opposition to one another, carried on an uninterrupted, now hidden, now open fight, that each time ended, either in the revolutionary reconstitution of society at large, or in the common ruin of the contending classes.

In the earlier epochs of history we find almost everywhere a complicated arrangement of society into various orders, a manifold gradation of social rank. In ancient Rome we have patricians, knights, plebeians, slaves; in the Middle Ages, feudal lords, vassals, guild masters, journeymen, apprentices, serfs; in almost all of these classes, again, subordinate gradations.

The modern bourgeois society that has sprouted from the ruins of feudal society has not done away with class antagonisms. It has but established new classes, new conditions of oppression, new forms of struggle in place of the old ones.

Our epoch, the epoch of the bourgeois, possesses, however, this distinctive feature: it has simplified the class antagonisms. Society as a whole is more and more splitting up into two great hostile camps, into two great classes directly facing each other: Bourgeoisie and Proletariat.

From the serfs of the Middle Ages sprang the chartered burghers of the earliest towns. From these burgesses the first elements of the bourgeoisie were developed.

The discovery of America, the rounding of the Cape, opened up fresh ground for the rising bourgeoisie. The East Indian and Chinese markets, the colonization of America, trade with the colonies, the increase in the means of exchange and in commodities generally, gave to commerce, to navigation, to industry, an impulse never before known, and thereby, to the revolutionary element in the tottering feudal society, a rapid development.

The feudal system of industry, under which industrial production was monopolized by close guilds, now no longer sufficed for the growing wants of the new markets. The manufacturing system took its place. The guild masters were pushed on one side by the manufacturing middle class; division of labor between the different corporate guilds vanished in the face of division of labor in each single workshop.

Meantime the markets kept ever growing, the demand ever rising. Even manufacture no longer sufficed. Thereupon steam and machinery revolutionized industrial production. The place of manufacture was taken by the giant, Modern Industry, the place of the industrial middle class, by industrial millionaires, the leaders of whole industrial armies, the modern bourgeois.

Modern industry has established the world's market, for which the discovery of America paved the way. The market has given an immense development to commerce, to navigation, to communication by land. This development has, in its turn, reacted on the extension of industry; and in proportion as industry, commerce, navigation, and railways extended, in the same proportion the bourgeoisie developed, increased its capital, and pushed into the background every class handed down from the Middle Ages.

We see, therefore, how the modern bourgeoisie is itself the product of a long course of development, of a series of revolutions in the modes of production and of exchange.

Each step in the development of the bourgeoisie was accompanied by a corresponding political advance of that class. An oppressed class under the sway of the feudal nobility, an armed and self-governing association in the medieval commune, here independent urban republic (as in Italy and Germany), there taxable "third estate" of the monarchy (as in France), afterwards, in the period of manufacture proper, serving either the semifeudal or the absolute monarchy as a counterpoise against the nobility, and, in fact, cornerstone of the great monarchies in general, the bourgeoisie has at last, since the establishment of modern industry and of the world's market, conquered for itself, in the modern representative state, exclusive political sway. The executive of the modern state is but a committee for managing the common affairs of the whole bourgeoisie.

The bourgeoisie, historically, has played a most revolutionary part.

The bourgeoisie, wherever it has got the upper hand, has put an end to all feudal, patriarchal, idyllic relations. It has pitilessly torn asunder the motley feudal ties that bound man to his "natural superiors," and has left remaining no other nexus between man and man than naked self-interest, callous "cash payment." It has drowned the most heavenly ecstasies of religious fervor, of chivalrous enthusiasm, of philistine sentimentalism, in the icy water of egotistical calculation. It has resolved personal worth into exchange value, and in place of the numberless indefeasible chartered freedoms, has set up that single, unconscionable freedom—Free Trade. In one word, for exploitation, veiled by religious and political illusions, it has substituted naked, shameless, direct, brutal exploitation.

The bourgeoisie has stripped of its halo every occupation hitherto honored and looked up to with reverent awe. It has converted the physician, the lawyer, the priest, the poet, the man of science, into its paid wage laborers.

The bourgeoisie has torn away from the family its sentimental veil, and has reduced the family relation to a mere money relation.

The bourgeoisie has disclosed how it came to pass that the brutal display of vigor in the Middle Ages, which reactionists so much admire, found its fitting complement in the most slothful indolence. It has been the first to show what man's activity can bring about. It has accomplished wonders far surpassing Egyptian pyramids, Roman aqueducts, and Gothic cathedrals; it has conducted expeditions that put in the shade all former exoduses of nations and crusades.

The bourgeoisie cannot exist without constantly revolutionizing the instruments of production, and thereby the relations of production, and with them the whole relations of society. Conservation of the old modes of production in unaltered forms, was, on the contrary, the first condition of existence for all earlier industrial classes. Constant revolutionizing of production, uninterrupted disturbance of all social conditions, everlasting uncertainty and agitation, distinguish the bourgeois epoch from all earlier ones. All fixed, fast-frozen relations, with their train of ancient and venerable prejudices and opinions, are swept away; all new-formed ones become antiquated before they can ossify. All that is solid melts into air, all that is holy is profaned, and man is at last compelled to face with sober senses his real conditions of life and his relations with his kind.

The need of a constantly expanding market for its products chases the bourgeoisie over the whole surface of the globe. It must nestle everywhere, settle everywhere, establish connections everywhere.

The bourgeoisie has through its exploitation of the world's market given a cosmopolitan character to production and consumption in every country. To the great chagrin of reactionists, it has drawn from under the feet of industry the national ground on which it stood. All old-established national industries have been destroyed or are daily being destroyed. They are dislodged by new industries, whose introduction becomes a life and death question for all civilized nations, by industries that no longer work up indigenous raw material, but raw material drawn from the remotest zones, industries whose products are consumed, not only at home, but in every quarter of the globe. In place of the old wants, satisfied by the productions of the country, we find new wants, requiring for this satisfaction the products of distant lands and climes. In place of the old local and national seclusion and self-sufficiency, we have intercourse in every direction, universal interdependence of nations. And as in material, so also in intellectual production. The intellectual creations of individual nations become common property. National one-sidedness and narrow-mindedness become more and more impossible, and from the numerous national and local literatures, there arises a world literature.

The bourgeoisie, by the rapid improvement of all instruments of production, by the immensely facilitated means of communication, draws all, even the most barbarian, nations into civilization. The cheap prices of its commodities are the heavy artillery with which it batters down all Chinese walls, with which it forces the barbarians' intensely obstinate hatred of foreigners to capitulate. It compels all nations, on pain of extinction, to adopt the bourgeois mode of production; it compels them to introduce what it calls civilization into their midst, *i.e.*, to become bourgeois themselves. In one word, it creates a world after its own image.

The bourgeoisie has subjected the country to the rule of the towns. It has created enormous cities, has greatly increased the urban population as compared with the rural, and has thus rescued a considerable part of the population from the idiocy of rural life. Just as it has made the country dependent on the towns, so it has made barbarian and semibarbarian countries dependent on the civilized ones, nations of peasants on nations of bourgeois, the East on the West.

The bourgeoisie keeps more and more doing away with the scattered state of the population, of the means of production, and of property. It has agglomerated population, centralized means of production, and has concentrated property in a few hands. The necessary consequence of this was political centralization. Independent, or but loosely connected provinces, with separate interests, laws, governments and systems of taxation, became lumped together into one nation, with one government, one code of laws, one national class interest, one frontier, and one customs tariff.

The bourgeoisie, during its rule of scarce one hundred years, has created more massive and more colossal productive forces than have all preceding generations together. Subjection of nature's forces to man, machinery, application of chemistry to industry and agriculture, steam navigation, railways, electric telegraphs, clearing of whole continents for cultivation, canalization of rivers, whole populations conjured out of the ground—what earlier century had even a presentiment that such productive forces slumbered in the lap of social labor?

We see then: the means of production and of exchange on whose foundation the bourgeoisie built itself up, were generated in feudal society. At a certain stage in the development of these means of production and of exchange, the conditions under which feudal society produced and exchanged, the feudal organization of agriculture and manufacturing industry, in one word, the feudal relations of property, became no longer compatible with the already developed productive forces; they became so many fetters. They had to be burst asunder.

Into their place stepped free competition, accompanied by a social and political constitution adapted to it, and by the economical and political sway of the bourgeois class.

A similar movement is going on before our own eyes. Modern bourgeois society with its relations of production, of exchange, and of property, a society that has conjured up such gigantic means of production and of exchange, is like the sorcerer, who is no longer able to control the powers of the nether world whom he has called up by his spells. For many a decade past the history of industry and commerce is but the history of the revolt of modern productive forces against modern conditions of production, against the property relations that are the conditions for the existence of the bourgeoisie and of its rule. It is enough to mention the commercial crises that by their periodical return put on its trial, each time more threateningly, the existence of the bourgeois society. In these crises a great part not only of the existing products, but also of the previously created productive forces, is periodically destroyed. In these crises there breaks out an epidemic that, in all earlier epochs, would have seemed an absurdity—the epidemic of overproduction. Society suddenly finds itself put back into a state of momentary barbarism; it appears as if a famine, a universal war of devastation had cut off the supply of every means of subsistence; industry and commerce seem to be destroyed; and why? because there is too much civilization, too much means of subsistence, too much industry, too much commerce. The productive forces at the disposal of society no longer tend to further the development of the conditions of bourgeois property; on the contrary, they have become too powerful for these conditions, by which they are fettered, and so soon as they overcome these fetters, they bring disorder into the whole of bourgeois society, endanger the existence of bourgeois property. The conditions of bourgeois society are too narrow to comprise the wealth created by them. And how does the bourgeoisie get over these crises? On the one hand by enforced destruction of a mass of productive forces; on the other, by the conquest of new markets, and by the more thorough exploitation of the old ones. That is to say, by paving the way for more extensive and more destructive crises, and by diminishing the means whereby crises are prevented.

The weapons with which the bourgeoisie felled feudalism to the ground are now turned against the bourgeoisie itself.

But not only has the bourgeoisie forged the weapons that bring death to itself; it has also called into existence the men who are to wield those weapons—the modern working class—the proletarians.

In proportion as the bourgeoisie, *i.e.,* capital, is developed, in the same proportion is the proletariat, the modern working class, developed; a class of laborers, who live only so long as they find work, and who find work only so long as their labor increases capital. These laborers, who must sell themselves piecemeal, are a commodity, like every other article of commerce, and are consequently exposed to all the vicissitudes of competition, to all the fluctuations of the market.

Owing to the extensive use of machinery and to division of labor, the work of the proletarians has lost all individual character, and, consequently, all charm for the workman. He becomes an appendage of the machine, and it is only the most simple, most monotonous, and most easily acquired knack, that is required of him. Hence, the cost of production of a workman is restricted almost entirely to the means of subsistence that he requires for his maintenance, and for the propagation of his race. But the price of a commodity, and therefore also of labor, is equal, in the long run, to its cost of production. In proportion, therefore, as the repulsiveness of the work increases, the wage decreases. Nay, more, in proportion as the use of machinery and division of labor increase, in the same proportion the burden of toil also increases, whether by prolongation of the working hours, by increase of the work exacted in a given time, or by increased speed of the machinery, etc. . . .

No sooner is the exploitation of the laborer by the manufacturer so far at an end that he receives his wages in cash, than he is set upon by the other portions of the bourgeoisie, the landlord, the shopkeeper, the pawnbroker, etc.

The lower strata of the middle class—the small tradespeople, shopkeepers, and retired tradesmen generally, the handicraftsmen, and peasants—all these sink gradually into the proletariat, partly because their diminutive capital does not suffice for the scale on which modern industry is carried on, and is swamped in the competition with the large capitalists, partly because their specialized skill is rendered worthless by new methods of production. Thus the proletariat is recruited from all classes of the population.

The proletariat goes through various stages of development. With its birth begins its struggle with the bourgeoisie. At first the contest is carried on by individual laborers, then by the workpeople of a factory, then by the operatives of one trade, in one locality, against the individual bourgeois who directly exploits them. They direct their attacks not against the bourgeois conditions of production, but against the instruments of production themselves; they destroy imported wares that compete with their labor, they smash to pieces machinery, they set factories ablaze, they seek to restore by force the vanished status of the workman of the Middle Ages.

At this stage the laborers still form an incoherent mass scattered over the whole country, and broken up by their mutual competition. If anywhere they unite to form more compact bodies, this is not yet the consequence of their own active union, but of the union of the bourgeoisie, which class, in order to attain its own political ends, is compelled to set the whole proletariat in motion, and is moreover yet, for a time, able to do so. At this stage, therefore, the proletarians do not fight their enemies, but the enemies of their enemies, the remnants of absolute monarchy, and land owners, the nonindustrial bourgeois, the petty bourgeoisie. Thus the whole historical movement is concentrated in the hands of the bourgeoisie; every victory so obtained is a victory for the bourgeoisie.

But with the development of industry the pro-

letariat not only increases in number; it becomes concentrated in greater masses, its strength grows and it feels that strength more. The various interests and conditions of life within the ranks of the proletariat are more and more equalized, in proportion as machinery obliterates all distinctions of labor, and nearly everywhere reduces wages to the same low level. The growing competition among the bourgeois, and the resulting commercial crises, make the wages of the workers ever more fluctuating. The unceasing improvement of machinery, ever more rapidly developing, makes their livelihood more and more precarious; the collisions between individual workman and individual bourgeois take more and more the character of collisions between two classes. Thereupon the workers begin to form combinations (trades' unions) against the bourgeois; they club together in order to keep up the rate of wages; they found permanent associations in order to make provision beforehand for these occasional revolts. Here and there the contest breaks out into riots.

Now and then the workers are victorious, but only for a time. The real fruit of their battles lies not in the immediate result but in the ever expanding union of the workers. This union is furthered by the improved means of communication that are created in modern industry and that place the workers of different localities in contact with one another. It was just this contact that was needed to centralize the numerous local struggles, all of the same character, into one national struggle between classes. But every class struggle is a political struggle. And that union, to attain which the burghers of the Middle Ages, with their miserable highways, required centuries, the modern proletarians, thanks to railways, achieve in a few years.

This organization of the proletarians into a class and consequently into a political party, is continually being upset again by the competition between the workers themselves. But it ever rises up again; stronger, firmer, mightier. It compels legislative recognition of particular interests of the workers, by taking advantage of the divisions among the bourgeoisie itself. Thus the Ten Hours' Bill in England was carried.

Altogether collisions between the classes of the old society further, in many ways, the course of the development of the proletariat. The bourgeoisie finds itself involved in a constant battle. At first with the aristocracy; later on, with those portions of the bourgeoisie itself whose interests have become antagonistic to the progress of industry; at all times with the bourgeoisie of foreign countries. In all these countries it sees itself compelled to appeal to the proletariat, to ask for its help, and thus to drag it into the political arena. The bourgeoisie itself, therefore, supplies the proletariat with weapons for fighting the bourgeoisie.

Further, as we have already seen, entire sections of the ruling classes are, by the advance of industry, precipitated into the proletariat, or are at least threatened in their conditions of existence. These also supply the proletariat with fresh elements of enlightenment and progress.

Finally, in times when the class struggle nears the decisive hour, the process of dissolution going on within the ruling class, in fact within the whole range of old society, assumes such a violent, glaring character, that a small section of the ruling class cuts itself adrift, and joins the revolutionary class; the class that holds the future in its hands. Just as, therefore, at an earlier period, a section of the nobility went over to the bourgeoisie, so now a portion of the bourgeoisie goes over to the proletariat, and in particular, a portion of the bourgeois ideologists, who have raised themselves to the level of comprehending theoretically the historical movement as a whole.

Of all the classes that stand face to face with the bourgeoisie today, the proletariat alone is a really revolutionary class. The other classes decay and finally disappear in the face of modern industry; the proletariat is its special and essential product. . . .

In the conditions of the proletariat, those of old society at large are already virtually swamped. The proletarian is without property; his relation to his wife and children has no longer anything in common with the bourgeois family relations; modern industrial labor, modern subjection to capital, the same in England as in France, in America as in Germany, has stripped him of every trace of national character. Law, morality, religion, are to him so many bourgeois prejudices, behind which lurk in ambush just as many bourgeois interests.

All the preceding classes that got the upper hand sought to fortify their already acquired status by subjecting society at large to their conditions of appropriation. The proletarians cannot become masters of the productive forces of society, except by abolishing their own previous mode of appropriation, and thereby also every other previous mode of appropriation. They have nothing of their own to secure and to fortify; their mission is to destroy all previous securities for, and insurances of, individual property.

All previous historical movements were movements of minorities, or in the interest of minorities. The proletarian movement is the self-conscious, independent movement of the immense majority, in the interest of the immense majority. The proletariat, the lowest stratum of our present society, cannot stir, cannot raise itself up, without the whole superincumbent strata of official society being sprung into the air.

Though not in substance, yet in form, the struggle of the proletariat with the bourgeoisie is at first a national struggle. The proletariat of each country must, of course, first of all settle matters with its own bourgeoisie.

In depicting the most general phases of the development of the proletariat, we traced the more or less veiled civil war, raging within existing society, up to the point where that war breaks out into open revolution, and where the violent overthrow of the bourgeoisie lays the foundation for the sway of the proletariat.

Hitherto every form of society has been based, as we have already seen, on the antagonism of oppressing and oppressed classes. But in order to oppress a class certain conditions must be assured to it under which it can, at least, continue its slavish existence. The serf, in the period of serfdom, raised himself to membership in the commune, just as the petty bourgeois, under the yoke of feudal absolutism, managed to develop into a bourgeois. The modern laborer, on the contrary, instead of rising with the progress of industry, sinks deeper and deeper below the conditions of existence of his own class. He becomes a pauper, and pauperism develops more rapidly than population and wealth. And here it becomes evident that the bourgeoisie is unfit any longer to be the ruling class in society and to impose its conditions of existence upon society as an overriding law. It is unfit to rule because it is incompetent to assure an existence to its slave within his slavery, because it cannot help letting him sink into such a state that it has to feed him instead of being fed by him. Society can no longer live under this bourgeoisie; in other words, its existence is no longer compatible with society.

The essential condition for the existence, and for the sway of the bourgeois class is the formation and augmentation of capital; the condition for capital is wage-labor. Wage-labor rests exclusively on competition between the laborers. The advance of industry, whose involuntary promoter is the bourgeoisie, replaces the isolation of the laborers, due to competition, by their revolutionary combination, due to association. The development of modern industry, therefore, cuts from under its feet the very foundation on which the bourgeoisie produces and appropriates products. What the bourgeoisie therefore produces, above all, are its own grave diggers. Its fall and the victory of the proletariat are equally inevitable.

II: Proletarians and Communists

In what relation do the communists stand to the proletarians as a whole?

The communists do not form a separate party opposed to other working-class parties.

They have no interests separate and apart from those of the proletariat as a whole.

They do not set up any sectarian principles of their own by which to shape and mold the proletarian movement.

The communists are distinguished from the other working-class parties by this only: 1. In the national struggles of the proletarians of the different countries, they point out and bring to the front the common interests of the entire proletariat, independently of all nationality. 2. In the various stages of development which the struggle of the working class against the bourgeoisie has to pass through, they always and everywhere represent the interests of the movement as a whole.

The communists, therefore, are on the one hand, practically, the most advanced and resolute section of the working-class parties of every country, that section which pushes forward all others; on the other hand, theoretically, they have over the great mass of the proletariat the advantage of clearly understanding the line of march, the conditions, and the ultimate general results of the proletarian movement.

The immediate aim of the communists is the same as that of all the other proletarian parties: formation of the proletariat into a class, overthrow of the bourgeois supremacy, conquest of political power by the proletariat.

The theoretical conclusions of the communists are in no way based on ideas or principles that have been invented, or discovered, by this or that would-be universal reformer.

They merely express, in general terms, actual relations springing from an existing class struggle, from a historical movement going on under our very eyes. The abolition of existing property relations is not at all a distinctive feature of communism.

All property relations in the past have continually been subject to historical change, consequent upon the change in historical conditions.

The French Revolution, for example, abolished feudal property in favor of bourgeois property.

The distinguishing feature of communism is not the abolition of property generally, but the abolition of bourgeois private property. But modern bourgeois private property is the final and most complete expression of the system of producing and appropriating products, that is based on class antagonisms, on the exploitation of the many by the few.

In this sense the theory of the communists may be summed up in the single sentence: abolition of private property.

We communists have been reproached with the desire of abolishing the right of personally acquiring property as the fruit of a man's own labor, which property is alleged to be the ground work of all personal freedom, activity, and independence.

Hard-won, self-acquired, self-earned property! Do you mean the property of the petty artisan and of the small peasant, a form of property that preceded the bourgeois form? There is no need to abolish that; the development of industry has to a great extent already destroyed it, and is still destroying it daily.

Or do you mean modern bourgeois private property?

But does wage-labor create any property for the laborer? Not a bit. It creates capital, *i.e.,* that kind of property which exploits wage-labor, and which cannot increase except upon condition of begetting a new supply of wage-labor for fresh exploitation. Property, in its present form, is based on the antagonism of capital and wage-labor. Let us examine both sides of this antagonism.

To be a capitalist, is to have not only a purely personal, but a social *status* in production. Capital is a collective product, and only by the united action of many members, nay, in the last resort, only by the united action of all members of society, can it be set in motion.

Capital is therefore not a personal, it is a social power.

When, therefore, capital is converted into common property, into the property of all members of society, personal property is not thereby transformed into social property. It is only the social character of the property that is changed. It loses its class character.

Let us now take wage-labor.

The average price of wage-labor is the minimum wage, *i.e.,* that quantum of the means of subsistence, which is absolutely requisite to keep the laborer in bare existence as a laborer. What, therefore, the wage-laborer appropriates by means of his labor, merely suffices to prolong and reproduce a bare existence. We by no means intend to abolish this personal appropriation of the products of labor, an appropriation that is made for the maintenance and reproduction of human life, and that leaves no surplus wherewith to command the labor of others. All that we want to do away with, is the miserable character of this appropriation, under which the laborer lives merely to increase capital, and is allowed to live only in so far as the interest of the ruling class requires it.

In bourgeois society living labor is but a means to increase accumulated labor. In communist society accumulated labor is but a means to widen, to enrich, to promote the existence of the laborer.

In bourgeois society, therefore, the past dominates the present; in communist society, the present dominates the past. In bourgeois society capital is independent and has individuality, while the living person is dependent and has no individuality.

And the abolition of this state of things is called by the bourgeois: abolition of individuality and freedom! And rightly so. The abolition of bourgeois individuality, bourgeois independence, and bourgeois freedom is undoubtedly aimed at.

By freedom is meant, under the present bourgeois conditions of production, free trade, free selling and buying.

But if selling and buying disappears, free selling and buying disappears also. This talk about free selling and buying, and all the other "brave words" of our bourgeoisie about freedom in general, have a meaning, if any, only in contrast with restricted selling and buying, with the fettered traders of the Middle Ages, but have no meaning when opposed to the communistic abolition of buying and selling, of the bourgeois conditions of production, and of the bourgeoisie itself.

You are horrified at our intending to do away with private property. But in your existing society private property is already done away with for nine tenths of the population; its existence for the few is solely due to its nonexistence in the hands of those nine tenths. You reproach us, therefore, with intending to do away with a form of property, the necessary condition for whose existence is the nonexistence of any property for the immense majority of society.

In one word, you reproach us with intending to do away with your property. Precisely so: that is just what we intend.

From the moment when labor can no longer be converted into capital, money, or rent, into a social power capable of being monopolized, *i.e.*, from the moment when individual property can no longer be transformed into bourgeois property, into capital, from that moment, you say, individuality vanishes!

You must, therefore, confess that by "individual" you mean no other person than the bourgeois, than the middle-class owner of property. This person must, indeed, be swept out of the way, and made impossible.

Communism deprives no man of the power to appropriate the products of society: all that it does is to deprive him of the power to subjugate the labor of others by means of such appropriation.

It has been objected, that upon the abolition of private property all work will cease, and universal laziness will overtake us.

According to this, bourgeois society ought long ago to have gone to the dogs through sheer idleness; for those of its members who work, acquire nothing, and those who acquire anything, do not work. The whole of this objection is but another expression of tautology, that there can no longer be any wage-labor when there is no longer any capital.

All objections against the communistic mode of producing and appropriating material products, have, in the same way, been urged against the communistic modes of producing and appropriating intellectual products. Just as to the bourgeois the disappearance of class property is the disappearance of production itself, so the disappearance of class culture is to him identical with the disappearance of all culture.

That culture, the loss of which he laments, is, for the enormous majority, a mere training to act as a machine.

But don't wrangle with us so long as you apply to our intended abolition of bourgeois property, the standard of your bourgeois notions of freedom, culture, law, etc. Your very ideas are but the outgrowth of the conditions of your bourgeois production and bourgeois property, just as your jurisprudence is but the will of your class made into a law for all, a will, whose essential character and direction are determined by the economical conditions of existence of your class.

The selfish misconception that induces you to transform into eternal laws of nature and of reason, the social forms springing from your present mode of production and form of property—historical relations that rise and disappear in the progress of production—the misconception you share with every ruling class that has preceded you. What you see clearly in the case of ancient property, what you admit in the case of feudal property, you are of course forbidden to admit in the case of your own bourgeois form of property. . . .

The communists are further reproached with desiring to abolish countries and nationality.

The workingmen have no country. We cannot take from them what they have not got. Since the proletariat must first of all acquire political supremacy, must rise to be the leading class of the nation, must constitute itself *the* nation, it is, so far, itself national, though not in the bourgeois sense of the word.

National differences and antagonisms between peoples are daily more and more vanishing, owing to the development of the bourgeoisie, to freedom of commerce, to the world's market, to uniformity in the mode of production and in the conditions of life corresponding thereto.

The supremacy of the proletariat will cause them to vanish still faster. United action, of the leading civilized countries at least, is one of the first conditions for the emancipation of the proletariat.

In proportion as the exploitation of one individual by another is put an end to, the exploitation of one nation by another will also be put an end to. In proportion as the antagonism between classes within the nation vanishes, the hostility of one nation to another will come to an end.

The charges against communism made from a religious, a philosophical, and, generally, from an ideological standpoint are not deserving of serious examination.

Does it require deep intuition to comprehend that man's ideas, views, and conceptions, in one word, man's consciousness changes with every change in the conditions of his material existence, in his social relations, and in his social life?

What else does the history of ideas prove, than that intellectual production changes its character in proportion as material production is changed? The ruling ideas of each age have ever been the ideas of its ruling class.

When people speak of ideas that revolutionize society they do but express the fact that within the old society the elements of a new one have been created, and that the dissolution of the old ideas keeps even pace with the dissolution of the old conditions of existence.

When the ancient world was in its last throes the ancient religions were overcome by Christianity. When Christian ideas succumbed in the eighteenth century to rationalist ideas, feudal society fought its death battle with the then revolutionary bourgeoisie. The ideas of religious liberty and freedom of conscience merely gave expression to the sway of free competition within the domain of knowledge.

"Undoubtedly," it will be said, "religious, moral, philosophical, and juridical ideas have been modified in the course of historical development. But religion, morality, philosophy, political science, and law, constantly survived this change.

"There are besides, eternal truths, such as Freedom, Justice, etc., that are common to all states of society. But communism abolishes eternal truths, it abolishes all religion and all morality, instead of constituting them on a new basis; it therefore acts in contradiction to all past historical experience."

What does this accusation reduce itself to? The history of all past society has consisted in the development of class antagonisms, antagonisms that assumed different forms at different epochs.

But whatever form they may have taken, one fact is common to all past ages, viz., the exploitation of one part of society by the other. No wonder, then, that the social consciousness of past ages, despite all the multiplicity and variety it displays, moves within certain common forms, or general ideas, which cannot completely vanish except with the total disappearance of class antagonisms.

The communist revolution is the most radical rupture with traditional property relations; no wonder that its development involves the most radical rupture with traditional ideas.

But let us have done with the bourgeois objections to communism.

We have seen above that the first step in the revolution by the working class is to raise the proletariat to the position of the ruling class; to win the battle of democracy.

The proletariat will use its political supremacy to wrest, by degrees, all capital from the bourgeoisie; to centralize all instruments of production in the hands of the state, *i.e.,* of the proletariat organized as the ruling class; and to increase the total of productive forces as rapidly as possible.

Of course, in the beginning this cannot be effected except by means of despotic inroads on the rights of property and on the conditions of bourgeois production; by means of measures, therefore, which appear economically insufficient and untenable, but which, in the course of the movement, outstrip themselves, necessitate further inroads upon the old social order and are unavoidable as a means of entirely revolutionizing the mode of production.

These measures will, of course, be different in different countries.

Nevertheless in the most advanced countries the following will be pretty generally applicable:

1. Abolition of property in land and application of all rents of land to public purposes.

2. A heavy progressive or graduated income tax.

3. Abolition of all right of inheritance.

4. Confiscation of the property of all emigrants and rebels.

5. Centralization of credit in the hands of the state, by means of a national bank with state capital and an exclusive monopoly.

6. Centralization of the means of communication and transport in the hands of the state.

7. Extension of factories and instruments of production owned by the state; the bringing into cultivation of waste lands, and the improvement of the soil generally in accordance with a common plan.

8. Equal liability of all to labor. Establishment of industrial armies, especially for agriculture.

9. Combination of agriculture with manufacturing industries: gradual abolition of the dis-

tinction between town and country, by a more equable distribution of the population over the country.

10. Free education for all children in public schools. Abolition of children's factory labor in its present form. Combination of education with industrial production, etc., etc.

When, in the course of development, class distinctions have disappeared and all production has been concentrated in the hands of a vast association of the whole nation, the public power will lose its political character. Political power, properly so called, is merely the organized power of one class for oppressing another. If the proletariat during its contest with the bourgeoisie is compelled, by the force of circumstances, to organize itself as a class, if, by means of a revolution, it makes itself the ruling class, and, as such, sweeps away by force the old conditions of production then it will, along with these conditions, have swept away the conditions for the existence of class antagonisms, and of classes generally, and will thereby have abolished its own supremacy as a class.

In place of the old bourgeois society with its classes and class antagonisms we shall have an association in which the free development of each is the condition for the free development of all. . . .

IV: Position of the Communists in Relation to the Various Existing Opposition Parties

Section II has made clear the relations of the communists to the existing working-class parties, such as the Chartists in England and the Agrarian Reformers in America.

The communists fight for the attainment of the immediate aims, for the enforcement of the momentary interests of the working class; but in the movement of the present, they also represent and take care of the future of that movement. In France the Communists ally themselves with the Social-Democrats, against the conservative and radical bourgeoisie, reserving, however, the right to take up a critical position in regard to phrases and illusions traditionally handed down from the great Revolution.

In Switzerland they support the Radicals, without losing sight of the fact that this party consists of antagonistic elements, partly of Democratic Socialists, in the French sense, partly of radical bourgeois.

In Poland they support the party that insists on an agrarian revolution as the prime condition for national emancipation, that party which fomented the insurrection of Cracow in 1846.

In Germany they fight with the bourgeoisie whenever it acts in a revolutionary way against the absolute monarchy, the feudal squirearchy, and the petty bourgeoisie.

But they never cease, for a single instant, to instill into the working class the clearest possible recognition of the hostile antagonism between bourgeoisie and proletariat, in order that the German workers may straightway use, as so many weapons against the bourgeoisie, the social and political conditions that the bourgeoisie must necessarily introduce along with its supremacy, and in order that, after the fall of the reactionary classes in Germany, the fight against the bourgeoisie itself may immediately begin.

The communists turn their attention chiefly to Germany, because that country is on the eve of a bourgeois revolution that is bound to be carried out under more advanced conditions of European civilization, and with a much more developed proletariat, than that of England was in the seventeenth, and of France in the eighteenth century, and because the bourgeois revolution in Germany will be but the prelude to an immediately following proletarian revolution.

In short, the communists everywhere support every revolutionary movement against the existing social and political order of things.

In all these movements they bring to the front, as the leading question in each, the property question, no matter what its degree of development at the time.

Finally, they labor everywhere for the union and agreement of the democratic parties of all countries.

The communists disdain to conceal their views and aims. They openly declare that their ends can be attained only by the forcible overthrow of all existing social conditions. Let the ruling classes tremble at a communistic revolution. The proletarians have nothing to lose but their chains. They have a world to win.

Workingmen of all countries, unite!

C.   BÜCHNER AND MATERIALISM

One of the earliest and most successful popularizations of the new scientific conclusions was *Force and Matter: Empirico-Philosophical Studies Intelligibly Rendered*, published in 1855 by the German physician, Ludwig Büchner (1824–99). This book caused Büchner's dismissal from the University of Tübingen, but it nevertheless received a wide audience, going through twenty-one German editions and later being translated into English.

The success of his book launched Büchner on a life-long career as publicist and agitator in what the Germans called "the battle of materialism." Selections from *Force and Matter* follow.[8]

Force and Matter

No force without matter—no matter without force! Neither can be thought of *per se;* separated, they become empty abstractions. Imagine matter without force, and the minute particles of which a body consists, without that system of mutual attraction and repulsion which holds them together and gives form and shape to the body; imagine the molecular forces of cohesion and affinity removed, what then would be the consequence? The matter must instantly break up into a shapeless nothing. We know in the physical world of no instance of any particle of matter which is not endowed with forces, by means of which it plays its appointed part in some form or another, sometimes in connection with similar or with dissimilar particles. Nor are we in imagination capable of forming a conception of matter without force. . . . Force without matter is equally an idle notion. It being a law admitting of no exception that force can only be manifested in matter, it follows that force can as little possess a separate existence as matter without force. . . .

What are the philosophical consequences of this simple and natural truth?

That those who talk of a creative power, which is said to have produced the world out of itself, or out of nothing, are ignorant of the first and most simple principle, founded upon experience and the contemplation of nature. How could a power have existed not manifested in material substance, but governing it arbitrarily according to individual views? Neither could separately existing forces be transferred to chaotic matter and produce the world in this manner; for we have seen that a separate existence of either is an impossibility. It will be shown in the chapter which treats of the imperishability of matter that the world could not have originated out of nothing. A nothing is not merely a logical but also an empirical nonentity. The world, or matter with its properties which we term forces, must have existed from eternity and must last for ever—in one word, the world cannot have been created. The notion "eternal" is certainly one which, with our limited faculties, is difficult of conception. The facts, nevertheless, leave no doubt as to the eternity of the world. . . .

Immortality of Matter

Matter is immortal, indestructible. There is not an atom in the universe which can be lost. We cannot, even in thought, remove or add an atom without admitting that the world would thereby be disturbed and the laws of gravitation and the equilibrium of matter interfered with. It is the great merit of modern chemistry to have proved in the most convincing manner that the uninterrupted change of matter which we daily witness, the origin and decay of organic and inorganic forms and tissues, do not arise, as was hitherto believed, from new materials, but that this change consists in nothing else but the constant and continuous metamorphosis of the same elementary principles, the quantity and quality of which ever is, and ever remains, the same. Matter has, by means of the scales, been followed in all its various and complicated transitions, and everywhere has it been found to emerge from any combination in the same quantity as it has entered. The calculations founded upon this law have everywhere proved to be perfectly correct. . . .

How can anyone deny the axiom that out of nothing, nothing can arise? The matter must be in existence, though previously in another form and combination, to produce or to share in any new formation. An atom of oxygen, of nitrogen, or of iron, is everywhere and under all circumstances the same thing, endowed with the same immanent qualities, and can never in all eternity become anything else. Be it wheresoever it will, it must remain the same; from every combination, however heterogeneous, must it emerge the self-same atom. But never can an atom arise anew or disappear: it can only change its combinations. For these reasons is matter immortal: and for this reason is it, as already shown, impossible that the world can have been created. How could any thing be created that cannot be annihilated? . . .

There exists a phrase, repeated *ad nauseam,* of "mortal body and immortal spirit." A closer examination causes us with more truth to reverse the sentence. The body is certainly mortal in its individual form, but not in its constituents. It changes not merely in death, but, as we have seen, also during life: however, in a higher sense it is immortal, since the smallest particle of which it is composed cannot be destroyed. On the contrary, that which we call "spirit" disappears with the dissolution of the individual material combination; and it must appear to any unprejudiced intellect as if the concurrent action of many particles of matter had produced an effect which ceases with the cause.

Dignity of Matter

To despise matter and our own body, because it is material—to consider nature and the world as dust which we must endeavor to shake off— nay, to torment our own body, can only arise from a confusion of notions, the result of ignorance or fanaticism. Different feelings animate him who has, with the eyes of an observer, followed matter in its recondite gyrations, who has marked its various and manifold phenomena. He has learned that matter is not inferior to but the peer of spirit; that one cannot exist without the other; and that matter is the vehicle of all mental power, of all human and earthly greatness. We may, perhaps, share with one of our greatest naturalists his enthusiasm for matter, "the veneration of which formerly called forth an accusation." Whoever degrades matter, degrades himself; who abuses his body, abuses his mind and injures himself to the same degree as, in his foolish imagination, he believed to have profited his soul. We frequently hear those persons contemptuously called materialists, who do not share the fashionable contempt for matter but endeavor to fathom by its means the powers and laws of existence; who have discerned that spirit could not have built the world out of itself, and that it is impossible to arrive at a just conception of the world without an exact knowledge of matter and its laws. In this sense, the name of materialist can nowadays be only a title of honor. It is to materialists that we owe the conquest over matter and a knowledge of its laws, so that, almost released from the chains of gravitation, we fly with the swiftness of the wind across the plain and are enabled to communicate, with the celerity of thought, with the most distant parts of the globe. Malevolence is silenced by such facts; and the times are past in which a world, produced by a deceitful fancy, was considered of more value than the reality. . . .

Increased knowledge has taught us to have more respect for the matter without and within us. Let us, then, cultivate our body no less than our mind; and let us not forget that they are inseparable, so that which profits the one, profits the other! *Mens sana in corpore sano.*

On the other hand, we must not forget that we are but a vanishing, though necessary, part of the whole, which sooner or later must again be absorbed in the universe. Matter in its totality is the mother, engendering and receiving again all that exists.

Immutability of the Laws of Nature

The laws according to which nature acts, and matter moves, now destroying, now rebuilding, and thus producing the most varied organic and inorganic forms, are eternal and unalterable. An unbending, inexorable necessity governs the mass. "The law of nature," observes Moleschott, "is a stringent expression of necessity." There exists in it neither exception nor limitation, and no imaginable power can disregard this necessity. A stone not supported will in all eternity fall toward the center of the earth; and there never was, and never will be, a command for the sun to stand still. The experience of thousands of years has impressed upon the investigator the firmest conviction of the immutability of the laws of nature, so that there cannot remain the least doubt in respect to this great truth.

Science has gradually taken all the positions of the childish belief of the peoples; it has snatched thunder and lightning from the hands of the gods; the eclipse of the stars, and the stupendous powers of the Titans of the olden time, have been grasped by the fingers of man. That which appeared inexplicable, miraculous, and the work of a supernatural power, has, by the torch of science, proved to be the effect of hitherto unknown natural forces. The power of spirits and gods dissolved in the hands of science. Superstition declined among cultivated nations, and knowledge took its place. We have the fullest right, and are scientifically correct, in asserting there is no such thing as a miracle; everything that happens does so in a natural way—*i.e.,* in a mode determined only by accidental or necessary coalition of existing materials and their immanent natural forces. No revolution on earth or in heaven, however stupendous, could occur in any other manner.

It was no mighty arm reaching down from the ether which raised the mountains, limited the seas, and created man and beast according to pleasure, but it was effected by the same forces which to this day produce hill and dale and living beings; and all this happened according to the strictest necessity. . . .

The fate of man resembles the fate of nature. It is similarly dependent on natural laws, and it obeys without exception the same stringent and inexorable necessity which governs all that exists. It lies in the nature of every living being that it should be born and die; none has ever escaped that law; death is the surest calculation that can be made, and the unavoidable keystone of every individual existence. The supplications of the mother, the tears of the wife, the despair of the husband, cannot stay his hands. "The natural laws," says Vogt, "are rude unbending powers, which have neither morals nor heart." No call can awaken from the sleep of death; no angel can deliver the prisoner from the dungeon; no hand from the clouds reaches bread to the hungry. . . .

Apparent exceptions from the natural order have been called miracles, of which there have been many at all times. Their origin must be ascribed partly to superstition, and partly to that strange longing after what is wonderful and supernatural, peculiar to human nature. It is somewhat difficult for man, however evident the facts, to convince himself of the conformity which surrounds him; it creates in him an oppressive feeling, and the desire never leaves him to discover something which runs counter to this conformity. This desire must have had a larger sphere among savage and ignorant tribes. We should only waste words in our endeavor to prove the natural impossibility of a miracle. No educated, much less a scientific, person, who is convinced of the immutable order of things, can nowadays believe in miracles. . . .

It is not within our province to concern ourselves with those who, in their attempts to explain the secret of existence, turn to faith. We are occupied with the tangible sensible world, and not with that which every individual may imagine to exist.

What this or that man may understand by a governing reason, an absolute power, a universal soul, a personal God, etc., is his own affair. The theologians, with their articles of faith, must be left to themselves; so the naturalists with their science: they both proceed by different routes. The province of faith rests in human dispositions, which are not accessible to science; and even for the conscience of the individual, it does not appear impossible to keep faith and science separate. A respectable naturalist recently gave the ingenuous advice that we should keep two consciences, a scientific and a religious conscience, which for the peace of our mind we should keep perfectly separate, as they cannot be reconciled. This process is now known by the technical expression of "bookkeeping by double entry." We said the advice was ingenuous, because he whose conviction permits him to keep such a conscience by double entry stands in no need of advice.

Periods of the Creation of the Earth

The investigations of geology have thrown a highly interesting and important light on the history of the origin and gradual development of the earth. It was in the rocks and strata of the crust of the earth, and in the organic remains, that geologists read, as in an old chronicle, the history of the earth. In this history they found the plainest indications of several stupendous successive revolutions, now produced by fire, now by water, now by their combined action. These revolutions afforded, by the apparent suddenness and violence of their occurrence, a welcome pretext to orthodoxy to appeal to the existence of supernatural powers, which were to have caused these revolutions in order to render, by gradual transitions, the earth fit for certain purposes. This successive periodical creation is said to have been attended with a successive creation of new

organic beings and species. The Bible, then, was right in relating that God had sent a deluge over the world to destroy a sinful generation. God with His own hands is said to have piled up mountains, planed the sea, created organisms, etc.

All these notions concerning a direct influence of supernatural or inexplicable forces have melted away before the age of modern science. Like astronomy, which with mathematical certainty has measured the spaces of the heavens, so does modern geology, by taking a retrospective view of the millions of years which have passed, lift the veil which has so long concealed the history of the earth and has given rise to all kinds of religious and mysterious dreams. It is now known that there can be no discussion about these periodic creations of the earth of which so much was said, and which to this day an erroneous conception of nature tries to identify with the so-called days of creation of the Bible, but that the whole past of the earth is nothing but an unfolded present.

However probable it may at first sight appear that the changes, the traces of which we find in the crust of the earth, must have resulted from sudden and violent convulsions, closer observation teaches, on the contrary, that the greater portion of these changes is merely the result of a gradual, slow action, continued through immeasurably long periods of time; and that this action may still be observed going on, though on so reduced a scale that the effects do not particularly strike us. "For the earth," says Burmeister, "is solely produced by forces which, with corresponding intensity, are still acting; it has never essentially been subjected to more violent catastrophes; on the other hand, the period of time in which the change was effected is immense, etc. What is really surprising and stupendous in the process of development is the immeasurable time within which it was effected." . . .

We see at present all these slow and local effects, which millions of years have produced in their entirety, and cannot, therefore, divest ourselves of the idea of a direct creative power, whilst we are merely surrounded by the natural effects of natural forces. The whole science of the conditions of development of the earth is, however, the greatest victory over every kind of faith in an extramundane authority. This science, supported by the knowledge of surrounding nature and its governing forces, is enabled to trace the history of what has happened in infinite periods of time with approximating exactness, frequently with certainty. It has proved that everywhere, and at all times, only those materials and natural forces were in activity by which we are at present surrounded. Nowhere was a point reached, when it was necessary to stop scientific investigation and to substitute the influence of unknown forces. Everywhere it was possible to indicate or to conceive the possibility of visible effects from the combination of natural conditions; everywhere existed the same law, and the same matter.

Personal Continuance

A spirit without body is as unimaginable as electricity or magnetism without metallic or other substances on which these forces act. We have equally shown that the animal soul does not come into the world with any innate intuitions, that it does not represent an *ens per se*, but is a product of external influences, without which it would never have been called into existence. In the face of all these facts, unprejudiced philosophy is compelled to reject the idea of an individual immortality and of a personal continuance after death. With the decay and dissolution of its material substratum, through which alone it has acquired a conscious existence and become a person, and upon which it was dependent, the spirit must cease to exist. All knowledge which this being has acquired relates to earthly things; it has become conscious of itself in, with, and by these things; it has become a person by its being opposed against earthly, limited individualities. How can we imagine it to be possible that, torn away from these necessary conditions, this being should continue to exist with self-consciousness and as the same person? It is not reflection but obstinacy, not science but faith, which supports the idea of a personal continuance. . . .

Free Will

Man is a product of nature in body and mind. Hence not merely what he is but also what he does, wills, feels, and thinks depends upon the same natural necessity as the whole structure of the world. Only a superficial observation of human existence could lead to the conclusion that the actions of nations and of individuals were the result of a perfectly free will. A closer inquiry teaches us, on the contrary, that the connection of nature is so essential and necessary, that free will, if it exist, can only have a very limited range; it teaches us to recognize in all these phenomena fixed laws which hitherto were considered as the results of free choice. "Human liberty, of which all boast," says Spinoza, "consists solely in this, that man is conscious of his will, and unconscious of the causes by which it is determined."

That this view is no longer theoretical, but sufficiently established by facts, is chiefly owing to that interesting new science [of] statistics, which exhibits fixed laws in a mass of phenomena that until now were considered to be arbitrary and accidental. The data for this truth are frequently lost in investigating individual phenomena, but taken collectively they exhibit a strict order, inexorably ruling men and humanity. It may, without exaggeration, be stated that at present most physicians and practical psychologists incline to the view in relation to free will that human actions are, in the last instance, dependent upon a fixed necessity, so that in every individual case free choice has only an extremely limited, if any, sphere of action. . . .

The conduct and actions of every individual are dependent upon the character, manners, and modes of thought of the nation to which he belongs. These again are, to a certain extent, the necessary product of external circumstances under which they live and have grown up. . . .

If the nations are thus in the aggregate, in regard to character and history, dependent upon external circumstances, the individual is no less the product of external and internal natural actions, not merely in relation to his physical and moral nature but in his actions. These actions depend necessarily, in the first instance, upon his intellectual individuality. But what is this intellectual individuality which determines man and prescribes to him, in every individual case, his mode of action with such force that there remains for him but a minute space for free choice; what else is it but the necessary product of congenital physical and mental dispositions in connection with education, example, rank, property, sex, nationality, climate, soil, and other circumstances? Man is subject to the same laws as plants and animals. . . .

An unprejudiced study of nature and the world, based upon innumerable facts, shows that the actions of individuals and of men in general are determined by physical necessities which restrict free will within the narrowest limits. Hence it has been concluded that the partisans of this doctrine denied the discernment of crime and that they desired the acquittal of every criminal, by which the state and society would be thrown into a state of anarchy. We shall presently return to the last reproach which has, by the way, thousands of times been made to natural science; as to the first, it is too absurd to deserve any refutation. No scientific system has rendered the necessity of social and political order more evident than that to which natural science owes its progress, nor has any modern naturalist denied to the state the right of legitimate defense against attacks on the well-being of society. What is true is that the partisans of these modern ideas hold different opinions as regards crime and would banish that cowardly and irreconcilable hatred which the state and society have hitherto cherished with so much hypocrisy as regards the malefactor. Penetrated by such ideas, we cannot help a feeling of commiseration for the offender, whilst we not the less abhor every action calculated to disturb society; a humane sentiment, which gives the preference to preventive measures over punishment. . . .

Concluding Observations

We must finally be permitted to leave all questions about morality and utility out of sight. The chief and indeed the sole object which concerned us in these researches is truth. Nature exists neither for religion, for morality, nor for human beings; but it exists for itself. What else can we do but take it as it is? Would it not be ridiculous in us to cry like little children because our bread is not sufficiently buttered?

Part III.   SCIENCE AND SOCIETY

In the second half of the nineteenth century the natural scientists moved "from small experiments to large conclusions," with thermodynamics, electro-magnetism, organic chemistry, and the theory of evolution, to name only a handful. The impact of these scientific syntheses was immediate but varied. One obvious effect was "the marriage of science and technology," as pure science was put to use in commerce and industry. Another was seen in the widespread scientific materialism of Büchner and others. Probably the most spectacular of the new scientific conclusions was the contribution made to the theory of biological evolution by Charles Robert Darwin (1809–92). Grandson of a noted eighteenth century scientist, Darwin commenced his career as a naturalist aboard the *Beagle* which voyaged from South America through the Pacific and Indian oceans in the years 1831–36. The data he collected in this trip led him to formulate his theory of evolution, but so averse were the scientists of his time to such general "speculations" that Darwin long withheld publication of his ideas. However in 1858 a fellow naturalist, Alfred Russel Wallace (1823–1913), sent Darwin a manuscript containing the identical theory which he had arrived at independently. Wallace and Darwin therefore announced their theory jointly. With his *On the Origin of the Species* (1859), Darwin put out an "imperfect abstract" of his main conclusions: that the old theory of evolution could be proved by inherited variations; that in the struggle for existence adaptability and natural selection determined the vast differences between species and their ultimate survival. Such doctrines, which altered man's whole ideas of the universe were not accepted without a struggle, especially by philosophers and theologians. And while Huxley and the other popularizers of Darwin were carrying the battle to the men of religion, they were also applying these new scientific theories to society and politics. The selections that follow are intended to display something of the impact of science on nineteenth-century thought and society.

A.   Comte and Positivism

Auguste Comte (1798–1857) was born in Montpelier, France, of Catholic royalist parents. By background and early training he reacted against the more individualistic, doctrinaire attitude of the Enlightenment in favor of a more ordered, historically rooted society. Yet he retained the *philosophe's* supreme confidence in progress and was determined to reorganize human society in accordance with a pattern wherein science played an increasingly dominant part. This led him to pioneer in the social sciences with the *System of Positive Philosophy* (6 vols., 1830–42) whose influence was in no way lessened by Comte's recourse in his later works to an elaborately organized religion of humanity as the ultimate capstone of his system. The following selections are from an English translation of the *System* (1856).[9]

In order to understand the true value and character of the Positive Philosophy, we must take a brief general view of the progressive course of the human mind, regarded as a whole; for no conception can be understood otherwise than through its history.

From the study of the development of human intelligence, in all directions, and through all times, the discovery arises of a great fundamental law, to which it is necessarily subject, and which has a solid foundation of proof, both in the facts of our organization and in our historical experience. The law is this: that each of our leading conceptions—each branch of our knowledge—passes successively through three different theoretical conditions: the Theological, or fictitious; the Metaphysical, or abstract; and the Scientific, or positive. In other words, the human mind, by its nature, employs in its progress three methods of philosophizing, the character of which is essentially different, and even radically opposed: viz., the theological method, the metaphysical, and the positive. Hence arise three philosophies, or general systems of conceptions on the aggregate of phenomena, each of which excludes the others. The first is the necessary point of departure of the human understanding; and the third is its fixed and definite state. The second is merely a state of transition.

In the theological state, the human mind, seeking the essential nature of beings, the first and final causes (the origin and purpose) of all effects —in short, Absolute knowledge—supposes all phenomena to be produced by the immediate action of supernatural beings.

In the metaphysical state, which is only a modification of the first, the mind supposes, instead of supernatural beings, abstract forces, veritable entities (that is, personified abstractions) inherent in all beings, and capable of producing all phenomena. What is called the explanation of phenomena is, in this stage, a mere reference of each to its proper entity.

In the final, the positive state, the mind has given over the vain search after Absolute notions, the origin and destination of the universe, and the causes of phenomena, and applies itself to the study of their laws—that is, their invariable relations of succession and resemblance. Reasoning and observation, duly combined, are the means of this knowledge. What is now understood when we speak of an explanation of facts is simply the establishment of a connection between single phenomena and some general facts, the number of which continually diminishes with the progress of science.

The Theological system arrived at the highest perfection of which it is capable when it substituted the providential action of a single Being for the varied operations of the numerous divinities which had been before imagined. In the same way, in the last stage of the Metaphysical system, men substitute one great entity (Nature) as the cause of all phenomena, instead of the multitude of entities at first supposed. In the same way, again, the ultimate perfection of the Positive system would be (if such perfection could be hoped for) to represent all phenomena as particular aspects of a single general fact—such as Gravitation, for instance.

The importance of the working of this general law will be established hereafter. At present, it must suffice to point out some of the grounds of it.

There is no science which, having attained the positive stage, does not bear the marks of having passed through the others. Some time since it was (whatever it might be) composed, as we can now perceive, of metaphysical abstractions; and, further back in the course of time, it took its form from theological conceptions. We shall have only too much occasion to see, as we proceed, that our most advanced sciences still bear very evident marks of the two earlier periods through which they have passed.

The progress of the individual mind is not only an illustration, but an indirect evidence of that of the general mind. The point of departure of the individual and of the race being the same, the phases of the mind of a man correspond to the epochs of the mind of the race. Now, each of us is aware, if he looks back upon his own history, that he was a theologian in his childhood, a metaphysician in his youth, and a natural philosopher in his manhood. All men who are up to their age can verify this for themselves. . . .

Though involved with the physiological, Social phenomena demand a distinct classification, both on account of their importance and of their difficulty. They are the most individual, the most complicated, the most dependent on all others; and therefore they must be the latest—even if they had no special obstacle to encounter. This branch of science has not hitherto entered into the domain of Positive philosophy. Theological and metaphysical methods, exploded in other departments, are as yet exclusively applied, both in the way of inquiry and discussion, in all treatment of Social subjects, though the best minds are heartily weary of eternal disputes about divine right and the sovereignty of the people. This is the great, while it is evidently the only gap which has to be filled, to constitute, solid and entire, the Positive Philosophy. Now that the human mind has grasped celestial and terrestrial physics—mechanical and chemical; organic physics, both vegetable and animal—there remains one science, to fill up the series of sciences of observation—Social physics. . . .

The philosophical principle of the science being that social phenomena are subject to natural laws, admitting of rational prevision, we have to ascertain what is the precise subject, and what the peculiar character of those laws. The distinction between the Statical and Dynamical conditions of the subject must be extended to social science. . . .

The statical study of sociology consists in the

investigation of the laws of action and reaction of the different parts of the social system—apart, for the occasion, from the fundamental movement which is always gradually modifying them. In this view, sociological prevision, founded upon the exact general knowledge of those relations, acts by judging by each other the various statical indications of each mode of social existence, in conformity with direct observation—just as is done daily in the case of anatomy. This view condemns the existing philosophical practice of contemplating social elements separately, as if they had an independent existence; and it leads us to regard them as in mutual relation, and forming a whole which compels us to treat them in combination. By this method, not only are we furnished with the only possible basis for the study of social movement, but we are put in possession of an important aid to direct observation; since many social elements which can not be investigated by immediate observation, may be estimated by their scientific relation to others already known. . . .

It follows from this attribute that there can be no scientific study of society, either in its conditions or its movements, if it is separated into portions, and its divisions are studied apart. . . . Materials may be furnished by the observation of different departments; and such observation may be necessary for that object; but it cannot be called science. The methodical division of studies which takes place in the simple inorganic sciences is thoroughly irrational in the recent and complex science of society, and can produce no results. The day may come when some sort of subdivision may be practicable and desirable; but it is impossible for us now to anticipate what the principle of distribution may be; for the principle itself must arise from the development of the science; and that development can take place not otherwise than by our formation of the science as a whole. The complete body will indicate for itself, at the right season, the particular points which need investigation; and then will be the time for such special study as may be required. By any other method of proceeding, we shall only find ourselves encumbered with special discussions, badly instituted, worse pursued, and accomplishing no other purpose than that of impeding the formation of real science. It is no easy matter to study social phenomena in the only right way—viewing each element in the light of the whole system. It is no easy matter to exercise such vigilance as that no one of the number of contemporary aspects shall be lost sight of. But it is the right and the only way; and we may perceive in it a clear suggestion that this lofty study should be reserved for the highest order of scientific minds, better prepared than others, by wise educational discipline, for sustained speculative efforts, aided by an habitual subordination of the passions to the reason. . . .

Though the statical view of society is the basis of sociology, the dynamical view is not only the more interesting of the two, but the more marked in its philosophical character from its being more distinguished from biology by the master-thought of continuous progress, or rather, of the gradual development of humanity. If I were writing a methodical treatise on political philosophy, it would be necessary to offer a preliminary analysis of the individual impulsions which make up the progressive force of the human race, by referring them to that instinct which results from the concurrence of all our natural tendencies, and which urges man to develop the whole of his life, physical, moral, and intellectual, as far as his circumstances allow. But this view is admitted by all enlightened philosophers; so that I may proceed at once to consider the continuous succession of human development, regarded in the whole race, as if humanity were one. For clearness, we may take advantage of Condorcet's device of supposing a single nation to which we may refer all the consecutive social modifications actually witnessed among distinct peoples. This rational fiction is nearer the reality than we are accustomed to suppose; for in a political view, the true successors of such or such a people are certainly those who, taking up and carrying out their primitive endeavors, have prolonged their social progress, whatever may be the soil which they inhabit, or even the race from which they spring. In brief, it is political continuity which regulates sociological succession, though having a common country must usually affect this continuity in a high degree. As a scientific artifice merely, however, I shall employ this hypothesis, and on the ground of its manifest utility.

The true general spirit of social dynamics then consists in conceiving of each of these consecutive social states as the necessary result of the preceding, and the indispensable move of the following, according to the axiom of Leibnitz—*the present is big with the future*. In this view, the object of science is to discover the laws which govern this continuity, and the aggregate of which determines the course of human development. In short, social dynamics studies the laws of succession, while social statics inquires into those of co-existence; so that the use of the first is to furnish the true theory of progress to political practice, while the second performs the same service in regard to order; and this suitability to the needs of modern society is a strong confirmation of the philosophical character of such a combination. . . .

The ancients used to suppose Order and Progress to be irreconcilable; but both are indispensable conditions in a state of modern civilization; and their combination is at once the grand difficulty and the main resource of every genuine political system. No real order can be established, and still less can it last, if it is not fully compatible with progress: and no great progress can be accomplished if it does not tend to the consolidation of order. Any conception which is so devoted to one of these needs as to prejudice the other, is sure of rejection, sooner or later, as mistaking the nature of the political problem. Therefore, these two conditions, which will be two aspects, constant and inseparable, of the same principles. Throughout the whole range of science, thus far, we have seen that the conditions of combination and of progress are originally identical: and I trust we shall see, after looking into social science in the same way, that the ideas of Order and Progress are in Social Physics, as rigorously inseparable as the ideas of Organization and Life in Biology; from whence, indeed they are, in a scientific view, evidently derived.

The misfortune of our actual state is that the two ideas are set up in radical opposition to each other—the retrograde spirit having directed all efforts in favor of Order, and anarchical doctrine having arrogated to itself the charge of Social Progress; and, in this state of things, the reproaches exchanged between the respective parties are only too well merited by both. In this vicious circle is society now confined; and the only issue from it is by the undisputed preponderance of a doctrine equally progressive and hierarchical . . .

All ideas of order in the political world are derived from the old doctrine of the theological and military system, regarded especially in its catholic and feudal constitution: a doctrine which from our point of view in this work, represents the theological state of social science: and, in the same way, all ideas of progress are still derived from the purely negative philosophy which, issuing from protestantism, assumed its final form and development in the last century, and which, applied to social affairs, constitutes the metaphysical state of politics. The different classes of society range themselves on the one side or the other, according to their inclination for conservatism or amelioration. With every new uprising of a social difficulty, we see the retrograde school proposing, as the only certain and universal remedy, the restoration of the corresponding part of the old political system; and the critical school referring the evil exclusively to the destruction of the old system not being complete. We do not often see the two doctrines presented without modification. They so exist only in purely speculative minds. But when we see them in monstrous alliance, as we do in all degrees of political opinion, we can not but know that such an alliance can not yield any virtue which its elements do not contain, and that it can only exhibit their mutual neutralization. We must here, it is clear, regard the theological and the metaphysical politics separately, in the first place, that we may afterward understand their present antagonism, and form an estimate of the futile combinations into which men have endeavored to force them. . . .

Regarded from the logical point of view, the problem of our social reorganization seems to me reducible to this one condition: to construct rationally a political doctrine which, in the whole of its active development, shall be always fully consequent of its own principles. . . .

B.   SPENCER AND THE PRINCIPLES OF SOCIOLOGY

Born and brought up in the philosophical radical tradition, Herbert Spencer (1820–1903) came to social philosophy after a career as an engineer and much reading in natural science and biology. Though his explanation of adaptation proved less satisfactory than Darwin's, Spencer had independently hit upon the idea of organic evolution and the survival of the fittest. On this scientific foundation was based his extensive work in social and political theory whose influence in the nineteenth century far outweighed their originality. The following selection is from his *Principles of Sociology* (3 vols., 1876–96).[10]

There are two ways in which men's actions, individual or social, may be regarded. We may consider them as groups of phenomena to be analyzed, and the laws of their dependence ascertained; or, considering them as causing pleasures or pains, we may associate with them approbation or reprobation. Dealing with its problems intellectually, we may regard conduct as always the result of certain forces; or, dealing with its problems morally, and recognizing its outcome as in this case good and in that case bad, we may allow now admiration and now indignation to fill our consciousness. Obviously, it must make a great difference in our conclusions whether, as in the one case, we study men's doings as those of alien creatures, which it merely concerns us to understand; or whether, as in the other case, we contemplate them as the doings of creatures like ourselves, with whose lives our own lives are bound up, and whose behaviour arouses in us, directly and sympathetically, feelings of love or hate.

Instead of passing over as of no account, or else regarding as purely mischievous, the superstitions of the primitive man, we must inquire what part they play in social evolution; and must be prepared, if need be, to recognize their usefulness. Already we have seen that the belief which prompts the savage to bury valuables with the corpse and carry food to the grave, has a natural genesis; that the propitiation of plants and animals, and the "worship of stocks and stones," are not gratuitous absurdities; and that slaves are sacrificed at funerals in pursuance of an idea which seems rational to uninstructed intelligence. Presently we shall have to consider in what way the ghost-theory has operated politically; and if we should find reason to conclude that it has been an indispensable aid to political progress, we must be ready to accept the conclusion.

Knowledge of the miseries which have for countless ages been everywhere caused by the antagonisms of societies, must not prevent us from recognizing the all-important part these antagonisms have played in civilization. Shudder as we must at the cannibalism which all over the world in early days was a sequence of war—shrink as we may from the thought of those immolations of prisoners which have, tens of thousands of times, followed battles between wild tribes—read as we do with horror of the pyramids of heads and the whitening bones of slain peoples left by barbarian invaders—hate, as we ought, the militant spirit which is even now among ourselves prompting base treacheries and brutal aggressions; we must not let our feelings blind us to the proofs that inter-social conflicts have furthered the development of social structures.

Moreover, dislikes to governments of certain kinds must not prevent us from seeing their fitness to their circumstances. Though, rejecting the common idea of glory, and declining to join soldiers and school boys in applying the epithet "great" to conquering despots, we detest despotism—though we regard their sacrifices of their own peoples and of alien peoples in pursuit of universal dominion as gigantic crimes; we must yet recognize the benefits occasionally arising from the consolidations they achieve. Neither the massacres of subjects which Roman emperors directed, nor the assassinations of relatives among potentates in the East, nor the impoverishment of whole nations by the exactions of tyrants, must so revolt us as to prevent appreciation of the benefits which have, under certain conditions, resulted from the unlimited power of the supreme man. Nor must the remembrances of tor-

turing implements, and oubliettes, and victims built into walls, shut out from our minds the evidence that abject submission of the weak to the strong, however unscrupulously enforced has in some times and places been necessary.

So, too, with the associated ownership of man by man. Absolute condemnation of slavery must be withheld, even if we accept the tradition repeated by Herodotus, that to build the Great Pyramid relays of a hundred thousand slaves toiled for twenty years; or even if we find it true that of the serfs compelled to work at the building of St. Petersburg, three hundred thousand perished. Though aware that the unrecorded sufferings of men and women held in bondage are beyond imagination, we must be willing to receive such evidence as there may be that benefits have resulted.

In brief, trustworthy interpretations of social arrangements imply an almost passionless consciousness. Though feeling cannot and ought not to be excluded from the mind when otherwise contemplating them, yet it ought to be excluded when contemplating them as natural phenomena to be understood in their causes and effects.

Maintenance of this mental attitude will be furthered by keeping before ourselves the truth that in human actions the absolutely bad may be relatively good, and absolutely good may be relatively bad.

Though it has become a commonplace that the institutions under which one race prospers will not answer for another, the recognition of this truth is by no means adequate. Men who have lost faith in "paper constitutions," nevertheless advocate such conduct towards inferior races, as implies the belief that civilized social forms can with advantage be imposed on uncivilized peoples; that the arrangements which seem to us vicious are vicious for them; and that they would benefit by institutions—domestic, industrial, or political—akin to those which we find beneficial. But acceptance of the truth that the type of a society is determined by the natures of its units, forces on us the corollary that a regime intrinsically of the lowest, may yet be the best possible under primitive conditions.

Otherwise stating the matter, we must not substitute our developed code of conduct, which predominantly concerns public relations. Now that life is generally occupied in peaceful intercourse with fellow-citizens, ethical ideas refer chiefly to actions between man and man; but in early stages, while the occupation of life was mainly in conflicts with adjacent societies, such ethical ideas as existed referred almost wholly to inter-social actions: men's deeds were judged by their direct bearings on tribal welfare. And since preservation of the society takes precedence of individual preservation, as being a condition to it, we must, in considering social phenomena, interpret good and bad rather in their earlier senses than in their later senses; and so must regard as relatively good, that which furthers survival of the society, great as may be the suffering inflicted on its members.

Another of our ordinary conceptions has to be much widened before we can rightly interpret political evolution. The words "civilized" and "savaged" must have given to them meanings differing greatly from those which are current. That broad contrast usually drawn wholly to the advantage of the men who form large nations, and to the disadvantage of the men who form simple groups, a better knowledge obliges us profoundly to qualify. Characters are to be found among rude peoples which compare well with those of the best among cultivated peoples. With little knowledge and but rudimentary arts, there in some cases go virtues which might shame those among ourselves whose education and polish are of the highest. . . .

"How is this conclusion to be reconciled with the conception of progress?" most readers will ask. "How is civilization to be justified if, as is thus implied, some of the highest of human attributes are exhibited in greater degrees by wild people who live scattered in pairs in the woods, than by the members of a vast, well-organized nation, having marvellously elaborated arts, extensive and profound knowledge, and multitudinous appliances to welfare?" The answer to this question will best be conveyed by an analogy.

As carried on throughout the animate world at large, the struggle for existency has been an indispensable means to evolution. Not simply do we see that in the competition among individuals of the same kind, survival of the fittest, has from the beginning furthered production of a higher type; but we see that to the unceasing warfare between species is mainly due both growth and organization. Without universal conflict there would have been no development of the active powers. The organs of perception and of locomotion have been little by little evolved during the interaction of pursuers and pursued. Improved limbs and senses have furnished better supplies to the viscera, and improved visceral structures have ensured a better supply of aerated blood to the limbs and senses; while a higher nervous system has at each stage been called into play for co-ordinating the actions of these more complex structures. Among predatory animals death by starvation, and among animals preyed upon, death by destruction, have carried off the least-favourably modified individuals and varieties. Every advance in strength, speed, agility, or sagac-

ity, in creatures of the one class, has necessitated a corresponding advance in creatures of the other class; and without never-ending efforts to catch and to escape, with loss of life as the penalty for failure, the progress of neither could have been achieved.

Mark now, however, that while this merciless discipline of Nature, "red in tooth and claw," has been essential to the progress of sentient life, its persistence through all time with all creatures must not be inferred. The high organization evolved by and for this universal conflict, is not necessarily for ever employed to like ends. The resulting power and intelligence admit of being far otherwise employed. Not for offense and defense only are the inherited structures useful, but for various other purposes; and these various other purposes may finally become the exclusive purposes. The myriads of years of warfare which have developed the powers of all lower types of creatures, have bequeathed to the highest type of creatures, the powers now used by him for countless objects besides those of killing and avoiding being killed. His limbs, teeth and nails are but little employed in fight; and his mind is not ordinarily occupied in devising ways of destroying other creatures, or guarding himself from injury by them.

Similarly with social organisms. We must recognize the truth that the struggles for existence between societies have been instrumental to their evolution. Neither the consolidation and re-consolidation of small groups into large ones; nor the organization of such compound and doubly compound groups; nor the concomitant developments of those aids to a higher life which civilization has brought; would have been possible without inter-tribal and inter-national conflicts. Social cooperation is initiated by joint defense and offense; and from the cooperation thus initiated, all kinds of cooperations have arisen. Inconceivable as have been the horrors caused by this universal antagonism which, beginning with the chronic hostilities of small hordes tens of thousands of years ago, has ended in the occasional vast battles of immense nations, we must nevertheless admit that without it the world would still have been inhabited only by men of feeble types, sheltering in caves and living on wild food.

But now observe that the inter-social struggle for existence which has been indispensable in evolving societies, will not necessarily play in the future a part like that which it has played in the past. Recognizing our indebtedness to war for forming great communities and developing their structures, we may yet infer that the acquired powers, available for other activities, will lose their original activities. While conceding that without these perpetual bloody strifes, civilized societies could not have arisen, and that an adapted form of human nature, fierce as well as intelligent, was a needful concomitant; we may at the same time hold that such societies having been produced, the brutality of nature in their units which was necessitated by the process, ceasing to be necessary with the cessation of the process, will disappear. While the benefits achieved during the predatory period remain a permanent inheritance, the evils entailed by it will decrease and slowly die out.

Thus, then, contemplating social structures and actions from the evolution point of view, we may preserve that calmness which is needful for scientific interpretation of them, without losing our powers of feeling moral reprobation or approbation.

C. THE STRUGGLE FOR EXISTENCE IN HUMAN SOCIETY

Thomas Henry Huxley (1825–95) was an excellent biologist in his own right, but he devoted a major share of his energies to publicizing evolution and applying biological theory to society. He dubbed himself "Darwin's bulldog." Among his voluminous writings is an essay entitled "The Struggle for Existence in Human Society" (1888), from which the following selection is taken.[11]

In the strict sense of the word "nature," it denotes the sum of the phenomenal world, of that which has been, and is, and will be; and society, like art, is therefore a part of nature. But it is convenient to distinguish those parts of nature in which man plays the part of immediate cause, as something apart; and, therefore, society, like art, is usefully to be considered as distinct from nature. It is the more desirable, and even necessary, to make this distinction, since society differs from nature in having a definite moral object; whence it comes about that the course shaped by the ethical man—the member of society or citizen—necessarily runs counter to that which the nonethical man—the primitive savage, or man as a mere member of the animal kingdom—tends to adopt. The latter fights out the struggle for existence to the bitter end, like any other animal; the former devotes his best energies to the object of setting limits to the struggle.

In the cycle of phenomena presented by the life of man, the animal, no more moral end is discernible than in that presented by the lives of the wolf and of the deer. However imperfect the relics of prehistoric men may be, the evidence which they afford clearly tends to the conclusion that, for thousands and thousands of years, before the origin of the oldest known civilizations, men were savages of a very low type. They strove with their enemies and their competitors; they preyed upon things weaker or less cunning than themselves; they were born, multiplied without stint, and died, for thousands of generations, alongside the mammoth, the urus, the lion, and the hyena, whose lives were spent in the same way; and they were no more to be praised or blamed on moral grounds than their less erect and more hairy compatriots.

As among these, so among primitive men, the weakest and stupidest went to the wall, while the toughest and shrewdest, those who were best fitted to cope with their circumstances, but not the best in any other sense, survived. Life was a continual free fight, and beyond the limited and temporary relations of the family, the Hobbesian war of each against all was the normal state of existence. The human species, like others, plashed and floundered amid the general stream of evolution, keeping its head above water as it best might, and thinking neither of whence nor whither.

The history of civilization—that is, of society—on the other hand, is the record of the attempts which the human race has made to escape from his position. The first men who substituted the state of mutual peace for that of mutual war, whatever the motive which impelled them to take that step, created society. But, in establishing peace, they obviously put a limit upon the struggle for existence. Between the members of that society, at any rate, it was not to be pursued *à outrance*. And of all the successive shapes which society has taken, that most nearly approaches perfection in which the war of individual against individual is most strictly limited. The primitive savage, tutored by Istar, appropriated whatever took his fancy, and killed whomsoever opposed him, if he could. On the contrary, the ideal of the ethical man is to limit his freedom of action to a sphere in which he does not interfere with the freedom of others; he seeks the common weal as much as his own; and, indeed, as an essential part of his own welfare. Peace is both end and means with him; and he founds his life on a more or less complete self-restraint, which is the negation of the unlimited struggle for existence. He tries to escape from his place in the animal kingdom, founded on the free development of the principle of nonmoral evolution, and to establish a kingdom of man, governed upon the principle of moral evolution. For society not only has a moral end, but in its perfection, social life, is embodied morality.

But the effort of ethical man to work toward a moral end by no means abolished, perhaps has hardly modified, the deep-seated organic impulses which impel the natural man to follow his nonmoral course. One of the most essential conditions, if not the chief cause, of the struggle for existence, is the tendency to multiply without limit, which man shares with all living things. It is notable that "increase and multiply" is a commandment traditionally much older than the ten; and that it is, perhaps, the only one which has been spontaneously and *ex animo* obeyed by the great majority of the human race. But, in civilized society, the inevitable result of such obedience is the re-establishment, in all its intensity, of that struggle for existence—the war of each against all—the mitigation or abolition of which was the chief end of social organization. . . .

Historians point to the greed and ambition of rulers, to the reckless turbulence of the ruled, to the debasing effects of wealth and luxury, and to the devastating wars which have formed a great part of the occupation of mankind, as the causes of the decay of states and the foundering of old civilizations, and thereby point their story with a moral. No doubt immoral motives of all sorts have figured largely among the minor causes of these events. But beneath all this superficial turmoil lay the deep-seated impulse given by unlimited multiplication. . . .

In the ancient world, and in a large part of that in which we live, the practice of infanticide was, or is, a regular and legal custom; famine, pestilence, and war were and are normal factors in the struggle for existence, and they have served, in a gross and brutal fashion, to mitigate the intensity of the effects of its chief cause.

But, in the more advanced civilizations, the progress of private and public morality has steadily tended to remove all these checks. We declare infanticide murder and punish it as such; we decree, not quite so successfully, that no one shall die of hunger; we regard death from preventible causes of other kinds as a sort of constructive murder, and eliminate pestilence to the best of our ability; we declaim against the curse of war, and the wickedness of the military spirit, and we are never weary of dilating on the blessedness of peace and the innocent beneficence of industry. In their moments of expansion, even statesmen and men of business go thus far. The finer spirits look to an ideal *civitas Dei;* a state when, every man having reached the point of absolute self-

negation and having nothing but moral perfection to strive after, peace will truly reign, not merely among nations but among men, and the struggle for existence will be at an end.

Whether human nature is competent, under any circumstances, to reach, or even seriously advance toward, this ideal condition, is a question which need not be discussed. It will be admitted that mankind has not yet reached this stage by a very long way, and my business is with the present. And that which I wish to point out is that, so long as the natural man increases and multiplies without restraint, so long will peace and industry not only permit, but they will necessitate, a struggle for existence as sharp as any that ever went on under the regime of war. . . .

There are now 36,000,000 of people in our British islands, and every year considerably more than 300,000 are added to our numbers. That is to say, about every hundred seconds, or so, a new claimant to a share in the common stock of maintenance presents him or herself among us. At the present time, the produce of the soil does not suffice to feed half its population. The other moiety has to be supplied with food which must be bought from the people of food-producing countries. That is to say, we have to offer them the things which they want in exchange for the things we want. And the things they want and which we can produce better than they can are mainly manufactures—industrial products.

The insolent reproach of the first Napoleon had a very solid foundation. We not only are, but, under penalty of starvation, we are bound to be, a nation of shopkeepers. But other nations also lie under the same necessity of keeping shop, and some of them deal in the same goods as ourselves. Our customers naturally seek to get the most and the best in exchange for their produce. If our goods are inferior to those of our competitors, there is no ground, compatible with the sanity of the buyers, which can be alleged why they should not prefer the latter. And, if that result should ever take place on a large and general scale, five or six millions of us would soon have nothing to eat. . . .

Judged by an ethical standard, nothing can be less satisfactory than the position in which we find ourselves. In a real, though incomplete, degree we have attained the condition of peace which is the main object of social organization; and, for argument's sake, it may be assumed that we desire nothing but that which is in itself innocent and praiseworthy—namely, the enjoyment of the fruits of honest industry. And lo! in spite of ourselves, we are in reality engaged in an internecine struggle for existence with our presumably no less peaceful and well-meaning neighbors.

We seek peace and we do not ensue it. The moral nature in us asks for no more than is compatible with the general good; the nonmoral nature proclaims and acts upon that fine old Scottish family motto, "Thou shalt starve ere I want." Let us be under no illusions, then. So long as unlimited multiplication goes on, no social organization which has ever been devised, or is likely to be devised, no fiddle-faddling with the distribution of wealth, will deliver society from the tendency to be destroyed by the reproduction within itself, in its intensest form, of that struggle for existence the limitation of which is the object of society. And however shocking to the moral sense this eternal competition of man against man and of nation against nation may be; however revolting may be the accumulation of misery at the negative pole of society, in contrast with that of monstrous wealth at the positive pole; this state of things must abide, and grow continually worse, so long as Istar holds her way unchecked. It is the true riddle of the Sphinx; and every nation which does not solve it will sooner or later be devoured by the monster itself has generated.

To this end, it is well to look into the necessary conditions of our salvation by works. They are two, one plain to all the world and hardly needing insistence; the other seemingly not so plain, since too often it has been theoretically and practically left out of sight. The obvious condition is that our produce shall be better than that of others. There is only one reason why our goods should be preferred to those of our rivals—our customers must find them better at the price. That means that we must use more knowledge, skill, and industry in producing them, without a proportionate increase in the cost of production; and, as the price of labor constitutes a large element in that cost, the rate of wages must be restricted within certain limits. It is perfectly true that cheap production and cheap labor are by no means synonymous; but it is also true that wages cannot increase beyond a certain proportion without destroying cheapness. Cheapness, then, with, as part and parcel of cheapness, a moderate price of labor, is essential to our success as competitors in the markets of the world.

The second condition is really quite as plainly indispensable as the first, if one thinks seriously about the matter. It is social stability. Society is stable, when the wants of its members obtain as much satisfaction as, life being what it is, common sense and experience show may be reasonably expected. Mankind, in general, care very little for forms of government or ideal considerations of any sort; and nothing really stirs the great multitude to break with custom and incur the manifest perils of revolt except the belief that misery in this world, or damnation in the next, or both, are threatened by the continuance of the state of things in which they have been brought up. But when they do attain that conviction, society becomes as unstable as a package of dynamite, and a very small matter will produce the explosion which sends it back to the chaos of savagery.

It needs no argument to prove that when the price of labor sinks below a certain point, the worker infallibly falls into that condition which the French emphatically call *la misère*—a word for which I do not think there is any exact English equivalent. It is a condition in which the food, warmth, and clothing which are necessary for the mere maintenance of the functions of the body in their normal state cannot be obtained; in which men, women, and children are forced to crowd into dens wherein decency is abolished and the most ordinary conditions of healthful existence are impossible of attainment; in which the pleasures within reach are reduced to bestiality and drunkenness; in which the pains accumulate at compound interest, in the shape of starvation, disease, stunted development, and moral degradation; in which the prospect of even steady and honest industry is a life of unsuccessful battling with hunger, rounded by a pauper's grave.

That a certain proportion of the members of every great aggregation of mankind should constantly tend to establish and populate such a slough of despond as this is inevitable, so long as some people are by nature idle and vicious, while others are disabled by sickness or accident, or thrown upon the world by the death of their breadwinners. So long as that proportion is restricted within tolerable limits, it can be dealt with; and, so far as it arises only from such causes, its existence may and must be patiently borne. But, when the organization of society, instead of mitigating this tendency, tends to continue and intensify it; when a given social order plainly makes for evil and not for good, men naturally enough begin to think it high time to try a fresh experiment. The animal man, finding that the ethical man has landed him in such a slough, resumes his ancient sovereignty, and preaches anarchy; which is, substantially, a proposal to reduce the social cosmos to chaos, and begin the brute struggle for existence once again.

Any one who is acquainted with the state of the population of all great industrial centers, whether in this or other countries, is aware that, amidst a large and increasing body of that population, *la misère* reigns supreme. I have no pretensions to the character of a philanthropist, and I have a special horror of all sorts of sentimental rhetoric; I am merely trying to deal with facts, to some extent within my own knowledge, and further evidenced by abundant testimony, as a naturalist, and I take it to be a mere plain truth that, throughout industrial Europe, there is not a single large manufacturing city which is free from a vast mass of people whose condition is exactly that described; and from a still greater mass who, living just on the edge of the social swamp, are liable to be precipitated into it by any lack of demand for their produce. And, with every addition to the population, the multitude already sunk in the pit and the number of the host sliding toward it continually increase.

Argumentation can hardly be needful to make it clear that no society in which the elements of decomposition are thus swiftly and surely accumulating can hope to win in the race of industries. Intelligence, knowledge, and skill are undoubtedly conditions of success; but of what avail are they likely to be unless they are backed up by honesty, energy, good will, and all the physical and moral faculties that go to the making of manhood, and unless they are stimulated by hope of such reward as men may fairly look to? And what dweller in the slough of want, dwarfed in body and soul, demoralized, hopeless, can reasonably be expected to possess these qualities?

Any full and permanent development of the productive powers of an industrial population, then, must be compatible with and, indeed, based upon a social organization which will secure a fair amount of physical and moral welfare to that population; which will make for good and not for evil. Natural science and religious enthusiasm rarely go hand in hand, but on this matter their concord is complete; and the least sympathetic of naturalists can but admire the insight and the devotion of such social reformers as the late Lord Shaftesbury, whose recently published *Life and Letters* gives a vivid picture of the condition of the working classes fifty years ago, and of the pit which our industry, ignoring these plain truths, was then digging under its own feet.

There is, perhaps, no more hopeful sign of progress among us, in the last half-century, than the steadily increasing devotion which has been and is directed to measures for promoting physical and moral welfare among the poorer classes. Sanitary reformers, like most other reformers whom I have had the advantage of knowing, seem to need a good dose of fanaticism, as a sort of moral coca, to keep them up to the mark, and, doubtless, they have made many mistakes; but that the endeavor to improve the condition under which our industrial population live, to amend the drainage of densely peopled streets, to provide baths, washhouses, and gymnasia, to facilitate habits of thrift, to furnish some provision for instruction and amusement in public libraries and the like, is not only desirable from a philanthropic point of view, but an essential condition of safe industrial development, appears to me to be indisputable. It is by such means alone, so far as I can see, that we can hope to check the constant gravitation of industrial society toward *la misère*, until the general progress of intelligence and morality leads men to grapple with the sources of that tendency. If it is said that the carrying out of such arrangements as those indicated must enhance the cost of production, and thus handicap the producer in the race of competition, I venture, in the first place, to doubt the fact; but if it be so, it results that industrial society has to face a dilemma, either alternative of which threatens destruction.

D. NATIONAL LIFE FROM THE STANDPOINT OF SCIENCE

Prominent among English scientists at the turn of the century was Karl Pearson (1857–1936), professor of applied mathematics at University College, London. In 1900, when England was having considerable difficulty in subduing the Boers in South Africa, Pearson delivered a lecture, "National Life from the Standpoint of Science," to the Literary and Philosophical Society of Newcastle. Selections from the lecture follow.[12]

History shows me one way, and one way only, in which a high state of civilization has been produced, namely, the struggle of race with race, and the survival of the physically and mentally fitter race. If you want to know whether the lower races of man can evolve a higher type, I fear the only course is to leave them to fight it out among themselves, and even then the struggle for existence between individual and individual, between tribe and tribe, may not be supported by that physical selection due to a particular climate on which probably so much of the Aryan's success depended. . . .

The struggle means suffering, intense suffering, while it is in progress; but that struggle and that suffering have been the stages by which the white man has reached his present stage of development, and they account for the fact that he no longer lives in caves and feeds on roots and nuts. This dependence of progress on the survival of the fitter race, terribly black as it may seem to some of you, gives the struggle for existence its redeeming features; it is the fiery crucible out of which comes the finer metal. You may hope for a time when the sword shall be turned into the ploughshare, when American and German and English traders shall no longer compete in the markets of the world for their raw material and for their food supply, when the white man and the dark shall share the soil between them, and each till it as he lists. But, believe me, when that day comes mankind will no longer progress; there will be nothing to check the fertility of inferior stock; the relentless law of heredity will not be controlled and guided by natural selection. Man will stagnate; and unless he ceases to multiply, the catastrophe will come again; famine and pestilence, as we see them in the East, physical selection instead of the struggle of race against race, will do the work more relentlessly, and, to judge from India and China, far less efficiently than of old. . . .

There is a struggle of race against race and of nation against nation. In the early days of that struggle it was a blind, unconscious struggle of barbaric tribes. At the present day, in the case of the civilized white man, it has become more and more the conscious, carefully directed attempt of the nation to fit itself to a continuously changing environment. The nation has to foresee how and where the struggle will be carried on; the maintenance of national position is becoming more and more a conscious preparation for changing conditions, an insight into the needs of coming environments. . . .

I have asked you to look upon the nation as an organized whole in continual struggle with other nations, whether by force of arms or by force of trade and economic processes. I have asked you to look upon this struggle of either kind as a not wholly bad thing; it is the source of human progress throughout the world's history. But if a nation is to maintain its position in this struggle, it must be fully provided with trained brains in every department of national activity, from the government to the factory, and have, if possible, a reserve of brain and physique to fall back upon in times of national crisis. . . .

We have to remember that man is subject to the universal law of inheritance, and that a dearth of capacity may arise if we recruit our society from the inferior and not the better stock. If any social opinions or class prejudices tamper with the fertility of the better stocks, then the national character will take but a few generations to be seriously modified. The pressure of population should always tend to push brains and physique into occupations where they are not a primary necessity, for in this way a reserve is formed for the times of national crisis. Such a reserve can always be formed by filling up with men of our own kith and kin the waste lands of the earth, even at the expense of an inferior race of inhabitants. . . .

You will see that my view—and I think it may be called the scientific view of a nation—is that of an organized whole, kept up to a high pitch of internal efficiency by insuring that its numbers are substantially recruited from the better stocks, and kept up to a high pitch of external efficiency by contest, chiefly by way of war with inferior races, and with equal races by the struggle for trade-routes and for the sources of raw material and of food supply. This is the natural history view of mankind, and I do not think you can in its main features subvert it. Some of you may refuse to acknowledge it, but you cannot really study history and refuse to see its force. Some of you may realize it, and then despair of life; you may decline to admit any glory in a world where the superior race must either eject the inferior, or, mixing with it, or even living alongside it, degenerate itself. What beauty can there be when the battle is to the stronger, and the weaker must suffer in the struggle of nations and in the struggle of individual men? You may say: Let us cease to struggle; let us leave the lands of the world to the races that cannot profit by them to the full; let us cease to compete in the markets of the world. Well, we could do it, if we were a small nation living on the produce of our own soil, and a soil so worthless that no other race envied it and sought to appropriate it. We should cease to advance; but then we should naturally give up progress as a good which comes through suffering. . . .

The man who tells us that he feels to all men alike, that he has no sense of kinship, that he has no patriotic sentiment, that he loves the Kaffir as he loves his brother, is probably deceiving himself. If he is not, then all we can say is that a nation of such men, or even a nation with a large minority of such men, will not stand for many generations; it cannot survive in the struggle of the nations, it cannot be a factor in the contest upon which human progress ultimately depends. The national spirit is not a thing to be ashamed of, as the educated man seems occasionally to hold. If that spirit be the mere excrescence of the music hall, or an ignorant assertion of superiority to the foreigner, it may be ridiculous, it may even be nationally dangerous; but if the national spirit takes the form of a strong feeling of the importance of organizing the nation as a whole, of making its social and economic conditions such that it is able to do its work in the world and meet its fellows without hesitation in the field and in the market, then it seems to me a wholly good spirit

—indeed, one of the highest forms of social, that is, moral instinct.

So far from our having too much of this spirit of patriotism, I doubt if we have anything like enough of it. We wait to improve the condition of some class of workers until they themselves cry out or even rebel against their economic condition. We do not better their state because we perceive its relation to the strength and stability of the nation as a whole. Too often it is done as the outcome of a blind class war. The coal owners, the miners, the manufacturers, the mill-hands, the landlords, the farmers, the agricultural laborers, struggle by fair means, and occasionally by foul, against each other, and, in doing so, against the nation at large, and our statesmen as a rule look on. That was the correct attitude from the standpoint of the old political economy. It is not the correct attitude from the standpoint of science; for science realizes that the nation is an organized whole, in continual struggle with its competitors. You cannot get a strong and effective nation if many of its stomachs are half fed and many of its brains untrained. We, as a nation, cannot survive in the struggle for existence if we allow class distinctions to permanently endow the brainless and to push them into posts of national responsibility. The true statesman has to limit the internal struggle of the community in order to make it stronger for the external struggle. We must reward ability, we must pay for brains, we must give larger advantage to physique; but we must not do this at a rate which renders the lot of the mediocre a wholly unhappy one. We must foster exceptional brains and physique for nation purposes; but, however useful prize cattle may be, they are not bred for their own sake, but as a step toward the improvement of the whole herd. . . .

Science is not a dogma; it has no infallible popes to pronounce authoritatively what its teaching is. I can only say how it seems to one individual scientific worker that the doctrine of evolution applies to the history of nations. My interpretation may be wrong, but of the true method I am sure; a community of men is as subject as a community of ants or as a herd of buffaloes to the laws which rule all organic nature. We cannot escape from them; it serves no purpose to protest at what some term their cruelty and their bloodthirstiness. . . .

Mankind as a whole, like the individual man, advances through pain and suffering only. The path of progress is strewn with the wreck of nations; traces are everywhere to be seen of the hecatombs of inferior races, and of victims who found not the narrow way to the greater perfection. Yet these dead peoples are, in very truth, the steppingstones on which mankind has arisen to the higher intellectual and deeper emotional life of today.

E.   FREUD AND PSYCHOANALYSIS

To a large extent the proliferation of scientific understanding in Europe since the Renaissance was based on the assumption that man through reason could achieve a rational explanation of himself and his universe. As the founder of psychoanalysis Sigmund Freud (1856–1939) introduced a new dimension to this process. He was working alone on the problem during the last years of the nineteenth century, but was soon joined by coworkers in Europe and America. The following selection is from Freud's *General Introduction to Psychoanalysis* (English Translation, 1920).[13]

This is the lacuna which psychoanalysis is striving to fill. It hopes to provide psychiatry with the missing psychological foundation, to discover the common ground on which a correlation of bodily and mental disorder becomes comprehensible. To this end it must dissociate itself from every foreign preconception, whether anatomical, chemical, or physiological, and must work throughout with conceptions of a purely psychological order, and for this very reason I fear that it will appear strange to you at first.

For the next difficulty I shall not hold you, your training or your mental attitude, responsible. There are two tenets of psychoanalysis which offend the whole world and excite its resentment; the one conflicts with intellectual, the other with moral and esthetic prejudices. Let us not underestimate these prejudices; they are powerful things, residues of valuable, even necessary, stages in human evolution. They are maintained by emotional forces, and the fight against them is a hard one.

The first of these displeasing propositions of psychoanalysis is this: that mental processes are essentially unconscious, and that those which are conscious are merely isolated acts and parts of the whole psychic entity. Now I must ask you to remember that, on the contrary, we are accustomed to identify the mental with the conscious. Consciousness appears to us as positively the characteristic that defines mental life, and we regard psychology as the study of the content of consciousness. This even appears so evident that any contradiction of it seems obvious nonsense to us, and yet it is impossible for psychoanalysis to avoid this contradiction, or to accept the identity between the conscious and the psychic. The psychoanalytical definition of the mind is that it comprises processes of the nature of feeling, thinking, and wishing, and it maintains that there are such things as unconscious thinking and unconscious wishing. But in doing so psychoanalysis has forfeited at the outset the sympathy of the sober and scientifically minded, and incurred the suspicion of being a fantastic cult occupied with dark and unfathomable mysteries. You yourselves must find it difficult to understand why I should stigmatize an abstract proposition, such as "The psychic is the conscious," as a prejudice; nor can you guess yet what evolutionary process could have led to the denial of the unconscious, if it does indeed exist, nor what advantage could have been achieved by this denial. It seems like an empty wrangle over words to argue whether mental life is to be regarded as co-extensive with consciousness or whether it may be said to stretch beyond this limit, and yet I can assure you that the acceptance of unconscious mental processes represents a decisive step towards a new orientation in the world and in science.

As little can you suspect how close is the connection between this first bold step on the part of psychoanalysis and the second to which I am now coming. For this next proposition, which we put forward as one of the discoveries of psychoanalysis, consists in the assertion that impulses, which can only be described as sexual in both the narrower and the wider sense, play a peculiarly large part, never before sufficiently appreciated, in the causation of nervous and mental disorders. Nay, more, that these sexual impulses have contributed invaluably to the highest cultural, artistic, and social achievements of the human mind.

In my opinion, it is the aversion from this conclusion of psychoanalytic investigation that is the most significant source of the opposition it has encountered. And are you curious to know how we ourselves account for this? We believe that civilization has been built up, under the pressure of the struggle for existence, by sacrifices in gratification of the primitive impulses, and that it is to a great extent for ever being re-created, as each individual, successively joining the community, repeats the sacrifice of his instinctive pleasures for the common good. The sexual are amongst the most important of the instinctive forces thus utilized: they are in this way sublimated, that is to say, their energy is turned aside from its sexual goal and diverted towards other ends, no longer sexual and socially more valuable. But the structure thus built up is insecure, for the sexual impulses are with difficulty controlled; in each individual who takes up his part in the work of civilization there is a danger that a rebellion of the sexual impulses may occur, against this diversion of their energy. Society can conceive of no more powerful menace to its culture than would arise from the liberation of the sexual impulses and a return of them to their original goal. Therefore society dislikes this sensitive place in its development being touched upon; that the power of the sexual instinct should be recognized, and the significance of the individual's sexual life revealed, is very far from its interests; with a view to discipline it has rather taken the course of diverting attention away from this whole field. For this reason, the revelations of psychoanalysis are not tolerated by it, and it would greatly prefer to brand them as aesthetically offensive, morally reprehensible, or dangerous. But since such objections are not valid arguments against conclusions which claim to represent the objective results of scientific investigation, the opposition must be translated into intellectual terms before it can be expressed. It is a characteristic of human nature to be inclined to regard anything which is disagreeable as untrue, and then without much difficulty to find arguments against it. So society pronounces the unacceptable to be untrue, disputes the results of psychoanalysis with logical and concrete arguments, arising, however, in affective sources, and clings to them with all the strength of prejudice against every attempt at refutation.

IX

The Dilemma of the Twentieth Century

Liberty is the right to discipline oneself in order not to be disciplined by others.

GEORGES CLEMENCEAU (1841–1929)

CONTENTS

[247]

QUESTIONS FOR STUDY

PART I

1. How did the Italian doctrine of Fascism come into being? How did Mussolini justify it?
2. What did Mussolini set forth as the ideals of Fascism?
3. What was the role of the state in Italian Fascism?
4. Analyze the principles of Nazism. How did Hitler define "true Germanic democracy"?
5. What are the historic origins of Hitler's concepts? Why did he consider these concepts the solution to Germany's problems?
6. Compare Franco's totalitarianism with those of Mussolini and Hitler. What are the points of similarity and difference?
7. What did Lenin consider to be the basic problems of man and society?
8. Why did he emphasize the dictatorship of the proletariat as a solution to these problems?
9. How did Lenin and Stalin employ the words "democracy" and "democratic"?
10. Why, according to the Communists, are the soviets and the dictatorship of the proletariat "democratic" institutions?
11. What is the role of the party in achieving Communist ideals? How does the party function?
12. Against the background of twentieth-century history, why do you believe that Lenin and Stalin interpreted Marxism as they did?
13. Analyze the basic international views of Communism.
14. Compare the totalitarianism of Communism and Integral Nationalism. Are they distinct developments or different aspects of the same phenomenon? What in the main accounts for their success or failure?

PART II

15. How does Slesser view the basic problems of liberalism in the twentieth century?
16. Does Attlee resolve any of Slesser's doubts? How far does he justify his statement, "Ours is a philosophy in its own right"?
17. Evaluate Churchill's faith in "the broad harmony of thought which prevails between the modern Tory democracy and the doctrines of the famous Liberal leaders of the past."
18. What are the old and new elements in Maritain's "Rights of Man"?
19. What does Meinecke consider to be the right program for the free Western states?
20. What does Fromm contribute toward a solution of the difficulties facing free men?
21. Analyze the goals of the United Nations and the methods prescribed for their accomplishment. Upon what principles are they based?
22. How far are they compatible with the international views of Communism?

PART III

23. What is Barker's thesis concerning the future of Europe and her culture?
24. Is his thesis supported by the condition of world affairs at mid-century?

The nineteenth century left to the twentieth a heritage rich in fruitful possibilities and fraught with dire perils. Of the many elements in the legacy of the past, two appeared at mid-century to have a particular significance.

The first was the economic system resulting from the industrial revolution. A spectacularly advancing technology—industrial, commercial, and financial—created an enormous productive capacity in the states of Western and Central Europe. Never before in history had there been so wealthy a civilization. Yet the speed of development outran the ability of society to cope with some of its undesirable consequences. Although the general standard of living continued to rise, the "less eligible" economic status of various segments in society still caused bilious unrest. Moreover, the whole economy was liable to extremes of "boom and bust," which had severe repercussions in every sphere of existence.

The second was the international system stemming from the post-unification period. The grouping of the major powers into two competing alliances, divided by nationalist and imperialist rivalries, led to heightened international tension. Each bloc grew ever more fearful of the other. Peace conferences at the Hague and unilateral efforts to reduce the strain had little result. The arms budgets of the great states doubled and trebled with the dawn of the new century.

The results of these twin legacies were fifty years of crisis, war, and economic depression relieved by only brief spurts of prosperity. In the course of catastrophe Western Europe lost her dominant position in global politics. Two massive conflicts involved nearly the whole world, and there were numerous localized outbreaks of hostility, civil or international, in almost every year. Between the great wars the uncertain boom of the 1920's was shattered by the deep depression of the following decade. In the aftermath of World War II arose a "cold war" between Russia and her communist satellites on the one hand and the democracies, led by the United States, on the other. The possibility of a third armageddon became an ever-present threat to civilization, for the invention of the atomic and hydrogen bombs unleashed incalculable powers of destruction.

From these conditions the world groped for relief. Statesmen explored every facet of the ideological past. Marxism grew into totalitarian Bolshevism. Nationalism gave birth to Nazism and Fascism. Liberalism expanded into the democratic welfare state. All experienced periods of failure and success, on their own terms, in different parts of the globe.

The rise of totalitarianism in its various forms represented a retrogression from the libertarian ideals which the West had long sought to implement everywhere. And totalitarianism was militarily strong, a menace to its free neighbors. Could it be destroyed only by the sword? So it seemed in 1914 and 1939. Was it possible for antagonistic systems to co-exist till the world could be peaceably won to freedom? Could the democracies continue to meet the pressing demands of fast changing society while in constant dread of subversion or attack? Totalitarianism sacrificed liberty in the name of order and survival. Its exponents, seeing no alternative in a chaotic world, cast freedom on the rubbish heap of outworn shibboleths. Must democracy follow suit? Or could the principles of democracy be adapted to modern conditions, at home and abroad, to effectuate its traditional ideals? Here was the dilemma of the twentieth century.

The documents which follow represent the different approaches to the dilemma. Against his knowledge of the historical background, the student should seek to understand the appeal of each ideology, the conditions of its success and failure, and the general character of the world situation at mid-century.

THE PROBLEM

Part I.   THE TOTALITARIAN SOLUTIONS

The emergence of totalitarian dictatorship was probably the outstanding political phenomenon in the first half of the twentieth century. By 1939 only nine of Europe's twenty-
seven states were truly democratic. Varying types of authoritarian regime prevailed in all
the rest. The materials in Part I provide an insight into the two most important forms:
the integral nationalism which incorporated the "leader principle" in Italy, Germany, and
Spain; and the "dictatorship of the proletariat" in Russia.

A.   INTEGRAL NATIONALISM

Ideological development and political experience in the nineteenth century worked for
the intensification of nationalism. In the chaos of the twentieth century there was a
strong urge to seek the solution to a country's ills in integral nationalism, first defined by
Charles Maurras as "the exclusive pursuit of national politics, the absolute maintenance
of national integrity, and the steady increase of national power."

1. *Il Duce in Italy*. Benito Mussolini (1883–
1945) began his career as a revolutionary
socialist. During World War I he broke with
his old associates and later formed his own
party, the *Fasci di Combattimento,* which
seized power by the famous "march on
Rome" in 1922. The Fascists under Mussolini's leadership ruled Italy until 1943, when
his regime crumbled before the allied invasion. The principles of his movement may
be observed in the following selection from
the article "Fascism" in the 1932 edition of
the *Encyclopedia Britannica,* prepared for
Mussolini's signature by the Italian philosopher, Giovanni Gentile (1875–1944).[1]

After the war, in 1919, socialism was already
dead as a doctrine: it existed only as a hatred.
There remained to it only one possibility of action, especially in Italy, reprisals against those
who had desired the war and who must now be
made to "expiate" its results. The *Populo d'Italia*
was then given the subtitle of "The Newspaper
of Ex-service Men and Producers," and the word
"producers" was already the expression of a mental attitude. Fascism was not the nursling of a doctrine worked out beforehand with detailed elabo-
ration; it was born of the need for action and it
was itself from the beginning practical rather
than theoretical; it was not merely another political party but, even in the first two years, in
opposition to all political parties as such, and itself a living movement. The name which I then
gave to the organization fixed its character. And
yet, if one were to reread, in the now dusty columns of that date, the report of the meeting in
which the *Fasci Italiana di Combattimento* were
constituted, one would there find no ordered ex-

pression of doctrine, but a series of aphorisms, an-
ticipations, and aspirations which, when refined
by time from the original ore, were destined after
some years to develop into an ordered series of
doctrinal concepts, forming the fascist political
doctrine—different from all others either of the
past or the present day.

"If the bourgeoisie," I said then, "think that
they will find lightning conductors in us, they
are the more deceived; we must start work at
once. . . . We want to accustom the working
class to real and effectual leadership, and also
to convince them that it is no easy thing to direct an industry or a commercial enterprise successfully. . . . We shall combat every retrograde
idea, technical or spiritual. . . . When the succession to the seat of government is open, we
must not be unwilling to fight for it. We must
make haste; when the present regime breaks
down, we must be ready at once to take its place.
It is we who have the right to the succession, because it was we who forced the country into the
war, and led her to victory. The present method
of political representation cannot suffice, we must
have a representation direct from the individuals
concerned. It may be objected against this program that it is a return to the conception of the
corporation, but that is no matter. . . . Therefore, I desire that this assembly shall accept the
revindication of national trades unionism from
the economic point of view." . . .

And above all, fascism, the more it considers
and observes the future and the development of
humanity quite apart from political considerations of the moment, believes neither in the possibility nor the utility of perpetual peace. It thus
repudiates the doctrine of pacifism—born of a renunciation of the struggle and an act of coward-

ice in the face of sacrifice. War alone brings up to its highest tension all human energy and puts the stamp of nobility upon the peoples who have the courage to meet it. All other trials are substitutes, which never really put men into the position where they have to make the great decision—the alternative of life or death. Thus a doctrine which is founded upon this harmful postulate of peace is hostile to fascism. And thus hostile to the spirit of fascism, though accepted for what use they can be in dealing with particular political situations, are all the international leagues and societies which, as history will show, can be scattered to the winds when once strong national feeling is aroused by any motive—sentimental, ideal, or practical. . . .

Such a conception of life makes fascism the complete opposite of that doctrine, the base of so-called scientific and Marxian socialism, the materialist conception of history; according to which the history of human civilization can be explained simply through the conflict of interests among the various social groups and by the change and development in the means and instruments of production. That the changes in the economic field—new discoveries of raw materials, new methods of working them, and the inventions of science—have their importance no one can deny; but that these factors are sufficient to explain the history of humanity excluding all others is an absurd delusion. Fascism, now and always, believes in holiness and in heroism; that is to say, in actions influenced by no economic motive, direct or indirect. And if the economic conception of history be denied, according to which theory men are no more than puppets, carried to and fro by the waves of chance, while the real directing forces are quite out of their control, it follows that the existence of an unchangeable and unchanging class war is also denied—the natural progeny of the economic conception of history. And above all fascism denies that class war can be the preponderant force in the transformation of society. These two fundamental concepts of socialism being thus refuted, nothing is left of it but the sentimental aspiration—as old as humanity itself—toward a social convention in which the sorrows and sufferings of the humblest shall be alleviated. But here again fascism repudiates the conception of "economic" happiness, to be realized by socialism and, as it were, at a given moment in economic evolution to assure to everyone the maximum of well-being. Fascism denies the materialist conception of happiness as a possibility, and abandons it to its inventors, the economists of the first half of the nineteenth century: that is to say, fascism denies the validity of the equation, well-being-happiness, which would reduce men to the level of animals caring for one thing only—to be fat and well-fed—and would thus degrade humanity to a purely physical existence.

After socialism, fascism combats the whole complex system of democratic ideology and repudiates it, whether in its theoretical premises or in its practical application. Fascism denies that the majority, by the simple fact that it is a majority, can direct human society; it denies that numbers alone can govern by means of a periodical consultation, and it affirms the immutable, beneficial, and fruitful inequality of mankind, which can never be permanently leveled through the mere operation of a mechanical process such as universal suffrage. The democratic regime may be defined as from time to time giving the people the illusion of sovereignty, while the real effective sovereignty lies in the hands of other concealed and irresponsible forces. Democracy is a regime nominally without a king, but it is ruled by many kings—more absolute, tyrannical, and ruinous than one sole king, even though a tyrant. This explains why fascism, having first in 1922 (for reasons of expediency) assumed an attitude tending toward republicanism, renounced this point of view before the march to Rome; being convinced that the question of political form is not today of prime importance, and after having studied the examples of monarchies and republics past and present reached the conclusion that monarchy or republicanism are not to be judged, as it were, by an absolute standard; but that they represent forms in which the evolution—political, historical, traditional, or psychological—of a particular country has expressed itself. . . .

Fascism has taken up an attitude of complete opposition to the doctrines of liberalism, both in the political field and the field of economics. There should be no undue exaggeration (simply with the object of immediate success in controversy) of the importance of liberalism in the last century, nor should what was but one among many theories which appeared in that period be put forward as a religion for humanity for all time, present and to come. Liberalism only flourished for half a century. . . .

Fascism uses in its construction whatever elements in the liberal, social, or democratic doctrines still have a living value; it maintains what may be called the certainties which we owe to history, but it rejects all the rest—that is to say, the conception that there can be any doctrine of unquestioned efficacy for all times and all peoples. Given that the nineteenth century was the century of socialism, of liberalism, and of democracy, it does not necessarily follow that the twentieth century must also be a century of socialism, liberalism, and democracy: political doctrines pass, but humanity remains; and it may rather be expected that this will be a century of authority, a century of the Left, a century of fascism. For if the nineteenth century was a century of individualism (liberalism always signifying individualism) it may be expected that this will be the century of collectivism, and hence the century of the state. . . .

In 1929, at the first five-yearly assembly of the fascist regime, I said:

"For us fascists, the state is not merely a guardian, preoccupied solely with the duty of assuring the personal safety of the citizens; nor is it an organization with purely material aims, such as to guarantee a certain level of well-being and peaceful conditions of life; for a mere council of administration would be sufficient to realize such objects. Nor is it a purely political creation, divorced from all contact with the complex material reality which makes up the life of the individual and the life of the people as a whole. The state, as conceived of and as created by fascism, is a spiritual and moral fact in itself, since its political, juridical, and economic organization of the nation is a concrete thing: and such an organization must be in its origins and development a manifestation of the spirit. The state is the guarantor of security both internal and external, but it is also the custodian and transmitter of the spirit of the people, as it has grown up through the centuries in language, in customs, and in faith. And the state is not only a living reality of the present, it is also linked with the past and above all with the future, and thus transcending the brief limits of individual life, it represents the immanent spirit of the nation. The forms in which states express themselves may change, but the necessity for such forms is eternal. It is the state which educates its citizens in civic virtue, gives them a consciousness of their mission and welds them into unity; harmonizing their various interests through justice, and transmitting to future generations the mental conquests of science, of art, of law and the solidarity of humanity. It leads men from primitive tribal life to that highest expression of human power which is empire: it links up through the centuries the names of those of its members who have died for its existence and in obedience to its laws, it holds up the memory of the leaders who have increased its territory and the geniuses who have illumined it with glory as an example to be followed by future generations. When the conception of the state declines, and disunifying and centrifugal tendencies prevail, whether of individuals or of particular groups, the nations where such phenomena appear are in their decline." From 1929 until today, evolution, both political and economic, has everywhere gone to prove the validity of these doctrinal premises. . . .

For fascism, the growth of empire, that is to say the expansion of the nation, is an essential manifestation of vitality, and its opposite a sign of decadence. Peoples which are rising, or rising again after a period of decadence, are always imperialist; any renunciation is a sign of decay and of death. Fascism is the doctrine best adapted to represent the tendencies and the aspirations of a people, like the people of Italy, who are rising again after many centuries of abasement and foreign servitude. But empire demands discipline, the coordination of all forces and a deeply felt sense of duty and sacrifice: this fact explains many aspects of the practical working of the regime, the character of many forces in the state, and the necessarily severe measures which must be taken against those who would oppose this spontaneous and inevitable movement of Italy in the twentieth century, and would oppose it by recalling the outworn ideology of the nineteenth century—repudiated wheresoever there has been the courage to undertake great experiments of social and political transformation: for never before has the nation stood more in need of authority, of direction, and of order. If every age has its own characteristic doctrine, there are a thousand signs which point to fascism as the characteristic doctrine of our time. For if a doctrine must be a living thing, this is proved by the fact that fascism has created a living faith; and that this faith is very powerful in the minds of men is demonstrated by those who have suffered and died for it.

Fascism has henceforth in the world the universality of all those doctrines which, in realizing themselves, have represented a stage in the history of the human spirit.

2. *Der Fuehrer in Germany*. In 1919 was founded at Munich the National Socialist German Workers Party. Its seventh member was an obscure Austrian ex-service man named Adolf Hitler (1889–1945). Hitler gradually assumed the leadership of the movement which, after several unsuccessful attempts, finally took control of the German government in 1933. Nazi rule was broken by the allied occupation of Germany in 1945. The ingredients of Nazism may be found in the following selections from Hitler's *Mein Kampf* and two of his speeches.[2]

[Mein Kampf]

German Austria must return to the great German motherland, and not because of economic considerations of any sort. No, no: even if from the economic point of view this union were unimportant, indeed, if it were harmful, it ought nevertheless to be brought about. *Common blood belongs in a common Reich.* As long as the German nation is unable even to band together its own children in one common state, it has no moral right to think of colonization as one of its political aims. Only when the boundaries of the Reich include even the last German, only when it is no longer possible to assure him of daily bread inside them, does there arise, out of the distress of the nation, the moral right to acquire foreign soil and territory. The sword is then the plow, and from the tears of war there grows the daily bread for the generations to come. . . .

The question of the "nationalization" of a people is first of all a question of creating sound social conditions as the fundamental possibility for educating the individual. For only those who, through education and schooling, get to know the cultural and economic, and above all the political, greatness of their own country can and will be proud of being allowed to call themselves members of this nation. Moreover, I can only fight for what I love; only love what I can respect; only respect what I know. . . .

Like a woman, whose psychic feeling is influenced less by abstract reasoning than by an undefinable, sentimental longing for complementary strength, who will submit to the strong man rather than dominate the weakling, thus the masses love the ruler rather than the suppliant, and inwardly they are far more satisfied by a doctrine which tolerates no rival than by the grant of liberal freedom; they often feel at a loss what to do with it, and even easily feel themselves deserted. They neither realize the impudence with which they are spiritually terrorized, nor the outrageous curtailment of their human liberties, for in no way does the delusion of this doctrine dawn on them. Thus they see only the inconsiderate force, the brutality and the aim of its manifestations to which they finally always submit. . . .

The Jewish doctrine of Marxism rejects the aristocratic principle in nature; instead of the eternal privilege of force and strength, it places the mass of numbers and its dead weight. Thus it denies the value of the individual in man, disputes the meaning of nationality and race, depriving mankind of the assumption for its existence and culture. As the basis of the universe it would lead up to the end of all order conceivable to man. And as in this greatest discernible organism only chaos could be the result of the application of such a law, so on this earth the decline of its inhabitants would be the result. . . .

Democracy of the west today is the forerunner of Marxism, which would be inconceivable without it. It is democracy alone which furnishes this universal plague with the soil in which it spreads.

In parliamentarianism, its outward form of expression, democracy created a "monstrosity of filth and fire" (*Spottgeburt aus Dreck und Feuer*) in which, to my regret, the "fire" seems to have burned out for the moment. . . .

The parliamentary principle of decision by majority, by denying the authority of the person and placing in its stead the number of the crowd in question, sins against the aristocratic basic idea of nature, whose opinion of aristocracy, however, need in no way be represented by the present-day decadence of our upper ten thousand. . . .

One thing we must and may never forget: here, too, a majority can never replace the Man. It is not only always a representative of stupidity, but also of cowardice. Just as a hundred fools do not make one wise man, an heroic decision is not likely to come from a hundred cowards. . . .

It will be easiest to understand this absurd and dangerous human error if one compares the democratic parliamentarianism with true Germanic democracy.

The characteristic of the first is that a number of, say five hundred, men, and recently also women, are elected, who are entrusted with the final decision on everything. They alone practically represent the government, for though they elect the cabinet which to all outward appearances seems to take on the guidance of the state's affairs, this is nevertheless mere pretense. In reality, this so-called government cannot take one step without having first obtained the consent of the general assembly. Therefore, it cannot be held responsible for anything at all, as it is not the government which has the ultimate decision, but the majority of parliament. In all cases, therefore, the government is only the executive of the will of the majority. We would judge its political ability only by the skill it shows either in adapting itself to the will of the majority, or in winning it over. But then it sinks from the height of a real government to that of a beggar appealing to the majority. Its most important task now consists of securing either the favor of the majority, from case to case, or of taking upon itself the formation of a more gracious new majority. If it succeeds in this, then it may continue to "rule" for a short time longer, but if it does not, it must go. Whether its intentions are right or not is of no consequence. . . .

This system is opposed by the true Germanic democracy of the free choice of a leader with the latter's obligation to take over fully all responsibility for what he does or does not do. There will be no voting by a majority on single questions, but only the decision of the individual who backs it with his life and all he has.

If the objection were raised that under such circumstances no one could be found ready to devote himself to such a hazardous task, there can be one reply:

God be thanked, this is just the meaning of Germanic democracy, that no unworthy climber or moral shirker can come in the back way to rule his fellow citizens, but that the greatness of the position to be assumed will discourage incompetents and weaklings. . . .

[Natural Selection Among Nations, January 15, 1928]

What is the most powerful force that dominates human life? First, it is the drive for momentary self-preservation, the satisfaction of hunger; second, the drive to propagate the race, the gratification of love. These two drives dominate the individual. They compel him to work. From this fact one thing in particular is apparent, namely, that when all living creatures in this world are motivated by the same drive—that is, the preservation of life at any price—then they are forced into a competitive struggle.

Man must make use of his powers. He must struggle and fight. There is no achievement without breaking down resistance. Every new deed of mankind signifies the conquest of a previous one. We see that in mankind individual giants continuously tower over the rest. There are always certain nations which proceed in advance of all the others, nations which in the eternal struggle with nature are able to discover her secrets and to make them available for the rest of humanity. These nations are thereby able to open the gates of culture for other peoples. . . . By means of this eternal struggle, the individual nations are sifted out. . . .

Why is the position of the German people so desperate? Because we need power for every enterprise. Force determines the way of life. Right exists only when it is created and protected by power and force. It bespeaks the greatness of a people if it can find the strength to raise itself upward. But when a people dances Negro dances and listens only to jazz music, then we need not be surprised if it should perish, and seek out parliamentary monstrosities. He who does not honor his past is not worthy of a better future. A people must be taught to struggle. Struggle must be brought to the realization of a people.

[Racial Purity, January 30, 1937]

The main plank in the National Socialist program is to abolish the liberalistic concept of the individual and the Marxist concept of humanity and to substitute therefor the folk community, rooted in the soil and bound together by the bond of its common blood. This is a very simple statement, but it involves a principle that has tremendous consequences. This is probably the first time and this is the first country in which the people are being taught to realize that, of all tasks which we have to face, the noblest and most sacred for mankind is that each racial species must preserve the purity of the blood which God has given it. . . . The greatest revolution which National Socialism has brought about is that it has rent asunder the veil which hid from us the knowledge that all human failures and mistakes are due to the conditions of the time and therefore can be remedied, but that there is one error which cannot be remedied once men have made it, namely, the failure to recognize the importance of conserving the blood and the race free from intermixture and thereby the racial aspect and character which are God's gift and God's handiwork. It is not for men to discuss the question of why Providence created different races, but rather to recognize the fact that it punishes those who disregard its work of creation.

Unspeakable suffering and misery have come upon mankind because they lost this instinct which was grounded in a profound intuition; and this loss was caused by a wrong and lopsided education of the intellect. Among our people there are millions and millions of persons living today for whom this law has become clear and intelligible. What individual seers and the still unspoiled natures of our forefathers saw by direct perception has now become a subject of scientific research in Germany. I can prophesy here that, just as the knowledge that the earth moves around the sun led to a revolutionary alteration in the general world-picture, so the blood-and-race doctrine of the National Socialist Movement will bring about a revolutionary change in our knowledge and therewith a radical reconstruction of the picture which human history gives us of the past and will also change the course of that history in the future.

This will not lead to an estrangement between nations; but, on the contrary, it will bring about for the first time a real understanding of one another. At the same time, however, it will prevent the Jewish people from intruding themselves among all the other nations as elements of internal disruption, under the mask of honest world-citizens, and thus gaining power over these nations.

We feel convinced that the consequences of this revolutionizing vision of truth will bring about a radical transformation in German life. For the first time in our history, the German people have found the way to a higher unity. . . . From that chaos of disunion which had been caused by tribal, dynastic, philosophical, religious, and political strife, the German nation has arisen and has unfurled the banner of a reunion which symbolically announces, not a political triumph, but the triumph of the racial principle. . . . The National Socialist Movement limits its sphere of internal activity to those individuals who belong to one people and it refuses to allow the members of a foreign race to wield an influence over our political, intellectual, or cultural life. We refuse to accord to the members of a foreign race any predominant position in our national economic system. In this folk-community, which is based on the bond of blood, and in the results which National Socialism has obtained by making the idea of this community understood among the public, lies the most profound reason for the marvelous success of our Revolution.

3. *El Caudillo in Spain.* In July 1936 a conservative revolt broke out against the Spanish Republic. Three months later the insurgents named as chief of state General Francisco Franco (1892–   ), a little known officer who had once been chief of staff. His forces gained control of Spain after three years of civil war, and his regime has endured to the present. Franco's leading ideas were set forth in a speech in January 1937, portions of which follow.[3]

Spain, Spain, Spain—land of heroic deeds, of heroic greatness, home of ascetics and of Quixotes, land of nobles, has awakened with new vitality and strength. It is a national movement, this wakening of a people who did not know themselves, and felt strange and out of place. Undermined by the hidden forces of revolution, little by little it was succumbing to the criminal designs of alien committees that, under the mask of democracy, and brandishing the strong weapon of materialism was undermining all there was of nobility and spirituality in our ancient homeland.

Liberty, fettered by the license of government partisans; equality, destroyed by those who in the government proclaimed themselves to be belligerents; fraternity, given the lie by daily assassinations of men of the opposition, with the complacency and complicity of the authorities and the government; these exist again.

Hidden pacts with Russian communism, secret agreements with foreign nations behind the back of the constitution and the laws, persecution of the constitution and the laws, persecution without truce of everything representing any spiritual or moral value, or that did not yoke itself to the tumbril of Muscovite revolution—this was the Spain of yesterday: the Spain of workers criminally exploited by their employers, of the tubercular without sanatoriums, of the hearths without fires, of political bosses, of social injustice, or children with no schools, of Spaniards without a fatherland, of men without a God.

For peace and the country's welfare, for the rational and just betterment of working and middle classes, for liberty of conscience and respect for religion and tradition, for the tranquillity and prosperity of the home, for our threatened civilization, and the prestige of our flag, for the independence of our country, for a new Spain, a free Spain, a great Spain, our soldiers are fighting today this Russo-communistic invasion.

This new Spain will represent a great national family, one without masters or vassals, without poor or potentate. Social justice will be the basis of our new empire, without destructive and suicidal class warfare, without meddlesome interferences from abroad that are so incompatible with our national dignity. We want a fraternal Spain, an industrious and working Spain, where parasites can find no lodging. A Spain without chains and tyrannies: a nation without destructive Marxism and communism: a state for the people and not a people for the state. A Spain without parties in continual conflict, without parliamentary preponderancies or irresponsible assemblies. We want a Spain great, strong, and united, one with authority, direction, and order. Our progress must be firm and unhesitating: and we must go progressively and constantly on to our goal of a great organic Spain. . . .

We must awaken in all Spaniards the love of country, pride in realizing their Spanish birth, by creating conditions of life for all social classes that will permit them to appreciate without pain or rancor the political greatness of the new state. . . .

This is our commission—love of our country, honor, love for the people, deep Catholic sentiment, and a complete faith in the destiny of Spain.

In the order of religion, to the angry persecution of the Marxists and communists of whatever represents the existence of spirituality, of faith, or of religious worship, we oppose the sentiment of a Catholic Spain, with her saints and martyrs, with her secular institutions, her social justice, her Christian charity, and that great comprehensive soul which, in the Golden Ages of our history when a vigorous and deep-rooted Catholicism was the reconstructing arm of our historic unity, suffered, under the tolerant guardianship of the Catholic state, the mosques and synagogues to be gathered within the soul of Catholic Spain.

This great national movement demands of everyone faith and enthusiasm, and includes the sacrifice of everything that in this holocaust of our land can be spared. If we are to make a Spain for everyone, everyone must sacrifice himself for Spain and put aside shades of difference and details that might roughen the facets that in a new Spain must be limpid and glittering.

Union and collaboration with the state must

be disinterested, self-sacrificing, without materialistic aims or self-seeking. Law and the family must be its principal cells. Family, laws, corporations, municipalities, province, region, will be the principal wheels of progress of this new state. . . .

This is the Spain that, honored by the recognition of those countries which understand the threat of communism and the sanctity of our crusade for the defense of civilization, salutes the world. Spain which nobly thanks those other na-

tions for their spiritual assistance, those other nations which, without official manifestation, weep for the profanation of churches and the martyrdom of our brethren at the hands of blood-maddened hordes, as if our churches were the very ones in which they kneel in worship and the blood of our martyred were that of their own.

Spain that unites in intimate communion with the plans of her chief!

Spaniards all: Long live Spain!

B.   COMMUNISM

The socialist and communist parties of Europe underwent many splits and reorganizations in the latter years of the nineteenth century. From the numerous factional disputes arose the Russian Bolshevik party, founded in 1903 by Vladimir Lenin (1870–1924). Upon the breakdown of Czarist rule in 1917, the Bolsheviki fought their way to dominance in the Russian empire, which they renamed the Union of Soviet Socialist Republics. Lenin retained the leadership till his death, when he was succeeded by Josef Stalin (1879–1953) who gradually established an iron dictatorship by "purging" all opposition. The soviet government still cleaves to the doctrines derived by Lenin and Stalin from the works of Karl Marx, and their ideas dominate the Communist regimes established in other lands since World War II.

1. *Leninism.* Following is a selection from Lenin's *State and Revolution*, written in 1919.[4]

The main point in the teaching of Marx is the class struggle. This has very often been said and written. But this is not true. Out of this error, here and there, springs an opportunist distortion of Marxism, such a falsification of it as to make it acceptable to the bourgeoisie. The theory of the class struggle was *not* created by Marx, but by the bourgeoisie *before* Marx and is, generally speaking, *acceptable* to the bourgeoisie. He who recognizes *only* the class struggle is not yet a Marxist; he may be found not to have gone beyond the boundaries of bourgeois reasoning and politics. To limit Marxism to the teaching of the class struggle means to curtail Marxism—to distort it, to reduce it to something which is acceptable to the bourgeoisie. A Marxist is one who *extends* the acceptance of class struggle to the acceptance of the *dictatorship of the proletariat.* Herein lies the deepest difference between a Marxist and an ordinary petty or big bourgeois. On this touchstone it is necessary to test a *real* understanding and acceptance of Marxism. . . .

Opportunism *does not lead* the recognition of class struggle up to the main point, up to the period of *transition* from capitalism to communism, up to the period of *overthrowing* and completely abolishing the bourgeoisie. In reality, this period inevitably becomes a period of unusually violent class struggles in their sharpest possible forms

and, therefore, the state during this period inevitably must be a state that is democratic *in a new way* (for the proletariat and the poor in general) and dictatorial *in a new way* (against the bourgeoisie).

Further, the substance of the teachings of Marx about the state is assimilated only by one who understands that the dictatorship of a *single* class is necessary not only for any class society generally, not only for the *proletariat* which has overthrown the bourgeoisie, but for the entire *historic period* which separates capitalism from "classless society," from communism. The forms of bourgeois states are exceedingly variegated, but their essence is the same: in one way or another, all these states are in the last analysis inevitably a *dictatorship of the bourgeoisie.* The transition from capitalism to communism will certainly bring a great variety and abundance of political forms, but the essence will inevitably be only one: *the dictatorship of the proletariat. . . .*

In capitalist society, under the conditions most favorable to its development, we have more or less complete democracy in the democratic republic. But this democracy is always bound by the narrow framework of capitalist exploitation, and consequently always remains, in reality, a democracy for the minority, only for the possessing classes, only for the rich. Freedom in capitalist society always remains just about the same as it was in the ancient Greek republics: freedom for the slaveowners. The modern wage slaves, owing to the conditions of capitalist exploitation, are so much crushed by want and poverty that "democracy is nothing to them," "politics is nothing to them"; that, in the ordinary peaceful course of events, the majority of the population is debarred from participating in social and political life. . . .

But from this capitalist democracy—inevitably narrow, subtly rejecting the poor, and therefore hypocritical and false to the core—progress does not march onward, simply, smoothly and directly, to "greater and greater democracy," as the liberal professors and petty-bourgeois opportunists would have us believe. No, progress marches onward, *i.e.* toward communism, through the dictatorship of the proletariat; it cannot do otherwise, for there is no one else and no other way to *break the resistance* of the capitalist exploiters.

But the dictatorship of the proletariat—*i.e., the* organization of the vanguard of the oppressed as the ruling class for the purpose of crushing the oppressors—cannot produce merely an expansion of democracy. *Together* with an immense expansion of democracy which *for the first time* becomes democracy for the poor, democracy for the people, and not democracy for the rich folk, the dictatorship of the proletariat produces a series of restrictions of liberty in the case of the oppressors, the exploiters, the capitalists. We must crush them in order to free humanity from wage slavery; their resistance must be broken by force; it is clear that where there is suppression there is also violence, there is no liberty, no democracy. . . .

Democracy for the vast majority of the people, and suppression by force, *i.e.*, exclusion from democracy, of the exploiters and oppressors of the people—this is the modification of democracy during the *transition* from capitalism to communism. . . .

Democracy is of great importance for the working class in its struggle for freedom against the capitalists. But democracy is by no means a limit one may not overstep; it is only one of the stages in the course of development from feudalism to capitalism, and from capitalism to communism. . . .

Democracy is a form of the state—one of its varieties. Consequently, like every state, it consists in organized, systematic application of force against human beings. This on the one hand. On the other hand, however, it signifies the formal recognition of the equality of all citizens, the equal right of all to determine the structure and administration of the state. This, in turn, is connected with the fact that, at a certain stage in the development of democracy, it first rallies the proletariat as a revolutionary class against capitalism, and gives it an opportunity to crush, to smash to bits, to wipe off the face of the earth the bourgeois state machinery—even its republican variety: the standing army, the police, and bureaucracy; then it substitutes for all this a *more* democratic, but still a state machinery in the shape of armed masses of workers, which becomes transformed into universal participation of the people in the militia. . . .

Accounting and control—these are the *chief* things necessary for the organizing and correct functioning of the *first phase* of communist society. *All* citizens are here transformed into hired employees of the state, which is made up of the armed workers. *All* citizens become employees and workers of *one* national state "syndicate." All that is required is that they should work equally, should regularly do their share of work, and should receive equal pay. The accounting and control necessary for this have been *simplified* by capitalism to the utmost, till they have become the extraordinarily simple operations of watching, recording and issuing receipts, within the reach of anybody who can read and write and knows the first four rules of arithmetic.

When the *majority* of the people begin everywhere to keep such accounts and maintain such control over the capitalists (now converted into employees) and over the intellectual gentry, who still retain capitalist habits, this control will really become universal, general, national; and there will be no way of getting away from it, there will be "nowhere to go."

The whole of society will have become one office and one factory, with equal work and equal pay.

But this "factory" discipline, which the proletariat will extend to the whole of society after the defeat of the capitalists and the overthrow of the exploiters, is by no means our ideal, or our final aim. It is but a *foothold* necessary for the radical cleansing of society of all the hideousness and foulness of capitalist exploitation, *in order to advance further*.

From the moment when all members of society, or even only the overwhelming majority, have learned how to govern the state *themselves*, have taken this business into their own hands, have "established" control over the insignificant minority of capitalists, over the gentry with capitalist leanings, and the workers thoroughly demoralized by capitalism—from this moment the need for any government begins to disappear. The more complete the democracy, the nearer the moment when it begins to be unnecessary. The more democratic the "state" consisting of armed workers, which is "no longer a state in the proper sense of the word," the more rapidly does *every* state begin to wither away.

For when *all* have learned to manage, and independently are actually managing by themselves social production, keeping accounts, controlling the idlers, the gentlefolk, the swindlers, and similar "guardians of capitalist traditions," then the escape from this national accounting and control will inevitably become so increasingly difficult, such a rare exception, and will probably be accompanied by such swift and severe punishment (for the armed workers are men of practical life, not sentimental intellectuals, and they will scarcely allow anyone to trifle with them), that very soon the *necessity* of observing the simple, fundamental rules of everyday social life in common will have become a *habit.*

The door will then be wide open for the transition from the first phase of communist society to its higher phase, and along with it to the complete withering away of the state.

2. *Stalinism.* The following are selections from two speeches delivered by Stalin in 1924.[5]

[Stalin on the Soviets]

The victory of the dictatorship of the proletariat signifies the suppression of the bourgeoisie, the destruction of the bourgeois state machinery, and the displacement of bourgeois democracy by proletarian democracy. That is clear. But what organizations are to be employed for this colossal undertaking? There can hardly be any doubt that the old forms of proletarian organization which grew up with bourgeois parliamentarism as their base are not equal to this task. What new forms of proletarian organization are required to break up the machinery, to displace bourgeois democracy by proletarian democracy, and, above all, to serve as the foundation of the state power of the proletariat?

This new form of organization of the proletariat is the soviets.

Why are the soviets stronger than the old forms of organization? Because the soviets are absolutely *all-embracing* mass organizations of the proletariat and because they and they alone embrace all workers without exception.

The soviets are the *only* mass organizations that take in all the oppressed and exploited, workers and peasants, soldiers and sailors; and for this reason the vanguard of the masses of the proletariat can most easily and most completely bring to fruition its political direction of the struggle of the masses.

The soviets are *the most powerful organs* of the revolutionary mass struggle, of the mass political demonstrations, and of the mass uprising; they are organs capable of breaking the omnipotence of finance capital and its political satellites.

The soviets are the organizations which organize the masses themselves directly, *i.e., the most democratic,* signifying the most authoritative, organizations of the masses, that provide them with the maximum facilities for participating in the building up of the new state and its administration; they develop to their fullest extent the revolutionary energy, the initiative and the creative faculties of the masses in the struggle for the destruction of the old system, in the struggle for the new proletarian system.

The soviet power is the unification and the crystallization of the local soviets into one general state organization, into a state organization of the proletariat as the vanguard of the oppressed and exploited masses and, as the ruling class, their unification into the soviet republic.

The soviet power is in essence the fact that the largest and most revolutionary mass organizations of precisely those classes that were oppressed by the capitalists and landed proprietors now constitute the "*permanent* and *sole* foundation of all state power, of the entire state apparatus"; . . .

For this reason the soviet power is a *new form* of state organization different in principle from the old bourgeois democratic and parliamentary form. . . .

The soviet power combines the legislative and executive functions in a single state body and replaces territorial electoral divisions by units of production, *i.e.,* factories and workshops, and thereby connects the workers and the laboring masses in general directly with the apparatus of state administration and teaches them how to administer the country. . . .

The soviet republic is thus the political form, so long sought and finally found, within the framework of which the economic emancipation of the proletariat and the complete victory of socialism is to be accomplished. The Paris Commune handed it down to us in embryonic form. The soviet power is its development and culmination.

[Stalin on the Party]

The Party must first of all constitute the *vanguard* of the working class. The Party must absorb all the best elements of the working class, their experience, their revolutionary spirit, and their unbounded devotion to the cause of the proletariat. But in order that it may really be the vanguard, the Party must be armed with a revolutionary theory, with a knowledge of the laws of the movement, with a knowledge of the laws of the revolution. . . . The Party cannot be a real party if it limits itself to registering what the masses of the working class think or experience, if it drags along at the tail of the spontaneous movement, if it does not know how to overcome the inertia and the political indifference of the spontaneous movement; or if it cannot rise above the ephemeral interests of the proletariat, if it cannot raise the masses to the level of the class interests of the proletariat. . . . The Party is the political leader of the working class. . . .

The Party is not only the vanguard of the working class. If it really desires to lead the struggle of the class it must at the same time be the *organized* detachment of its class. . . .

But the Party is not merely the *sum total* of Party organizations. The Party at the same time represents a single *system* of these organizations, their formal unification into a single whole, permitting of higher and lower organs of leadership of the submission of the minority to the majority, where decisions on questions of practice are obligatory upon all members of the Party. . . .

The Party is the organized detachment of the working class. But the Party is not the only organization of the working class. The proletariat has in addition a great number of other organizations which are indispensable in its struggle against the capitalist system. . . . Most of these organizations are nonparty. . . . The question then arises: Who is to determine the line, the general direction along which the work of all these organizations is to be conducted? Where is that central organization with the necessary experience to work out such a general line and also able, because of its authority, to prevail upon all these organizations to carry out this line, so as to attain unity of direction and preclude the possibility of working at cross purposes?

This organization is the Party of the proletariat. . . .

The Party is the highest form of class organization of the proletariat.

This does not mean, of course, that nonparty organizations like trade unions, operatives, etc., must be formally subordinated to Party leadership. It means simply that the members of the Party who belong to these organizations and doubtless exercise influence in them, should do all they can to persuade these nonparty organizations to draw nearer to the Party of the proletariat in their work and voluntarily accept its political guidance. . . .

The proletariat needs the Party not only to achieve the dictatorship, it needs it still more to maintain and extend its dictatorship in order to attain complete victory for socialism. . . .

Now what is meant by "maintaining" and "extending" the dictatorship? It means to imbue these millions of proletarians with the spirit of discipline and organization; it means making the proletarian masses immune against the deteriorating influences of petty-bourgeois spontaneity and petty-bourgeois habits: . . . it means assistance must be given to the masses of the proletarians in educating themselves so that they may become a force capable of abolishing classes and of preparing the ground for the organization of socialist production. But it is impossible to accomplish all this without a Party, which is strong by reason of its cohesion and discipline. . . .

The proletariat needs the Party *for* the achieving and maintenance of the dictatorship. The Party is the instrument of the dictatorship of the proletariat.

From this it follows that when classes disappear and the dictatorship of the proletariat will die out, the Party will also die out. . . .

Achievement and maintenance of the dictatorship of the proletariat are impossible without a party strong in its cohesion and iron discipline. But iron discipline in the Party is impossible without unity of will and without absolute and complete unity of action on the part of all members of the Party. This does not mean of course that there will never be any conflict of opinion within the Party. On the contrary, iron discipline does not preclude but presupposes criticism and conflicts of opinion within the Party. Least of all does it mean that this discipline must be "blind" discipline. On the contrary, iron discipline does not preclude but presupposes conscious and voluntary submission, for only conscious discipline can be truly iron discipline. But after a discussion has been closed, after criticism has run its course and a decision has been made, unity of will and unity of action become indispensable conditions without which Party unity and iron discipline in the Party are inconceivable. . . .

It follows that the existence of factions is incompatible with Party unity and with its iron discipline. . . .

The Party is synonymous with unity of will, which leaves no room for any factionalism or division of Party control.

    3. *Communist International Policy.* The attitude of Communist states toward other countries, though basically governed by party ideology, has undergone numerous changes since 1917. Following are representative pronouncements by Soviet spokesmen at critical points in international relations.

[Karl Radek, The Bases of Soviet Foreign Policy, January 1934]

Foreign policy is a function of domestic policy. It solves problems which result from the development of a given society, a given state, under definite historical conditions. . . .

It is silly to say that geography plays the part of fate, that it determines the foreign policy of a state. Czarist policy originated not in geographical conditions, but in the privileges of the Russian nobility and the demands of young Russian capitalism. The questions raised by geography are dealt with by each social formation in its own way; that way is determined by its peculiar economic and political aims. . . .

The main object for which Soviet diplomacy is fighting is *peace*. Now this term "peace" is much abused. There is no diplomat whose official pronouncements do not use this term reverently over and over again, even though he is a representative of one of those imperialistic nations which are most active in preparing war. But those who are incapable of understanding the specific place occupied by the struggle for peace in Soviet foreign policy are altogether incapable of understanding that policy in whole or in part. Why is the struggle for peace the central object of Soviet policy? Primarily because the Soviet Union—to use the expression of Lenin—"has everything necessary for the building up of a socialist society." . . .

Does the Soviet Union need war in order to build up socialism? It does not. Certain capitalist circles have stubbornly asserted since the Soviet Union was founded that it would seek a solution of its difficulties in war; these assertions are repudiated by the history of the Soviet Union during its sixteen years of life. Even at the moment when we were particularly ill equipped to undertake the building-up of socialism, immediately after we had assumed governmental responsibilities, we readily accepted the heaviest sacrifices in order to give peace to the country. We deeply believed—and this was of great importance—that we had in our hands everything necessary for building up a socialist society. Now we know that the problem of building socialism in the Soviet Union admits of a practical solution and that a considerable part of the problem has been already solved. The peace policy of the Soviet Union therefore rests on the granite foundation of triumphant socialist construction.

The enemies of the Soviet Union attempt to undermine the importance of this fact from two directions. Some of them accuse the Soviet Union of having given up its international aims. These aims, in their opinion, would demand military intervention by the Soviet Union to aid the emancipation of the international proletariat and of the colonial peoples. Others, on the contrary, maintain that, because the Bolshevik Party which controls the Soviet Union is inherently an international party, all the peace declarations of the Soviet Union are purely provisional and hence, that having reached a certain economic level which enables it to wage an aggressive war, the Soviet Union will repudiate its peace declarations and assume the initiative in a war. The best way of answering both these accusations is to quote the statement made by Stalin in December 1926: . . .

"And what is meant by 'victory on the world scale'? Does it mean that such a victory is equivalent to the victory of socialism in a single country? No, it does not. Lenin in his writings carefully distinguished the victory of socialism in a single country from victory 'on the world scale.' What Lenin really means when he speaks of 'victory on the world scale' is that *the success of socialism in our country, the victory of consolidating socialism in our country, has such an immense international significance that it (the victory) cannot be limited to our country alone but is bound to call forth a powerful movement toward socialism in all capitalist countries,* and even if it does not coincide with the victory of the proletarian revolution in other countries, it must in any event lead to a strong proletarian movement of other nations toward the victory of world revolution. Such is the revolutionary outlook according to Lenin, if we think in terms of the outlook for the victory of the revolution, which after all is the question in which we in the Party are interested." . . .

The Soviet Union is opposed to imperialism. It is opposed to an imperialistic war. It recognizes as equitable only one war, the war for the defense of socialism, the war of the enslaved peoples for their liberation. This point of view determines our attitude toward imperialism, as a system, and toward the consequences of its policy which find their expression in the preparation of a new war. It also dictates our attitude toward imperialistic alliances which evolve during the process of preparing a new war for the redistribution of the world.

The Soviet Union takes no part in the struggle for the redistribution of the world.

The words of Stalin at the sixteenth congress of the Communist Party of the Soviet Union—"We do not want a single bit of foreign land; but at the same time not an inch of our land shall ever be yielded to anyone else"—these words are the exact expression of the policy of the Soviet Union. . . .

The Soviet Union is confronted both in Europe and the Far East with hostile camps which are preparing war against one another. It holds toward them a position of neutrality, and endeavors to guarantee its own peace by a policy of noninterference in their affairs and by entering into mutual obligations of nonaggression with all sides. These obligations have been stated concretely and precisely in the pact containing the definition of the aggressor. The Soviet government has definitely undertaken not to move its armed forces by land, sea, or air across the frontiers of states which have assumed similar obligations, and also not to intervene directly or indirectly in their domestic affairs. All this indicates to the world that the policy of peace and neutrality on which the Soviet Union has embarked is not a mere diplomatic gesture, but a concrete political obligation in the earnestness of which should be beyond question. . . .

The Soviet Union does not close the door to the possibility of a deal, an agreement, with imperialistic powers which are waging a struggle against other imperialistic powers, if the latter attack the Soviet Union; but in entering into such an agreement the Soviet Union would not accept any responsibility for the specific purposes pursued by the imperialistic powers parties to the agreement. Never and under no conditions would it participate in the plundering of other nations, because participation in such a plunder would be contrary to the international solidarity of the workers. But against attacking imperialism an agreement is permissible with any opponent in order to defeat an enemy invading Soviet territory.

[Stalin, Interview with Elliott Roosevelt, December 1946]

Question: Do you consider it possible for such a democracy as the U. S. to live at peace side by side in this world with such a Communist form of state administration as exists in the Soviet Union, and that neither one side nor the other will make an attempt to intervene in the internal position or political affairs of the other side?

Answer: Yes, of course. This is not only possible, it is reasonable and fully realizable. At the most tense times during the war, differences in the form of government did not prevent our two countries from uniting and conquering our enemies. To an even greater degree it is possible to retain these relations in peacetime.

[Zhdanov, Cominform Declaration, September 1947]

The fundamental changes caused by the war on the international scene and in the position of individual countries has entirely changed the political landscape of the world. A new alignment of political forces has arisen. The more the war recedes into the past, the more distinct become two major trends in post-war international policy, corresponding to the division of the political forces operating on the international arena into two major camps; the imperialist and anti-democratic camp, on the one hand, and the anti-imperialist and democratic camp, on the other. The principal driving force of the imperialist

camp is the U. S. A. Allied with it are Great Britain and France.

The anti-fascist forces comprise the second camp. This camp is based on the USSR and the new democracies. It also includes countries that have broken with imperialism and have firmly set foot on the path of democratic development, such as Rumania, Hungary, and Finland . . .

The anti-imperialist camp is backed by the labor and democratic movement and by the fraternal Communist Parties in all countries, by the fighter for national liberation in the colonies and dependencies, by all progressive and democratic forces in every country. The purpose of this camp is to resist the threat of new wars and imperialist expansion, to strengthen democracy and to extirpate the vestiges of fascism.

. . . The change in the general alignment of forces between the capitalist world and the Socialist world brought about by the war has still further enhanced the significance of the foreign policy of the Soviet state and enlarged the scope of its activity on the international arena.

[Burdzhalov, International Significance of Historical Experience of Bolshevik Party, September 1948]

The defense tactics, from the point of view of the Bolsheviks, are a means for preserving the cadres and building up strength in anticipation of coming battles. The party avoided a decisive encounter whenever it was not yet ready for combat. But the Bolshevik Party never overlooked a single advantageous opportunity to engage the enemy in combat when it was to the enemy's disadvantage. It kept the enemy constantly tense: it disorganized and demoralized his forces, and at the same time it tempered and increased its own forces in daily battles with the enemy. Comrade Stalin called these the tactics of active defense . . .

The Bolshevik Party sought to occupy positions on all combat sectors and to put into combat readiness all types of armaments, for it is impossible to know beforehand what means of combat will prove to be the most advantageous for achieving a given end. Lenin remarked that the revolutionary class must first master all methods of combat without any exception whatsoever, and, second, must be ready for the most rapid and least expected substitution of one combat method for another. This also constitutes the chief rule of tactical leadership.

[Pravda Article, October 1948]

Lenin and Stalin teach that every country will traverse the road toward Socialism taking into account the peculiarities of its historical development. Notwithstanding all these peculiarities, however, the policy of the Communist parties of the countries of people's democracy is determined by the laws of the transition period from capitalism to socialism which were discovered by Lenin and Stalin on the basis of generalization from the practical experience of Socialist construction in the USSR.

. . . The transition from capitalism to socialism in the countries of people's democracy can be effected successfully only with the assistance of the Soviet Union and in close friendship with the Soviet Union . . . Only those are true proletarian internationalists who base their activity on the principles of Marxism-Leninism, who take as their starting point the experience of the USSR and of the Communist party of the Soviet Union, who understand the leading role of the Soviet Union . . . in the world's anti-imperialist camp, who unconditionally uphold and defend the USSR and who firmly and consistently pursue a policy of cooperation and friendship with the first country of victorious Socialism in the world.

[Vishinsky, Communism and Motherland, 1948]

At present the only determining criterion of revolutionary proletarian internationalism is: are you for or against the USSR, the motherland of the world proletariat? An internationalist is not one who verbally recognizes international solidarity or sympathizes with it. A real internationalist is one who brings his sympathy and recognition up to the point of practical and maximal help to the USSR in support and defense of the USSR by every means and in every possible form. Actual cooperation with the USSR, the readiness of the workers of any country to subject all their aims to the basic problem of strengthening the USSR in their struggle—this is the manifestation of revolutionary proletarian internationalism on the part of workmen in foreign countries . . .

. . . The defense of the USSR, as of the socialist mother land of the world proletariat, is the holy duty of every honest man everywhere and not only of the citizens of the USSR.

Part II.   THE DEMOCRATIC APPROACH

During the last years of the nineteenth century many liberal thinkers had come, like John Stuart Mill, to regard their institutions as "merely provisional." They had ceased to be doctrinaires. They were willing to experiment freely with social arrangements, and to revaluate their methods frequently, in order to reach their ideal of a free and peaceful world. The pressure of war and economic distress in the twentieth century urged the democracies on to broader and deeper reconsideration of their basic problems. The documents in Part II reveal the lines of thought and action followed by their leaders in these years.

A.   GREAT BRITAIN

The political history of Britain in the twentieth century has been marked chiefly by the decline of the Liberal party, the rise of Labour, and the steady persistence of the Conservatives. The Liberals led the country far along the path of social reform from 1906 to 1914 and then were reduced to a small splinter group in the interwar years. In their place grew the Labour Party, to give Britain a period of socialist reform from 1945 to 1951. The Conservatives dominated the scene most of the rest of the time. In the documents below prominent members of each party give their estimates of British democracy.

1. *Liberalism.* The Rt. Hon. Sir Henry Slesser (1883–   ), a Liberal lawyer and judge, published in 1944 *A History of the Liberal Party* as a survey of the Liberal past and an endeavor to assess the potency of liberalism in his own time. In the following selection Slesser states his conclusions.[7]

Three reasons, perhaps incompatible, have been advanced to account for the disappearance of the Liberal Party as an effective force in poli-

tics. The first, and more superficial, is to assert that the purposes for which the Whigs and their successors stood have been fully achieved: the relations of Crown and Parliament have been finally determined, the rule of law has been irrevocably established, and the Commons, under adult suffrage, have been finally accepted as the rulers of the nation, to govern according to the people's will; there is nothing more for Liberalism to do. They have perished of success; their work is done.

Another explanation for their failure to continue as a party with any reasonable prospect of power lies in the assertion that the ideal for which Liberalism contended is spent. Sociology, it is said, has exploded the notion of the free autonomous individual—man is but the creature of his race and environment; the exact influences of each may be a subject of dispute, but essentially he is but a unit in society—we are back with Plato and Hegel.

In this latter view, planning by competent authority must be the prime concern of governments and society. Irresponsible plutocrats are to be condemned as much as eccentric anarchs; both distract the community from its essential purpose, to breed, educate, and sustain functionaries to serve and fight for the nation—all else is futile and may be dangerous. Liberalism is negative, it relies upon the notion of liberty; social purpose, not freedom, is the modern ideal; from this standpoint, fascism and communism are but extreme illustrations of the good life—even a religious sanction can be found in the notion of uncritical dedication to service.

Whether, therefore, a resurrection of Liberalism is probable may depend upon the possibility of the recapture of the vision of the basic invaluable quality of personality. If the present collective outlook persists or develops, the very notion may be incomprehensible to future generations. Recurrent war has done much to destroy Liberalism. It is not an accident that Asquith, the last Liberal leader, was unable to weather the upheaval of 1914. As has been said, his prejudices against conscription and compulsory labor delayed the passing of the Military Service Acts.

As to the common law, for which the first Liberal parliamentarians contended, ever since the introduction of the National Insurance Acts, one civic function after another has been withdrawn from juridical determination. The decision of the House of Lords in a recent case, that a minister has but to state that he has reasonable grounds for the exercise of his powers under some statute or regulation to justify detentions without trial, opens up a possibility of autocracy which need not necessarily be confined to the exigencies of war.

The decay of party government may assist the progress of benevolent surveillance; in the Middle Ages, the cities of Italy won their freedom through the contending claims of Pope and emperor—when all are agreed how to organize and educate the citizen, his prospects of independence are poor.

At the same time it must be confessed that the present program of the Liberals, as exemplified in the publications of Ramsay Muir, their political philosopher, is very inconclusive. In 1920, under the title, *Liberalism and Industry*, he wrote: "Real liberty is not mere absence of restraint, it is security in doing, by a man's free choice, all or any of the things that are worth doing and that are not harmful to his neighbors—first and foremost the Liberal concern is to preserve or increase human liberty—Liberalism attaches an infinite value to human personality." . . .

This is very fine, no instructed civilized man could dissent from it. He goes on to point out how nineteenth-century Liberalism, in its limited advocacy of the mere removal of restriction in the economic sphere, meant that "the rich were left free to employ the power that their riches gave them over the unprotected poor." . . .

"Liberals, nevertheless," he declares, "believe in a man being allowed to save what he earns." . . . "Far from agreeing to the abolition of the ownership of capital, the Liberal would desire to extend it more widely. In the ideal Liberal state everybody would have the chance of creating capital by thrift." . . . This kind of capitalism, it appears, Liberals still defend. In conclusion, the author, not very convincingly, asserts that "modern Liberalism is not merely helpless and bewildered in face of the problems which surround us." Those not in the Liberal assembly may be less sure.

Yet a third suggestion which has been advanced to account for the fact that in this present age few boys and girls are "born little Liberals" (or become so) is that liberalism has so converted the other two parties that the modern Conservative and supporter of labor alike accept all Mr. Muir's assumptions. There is much to be said for this view. If it be correct, the fall of the Liberal Party is but an incident in the general acceptance of libertarian ideals; if it be false, the failure of liberalism may prove to be an unqualified disaster.

2. *Labour.* The Rt. Hon. Clement R. Attlee (1883–   ) was socialist prime minister from 1945 to 1951. In the following selection from a radio address made in January 1948 Mr. Attlee explains the philosophy of his party.[8]

Mr. Walter Elliott a fortnight ago said that we wanted a restatement of the old controversy between freedom and order, liberty and authority. What is needed is not so much a restatement as a reconciliation for we need both authority and liberty.

My contention is that this reconciliation can only be achieved through the application of the principles of democratic socialism, of which the British Labour Party is the outstanding champion. I claim that here in Britain the British people through the Labour government are giving a practical lead to the world, a lead which is needed today in order to preserve our heritage of European civilization, a lead which cannot be given by a Conservative or Liberal government.

In the nineteenth century the contest between liberal and authority was fought largely on political issues. Liberalism rendered a great service to the world in fighting for freedom of democracy, but it failed to deal with the problem of economic freedom. In the name of freedom it left in the hands of the few the power which the possession of land and capital gives to its possessors over the many. Therefore when the struggle passed from the political to the economic field the Liberal Party was superseded. It had finished its task. The freedoms which it won are cherished today in this country not only by the Labour Party but also by its old opponents the Conservatives who have to a large extent accepted its political principles. That is why the Liberal Party is reduced so low today. What is true and vital in liberalism has become the common doctrine of all democratic parties. But liberalism which triumphed in western Europe was never really accepted or put into practice in eastern Europe. Today in eastern Europe the Communist Party while overthrowing an economic tyranny of landlordism and capitalism has renounced the doctrines of individual freedom and political democracy and rejected the whole spiritual heritage of western Europe.

The history of Soviet Russia provides us with a warning here—a warning that without political freedom, collectivism can quickly go astray and lead to new forms of oppression and injustice. For political freedom is not merely a noble thing in itself, essential for the full development of human personality—it is also a means of achieving economic rights and social justice, and of preserving these things when they have been won. Where there is no political freedom privilege and injustice creep back. In communist Russia "privilege for the few" is a growing phenomenon, and the gap between the highest and lowest incomes is constantly widening. Soviet communism pursues a policy which threatens with a new form of imperialism—ideological, economic, and strategic —the welfare and way of life of the other nations of Europe.

At the one end of the scale are the communist countries; at the other end the United States of America stands for individual liberty in the political sphere and for the maintenance of human rights. But its economy is based on capitalism with all the problems which it presents and with the characteristic extreme inequality of wealth in its citizens. As a new country with immense resources it has not yet had to face the acute problems which have arisen in the other capitalist countries.

Great Britain like the other countries of western Europe is placed geographically and from the point of view of economic and political theory between these two great continental states. That is not to say that our ideas are in any sense "watered-down capitalism" or "watered-down communism" or that they constitute a temporary halting-place on a journey from one creed to the other. Ours is a philosophy in its own right. Our task is to work out a system of a new and challenging kind which combines individual freedom with a planned economy, democracy with social justice. This task which faces not only ourselves but all the Western democracies requires a government inspired by a new conception of society with a dynamic policy in accord with the needs of a new situation. It could not be accomplished by any of the old parties nor by a totalitarian party whether fascist or communist.

> 3. *Conservatism.* Sir Winston L. S. Churchill (1874–   ) has been a member of both Liberal and Conservative parties. As wartime premier of Britain from 1940–1945 he came to be the very symbol of Conservatism, John Bull himself. In 1951 he returned to office and retired in 1955. Following is a portion of an election address made by Churchill during his last campaign as party leader.[9]

Let me mention to you some of the great issues on which Conservatives and Liberals are agreed, and which constitute the elements of the common cause vital to our national welfare. First, we proclaim that the state is the servant and not the master of the people. We reject altogether the socialist conception of a division of society between officials and the common mass. We repudiate their policy of leveling down to a minimum uniformity, above which only politicians and their agents may rise. We stand for the increasingly higher expression of individual independence. We hold most strongly to the Declaration of Human Rights, as set forth by the United Nations at Geneva. . . .

No doubt there are other points upon which Liberals and Conservatives do not agree. But how small they are in scale and importance compared to the great body of fundamental principles and practical schemes of application on which both anti-Socialist parties are in accord, and which are now supported by a large majority of electors all over the country. There is a wide overlap of agreement, both in doctrine and in action, between those who have hitherto been brought up to regard themselves as political opponents. But now the times are very grave, and it is the duty of every man and woman who agrees upon so large a proportion of the main principles and practical steps, to make sure that these are not overwhelmed by the ignorant and obsolete doctrine of Socialism, against which the British nation stands today in marked recoil. . . .

More than 40 years ago I sat myself in a Left-wing Government with a great majority, and I was one of their most prominent and controversial figures. . . . The Liberal Government of 1906 was built around and upon those great principles of liberalism, which have since passed into the possession of every party except the Communists, and are still spreading with irresistible appeal throughout the world. But now our opponents are not ranged around the great truths of liberalism; they are ranged around the fallacy of socialism, which is in principle contrary to human nature and which I believe can only be enforced upon nations in its entirety in the wholesale fashion of communism. . . .

I find comfort in the broad harmony of thought which prevails between the modern Tory democracy and the doctrines of the famous Liberal leaders of the past. I am sure that in accord with their speeches and writings, men like Asquith, Morley and Grey whom I knew so well in my youth, would have regarded the establishment of a Socialist State and the enforcement of the collectivist theory as one of the worst evils that could befall Britain and her slowly evolved, long-cherished way of life. . . .

The supreme question is, are we after our experiences of the last six years to take another deep plunge into socialism or regain the high road, which all the rest of the English-speaking world are now treading, of free enterprise and opportunity for all, and of the strong helping the weak? It is better for the strong to help the weak, than for the weak to hinder the strong. Basic standards of life and labor must be secured in our society and civilization, and on this foundation everyone should be free to use his or her gifts and qualities to the full. In this way alone can our 50 millions, crowded in our island, safeguard their food, their work and their homes.

But beware! For we may be at the parting of the ways. The wisdom of our ancestors for more than 300 years has sought the division of power in the constitution. Crown, Lords and Commons have been checks and restraints upon one another. The limitation of the power of the monarchy was the cause for which, as Liberals used to say, "Hampden died in the field and Sidney on the scaffold." The concentration of all power over the daily lives of ordinary men and women in what is called "the state," exercised by what

is virtually single-chamber government, is a reactionary step contrary to the whole trend of British history and to the message we have given to the world.

The British race have always abhorred arbitrary and absolute government in every form. The great men who founded the American Constitution embodied this separation of authority in the strongest and most durable form. Not only did they divide executive, legislative and judicial functions, but also by instituting a federal system they preserved immense and sovereign rights to local communities, and by all these means they have preserved—often at some inconvenience—a system of law and liberty under which they have thrived and reached the leadership of the world.

The socialist conception of the all-powerful state entering into the smallest detail of the life and conduct of the individual and claiming to plan and shape his work and its rewards is odious and repellent to every friend of freedom. These absolute powers would make the group of politicians who obtained a majority of seats in Parliament the masters and not the servants of the people and would centralize all government in Whitehall. . . .

The worship of an all-powerful state, beneath which the ordinary mass of citizens lies prostrate, is one of the most deadly and insidious delusions by which a free people, as we still are, can cast away rights and liberties, which for their own sake and the sake of their children, they ought to hold dearer than life itself. The British nation now has to make one of the most momentous choices in its history.

That choice is between two ways of life; between individual liberty and state domination; between the concentration of ownership in the hands of the state and the extension of a property-owning democracy; between a policy of increasing control and restriction, and a policy of liberating energy and ingenuity; between a policy of levelling down and a policy of finding opportunity for all to rise upwards from a basic standard. . . .

We must not lose faith in our race and in our destiny. We are the same people, in the same island, as we were in the great days we can all remember. Our spirit is unconquerable, our ingenuity and craftsmanship unsurpassed. Our latent resources are unmeasured. Our underlying unities are enduring. We have but to cast away by an effort of will the enfeebling tendencies and mental infirmities of Socialism and free ourselves from Socialist rule to stand erect once more and take our place amongst the great powers of the world.

B.   FRANCE

The collapse of the Third Republic amid military defeat in 1940 annihilated French political parties and called into question the validity of liberal doctrine. Pétain reigned at Vichy in the shadow of the German army, and totalitarianism seemed triumphant. But French liberals sought a revaluation of their ideals in the hour of defeat, and notable among their new tracts was *The Rights of Man and Natural Law* by Jacques Maritain (1882–   ), a Catholic liberal who sought hope for his country in a combination of liberalism with the religion of the majority of his countrymen. Selections from Maritain's work follow.[10]

One of the causes of the debilities and weaknesses from which the democracies suffered at the beginning of the war was that they partly lost faith in themselves. In the midst of disaster they have now regained a belief in their principles. At the same time they fully realize that they must profoundly revivify their philosophy to put themselves in a position to accomplish what the world expects of them. Peace will be won and civilization reconstructed only if the free peoples are clearly aware of their principles and their aims, and only if a strong and generous hope animates the desire for their realization.

Of particular concern for France is the fact that among the French people a profound disgust for all previous political organizations is joined with a love of liberty which is stronger than ever before. Military defeat, then the armistice and capitulation, then the policy of collaboration have successfully liquidated all parties. Abandoned by their leaders and their government, the French people can rely on none but themselves; and when they have regained their liberty, they will have to construct a wholly new edifice.

The new declaration of rights will be their work. The political and social institutions of the France of tomorrow will be the result of an infinitely bitter experience. . . . If one may take it for granted that the French people will not return to the particular forms of the prewar regime, everything that we know indicates that they aspire to a regime whose new forms will realize better and more completely an ideal democracy, both in the social and political order. In an abyss of suffering, France has taken up again her true vocation, that vocation which has its source in the Gospel and in reason, that vocation which is essentially one of liberation. It is fidelity to this mission of freedom—the instinct for justice, the knowledge of the rights of the human individual, of liberty, equality, and fraternity—which has inspired the mass of the people to run every risk in resisting the yoke of foreign domination. But to succeed in their heroic task, they will need a revivified vocabulary and ideology. . . .

We have not discussed in this study the rights concerned with the international order, whose consideration belongs to a special field, and among which the most important are the right of each state, large or small, to freedom and respect for its autonomy, the right to the respecting of solemn oaths and the sanctity of treaties, the right to peaceful development (a right which, being valid for all, requires for its own development the establishment of an international community having juridical power, and the development of federative forms of organization). It may not be altogether unnecessary at this point to make a summary list of those rights of which we have spoken.

Rights of the Human Person as Such—The Right to Existence

The right to personal liberty or the right to conduct one's own life as master of oneself and of one's acts, responsible for them before God and the law of the community. The right to the pursuit of the perfection of rational and moral human life. The right to the pursuit of eternal life along the path which conscience has recognized as the path indicated by God. The right of the Church and other religious families to the free exercise of their spiritual activity. The right of pursuing a religious vocation; the freedom of religious orders and groups. The right to marry according to one's choice and to raise a family, which will in its turn be assured of the liberties due it; the right of the family society to respect for its constitution, which is based on natural law, not on the law of the state, and which fundamentally involves the morality of the human being. The right to keep one's body whole. The right to property. Finally, the right of every human being to be treated as a person, not as a thing.

Rights of the Civic Person

The right of every citizen to participate actively in political life, and in particular the right of equal suffrage for all. The right of the people to establish the constitution of the state and to determine for themselves their form of government. The right of association, limited only by the juridically recognized necessities of the common good, and in particular the right to form political parties or political schools. The right of free investigation and discussion (freedom of expression). Political equality, and the equal right of every citizen to his security and his liberties within the state. The equal right of every one to the guarantees of an independent judiciary power. Equal possibility of admission to public employment and free access to the various professions.

Rights of the Social Person, and More Particularly of the Working Person

The right freely to choose his work. The right freely to form vocational groups or trade unions.

The right of the worker to be considered socially as an adult. The right of economic groups (trade unions and working communities) and other social groups to freedom and autonomy. The right to a just wage. The right to work. And wherever an associative system can be substituted for the wage system, the right to the joint ownership and joint management of the enterprise, and to the "worker's title." The right to relief, unemployment insurance, sick benefits, and social security. The right to have a part, free of charge, depending on the possibilities of the community, in the elementary goods, both material and spiritual, of civilization.

C. GERMANY

The destruction of the Third Reich in 1945 left Germany split into two sections, one occupied by the Western allies, the other by the Russians. Helpless and divided, Germans found it as hard to evaluate their historical experience as to plan for their future. One articulate voice was that of Friedrich Meinecke (1862–1954), one of Germany's most distinguished historians. In *The German Catastrophe*, published in 1946, he sought to apply the lessons of the past to solve the problems of his country. Selections from his work follow.[11]

To be defenseless now does not mean that we shall always be defenseless. It is humiliating enough for us that when we may enjoy the rights of a free nation depends on the decision of foreign powers. Today, however, the anger over our humiliation should be turned primarily against those who are to blame for it, against the overweening pride of those who led us to the abyss, and against the lack of judgment of those who subjected themselves to this leadership without any inner protest.

The radical break with our military past that we must now accept faces us with the question about what is to become of our historical traditions in general. It would be impossible and suicidal to throw them wholesale into the fire and behave as apostates. But our customary picture of the history under which we grew to greatness needs at any rate a fundamental revision in order to discriminate between what was valuable and what was valueless. To do this, according to our conviction, only that type of historical thinking is adequate which perceives the close demonic connection between the valuable and the valueless in history. To "the eternal, iron, great laws" of our existence, of which Goethe spoke in his ode *Das Göttliche*, belongs, we believe, our impression that good and bad, divine and demonic, so often seem to grow into one another. Goethe said in the ode: "Man alone is capable of the impossible. He discriminates,

chooses, judges." How the apparently impossible nevertheless becomes possible, how we in our observation so often see good and evil growing into one another and in our moral actions are able to discriminate and work for the good—that can never be fully comprehended through logic, but must be experienced in life in order to be understood. If then observation ventures the task of discriminating between the good and the bad, between the higher and the lower in our historical past and of replacing traditional accounts of the past by new evaluations, then the observer must remain aware that he is dealing with the work of mortal man and that he is bound by the momentary spirit of the age. And yet the venture must be made! Made with a sense of responsibility, with a pure, humane, and patriotic feeling. . . .

Even a partitioned Germany robbed of her national political existence, which is our lot today, ought to remember with sorrowful mourning the unity and strength that she previously enjoyed. Her former striving for unity and strength was not merely, as Burckhardt saw it in his *Reflections on History*, a blind striving of the masses to whom culture meant nothing. Rather was it borne along, as Burckhardt was not quite fully able to understand, by that great idea of an inner union of spirit and power, by humanity and nationality. Great cultural values emerged for us from it. But this union, as we must make clear to ourselves, was disrupted through our own fault. Now the question arises, shall we immediately work for it anew? In the first place, we are at present prevented from doing so by the external control by foreign powers. To attempt at present to win back a part of the strength of such a union would today lead only to impotent convulsions. For inner reasons also, it must be renounced at present. Our conception of power must first be purified from the filth which came into it during the Third Reich before it can again be capable of forming a union with spirit and culture. The purpose of power must be reflected upon and wisely limited. The desire to become a world power has proven to be a false idol for us. Our geopolitical and geophysical situation alone forbids it. To be a world power is furthermore an adventure which cuts in two directions leading to temptations in which culture is too much the loser. . . .

The historian has only to write down and evaluate the course of events, and not to take part in determining them. But times of great crisis lead him beyond this mission. Therefore let us state our view of the part that power is to play in our future existence, an existence which at present is so powerless. We can win back power only as a member of a future federation, voluntarily concluded, of the central and west European states. Such a United Nations of Europe will naturally accept the hegemony of the victor powers.

The time has not yet come to consider more closely the problems that will grow out of such a federation. But a look at our small Germanic neighboring peoples can teach us some lessons. Sweden and Holland were once great European powers and Switzerland at the beginning of the sixteenth century carried on a policy something like that of a great power. Today they have enough power so that if attacked they could fight manfully. Their defense spirit has remained sound and alive. They would be able to maintain themselves successfully in such a fight, to be sure, only by leaning upon at least one of the great powers. That also will be our destiny in the future.

We have therefore come into the position of these three peoples, of being like burnt-out craters of great power politics, and yet of feeling within ourselves the appeal to remain brave and capable of self-defense. These three peoples have also given evidence of an inner vitality in their whole cultural life. They do not suffer more, or more severely, than we under the problems of the modern age, when the spontaneous spiritual creative power of the individual has to struggle against the pressure of the masses and the flattening effects of technology. All three in recent generations have given us the most beautiful and peculiarly irreplaceable fruits of their poetry, science, and art. I will name only in my own field of science the three names of Jakob Burckhardt, Huizinga, and Kjellén. No one of these three nations—Sweden, Holland, Switzerland—has forgotten the days in which it fought its battles. Each honors and loves its former heroes, even when today there is no place for heroism of the same kind. Such an existence as these three peoples live today is more for them than a kind old-age allotment apportioned to aged peasant parents. All the moral forces and energies of man find room for expression. Let us resolve to follow their example.

On the basis of what we have already said, we shall be asked: How about that intermingling of the great tendencies of the age, the two waves of the nationalist and socialist movements? We reply that the intermingling cannot be a matter of conscious rational planning, but can only proceed by a gradual evolution and in a particular manner for each people. In England, for example, the existence, attitude, and success of the Labour party today proves that it is possible to combine a strong national feeling with a strong socialistic resolve. The reason that Hitler's National Socialist experiment was so unsound was that it threw into the mixing pot the national element only in its most frightful form of a degenerate and unbridled nationalism and a racial madness. As a result, the socialist element that was thrown in from the other side was denatured and robbed of its best content. To be socialist and socialist-minded today and to act accordingly means nothing else but the following of a general humane ideal. It means applying the concept of humanity in a concrete way in modern society— and this humanity is to benefit not only one's own country but also the human community in general. To be socially and humanely minded is one and the same thing at the present stage of Occidental development, when the increased masses of the population admonish us to be so. Then, when a truly healthy intermingling of the nationalist and socialist movements has come about, it must again free us from nationalist excesses and humanize us. *Ritornar al segno* is the watchword for us and for *all* the peoples of the Occident! Did not Herder, when he arose to create a new epoch, proclaim both humanity and nationality?

D.   A PSYCHOLOGIST'S VIEW

In the western democracies the problem of individual freedom was something more than a national question. The work of Freud had revealed aspects of the being Man, undreamed of by early liberals, which could not be left out of consideration. One of the most eminent of twentieth-century psychologists who have analyzed the problem of man in society is Erich Fromm (1900–   ), a German scholar who migrated to the United States at the advent of the Nazi regime. Following is a portion of his work, *Escape from Freedom,* published in 1944.[12]

In the course of modern history the authority of the Church has been replaced by that of the State, that of the State by that of conscience, and in our era, the latter has been replaced by the anonymous authority of common sense and public opinion as instruments of conformity. Because we have freed ourselves of the older overt forms of authority, we do not see that we have become the prey of a new kind of authority. We have become automatons who live under the illusion of being self-willing individuals. This illusion helps the individual to remain unaware of his insecurity, but this is all the help such an illusion can give. Basically the self of the individual is weakened, so that he feels powerless and extremely insecure. He lives in a world to which he has lost genuine relatedness and in which everybody and everything has become instrumentalized, where he has become a part of the machine that his hands have built. He thinks, feels, and wills what he believes he is supposed to think, feel, and will; in this very process he loses his self upon which all genuine security of a free individual must be built.

The loss of the self has increased the necessity to conform, for it results in a profound doubt of one's own identity. If I am nothing but what I believe I am supposed to be—who am "I"? We have seen how the doubt about one's own self started with the breakdown of the medieval order in which the individual had had an unquestionable place in a fixed order. The identity of the individual has been a major problem of modern philosophy since Descartes. Today we take for granted that we are we. Yet the doubt about ourselves still exists, or has even grown. In his plays Pirandello has given expression to this feeling of modern man. He starts with the question: Who am I? What proof have I for my own identity other than the continuation of my physical self? His answer is not like Descartes'—the affirmation of the individual self—but its denial: I have no identity, there is no self excepting the one which is the reflex of what others expect me to be: I am "as you desire me."

This loss of identity then makes it still more imperative to conform; it means that one can be sure of oneself only if one lives up to the expectations of others. If we do not live up to this picture we not only risk disapproval and increased isolation, but we risk losing the identity of our personality, which means jeopardizing sanity.

By conforming with the expectations of others, by not being different, these doubts about one's own identity are silenced and a certain security is gained. However, the price paid is high. Giving up spontaneity and individuality results in a thwarting of life. Psychologically the automaton, while being alive biologically, is dead emotionally and mentally. While he goes through the motions of living, his life runs through his hands like sand. Behind a front of satisfaction and optimism modern man is deeply unhappy; as a matter of fact, he is on the verge of desperation. He desperately clings to the notion of individuality; he wants to be "different," and he has no greater recommendation of anything than that "it is different." We are informed of the individual name of the railroad clerk we buy our tickets from; handbags, playing cards, and portable radios are "personalized," by having the initials of the owner put on them. All this indicates the hunger for "difference" and yet these are almost the last vestiges of individuality that are left. Modern man is starved for life. But since, being an automaton, he cannot experience life in the sense of spontaneous activity he takes as surrogate any kind of excitement and thrill: the thrill of drinking, of sports, of vicariously living the excitements of fictitious persons on the screen.

What then is the meaning of freedom for modern man?

He has become free from the external bonds that would prevent him from doing and thinking as he sees fit. He would be free to act according to his own will, if he knew what he wanted, thought, and felt. But he does not know. He conforms to anonymous authorities and adopts a self which is not his. The more he does this, the more powerless he feels, the more is he forced to conform. In spite of a veneer of optimism and initiative, modern man is overcome by a profound feeling of powerlessness which makes him gaze toward approaching catastrophes as though he were paralyzed.

Looked at superficially, people appear to function well enough in economic and social life; yet it would be dangerous to overlook the deep-seated unhappiness behind that comforting veneer. If life loses its meaning because it is not lived, man becomes desperate. People do not die quietly from physical starvation; they do not die quietly from psychic starvation either. If we look only at the economic needs as far as the "normal" person is concerned, if we do not see the unconscious suffering of the average automatized person, then we fail to see the danger that threatens our culture from its human basis: the readiness to accept any ideology and any leader, if only he promises excitement and offers a political structure and symbols which allegedly give meaning and order to an individual's life. The despair of the human automaton is fertile soil for the political purposes of Fascism. . . .

We believe that there is a positive answer, that the process of growing freedom does not constitute a vicious circle, and that man can be free and yet not alone, critical and yet not filled with doubts, independent and yet an integral part of mankind. This freedom man can attain by the realization of his self, by being himself. What is realization of the self? Idealistic philosophers have believed that self-realization can be achieved by intellectual insight alone. They have insisted upon splitting human personality, so that man's nature may be suppressed and guarded by his reason. The result of this split, however, has been that not only the emotional life of man but also his intellectual faculties have been crippled. Reason, by becoming a guard set to watch its prisoner, nature, has become a prisoner itself; and thus both sides of human personality, reason and emotion, were crippled. We believe that the realization of the self is accomplished not only by an act of thinking but also by the realization of man's total personality, by the active expression of his emotional and intellectual potentialities. These potentialities are present in everybody; they become real only to the extent to which they are expressed. In other words, positive freedom consists in the spontaneous activity of the total, integrated personality. . . .

Why is spontaneous activity the answer to the problem of freedom? We have said that negative freedom by itself makes the individual an isolated being, whose relationship to the world is distant and distrustful and whose self is weak and constantly threatened. Spontaneous activity is the one way in which man can overcome the terror of aloneness without sacrificing the integrity of his self; for in the spontaneous realization of the self man unites himself anew with the world —with man, nature, and himself. Love is the foremost component of such spontaneity; not love as the dissolution of the self in another person, not love as the possession of another person, but love as spontaneous affirmation of others, as the union of the individual with others on the basis of preservation of the individual self. The dynamic quality of love lies in this very polarity: that it springs from the need of overcoming separateness, that it leads to oneness— and yet that individuality is not eliminated. Work is the other component; not work as a compulsive activity in order to escape aloneness, not work as a relationship to nature which is partly one of dominating her, partly one of worship of and enslavement by the very products of man's hands, but work as creation in which man becomes one with nature in the act of creation. What holds true of love and work holds true of all spontaneous action, whether it be the realization of sensuous pleasure or participation in the political life of the community. It affirms the individuality of the self and at the same time it unites the self with man and nature. The basic dichotomy that is inherent in freedom—the birth of individuality and the pain of aloneness—is dissolved on a higher plane by man's spontaneous action. . . .

If the individual realizes his self by spontaneous activity and thus relates himself to the world, he ceases to be an isolated atom; he and the world become part of one structuralized whole; he has his rightful place, and thereby his doubt concerning himself and the meaning of life disappears. This doubt sprang from his separateness and from the thwarting of life; when he can live, neither compulsively nor automatically but spontaneously, the doubt disappears. He is aware of himself as an active and creative individual and recognizes that there is only one meaning of life: the act of living itself.

If the individual overcomes the basic doubt concerning himself and his place in life, if he is related to the world by embracing it in the act of spontaneous living, he gains strength as an individual and he gains security. This security, however, differs from the security that characterizes the preindividualist state in the same way in which the new relatedness to the world differs from that of the primary ties. The new security is not rooted in the protection which the individual has from a higher power outside of himself; neither is it a security in which the tragic quality of life is eliminated. The new security is dynamic; it is not based on protection, but on man's spontaneous activity. It is the security acquired each moment by man's spontaneous activity. It is the security that only freedom can give, that needs no illusions because it has eliminated those conditions that necessitate illusions. . . .

It has been the thesis of this book that freedom has a twofold meaning for modern man: that he has been freed from traditional authorities and has become an "individual," but that at the same time he has become isolated, powerless, and an instrument of purposes outside of himself, alienated from himself and others; furthermore, that this state undermines his self, weakens and frightens him, and makes him ready for submission to new kinds of bondage. Positive freedom on the other hand is identical with the full realization of the individual's potentialities, together with his ability to live actively and spontaneously. Freedom has reached a critical point where, driven by the logic of its own dynamism, it threatens to change into its opposite. The future of democracy depends on the realization of the individualism that has been the ideological aim of modern thought since the Renaissance. The cultural and political crisis of our day is not due to the fact that there is too much individualism but that what we believe to be individualism has become an empty shell. The victory of freedom is possible only if democracy develops into a society in which the individual, his growth and happiness, is the aim and purpose of culture, in which life does not need any justification in success or anything else, and in which the individual is not subordinated to or manipulated by any power outside of himself, be it the State or the economic machine; finally, a society in which his conscience and ideals are not the internalization of external demands, but are really

his and express the aims that result from the peculiarity of his self. These aims could not be fully realized in any previous period of modern history; they had to remain largely ideological aims, because the material basis for the development of genuine individualism was lacking. Capitalism has created this premise. The problem of production is solved—in principle at least—and we can visualize a future of abundance, in which the fight for economic privileges is no longer necessitated by economic scarcity. The problem we are confronted with today is that of the organization of social and economic forces, so that man—as a member of organized society—may become the master of these forces and cease to be their slave. . . .

Only if man masters society and subordinates the economic machine to the purposes of human happiness and only if he actively participates in the social process, can he overcome what now drives him into despair—his aloneness and his feeling of powerlessness. Man does not suffer so much from poverty today as he suffers from the fact that he has become a cog in a large machine, an automaton, that his life has become empty and lost its meaning. The victory over all kinds of authoritarian systems will be possible only if democracy does not retreat but takes the offensive and proceeds to realize what has been its aim in the minds of those who fought for freedom throughout the last centuries. It will triumph over the forces of nihilism only if it can imbue people with a faith that is the strongest the human mind is capable of, the faith in life and in truth, and in freedom as the active and spontaneous realization of the individual self.

E. THE DEMOCRATIC INTERNATIONAL IDEAL

Attempts at international organization for the settlement of disputes among states were carried on from the nineteenth century into the twentieth. The Permanent Court of Arbitration established at The Hague in 1908 provided a tribunal to which nations might voluntarily bring their differences for peaceful solution. The League of Nations was a more ambitious effort to secure world peace and cooperation. Its failure did not deter the victorious powers in World War II from a similar venture, the United Nations, founded at San Francisco in 1945. The new organization was broader in scope, as experience had taught the world that the problems of peace and freedom were many-sided. Following is a selection from the U. N. Charter.[13]

THE CHARTER OF THE UNITED NATIONS

We, the peoples of the United Nations, determined
—to save succeeding generations from the

scourge of war, which twice in our lifetime has brought untold sorrow to mankind, and
—to reaffirm faith in fundamental human rights, in the dignity and worth of the human person, in the equal rights of men and women and of nations large and small, and

—to establish conditions under which justice and respect for the obligations arising from treaties and other sources of international law can be maintained, and

—to promote social progress and better standards of life in larger freedom,
And For These Ends

—to practice tolerance and live together in peace with one another as good neighbors, and

—to unite our strength to maintain international peace and security, and

—to insure, by the acceptance of principles and the institution of methods, that armed force shall not be used, save in the common interest, and

—to employ international machinery for the promotion of the economic and social advancement of all peoples,
Have Resolved To Combine Our Efforts To Accomplish These Aims.

Accordingly, our respective governments, through representatives assembled in the City of San Francisco, who have exhibited their full powers found to be in good and due form, have agreed to the present Charter of the United Nations and do hereby establish an international organization to be known as the United Nations.

Chapter I

PURPOSES AND PRINCIPLES

ARTICLE 1

The purposes of the United Nations are:

1. To maintain international peace and security, and to that end: to take effective collective measures for the prevention and removal of threats to the peace and for the suppression of acts of aggression or other breaches of the peace, and to bring about by peaceful means, and in conformity with the principles of justice and international law, adjustment or settlement of international disputes or situations which might lead to a breach of the peace;

2. To develop friendly relations among nations based on respect for the principle of equal rights and self-determination of peoples, and to take other appropriate measures to strengthen universal peace;

3. To achieve international cooperation in solving international problems of an economic, social, cultural, or humanitarian character, and in promoting and encouraging respect for human rights and for fundamental freedoms for all without distinction as to race, sex, language, or religion; and

4. To be a center for harmonizing the actions of nations in the attainment of these common ends.

ARTICLE 2

The Organization and its Members, in pursuit of the Purposes stated in Article 1, shall act in accordance with the following Principles.

1. The Organization is based on the principle of the sovereign equality of all its Members.

2. All Members, in order to ensure to all of them the rights and benefits resulting from membership, shall fulfill in good faith the obligations assumed by them in accordance with the present Charter.

3. All Members shall settle their international disputes by peaceful means in such a manner that international peace and security, and justice, are not endangered.

4. All Members shall refrain in their international relations from the threat or use of force against the territorial integrity or political independence of any state, or in any other manner inconsistent with the purposes of the United Nations.

5. All Members shall give the United Nations every assistance in any action it takes in accordance with the present Charter, and shall refrain from giving assistance to any state against which the United Nations is taking preventive or enforcement action.

6. The Organization shall ensure that states which are not Members of the United Nations act in accordance with these Principles so far as may be necessary for the maintenance of international peace and security.

7. Nothing contained in the present Charter shall authorize the United Nations to intervene in matters which are essentially within the domestic jurisdiction of any state or shall require the Members to submit such matters to settlement under the present Charter; but this principle shall not prejudice the application of enforcement measures under Chapter VII. . . .

Chapter VI

PACIFIC SETTLEMENT OF DISPUTES

ARTICLE 33

1. The parties to any dispute, the continuance of which is likely to endanger the maintenance of international peace and security, shall, first of all, seek a solution by negotiation, enquiry, mediation, conciliation, arbitration, judicial settlement, resort to regional agencies or arrangements, or other peaceful means of their own choice.

2. The Security Council shall, when it deems necessary, call upon the parties to settle their dispute by such means.

ARTICLE 34

The Security Council may investigate any dispute, or any situation which might lead to international friction or give rise to a dispute, in order to determine whether the continuance of the dispute or situation is likely to endanger the maintenance of international peace and security.

ARTICLE 35

1. Any Member of the United Nations may bring any dispute or any situation of the nature referred to in Article 34 to the attention of the Security Council, or of the General Assembly.

2. A state which is not a Member of the United Nations may bring to the attention of the Security Council or of the General Assembly any dispute to which it is a party, if it accepts in advance, for the purposes of the dispute, the obligations of pacific settlement provided in the present Charter.

3. The proceedings of the General Assembly in respect of matters brought to its attention under this Article will be subject to the provisions of Articles 11 and 12.

ARTICLE 36

1. The Security Council may, at any stage of a dispute of the nature referred to in Article 33, or of a situation of like nature, recommend appropriate procedures or methods of adjustment.

2. The Security Council should take into consideration any procedures for the settlement of the dispute which have already been adopted by the parties.

3. In making recommendations under this Article the Security Council should also take into consideration that legal disputes should as a general rule be referred by the parties to the International Court of Justice in accordance with the provisions of the Statute of the Court.

ARTICLE 37

1. Should the parties to a dispute of the nature referred to in Article 33 fail to settle it by the means indicated in that Article, they shall refer it to the Security Council.

2. If the Security Council deems that the continuance of the dispute is in fact likely to endanger the maintenance of international peace and security, it shall decide whether to take action under Article 36 or to recommend such terms of settlement as it may consider appropriate.

ARTICLE 38

Without prejudice to the provision of Articles 33–37, the Security Council may, if all the parties to any dispute so request, make recommendations to the parties with a view to a pacific settlement of the dispute.

Chapter VII

ACTION WITH RESPECT TO THREATS TO THE PEACE, BREACHES OF THE PEACE, AND ACTS OF AGGRESSION

ARTICLE 39

The Security Council shall determine the existence of any threat to the peace, breach of the peace, or act of aggression and shall make recommendations, or decide what measures shall be taken in accordance with Articles 41 and 42, to maintain or restore international peace and security.

ARTICLE 40

In order to prevent an aggravation of the situation, the Security Council may, before making the recommendations or deciding upon the measures provided for in Article 41, call upon the parties concerned to comply with such provisional measures as it deems necessary or desirable. Such provisional measures shall be without prejudice to the rights, claims, or position of the parties concerned. The Security Council shall duly take account of failure to comply with such provisional measures.

ARTICLE 41

The Security Council may decide what measures not involving the use of armed force are to be employed to give effect to its decisions, and it may call upon the Members of the United Nations to apply such measures. These may include complete or partial interruption of economic relations and of rail, sea, air, postal, telegraphic, radio, and other means of communication, and the severance of diplomatic relations.

ARTICLE 42

Should the Security Council consider that measures provided for in Article 41 would be inadequate or have proved to be inadequate, it may take such action by air, sea, or land forces as may be necessary to maintain or restore international peace and security. Such action may include demonstrations, blockade, and other operations by air, sea, or land forces of Members of the United Nations.

ARTICLE 43

1. All Members of the United Nations, in order to contribute to the maintenance of international peace and security, undertake to make

available to the Security Council, on its call and in accordance with a special agreement or agreements, armed forces, assistance, and facilities, including rights of passage, necessary for the purpose of maintaining international peace and security.

2. Such agreement or agreements shall govern the numbers and types of forces, their degree of readiness and general location, and the nature of the facilities and assistance to be provided.

3. The agreement or agreements shall be negotiated as soon as possible on the initiative of the Security Council. They shall be concluded between the Security Council and Members or between the Security Council and groups of Members and shall be subject to ratification by the signatory states in accordance with their constitutional processes.

ARTICLE 44

When the Security Council has decided to use force it shall, before calling upon a Member not represented on it to provide armed forces in fulfillment of the obligations assumed under Article 43, invite that Member, if the Member so desires, to participate in the decisions of the Security Council concerning the employment of contingents of that Member's armed forces.

ARTICLE 45

In order to enable the United Nations to take urgent military measures, Members shall hold immediately available national air-force contingents for combined international enforcement action. The strength and degree of readiness of these contingents and plans for their combined action shall be determined, within the limits laid down in the special agreement or agreements referred to in Article 43, by the Security Council with the assistance of the Military Staff Committee.

ARTICLE 46

Plans for the application of armed force shall be made by the Security Council with the assistance of the Military Staff Committee.

ARTICLE 47

1. There shall be established a Military Staff Committee to advise and assist the Security Council on all questions relating to the Security Council's military requirements for the maintenance of international peace and security, the employment and command of forces placed at its disposal, the regulation of armaments, and possible disarmament.

2. The Military Staff Committee shall consist of Chiefs of Staff of the permanent members of the Security Council or their representatives. Any

Member of the United Nations not permanently represented on the Committee shall be invited by the Committee to be associated with it when the efficient discharge of the Committee's responsibilities requires the participation of that Member in its work.

3. The Military Staff Committee shall be responsible under the Security Council for the strategic direction of any armed forces placed at the disposal of the Security Council. Questions relating to the command of such forces shall be worked out subsequently.

4. The Military Staff Committee, with the authorization of the Security Council and after consultation with appropriate regional agencies, may establish regional subcommittees.

ARTICLE 48

1. The action required to carry out the decisions of the Security Council for the maintenance of international peace and security shall be taken by all the Members of the United Nations or by some of them, as the Security Council may determine.

2. Such decisions shall be carried out by the Members of the United Nations directly and through their action in the appropriate international agencies of which they are members.

ARTICLE 49

The Members of the United Nations shall join in affording mutual assistance in carrying out the measures decided upon by the Security Council.

ARTICLE 50

If preventive or enforcement measures against any state are taken by the Security Council, any other state, whether a Member of the United Nations or not, which finds itself confronted with special economic problems arising from the carrying out of those measures shall have the right to consult the Security Council with regard to a solution of those problems.

ARTICLE 51

Nothing in the present Charter shall impair the inherent rights of individual or collective self-defense if an armed attack occurs against a Member of the United Nations, until the Security Council has taken the measures necessary to maintain international peace and security. Measures taken by Members in the exercise of this right of self-defense shall be immediately reported to the Security Council and shall not in any way affect the authority and responsibility of the Security Council under the present Charter to take at any time such action as it deems necessary in order to maintain or restore international peace and security. . . .

Chapter IX

INTERNATIONAL ECONOMIC AND SOCIAL COOPERATION

ARTICLE 55

With a view to the creation of conditions of stability and well-being which are necessary for peaceful and friendly relations among nations based on respect for the principle of equal rights and self-determination of peoples, the United Nations shall promote:

a. higher standards of living, full employment, and conditions of economic and social progress and development;
b. solutions of international economic, social, health, and related problems; and international cultural and educational cooperation; and
c. universal respect for, and observance of, human rights and fundamental freedoms for all without distinction as to race, sex, language, or religion.

ARTICLE 56

All Members pledge themselves to take joint and separate action in cooperation with the Organization for the achievement of the purposes set forth in Article 55.

ARTICLE 57

1. The various specialized agencies, established by inter-governmental agreement and having wide international responsibilities, as defined in their basic instruments, in economic, social, cultural educational, health, and related fields, shall be brought into relationship with the United Nations in accordance with the provisions of Article 63.
2. Such agencies thus brought into relationship with the United Nations are hereinafter referred to as "specialized agencies."

ARTICLE 58

The Organization shall make recommendations for the coordination of the policies and activities of the specialized agencies.

ARTICLE 59

The Organization shall, where appropriate, initiate negotiations among the states concerned for the creation of any new specialized agencies required for the accomplishment of the purposes set forth in Article 55.

ARTICLE 60

Responsibility for the discharge of the functions of the Organization set forth in this Chapter shall be vested in the General Assembly and, under the authority of the General Assembly, in the Economic and Social Council, which shall have for this purpose the powers set forth in Chapter X. . . .

Chapter XIV

THE INTERNATIONAL COURT OF JUSTICE

ARTICLE 92

The International Court of Justice shall be the principal judicial organ of the United Nations. It shall function in accordance with the annexed Statute, which is based upon the Statute of the Permanent Court of International Justice and forms an integral part of the present Charter.

ARTICLE 93

1. All Members of the United Nations are *ipso facto* parties to the Statute of the International Court of Justice.
2. A state which is not a Member of the United Nations may become a party to the Statute of the International Court of Justice on conditions to be determined in each case by the General Assembly upon the recommendation of the Security Council.

ARTICLE 94

1. Each Member of the United Nations undertakes to comply with the decision of the International Court of Justice in any case to which it is a party.
2. If any party to a case fails to perform the obligations incumbent upon it under a judgment rendered by the Court, the other party may have recourse to the Security Council, which may, if it deems necessary, make recommendations or decide upon measures to be taken to give effect to the judgment.

ARTICLE 95

Nothing in the present Charter shall prevent Members of the United Nations from entrusting the solution of their differences to other tribunals by virtue of agreements already in existence or which may be concluded in the future.

ARTICLE 96

1. The General Assembly or the Security Council may request the International Court of Justice to give an advisory opinion on any legal question.
2. Other organs of the United Nations and specialized agencies, which may at any time be so authorized by the General Assembly, may also request advisory opinions of the Court on legal questions arising within the scope of their activities.

Part III.   EPILOGUE: EUROPE IN PERSPECTIVE

> The realization that Europe no longer holds the dominant position in global politics has led statesmen and scholars to reconsider her role in world civilization. What is to become of the great western heritage with which Europe has endowed all other lands? And what is to be the future of the great seed-bed of world culture? One answer to these challenging questions is given by Sir Ernest Barker (1874–   ), noted British historian, in the following selection from *The European Inheritance* (1954).[14]

If we seek to look in conclusion at the tendencies of the times, it might seem at first sight as if Europe, unable to remain European, were dubiously poised in the balance between the USSR and the U. S. A., and were destined either to be Russianized or cut to the American pattern. It is true that a highly variegated Europe is standing at the moment between two massive uniformities; and the odds may be held to be in favor of the great uniformities. But the variegation of Europe is a strength as well as a weakness, and a strength even more than a weakness. The many nations of peninsular Europe, with their many languages and literatures, and all their various schemes both of social life and political structure, provide a rich sum of patterns and types which are not only a stimulus to one another but also serve as a store of examples on which the rest of the world can draw. The different common forces at work in this variegated system—the force of nationalism, the force of liberalism, the force of socialism—enter here into various combinations which make peninsular Europe a laboratory for the world. Great Britain, for instance, has been attempting, in the course of the last few years, a combination of liberalism and socialism, and a reconciliation of nationalized production with private enterprise, which is something new in its kind; and similar movements have been afoot in other parts of western Europe. There is something here which is precious in its kind. Can we say to it *Esto Perpetua,* and, if so, on what conditions is its perpetuity possible?

We have to begin by admitting that the Great Europe of the geographers—the Europe which stretches from the west coast of Ireland to the Urals, and from the North Cape to the south coast of Sicily—has always been a spatial rather than a mental and historical unit. It has already been noticed, in the first section of this review, that whether we look at Europe in terms of the south and the Mediterranean or whether we regard it from a northern point of view there has always been a cleavage between an eastern and a western half. This cleavage is still with us; and it weighs the more heavily on our minds

today because it is newly deepened for us by the ideological difference of communism and liberalism, and because we feel it freshly accentuated by the demographic factor of the great growth of population in the Slavonic east. But there is some comfort in the reflection that there is nothing new in kind, even if there is a difference of degree, in a cleavage between two Europes which is almost as old as time. There is a further and greater comfort in the reflection that a process of cross-fertilization between its different elements has always been a great factor in the general inheritance of Europe and the transmission of that inheritance. It is true that there is little contact today along the "marches" of the border-area which runs down through the middle of Europe; it is true that a curtain seems to have descended, and that an ancient instinct of xenophobia seems to be stronger than ever in the east; it is true that the eastern land-mass appears to be drawn together in a common aversion from the west. Even natural science has lost its fraternity, splitting as it were into different species; and if there is still some exchange of commodities, it is almost a grudging exchange. The omens are not propitious. But it is one of the lessons of history that adjoining civilizations must in the long run come into contact and even begin to "cross." The process, when it begins, will naturally be strongest in the debatable land between the eastern Baltic and the Aegean Sea. The west will be wise to be patient. This is one of the conditions of its own perpetuity. If its liberalism and its nationalism and its socialism, each mixed with and each moderating the other, have something to give to the border-area of eastern Europe, they will give it in time, and by virtue of patience, when once there is any desire to receive. And that desire may emerge, even sooner than we expect.

There is a still further and greater condition of the perpetuity of western Europe. Eastern Europe has drawn itself together, or at any rate it has been drawn together by its directing center, in a common scheme of policy and structure which runs through all its states. The USSR—itself in form a federal state, if in fact a centralized mechanism—has imposed the fact of a semi-federal direction on the associated states of eastern Europe, though it has left them the form and status of independent sovereigns. Here, therefore, the new force of federalism has been added to the three old forces of nationalism, liberalism, and socialism which have hitherto directed the movement of Europe. That new force has also to be added, and indeed is now being added, in the Europe of the west, which is thus beginning to answer the integration of the east by a similar, and yet different, integration of its own. The growth of "Western Union," which in its broader form has already moved to the idea and practice of a "Council of Europe," began in 1947, and is proceeding steadily if slowly. It differs from the integration of the east in being a voluntary movement, based on the free adhesion of each consenting state. It differs again, and in consequence, in not being inimical either to the idea of nationalism or to the principles of liberalism: on the contrary it can include and enlist both, as it can also include and enlist the ideas and principles of socialism—not indeed as a *sine qua non* which all states must adopt (though some statesmen have sought to follow that line), but rather as a possible ingredient which may or may not be added in each particular case by the free choice of each participant. This growth of "union" and this institution of a common "council" is not, in itself, the adoption of a federal system or the constitution of a federal state. Such a consummation is unlikely in view of the different national traditions and the general variegation of pattern which distinguishes western Europe from all the regions or territories which have hitherto adopted the logic of a full federal system. What is happening is rather a movement of the guiding idea of federalism than an adoption of actual federalism; but already the movement has gone far enough to result in proposals for a bicameral European legislature, making "rules" for Europe (the Europe of the west) with the assent of all member states, and for an executive organ connected with the legislature which would give effect and force to those "rules."

Europe—the peninsular Europe of the west—can endure and prosper, and maintain the perpetuity of her inheritance, if she can mix some new and experimental form of federalism, suited to her own peculiar needs, with the other forces which have been, and still are, active in determining her life. On this condition she can retain the riches of a variegated pattern of different national idiosyncrasies; on this condition she can remain the laboratory of the world, searching out new ideas and new combinations of ideas; on this condition she can offer and inspire resistance to that movement towards a drab technological (or "technocratic") universalism which might otherwise overwhelm the whole of the human race. There remains, indeed, the peril which must always be present in a system of two Europes: the peninsular Europe of the west, and the Europe of the eastern land-mass which is Eurasian as well as European. The peril may seem to be accentuated if each of these Europes draws itself together, federally or quasi-federally, and the two thus confront one another as separate collectivities growing more and more collective. But the idea of balance is an old idea in Europe, which has done some service in the past, and may, in new forms and with a new grouping of forces, do service in the present and the future. There have been two Europes in the past, and they have managed to live together, or at any rate side by side. There has been a Holy Roman empire of the west by the side of an east Roman emperor, and a Latin Christianity by the side of Greek Orthodoxy. The form and substance of the old division have both changed greatly in our generation; but however different both in form and substance, the old division still remains Our predecessors faced the division. We can only do the same.

Meanwhile the great fact remains—and it is consoling as well as great—that Europe is something more than the peninsula of Europe. Overseas Europe—the Europe that has crossed the oceans since the beginning of the sixteenth century—is still a part of Europe, and still helps to determine its balance and system. To think merely in terms of the land-space of Europe is to think in terms far too narrow. Europe exists and acts in all the continents—no longer in the guise of a conqueror, or as an imperialist power, but rather as a habit of mind and a tradition of civilization. Old political bonds between Europe and its off-shoots beyond the seas have either now been broken or are now being steadily loosed. But politics is not everything, and other bonds remain—the firmer and more enduring just because they are looser. The two Americas, that of the Anglo-Saxon north and that of the Latin center and south, belong to Europe as well as themselves; and if they are separated from it both by the Atlantic Ocean and by a century and more of political independence, they are still connected with it by their civilization and culture. The British Commonwealth—so broad and so mixed in its nature that it now begins to shed the appellation of "British" and to style itself simply "the Commonwealth"—carries Europe into every continent, and mixes, in the south of Asia, European traditions of language, literature, and government with the ancient and indigenous traditions of eastern civilizations. The continent of Africa, in the course of the last hundred years, has been drawn into the orbit of Europe; it is being stirred into self-conscious development by the parliamentary methods and the political ideas of Europe; and it is bringing its resources and its economic weight into the general maintenance of a European system and balance.

The connection of the two Americas with the peninsula of Europe is real, and yet also difficult. The difficulty is not only geographical: it is also a matter of the development of another temper— go-ahead, confident, inventive, electric—under the conditions of a new life, moving at a rapid pace, on a new soil and among new resources. Under such conditions, as ancient Greece had already learned, a difference naturally develops between the more static character of the old metropolitan centres and the more mobile and experimental quality of the new overseas communities. In the United States this difference has been further accentuated both by the fusing of different stocks in the crucible of one nation, producing a new mixed national type, and by a great technological development of unique di-

mensions and strength. It may thus appear, on the surface, that the "New World" is a different thing from the "Old World" of the European pattern; and while the New World may feel that the Old World is frozen and fixed in an outmoded pattern of traditional varieties, the Old World may feel, on its side, that the New World, in spite of its marvels and mechanism, is still fluid, still in the making, and still in search of a pattern. It is necessary to face and feel these differences of outlook. Unless they are faced and felt, there can be no true understanding, and no full cooperation. But the differences are only differences within a fundamental identity. The settlers in the New World have always carried with them the inheritance of Europe; and they still retain that inheritance. That is the bond which must always connect them, whatever their differences may be, with the fate and the fortunes of the Europe from which they brought the inheritance.

NOTES

NOTES TO PROBLEM I

The quotations on the title page are from Cicero, *Tusculan Disputations* V, iv, 10 and Diogenes Laertius, *Lives of the Philosophers* II, 20.

[1] Herodotus VII, 102–104 (tr. A. de Selincourt, Penguin Books: Harmsworth, 1954).

[2] *Ibid.*, IV, 231; IX, 71.

[3] Sophocles, *Antigone,* 1–48; 61–79 (tr. Elizabeth Wyckoff, in "The Complete Greek Tragedies," edited by David Greene and Richmond Lattimore, University of Chicago Press, 1954).

[4] *Ibid.*, 175–214.

[5] *Ibid.*, 446–70; 480–525.

[6] Thucydides II, 35–43 (tr. Benj. Jowett, 1881).

[7] Aristophanes, *Clouds, passim* (tr. B. B. Rogers, London: Bell, 1902–16, reprinted in Loeb Classical Library, 1924).

[8] Diogenes Laertius, *Lives of the Philosophers* II, 40.

[9] Plato, *Apology, passim* (tr. Benj. Jowett, ed. 3, 1892).

[10] *Ibid.*

[11] Plato, *Crito, passim* (tr. Benj. Jowett, ed. 3, 1892).

[12] Plato, *Phaedo,* 116–118 (tr. Benj. Jowett, ed. 3, 1892).

NOTES TO PROBLEM II

The quotations on the title page are from Cicero, *Defense of Cluentius,* 146; Vergil, *Aeneid* IV, 847–53 (tr. C. Day Lewis, London: Hogarth Press, 1952); Aldous Huxley, *Eyeless in Gaza,* Harper and Brothers, 1936, pp. 120–21.

[1] Scriptores Historiae Augustae, *Hadrian,* 8, 3.

[2] Polybius, *Histories* VI, Preface (tr. W. R. Paton, Loeb Classical Library, 1923).

[3] *Ibid.* VI, 11–18.

[4] Livy VIII, vi–x (tr. B. O. Foster, Loeb Classical Library, 1926).

[5] Sallust, *War with Jugurtha,* ii–iv, xli (tr. J. C. Rolfe, Loeb Classical Library, 1921).

[6] Lucretius, *On the Nature of Things* II, 1–61 (tr. W. E. Leonard, Everyman Edition, 1921).

[7] Cicero, *Republic* V, 1–2 (tr. C. W. Keyes, Loeb Classical Library, 1928).

[8] *Ibid.* I, 1–9.

[9] *Ibid.* I, 39.

[10] *Ibid.* I, 42–43, 69; II, 57.

[11] Cicero, *Laws* I, 19 (tr. C. W. Keyes, Loeb Classical Library, 1928).

[12] Cicero, *Republic* III, 33; *Laws* I, 23, 28–29, 34, 43.

[13] Caesar, *Commentaires on the Civil War* I, 2–8 (tr. Somerset de Chair, London: Golden Cockerel Press, 1951).

[14] Cicero, *Letters to Friends* XVI, 11 (tr. W. G. Williams, Loeb Classical Library, 1929).

[15] Cicero, *Letters to Atticus* VII, 11 (tr. E. O. Winstedt, Loeb Classical Library, 1928).

[16] *Ibid.* VIII, 2.

[17] *Ibid.* VIII, 11.

[18] *Ibid.* VIII, 13.

[19] *Ibid.* IX, 10.

[20] *Ibid.* IX, 6a.

[21] *Ibid.* IX, 11a.

[22] *Ibid.* IX, 16.

[23] *Ibid.* IX, 18.

[24] *Ibid.* X, 4.

[25] Cicero, *Philippic* II, 113–16 (tr. W. C. A. Ker, Loeb Classical Library, 1926).

[26] Augustus, *Res Gestae* (Monumentum Ancyranum).

[27] Tacitus, *Annals* I, 2–10 (tr. Church and Brodribb, London, 1877).

[28] The so-called *Laudatio Turiae.*

[29] Pliny the Younger, *Panegyric of Trajan, passim.*

[30] *New Testament: The Gospel According to John* 18, 28–19, 16; (Revised Standard Version, New York: Thomas Nelson and Sons, 1946).

[31] *New Testament: The Acts of the Apostles* 21, 30–33; 22, 22–29; 25, 6–16; 25, 21; 28, 30.

[32] Tacitus, *Annals* XV, 38, 44 (tr. Church and Brodribb, London, 1877).

[33] Tertullian, *To the Martyrs* 1–2 (tr. S. Tholwall, in Ante-Nicene Christian Library, Vol. XI, Edinburgh, 1869).

[34] Eusebius, *Oration in Praise of the Emperor Constantine* III, 5–6; VII, 12–13; XVI, 2–7 (tr. E. C. Richardson, Nicene and Post-Nicene Fathers, Second Series, Vol. I, New York: The Christian Literature Co., 1890).

NOTES TO PROBLEM III

The quotation on the titlepage of this Problem is from Arnold J. Toynbee, *A Study of History, Abridgement of Volumes I–VI by D. C. Somervell* (Oxford, 1947), pp. 352–53. Reprinted by permission of Oxford University Press, New York.

[1] J. M. Thompson and E. N. Johnson, *An Introduction to Medieval Europe* (New York: Norton, 1937), p. 373.

[2] C. Mirbt, *Quellen zur Geschichte des Papsttums* (Tubingen, 1911), p. 107. Translation in R. G. D. Laffan, *Select Documents of European History* (New York, 1930), pp. 21–22. Reprinted by permission of Methuen & Co., Ltd.

[3] E. Bernheim, *Quellen zur Geschichte des Investitursteits* (Leipzig, 1907), I, 12–14 and 14–17. Translation in Laffan, *Select Docs.*, pp. 23–24, and E. F. Henderson, *Select Historical Documents of the Middle Ages* (London, 1896), p. 364. Reprinted by permission of G. Bell & Sons, Ltd.

[4] From B. J. Kidd, *Documents Illustrative of the History of the Early Church* (London, 1941), III, 123–24. By permission of The Macmillan Company, publishers.

[5] Migne, Patrologia; *Cursus completus patrologia latina* (Paris, 1852), vol. 148, cols. 289 f. Translation in Thatcher and McNeal, *Source Book,* pp. 142–43. Reprinted by permission of Charles Scribner's Sons.

[6] E. Caspar, *Das Register Gregors VII in Monumenta Germaniae Historica . . . Epistalae selectae* (Balm, 1920–23), p. 188. Translation in Kidd, *Documents,* p.

126. By permission of The Macmillan Company, publishers.

⁷ Reprinted from *The Correspondence of Pope Gregory VII*, translated with an introduction by Ephraim Emerton. No. XIV of the series Records of Civilization: Sources and Studies. Copyright 1932 by Columbia University Press, pp. 11–12.

⁸ *Ibid.*, pp. 46–48.

⁹ Bernheim, *Quellen, I*, 40–43. Translations in Thatcher and McNeal, *Source Book*, pp. 134–35 (reprinted by permission of Charles Scribner's Sons) and Laffan, *Select Docs.*, p. 26. Reprinted by permission of Methuen & Co., Ltd.

¹⁰ Ekkehard, *Chronicon universale*, ad. an. 105–07 et seq. in H. Pertz, ed. *Monumenta Germaniae Historica*, VI, 198 et seq. Translation in J. H. Robinson, *Readings in European History* (New York, 1904), I, 266–71. Reprinted by permission of Ginn & Company.

¹¹ Emerton, *Correspondence*, pp. 81–83. Reprinted by permission of Columbia University Press.

¹² *Ibid.*, pp. 18–19.

¹³ *Ibid.*, pp. 8 and 15–16.

¹⁴ *Ibid.*, pp. 80–81 and 86–90.

¹⁵ Bernheim, *Quellen*, I, 70–71. Translation in Thatcher and McNeal, *Source Book*, pp. 151–52. Reprinted by permission of Charles Scribner's Sons.

¹⁶ Emerton, *Correspondence*, pp. 90–91. Reprinted by permission of Columbia University Press.

¹⁷ Bernheim, *Quellen*, I, 73–77. Translation in Laffan, *Select Docs.*, pp. 30–33. Reprinted by permission of Methuen & Co., Ltd.

¹⁸ Bernheim, *Quellen*, I, 78–80. Translation in Henderson, *Select Hist. Docs.*, pp. 377–79. Reprinted by permission of G. Bell & Sons, Ltd.

¹⁹ Bernheim, *Quellen*, I, 68, translation in Laffan, *Select Docs.*, pp. 26–29 (reprinted by permission of Methuen & Co., Ltd.) and Thatcher and McNeal, *Source Book*, p. 155. Reprinted by permission of Charles Scribner's Sons.

²⁰ Emerton, *Correspondence*, pp. 102–05. Reprinted by permission of Columbia University Press.

²¹ *Ibid.*, pp. 105–107.

²² The various translations of the chroniclers concerning Canossa are reprinted from F. Duncalf and A. C. Krey, *Parallel Source Problems in Medieval History* (New York: Harper, 1912), pp. 56–59 and 75–77. Reprinted by permission of Harper & Brothers.

²³ Bernheim, *Quellen*, I, 86–87. Translation in Henderson, *Select Hist. Docs.*, pp. 384–85. Reprinted by permission of G. Bell & Sons, Ltd.

²⁴⁻³⁰ As in note 22 above the translations of the chroniclers are reprinted from Duncalf and Krey, *Parallel Source Problems*, pp. 40–56, 59–71, 77–87.

³¹ Emerton, *Correspondence*, pp. 111–13. Reprinted by permission of Columbia University Press.

NOTES TO PROBLEM IV

The quotation on the title page of this Problem is taken from J. H. Robinson and H. W. Rolfe, *Petrarch, The First Modern Scholar and Man of Letters* (N. Y., 1914), p. 452. Translation is based on the 1496 edition of Petrarch's *Secretum*. Reprinted by permission of G. P. Putnam's Sons.

¹ W. K. Ferguson, *The Renaissance* (N. Y., 1940),

p. 2. Reprinted by permission of Henry Holt & Co., Inc., publishers.

² Ferdinand Schevill, *The First Century of Italian Humanism* (N. Y.: F. S. Crofts & Co., 1928), pp. 51–53. Translation based on *Der Briefwechsel des E. S. Piccolomini, herausgegeben von R. Wolkan. Fontes Rerum Austricarum*, II Abtheilung, LXI, 7.

³ M. Whitcomb, *A Literary Source-Book of the Renaissance* (Philadelphia, 1900), pp. 13–15. Reprinted by permission of University of Pennsylvania Press. Translation based on text of Petrarch's *Epistolae de Rebus Familiaribus et Variae*, ed. G. Fracasetti (Florence, 1859–63).

⁴ J. H. Robinson and H. W. Rolfe, *Petrarch, The First Modern Scholar and Man of Letters* (N. Y., 1914), pp. 275–78. Reprinted by permission of G. P. Putnam's Sons. Translation based on text in Fracasetti's edition of *Epistolae de Rebus Familiaribus et Variae*.

⁵ Robinson and Rolfe, *Petrarch*, 245.

⁶ Ephraim Emerton, *Humanism and Tyranny* (Cambridge, 1925), pp. 312, 320. Reprinted by permission of Harvard University Press. Text in F. Novati, *Epistolario di Coluccio Salutati* (Rome, 1891–1911), IV, 170.

⁷ Ferdinand Schevill, *First Century of Italian Humanism* (N. Y.: F. S. Crofts & Co., 1928), pp. 44–45. Translation based on text in *Rerum Italicarium Scriptores*, ed. Muratori (Milan, 1731), XIX, 920.

⁸ W. G. and E. Waters, *The Vespasiano Memoirs* (London, 1926), pp. 102–05. Reprinted by permission of George Routledge & Sons, Ltd. Text of *Vite di Uomini Illustri del Secolo XV* edited by L. Frati (Bologna, 1892–93).

⁹ W. H. Woodward, *Vittorino da Feltre and Other Humanist Educators* (Cambridge, 1905), pp. 161–78. Reprinted by permission of University Press, Cambridge.

¹⁰ R. H. H. Cust, *The Life of Benvenuto Cellini* (London, 1910), I, 93–96; II, 296–303. Reprinted by permission of G. Bell & Sons, Ltd. Cust's translation is based on the Italian text edited by O. Bacci (Florence, 1901).

¹¹ J. H. Robinson, *Readings in European History* (Boston, 1904), I, 532–34. Reprinted by permission of Ginn and Company. Text in the edition of O. Bacci (Florence, 1901).

¹² From *The Man of the Renaissance* by Ralph Roeder, copyright 1933 by Ralph Roeder. By permission of The Viking Press, Inc., New York, N. Y., pp. 503–05, 505–06. Text in F. Nicolini's edition of Aretino's *Lettere* (Bari, 1913–16).

¹³ Cust, *Life of Cellini*, I, 1–7. Reprinted by permission of G. Bell & Sons, Ltd.

¹⁴ Giorgio Vasari, *Lives of Seventy of the Most Eminent Painters, Sculptors, and Architects*, ed. E. H. and E. W. Blashfield and A. A. Hopkins (N. Y., 1896), II, 49–61. Reprinted by permission of Charles Scribner's Sons. Text of Vasari's works edited by G. Masselli (Florence, 1832–38).

¹⁵ Waters, eds., *Vespasiano Memoirs*, pp. 181–83. Reprinted by permission of George Routledge & Sons, Ltd.

¹⁶ L. E. Opdycke, *The Book of the Courtier by Count Baldesar Castiglione* (N. Y., 1903), pp. 19, 22–24, 25–32, 59, 62–63, 65–66. Reprinted by permis-

sion of Charles Scribner's Sons. Translation based on
V. Cian's edition of the text (Florence, 1894).

NOTES TO PROBLEM V

The quotation of the title page of this Problem
is from Lord Acton, *Lectures on Modern History*
(London, 1906), pp. 50–51. By permission of The
Macmillan Company, publishers.

1 Taken from *The Prince*, by N. Machiavelli, translated by W. K. Marriott (London, 1908). Published
by E. P. Dutton & Co., Inc., New York, pp. 53–63, 91,
121–23, 127–29, 133–36, 141–45, 149–54, 163, 177–93,
203–07.
2 F. W. Coker, *Readings in Political Philosophy*
(New York: Macmillan, 1938), pp. 374–80. The translation is by Professor Coker.
3 Translation in Martin Luther, *Works* (Philadelphia, 1915ff.), III, 236, 237–38, 239–40, 251. Reprinted
by permission of Muhlenberg Press, Philadelphia, Pa.
4 *Institutes of the Christian Religion by John Calvin. Translated from the Latin and Collated with the
Author's Last Edition in French*, et. John Allen
(Philadelphia, 7th American edition, 1936), II, 770,
772–73, 791, 802–03, 804–05.
5 John Knox, *The History of the Reformation in
Scotland*, ed. W. M'Gavin (Glasgow, 1832), pp. 250,
252, 253.
6 *Statutes of the Realm* (London, 1810–18), IV, 350.
Reprinted in G. B. Adams and H. M. Stephens, *Select Documents of English Constitutional History*
(New York, 1902), pp. 296–302.
7 J. Dumont, *Corps Universal Diplomatique du
Droit des Gens* (Amsterdam, 1726–31), V, 544ff. Translated in Ann Maury, ed., *Memoirs of a Huguenot Family* (New York, 1853), pp. 453–96.
8 *Novisima Recopilacion de las Leyes de España*
(Paris, 1846), I, 5–6. Translated by Professor José
Arrom; F. Colin, *Labor Evangélica* (Barcelona, 1900–
02), III, 674–97. Translated in E. H. Blair and J. A.
Robertson, *The Philippine Islands* (Cleveland, 1905),
XXI, 19–31. Reprinted by permission of The Arthur
H. Clark Company.

NOTES TO PROBLEM VI

The quotation on the title page of this Problem is
from *The Complete Works of G. Savile, First Mar-
quess of Halifax*, ed. Sir Walter Raleigh (Oxford:
Clarendon Press, 1912), p. 183.

1 G. Burnet, *Bishop Burnet's History of His Own
Time* (London, 1724–34), I, 611–13. Reprinted in
D. N. Smith, *Characters from the Histories and Memoirs of the Seventeenth Century* (Oxford, 1918), pp.
218–20.
2 Burnet, *History*, I, 168–70. Reprinted in Smith,
Characters, pp. 253–56.
3 F. A. M. Mignet, *Négociations Relatives à la Succession d'Espagne sous Louis XIV* (Paris, 1835–42), III,
187–97. Translation in D. Ogg, *England in the Reign
of Charles II* (Oxford, 1934), I, 344–46. Reprinted by
permission of The Clarendon Press.
4 F. Bate, *The Declaration of Indulgence* (London,
1908), pp. 76–78. Reprinted by permission of University Press of Liverpool.

5 *Privy Council Register* (Ms), LXIII, 195; printed
in T. G. Stone, *England under the Restoration* (London, 1923), pp. 34–35. Reprinted by permission of
Longmans, Green & Co., Inc.
6 *The Parliamentary Diary of Sir Edward Dering
1670–1673*, ed. B. D. Henning (New Haven, 1940), pp.
114–18. Reprinted by permission of Yale University
Press; *Journals of the House of Commons* (London,
1803–63), IX, 252, 256, 257; *Journals of the House of
Lords* (London, ?–1887), XII, 549. The selections from
the *Journals* are reprinted in C. Stephenson and F. G.
Marcham, *Sources of English Constitutional History*
(N. Y., 1937), pp. 567–69.
7 *Statutes of the Realm* (London, 1810–18), V,
782–83. Reprinted in Stephenson and Marcham,
Sources, pp. 555–56.
8 Anchitel Grey, *Debates of the House of Commons
from the Year 1667 to the Year 1694* (London, 1769),
II, 197–209. Reprinted in Stone, *England*, 36–38;
Commons Journals, IX, 298, 299.
9 G. Chalmers, *A Collection of Treaties between
Great Britain and Other Powers* (London, 1790), I,
172. Reprinted in Stone, *England*, pp. 39–40.
10 Grey, *Debates*, VIII, 353–62.
11 T. B. Howell, *A Complete Collection of State
Trials to 1783* (London, 1816–26), XI, 1197–98. Reprinted in Stephenson and Marcham, *Sources*, pp.
582–83.
12 Burnet, *History* (second edition, 1833), III, 108–
09, 146–58.
13 *Privy Council Register* (Ms), LXXXII, 1. Printed
in Stone, *England*, pp. 122–23. Reprinted by permission of Longmans, Green & Co., Inc.
14 *Memoirs of Sir John Reresby*, ed. A. Browning
(Glasgow, 1936), pp. 478–79. Reprinted by permission
of Jackson, Son & Co.
15 *Diary of John Evelyn*, ed. H. B. Wheatley (London, 1906), III, 46–50.
16 Sir J. Dalrymple, *Memoirs of Great Britain and
Ireland* (London, 1771–73), I, app., pp. 228–31. Reprinted in Stone, *England*, pp. 80–81.
17 *Statutes of the Realm*, VI, 23. Also reprinted in
C. G. Robertson, *Select Statutes, Cases and Documents to Illustrate English Constitutional History*
(London, 1935), pp. 105–06.
18 A. P. Cheyney, *Readings in English History*
(N. Y., 1922), pp. 545–47. Reprinted by permission of
Ginn and Company.
19 *Ibid.*, pp. 549–50.
20 *Statutes of the Realm*, VI, 74–76. Also reprinted
in Robertson, *Select Stat.*, pp. 124–26, 128.
21 *Statutes of the Realm*, VII, 636–38. Also reprinted in Robertson, *Select Stat.*, pp. 152–56.
22 John Locke, *Two Treatises on Civil Government*
(London, 1690), pp. 219–25, 230–32, 241–46, 249–51,
265–69, 273, 281–82, 305–06, 316–17, 319–20, 345–47,
350, 423–24, 441–43.

NOTES TO PROBLEM VII

The text of the Marseillaise on the title page has
been taken from Granville Bantock, *National Airs of
the Allies* (London, 1940), p. 8. Reprinted by permission of W. Paxton and Company, Ltd.

1 The translation is by Thomas Paine, *The Rights
of Man* (London, 1791), pp. 116–19.

[2] Paris, *Moniteur*, II, 123.

[3] The records of the Paris *Commune* are from P. J. B. Buchez and P. C. Roux-Lavergne, *Histoire parlementaire de la révolution française* (Paris, 1834–38), IX, 444–45; the speech on the *Loi le Chapelier* is from the *Moniteur*, VII, 661–62.

[4] A. Young, *Travels in France and Italy* (London, 1915), pp. 124–25. Published by Everyman's Library, E. P. Dutton and Company, Inc., New York.

[5] F. de la Fontainerie, ed., *French Liberalism and Education in the Eighteenth Century* (N. Y., 1922), pp. 323–56 *passim*. Reprinted by permission of McGraw-Hill Book Company, Inc.

[6] J. B. Duvergier et al., *Collection complète des lois, décrets, ordonnances, règlements, avis du Conseil d'état* (Paris, 1834), I, 63.

[7] *Ibid.*, I, 73–78.

[8] E. L. Higgins, *The French Revolution as Told by Contemporaries* (Boston, 1938), pp. 411–30. Reprinted by permission of Houghton Mifflin Company.

[9] *Ibid.*, pp. 153–55.

[10] *Moniteur*, XII, 188.

[11] Higgins, *op. cit.*, pp. 432–37. Reprinted by permission of Houghton Mifflin Company.

[12] *Moniteur*, XIX, 401–02. (R. B. Palmer, transl., *Twelve Who Ruled*, 275–6, Princeton, 1941.)

[13] Buchez and Roux, *Histoire Parlementaire*, XXIX, 159–72.

[14] *Moniteur*, XIX, 51.

[15] Decree creating the Committee of Public Safety is in Duvergier, *Collection complète*, V, 248; decree on revolutionary government, in Buchez and Roux, *Histoire parlementaire*, XXIX, 172; decree on representatives on mission, in Duvergier, *Collection complète*, V, 243; notes on the Perpignan Jacobin Club, in C. C. Brinton, *The Jacobins* (N. Y., 1930), pp. 99–100, copyright, 1930, by The Macmillan Company and used with their permission; letter from Chaumette, in Aulard, *Recueil des actes du comité du salût public* (Paris, 1889–1933), X, 680–81.

[16] The *Levée en Masse* is from F. M. Anderson, *The Constitutions and Other Select Documents Illustrative of the History of France, 1789–1907*, 2d ed. (Minneapolis, 1908), pp. 184–85, reprinted by permission of the H. W. Wilson Company; Law of Suspects, *Ibid.*, pp. 186–87; the letter of young conscript is from H. F. Stewart and P. Desjardins, *French Patriotism in the Nineteenth Century (1814–1833)* (Cambridge, 1925), pp. 21–23. Reprinted by permission of University Press, Cambridge.

[17] Chaumette's speech is from A. Mathiez, *La vie chère et le mouvement social sous le Terreur* (Paris, 1927), p. 160; Robespierre's speech, from *Moniteur*, XIV, 636; Herault de Seschelles' speech, from Mathiez, *La vie chère*, pp. 307–08; report by Couppé (de l'Oise), from *Moniteur*, XVII, 775; the selection from the Law of the Maximum, from Anderson, *Constitutions*, pp. 188–89, reprinted by permission of the H. W. Wilson Company.

[18] *Moniteur*, XV, 838.

[19] The order of the Committee of Public Safety is from A. Aulard, *Recueil*, XI, 157; Barère's speech, from *Moniteur*, XIX, 317–20; the account of the youth festival, from J. M. Thompson, *English Witnesses of the French Revolution* (Oxford, 1938), pp.

263–64, reprinted by permission of Basil Blackwell and Mott, Ltd.

[20] Decree for proclaiming the liberty and sovereignty of all peoples is from Anderson, *Constitutions*, 130–32, reprinted by permission of the H. W. Wilson Company; the Carnot report is from H. Carnot, *Mémoires sur Carnot* (Paris, 1861), I, 296–301.

[21] Stewart and Desjardins, *op. cit.*, pp. 49–51. Reprinted by permission of University Press, Cambridge.

NOTES TO PROBLEM VIII

The quotation on the title page is from A. N. Whitehead, *Science and Modern World* (N. Y., 1925), p. 282. Reprinted by permission of the Macmillan Company.

[1] Adam Smith, *An Inquiry into the Nature and Causes of the Wealth of Nations* (London, 1786), Book I, Chapter 10; Book II, Chapters 3 and 4; Book IV, Introduction and Chapters 1, 2, and 9.

[2] The material to the second ellipsis is taken from the 1st edition of Malthus' *Essay on the Principle of Population* (London, 1798), pp. 1–17; from the second ellipsis to the end of the selection the material is taken from the 6th edition (London, 1826), I, 12–17.

[3] J. Bowring, ed., *The Works of Jeremy Bentham* (Edinburgh, 1843), I, 1–4.

[4] *Ibid.*, 33, 35.

[5] John Stuart Mill, *Autobiography* (London, 1873), pp. 230–34.

[6] Lord Acton, *The History of Freedom and Other Essays* (London, 1907), pp. 288–89, 292–93, 299–300.

[7] Karl Marx and Friedrich Engels, *Manifesto of the Communist Party* (Chicago, 1888), pp. 1–23, 24–39, 41–47, 62–64.

[8] Ludwig Buchner, *Force and Matter: Empirico-Philosophical Studies Intelligibly Rendered*, trans. by J. F. Collingswood (London, 1870), pp. 2–5, 9–10, 12–13, 28–30, 33–35, 43, 56–59, 196–97, 239–40, 242–43, 246–47, 257.

[9] *The Positive Philosophy of Auguste Comte*, as freely translated and condensed by Harriet Martineau (N. Y., 1855).

[10] Herbert Spencer, *The Principles of Sociology* (N. Y., 1897), 229–34, 239–42.

[11] Thomas H. Huxley, *Evolution and Ethics*, and Other Essays (London, 1894), pp. 202–18.

[12] Pearson, *National Life from the Standpoint of Science*, 2d ed. (Cambridge, 1919), pp. 21–22, 26–27, 36–37, 43–47, 52–54, 62–64.

[13] Sigmund Freud, *A General Introduction to Psychoanalysis* (N. Y., 1938), pp. 22–24.

NOTES TO PROBLEM IX

The quotation on the title page is cited by C. L. Sulzberger in the *New York Times*, October 29, 1955.

[1] *Enciclopedia Italiana* (Milan, 1932), XIV, 847–51.

[2] A. Hitler, *Mein Kampf* (Houghton Mifflin, N. Y., 1939), pp. 3, 44, 56, 83–4, 99, 103, 105, 111–12, 116–17. Gordon W. Prange, ed., *Hitler's Words* (Washington, 1934), pp. 7, 80–81. Reprinted by permission of the American Council on Foreign Affairs.

[3] G. Rotrand, *Franco Means Business* (N. Y., n.d.),

pp. 56–62. Reprinted by permission of the Devin-Adair Company, Publishers.

4 V. I. Lenin, *State and Revolution* (N. Y., 1932), pp. 30–31, 71–72, 73, 82–85.

5 J. Stalin, *Foundations of Leninism* (N. Y., 1932), pp. 14–16, 17–20.

6 *Foreign Affairs*, XII, 193, 195–96, 198–99, 201, 203–4, 205 (complete text reprinted in *The Foreign Affairs Reader* (N. Y., 1947), Harper and Brothers for Council in Foreign Relations); *Communist Perspective* (External Research Staff, Office of Intelligence Research, Department of State, n.d.), pp. 273, 278, 380, 401, 479.

7 Sir Henry Slesser, *A History of the Liberal Party* (London, 1944), pp. 163–65. Reprinted by permission of Hutchinson and Company, Limited.

8 Radio Address of January 3, 1948, by the Rt. Hon. Clement R. Attlee over the BBC, by courtesy of the British Information Service and reprinted with the permission of Mr. Attlee.

9 Address of the Rt. Hon. Winston Churchill to the Conservative Electors of the Colne Valley, October 1951.

10 Jacques Maritain, *Les Droits de l'homme et la loi naturelle* (N. Y., 1942), pp. 7–10, 111–14. Reprinted by permission of Charles Scribner's Sons.

11 Friedrich Meinecke, *The German Catastrophe* (trans. S. B. Fay, Cambridge, Mass., 1950), pp. 106–7, 108–9, 110–12. Reprinted by permission of Harvard University Press.

12 Erich Fromm, *Escape from Freedom* (N. Y., 1941), pp. 253–56, 257–58, 260–61, 262–63, 270–71, 276. Reprinted by permission of Rinehart & Co., Inc.

13 *The Charter of the United Nations*, Preamble, Chs. I, VI, VII, IX, XIV.

14 Sir Ernest Barker, *et al., The European Inheritance* (Oxford, 1954), pp. 346–50. Reprinted by permission of Clarendon Press.